THE OXFORD HANDBOOK OF

MUSIC IN CHINA AND THE CHINESE DIASPORA

THE OXFORD HANDBOOK OF

MUSIC IN CHINA AND THE CHINESE DIASPORA

Edited by
YU HUI
and
JONATHAN P. J. STOCK

Oxford University Press is a department of the University of Oxford. It furthers
the University's objective of excellence in research, scholarship, and education
by publishing worldwide. Oxford is a registered trade mark of Oxford University
Press in the UK and certain other countries.

Published in the United States of America by Oxford University Press
198 Madison Avenue, New York, NY 10016, United States of America.

© Oxford University Press 2023

All rights reserved. No part of this publication may be reproduced, stored in
a retrieval system, or transmitted, in any form or by any means, without the
prior permission in writing of Oxford University Press, or as expressly permitted
by law, by license, or under terms agreed with the appropriate reproduction
rights organization. Inquiries concerning reproduction outside the scope of the
above should be sent to the Rights Department, Oxford University Press, at the
address above.

You must not circulate this work in any other form
and you must impose this same condition on any acquirer.

Library of Congress Cataloging-in-Publication Data
Names: Yu Hui (Ethnomusicologist) author. | Stock, Jonathan P. J.; 1963– author.
Title: The Oxford handbook of music in China and the Chinese diaspora /
[edited by] Yu Hui, Jonathan P.J. Stock.
Description: [1.] | New York, NY : Oxford University Press, 2023. |
Series: Oxford handbooks series | Includes bibliographical references and index.
Identifiers: LCCN 2022045586 (print) | LCCN 2022045587 (ebook) |
ISBN 9780190661960 (hardback) | ISBN 9780190661991 |
ISBN 9780190661984 (epub)
Subjects: LCSH: Music—China—History and criticism. |
Chinese—Music—History and criticism.
Classification: LCC ML336 .O94 2023 (print) | LCC ML336 (ebook) |
DDC 780.951—dc23/eng/20220920
LC record available at https://lccn.loc.gov/2022045586
LC ebook record available at https://lccn.loc.gov/2022045587

DOI: 10.1093/oxfordhb/9780190661960.001.0001

Printed by Integrated Books International, United States of America

Contents

List of Figures and Tables ... ix
Acknowledgments ... xv
Note on Glossaries ... xvii
List of Contributors ... xix

1. Introduction: Frames of Reference for the Study of Music in China and Its Diaspora ... 1
   YU HUI AND JONATHAN P. J. STOCK

PART I NEW DIRECTIONS IN HISTORY AND THEORY

2. Musical Archaeology and the Prehistory of Chinese Music ... 9
   YANG YUANZHENG

3. Theorizing "Natural Sound": Ancient Chinese Music Theory and Its Contemporary Applications in the Study of *Guqin* Intonation ... 30
   YU HUI AND CHEN YINGSHI

4. The *Huxuan* and *Huteng* Dances: Foreign Musical Dances in Chinese History ... 47
   ZHAO WEIPING

5. *Kunqu* from Analytical Perspectives: A Focus on "Feng ru song" ... 63
   KAR LUN ALAN LAU

6. Why and How Do Chinese Sing *Shijing* Songs? ... 99
   JOSEPH S. C. LAM

7. Music History and Historiography in the Chinese Context ... 134
   HON-LUN HELAN YANG

8. Chinese Music Modernities ... 155
   FREDERICK LAU

PART II MUSIC GENRES AND PRACTICES IN EVOLVING CONTEXTS

9. Traditional Instruments and Heterophonic Practice 179
   ALAN R. THRASHER

10. Jiangnan *Sizhu* in the Greater Suzhou Area: Repertoire, Revitalization, and Sustainability 199
    MERCEDES M. DUJUNCO

11. Social Change and the Maintenance of Musical Tradition among the Western Yugurs 229
    DU YAXIONG

12. The Making of a Music Community as a Manifestation of Nationalism: The Jinyu Qinshe Society in 1930s China 247
    YU HUI

13. A Multimodal and Interdisciplinary Approach to Luo Yusheng's Video Performance of *Choumo yinchu* (*At Break of Day*) 271
    FRANCESCA R. SBORGI LAWSON

14. The Emergence of Taiwanese New *Xiqu*: A Case Study on Chichiao Musical Theater 292
    HSIEH HSIAO-MEI

15. Hybridity in the Modern Chinese Orchestral Music (*Guoyue*) of Taiwan 310
    CHING-YI CHEN

16. Trends in the Globalization of *Pipa* Music 329
    BEN WU

PART III CROSS-CUTTING ISSUES IN CONTEMPORARY SETTINGS

17. Humanism in Red: A New Mainstream Narrative in the Pop Songs of 1980s China 353
    LIJUAN QIAN

18. Staging Race and Sexuality Across Borders: Marketing Pop Singer
    Coco Lee 373
    GRACE WANG

19. Re-Imagining China's Women Pianists: Yuja Wang and
    Zhu Xiao-Mei 391
    SHZR EE TAN

20. Liveness and Mediation in Chinese Art Music: From *The Map* to the
    Qingming Festival 416
    GERMÁN GIL-CURIEL

21. The Amateur and the Professional in Wuhan's Park Pop 431
    SAMUEL HORLOR

22. "Minorities" and the Mainstream: The Musical Place of the
    Non-Han Peoples in Modern China 452
    CHUEN-FUNG WONG

23. "Kita Anak Malaysia" ("We are the Children of Malaysia"):
    Performing Multicultural Chinese Identities 468
    TAN SOOI BENG

24. Conclusions: New Directions in Chinese Music Research 491
    JONATHAN P. J. STOCK

Index 511

List of Figures and Tables

Figures

2.1. Woodblock facsimile of a rubbing of the inscription on the lower portion of the front of Anlu Bell 1. Source: Wang, 1802: fol. 31v. — 13

2.2. Woodblock facsimile of a rubbing of the inscription on the lower portion of the back of Anlu Bell 1. Source: Wang, 1802: fol. 32r. — 14

2.3. Line drawings of the ten-stringed *qin* from the tomb of Marquis Yi of Zeng, Suizhou, Hubei province (above), and the highly decorated ten-stringed *qin* excavated from Jiuliandun tomb no. 1, Hubei province (below). Source: drawing by Yang Yuanzheng. — 17

2.4. Line drawings of the seven-stringed *qin* from Guodian tomb no. 1, Hubei province (above); Changsha tomb no. 1195, Wulipai, Hunan province (middle); and Mawangdui tomb 3, Changsha, Hu'nan province (below). Source: drawing by Yang Yuanzheng. — 17

2.5. Line drawings of the seven-stringed *qin* excavated from Liu He's tomb, Nanchang, Jiangxi province; *qin* 1 (M1: 561), front and back plates, top view. Source: drawing by Yang Yuanzheng. — 18

2.6. Line drawings of the fragments of *qin* excavated from Liu He's tomb: *qin* 2 (M1: 342 and M1: 366), *qin* 3 (M1: 473), *qin* 4 (M1: 481), *qin* 5 (M1: 656), all viewed from above and below. Source: drawing by Yang Yuanzheng. — 19

3.1. The first five overtones in a harmonic series when the fundamental note is C. — 35

3.2. Marker positions on the surface of the *guqin* fingerboard. — 36

4.1. Picture of dancing figures on the stone doors to Grave M6, Yanchi, Ningxia (copy painted by Zhou Chanling). — 52

4.2. Dance picture on Han Xiu's tomb (detail), Guoxin village, Xi'an (copy painted by Zhou Chanling). — 53

4.3. Detail of early Tang-dynasty painting of dancing from Cave 220 north wall, Dunhuang (copy painted by Zhou Chanling). — 54

4.4. Sketch of a Tang-dynasty figurine of a *huteng* dancer (Shandan County Museum, Gansu province) (copy painted by Zhou Chanling). — 58

LIST OF FIGURES AND TABLES

5.1.	Four tones in Mandarin.	65
5.2.	Vocal *qupai* paradigm.	66
5.3.	Textual *qupai* template of "Feng ru song."	67
5.4.	Three-part *kunqu* creative process.	69
5.5.	Multiple definitions of *Zhongzhou yun* and stylistic division within *kunqu*.	70
5.6.	(a) Comparison between singing and (b) recitation in the first "Feng ru song" aria.	72
5.7.	Tonal contours of southern *kun* singing and recitation of "Feng ru song," Phrase 3.	74
5.8.	Tonal contours of the recitations of "Feng ru song," Phrases 3 and 4, in southern *kun* style, Standard Mandarin, and Suzhou Wu dialect.	74
5.9.	Tonal contours of northern and southern *kun* recitation of "Feng ru song," Phrases 3 and 4.	74
5.10.	Tone categorization of "Feng ru song," Phrase 4, based on *Hongwu zhengyun* and *Zhongyuan yinyun*.	75
5.11.	Tonal contours from historical and regional sources and the melodic contour of "Feng ru song," Phrase 4.	75
5.12.	Vocal melody and non-theatrical recitation in Standard Mandarin and the Suzhou dialect of "Feng ru song," Phrase 4.	76
5.13.	Visual discrepancies between tonal contour and symbolic representation of music and language in "Feng ru song," Phrase 4.	76
5.14.	Syllable sets from Phrases 3 and 4.	77
5.15.	Voice-leading rules for "Feng ru song," Phrases 3 and 4.	78
5.16.	Tone-pitch relationships in Phrase 4 syllable set.	78
5.17.	Tone-pitch relationships in Phrase 3 syllable set.	78
5.18.	Temporal relationships in music and language, Phrase 4 syllable set.	79
5.19.	Melodic diversity and stability of "Feng ru song" arias, Phrase 4.	80
5.20.	Historical and contemporary sources ("Feng ru song," Phrase 3, female role, from *Hongli ji*).	82
5.21.	Historical sources and contemporary performances ("Feng ru song," Phrase 4).	83
5.22.	Reductive analysis of "Feng ru song" arias, Phrase 4.	84
5.23.	Typical placement of syllables, *ban*, and melisma in "Feng ru song," Phrase 4, from "Sao song."	84
5.24.	First "Feng ru song" aria from "Sao song," Phrase 4, as a compound melody.	85
5.25.	Two-voice reductive analysis of "Feng ru song," Phrase 4, from "Sao song."	86

5.26.	Two-voice reductive analysis of "Feng ru song" arias, Phrase 4.	87
5.27.	Structural organization and temporal progression ("Feng ru song," Phrase 4, from "Sao song").	88
5.28.	Melodic diversity and stability in various "Feng ru song" arias, Phrase 4.	89
5.29.	Multidomain interactions in the first "Feng ru song" aria, "Sao song," Phrase 4.	89
5.30.	Complexities in *kunqu* creation and the *qupai* paradigm.	90
5.31.	Instrumental "Feng ru song" for *suona*.	91
6.1.	Four musical versions of "Guanju"	102
9.1.	Chaozhou *xianyue*, *Hanya Xishui*, reflecting moderate heterophonic interaction among the four instruments. (Excerpt from 1986 field tape.)	183
9.2.	Jiangnan *sizhu*, *Zhonghua Liuban*, showing an active heterophonic texture based upon differing idiomatic techniques and ensemble interaction. (Excerpt from 1989 field tape.)	186
9.3.	Fujian *nanyin* suite, *Bazhan Wu*, heterophonic excerpt from metered Section 1, showing a minimally ornamented *pipa* realization of the skeletal melody and a highly ornamented *dongxiao* realization. (Excerpt from 1979 field tape.)	187
10.1.	Map showing the extents of the Jiangnan region from different perspectives.	201
10.2.	Area of Jiangsu province showing the Suzhou metropolitan area, which includes the county-level cities of Taicang (encircled) and Kunshan in relation to Shanghai.	205
10.3.	(a–b) Two versions of *Liuhua liujie*.	209
10.4.	*Sizhu* instrumentalists of the Donghong Yishutuan performing one of the revived "Ten Great Pieces" of Jiangnan *sizhu*.	214
10.5.	Gu Family Music Troupe (Gujia Yinyue Ban) performing Jiangnan *sizhu* at a wedding in Tianchi village, Suzhou.	216
10.6.	Gu Family Music Troupe leading the wedding procession from the groom's house to fetch the bride. (Instruments used are two *suona*, cymbals, gong, drum, and *haotong*.)	217
11.1.	Yugur singers with researcher Du Yaxiong (standing, third from right).	239
12.1.	Gathering in the Yiyuan 怡园 garden in Suzhou, October 6, 1935 (JYQK, 2018: 6 [pictures]; credit: Jinyu Qinshe, 1938).	256
12.2.	A gathering in Suzhou celebrating Li Zizhao's birthday, June, 1936 (JYQK: 6 [pictures]; credit: Jinyu Qinshe, 1938).	261

12.3.	The cover of *Jinyu qinkan*	263
13.1.	Melody and song text marked with speech tone, *Choumo yinchu* lines T-3, T-4, T-5, and T-6, as sung by Luo Yusheng, 1960.	283
13.2.	Line B-1 from *Choumo yinchu*, sung by Luo Yusheng, 1960.	284
13.3.	Line B-2 from *Choumo yinchu*, sung by Luo Yusheng, 1961.	284
13.4.	Luo Yusheng's *Choumo* performance in front of a painting that depicts a morning scene.	287
15.1.	Cheng Si Sum 鄭思森 conducting a school orchestra in a national *guoyue* competition, 1973.	318
15.2.	Taipei Chinese Orchestra performing at the National Concert Hall, 2019.	319
15.3.	Tainan City Traditional Orchestra in musical-theater crossover performance "First Street Episode," Concert Hall of Tainan Municipal Cultural Center, October 1–2, 2016.	320
17.1.	Rhythmic mode in "Blood-Stained Dignity."	357
17.2.	"Blood-Stained Dignity," measures 1–24 (Li, 1992: 183–84).	357
17.3.	Voice and *erhu* interaction in "Blood-Stained Dignity," measures 13–20.	358
17.4.	Lyrics to "Fill the World with Love" (Lin, 1994: 667–70).	361
17.5.	Meng Guangzheng in Damucang salon.	365
17.6.	Xu Peidong (right) in Damucang salon.	366
19.1.	Criticism of Yuja Wang on YouTube.	407
19.2.	Zhihu discussion thread on Zhu Xiao-Mei's interpretation of the "Goldberg Variations."	409
20.1.	On-site musicians interact with on-screen ethnic-minority performers, for an audience of more than 30,000 villagers.	420
20.2.	The Magnificent City Gates (detail from *Along the River During the Qing Ming Festival*), musically rendered by *suona* in the *Qingming Symphonic Picture*.	425
21.1.	One of the *jiqing guangchang* stages in Nan'anzui Riverside Park, with a pre-show video playing on the screens.	436
21.2.	Refreshment stall and pool tables under the bridge at the entry to Nan'anzui Riverside Park.	441
23.1.	Typical *dondang sayang* melodic introduction from *Dondang Sayang Tanaman 1* (Pagoda V3770), sung by Miss Piah, Mr. Poh Tiang Swee, and Mr. Koh Hoon Teck.	472
23.2.	Score of voice and violin performing in heterophony and accompanied by the *asli* rhythmic pattern in *Dondang Sayang Tanaman 1* (Pagoda V3770), sung by Miss Piah, Mr. Poh Tiang Swee, Mr. Koh Hoon Teck.	473

23.3. (a–b) Handwritten musical score of *Kronchong Weltevreden* for violin or mandolin with guitar accompaniment, published in *Penghiboran Hati* (H.S.L. 1924). 475

23.4. Notation of four measures of *Joget Anak Udang* showing the use of three against two notes and simple triads. 481

23.5. Multiethnic characters and costumes in localized Potehi glove-puppet theater, representing the children of Malaysia. 486

Tables

3.1. The ratios of the string lengths marked by the thirteen markers and the pitch intervals of stopped and harmonic notes generated at the marker positions. 37

3.2. Pitches of stopped notes and harmonics produced from the thirteen inlay markers when the open strings of the *guqin* are tuned in *sanfen sunyi* tuning. 40

Acknowledgments

Our thanks go to our contributing authors for their dedication to filling the chapters with their invaluable research expertise and for their patience in waiting for the final publication, which has taken longer than expected due partially to global lockdowns against the COVID-19 pandemic. We would also like to warmly acknowledge the input of peers across (and beyond) Chinese music studies who provided insightful reviews and other guiding input at all stages of the work. Our special thanks go to Dr. Samuel Horlor, who spared neither time nor effort in helping us review and edit the manuscripts in the last stages of work on the volume during his stay in China as a postdoctoral fellow, working with the ethnomusicology team at Yunnan University. Colleagues and students at each of our institutions, Yunnan University in China and University College Cork in Ireland, have helped us in a myriad of ways, from offering flexibility in scheduling to allow for moments of editorial focus to providing a stimulating environment for dialogue on Chinese music research and its future prospects. We thank our respective families for their patience and support during the evenings and weekends of our absence, which are inevitably involved in editing a work like this. Finally, we acknowledge the assistance of the Key Project of Arts of China National Fund for Social Sciences (14ZD02) in supporting this book project.

Yu Hui
Kunming, 2021

Jonathan P. J. Stock
Cork, 2021

Note on Glossaries

EACH chapter of this book is accompanied by a Glossary that shows the pinyin romanization used for the primary terms found in the chapter, its writing in full-form Chinese characters, and a brief reminder of its meaning and usage in the chapter. A small number of terms have non-*pinyin* romanizations, for instance those for Taiwanese, Cantonese, Korean, or Japanese names. A small number of terms have also acquired divergent meanings over the history of Chinese musical culture, and so they may be glossed differently from one chapter to another. Many composite terms in Chinese are assembled from more than one character, and ordering is conventionally handled alphabetically by character (and then by speech tone and number of brush strokes) rather than alphabetically by letter alone. This is idiomatic for readers of Chinese, but readers of English will need to know that an entry for *huju* 滬劇 (Shanghai traditional opera) would appear above that for Hua Yanjun 華彥均 (folk musician, *c.* 1893–1950). The latter readers may need to scan further up or down the list to find the term they are seeking.

Contributors

Ching-Yi Chen is Co-Principal Investigator for several research projects at the Graduate Institute of Tainan National University of the Arts, Taiwan.

Chen Yingshi was Professor of Musicology at the Shanghai Conservatory of Music, China.

Du Yaxiong is Professor of Musicology at China Conservatory of Music.

Mercedes M. Dujunco is Senior Lecturer in the Division of Humanities at the Hong Kong University of Science and Technology.

Germán Gil-Curiel is a research associate in the Department of Music at University College Cork, Ireland.

Samuel Horlor is Postdoctoral Fellow at the Center for Ethnomusicology, Yunnan University, China.

Hsieh Hsiao-Mei is Associate Professor and Chair of the Department of Drama and Theatre at the National Taiwan University, Taiwan.

Joseph S. C. Lam is Professor of Musicology at Michigan University, United States.

Frederick Lau is Professor of Ethnomusicology at the Chinese University of Hong Kong.

Kar Lun Alan Lau is an independent scholar, composer, and MD candidate at the University of British Columbia, Canada.

Francesca R. Sborgi Lawson is Marshall Professor and Humanities Center Fellow at Brigham Young University, United States.

Lijuan Qian is Senior Lecturer in Music at University College Cork, Ireland.

Jonathan P. J. Stock is Professor of Music at University College Cork, Ireland.

Shzr Ee Tan is Senior Lecturer in the Music Department at Royal Holloway University of London, United Kingdom.

Tan Sooi Beng is Professor of Music at Universiti Sains Malaysia.

Alan R. Thrasher is Professor Emeritus of Ethnomusicology at University of British Columbia, Canada.

Grace Wang is Associate Professor in the American Studies Department at the University of California, Davis, United States.

Chuen-Fung Wong is Associate Professor of Music at Macalester College, United States.

Ben Wu is an independent scholar currently residing in the United States.

Hon-Lun Helan Yang is Professor of Music at Hong Kong Baptist University.

Yang Yuanzheng is Professor of Music at the University of Hong Kong.

Yu Hui is a Changjiang Scholar Distinguished Professor of the Chinese Ministry of Education at Yunnan University and Professor at Nanjing Normal University, China.

Zhao Weiping is Professor of Musicology at the Shanghai Conservatory of Music, China.

CHAPTER 1

INTRODUCTION

Frames of Reference for the Study of Music in China and its Diaspora

YU HUI AND JONATHAN P. J. STOCK

As a reflection of a major civilization in the development of human history, Chinese communities have contributed to the world's musical culture a diverse range of performance genres, unique music aesthetics, distinctive philosophical notions, multilayered musical lives, and in-depth academic discourses. The research field is increasingly dynamic and absorbing for those interested in the musical cultures of the current territory of the People's Republic of China (PRC) and its diasporas overseas, with music scholars in many parts of the world attracted to the interpretation and analysis of historical developments, cultural characteristics, and philosophical implications from countless different perspectives.

One possible premise is that the concept of "Chinese music" is self-evident; however, due to consistent shifts in geographic territories throughout history and the migration and spread of diaspora communities worldwide, delineating the notion of "Chinese music" actually proves a complex task. On the one hand, there are still disputes over some parts of the borders of the PRC as recognized by the United Nations. And many music genres are shared by people who live on opposite sides of national boundaries. On the other hand, not only is the PRC multiethnic but also there is a vast number of Han Chinese people living outside of its sovereign territory. Likewise, many ethnic minority people, such as Mongolians, Uyghurs, and Tibetans, who may or may not live inside the current boundaries of the PRC, have created and sustained rich music genres and musical cultures through contact and interaction with the Han Chinese people throughout history. This all makes Chinese people and Chinese lands not entirely equivalent ideas. "Music in China and Its Diaspora" therefore seems a more suitable title for this volume than "Chinese Music," and we hope this choice may also help readers to navigate some of the related academic and political entanglements arising, while also reflecting our authors' academic insights into their subjects.

This volume focuses on the musical heritage of the cultures created by the Han Chinese—bearing the cultural elements of language, lifestyle, and religious beliefs from Confucianism, Daoism, and Mahayana Buddhism—as well as the music of ethnic minorities living inside the current territory of the PRC. The content ranges from introducing key musical eras and contexts of performance, via selected studies of China's musical material and expressive cultures, to the discussion of representative protagonists in Chinese music. Each chapter offers in-depth and individual nuance on a pertinent case, including through the analysis of long-standing aspects of musical culture and exploration of significant recent developments. They provide basic musical information and introductions to the current academic study of their particular topics, making them suitable both for entry-level scholars interested in following present research trends and for specialists looking for deeper insights into specific and complex issues. We intend to expand our reader's horizons on recent international scholarship of musical cultures in Chinese communities around the world, presenting the music and musical cultures of these communities from three distinctive perspectives: "New Directions in History and Theory," "Music Genres and Practices in Evolving Contexts," and "Cross-Cutting Issues in Contemporary Settings." The titles of the three parts are intended not as scientific classifications but rather as crucial perspectives for looking into the limitless phenomena emerging in the musical cultures of communities in China and its diaspora.

In our view, contemporary scholarship on Chinese music can be thought of as having grown up in relation to three realms, each with distinctive legacies and frontiers. The first realm is the historical legacies, recorded in the treatises of Chinese historical literature in philosophy, history, literature, acoustics, and music theory. The contemporary interpretation of this historical literature, including music scores, furthers this inheritance in East Asia and in the West. The second realm is modern music scholarship in mainland China, Taiwan, Hong Kong, and in Chinese communities in other Asian regions; this focuses on analytical approaches and musicological methods. The third realm is represented by the growing number of publications, primarily by Western scholars, written in non-Chinese languages. While European scholarship inherits approaches from its traditions in sinology and comparative musicology, its American counterparts have had particularly heavy effects on trends in China through the disciplines of anthropology and Asian studies.

Regarding the first category, music scholarship in China can be traced back to early antiquity. The *Shijing* 詩經, a song collection that Confucius (551–479 BCE) compiled and used to teach his humanist ideals, recorded various musical activities and the social functions of different music genres. The inscriptions on the bronze bell set excavated in the tomb of Zeng Houyi 曾侯乙 (Marquis Yi of the Zeng kingdom, *c.* 475–433 BCE) recorded the earliest functional system of musical theory in relation to scales and intonations, with their contents still essential topics in modern discussions around Chinese music theory. Many of the treatises emerging from the philosophical branches of the so-called "one hundred schools" in the Spring and Autumn and Warring States periods (770–221 BCE) contain ideas about the social functions of music in society. Among them, *Guanzi* 管子 (*Book of Master Guan*) of the Warring States period (475–221 BCE) recorded a method of adding and subtracting one-third to a vibration object as a way of calculating the pentatonic scale, comparable to the Pythagorean system in the West. Over the next two millennia, Chinese philosophers, scientists, and court scholars—including Jing Fang 京房, Zhu Xi 朱熹, Shen Kuo 沈括, Cai Yuanding 蔡元定, and Zhu Zaiyu 朱載堉—made enormous progress discussing music from the perspectives of philosophy, aesthetics, and acoustics, thus contributing to our understanding of music both as a part of human life and as a natural acoustic phenomenon. The discovery of a mathematical solution for equal temperament by Prince Zhu Zaiyu in the Ming dynasty became a source of national pride in China.

After Western music and Western systems of music education were introduced to China with government sponsorship in the 1920s, traditional Chinese music theory and practical courses gradually came to be taught in conservatories modeled on Western forebears. An undergraduate major called *minzu yinyue lilun* 民族音樂理論 ("national music theory") was created in the early 1960s at the Shanghai Conservatory of Music, training the first generation of students specializing in research on traditional Chinese music to harness methodologies of Western classical musicology and music theory. Meanwhile in the Chinese communities in Taiwan, Hong Kong, and Southeast Asian countries, music scholarship made much progress integrating Western musicology and ethnomusicology methodologies for investigating the traditional music of the Han people and indigenous communities. Many of the musical traditions of the Han Chinese have been preserved relatively intact in these areas. At the same time, political movements in mainland China, including the Cultural Revolution, caused catastrophic damage to living musical traditions, either permanently or intermittently.

While research on historical music continued to produce fruitful results in Taiwan, Hong Kong, Korea, and Japan in the latter half of the twentieth century, scholars in mainland China also made enormous progress in this area before and after the Cultural Revolution. In 2005, musicologists from mainland China and South Korea established the Dongya Yuelü Xuehui 東亞樂律學會 (East Asian Society for Music Theory and Intonation), which convenes every year in one of the two countries to exchange research on music traditions of East Asia.

The introduction of Western ethnomusicology into Asia changed the overall landscape of traditional music research in mainland China from the early 1980s, when research on people making music became normal, no longer a novelty. Many scholars adopted anthropological methods, focusing on social and cultural dimensions. In the meantime, as it has become clear that many new students in the field of traditional music research lack intensive training in analytical skills and the ability to interpret historical music literature, some scholars have begun to worry about the future directions of Chinese music scholarship in China, where the legacies of traditional methods are not as valued as they once were.

For European languages, Marco Polo left probably the earliest historical literature on Chinese music. Later, missionaries provided more detailed accounts of Chinese music to the West, and several also introduced Western music and musical instruments to

China during their sojourns. Some twentieth-century Western scholars pioneered the in-depth and comprehensive research of ancient musical inheritances, including their literature and music scores. This pushed ethnomusicological work in the West into new territories, drawing in subsequent generations of followers, some of whom devoted themselves to the study of historical music while others broadened their foci toward anthropological perspectives on living traditions, popular music, and contemporary musical creations. Taking advantage of plentiful historical resources in the libraries and museums outside of China, readily available interdisciplinary collaborations, and fewer political restrictions, Chinese music research in the West has reached a high point since the Internet became widely available at the end of the twentieth century. Many monographs on Chinese music are being published, more university courses on the subject are offered, and an increasing number of PhD dissertations on Chinese music are completed.

Bringing together current developments in the aforementioned three branches of scholarship, we hope this book produces a frame of reference for Chinese music scholarship worldwide, inspiring further endeavor in this research field, especially on its complex subjects with their interdisciplinary dimensions. The contributors to this anthology come from around the world—Asia, North America, and Europe—bringing to their work different levels of seniority, multiple perspectives on the musical phenomena considered, and varying depths and breadths of approach. We hope the volume objectively reflects the current state of this field of research around the world.

We also hope the publication of such a volume is timely because of the absence of an English-language work exclusively dedicated to providing a holistic account of Chinese music and music scholarship in general. There is, meanwhile, a growing global interest in China, one no longer solely focused on its economic aspects but increasingly attuned to matters of cultural significance. Alongside the inherent value of this book as a compilation of new research perspectives, we believe that benefits on the level of intercontinental scholarly cooperation will ensue from the work entailed to produce it, undoubtedly leading to promising scholarly undertakings in the years ahead.

As coeditors of this volume, we harness a combination of insider and outsider perspectives, from the points of view of the musical cultures we grew up in. Nevertheless, like any specialists in a narrow field of academic research, we understand that we both bring strengths and weaknesses when observing from our particular angles. We seek to overcome the limitations by combining our knowledge base with those of our contributors, Chinese music specialists worldwide, to present this up-to-date view of Chinese music research. We hope this structure allows for both the use of the book as a reference work for quick scholarly access, and "cover-to-cover" reading for those less familiar, or not at all familiar, with Chinese music. Thus, we aim to satisfy the needs of students in ethnomusicology, Chinese music and culture, and Asian studies to grasp important issues in current research, as well as those of Chinese music specialists who intend to expand their expertise in this field.

Glossary

Cai Yuanding 蔡元定, court scholar (1135–1198)
Dongya Yuelü Xuehui 東亞樂律學會, East Asian Society for Music Theory and Intonation
Guanzi 管子, *Book of Master Guan*, written during the Warring States period (475–221 BCE)
Jing Fang 京房, court scholar (77–33 BCE)
minzu yinyue lilun 民族音樂理論, "national music theory," course of study
Shen Kuo 沈括, scholar (*c.* 1031–*c.* 1095)
Shijing 詩經, song collection compiled by Confucius (551–479 BCE)
Zeng Houyi 曾侯乙, Marquis Yi of the Zeng kingdom (*c.* 475–433 BCE)
Zhu Xi 朱熹, court scholar (1130–1200)
Zhu Zaiyu 朱載堉, court scholar (1536–1611)

PART I

NEW DIRECTIONS IN HISTORY AND THEORY

CHAPTER 2

MUSICAL ARCHAEOLOGY AND THE PREHISTORY OF CHINESE MUSIC

YANG YUANZHENG

INTRODUCTION

IN a 1925 seminar class at the Tsinghua University Institute of National Studies entitled "Gushi xinzheng" 古史新證 ("New Evidence on Ancient History"), Wang Guowei 王國維 (1877–1927) explained:

> I can only live in the present, and luckily nowadays in addition to textual sources, there are also excavated remains. From using these materials, my generation can find evidence to supplement written sources, and can prove whether a part of an ancient text is a genuine account of events, and establish whether the other hundred schools still contain a facet of truth. This dual method of investigation can only be carried out in the new atmosphere there is today, and although some ancient books may not yet have secured proof of their veracity, it is not possible to deny their value; and those that have already shown their worth can be wholly given an affirmation; this can be said with certainty (Wang, 1997: 2).

Wang Guowei was a specialist in the study of ancient history, epigraphy, and philology, and a literary figure, so it is unsurprising that his methodology focused on the value of archaeology to textual studies.[1] For him, "textual sources" included the seminal collections of historical texts passed down through the generations while "excavated remains" encompassed ancient writings, oracle bones, manuscripts written on silk, and even the Dunhuang manuscripts in multiple languages. For the music historian, "excavated remains" can be expanded to include musical instruments and the tools used to play them, as well as other aspects of the ceremonial employed in connection to them.

The twentieth century saw much pioneering archaeological excavation of these musical artifacts (Li, 1996). This chapter presents two case studies that shed light on different interactions between new archaeological evidence and already established historical paradigms. In the first, timely unearthing of *zhong* 鐘 bell sets from Bronze Age tombs confirmed a hypothesis that had only just been put forward in the scholarly literature, namely that ancient bells could be sounded with two different tones, even though evidence suggesting this feature had been available, but largely ignored, for more than eight hundred years. Confusion regarding these bells and their sounding pitches was suddenly lifted by those that came from the tombs, and the evidence was almost immediately accepted unequivocally by the scholarly community. In the second, the unprecedented excavation of ancient *qin* 琴 from grave sites caused an entirely new history of the instrument to be written, defining the ancient version as completely different in structure from its classical counterpart. Here, the evidence has been slower in accumulating as more instruments have been unearthed, and its persuasiveness has increased proportionally; only since 2015 has the number of excavated ancient *qin* reached double figures. The acceptance of this new paradigm has also proceeded at an equivalent pace, and arguments still rage.

Bells

An essay by Huang Xiangpeng 黃翔鵬 (1927–97), "Evidence of Pitch in the Neolithic and Bronze Ages and Its Bearing on the History and Development of Chinese Musical Scales" ("Xinshiqi he qingtong shidai de yizhi yinxiang ziliao yu woguo yinjie fazhanshi de wenti") was the first occurrence in the history of Chinese musicology of a scholar postulating the existence of two pitches (henceforth called A- and B-tones) that could be produced by the same Bronze Age bell. The essay was published in two installments, the first in the inaugural issue of the *Collection of Dissertations on Music* (*Yinyue luncong*) in 1978 (Huang, 1978) and the second in the third issue in 1980 (Huang, 1980). It was first completed, however, in 1977 (Huang, 1980: 161), but resistance to its ground-breaking hypothesis was so fierce, in particular from Yang Yinliu 楊蔭瀏 (1899–1984), the director of the Institute of Music Research in Beijing, that it was split into two portions and not published in consecutive issues of the series (Feng, 2007: 60).

In 1978, the unearthing of bell sets from the tomb of Marquis Yi of Zeng 曾侯乙 and the deciphering of their inscriptions immediately confirmed that Huang Xiangpeng's theory was entirely substantiated by archaeological evidence (Hubeisheng bowuguan, 1989: 76–134). A footnote at the end of the second installment of Huang's essay declares: "This essay was first completed in September 1977 and many of the conjectures in it were confirmed by the bell sets [just] excavated from the Marquis Yi of Zeng's tomb" (Huang, 1980: 161). In fact, the practical experience of musicians had already presaged Huang Xiangpeng's discovery by two decades. Bells excavated in Xinyang 信陽 in the state of Chu 楚 were used in a broadcast on the eve of the Chinese New Year in 1958 where the requirement was for the melody "Dongfang hong" 東方紅 ("The East is Red") to be performed (Henansheng wenwu yanjiusuo, 1986: 22). Striking the bells on only the central axis, one note, E#, was still missing from the tune, but the wily musician discovered that it could be produced by striking one of the bells on one side, thus rendering the melody complete (Huang, 1980: 149). That something so readily discovered by a performing musician could have eluded the attention of scholarly circles is a remarkable phenomenon and one that deserves further explanation.

The bells excavated from the tomb of the Marquis Yi of Zeng uniquely have the striking points for both the A- and B-tones marked with gold-inlaid characters that name the pitches sounded, and when they are struck, they still produce the notes given by the characters (Hubeisheng bowuguan, 1989; Cui, 1997; Zou and Tan, 2015). Here was immediate confirmation of Huang Xiangpeng's theory, yet why had it taken more than two thousand years for scholars to become aware that a bell could produce two tones? Was it simply because clear-cut evidence had not appeared until 1978? In fact, at least eight hundred years earlier, proof had already emerged, yet it was not accepted.

The largest *bo* bell in the Marquis Yi of Zeng's tomb hangs on the lowest spar of one of the racks and is furnished with an inscription, which details that it was made by the ruler of Chu for Marquis Yi:

> In the fifty-sixth year in the reign of the ruler [433 BCE] on receiving news from Xiyang [of the death of Marquis Yi of Zeng, *c.* 477–*c.* 433 BCE], the ruler of Chu, Yan Zhang 酓章 [King Hui of Chu, r. 488–432 BCE], had a set of bronze vessels cast for the Marquis Yi of Zeng for use in sacrificial ceremonies for the worship of ancestors, desiring they be positioned in Xiyang for the eternal use and enjoyment of his house (Hubeisheng bowuguan, 1989: 87).

Some 1,500 years later in the Northern Song dynasty (960–1127), two bells were discovered and had the exact same inscription on them. They were unearthed in Anlu (present-day Xiaogan) in Hubei province and passed into the keeping of a Mr. Fan 范 of Fangcheng (henceforth Anlu Bell 1 and Anlu Bell 2). On one the inscription was entirely legible, whereas on the other it had only survived in part. That which was preserved intact was recorded in the *Zhong ding kuanzhi* 鐘鼎款識 (*Zhong Bells and Ding Tripod Inscriptions*) of Wang Houzhi 王厚之 (1131–1204) (Wang, 1802: fols. 31v–32v). Not actually a book in its own right, more a collection of rubbings and related material on album leaves, this volume passed through a distinguished lineage of literati collectors: Xiang Yuanbian 項元汴 (1525–90) who obtained it in 1572 from a Mr. Xu 徐 of Suzhou, then his grandson Xiang Shengmo 項聖謨 (1597–1658), Cao Rong 曹溶 (1613–85), Zhu Yizun 朱彝尊 (1629–1709), Ma Sizan 馬思贊 (1669–1722), Wang Sen 汪森 (1653–1726), and Lu Gong 陸恭 (1741–1818), finally ending up, in 1802, in the hands of Ruan Yuan 阮元 (1764–1849) who published a woodblock facsimile of it (Rong, 1964: 88). The total number of bronzes represented is fifty-nine, though one bell is duplicated (not the bell under discussion here), so the exact number of items is fifty-eight. Rubbings of the fifty-nine are divided into three categories: the lion's share, rubbings 1 through 42, were in Wang Houzhi's own collection; rubbings 43 through 57 were possessions of the son (Qin Xi 秦熺, 1117–61) of the chancellor of the Song-dynasty, Qin Hui 秦檜 (or Qin Kuai, 1091–1155); and the rubbings of the remaining items, 58 and 59, belonged to Shi Gongbi 石公弼 (1061–1115) before being passed on to Wang Houzhi. The fifty-eighth item is the bell whose rubbings are pertinent to the discussion here.

Wang Houzhi's original volume was destroyed in a fire in Ruan Yuan's library in 1843, but the woodblock facsimile survives to this day. Two rubbings were taken of the relevant bell, one of the lower portion of its front (Figure 2.1) and the other of the equivalent portion of its reverse (Figure 2.2). The inscription on the front is identical to that translated above. Underneath the inscription is a *gukui* 顧夔 pattern, which is also to be found in the same position on the reverse of the bell, and this is where the characters denoting the striking points are inscribed: two *shang* 商 characters indicating the A-tone both above and below the *gukui* pattern (that below is situated extremely close to the bottom rim of the bell), while the character *mu* 穆, to the right of the bell, is the B-tone striking point.

In the mid-twentieth century, Rong Geng 容庚, an expert on ancient inscriptions, expressed doubts regarding the veracity of this illustration. An absence of corroborating bells with inscriptions in similar places led him to suggest that either Ruan Yuan had moved its position from elsewhere on the bell or that the inscription was itself an outright forgery (Rong, 1964: 88). However, in 1978 in Baoji, in modern Shaanxi province, a *bo* bell of the duke of Qin 秦 was excavated with inscriptions in the selfsame place (Li, 1984: 88), so these suspicions were allayed.

Although neither of the two bells unearthed in the Northern Song dynasty has survived, and the rubbings for only the one bell whose inscription was complete were preserved by Wang Houzhi, the inscriptions on both bells, both the complete and the partially complete, were copied into a book by Xue Shanggong 薛尚功 titled *Lidai zhongding yiqi kuanzhi fatie* 歷代鐘鼎彝器款識法帖 (*Model Calligraphy of Inscriptions on Bronzes of Successive Dynasties*), published in 1144. The characters that form both inscriptions are present in this volume but no longer as rubbings, so their positions have been substantially altered. The partially complete inscription on the second bell is identical to the second half of the complete inscription on the first bell, but the characters denoting the sounding pitches of the bell on the reverse are different. On the second bell, they are *shao yu fan* 少羽反 and *gong fan* 宮反, and they are written in one vertical column next to the transcription of the inscription; a reasonable assumption is that these correspond to the *shang* and *mu* on the reverse of the first bell. Given the concordance in inscription between the two bells unearthed in the Northern Song dynasty and the *bo* bell in Marquis Yi's tomb, the likelihood is that all three formed part of a set of many bells presented by Yan Zhang to Marquis Yi in 433 BCE (Li, 1984: 88). Apart from the *bo* bell in Marquis Yi's tomb, all others in this set, of which those unearthed in the Northern Song dynasty were but two, would have also had both A- and B-tone pitches inscribed on them. Xue Shanggong explains this phenomenon thus:

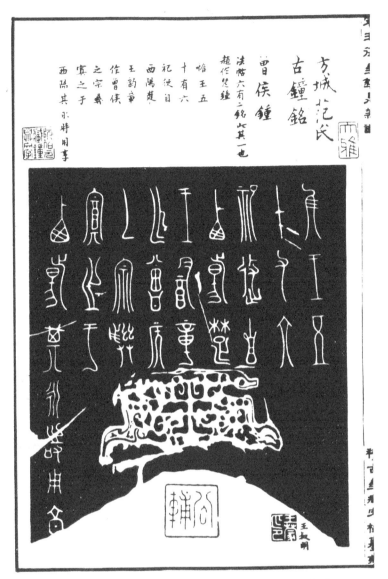

FIGURE 2.1. Woodblock facsimile of a rubbing of the inscription on the lower portion of the front of Anlu Bell 1.

Source: Wang, 1802: fol. 31v.

On the reverse of the first bell are the *mu* character and two *shang* characters, while on the reverse of the second bell are *shao yu fan* and *gong fan* [in total] five characters, whose meaning cannot yet be determined, however, perhaps *gong* and *shang* are relevant to the pitches the bells produce (Xue, 1634: fascicle 6, fols. 53r–54v).

As Xue has selected only one pitch to represent each bell, he appears to have perceived each bell as capable of reproducing only that one pitch—that is, the A-tone.

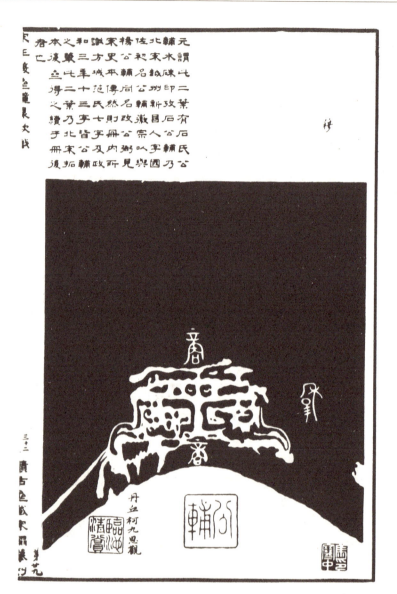

FIGURE 2.2. Woodblock facsimile of a rubbing of the inscription on the lower portion of the back of Anlu Bell 1.

Source: Wang, 1802: fol. 32r.

Some explanation for the double appearance of the *shang* pitch on the reverse of the first bell is required. Of the two *shang*, by comparison with that above the *gukui* pattern, that situated on the bottom rim seems rather squashed, so perhaps clarity dictated that the manifestation on the rim needed a second imprint above (Fang, 2015: 62). Interpretations of the pitch denoted by the *mu* character vary, but it is either another note or an interval relative to the *shang* pitch, probably a minor third higher. On the second bell, the A-tone *yu* pitch is produced by the central striking point and the B-tone *gong* pitch by the striking point on one side, so thus also a minor third higher in pitch; the characters denoting both pitches are supplied with the suffix *fan*, which puts them up an octave, and defined by the *shao*, which governs both pitches and also indicates the higher octave.

Of the sixty-five bells excavated from the tomb of Marquis Yi, six have the same two-tone pitch arrangement as the second of the bells that emerged in the Northern Song dynasty—that is, the *shao yu* characters inscribed at the A-tone striking point and *gong fan* inscribed into the B-tone striking point (Fang, 2015: 62). Taking one of these six as an example, given that there are three bell racks and three spars to each rack, it is catalogued as bell four (rack one, middle spar). Identically to Anlu Bell 1, fourteen of the Marquis Yi bells also have the pitch *shang* inscribed at their A-tone striking point, and all of these have the pitch *qing jue* 清角 inscribed at their B-tone striking point too; that pitch is a minor third higher than the *shang* pitch (Wang, 2015: 12–20), confirming that the *mu* character at the B-tone striking point of Anlu Bell 1 also indicated a minor third higher.

Similar evidence had emerged both in the Northern Song dynasty and in 1978 indicating that ancient bells could be sounded with two tones. Yet while Song-dynasty campanologists did not notice the phenomenon, more recent scholars did, so some explanation for this discrepancy should be sought. In fact, Northern Song–dynasty scholars were fully conversant with ancient texts and Han dynasty (202 BCE–220 CE) commentaries on them, and they were riding on a wave of enthusiasm for archaeological discovery and of an attitude promoting resurgence of ancient practice. Many bell sets were manufactured in this period in imitation of pre-Qin dynasty models, and inscribed with the pitches they played, but always with only one pitch at the A-tone striking point and never two (Watt, 1996: 222–28).

The issue of the extent to which actual objects should be brought into the discussion, as opposed to there being reliance on text alone, was one Northern Song–dynasty scholars were prepared to consider. Ouyang Xiu 歐陽修 (1007–72) in 1064 succinctly criticizes over-reliance on text:

> As for Confucian researchers into ritual, simply to rely on information transmitted by the written word and not to look at the objects themselves is doomed to give rise to a situation by which the objects exist in name only but in reality are misunderstood (Ouyang, 1929: fascicle 134, fols. 9r–v).

In a similar vein, Lin Xiyi 林希逸 (1193–1271), in his *Kaogong ji jie* 考工記解 (*Commentary on Records of the Examination of Craftsmanship*), quotes Lin Guangzhao 林光朝 (1114–78, pseudonym Aixuan):

> Aixuan says: *Bogu tu* 博古圖 [*Pictures of a Myriad of Ancient Objects*] had its inception in the Xuanhe era [1119–1125] and was not available in the Han and Jin dynasties. Those ancient objects that had been unearthed down the centuries were first recorded in pictures in the Xuanhe era in order to make them available to later generations, and had not been seen by the Confucianists of the Han and Jin

dynasties, so they are not to be blamed for being ignorant of them. Therefore, Nie Chongyi's 聶崇義 *San li tu* 三禮圖 [*Illustrations to the Three Canons of Confucian Classics Dealing with Ritual*] had nothing that preceded it, and a jade millet circlet is illustrated with a rice stalk and a jade bulrush circlet with a reed, both images entirely derived from his understanding of the meaning of the characters, but he was ignorant of the fact that a jade millet circlet is like a jade belt of today on which patterns of ears of millet have been carved, as can be seen by perusing the *Bogu tu* (Lin, 1969: 16,435).

In fact, Lin Xiyi positions this section precisely at a point preceding discussion of the manufacture of bells, which imbues it with added significance.

Taking a corpus of this type of revivalist book—for example, Lü Dalin's 呂大臨 (1044-91) *Kaogu tu* 考古圖 (*Examining Antiquities in Pictures*, 1092),[2] Wang Fu's 王黼 (1079-1126) *Xuanhe bogu tu* (1123),[3] Xue Shanggong's *Lidai Zhongding yiqi kuanshi fatie* (1144), Wang Qiu's 王俅 *Xiao tang jigu lu* 嘯堂集古錄 (*Records of the Wailing Hall's Collection of Ancient Bronzes*, 1176),[4] and Wang Houzhi's *Zhong ding kuanzhi*—the direction of the argument remains throughout that actual objects are to be used only to demonstrate what is described in ancient text, and the objects themselves remain relegated to this junior role. In other words, writers were aware of potential contradictions between object and text, but their paradigm was governed by the overriding purpose of providing exegesis to ancient text, and by the conviction that examining objects themselves was only useful insofar as it served this role. A case in point is the cross section of ancient bells. In order to produce the required two tones, they have to be cast with a cross section that is almond- or oval-shaped and not one that is circular. Scholars of the Song dynasty were well aware of the shape of the ancient prototypes they copied, and this shape is also described in ancient texts, but they did not associate it with producing two tones as there was no mention of this therein.

THE QIN

Issues surrounding bells and their usage had been present in the scholarly ether for more than eight hundred years, and the solution came suddenly and comprehensively in 1978 with the excavation of the Marquis Yi of Zeng's tomb in Leigudun. By comparison, no one had suggested that the classical *qin* was anything other than the ancient *qin* until archaeology first unearthed a specimen. This happened in 1973, and it is from that date that the revisionist view of the history of the *qin* had its inception. The *qin* in question (Figure 2.4) was excavated from a tomb in Mawangdui near Changsha (Hunansheng bowuguan and Zhongguo kexueyuan kaogu yanjiusuo, 1974; Hunansheng bowuguan and Hunansheng wenwu kaogu yanjiusuo, 2004: 43–73; Yang, 2012: 196, 206; and Yang, 2020: 46–47), and to the surprise of all concerned it was completely different from the classical image of the instrument as promulgated by countless illustrations from the

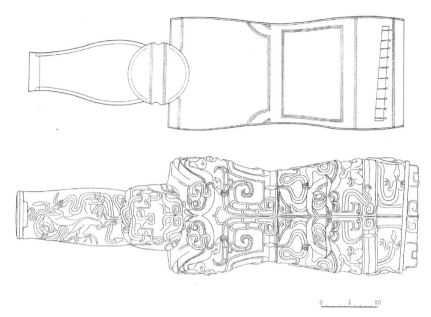

FIGURE 2.3. Line drawings of the ten-stringed *qin* from the tomb of Marquis Yi of Zeng, Suizhou, Hubei province (above), and the highly decorated ten-stringed *qin* excavated from Jiuliandun tomb no. 1, Hubei province (below).

Source: drawing by Yang Yuanzheng.

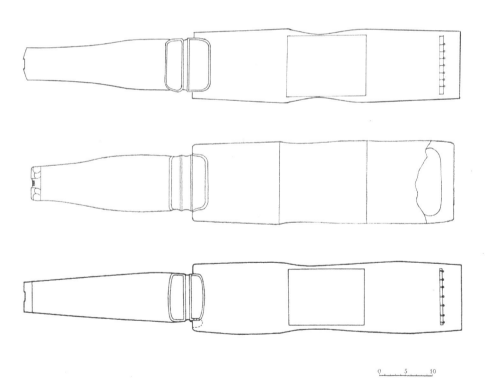

FIGURE 2.4. Line drawings of the seven-stringed *qin* from Guodian tomb no. 1, Hubei province (above); Changsha tomb no. 1195, Wulipai, Hunan province (middle); and Mawangdui tomb 3, Changsha, Hunan province (below).

Source: drawing by Yang Yuanzheng.

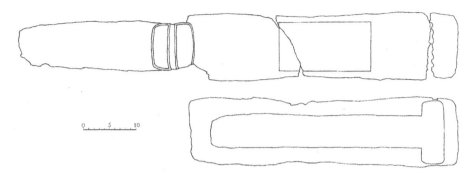

FIGURE 2.5. Line drawings of the seven-stringed *qin* excavated from Liu He's tomb, Nanchang, Jiangxi province; *qin* 1 (M1: 561), front and back plates, top view.

Source: drawing by Yang Yuanzheng.

Song dynasty onward (Yang, 2012). Since then, a total of five ancient *qin* (Figures 2.3 and 2.4) have been unearthed in various locations,[5] but most significantly, another five (Figures 2.5 and 2.6) have emerged since 2015 from a single tomb, that of Liu He 劉賀 (92–59 BCE), latterly the Marquis of Haihun 海昏. This reservoir provides the scholar with a total of ten instruments from which to draw conclusions, and the inescapable indication is that ancient *qin* conformed to a completely different range of specifications from those of the classical version.

At the heart of the definition of the ancient *qin* is its division into five registers rather than the whole being considered a unified item, as is the case with the classical *qin*. Moving down the instrument, the first three registers comprise the hollow sound-box, at first with its sides parallel (the first register), then its sides indented (the second register), and finally its sides parallel once more (the third register). The fourth register is a joint that connects to the fifth register, the tail, which is solid (Yang, 2016).

The significance of the Mawangdui instrument was recognized by the archeologists responsible for its excavation. In the *Archaeological Fieldwork Excavation Report* issued afterward, they muse: "Does this *qin* represent a type which was widely played at the time? Or was it simply an aberration? Or perhaps it is a specimen much earlier than the tomb itself. These are all questions that are worth considering" (Hunansheng bowuguan and Hunansheng wenwu kaogu yanjiusuo, 2004: vol. 1, 182).

The first reactions of scholars in the field were not only doubt and amazement but also a desire to position the new discovery within already existing paradigms. Thus, there evolved a mainstream view that regarded the *qin* in ancient textual sources as undoubtedly indigenous to the central plains, but this instrument was from the outlying Chu region of southern China, so not mentioned in the texts, and was by definition a rare variant confined to this area; the classical *qin* was a descendant of the *qin* of the central plains and not this evolutionary dead end. For example, Wang Zichu 王子初 posed the question: "Did the modern *qin* that is seen today whose sound-box extends for the length of the instrument evolve directly from this 'Chu'-style instrument?" To which, he answers:

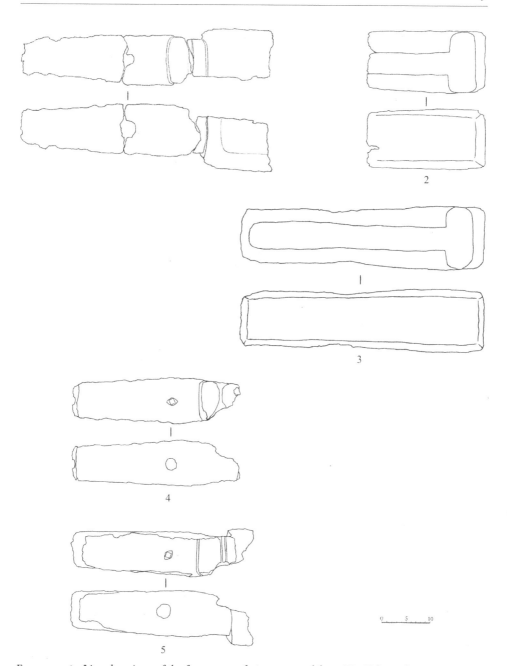

FIGURE 2.6. Line drawings of the fragments of *qin* excavated from Liu He's tomb: *qin* 2 (M1: 342 and M1: 366), *qin* 3 (M1: 473), *qin* 4 (M1: 481), *qin* 5 (M1: 656), all viewed from above and below.

Source: drawing by Yang Yuanzheng.

The vast majority of *qin* recorded in ancient texts were likely to have been those that were played most widely in the central plains, which were of a type to be differentiated from that excavated in Mawangdui, the Chu-style *qin*.... The Mawangdui specimen is a "half sound-box" *qin*, and the extent of its cultural dispersal strictly limited. The reason why the "half sound-box" *qin* was not seen in later generations can only be explained in the following ways: either after the Western Han dynasty [206 BCE–8 CE], it gradually disappeared into the wider flow of history, or it had already been absorbed into the *qin* of the central plains, which had subsequent manifestation in the instrument styles of later eras (Wang, 2005: 42–43).

Similarly, Zheng Minzhong 鄭珉中, when discussing the Mawangdui *qin*, as well as two later unearthed in Guodian and Leigudun, summarizes:

> The three places where the three *qin* were excavated are all in the Chu region, so they are undoubtedly of the type found in that area. Using the vocabulary of the state of Jin 晉, they could be regarded as "southern *qin*" or "aboriginal *qin*." Aboriginal *qin* are naturally to be distinguished from the seven-string *qin* of the state of Jin (Zheng, 2006: 19).

Conveniently for proponents of this hypothesis, owing to geological and climatic factors, tombs of the central plains are unlikely to preserve lacquered wooden grave goods, and no *qin* have yet been excavated from this region.

Two texts are crucial to illuminating this issue. The first is a poem "Qifa" 七發 ("Seven Stimuli") by Mei Sheng 枚乘 (d. 140 BCE), written to expel apathy and depression suffered by Liu Wu 劉武 (d. 144 BCE), ruler of the royal fiefdom of Liang 梁. The following lines of the poem are relevant:

> The Dragon Gate Mountain's *tong* tree
> In height, a hundred *chi* feet and without branches
> ...
> Let Master Craftsman Zhi 摯 fell the tree and carve it into a *qin*
> Taking silk of wild cocoons to make the strings
> An orphan's decorated belt hook for a bridge
> A nine-times widow's ear pendants as *yue* 約 tuning pins[6]

The second important text is composed of two passages from the Prince of Huainan Liu An's 劉安 (179–122 BCE) eponymous text, *Huainanzi* 淮南子. The first passage is found in the chapter "Cultivating Effort" (phrases in the text are numbered for ease of discussion below):

> (1) There are those who are blind, (2) whose eyes are unable to differentiate between day and night, (3) or distinguish between white or black, (4) however, when they play the *qin* and stroke the strings, (5) right hand repeatedly plucking, left hand executing glissandos back and forth, (6) a myriad of finger techniques, (7) their hands exhibit virtuoso vivacity, (8) neither missing a single note nor a single string.[7]

The second passage is found in the chapter "The Ruler's Techniques":

> (9) Zou Ji 鄒忌 [d. *c*. 341 BCE] played on note on his *qin*, (10) and King Wei 威 of Qi 齊 [r. 356–320 BCE] was mournful all evening in response to its sadness.[8]

In support of Wang Zichu and Zheng Minzhong's interpretation, these two texts might be given explanation such as that provided by the philologist Rao Zongyi 饒宗頤, who cites the Tang-dynasty exegete Li Shang's 李善 (630–89) annotations to Mei Sheng's poem by which the *yue* [tuning pins] are regarded as *hui* nodes of vibration. With respect to phrases (5) and (9) of *Huainanzi*, where the original texts are "*san tan fu hui*" 參彈復徽 and "*Zou Ji yi hui*" 鄒忌一徽, Rao Zongyi notices that:

> The phrase "*fu hui*" describes a repeated movement back and forth at the *hui* nodal point, and [the term *hui*] is being used as a noun. In the phrase "*yi hui*," [the term *hui*] is being used as a verb, meaning to "stop a string at the position of a certain *hui* nodal point." ... Therefore, *qin* had *hui*, and this was already a fact in the Western Han dynasty. Although the *qin* excavated in Mawangdui is not furnished with *hui*, not to interpret in this way, but to go as far as to state that in the Han dynasty there were no *hui* and to regard *The Huainanzi* with suspicion, is a viewpoint entirely without foundation. (Rao, 1987: 5–6)

Taking an opposite point of view, Wu Zhao 吳釗 reflects that: "From the perspective of the categorization of tools," the ten-stringed instrument from Leigudun and seven-stringed version from Mawangdui can be compared with the present-day *qin* as follows:

> in spite of the severing of the tradition at various points and although a direct evolutionary descent through a series of distinct developments cannot be traced, in terms of fundamental construction—head, shoulders, waist, tail, and "nut" (at the far end of the tail)—it is in substance the same instrument. (Wu, 1989: 33)

Bo Lawergren in his essay on the subject goes as far as to classify the *qin* from after approximately 500 CE as "the classical *qin*" and that from before as "the ancient *qin*" and propounds: "These ancient instruments are ancestors of the later classical *qin*" (2000: 74). He criticizes scholars who "refuse to accept that the two have a direct relationship and persist in clinging to the view that the ancient *qin* is only an aberration of the Chu region" as "conservatives" while stating that the process of evolution of the ancient *qin* to the classical *qin* is furnished with ample proof by depictions found on the reverse sides of bronze mirrors (Lawergren, 2008: 127–28). Meanwhile, Zheng Zuxiang 鄭祖襄 further amplifies Guo Moruo's 郭沫若 (1892–1978) view that "*qin* and *se* zithers were new instruments that came into the territory of the Zhou dynasty empire from outside during its later years" (Guo, 1982: vol. 2, 278–311), and proposes: "The *qin* was originally an instrument of the Miao 苗 barbarian confederacy and belonged to ancient Chu culture. It came into the mainstream of Chinese culture from Chu culture" (Zheng, 2008: 52).

With regard to the Western Han–dynasty texts "Qifa" and *Huainanzi*, Zheng Zuxiang (1986: 25–26), Xu Jian 許健 (1988: 114–15), and Feng Jiexuan 馮潔軒 (1988: 74–77) all consider it inappropriate to take as gospel the explanatory notes of Li Shan, compiled eight hundred years subsequent to the original writing of the texts, and instead lend more weight to those closer in time, for example Xu Shen 許慎 (58 CE–147 CE) and Gao You 高誘 (active 205–212 CE). To the phrase (9) of *Huainanzi*, Xu Shen's note adds: "When playing the *qin*, sliding along the strings is known as '*hui*'" (Li, 1977: 242). Gao You's note to the phrase (5) suggests: "'*San tan*' means '[with the right hand, pluck the] strings together'; '*fu hui*' means '[slide repeatedly] back and forth along the strings with the [left] hand.'" And Gao states further that the character *hui* in this usage should be pronounced "suī" 繀 instead of "huī" 徽 (Gao, 1936: 175). Zheng Zuxiang summarizes:

> Therefore, from Liu An of the Western Han dynasty down to Xu Shen and Gao You of the Eastern Han dynasty [25–220 CE], the character "*hui*" with respect to performance on the *qin* pertains either to moving the left hand fingers along the strings while plucking them or plucking them vigorously at a swift tempo, and does not refer to the *hui* nodes of vibration of later eras (Zheng, 1986: 26).

Without doubt, the shape and construction of the excavated *qin* are extremely different from those of the classical *qin*. The two opinions cited above diverge from each other in explaining these discrepancies in the following ways: Wu Zhao and others regard them as products of stages in the evolution of the instrument, while Wang Zichu spearheads a desire to explain them simply as regional aberrations and considers the excavated *qin* to be representatives of a Chu region variant recorded in ancient documents—in other words, Zheng Minzhong's "southern *qin*" or "aboriginal *qin*."

Given that the occupant of the Mawangdui tomb was a son of the Minister of the state of Changsha, an individual called Li Cang 利蒼, and also that he died in 186 BCE while the state of Changsha was still under the sway of Wu-surnamed rulers unrelated to the Liu-surnamed emperors of the Han dynasty, the notion that he might still have been buried with a "Chu"-style *qin* still has a degree of forced logic. By comparison, Liu He, in his erstwhile capacity of ruler of Changyi 昌邑, had buried with him many lacquered grave goods and instruments that had come from his former territory of Changyi in modern Shandong province, well away from the Chu sphere of influence. This being so, simply owing to the location of his tomb on the marches separating the regions of Wu 吳 and Chu, to define the *qin* buried therein as "Chu *qin*," "southern *qin*," or "aboriginal *qin*" is palpably absurd. From the joint perspectives of materials used and craftsmanship, the surviving fragments of the five *qin* that were excavated there were self-evidently not of instruments made at the same time. Still more, they could not possibly have all been carved from felled timber into finished items in the narrow window of four years when Liu He was in Yuzhang, between the third year of the Yuankang 元康 era (63 BCE) when he was ennobled (or banished) as the Marquis of Haihun to the third year of the Shenjue 神爵 era (59 BCE) when he died. Their position in the tomb also strongly suggests that they were not for the use of professional musicians but were instead played by Liu He himself for personal entertainment and enlightenment. If this was indeed the case, how could the instruments that Liu He had played in Changyi in modern Shandong province be so-called "Chu *qin*"?

In fact, in construction, the five lacquered *qin* excavated from the tomb of Liu He are extremely similar to those found in Guodian (mid-Warring States period), Wulipai (late Warring States period), and Mawangdui (early Western Han dynasty), to a degree sufficient to overturn completely the idea that this corpus might be "southern *qin*" or "aboriginal *qin*"; instead, they are unquestionably the "elegant" or "courtly" *qin* of the Han era. *Huainanzi* was completed before 139 BCE and "Qifa" written to admonish the ruler of the state of Liang, an individual called Liu Wu, so both belong to a period slightly later than the seven-stringed *qin* in the Mawangdui tomb of the early Western Han dynasty yet before Liu He's burial together with five specimens of seven-stringed *qin* in the mid-Western Han dynasty. These latter six *qin* represent a sufficiently critical mass of evidence to confirm that the exegesis of Xu Shen and Gao You of the Eastern Han dynasty, regarding interpretation of the character *hui*, is reliable, and to demonstrate that Li Shan's explanation of *yue* as *hui* nodes of vibration was simply a misunderstanding circumscribed by his direct knowledge only of *qin* of the Sui and Tang dynasties (581–907).

Conclusions

Wang Guowei's paradigm was for archaeology to supplement and provide evidence for what was already available in text. The discovery of the two-tone bells in the Marquis of Zeng's tomb indicated that archaeology could act independently and provide something entirely new. This was an exponential expansion of the value of archaeology to historical enquiry. Nothing in the ancient texts had suggested that the ancient *qin* was different from the classical *qin*, yet again it was excavations that caused the history to be completely rewritten. Resistance to paradigm change is always likely, and in this case such resistance has been, and still is, slow in dissolving. But here once more, excavated finds have transformed archaeology from Wang Guowei's junior player in the service of textual exegesis to the driving force of new discovery.

Glossary

Cao Rong 曹溶, scholar-official (1613–85)
Chu 楚, a Zhou-dynasty vassal state
"Dongfang hong" 東方紅, "The East is Red," revolutionary song
Feng Jiexuan 馮潔軒, musicologist
Gao You 高誘, scholar and bureaucrat (active 205–212 CE)
gong fan 宮反, a scale degree
gukui 顧夔, decorative pattern
Guo Moruo 郭沫若, author, historian, and government official (1892–1978)
Huang Xiangpeng 黃翔鵬, musicologist (1927–97)
hui 徽, marked nodes on the *qin* that guide finger placement

Li Cang 利蒼, minister of the state of Changsha (d. 186 BCE)
Li Shang 李善, scholar and commentator (630–89)
Lin Xiyi 林希逸, scholar-official (1193–1271)
Lin Guangzhao 林光朝, scholar-official (1114–78)
Liu An 劉安, Prince of Huainan (179–122 BCE)
Liu He 劉賀, Marquis of Haihun (92–59 BCE)
Liu Wu 劉武, Prince Xiao of Liang (d. 144 BCE)
Lu Gong 陸恭, painter and collector (1741–1818)
Lü Dalin 呂大臨, paleographer (1044–91)
Ma Sizan 馬思贊, book collector (1669–1722)
Mei Sheng 枚乘, poet (d. 140 BCE)
Miao 苗, barbarian confederacy
mu 穆, a scale degree
Nie Chongyi 聶崇義, Confucian classist
Ouyang Xiu 歐陽修, scholar-official (1007–72)
Qi Weiwang 齊威王, King Wei of Qi (r. 356–320 BCE)
Qi 齊, a Zhou-dynasty vassal state
qin 琴, zither
Qin 秦, a Zhou-dynasty vassal state
Qin Hui 秦檜, a chancellor of the Song dynasty (1091–1155)
Qin Xi 秦熺, the son of Qin Hui
qing jue 清角, a scale degree
Rao Zongyi 饒宗頤, historian
Ruan Yuan 阮元, scholar-official (1764–1849)
shang 商, a scale degree
shao yu fan 少羽反, a scale degree
Shenjue 神爵, era (61–58 BCE)
sui 繀, to reel silk
Wang Fu 王黼, politician (1079–1126)
Wang Guowei 王國維, historian (1877–1927)
Wang Houzhi 王厚之, paleographer (1131–1204)
Wang Qiu 王俅, paleographer
Wang Sen 汪森, literatus (1653–1726)
Wu 吳, a Zhou-dynasty vassal state
Wu Zhao 吳釗, musicologist
Xiang Shengmo 項聖謨, painter (1597–1658)
Xiang Yuanbian 項元汴, collector (1525–90)
Xu Jian 許健, musicologist
Xu Shen 許慎, philologist (58–147 CE)
Xue Shanggong 薛尚功, paleographer (fl. 1144)
Yan Zhang 酓章, King Hui of Chu (r. 488–432 BCE)
Yang Yinliu 楊蔭瀏, musicologist (1899–1984)
Yuankang 元康, era (65–61 BCE)
yue 約, tuning pins
Zeng Hou Yi 曾侯乙, Marquis Yi of Zeng (d. 433 BCE)
Zheng Minzhong 鄭珉中, calligrapher and art historian
Zheng Zuxiang 鄭祖襄, musicologist

Zhi 挚, master craftsman
Zou Ji 鄒忌, politician (d. *c.* 341 BCE)
zhong 鐘, bell
Zhu Yizun 朱彝尊, author and poet (1629–1709)

Notes

1. The research for this essay was supported by the General Research Fund of the University Grants Committee of Hong Kong, the Cross-national Interdisciplinary Research Grant of Harvard-Yenching Institute, and the Hsu Long-sing Research Fund.
2. For a facsimile edition, see Lü, 1987.
3. For a facsimile edition, see Wang, 1969.
4. For a facsimile edition, see Wang, 1983. The outline copy of the inscriptions on the back and front of Anlu Bell 1 appears on pages 185–186.
5. The second specimen of ancient *qin* was excavated in Marquis Yi's tomb (early Warring States period), see Hubeisheng bowuguan, 1989: 166–67; Lawergren, 1997 and 2000; Li, 1996: 448–50; Li, 2010: 48–52; Yang, 2012; and Yang, 2020: 29–31. The third specimen was excavated in Wulipai 五里牌 (late Warring States period), see Changshashi wenwu gongzuodui, 1982: 34; Huang, 1984; Hunansheng bowuguan, 2000: vol. 1, 53 and 56; and Yang, 2020: 43–45. The fourth specimen was excavated in Guodian 郭店 (mid-Warring States period), see Zhongguo yinyue wenwu daxi bianjibu, 1996: 144; Hubeisheng Jingmenshi bowuguan, 1997: 45; Jianbo shufa xuan bianjizu, 2002: 43–68; and Yang, 2020: 42–43. The fifth specimen was excavated in Jiuliandun 九連墩 (mid-Warring States period), see Hubeisheng bowuguan, 2007: i; Shenzhen bowuguan, 2010: 12 and 16; Hubeisheng wenwu kaogu yanjiusuo, 2003; Yang, 2015; and Yang, 2020: 32–41.
6. For the Chinese text of the entire poem, see Ju, 1979: 6–25. For an English translation of the complete text by Douglass A. White, see Victor, 1994: 411–28.
7. For the Chinese text of the quotation, see Liu et al., 1989: 213. For an English translation of the complete chapter, see Major et al., 2010: 757–88.
8. For the Chinese text of the quotation, see Liu et al., 1989: 87. For an English translation of the complete chapter, see Major et al., 2010: 289–340.

References

Changshashi wenwu gongzuodui 長沙市文物工作隊 [Changsha Municipal Institute of Cultural Relics and Archaeology]. (1982). "Changshashi Wulipai Zhanguo muguo mu" "長沙市五里牌戰國木槨墓" [A Tomb with Wooden Outer Coffin of Zhanguo Era in Wulipai, Changsha City]. *Hunan kaogu jikan* 湖南考古輯刊 [Hunan Archaeology] 1: 32–38.

Cui Xian 崔憲. (1997). *Zenghou Yi bianzhong zhongming jiaoshi jiqi lüxue yanjiu* 曾侯乙編鐘鐘銘校釋及其律學研究 [Inscriptions on the Chime Bells of the Marquis Yi of Zeng: Critical Edition and Study of Temperament]. Beijing: Renmin yinyue chubanshe.

Fang Jianjun 方建軍. (2015). "Chuwang Yan Zhang zhong shang shang mu shijie" "楚王酓章鐘'商商穆'試解" [A Tentative Interpretation of the "*Shang Shang Mu*" Inscription on the Bells of King Yan Zhang of Chu]. *Huangzhong* 黃鐘 [Journal of Wuhan Conservatory of Music], no. 1: 60–63.

Feng Jiexuan 馮潔軒. (1988). "Shuo hui: jianyi Zheng Rao er wen" "說徽: 兼議鄭、饒二文" [On the Question of *Hui*: An Appraisal of Zheng Zuxiang and Rao Zongyi's Opinions]. *Zhongguo yinyue xue* 中國音樂學 [Musicology in China], no. 4: 74-92.

Feng Jiexuan 馮潔軒. (2007). "Jinian Huang Xiangpeng xiansheng faxian yi zhong shuang yin sanshi zhounian" "紀念黃翔鵬先生發現一鐘雙音三十周年" [The 30th Anniversary of Mr. Huang Xiangpeng's Discovery of the Two-tone Bells]. *Yinyue yishu* 音樂藝術 [Art of Music], no. 4: 57-61.

Gao You 高誘, commentator. (1936). *Hainanzi* 淮南子. Shanghai: Zhonghua shuju.

Guo Moruo 郭沫若. (1982). "Shi pipan shu houji" "十批判書後記" [Ten Critiques: Epilogue]. In *Guo Moruo quanji (Lishi bian)* 郭沫若全集 (歷史編) [Complete Works of Guo Moruo (Historical Studies)], vol. 2, 278-311. Beijing: Renmin chubanshe.

Henansheng wenwu yanjiusuo 河南省文物研究所 [Henan Provincial Institute of Archaeology], ed. (1986). *Xinyang Chu mu* 信陽楚墓 [Two Tombs of the Chu State at Xinyang]. Beijing: Wenwu chubanshe.

Huang Gangzheng 黃綱正. (1984). "Changsha chutu de Zhanguo qin" "長沙出土的戰國琴" [A *Qin* of the Zhanguo Era Excavated in Changsha]. *Yueqi* 樂器 [Musical Instruments] 54: 19-20, and plates 1-5.

Huang Xiangpeng 黃翔鵬. (1978). "Xinshiqi he qingtong shidai de yizhi yinxiang ziliao yu woguo yinjie fazhan shi de wenti (I)" "新石器和青銅時代的已知音響資料與我國音階發展史問題 (上)" [Evidence of Pitch in the Neolithic and Bronze Ages and Its Bearing on the History and Development of Chinese Musical Scales, part 1]. *Yinyue luncong* 音樂論叢 [A Collection of Dissertations on Music] 1: 184-206.

Huang Xiangpeng 黃翔鵬. (1980). "Xinshiqi he qingtong shidai de yizhi yinxiang ziliao yu woguo yinjie fazhan shi de wenti (II)" "新石器和青銅時代的已知音響資料與我國音階發展史問題 (下)" [Evidence of Pitch in the Neolithic and Bronze Ages and Its Bearing on the History and Development of Chinese Musical Scales, part 2]. *Yinyue luncong* 音樂論叢 [A Collection of Dissertations on Music] 3: 126-61.

Hubeisheng bowuguan 湖北省博物館 [Hubei Provincial Museum], ed. (1989). *Zenghou Yi mu* 曾侯乙墓 [Tomb of Marquis Yi of Zeng], 2 vols. Beijing: Wenwu chubanshe.

Hubeisheng bowuguan 湖北省博物館 [Hubei Provincial Museum], ed. (2007). *Jiuliandun: Changjiang zhongyou de Chuguo guizu damu* 九連墩: 長江中游的楚國貴族大墓 [Jiuliandun: Large Tombs of a Chu Noble in the Middle Reaches of the Yangtze]. Beijing: Wenwu chubanshe.

Hubeisheng Jingmenshi bowuguan 湖北省荊門市博物館 [Jingmen City Museum, Hubei Province]. (1997). "Jingmen Guodian 1 hao Chu mu" "荊門郭店一號楚墓" [Chu Tomb no. 1 at Guodian, Jingmen]. *Wenwu* 文物 [Cultural Relics] 494: 35-48.

Hubeisheng wenwu kaogu yanjiusuo 湖北省文物考古研究所 [Hubei Provincial Archaeological Research Institute]. (2003). "Hubei Zaoyangshi Jiuliandun Chu mu" "湖北棗陽市九連墩楚墓" [Chu Tombs at Jiuliandun, Zaoyang City, Hubei Province]. *Kaogu* 考古 [Archaeology] 430: 11-12.

Hunansheng bowuguan 湖南省博物館 [Hunan Provincial Museum]. (2000). *Changsha Chu mu* 長沙楚墓 [Changsha Chu State Tombs], 2 vols. Beijing: Wenwu chubanshe.

Hunansheng bowuguan 湖南省博物館 [Hunan Provincial Museum] and Hunansheng wenwu kaogu yanjiusuo 湖南省文物考古研究所 [Institute of Archaeology of Hunan Province]. (2004). *Changsha Mawangdui er san hao Han mu, di yi jun, tianye kaogu fajue baogao* 長沙馬王堆二、三號漢墓，第一卷: 田野考古發掘報告 [Tombs 2 and 3 of the

Han Dynasty at Mawangdui, Changsha: Report on Excavation, vol. 1]. Beijing: Wenwu chubanshe.

Hunansheng bowuguan 湖南省博物館 [Hunan Provincial Museum] and Zhongguo kexueyuan kaogu yanjiusuo 中國科學院考古研究所 [Institute of Archaeology, Chinese Academy of Sciences]. (1974). "Changsha Mawangdui er san hao Han mu fajue jianbao" "長沙馬王堆二、三號漢墓發掘簡報" [Brief Report on the Excavation of Tombs 2 and 3 of the Han Dynasty at Mawangdui, Changsha]. *Wenwu* 文物 [Cultural Relics] 218: 39–48.

Jianbo shufa xuan bianjizu 簡帛書法選編輯組 [Editorial Board of Selected Calligraphy of Bamboo Slips and Silk Manuscripts]. (2002). *Guodian Chu mu zhujian: Laozi jia* 郭店楚墓竹簡：老子甲 [Bamboo Slips of Guodian Chu Tomb: The Book of Laozi, Version One]. Beijing: Wenwu chubanshe.

Ju Duiyuan 瞿蛻園, ed. (1979). *Han Wei Liuchao fu xuan* 漢魏六朝賦選 [Selected Rhapsodies from the Han, Wei, and the Six Dynasties]. Shanghai: Shanghai guji chubanshe.

Lawergren, Bo. (1997). "To Tune a String: Dichotomies and Diffusions between the Near and Far East." In *Ultra Terminum Vagari: Scritti in onore di Carl Nylander*, edited by Börje Magnusson et al., 175–92. Rome: Edizioni Quasar.

Lawergren, Bo. (2000). "Strings." In *Music in the Age of Confucius*, edited by Jenny F. So, 65–86. Washington, DC: Freer Gallery of Art and Arthur M. Sackler Gallery.

Lawergren, Bo. 勞鏄. (2008). "Qinshi: Gongyuanqian 433 nian qianhou de qin" "琴史：公元前433年前後的琴" [The History of the *Qin*: The *Qin* at 433 BCE]. *Zhongming huanyu* 鍾鳴寰宇 [Bells Resonating through the Universe], edited by Li Youping 李幼平, 125–42. Wuhan: Wuhan chubanshe.

Li Chunyi 李純一. (1996). *Zhongguo shanggu chutu yueqi zonglun* 中國上古出土樂器綜論 [Survey of the Excavated Musical Instruments of Ancient China]. Beijing: Wenwu chubanshe.

Li Guangming 李光明. (2010). "Zenghou Yi mu shi xian qin xianzhen tiaoxian fangfa kaobian" "曾侯乙墓十弦琴弦軫調弦方法考辨" [An Examination of the Tuning Method of the Ten-stringed *Qin* Excavated from the Tomb of the Marquis Yi of Zeng]. *Yinyue yanjiu* 音樂研究 [Music Research] 144: 48–52.

Li Ling 李零. (1984). "Songdai chutu de Chuwang Yan Zhang zhong" "宋代出土的楚王酓章鐘" [King Yan Zhang of Chu's Bells Unearthed in the Song Dynasty]. *Jianghan kaogu* 江漢考古 [Jianghan Archaeology], no. 1: 88–89.

Li Shang 李善, commentator. (1977). *Wenxuan* 文選 [Selections of Refined Literature]. Beijing: Zhonghua shuju.

Lin Xiyi 林希逸. (1969). "Kaogong ji jie" "考工記解" [Commentary on Records of the Examination of Craftsmanship]. In *Tongzhi tang jingjie* 通志堂經解 [Commentaries to the Classics from the Hall of the Free Mind], edited by Nalan Xingde 納蘭性德, vol. 29, 16409–16495. Taipei: Datong shuju.

Liu An 劉安, et al. (1989). *Huainanzi* 淮南子. Shanghai: Shanghai guji chubanshe.

Lü Dalin 呂大臨. (1987). *Kaogu tu* 考古圖 [Examining Antiquities in Pictures]. Beijing: Zhonghua shuju.

Mair, Victor, ed. (1994). *The Columbia Anthology of Traditional Chinese Literature*. New York: Columbia University Press.

Major, John S., et al., trans. (2010). *The Huainanzi: A Guide to the Theory and Practice of Government in Early Han China*. New York: Columbia University Press.

Ouyang Xiu 歐陽修. (1929). *Ouyang Wenzhonggong ji* 歐陽文忠公集 [Collected Works of Ouyang Xiu]. Shanghai: Shangwu yinshuguan.

Rao Zongyi 饒宗頤. (1987). "Shuo qin hui: da Ma Shunzhi jiaoshou shu" "說琴徽: 答馬順之教授書" [On the Question of *Qin Hui*: In Answer to Prof. Ma Shunzhi]. *Zhongguo yinyue xue* 中國音樂學 [Musicology in China], no. 3: 4–7.

Rong Geng 容庚. (1964). "Songdai jijin shuji shuping (xu)" "宋代吉金書籍述評（續）" [Study of the Antiquarian Catalogs of the Song Dynasty, part 2], *Xueshu yanjiu* 學術研究 [Academic Research], no. 1: 85–102.

Shenzhen bowuguan 深圳博物館 [Shenzhen City Museum], ed. (2010). *Jianwu Chu tian: Hubei chutu Chu wenwu zhan tulu* 劍舞楚天: 湖北出土楚文物展圖錄 [Sword Dance of Chu: Exhibition Catalogue of Chu Cultural Relics from Hubei Province]. Beijing: Wenwu chubanshe.

Wang Fu 王黼. (1969). *Xuanhe bogu tu* 宣和博古圖 [Pictures of a Myriad of Ancient Objects in the Xuanhe Collection]. Taipei: Xinxing shuju.

Wang Guowei 王國維. (1997). "Gushi xinzheng" "古史新證" [New Evidence on Ancient History]. In *Wang Guowei wenji* 王國維文集 [Collected Essays of Wang Guowei], edited by Yao Ganming 姚淦銘 and Wang Yan 王燕, vol. 4, 1–32. Beijing: Zhongguo wenshi chubanshe.

Wang Houzhi 王厚之. (1802). *Zhong ding kuanzhi* 鐘鼎款識 [*Zhong* Bells and *Ding* Tripod Inscriptions]. Yangzhou: Jiguzhai.

Wang Qiu 王俅. (1983). *Xiao tang jigu lu* 嘯堂集古錄 [Records of the Wailing Hall's Collection of Ancient Bronzes]. Beijing: Zhonghua shuju.

Wang Zichu 王子初. (2005). "Mawangdui qixian qin he zaoqi qinshi wenti" "馬王堆七弦琴和早期琴史問題" [The Seven-stringed Mawangdui *Qin* and Historical Questions Raised Regarding the Ancient *Qin*]. *Shanghai wenbo luncong* 上海文博論叢 [Shanghai Archaeology and Museology Papers], no. 4: 40–45.

Wang Zichu 王子初. (2015). "Lun Songdai Anlu chutu Zenghou zhong zhi yuelü biaoming" "論宋代安陸出土曾侯鐘之樂律標銘 [On the Musical Inscriptions on the Marquis of Zeng's Bells Excavated in Anlu]. *Yinyue yanjiu* 音樂研究 [Music Research], no. 3: 12–20.

Watt, James C. Y. (1996). "Antiquarianism and Naturalism." In *Possessing the Past: Treasures from the National Palace Museum, Taipei*, edited by Wen Fong and James C. Y. Watt, 219–55. New York: Metropolitan Museum of Art.

Wu Zhao 吳釗. (1989). "釋徽: 與馮潔軒君商榷" [Explaining *Hui*: Discussion with Feng Jiexuan]. *Zhongguo yinyue xue* 中國音樂學 [Musicology in China], no. 3: 32–35.

Xu Jian 許健. (1988). "Xi Han you qinhui ma? Yu Rao Zongyi jiaoshou shangque" "西漢有琴徽嗎？與饒宗頤教授商榷" [Were There *Qin Hui* in the Western Han Dynasty? Discussions with Rao Zongyi]. *Zhongguo yinyue xue* 中國音樂學 [Musicology in China], no. 1: 114–17.

Xue Shanggong 薛尚功. (1634). *Lidai zhongding yiqi kuanzhi fatie* 歷代鐘鼎彝器款識法帖 [Model Calligraphy of Inscriptions on Bronzes of Successive Dynasties]. Nanchang: Zhu Mouyin.

Yang Yuanzheng. (2012). "Inventing the Fuxi Style of *Qin*." In *Studien zur Musikarchäologie VIII*, edited by Ricardo Eichmann, Fang Jianjun, and Lars-Christian Koch, 195–206. Rahden: M. Leidorf.

Yang Yuanzheng. (2015). "*Taotie*, Dragon, Phoenix, and Farmer: A Highly Decorated *Qin* Excavated from Jiuliandun." *Early China* 38: 129–150.

Yang Yuanzheng. (2016). "Typological Analysis of the Chinese *Qin* in the Late Bronze Age." *Galpin Society Journal* 69: 137–151.

Yang Yuanzheng. (2020). *Dragon's Roar: Chinese Literati Musical Instruments in the Freer and Sackler Collections*. Washington, DC: Freer Gallery of Art and Arthur M. Sackler Gallery.

Zheng Minzhong 鄭珉中, ed. (2006). *Gugong guqin* 故宮古琴 [Antique *Qin* in the Collection of the Palace Museum]. Beijing: Zijincheng chubanshe.

Zheng Zuxiang 鄭祖襄. (1986). "Hui zi yu huiwei: jiankao guqin huiwei chansheng de lishi niandai" "徽字與徽位：兼考古琴徽位產生的歷史年代" [The Character *Hui* and Its Position: An Examination through the Dynasties] *Zhongyang yinyue xueyuan xuebao* 中央音樂學院學報 [Journal of the Central Conservatory of Music], no. 4: 25–27.

Zheng Zuxiang 鄭祖襄. (2008). "Zaoqi qin de chuanshuo yu xinshi" "早期琴的傳說與信史" [The Ancient *Qin*: Fact and Fiction], *Xinghai yinyue xueyuan xuebao* 星海音樂學院學報 [Journal of Xinghai Conservatory of Music], no. 4: 51–56.

Zhongguo yinyue wenwu daxi zongbianjibu 中國音樂文物大系總編輯部 [Editorial Board of Archaeological Collection of Chinese Music]. (1996). *Zhongguo yinyue wenwu daxi: Hubei juan* 中國音樂文物大系: 湖北卷 [Archaeological Collection of Chinese Music: Book of Hubei]. Zhengzhou: Daxiang chubanshe.

Zou Heng 鄒衡, and Weisi Tan 譚維四, eds. (2015). *Zenghou Yi bianzhong* 曾侯乙編鐘 [The Chime Bells of Marquis Yi of Zeng], 4 vols. Beijing: Xiyuan chubanshe.

CHAPTER 3

THEORIZING "NATURAL SOUND"

Ancient Chinese Music Theory and Its Contemporary Applications in the Study of Guqin Intonation

YU HUI AND CHEN YINGSHI

YUELÜ XUE: THE CHINESE SCHOLARLY TRADITION OF MUSIC THEORY

THE music theory of the Han people in China, called *yuelü xue* 樂律學 (the study of *yuelü*), comprises two major branches, the study of *yue* 樂 (music) and the study of *lü* 律 (musical pitch).[1] The term *yuelü* comes originally from two chapters, the "Yueshu" 樂書 ("Book of Music") and "Lüshu" 律書 ("Book of Musical Pitches"), both found in the *Shiji* 史記 (*Historical Records*, c. 104–91 BCE) compiled by Sima Qian 司馬遷, the first-known official historian of ancient China. Following this precedent, most official history books of the following dynasties contain chapters on "Yuezhi" 樂志 ("Musical Records"), "Liyue zhi" 禮樂志 ("Ritual and Music Records"), and "Lüli zhi" 律曆志 ("Record of Musical Pitches and the Calendar"). After the Han dynasty (202 BCE–220 CE), scholars took the first part from each of the two terms, *yue zhi* and *lüli zhi*, and used them in historical literature. The term *yuelü* then appeared as part of the titles of books and articles such as *Yuelü yi* 樂律義 ("Meaning of *Yuelü*") by Shen Zhong 沈重 (c. 570 CE), *Mengxi bitan yuelü* 夢溪筆談·樂律 ("*Dreaming Stream Narratives*: Yuelü Chapter") by Shen Kuo 沈括 (1031–95 CE), *Yuelü juyao* 樂律舉要 ("Summary of *Yuelü*") by Han Bangqi 韓邦奇 (c. 1504 CE), *Yuelü quanshu* 樂律全書 ("*Yuelü* Encyclopedia") by Prince Zhu Zaiyu 朱載堉 (1595 CE), *Yuelü kao* 樂律考 ("*Yuelü* Verification," c. 1870 CE) by Xu Hao 徐灝, and *Yuelü kaoyuan* 樂律考源 ("Origin of *Yuelü*," 1894 CE) by Zhu Jijing 朱繼經. Thus, the word *yuelü* became a generic term commonly referred to in ancient Chinese music theory, and *yuelü xue* stood for the theoretical study of musical phenomena. In early research, *yuelü xue* also involved the academic study of mathematics, meteorology, the astronomical calendar, the philosophy of *yin-yang* and the five elements, phonology, and other disciplines.

The study of musical tuning and temperament is called *lüxue* 律學, and as one of the two core areas of *yuelü xue* scholarship, it was acoustically and philosophically significant in ancient China. Its focus is *lü*, the term referring to musical pitches. Beginning with the *Hou hanshu* 後漢書 (*History of the Later Han Dynasty*, [432–45 CE]), musical pitches and astronomy were treated as one subject in official histories. The twelve pitches of the chromatic scale were always considered related to the months and hours; a year was divided into twelve lunar months, a day into twelve double hours, and an octave into twelve notes. These divisions were all thought of as connected to society's order and rules. Therefore, musical tuning was considered as important as the calendar system and treated as a system of measurement akin to length, volume, and weight. Each Chinese dynasty published standards of musical pitches, lengths, volumes, and weights, with pitch taking pride of place. In ancient Chinese music literature, intonation was above ordinary things, existing on the same plane as heaven and earth. The chapter "Shundian" 舜典 ("The Canon of Shun") in *Shangshu* 尚書 (*Esteemed Documents*), one of the five classics of ancient Chinese literature, mentions, for instance, "harmonizing time by adopting the right calendar, unifying the measurement of musical pitch, length, volume, and weight."[2] Later on, Liu Xin 劉歆 (c. 50 BCE–23 CE) of the Han dynasty classified this research area into five parts in *Zhonglü shu* 鐘律書 (*Book on Bell Pitches*, c. 5 CE): "preparing numbers, harmonizing sound, judging length, propitiating volume, and comparing weight."[3] In *Qin tong* 琴統 ("*Qin* Tradition"), written in 1268, Xu Li 徐理 of the Song dynasty (960–1279 CE) wrote:

> wherever there is heaven and earth there are pitches; wherever there are pitches there are notes; wherever there are notes there are *zhun* [zither-like instruments used to provide standard pitches]. Although *zhun* had not yet been made in the early days of pitches, the importance of *zhun* precedes the *guqin*.[4]

In classical Chinese tuning studies, a method known as *sanfen sunyi* 三分損益 (one-third deduction and addition) was treated as the only way of producing musical scales—the method primarily comprises generating successive tones at intervals of perfect fifths by reducing or extending the length of a vibrating string to two-thirds or four-thirds of the original. It divides the string length into three equal parts; if the whole is taken as a fundamental note, shortening the length by a third produces a note that is a pure fifth higher, and lengthening by a third produces a note a pure fifth lower. When limited to five pitches, the *sanfen sunyi* method produces intervals equivalent to a Pythagorean scale, and both are called "cyclic tuning" or tuning of the "cycle of fifths" (McClain, 1979). Since *sanfen sunyi* uses perfect fifths upward and downward, it is sometimes also called "up and down tuning" (Kuttner, 1975).

The *sanfen sunyi* method made its first appearance in *Guanzi* 管子 (*Book of Master Guan*) of the Warring States period (475–221 BCE), which mentions adding and subtracting one-third to calculate the five notes of the pentatonic scale of *gong* 宮, *shang* 商, *jue* 角, *zhi* 徵, and *yu* 羽, beginning with increasing the length by a third. In *Lüshi chunqiu* 呂氏春秋 (*Master Lü's Spring and Autumn Annals*, 239 BCE), the method was used to calculate twelve pitches instead of five. In the *Huainanzi* 淮南子 (*Book of the Prince of Huainan*) written by Liu An 劉安 (179–*c*. 122 BCE), the method had reached its final form, in which, however, the first operation was to deduct, instead of to increase, a third of the length.

Links between the study of musical pitches, astronomy, and calendar-making proved an important stimulus for the study of tuning systems as scholars discovered that the movement of heavenly bodies, the sequence of the seasons, and the succession of night and day all returned to their starting points, but a scale calculated using the *sanfen sunyi* method did not. This is partly because of the fundamental difference between *sanfen sunyi* and Pythagorean methods. The latter is called "3-limit" tuning because the ratios can be expressed as a product of integer powers of whole numbers less than or equal to 3, including 2, a number that generates octaves. But in *sanfen sunyi*, 3 is the only integer power of a number used to generate the interval of a perfect fifth. Unlike the Pythagorean method, the *sanfen sunyi* method does not produce pure fourth and octave intervals. Therefore, the notes *zhonglü* 仲呂[5] and *qing huangzhong* 清黃鐘 (one octave higher than the fundamental *huangzhong* 黃鐘 note) are about 23.46 cents[6] (a Pythagorean comma)[7] higher than their Pythagorean equivalents. Since the Han dynasty, scholars have searched for ways to close the gap generated by this *sanfen sunyi* method, to make the starting pitch of the cycle return to its origin.

Jing Fang 京房 (77–33 BCE) used the *sanfen sunyi* method to produce sixty pitches, one for each year in the traditional calendar. The proposal brought the fifty-third pitch very close to the fundamental note of *huangzhong*, with the difference only 3.615 cents (known as "Jing Fang's comma" in China and the "Mecarto comma" in the West; see Yu, 2021). In the Yuanjia 元嘉 period of the Southern Liu Song dynasty (424–53 CE), Qian Lezhi 錢樂之 used the method to calculate 360 standard pitches, one for each day of the ancient calendar, cutting Jing Fang's comma in half to 1.8 cents. The scholars He Chengtian 何承天 (370–447 CE, a contemporary of Qian Lezhi), Wang Pu 王樸 (906–59 CE), and Cai Yuanding 蔡元定 (1135–98 CE) also proposed their own mathematical solutions to have *qing huangzhong* return to the original note of *huangzhong*.

The breakthrough for Chinese studies of tuning was the discovery of the equal-temperament solution by the Ming-dynasty prince Zhu Zaiyu (1536–1611 CE). In his treatise *Lüxue xinshuo* 律學新說 (*New Report on Lüxue*) published in 1584, one year before a similar discovery in Europe by the Dutch engineer Simon Stevin, Zhu calculated the twelfth root of 2 by taking the square root four times of the cube root, closing the gap of the Pythagorean comma. Zhu is therefore credited by most scholars as the first person in the world to discover the mathematical solution of equal temperament. While Simon Stevin's contribution was framed in the West as discovery of a mathematical formula with practical uses in keyboard instrument construction, Zhu considered his main contribution to be successfully closing the theoretical gap in the *sanfen sunyi* system. As such, his calculation was "a brilliant solution remaining an enigma as Chinese musical instrument constructions did not have any practical need to use equal temperament" (Barbour, 1951: 7)—it primarily highlighted discrepancies between theoretical work in *lüxue* study and music practices in China.

Studies of "Natural Sound" and the Theory of Just Intonation in China

Although Zhu's discovery did not cause music that used a chromatic scale to become prevalent in China during and following his time, subsequent Chinese scholars gradually realized that other tuning systems had existed in Chinese music practice for thousands of years, albeit not fitting well into the orthodox frame of *sanfen sunyi* tuning. As mentioned, the discovery of the equal-temperament solution was prompted by the need to resolve problems inherent to the *sanfen sunyi* method; Zhu's research was itself carried out using this method and he did not propose a new equal-temperament tuning system. Some scholars have speculated that this was because any new suggestions not in line with *sanfen sunyi* would have attracted criticism from traditionalists. Fritz Kuttner suggests that Zhu, to protect himself against criticism, intentionally attributed his discoveries to such time-honored and highly respected sources as *Huainan zi*; he may have felt he needed to "cover himself against a possible charge by ardent traditionalists that he advocated a tuning system at odds with a tradition of 17 centuries" (Kuttner, 1975: 182).

In fact, Zhu's idea to modify the *sanfen sunyi* method comes from his realization of discrepancies existing between *guqin* music practices and orthodox tuning. The tuning from "an unknown source" used in *guqin* music encouraged him to use in his calculation a perfect fifth of today's 700 cents instead of the then-standard 702 cents. He described his work with *guqin* music in *Lüxue xingshuo*:

> I once followed the theory of Zhu Xi, calculating the *guqin* inlay markers according to the *sanfen sunyi* method, but I noticed that the notes of the *guqin* were not in consonance with the positions of the standard pitches, and suspicions therefore arose in my mind. Night and day I searched for a solution and studied exhaustively. Suddenly early one morning I reached a perfect understanding of it and realized for the first time that the four ancient sorts of standard pitches[8] all gave mere approximations to the notes, and *lüxue* scholars were unaware of this for 2000 years. . . . Only the makers of the *guqin* in their method of placing the markers at three-quarters or two-thirds had, as common artisans, transmitted by word of mouth from an unknown source. I think that probably the men of old handed down the system in this way, only it is not recorded in literary works.[9]

In this passage, Zhu attributed the "method of placing the markers," which made *guqin* intonation different from the traditional *sanfen sunyi*, to "an unknown source."

What he did not realize, however, was that the *guqin* tuning system was actually that called "just intonation," as initially theorized by his contemporary, the Italian music theorist Gioseffo Zarlino (1517–90 CE); it is a tuning system that had existed in China's music practices for thousands of years before Zhu's time.

In his book *Sopplimenti musicali*, Zarlino observed that the mathematical deduction of consonant intervals affords a different distribution of these intervals within the octave, known today as "just intonation." It shifted the boundaries of consonance, now encompassing thirds and sixths, which were considered dissonant in the Pythagorean scale. And "all the consonances of the scale were just, i.e., defined by ratios between simple whole numbers ranging from 1 to 6 (*senario*): besides octave, fifth and fourth, thirds too, major C-E = 5/4, and minor A-c = 6/5, and sixths, major C-A= 5/3 and minor E-c = 8/5."[10] Zarlino argued that "the forms of the consonances and other intervals that we use in our times in vocal and *natural* compositions are not products of art nor inventions of man but primarily of *nature* itself . . . They are then ordered and rediscovered by art in the species that I call and shall always call *natural*" (Palisca, 1986: 272, emphasis added).

What Zarlino referred to as "natural" were the intervals of thirds and sixths, parts of the natural harmonic series that were not included in the Pythagorean system. In Zarlino's scheme, all have the number 5 in the ratios of the frequencies of string vibrations. This system is therefore called "5-limit" tuning, based on string-length ratios featuring the number 5 and its powers not existing in either the Pythagorean or the *sanfen sunyi* systems. As a method to obtain a just-intonation scale, this system was not recorded in any historical Chinese literature even though it has existed in Chinese music practices of *guqin* and bell sets since ancient times, as will be discussed later in this chapter.

The intervals of the third and sixth in just intonation are called "just intervals" or "just thirds" and "just sixths." They are considered pure like the intervals of a perfect fifth, perfect fourth, and the octave, as they are all the members of a single harmonic series, and no beating is heard when they are sounded. Figure 3.1 shows the first four harmonic overtones produced from the pitch of C.

In this example, the first harmonic overtone, whose frequency is twice the fundamental, sounds an octave higher; the second harmonic, three times the frequency of the fundamental, sounds a perfect fifth above the first harmonic; the third harmonic, which vibrates at four times the frequency of the fundamental, sounds a perfect fourth above the second harmonic and another octave higher than the fundamental; finally, the fourth harmonic, which vibrates at five times the frequency of the fundamental, sounds a major third (386 cents) above the third harmonic. This fourth overtone is the main element constituting the just intonation scale that Zarlino proposed.

Although Chinese music scholarship does not have a tuning theory parallel to just intonation in the West, Chinese scholars gradually realized that other ratios of the string lengths in addition to the perfect fifth in the *sanfen sunyi* method can also generate musical intervals. Historical literature since the Song dynasty recorded scholarly discourses on harmonic overtones through the ratios of string length, which are the inversion of

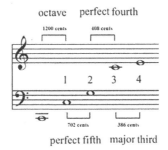

FIGURE 3.1. The first five overtones in a harmonic series when the fundamental note is C.

Notes: a. (Stopped notes): By converting the different lengths of the strings into cent values, addition and subtraction can be substituted for multiplication and division in the mathematical calculation, making the sizes of intervals more comprehensible.

b. (Octaves reduced rows): Simplified numbers of cent values for the pitches at each of the thirteen markers are derived by treating notes separated by one or more octaves as examples of "equivalence."

the ratios of vibration frequencies. In his article "Qinjian" 琴箋 ("Annotation of *Guqin*"), Cui Zundu 崔尊度 (953–1020) wrote that the musical pitches could be generated on a single *guqin* string at different ratios. He called the thirteen inlay markers on the fingerboard of a *guqin* "natural joints" but believed there were in fact twenty-three nodes, not the thirteen marked along the string (see Zha and Wu, 1980–2010: vol. 5, p. 25). In his article "Qin tong," Xu Li mentioned that overtones could be made on all nodes where the strings are divided and that harmonics could be produced at all equally spaced nodes. In the section "Ten Divisions" (十則), he listed details of the positions of each node from the second to the tenth division on a string and concluded that "the string on the *guqin* can be divided into ten sections with forty-five nodes. Excluding fourteen redundancies, there are thirty-one of them."[11] The pitches discovered on the thirty-one nodes, plus the base notes, comprise the harmonic series from the first to the tenth. The discovery of the "natural joints" prompted further study into *guqin* tuning systems during and after the Song dynasty.

THE STUDY OF *GUQIN* INTONATIONS AND ITS CONTEMPORARY SIGNIFICANCES

Chinese tuning studies classify musical pitches into different categories, according to the sound-producing body of the instrument in question. For example, pitches produced on *guqin* strings are called *qinlü* 琴律; those from tubes are called *guanlü* 管律; and *zhonglü* 鐘律 refers to pitches produced from bell sets. Classical studies of each category involved different methods of calculation according to relevant acoustic principles. The term *qinlü* emerged about the tenth century of the Song dynasty, when Zhu Xi 朱熹 (1130–1200) first used it in his treatise *Qinlü shuo* 琴律說 ("*Qin* Intonation," c. 1190 CE), although, as mentioned above, earlier scholars had also discussed issues surrounding musical pitches produced on monochord strings.

While Prince Zhu Zaiyu discovered the equal-temperament solution in China without practical need for it in instrument construction, the features of the *guqin*'s instrumental form prompted the theoretical investigation of just intonation in China. This is partly because of the fact that *guqin* is one of the very few musical instruments in the world that can produce just intonation, and *guqin* tablature is unique in being able to notate very minor intonation variances, reflecting features of the instrument's construction.

Figure 3.2 shows the marker positions on the surface of the fingerboard designed to guide the player in placing left-hand fingers when touching and stopping strings. Table 3.1 shows these marker positions, the corresponding string-length ratios, and the pitch intervals produced when the marker positions are touched or stopped.

The markers on the fingerboard of the *guqin* show positions where harmonics and stopped notes can be produced. The discrepancies between the traditional theory of *sanfen sunyi* and *guqin* music practice, which uses just intervals, are apparent. When stopping or touching the third, sixth, eighth, and eleventh markers, only intervals in the just intonation of the 386 cents of a major third, and the 884 cents of a major sixth can be produced. From Table 3.1, we see that the string ratios of 1/5, 2/5, 3/5, 4/5, and 5/6 are used on the third, sixth, eighth, eleventh, and twelfth stopped notes respectively. All of these ratios belong to the "5-limit" just-intonation system, as they contain the number 5. Just as Zarlino pointed out, the intervals of major thirds and sixths, and their inversions, are "natural" sounds of the harmonic series. Due to the hegemony of the orthodox *sanfen sunyi* tuning, Chinese scholars did not propose or discover any other tuning system theory equivalent to just intonation. Even Prince Zhu Zaiyu "was still fairly ignorant of some basic facts of his nation's two tuning systems and their differences. Otherwise, he could not have been so surprised and pleased upon discovering that the just ch'in [*guqin*] pitches were 'mere approximations' to the frequencies of the up-and-down principle" (Kuttner, 1975: 198).

It was not until the early to mid-twentieth century that Zarlino's theory began to circulate in China. Musicologists Wang Guanqi 王光祈 and Miao Tianrui 繆天瑞 were

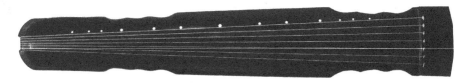

FIGURE 3.2. Marker positions on the surface of the *guqin* fingerboard.

Notes: a. Converting the different lengths of the strings into cent values allows addition and subtraction to be substituted for multiplication and division in the mathematical calculation, making the sizes of intervals more comprehensible.

b. By treating notes separated by one or more octaves as examples of "equivalence," we can derive simplified numbers of cent values for the pitches at each of the thirteen markers.

Table 3.1. The ratios of the string lengths marked by the thirteen markers and the pitch intervals of stopped and harmonic notes generated at the marker positions.

Marker position open string	13	12	11	10	9	8	7	6	5	4	3	2	1
Length ratio	7/8	5/6	4/5	3/4	2/3	3/5	1/2	2/5	1/3	1/4	1/5	1/6	1/8
Stopped notes[a]	231	316	386	498	702	884	1200	1586	1902	2400	2786	3102	3600
(octaves reduced)[b]	231	316	386	498	702	884	±0	386	702	±0	386	702	±0
Harmonic notes	3600	310	278	240	1902	786	1200	2786	1902	2400	2786	3102	3600
(octaves reduced)	±0	702	386	±0	702	386	±0	386	702	±0	386	702	±0

among the first scholars to introduce just intonation. The earliest Chinese literature mentioning just intonation, as far as the authors of the current chapter are aware, is Wang Guangqi's book *Dongxi yuezhi zhi yanjiu* 東西樂制研究 (*Musical Systems in the East and West*) published in 1926. Here Wang mentioned Zarlino's proposal in a chapter introducing Western theories of tuning and temperament but did not mention its occurrence in Chinese music practice (Wang, 1926: 188–96). In an article "On Harmonics" 泛音論 published in *Jinyu qinkan* 今虞琴刊, Yu Dishan 余地山, once a lieutenant-general of the Republic of China, discussed the overtones produced on the instrument and the specific string ratios of each inlay marker but, again, without mentioning the just-intonation tuning system (Yu, [1937] 2018).

In his influential book *Lüxue* 律學 (*The Study of Musical Pitches*), Miao Tianrui commented that the string ratios used to place the markers on the instruments made just intonation possible (Miao, 1950: 60). Subsequently, the musicologists Yang Yinliu 楊蔭瀏 (Yang, 1981: 1015) and Shen Zhibai 沈知白 (Shen, 1982: 50) also suggested that just intonation might have been used in the history of *guqin* music.

In the 1970s, Chinese musicologists discovered elements of just intonation in use historically from inscriptions on the bell set excavated in the tomb of Zeng Hou Yi 曾侯乙, Marquis Yi of the Zeng kingdom (*c.* 475–433 BCE), and from precise measurement of the acoustic capabilities of the instruments (Huang, 1981). The discovery verified that another tuning system was used in Chinese music practices thousands of years ago, and it has led to the flourishing of the study of *guqin* intonation since the 1980s. A large number of research papers have been published in Chinese musicological periodicals discussing ancient musical literature since then, which expands the horizons of historical music research in China from various new perspectives. In the meantime, the research has served the practical needs of contemporary *guqin* players as they creatively reinterpret *guqin* tablature, a process called *dapu* 打譜 in which rhythmic components are created for the tablature.

By investigating historical *guqin* tablature for the piece *Youlan* 幽蘭 (*Solitary Orchid*) from the earliest *wenzipu* 文字譜 (full-ideogram notation) tablature and from manuals printed in later dynasties, scholars have developed two theories regarding the tuning systems of the instrument. One asserts that the tuning of the *guqin* music recorded in early tablature, that from before the Ming dynasty, was all in just intonation, including for pieces such as *Youlan*, *Guanling san* 廣陵散 (*Guangling Melody*), and many other popular music pieces that have been recreated by master *guqin* players. This theory was strongly supported by the prominent scholar Yang Yinliu, who held that: "From the countless *guqin* tablatures which exist, we may at least confidently deduce that from the sixth century until the sixteenth century, a period of over a thousand years, China's *guqin* players continuously used just temperament, entire and unmodified" (Yang, 1981: 1015).

Yang points to *Youlan* as a fitting example of a sixth-century piece, with its transcription in full-ideogram notation currently preserved in the Tokyo National Museum, in Ueno Park. Yang's mention of the sixteenth century at the more recent end of his date range acknowledges the supposed transformation in the notation style of *guqin* tablature at this time: ten equal divisions called *fen* 分 began to be used between the inlay markers on the fingerboard, numbered from right to left. *Guqin* tablature began to contain notation indicating stopped notes at positions such as the second marker plus nine *fen* (2.9, a point nine-tenths of the way from the second marker to the third, where the note is slightly higher than the one at the third marker), the fifth marker plus nine *fen* (5.9), the seventh marker plus nine *fen* (7.9), and the tenth marker plus eight *fen* (10.8). None of these positions coincide with string ratios divided by whole numbers, and, being slightly off the third, sixth, eighth, and eleventh markers respectively, it indicates that the intervals of the *sanfen sunyi* tuning were being used.

Some musicologists have pointed out that altering the marker positions was inappropriate as the original positions reflected the sounds of just intonation used in earlier times. And it is suggested that when interpreting ancient *guqin* tablature, players should pay attention to the differences between the two tuning systems and take care to alter the marker positions so as to produce the natural sounds of ancient *guqin* music in just intonation (Chen, 1983; 1985). Nevertheless, some *guqin* players have argued that the interpretation of *guqin* tablature needs to be based on modern musical ears rather than the historical record, which might not be sufficiently reliable and accurate to guide current creative musical activities; the mathematical calculation of music pitches cannot replace musical originality (Wang, 1991; Cheng, 1992). Other *guqin* practitioners consider tuning systems an essential body of knowledge in both *guqin* practice and theory (Chen, 2012: 59–206).

The musicologist Huang Xiangpeng proposed that *guqin* music use a compound tuning system comprising both *sanfen sunyi* and just-intonation tuning (Huang,

1983). But other scholars disagree, arguing that pitches in a musical scale should not be generated and varied arbitrarily and that musical tuning should follow the rules of one system, not multiple ones (Chen, 1996).

It seems that two issues need to be clarified. First, is it appropriate to conclude that the music is in just intonation whenever a marker position producing a just interval is found in tablature? Then, can the historical division of tuning systems emerging in records be generalized to all musical pieces? In other words, are we to extrapolate that no pieces of music used just intonation after the Ming dynasty and that none used *sanfen suniyi* before then? Investigation of pieces in *guqin* manuals has become the key to understanding the historical situation of *guqin* intonation. Among the hundreds of existing historical manuals, the earliest extant *guqin* tablature collection, *Shenqi mipu* 神奇秘譜 (*Exact Tablatures for Treasured and Beautiful Melodies*), became the focus for clarifying the two issues mentioned. A new suggestion was made: to decipher the intonation used in the tablatures in *Shenqi mipu*, there should be comprehensive analysis of multiple elements of relevance to the intonations of *guqin* music (see Yu, 1997). Rather than looking at only one element, it is now common to consider the following four elements, which in combination determine the tuning system:

The first and the most essential is—as already discussed—the features of instrument construction, in the location of the thirteen inlays. As indicated in Table 3.1, the string ratios used to place the thirteen markers prove that a scale with just intonation can be generated. If tablature shows that markers producing intervals of just thirds and sixths were used, a just-intonation scale was possible. This is the logical basis of older research, but it is not a guarantee, as other elements also play a part in determining *guqin* intonation.

The second is how the seven open strings are tuned in relation to each other. If, for example, the third and sixth intervals between the open strings are tuned at 386 and 886 cents respectively, a just-intonation scale is most likely used, and vice versa. The traditional procedure to tune the seven open strings is based on the principle that a note produced by stopping one string at an inlay marker matches another open string. Thus, the inlay markers used in the tuning process decide the relations of the open strings. Historical literature records that several tuning procedures have been used in *guqin* practices. One involves generating *sanfen sunyi* tunings for the open strings based on matches with the perfect fifth at the ninth marker and the perfect fourth at the tenth marker, producing a scale with a major third interval of 408 cents. The other procedure produces a just-intonation scale among the open strings by using the major third interval of 386 cents at the eleventh marker and the perfect fourth at the tenth marker.

Thirdly, we also need to consider how the inlay markers are used when notes are fingered. Although the positions at the third, sixth, eighth, and eleventh inlay markers only produce just intervals, if those markers are never used in a piece of music, just-intonation tuning may not be implied. As indicated in Table 3.2, multiple positions on different strings can produce the same note but with different tunings. Here, the open

Table 3.2. Pitches of stopped notes and harmonics produced from the thirteen inlay markers when the open strings of the *guqin* are tuned in *sanfen sunyi* tuning.

Stopped Notes

open string	12	11	10	9	8	7	6	5	4	3	2	1
C	#D	E	#E	G	A̱	C	E	G	C	E	G	C
D	#E	♭G	G	A	♭C̱	D	♭G	A	D	♭G	A	D
E	G	#G	A	♭C	#C̱	E	#G	♭C	E	#G	♭C	E
G	#A	♭C	C	D	E̱	G	♭C	D	G	♭C	D	G
A	C̱	#C	D	E	♭C̱	A	#C	E	A	#C	E	A

Harmonics

open string	13	12	11	10	9	8	7	6	5	4	3	2	1
C	C	G	E̱	C	G	E̱	C	E̱	G	C	E̱	G	C
D	D	A	♭G	D	A	♭G	D	♭G	A	D	♭G	A	D
E	E	♭C	#G̱	E	♭C	#G̱	E	#G̱	♭C	E	#G̱	♭C	E
G	G	D	♭C̱	G	D	♭C̱	G	♭C̱	D	G	♭C̱	D	G
A	A	E	#C̱	A	E	#C̱	A	#C̱	E	A	#C̱	E	A

strings are tuned into a pentatonic scale. The letter names C, D, E, F, and A are used to represent the Chinese pentatonic notes of *gong, shang, jue, zhi,* and *yu* respectively, with the underscore indicating notes of just intervals (i.e., those that are lower by a comma than their equivalents in *sanfen sunyi* and Pythagorean tuning).

In this example, when the scale of the open strings employs Pythagorean tunings, some just intervals can still be produced. Both the Pythagorean pitches C, ♭C, and E and the just-intonation pitches C̱, ♭C̱, and E̱ can be produced, depending on which fingering positions are used. Therefore, the marker position employed in the tablature is an element that also decides the tuning system used in *guqin* music.

Finally, the tonality of the music pieces also shapes the tuning system in *guqin* music, as modulation and transmutation of keys alters the scale structure. In pieces in *Shenqi mipu*, there are many variants of the just-intonation scales that are different from the heptatonic scale proposed by Zarlino.

Through deciphering the intonation information contained in the *jianzi pu* 減字譜 characters in *Shenqin mipu*, we discovered that the tuning systems of *guqin* music are far more complex than previously understood (see Yu, 1997). Both just intonation—in many variations—and *sanfen sunyi* tunings were used in the Ming dynasty, and it is possible that the transformation of *guqin* tunings from just intonation to *sanfen sunyi*, if it did happen, took place more slowly than usually assumed. So, these findings represent a challenge to the key theory that *guqin* music did not use the *sanfen sunyi* system before the Ming dynasty. Other issues, however, remain unresolved—including the question of how these complex tuning phenomena came about and whether they reflect different personal, regional, or historical musical styles.

Further studies of *guqin* intonation have also challenged the Chinese concept of just intonation as proposed by Zarlino and first introduced by Wang Guangqi and Miao Tianrui. One argument is that any scale using just intervals, especially the just third and sixth, could be considered in just-intonation tuning (see Yu, 2014). This judgment could expand the repertoire of *guqin* music categorized as using just intonation. In fact, finding a *guqin* piece that uses a scale structure precisely reflecting Zarlino's theory presents a theoretical struggle for Chinese musicologists. One reason is that Chinese music mostly uses pentatonic scales in which only one interval of a major third exists, while Zarlino's theory was geared toward a heptatonic scale, which includes three major-third intervals in its structure. This presents another discrepancy of just intonation between music in China and the West.

Conclusion

Recent research into tuning systems in *guqin* music challenges doctrines of Chinese music theory based solely on *sanfen sunyi* tuning, which has occupied an orthodox place in Chinese scholarship from antiquity because of its relationship to research in disciplines such as mathematics, calendar-making, and astronomy. Analysis of *guqin* intonation opens up a new area of musical scholarship in modern China, making *guqin* practitioners aware of discrepancies between traditional *yuelü xue* notions and music practice. Although the just-intonation tuning used in *guqin* music is not as precise as that proposed and defined in the West, this system has been used in China for millennia without clear theorization from either *guqin* players or music scholars and without a place in the literature of the Confucian classics.

Musical scales represent sounds that humans select from the natural world, following the rules of the harmonic series rather than purely theoretical calculation. Thus, although the equal temperament of twelve chromatic notes allows for the fundamental note to return to its origin, it is an artificially created scale that is not "natural" in the same sense. The ancient Greek philosopher Aristoxenus once contended to the disciples of Pythagoras that the judgment of the ear was superior to mathematical ratios: "[A]re the cogitations of theorists as important as the observations of musicians themselves?" (see Barbour, 1951: 2).

Chinese scholars have long been perplexed by discrepancies between the orthodox *sanfen sunyi* theory and *guqin* music practice; the former does not explain the complex realities of musical traditions. But this method did finally help Prince Zhu Zaiyu find the mathematical solution for equal temperament. It was misunderstood for millennia before the theory of just intonation was introduced into China and *guqin* players gradually realized that both *sanfen sunyi* tuning and just intonation have existed in *guqin* music since ancient times. Depending on our ideals concerning how centrally to keep in mind the original composers or transcribers, when reviving partially lost ancient music, we can either seek to keep to the transcribed sound as accurately as possible or to prioritize musical originality and creativity.[12] Therefore, when reinterpreting ancient *guqin* music, on the one hand, we may choose not to be restricted by the position markers on the tablature and to make the ancient music more acceptable to the ears of contemporary listeners. On the other hand, we might avoid unnecessary alteration of fingerboard position markers and represent the acoustic features of "natural" sound by giving new life to historical Chinese *yuelü xue* scholarship.

Glossary

Cai Yuanding 蔡元定, Song-dynasty scholar (1135–98)

Cui Zundu 崔尊度, Northern Song–dynasty court official, scholar, and *guqin* practitioner (954–1020)

gong 宮, first note of Chinese pentatonic scale

Guanling san 廣陵散, *Guangling Melody*, a composition for *guqin*

guanlü 管律, musical pitches produced from pipes

Han Bangqi 韓邦奇, Ming-dynasty scholar, politician (1479–*c*. 1556)

He Chengtian 何承天, mathematician, astronomer, historian of the Northern and Southern dynasties (370–447)

Hou hanshu 後漢書, *History of the Later Han Dynasty* (432–445 CE), compiled by Fan Ye 范曄 and others

Huainanzi 淮南子, *Book of the Prince of Huainan*, collection of scholarly writings at the court of Liu An, compiled before 139 BCE

huangzhong 黃鐘, first pitch of ancient Chinese chromatic scale

jianzi pu 減字譜, traditional tablature for *guqin*, composed of strokes derived from Chinese characters

Jing Fang, 京房, music theorist, mathematician, and astrologer (*c*. 78–37 BCE)

Jinyu qinkan 今虞琴刊, *Journal of the Jinyu Guqin Society* (1936–37)

jue 角, third note of the Chinese pentatonic scale

Liu An 劉安, Han-dynasty Chinese prince, ruling the Huainan kingdom (*c*. 179–122 BCE)

Liu Xin 劉歆, a Chinese astronomer, mathematician, historian, librarian, and politician (*c*. 50 BCE–23 CE)

Liyue zhi 禮樂志, *Ritual and Music Records*

lü 律, musical pitch

Lüli zhi 律曆志, *Record of Musical Pitches and the Calendar*

Lüshi chunqiu 呂氏春秋, *Master Lü's Spring and Autumn Annals*, encyclopedic classic text compiled under the patronage of Qin-dynasty chancellor Lü Buwei (*c*. 239 BCE)

"Lüshu" 律書, "Book of Musical Pitches"

Lüxue 律學, *The Study of Musical Pitches*, a study by Miao Tianrui of tuning systems and temperaments

Mengxi bitan yuelü 夢溪筆談•樂律, *Dreaming Stream Narratives: "Yuelü* Chapter" by Shen Kuo (1088)

Miao Tianrui 繆天瑞, musicologist (1908–2009)

Qian Lezhi 錢樂之, scholar of music tuning systems and astronomy (424–53)
"Qinjian" 琴箋, "Annotation of *Guqin*," article by Cui Zundu
qinlü 琴律, pitches produced on *guqin*
Qinlü shuo 琴律說, "*Qin* Intonation," written by Zhu Xi (c. 1190)
"Qin tong" 琴統, "*Qin* Tradition," study written by Xu Li (1268)
qing huangzhong 清黃鐘, a pitch one octave higher than the fundamental in the chromatic scale
sanfen sunyi 三分損益, "one-third deduction and addition"
shang 商, second note of Chinese pentatonic scale
Shen Zhong 沈重, philologist (c. 570)
Shen Kuo 沈括, polymath, scientist, and statesman (1031–95)
Shen Zhibai 沈知白, musicologist (1904–68)
Shenqi mipu 神奇秘譜, *Exact Tablatures for Treasured and Beautiful Melodies*, earliest existent collection of *guqin* tablature (compiled 1425)
"Shi ze" 十則, "Ten Divisions," a section of the article "Qin tong" by Xu Li
Shiji 史記, *Historical Records* (c. 104–91 BCE), compiled by Sima Qian
"Shundian" 舜典, "The Canon of Shun" chapter in *Shangshu*, by Confucius
Sima Qian 司馬遷, historian of the early Han dynasty (c. 145–c. 86 BCE)
Wang Guanqi 王光祈, musicologist and social activist (1892–1936)
Wang Pu 王樸, court official, scholar, and music theorist (906–59)
wenzipu 文字譜, full-ideogram tablature for *ququin*
Xu Hao 徐灝, Qing-dynasty scholar (1809–79)
Xu Li 徐理, *guqin* scholar of the Southern Song dynasty
Yang Yinliu 楊蔭瀏, Chinese musicologist (1899–1984)
Youlan 幽蘭, *Solitary Orchid*, composition for *guqin*
Yu Dishan 余地山, lieutenant-general and member of the Jinyu Qinshe (*Guqin* Society of Today's Yushan 虞山 School) (early twentieth century)
yu 羽, fifth note of Chinese pentatonic scale
Yuanjia 元嘉, a period of the Southern Liu Song dynasty (424–453)
yue 樂, music
Yuelü juyao 樂律舉要, "Summary of *Yuelü*" by Han Bangqi of the Ming dynasty
Yuelü kao 樂律考, "*Yuelü* Verification" by Xu Hao (c. 1870)
Yuelü quanshu 樂律全書, "*Yuelü* Encyclopedia" by Zhu Zaiyu
yuelü xue 樂律學, tradition of studies on musical forms and intonations
Yuelü Yi 樂律義, "Meaning of *Yuelü*" by Shen Zhong
"Yueshu" 樂書, "Book of Music"
"Yuezhi" 樂志, "Musical Records"
Zeng Hou Yi 曾侯乙, Marquis Yi of the Zeng kingdom (c. 475–433 BCE)
zhi 徵, fifth note of Chinese pentatonic scale
Zhonglü shu 鐘律書, *Book on Bell Pitches*, by Han-dynasty scholar Liu Xin
zhonglü 鐘律, pitches produced from bells
zhonglü 仲呂, sixth pitch of ancient Chinese chromatic music scale
Zhu Xi 朱熹, Confucian scholar-philosopher and government official of Song-dynasty China (1130–1200)
Zhu Zaiyu 朱載堉, music theorist, mathematician, physicist, and Ming-dynasty prince (1536–1611)

Notes

1. Chen Yingshi formulated the initial draft (in Chinese) of this chapter, entitled "*Yuelü and Yuelü Xue*," providing an overview of ancient Chinese musical theory in general. Although he discussed the original plan with Yu and drafted several of the opening passages of the current chapter, unfortunately, Chen passed away in 2020. Yu has thus completed the chapter, developing the focus of the topic with new arguments and placing it under a new title.
2. "協時月正日，同律度量衡"; see Confucius, 2018: 12.
3. "備數、和聲，審度，嘉量，權衡"; see Qiu, 1999: 137.
4. "蓋有天地則有是律，有是律則有是聲，有是聲則有是准，准之器難未作於有律之初，准之意已默存於有琴之先"; see Zha and Wu, 1980–2010: vol. 3, p. 16.
5. The Chinese terms for the twelve notes, *shier lü* 十二律, in one octave are *huangzhong* 黃鐘, *dalü* 大呂, *taicu* 太簇, *jiazhong* 夾鐘, *guxian* 姑洗, *zhonglü* 仲呂, *ruibin* 蕤賓, *linzhong* 林鐘, *yize* 夷則, *nanlü* 南呂, *wuyi* 無射, and *yingzhong* 應鐘.
6. The cent is a logarithmic unit of measure used for musical intervals first used by Alexander J. Ellis (1814–90); in twelve-tone equal temperament, the octave divides into twelve semitones of 100 cents each (see Ellis, 1874).
7. The Pythagorean comma is the small interval (or comma) existing in Pythagorean tuning between two enharmonically equivalent notes, such as C and B♯, or D♭ and C♯.
8. Chinese historical literature recorded four different sets of numbers for the twelve pitches of the *sanfen sunyi* tuning.
9. "臣嘗宗朱熹之說，依古三分損益之法以求琴之律位，見律位與琴音不相協而疑之。晝夜思索，窮就此理，一旦豁然有悟，始知古四種律皆近似之音耳。此乃二千年間言律學者之所未覺。惟琴家安徽，其法四折去一，三折去一一，俗工口傳，莫知從來，疑必古人疑法如此，特未記載於文字耳。" (Zhu, 1986: 18)
10. Gioseffo Zarlino, *Sopplimenti musicali* (Venice: Francesco de' Franceschi Sanese, 1588), 8; cited in Palisca, 1986: 272.
11. "琴有十則，第四十五，同者十有四，得位者三十有一"; see Zha and Wu, 1980–2010: vol. 3, p. 11.
12. As there are no rhythmic indicators in *guqin* tablature, it is likely that the loss of rhythmic features is permanent and cannot be retrieved accurately through contemporary *dapu* re-creation.

References

Barbour, Murray. (1951). *Tuning and Temperament: A Historical Survey*. East Lansing: Michigan University.

Chen Changlin 陳長林. (2012). *Chen Changlin guqin wenji* 陳長林琴學文集 [Essays on *Guqin* Studies by Chen Changlin]. Beijing: Wenhua yishu chubanshe.

Chen Yingshi 陳應時. (1983). "*Qinqu* 'Guangling san' pulüxue kaoshi" "琴曲《廣陵散》譜律學考釋" [Examination of the Intonation of the *Guqin* Piece *Guanling san*]. *Zhongguo yinyue* 中國音樂 [Chinese Music], no. 3: 38–41.

Chen Yingshi 陳應時. (1985). "Ping guan pinghu yanzou ben 'Guangling san' pu" "評管平湖演奏本《廣陵散》譜" [Comments on Guan Pinghu's Version of *Guangling san*]. *Yinyue yishu* 音樂藝術 [Musical Art], no. 3: 18–23, 33.

Chen Yingshi 陳應時. (1996). "Ping 'Fuhe lüzhi'" "評'複合律制'" [Comments on the 'Compound Tuning System']. *Yinyue yishu* 音樂藝術 [Musical Art], no. 2: 5–13.

Cheng Gongliang 成公亮. (1992). "Cunjian mingdai *guqin* pu zhong you chunlü tiaoxianfa ma?" "存見明代古琴譜中有純律調弦法嗎?" [Is There Any Just Intonation Tuning Procedure in the Extant *Guqin* Tablature from the Ming Dynasty?]. *Zhongguo yinyuexue* 中國音樂學 [Musicology in China], no. 2: 101–6.

Confucius 孔夫子, ed. (2018). *Shangshu* 尚書 [Esteemed Documents]. Annotated by Wang Shishun王世舜 and Wang Cuiye王翠叶. Beijing: Zhonghua shuju.

Ellis, Alexander J. (1874). "Illustrations of Just and Tempered Intonation." *Proceedings of the Musical Association* 1: 159–165.

Huang Xiangpeng 黃翔鵬. (1981). "Zeng Hou Yi zhong qing mingwen yuexue tixi chutan" "曾侯乙鐘、磬銘文樂學體系初探" [Preliminary Discussion of the System of Music Theory in the Inscriptions on the Bells and Chimes from the Tomb of the Marquis Yi of the Zeng Kingdom]. *Yinyue yanjiu* 音樂研究 [Music Research], no. 1: 24–55.

Huang Xiangpeng 黃翔鵬. (1983). "Zhongguo gudai lüxue yizhong juyou minzu wenhua tedian de kexue yichan" "中國古代律學——一種具有民族文化特點的科學遺產" [Chinese Ancient Studies of *Lüxue*: A Scientific Heritage with National Cultural Characteristics]. *Yinyue yanjiu* 音樂研究 [Music Research], no. 4: 112–20.

Jinyu Qinshe 今虞琴社, ed. ([1937] 2018). *Jinyu Qinkan* 今虞琴刊 [Journal of the Jinyu *Guqin* Society]. Reprint, Shanghai: Shanghai shehui kexueyuan chubanshe.

Kuttner, Fritz. (1975). "Prince Chu Tsai-Yü's Life and Work: A Re-Evaluation of His Contribution to Equal Temperament Theory." *Ethnomusicology* 19 (2): 163–206.

McClain, Ernest G., with translations by Ming Shui Hung. (1979). "Chinese Cyclic Tunings in Late Antiquity." *Ethnomusicology* 23 (2): 205–24.

Miao Tianrui 繆天瑞. (1950). *Lüxue*律學 [The Study of Musical Pitches]. Shanghai: Wanye shudian.

Palisca, Claude V. (1986). *Humanism in Italian Renaissance Musical Thought*. New Haven: Yale University Press.

Qiu Qiongsun 丘瓊蓀. (1999). *Lidai yuezhi lüzhi jiaoshi (diyi fence)* 歷代樂制律志校釋 (第一分冊) [Annotated Records of Music and Records of Pitches of the Past Dynasties (Volume 1)]. Beijing: Renmin yinyue chubanshe.

Shen Zhibai 沈知白. (1982). *Zhongguo yinyueshi gangyao* 中國音樂史綱要 [Outline of Chinese Music History]. Shanghai: Shanghai wenyi chubanshe.

Wang Di王迪. (1991). "Youguan *guqin* lüzhi de duandai wenti" "有關古琴律制的斷代問題" [Issues of Periodization in *Guqin* Intonation]. *Yinyue yanjiu* 音樂研究 [Music Research], no. 4: 39–43.

Wang Guangqi 王光祈. (1926). *Dongxi yuezhi zhi yanjiu* 東西樂制之研究 [Musical Systems in the East and West]. Shanghai: Shanghai zhonghua shuju.

Yang Yinliu 楊蔭瀏. (1981). *Zhongguo gudai yinyue shigao* 中國古代音樂史稿 [A Draft History of Ancient Chinese Music]. Beijing: Renmin yinyue chubanshe.

Yu Dishan 余地山. ([1937] 2018). "Fanyin lun" "泛音論" [On Harmonics]. *Jinyu qinkan* 今虞琴刊 [Journal of the Jinyu Guqin Society]: 85–97. Reprint, Shanghai: Shanghai shehui kexueyuan chuban she.]

Yu Hui 喻輝. (1997). "Discontinuity in *Guqin* Temperament Prior to the 15th Century: An Investigation of Temperament of *Guqin* Music as Evidenced in *Shen Qi Mi Pu*." *CHIME* 磬, nos. 10–11: 79–110.

Yu Hui 喻輝. (2014). "Cong zhalinuo yinjie de shijian kan *guqin* yinyu de chunlü yu 'fuhe lüzhi' wenti" "從紮利諾音階的實踐看古琴音樂的純律與'複合律制'問題" [Investigation of the Issues of Just Intonation and Compound Tuning Systems on the *Guqin* from the

Practical Perspective of Zarlino's Scale]. *Zhongguo yinyuexue* 中國音樂學 [Musicology in China], no. 2: 104–9.

Yu Hui 喻輝. (2021). "Quanqiu shiye xia jingfang 'yiri yincha' faxian de zhongda lishi yiyi" "全球視野下京房'一日音差'發現的重大歷史意義" [The Historical Significance of the Discovery of the "Yiri Comma" by Jing Fang]. *Zhongyang yinyue xueyuan xuebao* 中央音樂學院報 [Journal of the Central Conservatory of Music], no. 2: 43–59.

Zha Fuxi 查阜西, Wu Zhao 吳釗, et al. (1980–2010). *Qinqu jicheng* 琴曲集成 [Collection of *Guqin* Pieces]. Beijing: Zhonghua shuju.

Zhu Zaiyu 朱載堉. (1986). *Lüxue xinshuo* 律學新說 [New Report on *Lüxue*]. Annotated by Feng Wenci 馮文慈. Beijing: Renmin yinyue chubanshe.

CHAPTER 4

THE *HUXUAN* AND *HUTENG* DANCES

Foreign Musical Dances in Chinese History

Zhao Weiping

Introduction

Yayue 雅樂 (literally, "elegant music") appeared early in the Western Zhou dynasty (mid-eleventh century–771 BCE) and became a dominant category of court ritual music using the combined media of singing, dancing, and instrumental performance. Before the emperor Qin Shi Huang (259–210 BCE) conquered the other six states to form a unified China in 221 BCE, there had evolved a rich and complete array of musical forms in the central plains area, among them folk music genres such as *zheng sheng* 鄭聲, a secular genre noted for its evocative performance style.[1] Following the Han dynasty (206 BCE–220 CE), and together with the formation of the Silk Route linking the Chinese heartlands with Central Asia and beyond, foreign culture and music began to be introduced and spread to the central plains, inspiring further change among native Chinese musical forms, especially in folk music contexts. Over the thousand years from the Han to the Tang dynasty (618–907 CE), a long process occurred in which foreign and Chinese native musical forms developed from entirely independent systems to ones that were accepted alongside one another and then to those with shared and integrated features. Good examples include the Sui (581–618) and Tang dynasties' "seven bureaus of performance" (*qibuji* 七部伎) and "nine bureaus of performance" (*jiubuji* 九部伎) and the Tang "ten bureaus of performance" (*shibuji* 十部伎), each of which integrated Chinese native dances with foreign ones. Questions that arise include: where did these foreign dances come from, in what situations were they performed, and what influence did they exert on native Chinese genres? This chapter applies these questions to two historical dances, the *huxuan* 胡旋 and *huteng* 胡騰, treating them as case studies in an overall investigation on how the foreign dances and their music were accepted by and integrated with Chinese music and gradually localized. This chapter is thus a study of two partially contrasting kinds of interculturation and localization. First of all, I focus on the origins of these two kinds of exotic music, their dance forms, their styles, and their influences.

THE *HUXUAN* DANCE

The *huxuan* dance was a folk musical dance introduced from the western regions at the time of the formation of the Silk Road. It became one of the most popular dances in the Sui and the Tang dynasties. Numerous historical records show that this dance came from the nomadic peoples who inhabited the western regions, known in Chinese as the Hu. The term *xuan* means "whirl," suggesting a dance of bright and cheerful tempo based on whirling and stomping footwork. Most of the *huxuan* dancers shown in historical sources are female. Wearing light and thin garments with long sleeves and ribbons and long skirts with wide hemlines, in addition to being adorned with jewelry, these *huxuan* girls are shown dancing in a scene of flying skirts, sleeves, and ribbons, just like snowflakes flying in the sky. The dance is mainly accompanied by percussion and strings to fit its style of quick and vigorous whirling steps (Du, [801] 1984: 763).

Ouyang Xiu 歐陽修 wrote about the form and the origin of the *huxuan* dance in the "Treatise of the Five Phases" ("Wu xing zhi" 五行志, part of the *New Book of the Tang* [*Xin Tang shu* 新唐書], completed in 1080 CE). He recorded that: "The *huxuan* dance originated from Kangju; it took the quick whirl as its main skill, and was a fashionable dance at that time" (Ouyang, [1080] 1975: treatise 25). Meanwhile, Du You 杜佑 in Volume 146 of the *Comprehensive Institutions* (*Tongdian* 通典, completed in 801) had recorded the following detail: "The dance is performed just like a whirling wind, after which it is named" (Du, [801] 1984: 763). These two records indicate that the *huxuan* dance came from Kangju, later called the kingdom of Kang, which bordered the kingdoms of Lige and Yilie and belonged to the realm of Sogdiana (in the area of Samarkand in present-day Uzbekistan). In the Tang dynasty, it came under Chinese control, and a local administrative institution named the Dudufu was set up to govern this area. Other historic documents have shown that people in the kingdom of Kang were habitually fond of drinking, often singing and dancing in the streets, and were especially charmed by the *huxuan* dance. According to the "Chronicle of the Western Regions" of the *New Book of the Tang* (*Xin Tang shu*, "Xicheng zhuan" 新唐書·西域傳), the Kang, Shi, Mi, Jumi, and other kingdoms in the western regions all presented *huxuan* girls to the court of the Tang empire at this time (Ouyang, [1080] 1975: 6243–66). An outcome was that, in the capital of Chang'an, the *huxuan* dance became all the rage—the most popular and fashionable dance of its day.

Apart from these formal records, some literary works also retain evidence about the H*huxuan* dance. For instance, the famous Tang-dynasty poet Yuan Zhen 元稹

(779–831), described the *huxuan* dance rather vividly in his poem, "In Response to Li Jiaoshu's New Poems, The Twelve *Yuefu*: *Huxuan* Girl" ("He Li Jiaoshu xin ti yuefu shi'er shou yuefu: Huxuan nü" 和李校書新題樂府十二首·胡旋女):

When Tianbao was about to end and barbarians about to revolt,
Barbarians presented girls who could dance with whirls.
The emperor was infatuated without knowing,
And the barbarians marched into Longevity Palace.
...
Jewelry and earrings shine like twinkling stars,
Light chiffons and long scarves dance like a flickering rainbow.
It seems as if a whale makes the sea's waves high and low,
It looks like a whirlwind tosses countless pearls round in the sky.
...
Silk ribbons loosely twine her soft waistline,
Dazzling bracelets circle her waving arms (Peng et al., [1705] 1960: vol. 419, p. 11).

This poem not only suggests the prevalence of *huxuan* dance in the last years of the Tang Tianbao reign period (742–56) but also vividly depicts the dancing posture of *huxuan* female dancers. This can be seen as evidence that the *huxuan* dance, as a foreign form that combined musical performance and dance featuring fast whirls, was widespread in the Tianbao period. Bai Juyi 白居易 (772–846), another famous Tang-dynasty poet, wrote the following lines in his poem, "*Huxuan* Girl: Against This Bad Social Custom" ("Huxuan nü: Jie jin xi ye" 胡旋女: 戒近习也):

Whirling dancing girl, whirling dancing girl. Heart as strings, hands as drums. Strings and drum, with one voice both sleeves raised, spinning round as blowing snow, her skirt fluttering.

Spinning left and turning right she never seemed to tire, thousand times rounds ten thousand more, never to stop. Nothing like it in the world of men, like a spinning wheel slow were the winds round her.

The song over, she thanked our Son of Heaven twice fold, the Son of Heaven opened his mouth part way to speak of it all. This whirling dancing girl of the Kangqu [Kangju] tribe, she travelled in vain from thousands of miles to the east. Ever since the Central Plains had its own whirling dancing girl, even [generals] of tremendous battle prowess could never compare.

In the seasons of the Heaven's Jewel [Tianbao] reign he desired a change, ministers and consorts alike learned this spinning dance. Taizhen [Consort Yang] within the palace, An Lushan outside. These very two their whirling dance so authentic. Amidst the Pear Blossom Gardens she became his queen, and Lushan, ever the Golden Pheasant was adopted as her son.

Lushan's whirling dance mystified our lord's eyes, soldiers crossed the Yellow
River without resistance. Consort Yang's whirling dance deluded our lord's heart, dead and abandoned at Mawei his yearning only grew deeper.

Alas, since then the Earth kept on spinning and the Heavens revolved; for fifty years, no imperial edict was ever issued to ban it. Oh whirling dancing girl, please do not dance in vain. Just sing this song a few times to awaken our bright lord. (translated by Gwyther, 2013: 58–59, Chinese text deleted)

"*Huxuan* Girl: Against This Bad Social Custom" gives a comprehensive account of what the *huxuan* dance was like, the way it was received in the highest echelons of Tang society, and the serious harm (so Bai alleged) that it brought to society as it spread from the court to the folk. The first lines describe the characteristics of the *huxuan* dance and emphasize the amazing skill of the female dancer with rhetorical exaggeration, highlighting her rapid whirls. The line beginning "the Son of Heaven opened his mouth" is a transition, literally reflecting the emperor's appreciation of the dance, implying in fact a criticism of the emperor's indulgence in it and his excessive tolerance of Consort Yang and An Lushan, who were both known for being good *huxuan* dancers, which led to the decline of the Tang empire. Lines from "This whirling dancing girl of the Kangqu tribe" to "abandoned at Mawei his yearning only grew deeper" describe the emperor Xuanzong's favor for Yang Yuhuan and An Lushan, which led to the An Lushan Rebellion. As tributes to the emperor of the Tang from Kangju, which was a small country thousands of miles distant, these *huxuan* dancers had formerly found few chances to compete with dancers in the central plains. However, in the last years of the Tianbao era, learning the *huxuan* dance suddenly became a new fashion among officials and commoners, just as the poem describes. The verses point to the monarch's personal fascination with the dance, which is presented as the root cause of this new vogue for Hu culture. The line "His yearning only grew deeper" implies not only that the emperor's subsequent decision to execute Consort Yang was made in desperation but also that his indulgence in singing and dancing ended up both harming the country and himself. Bai Juyi's poem thus warns how far-reaching the consequences can be when the state takes up the culture of neighboring peoples, such as those whom Bai perceived as less civilized.

But was the *huxuan* dance introduced from the western regions into the central plains to cover up an incipient rebellion? Bai Juyi's poem specifically presents the end of the Tianbao reign period as a turning point in acceptance of the dance. Yuan Zhen's poem quoted just above also suggested that the presentation of *huxuan* girls to the court occurred only in the mid-Tianbao phase as a calculated distraction from the planned rebellion. In fact, historical records including the already cited "Chronicle of the Western Regions" of the *New Book of the Tang* had many times noted the presentation of *huxuan* dancing girls as tribute to the empire of Tang during the preceding Kaiyuan reign phase (713–41). Entries for the kingdoms of the Kang, Mi, and Jumi in the "Historical Biography" ("Liezhuan" 列傳) component of the *New Book of the Tang*, record the tribute as follows:

Early Kaiyuan: (the kingdom of Kang) sent armor, crystal cups, agate bottles, ostrich eggs, textiles, dwarves, and *huxuan* girls.
    The kingdom of Mi, or Mimo . . . presented jade, a dancing stage, lions, and *huxuan* girls.

The kingdom of Jumi ... sent envoys to the imperial court in the 16th year of Zhenguan ... and presented *huxuan* girls in the mid-Kaiyuan years.

The kingdom of Shi, or Qusha.... King Hubiduo presented dancing girls and leopards in the 15th year of Kaiyuan (Ouyang, [1080] 1975: 6243–66).

In fact, before the Tang dynasty, associations between the peoples of the central plains and those of the kingdoms in the western regions already existed, including the practice of strategic intermarriage. According to a passage in volume 10 of the *Histories of the North* (*Bei shi* 北史, completed in 659) (Li, [659] 1974: 528–29), in March of 565, the emperor Wu of the Northern Zhou dynasty sent envoys from Yumen Pass with large gifts to propose to the Tujue princess Ashina. At that time the Tujue were a strong tribe in the Junggar Basin area, controlling the kingdoms in the western regions. Trying to connect closely with the strong Northern Zhou empire, the Turkic Khan accepted the marriage proposal, and the two wedded in 568. Because his daughter loved music, the Khan sent a large band of the western region's musicians and dancers as part of the dowry, which comprised three hundred people from Shule, Anguo, Kang, and other kingdoms. Among those sent to the Zhou capital of Chang'an were famous Kuche musicians such as Su Qipo 苏祇婆, Bai Mingda 白明达, and Bai Zhitong 白智通, as well as many dancing girls, who brought the instruments of the western regions, such as a five-stringed form of the lute *pipa* 琵琶, the vertical harp *shukonghou* 竖箜篌, transverse flute *hengdi* 横笛, and the skin drum *jiegu* 羯鼓. It is likely that the *huxuan* dance was also brought into central China then but that it did not become popularized over that region until the Kaiyuan or Tianbao years. Thus occurred the scenes described in the poems cited above, of dramatically changing dance fashions in that period.

In addition to these literary records, a great number of pictures of the *huxuan* dance have been preserved in Sogdian tombs and in Dunhuang frescoes. These exhibit various forms and styles, including solo and duo dances. As for the solo dance, we can take the musical dance on the stone gate of the Tang tomb in Yanchi, Ningxia province, as an example. The owner of the tomb was a Sogdian surnamed He, who lived in a prosperous period of the Tang dynasty. A male dancer is carved on each of the left and right stone doors of Grave M6 (Figure 4.1). The compilers of a report on the excavation of this tomb describe the dancers as follows:

The male carved on the right door wears a round cap, a long skirt with a round neckline and narrow sleeves, and soft shoes. The other male, on the left door, wears a long gown with a rectangular neckline. His cap and shoes are the same as the other's. Each of them stands on a small felt, with one leg in a prance, arms raised, waving ribbons in a dancing position. The background seems to be decorated as rolling clouds, on which each man dances (Ningxia, 1988: 52).

The dancers wear a typical Sogdian costume: a long, tight gown; a round cap; and soft shoes. The dancing posture of standing on a small, round piece of felt, the legs prancing, and the movement of waving ribbons are consistent with the performance of the *huxuan* dance described in literary sources. The text of the *New Book of the Tang* notes: "While

FIGURE 4.1. Picture of dancing figures on the stone doors to Grave M6, Yanchi, Ningxia (copy painted by Zhou Chanling).

dancing the *huxuan*, the dancer stands on a carpet, whirling like the wind" (Ouyang, [1080] 1975: 6244–55). Meanwhile, Duan Anjie 段安節, in the entry "Singer and Dancer" ("Pai you" 俳優) of his *Miscellanea on Music* (*Yuefu za lu* 樂府雜錄), writes: "The dancer of . . . the *huxuan* dances on a small carpet, jumping or whirling on their feet on the carpet. What a wonderful dance!" (Duan, [c. 880] 1988: 21–22).

Turning now to the duo format of the *huxuan* dance, the "Music Volume" ("Yinyue zhi" 音樂志) of the *Old Book of the Tang* (*Jiu Tang shu* 舊唐書) records the following information:

> Each of two dancers wears a dark red coat with a cotton collar, green silk-made trousers, and a pair of red leather boots. Carrying a white bag on their girdles, they whirl quickly like the wind. This is called *huxuan*. The accompaniment music is played by two flutes, a main drum, an assistant drum, and a cymbal. (Liu, [945] 1975: 1070–71)

The record above shows us the general appearance of the *huxuan* duo dance: wearing Hu clothing, the performers dance quickly in a whirl. This kind of *huxuan* dance is accompanied by a small-scale ensemble from the kingdom of Kang, which drew from the instrumental branches of both India and Persia. The exact instrumental configuration is based on percussion and so has a certain connection with the shape of the Medicine Buddha band of the Tang dynasty, which can also be seen in the Dunhuang cave murals. Thus, this form of musical dance is already permeated by multicultural impacts from Persia, India, and Sogdiana itself. After analyzing the music and dance paintings in the Tang-dynasty Dunhuang murals, Wang Kefen (Wang, 1987: 1070–71),

Luo Feng, Chen Haitao, and other scholars identified the images of Cave 331 as early Tang, Cave 214 and 215 as high Tang, and Cave 197 as mid-Tang depictions of *huxuan* dance, in which dancers wearing tight skirts and waving ribbons are rotating on a round carpet. Matching this are paintings of dances found in the frescoes of Tang-dynasty tombs. For example, the fresco on the north wall of Li Ji's tomb in Xianyang city, Shaanxi province, shows a pair of female dancers, side-by-side. Their hair is combed in a style called dual-circle hair buns, and they wear red shirts with sleeves and black-and-white striped skirts. Raising their arms and with legs leaping, while their skirt hemlines appear to whirl, they take on a distinct posture that evokes a whirling dance. This duo posture is consistent with the description of the *huxuan* dance as given in the *Old Book of the Tang* and the Tang-dynasty poems already cited. Beside this, on the tomb's east wall, there is another fresco in which the image of one of three dancers has been very damaged. The two that are undamaged play *paixiao* 排簫, an alternate name for the vertical flute *xiao*, and the transverse flute *hengdi* 橫笛 respectively. Together with the dancer, they form a small dance ensemble suggestive of a process of ongoing integration between Hu and native Chinese music.

In recent years, new evidence about the *huxuan* dance has emerged from further archaeological discoveries. In 2014, another picture of this dance was discovered in the tomb of Han Xiu (673–740), the prime minister of the emperor Tang Xuanzong, in Xi'an, Shaanxi province. The picture on the middle section of the tomb's east wall shows two groups of musicians on rugs, with a male and female dancer on round carpets in between the instrumentalists (Figure 4.2). The two dancers mirror each other's postures in a contradance. The female dancer on the left looks plump, wearing a shirt with long sleeves and with hair combed in a style called *woduoji*, typical of women of the Tang dynasty, and so appears to be a Han. The male dancer on the right has heavy eyebrows and a full beard, obvious markers of Hu identity. He wears a soft head cloth (*futou* 襆頭) and

FIGURE 4.2. Dance picture on Han Xiu's tomb (detail), Guoxin village, Xi'an (copy painted by Zhou Chanling).

a long robe with a round neckline. Both the two raise their arms and hold their legs in a whirling dancing position, in accordance with the characteristics of the *huxuan* dance (Cheng, 2016: 131).

The accompaniment ensemble comprises eight instrumentalists playing zither (*zheng* 箏), clappers (*paiban* 拍板), mouth organ (*sheng* 笙), *shukonghou*, *pipa*, reed pipe (*bili* 篳篥), vertical *xiao* flute (*paixiao*), and cymbals (*tongbo* 銅鈸). Among these, instruments with Hu origins are the *shukonghou*, *pipa*, *bili*, and *tongbo*; those native to China are the *zheng*, *paiban*, *sheng*, and *paixiao*. The Tang musicians, mainly female, are on the left while the male-dominated Hu musicians are on the right. We might interpret the mural as showing local Tang people learning and imitating Hu people's music and dance, as shown on the right, or even competing in the performance of the *huxuan* dance with the latter. In either interpretation, the painting vividly reflects the active attempts of Tang people to absorb the popular *huxuan* dance into their own costuming and musical norms, and it clearly depicts how Hu and Han music and people began to integrate with one another by the mid-Tang period. It also suggests some artistic transformations that emerged from this process of integration after the *huxuan*'s eastward spread to the central plains: the combination of male and female dancers, the interplay of Hu and Han performers, and reliance upon both sitting and standing postures—these changes may be emblematic of the hybridized Hu and Han music of the Kaiyuan period more generally.

Another characteristic of the *huxuan* dance is its symmetry. In an early Tang illustration at Cave 220, Dunhuang, two pairs of dancers are painted in pictures placed side-by-side on the north wall at the center of a fresco of the Medicine Buddha

FIGURE 4.3. Detail of early Tang-dynasty painting of dancing from Cave 220 north wall, Dunhuang (copy painted by Zhou Chanling).

(Figure 4.3).[2] All four dancers are female. In the left-hand picture, the pair dance on small, round blankets. Dressed in shirts and skirts, adorned with jewelry, and waving colored ribbons, they raise their arms and stamp their feet in a vigorous dancing posture, which can be inferred as representative of the *huteng* dance. In the right-hand picture, the two dancers on round blankets are dancing back-to-back. Their dancing posture shows their outstretched arms entwined with light ribbons and flying skirt hemlines as they whirl quickly and so identifies the *huxuan* dance. One point that emerges from the analysis of these paintings of the *huxuan* dance in duo and quartet format is the importance of pairing, which allows a symmetric aesthetic viewpoint, with dancers turned away from one another even as they whirl around. Meanwhile, Cave 220's pairing of contrasting paired dance scenes exemplifies how the *huxuan* existed in combination with other dances from Central Asia, notably the *huteng* dance.

Overall, there appears a clear track along which the *huxuan* dance developed in China: first, a simple type of foreign dance was introduced in the early Northern Zhou; then, a more comprehensive type of dance took shape, with its own characteristic instrumental resources. Finally, the *huxuan* gradually reached a creative peak, becoming thoroughly integrated into China's native musical culture and a favorite dance of the court-banquet musical entertainments in the Tang dynasty.

The *Huteng* Dance

During or before the Northern Qi dynasty (550–577), the *huteng* dance, which was as famous as the *huxuan* dance, was introduced to the central plains from the western regions. In 1971, a yellow-glazed flat ceramic pot dated to 575 was unearthed in the Fancui Tomb of Anyang county, Henan province. The pot's body is carved with a scene of music and dance; in the center is a male *huteng* dancer. Meanwhile there are also many descriptions of the *huteng* dance in Tang poems, such as "Watching the *Huteng* Dance at Night in Assistant Secretary Wang's Mansion" ("Wang Zhongcheng zhai ye guan wu Huteng" 王中丞宅夜觀舞胡騰) by Liu Yanshi 劉言史 (c. 742–813):

> The Shi people are very rare among Hu musicians, this dancer [from Shi kingdom] squats and dances as fast as a bird in front of the banquet.
> He wears a pointed hat, and a thin shirt with small sleeves.
> He throws the grape bowl, looking west, as if thinking deeply of his home town.
> He jumps and spins like a wheel, his belts ringing, his boots dazzling.
> Everyone is silent and stunned, the *hengdi* and *pipa* accelerating.
> He dances until the woolen blanket flies like a snowflake, petals falling like a melting candle.
> When the music and dance ends with the banquet, in the west the hibiscus faces a waning moon. (Peng, [1705] 1960: vol. 468, p. 11)

From this we know that the *huteng* dance combines the postures of squatting and standing (and movements associated with these alternations of posture) with an accompaniment played by instruments from western regions, including transverse flute (*hengdi*) and *pipa*, suggesting a distinctive Hu style. In Liu's poem, the *huteng* dance is dominated by fast and vigorous movements. Another Tang poem, "Huteng Boy" ("Huteng er" 胡騰兒) by Li Duan 李端, also describes the dance:

> The dancer of *huteng* is a boy from Liangzhou:
> His body is [as pale] as jade, and his nose [as sharp] as an awl.
> Wearing a white-colored light robe, the front and back [of the robe] is rolled up;
> Wearing a purple-colored long belt, one end [of the belt] is hanging.
> ...
> He lifts his eyebrows, moves his eyes, and steps on the flowery carpet;
> He sweats heavily and his pearl hat inclines aside.
> He [seems to be] drunk, teetering toward the east and then the west;
> His boots are softly [wandering] in front of the lamps.
> He walks in a circle or treads fast, all conforming to the beat;
> He puts his hands reversely on his waist, like a semicircular moon.
> (translation in Sha, 2016: 29)

The dancer is described as pale-skinned and has a high-bridged nose, indicating someone from the western regions. The dance is described as both dazzling and steady. Liu's poem above also identifies the accompanying instruments as those from western regions, including the *hengdi* and the *pipa*, both performed with a distinctive Hu style.

Where did the *huteng* dance come from? Liu Yanshi's poem refers to the Sogdian kingdom of Shi, which was located on the south bank of the Tarim river (in the region of the present-day city of Tashkent, Uzbekistan). As a pivotal point of connection between the eastern and western cultures on the Silk Road, the court there was in regular contact with its Chinese counterpart. The "Border Defense 9" ("Bianfang jiu" 邊防九) scroll of the *Tongdian* has a detailed record: "The kingdom of Shi was affiliated to the Sui dynasty.... In the fifth year of the Daye reign period [i.e., 609] in the Sui dynasty and in the eighth year of the Zhenguan reign period [634] in the Tang dynasty, it sent messengers to pay tribute" (Du You, [801] 1984: vol. 193). Through trade and cultural exchanges from Shi, the *huteng* dance was introduced into the central plains.

As for the time when the *huteng* dance was introduced into the central plains, the above-mentioned yellow-glazed pot, made in the sixth year of the Wuping reign of the Northern Qi dynasty (575), confirms that the *huteng* dance had been introduced into the central plains from Central Asia by at least that time. On the pot, the dancer stands on a lotus pedestal, raising his right arm and stretching his left arm downward with his left palm inverted. This backward-looking posture is consistent with descriptions of the *huteng* dance in Tang poetry.

Accompaniment instruments shown on the pot are a five-string *pipa*, a flute of Indian style, and West Asian cymbals. This suggests that such small ensembles of Hu instruments originally played for this kind of dance, and most of these early sources show no more than four or five performers together. Later, in the Tang dynasty, as banquets with singing and dancing became fashionable and training schools were established for both musical and operatic performance (the famous Jiaofang 教坊 and Liyuan 梨園), the *huteng* dance developed further, gaining a larger scale of performance and more potential for variation in its performance structures.

This kind of dance also appears on the tomb frescoes of Sogdians who had settled in what is now Daminggong county, Weiyang district, north of Xi'an in the period from the Northern Zhou dynasty to the Sui dynasty. In the frescoes of Anga's tomb and in those of Yu Hong's tomb from the Sui dynasty, there are scenes of banqueting among which the *huteng* dance is performed. Most of the dancers are male Hu with high noses and deep-set eyes, and they are dressed in Hu costumes. Again, the costumes and postures of dancers in these images are basically consistent with those of the *huteng* dance described in literature.

The *huteng* dance is mainly a solo dance. Frescoes of this type have been discovered adorning tombs of the royal family and aristocrats of the Tang dynasty, among which the most typical is a painting in the east wall in Su Sixu's tomb, which dates from the Tianbao years of the Tang dynasty. In the painting, there is a male dancer with a high nose, deep-set eyes, and long sideburns, wearing a tall and pointed "barbarian-type" cap, a long robe with a round neckline, and a pair of soft boots made from brocade. His stance suggests a curving sway, and he is placed on a carpet. Looking backward while waving backhandedly, he seems to move his eyeballs with emotion. All these characteristics exactly match those of the *huteng* dance described in the Tang poems.

In the picture at Su Sixu's tomb, nine accompaniment instruments and what appear to be two vocalists are arranged on each side of the dancer: *pipa*, *sheng*, *bo*, *zhudi*, *shukonghou*, *zheng*, *bili*, and *paixiao* (see Huang, 2000: 147–48). The grouping shows that the accompaniment of the *huteng* dance in the Tang dynasty had gradually incorporated instruments native to China among those from the western regions. The larger ensemble also suggests an integration between Hu music and Chinese music with increased resources for an art form combining dance, singing, instrumental melody, rhythm, and varied textures and patterns in the accompaniment.

This kind of *huteng* dance can also be seen in the Tang-dynasty murals of the Dunhuang caves. In the painting of a dance on the north wall of Cave 320, a male dancer performs in the center of a square blanket, waving a long ribbon in the air: the image can be speculated as revealing a quick curveting movement characteristic of the *huteng* dance. The accompaniment ensemble comprises ten players divided into groups arranged on each side of the dancer. The players on the left play *paiban*, *bili*, *sheng*, *pipa*, and *shukonghou* respectively; those on the right play *bili*, *hengdi*, vertical flute (*shudi* 豎笛), *paixiao*, and the stone chimes (*fangxiang* 方響) (see further, Gao, 2008: 91).[3] Wind instruments, six in all, dominate the ensemble; the rest being two plucked stringed instruments and two percussion instruments. Hu and native Chinese instruments, five each, strike up a perfect balance in number, suggesting deep integration of Hu and Chinese musical traditions, a development which is also evidenced in other mid-Tang-dynasty murals.

In the Tang period, with the increasing interaction between the Han Chinese and the peoples of the western regions, a large number of figurines were produced that depict Hu people, including dancers and musicians. Among them is a gilded copper figurine of a *huteng* dancer, the only such figurine surviving from the Tang dynasty discovered so far, which is of great significance in the analysis of *huteng* dance from that period (Figure 4.4). The male Hu dancer wears the now customary "barbarian-style" Hu

FIGURE 4.4. Sketch of a Tang-dynasty figurine of a *huteng* dancer (Shandan County Museum, Gansu province) (copy painted by Zhou Chanling).

clothes and Central Asian boots. His left foot stands on a lotus stage and he raises up his right leg in a curve, his left hand on his hip and right arm stretching up. The whole body takes up a prancing posture. All these features are consistent with written descriptions from contemporaneous documents and with the images found among the frescoes in Sogdian tombs.

From the yellow-glazed flat pot unearthed in Anyang and the dance's popularity in poems and murals, it can be inferred that the *huteng* dance had been introduced into the central plains in the second half of the sixth century, at the latest. Artifacts like the gilded-copper dance figurine vividly describe the dynamic image of the *huteng* dance and the character of Hu performers. The fact that *huteng* dance became a subject for art works like this underscores the important position it achieved in Tang culture more generally.

Conclusions

The *huxuan* and *huteng* dances became fashionable in the period from the Northern and Southern dynasties to the Sui and Tang dynasties and had a profound impact on the culture of the central plains. Du You, in Volume 142 of the *Comprehensive Institutions* recorded the evolutionary process of Hu dances: "Hu music became popular in the Xuanwu period.... Kucha *pipa*, five-string *pipa*, and *konghou*.... Hu dance is so sonorous and forceful that it startles one's heart and ears." The "Music Volume" of the *Old Book of the Tang* also recorded that the "Kucha *pipa*, five-string *pipa*, and song-and-dance performances (*gewuji* 歌舞伎) were new interests of the Wenxiang period, and had been frequently learned and practiced especially since the Heqing year [562]." It can be seen from these records that the music and dance of Hu had tremendous influence over music in the central plains.

Based on historical documents and archaeological evidence from the Northern and Southern dynasties to the high-Tang period, this chapter provides a discussion of the *huxuan* and *huteng* dances and their accompanying ensembles, exploring the performances, sources, influences, and localization process of each of the two dances. The *huxuan* dance, in the form of symmetrical duos or quartets danced by females, originated from the western regions in the Northern Zhou dynasty and prevailed in the years of Kaiyuan and Tianbao of the Tang dynasty. Both its dance and music were localized during the high-Tang period, with Hu instruments and local ones used in tandem in the accompaniment. The *huteng* dance, characterized by squatting and jumping, and often involving the posture of the right arm raised and the left arm held akimbo, was a powerful dance performed mainly in solo format. The accompaniment ensemble of the *huteng* dance was small when it was first introduced to the central plains. In the Tang dynasty, however, the proportion of Chinese native instruments increased, as did the scale of the ensemble. During the process of integration of Hu and local music, the *huteng* dance reached its creative peak.

In the Jiaofang and Liyuan training schools of the Tang dynasty, both the *huxuan* and *huteng* dances were classified as, literally, "energetic dances" (*jianwu* 健舞), implying the vigorous and powerful character of horsemen of northern China, and forming an aesthetic concept that could be opposed to other, "softer" styles of dance. The two dances followed a similar pattern of great development in their accompaniment and presumably their sound character when they entered the central plains, beginning with a small group of Hu instruments and becoming a more integrated, larger ensemble that included native Chinese instruments. The Chinese empire was clearly willing to accept foreign culture, assimilating and integrating it with existing Chinese resources, and providing an essential condition that allowed these two kinds of dances to occupy an important artistic position in the Sui and particularly the Tang dynasty. In analyzing the origins, the forms, the styles, and the cultural significance of these two dances, this chapter showcases how deeply and for how long in history Chinese music has been inseparable from cultural and political exchanges between China and other civilizations.

Funding Acknowledgment

This chapter is supported by the Key Project in the Arts, 2019, Project No. 19ad003, National Social Science Foundation of China.

Glossary

Bai Juyi 白居易, poet (772–846)
Bai Mingda 白明達, sixth-century musician
Bai Zhitong 白智通, sixth-century musician
bili 篳篥: reed pipe
"Bianfang jiu" 邊防九, "Border Defense 9," scroll that is part of the *Comprehensive Institutions* by Du You (801)
Du You 杜佑, historian and politician (735–812)
fangxiang 方響, suspended stone chimes
futou 襆頭, head cloth
gewuji 歌舞伎, song-and-dance performances
"He Li Jiaoshu xin ti yuefu shi'er shou yuefu: Huxuan nü" 和李校書新題樂府十二首·胡旋女, "In Response to Li Jiaoshu's New Poems, The Twelve *Yuefu: Huxuan* Girl," poem by Yuan Zhen
hengdi 橫笛, transverse flute
huteng 胡騰, dance genre
huxuan 胡旋, dance genre
"Huxuan nü: Jie jin xi ye" 胡旋女: 戒近習也, "*Huxuan* Girl: Against This Bad Social Custom," poem by Bai Juyi
huyueqi 胡樂器, "foreign" instruments
jianwu 健舞, category of energetic dances recognized by court training organizations
Jiaofang 教房, court music academy
jiegu 羯鼓, skin drum

jiubuji 九部伎, "nine bureaus of performance," Sui and Tang division of court entertainments
Li Duan 李端, poet (743–82)
Liyuan 梨园, court traditional-opera academy
"Liezhuan" 列傳, "Historical Biography," part of the *New Book of the Tang* (1080)
Liu Yanshi 劉言史, poet (*c.* 742–813):
Ouyang Xiu 歐陽修, historian (1007–72)
"Pai you" 俳優, "Singer and Dancer" section of Duan Anjie's *Miscellanea on Music* (*c.* 880)
paiban 拍板, wood clappers
paixiao 排簫, alternate name for the vertical flute *xiao* 簫
pipa 琵琶, lute
qibuji 七部伎, "seven bureaus of performance," Sui and Tang divisions of court entertainments
sheng 笙, mouth organ
shibuji 十部伎, "ten bureaus of performance," Tang division of court entertainments
shudi 豎笛, vertical flute
shukonghou 豎箜篌, vertical harp
Su Qipo 苏祇婆, sixth-century musician
tongbo 銅鈸, cymbals
"Wang Zhongcheng zhai ye guan wu Huteng" 王中丞宅夜觀舞胡騰, "Watching the Huteng Dance at Night in Assistant Secretary Wang's Mansion," poem by Liu Yanshi
"Wu xing zhi" 五行志, "Treatise of the Five Phases," part of the *New Book of the Tang* (1080)
"Xicheng zhuan" 西域傳, "Chronicle of the Western Regions," part of the *New Book of the Tang* (1080)
yayue 雅樂, "elegant music," category of court music and ritual
Yuan Zhen 元稹, poet (779–831)
zheng 箏, zither
zheng sheng 鄭聲, secular performance genre of antiquity

Notes

1. *Zheng sheng* is the general name in the Spring and Autumn period for the music of the countries of Zheng and Wei, now the area of Xinzheng and Huaxian in Henan. It was a folk music that was active and full of vitality, and its musical content and character were in sharp contrast to the court's elegant music (*yayue*). Although *zheng sheng* was strongly opposed by Confucianism, it nevertheless interacted with *yayue*, with developments in the one being echoed in the other, leading Confucius to accuse it in his *Analects* of destroying *yayue*.
2. This fresco, and the whole cave, can be explored online at https://www.e-dunhuang.com/cave/10.0001/0001.0001.0220, accessed January 9, 2019.
3. Further examples of this kind of dance among the Dunhuang grotto pictures appear in Caves 129 and 231, which both date from the mid-Tang period.

References

Cheng Xu 程旭. (2016). *Tangyun hufeng: tangmu bihua zhongde wailai wenhua yinsu jiqi fanying de minzu guanxi* 唐韻胡風—唐墓壁畫中的外來文化因素及其反映的民族關係

[Tang Rhythm and Hu Style: Foreign Cultural Factors and the Relationship between the Different Nationalities in Tomb Frescoes of the Tang Dynasty]. Beijing: Wenwu chubanshe.

Du You 杜佑. ([801] 1984). *Tongdian* 通典 [Comprehensive Institutions]. Beijing: Zhonghua shuju.

Duan Anjie 段安節. ([c. 880] 1988). *Yuefu za lu* 樂府雜錄 [Miscellanea on Music]. Shenyang: Liaoning jiaoyu shubanshe.

Gao Dexiang 高德祥. (2008). *Dunhuang gudai yuewu* 敦煌古代樂舞 [Dunhuang's Ancient Music and Dance]. Beijing: Renmin yinyue chubanshe.

Gwyther, Jordan A. (2013). *"Bai Juyi and the New Yuefu Movement."* MA thesis, University of Oregon.

Huang Xiangpeng 黃翔鵬. (2000). *Zhongguo yinyue wenwu daxi (Shaanxi juan)* 中國音樂文物大系 (陝西卷) [An Expanded Family of Chinese Musical Relics, Shaanxi Volume]. Zhengzhou: Daxiang chubanshe.

Li Yanshou 李延壽, ed. ([659] 1974). *Bei shi* 北史 [Histories of the North]. Beijing: Zhonghua shuju.

Liu Xi 劉昫. ([945] 1975). "Yinyue zhi" 音樂志 [Music Volume]. In *Jiu Tang shu* 舊唐書 [Old Book of the Tang], vol. 29. Beijing: Zhonghua shuju.

Ningxia Huizu zizhiqu bowuguan 寧夏回族自治區博物館. (1988). "Ningxia Yanchi Tangmu fajue jianbao" "寧夏鹽池唐墓發掘簡報" [Brief Report on Excavation of the Tang Tomb in Yanchi of Ningxia]. *Wenwu* 文物 [Cultural Relics], no. 9: 43–56.

Ouyang Xiu 歐陽修. ([1080] 1975). *Xin Tang shu* 新唐書 [New Book of the Tang]. Beijing: Zhonghua shuju.

Peng Dingqiu 彭定求 et al., eds. ([1705] 1960). *Quan Tang shi* 全唐詩 [Complete Poetry of the Tang]. Beijing: Zhonghua shuju.

Sha Wutian. (2016). "An Image of Nighttime Music and Dance in Tang Chang'an: Notes on the Lighting Devices in the Medicine Buddha Transformation Tableau in Mogao Cave 220, Dunhuang," translated by Anne Ning Feng. *The Silk Road* 14: 19–41.

Wang Kefen 王克芬. (1987). *Zhongguo wudao shi (Sui, Tang, Wudai bufen)* 中國舞蹈史 (隋、唐、五代部分) [The History of Chinese Dance (in the Sui, Tang, and the Five Dynasties)]. Beijing: Beijing Wenhua yishu chubanshe.

CHAPTER 5

KUNQU FROM ANALYTICAL PERSPECTIVES

A Focus on "Feng ru song"

KAR LUN ALAN LAU

INTRODUCTION

ONE outstanding feature of *kunqu* 崑曲 is its highly theorized and intellectual nature, evidenced by the abundance of compositional procedures and treatises, as cultivated by generations of writers and scholars, or the *wenren* 文人 ("literati").[1] An operatic style originally practiced in the Kunshan 崑山 area during the Ming dynasty, *kunqu* was descended from the Yuan-dynasty *nanxi* 南戲 ("southern drama"), but had over the course of its development acquired repertoires and arias, as well as linguistic and literary elements, from the *beiju* 北劇 ("northern theater") tradition. Codified by Wei Liangfu 魏良輔 (c. 1489–c. 1566) in *Qulü* 曲律 (*Rules for Singing* Qu [*Poetry*]), *kunqu* was subsequently elevated from a regional style to national prominence, emerging as an important artistic medium for the literati during the Ming and Qing dynasties. Within the boundaries and confines determined by the concept of *qupai* 曲牌 ("labeled tunes"), the literati were able to exercise not only their creativity and imagination in terms of lyrics and storyline but also the freedom to devise their own, often elaborate, rules and templates, to manipulate the *presumed* relationships between music, language, and literary forms; the decline in popularity of *kunqu* with the rise of Beijing opera during the mid-Qing dynasty could be viewed as a reaction by the general public against this highly specialized and elitist practice, in favor of artistic expressions that were more direct and accessible.

Despite the close association between the musical, linguistic, and textual domains, elements of artificiality and disconnect were inevitably introduced into *kunqu*, a "composed tradition," as poetry and lyrics written by literati/librettists were passed to musicians/composers, and then to singers/performers.[2] Any attempt to study these multidomain relationships can therefore be challenging, as the interactions are often not straightforward and can be further obscured by various transformative forces as part of the dynamic nature of musical and linguistic evolution. Research efforts may also be limited by a scarcity of field recordings, a lack of early notations, and a general shortage of music-oriented resources stemming from the heavy inclination toward the literary and linguistic aspects of *kunqu* in both historical and contemporary discourses.

In light of the vastness and complexity of *kunqu* music as a phenomenon, a narrower scope is adopted here. Focusing on the *nanqu* 南曲 ("southern song") aria of "Feng ru song" 風入松, two important aspects of *kunqu* music are examined: 1) interactions between linguistic tones and musical pitches; 2) melodic relationships among different versions of the same vocal aria. Important features of the "*qupai* paradigm" will also be introduced. It is hoped that investigations into much debated topics, such as *Zhongzhou yun* 中州韻 and *zhuqiang* 主腔, will lead not only to new insights into *kunqu* but also to a better reconciliation between traditional notions and empirical or analytical evidence.

Theoretical Background

The strong emphasis on the relationship between language and music in *kunqu*, and in most Chinese vocal music, can be traced back to the "tonal nature" of the Sinitic languages. A central premise is that a speech sound may convey different meanings, depending on 1) the pitch (acoustic frequency) at which it is produced relative to adjacent speech sounds, and/or 2) its particular pitch or "tonal" contour. Figure 5.1 illustrates how the sound *shi* varies depending on the four tones (*sisheng* 四聲) in Standard Mandarin[3] and introduces tone symbols and linguistic terminology used throughout this chapter.

Of particular interest are the discrepancies between the typical labeling of linguistic tones (*shengdiao* 聲調), a somewhat archaic system based on earlier forms of Chinese languages and the actual tonal contours as observed in Standard Mandarin. For instance, despite its upward intonation, Tone 2 is referred as the *yangping* 陽平 ("low-level") tone, whereas *shang* 上 ("rising") is used to describe the "dipping" profile of Tone 3.[4] It should also be noted that *ru* 入 ("entering" or "checked tone") is technically not a tone category, as it does not refer to any particular pitch contour. Rather, "checked tone" refers to speech sounds with unreleased stop consonant endings /p/, /t/, and /k/, which have largely disappeared in northern languages such as Mandarin and have been reduced to the glottal stop /ʔ/ in Wu 吳 Chinese.[5]

The inherent tonal and "musical" nature of the Chinese languages provides the basis for the traditional notion of a close correspondence—or even an ideal "oneness"—between music and language, as can be seen in the practice of singing, or "musically reciting" (*yinchang* 吟唱) various poetic forms throughout history, from the mostly equal-phrased *shi* 詩 of Tang and earlier periods, to *ci* 詞 poetry with irregular phrasing popular during the Song dynasty, and to the even more flexible *qu* 曲 format that flourished throughout the Yuan, Ming, and Qing periods. A musically oriented term denoting "song" or "tune", *qu* was the main poetic form for the creation of *kunqu* arias, which allowed for the use of added *chenzi* 襯字 ("padding syllables"). The prevalence of

KUNQU FROM ANALYTICAL PERSPECTIVES   65

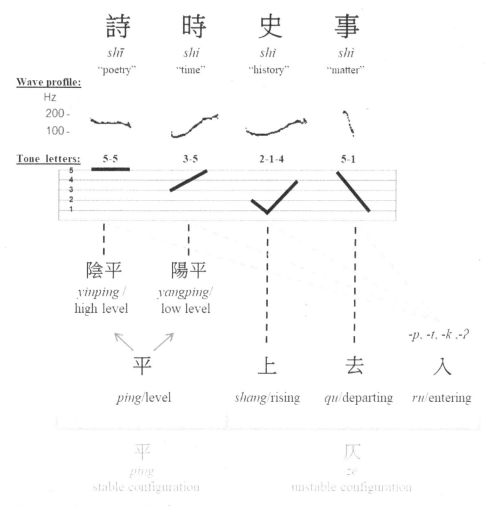

FIGURE 5.1. Four tones in Mandarin.

Note: Depending on its tone, the sound *shi* (in pinyin) may convey different meanings, including "poetry" 詩, "time" 時, "history" 史, and "matter" 事. Wave profile generated from recitation in Standard Mandarin by the *kunqu* performer Chen Rui, using WaveSurfer software (recorded in Vancouver, Canada, April 2018). Tone diagram based on tone letter system introduced by Chao Yuen-Ren (1930), and classification system adapted from Yang Yinliu (1983).

text-only *pu* 譜 ("notations") of *qu* poetry and operatic lyrics, with little mention of the musical aspects beyond the tune titles (as in Figure 5.3), thus reinforces the perceived "blurring" between the musical and language/literary domains.

The Qupai Paradigm

A multidomain approach to music making, especially in the creation of vocal or operatic music gave rise to the concept of *qupai*. Regarded as a "fundamental unit in Chinese music" (Qiao, 1994), *qupai* refers to recognizable instrumental or vocal tunes (or segments thereof), generally of considerable brevity, that are routinely used, referenced, and manipulated in order to serve a variety of musical or functional purposes (Lau, 2016; see further Thrasher, 2016). There also exists, however, a literary and textual definition of *qupai*, which the literati were more acquainted with, consisting of patterns and schemes of linguistic tone and rhyme used to guide poets and playwrights to select appropriate syllables or characters in a process known as *tianci* 填詞 ("filling in text"); visual representations of two literary *qupai*, in the form of an actual operatic text, and as instructional symbols are shown in Figure 5.3.

Under this dual music-literary *qupai* definition, there is but an ideal and tight connection between the musical and language/textual domains and a close mirroring between melodic movement and tonal contour. Structurally speaking, linguistic tones serve as the modulator of musical pitches, which are in turn organized into melodies and extend linearly along the time dimension. Music-text correspondence continues at higher levels, for example, between the often-irregular phrasing of the *qu* poetry text and musical phrases, and rhythmically, through the temporal punctuation of rhyme syllables by the *ban* 板 beat at phrase endings. Such theoretical *qupai* interactions are summarized in Figure 5.2.

At a conceptual level, and as a third definition, it is possible to regard *qupai* as a set of instructions or "schema," containing not only the aforementioned musical and linguistic/textual information but also *diangu* 典故 ("historical anecdotes"), in addition to other characteristics generally associated with a particular *qupai*—all readily accessible by poets and musicians upon the active citing or referencing of the *qupai* name in their works. The block-like symbolization of the word *qupai* is therefore not coincidental but rather reflects how concepts and ideas can be transmitted via *qupai* as "informational packages," from generation to generation, and across regions and cultures.

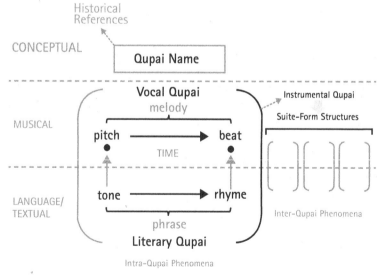

FIGURE 5.2. Vocal *qupai* paradigm.

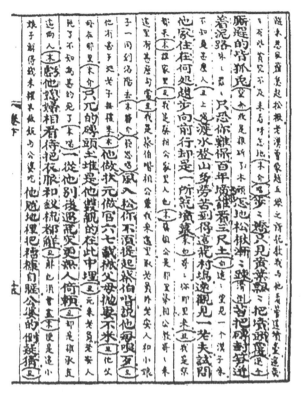

1. X 平 X 仄 仄 平 平 △   不 須 提 起 蔡 伯 喈，
2. X 仄 平 X 平 平 △   說 着 他 們 忒 歹。
3. X 平 仄 仄 平 平 去 △   他 去 做 官 [有] 六 七 載，
4. X 平 仄 平 平 平 去 △   撇 父 母 拋 妻 不 睬。
5. X 仄 平 平 仄 平 △   兀 的 [這] 磚 頭 土 堆，
6. X 平 仄 仄 平 平 △   [是 他] 雙 親 喪 [在] 此 中 埋。

FIGURE 5.3. Textual *qupai* template of "Feng ru song."
Notes: Upper left: Qing-dynasty version of *Pipa ji* (*Xinkan yuanben Cai Bojie Pipa ji* 新刊元本蔡伯喈琵琶記), with details of the first "Feng ru song" aria enlarged on the upper right (image source: Internet Archive).
Lower left: Underlined tone symbols in the tone and rhyme scheme (based on Wang, 1997) are optional and can be altered.
Lower right: Lyrics, with padding syllables marked by brackets [].

The so-called "*qupai* paradigm" can then be defined, first, as structural organization principles that utilize *qupai* or labeled tunes as a basic unit of music construction (as an "inter-*qupai*" phenomenon),[6] and second, at the "intra-*qupai*" level, as an approach to music making that emphasizes the interaction between the musical, linguistic/textual, and conceptual cognitive domains, with the concept of *qupai* itself serving as a medium or platform upon which such interfacings occur. The *qupai* paradigm (Figure 5.2) thus entails the "translation" of linguistic/textual "codes" into musical pitches and the subsequent "transcription" of the resulting musical materials across the vocal and instrumental domains. Based on this model, this chapter follows a specific pathway, from the tone-and-pitch interface to pitch relationships within the melodies of a single *qupai*.

Textual Qupai *and* Kunqu *Composition*

The *qupai* name "Feng ru song" 風入松 (literally, "Wind Entering Through the Pines") is said to be derived from either the title of a piece for the *qin* 琴 zither by the Jin-dynasty musician, Ji Kang嵇康 (*c.* 223–*c.* 262), or a poem by the Tang poet, Li Bai李白 (701–62): 風入松下清, 露出草間白.[7] This study primarily focuses on the first "Feng ru song" aria from the act, "Sao song" 掃松 ("Sweeping [Under] the Pines") of the *nanxi* ("southern drama"), *Pipa ji* 琵琶記 (*Tale of the Lute*).[8] Written by Gao Ming 高明 (*c.* 1305–*c.* 1370) toward the end of the Yuan dynasty, *Pipa ji* has been absorbed into *kunqu* and continues to be performed as part of the *nanqu* repertoire. The typical *qu* poetic structure of "Feng ru song" is shown in Figure 5.3 and consists of six phrases (three phrase pairs) of irregular length, each containing either six or seven syllables/characters. Rhyme syllables usually occur at the end of every phrase, sometimes with the exception of Phrase 5, and padding syllables may be inserted to expand the length of each phrase to create an almost prose-like effect.

During the creation of *qu* poetry, the writer selected a literary *qupai* template with desirable textual/linguistic characteristics, historical anecdotes, and artistic associations, and filled-in the template with lyrics that matched its tone and rhyme requirements. Despite the prestige the literati enjoyed, their involvement was often limited to textual and literary aspects of *kunqu* composition. According to *sandu chuangzuo* 三度創作, the three-part model of *kunqu* creation (Li, 2008), musicians, who were generally of a lower social status, then set the text to music in a rather systematic fashion. They would, for example, align important text and rhyme syllables at phrase endings to the strong *ban* beats, in a process known as *zhiqu* 製曲 ("song creation").[9] Musical pitches were then assigned based on the tonal nature of the text. The third step of the process involved the (re)interpretation of the musical notation by professional performers or amateur singers. This three-part process is summarized in Figure 5.4 and can be seen as an alternate representation of the conceptual *qupai* model introduced in Figure 5.2. The temporal-metrical framework that dictates the placement of rhyme syllables and the musical *ban* beats could in fact be viewed as a fourth definition or dimension of *qupai*.

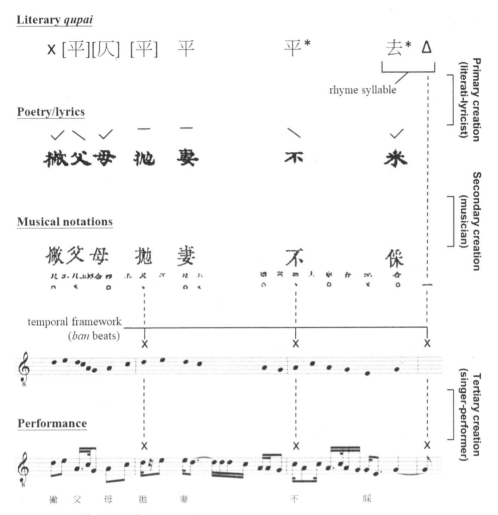

FIGURE 5.4. Three-part *kunqu* creative process.

Note: From top to bottom, the products from the various stages of the composition of the "Feng ru song" aria are: a) tone-and-rhyme scheme; b) textual version, from the *Xinkan yuanben Cai Bojie Pipa ji* (image source: Internet Archive); c) *gongche* 工尺 musical notation, from *Nashuying qupu* 納書楹曲譜 (Ye, 1792) (image source: Internet Archive); and d) actual performance version (transcribed from a demonstration by Chen Rui).

For the tone-and-rhyme scheme, X indicates an unspecified linguistic tone; [] marks non-mandatory tones; Δ shows rhyme syllables; * indicates discrepancy between tone symbols and text.

Music-Language Interactions in *Kunqu*

The preceding overview has set forth some of the theoretical basis of music-language interactions in *kunqu*. Yet in actual practice, these relationships are not always as simple and clear-cut. As to be explored throughout this chapter, while both being temporal processes, music and language are intrinsically different in many ways and a perfect correspondence between the two phenomena is often infeasible. The disconnection can be further exacerbated by the compartmentalization of the creative process, as well as variations introduced by musicians and performers during aural and written transmission and at both an individual and a collective level, leading to complexities and ambiguities that cannot be explained using singular perspectives.

One example of such ambiguity involves the concept of *Zhongzhou yun* 中州韻 (literally, "rhymes of the central plains"), the phonological standards of *guanhua* 官話 ("official speech"), or *lingua franca*, spoken in the central Chinese region (around today's Henan province) upon which *kunqu* composition, singing, and recitation are supposed to be based.[10] Controversies regarding *Zhongzhou yun* stem from its ever-evolving nature and complex mode of dissemination. As a manner of enunciating the "proper" northern language, *Zhongzhou yun* as presented in *kunqu* today has likely undergone substantial changes relative to its Ming and Qing-dynasty predecessors. Further confusions arise from the various standards of *Zhongzhou yun* used in *beiqu* 北曲 ("northern song") and *nanqu*, in addition to the disparities between singing and recitation. These differences are then subject to regional diversification, giving rise to *beikun* 北崑 and *nankun* 南崑, the northern and southern *kun* styles, not to be confused with the *beiqu* and *nanqu* repertoires.

Within these stylistic divides, further convergent and divergent forces are at work. For example, regional diversification can be countered by assimilation tendencies toward the *lingua franca* of the time. *Kunqu* performers may also employ different styles of singing and recitation along the *Zhongzhou yun*–dialect continuum depending on their dramatic role, their own interpretation, and the theatrical situation. The summary in Figure 5.5 thus illustrates not only the linguistic and musical divisions under the umbrella term of *Zhongzhou yun* but also the overall stylistic dynamics within *kunqu*.[11]

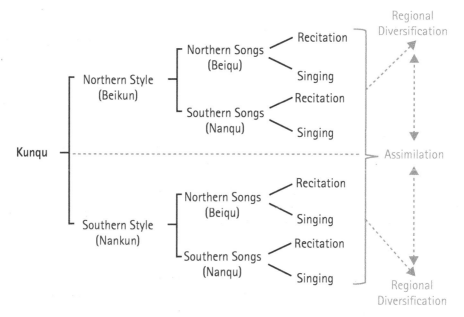

FIGURE 5.5. Multiple definitions of *Zhongzhou yun* and stylistic division within *kunqu*.

In the following sections, a three-part analysis will be conducted with increased levels of magnification. The aim is to investigate the various music-language interactions within the "Feng ru song" aria, from an overview of the differences between *kun* singing and recitation, to the relationships between melodic movement and historical/regional phonologies at the phrasal level, followed by an in-depth examination of various intra- and inter-syllabic phenomena.

Kun *Recitation and Singing*

Figure 5.6 contains a transcription of the first "Feng ru song" aria from *Sao song*, based on an unaccompanied demonstration by a southern *kun* performer, Chen Rui 陳睿, and is juxtaposed with a tonal contour profile of the recitation of the same lyrics (*nianbai* 念白, or more specifically *yunbai* 韻白 in the context of *kunqu*), also performed by Chen.[12]

Initial examination shows several differences between *kun* singing and recitation in duration, rhythm, and pitch. First, singing generally unfolds over a longer timespan than the recitation of the same text. The different distribution of durations, especially the use of short-long rhythms, in recitation, contributes a sense of recurring syncopation, which is largely absent in the melodic version. Second, continuous pitch changes or "glidings" are common within individual recited syllables, whereas singing often features discrete pitch successions in stepwise or leap motions.[13] The most significant observation, however, is the discrepancy between the tonal contour of the recitation and the corresponding melodic movement, with the recitation contour often operating in opposite directions from the melody (Figure 5.7), especially in Phrase 3, a surprising finding considering that both *kun* singing and recitation are supposed to reflect the tonal nature of *Zhongzhou yun*.

According to Yu Zhenfei 俞振飛 (1982), such discrepancies can be explained by the fact that *kun* recitation and singing are generally practiced as two separate disciplines (an observation confirmed by Chen Rui based on his own aural training).[14] Thus, *kun* recitation and singing have likely undergone relatively independent courses of development, and as a result, acquired different linguistic features and influences. In particular, Yu believes that *kun* recitation has preserved southern phonology (especially that of the Suzhou dialect of Wu Chinese) to a greater extent compared to singing, whereas Yang Yinliu 楊蔭瀏 (1983) considers both *kun* recitation and singing to have developed affinities toward northern phonology. As shown in Figure 5.8, certain northern and southern linguistic characteristics can be observed in the southern-style recitation of Phrases 3 and 4. While the recitation contour of 他去做官 largely complies with the Suzhou dialect, the falling-rising contour of 載 seems to echo that of Tone 3 in Standard Mandarin. Dissimilarities are also present, as in the case of 六 and 不, in which the tonal contours not only are opposite from those in Mandarin but also lack the glottal stop expected in the Wu language. Likewise, neither Mandarin nor the Suzhou dialect is implicated by the rising-falling contour of 睬.

As a point of interest, northern and southern styles of *kun* recitation have also been compared (Figure 5.9), with both versions displaying similar tonal contours. According to Chen Rui, northern-style recitation is strongly influenced by Beijing opera.

FIGURE 5.6. (a) Comparison between singing and (b; opposite side) recitation in the first "Feng ru song" aria.

Note: Both versions are performed by Chen Rui. The tonal profile of the recitation is generated by the WaveSurfer software. IPA symbols are used for the lyrics in both versions; vocables are marked by < >; [] indicates padding syllables.

Specifically, northern recitation of Phrase 3 appears to be more rhythmic and animated, in part due to the use of the vocable *le* 了 (in Mandarin) and the short-long syncopation of 不睬 at the end of Phrase 4.[15] More research is needed to discern between the effects of regional variations and personal interpretation in the above differences.

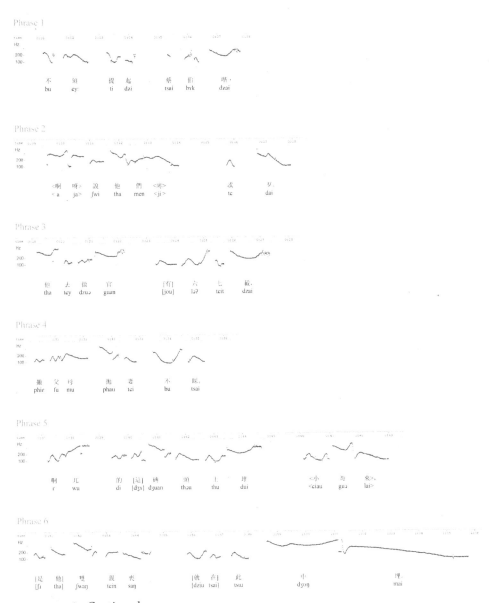

FIGURE 5.6. Continued

Historical and Regional Perspectives

The preceding section suggests a general lack of correlation between the tonal contour of *kun* recitation and its arias. Attention thus shifts toward the relationships between *kunqu* melodies and historical and regional phonologies. As previously noted, the use of different linguistic standards remains a major challenge in *kunqu* research. For instance, it is generally believed that the Yuan-dynasty rhyme dictionary, *Zhongyuan yinyun* 中原音韻 (Zhou, 1324) provides the phonological basis for the creation of *beiqu* arias, with tone categorization showing striking similarities to that of modern Mandarin. In

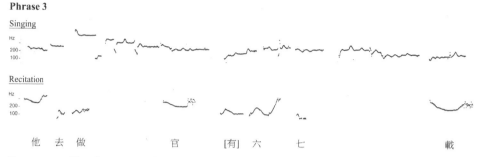

FIGURE 5.7. Tonal contours of southern *kun* singing and recitation of "Feng ru song," Phrase 3.

Note: The position of each syllable in the recitation has been adjusted to align with vocal melody; the duration of each syllable has not been altered.

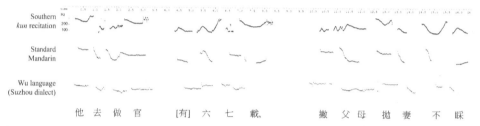

FIGURE 5.8. Tonal contours of the recitations of "Feng ru song," Phrases 3 and 4, in southern *kun* style, Standard Mandarin, and Suzhou Wu dialect.

Note: The position of each syllable in Mandarin and Suzhou recitations has been adjusted to align with the *kun* recitation without changes in syllabic duration.

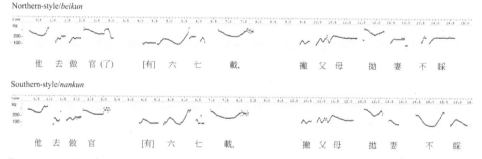

FIGURE 5.9. Tonal contours of northern and southern *kun* recitation of "Feng ru song," Phrases 3 and 4.

contrast, *Hongwu zhengyun* 洪武正韻 (Yue, Song, et al., 1375), the supposed standard for *nanqu*, is said to have preserved characteristics of an older form of Chinese, most notably, the entering/*ru* 入 "tone" (stop consonants or glottal stops) that ceased to exist in northern languages. Yet, as illustrated in Figure 5.10, the tone categorization from these two dictionaries can overlap significantly and neither volume provides the crucial information about the actual shape of the tonal contours.[16]

	撇	父	母	拋	妻	不	睬
Hongwu Zhengyun 洪武正韻	入 *ru* [entering]	去 *qu* [falling]	上 *shang* [rising]	平 *ping* [level]	平 *ping* [level]	入 *ru* [entering]	上 *shang* [rising]
Zhongyuan Yinyun 中原音韻	上 *shang* [rising]	去 *qu* [falling]	上 *shang* [rising]	陰平 *yinping* [high level]	陰平 *yinping* [high level]	上 *shang* [rising]	上 *shang* [rising]

FIGURE 5.10. Tone categorization of "Feng ru song," Phrase 4, based on *Hongwu zhengyun* and *Zhongyuan yinyun*.

FIGURE 5.11. Tonal contours from historical and regional sources and the melodic contour of "Feng ru song," Phrase 4.

Note: Linguistic tone patterns based on Ning (1985) for *Zhongyuan yinyun*, Shibles (1994) for Standard Mandarin, Gao (2009) for Qing-dynasty *nanqu* phonology, and Shi (2007) for *Zhongzhou yun* as used in Suzhou-style *kun* recitation.

To remedy this limitation, reconstructions of historical tone patterns along with those compiled from contemporary language and dialect sources are compared with the melodic contour of "Feng ru song," Phrase 4 (Figure 5.11).[17]

Overall, greater language-music correspondence can be seen with *Zhongyuan yinyun*, southern tone reconstruction, and Standard Mandarin, as opposed to Suzhou-style *Zhongzhou yun* (which is strongly influenced by the Suzhou dialect). The *shang* tone (falling-rising in Ning, Gao, and Standard Mandarin) in particular, is rather consistently matched by the ascending melodic motions in Phrase 4. Since Gao's reconstruction is extracted from the analysis of *nanqu* melodies from the mid-Qing-dynasty *Jiugong dacheng* 九宮大成 compendium (Zhou, Zou, et al., 1746), the strong correlation between Gao's southern tone reconstruction and the tonal patterns in Mandarin (or *Zhongyuan yinyun*) thus seems to support Yang Yinliu's assertion of the assimilation

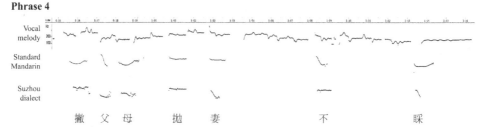

FIGURE 5.12. Vocal melody and non-theatrical recitation in Standard Mandarin and the Suzhou dialect of "Feng ru song," Phrase 4.

FIGURE 5.13. Visual discrepancies between tonal contour and symbolic representation of music and language in "Feng ru song," Phrase 4.

of northern phonologies into *nanqu* as noted above. Based on this reasoning, the *duanqiang* 斷腔 ("melodic pause") that accompanies the glottal stop in 不 could be potentially viewed as a southern linguistic feature (artificially) introduced within a predominantly northern scheme.

Interestingly, wave-contour analysis of the Phrase 4 melody (Figure 5.12) fails to reveal the same level of visual correspondence with either Standard Mandarin or the Suzhou dialect as compared to Figure 5.11, which highlights the difference between music and language as distinct temporal processes.[18] As illustrated in Figure 5.13, whereas correlation does exist, for example, between the *shang* tone (in Mandarin) and melodic motion, the falling-rising linguistic contour is not mimicked on a pitch-by-pitch basis but is instead approximated as stepwise ascending melodic motions involving two to three discrete pitches.[19]

Language-Music Interactions

With a certain level of correspondence established between Phrase 4 melodic movement and northern phonology in particular, the investigation now focuses on the relationships between individual linguistic tones and musical pitches. For this purpose, two sets of syllables, 有六七 ("being six and seven [years]") and 撇父母 ("abandoning [one's] parents") have been selected from Phrases 3 and 4 respectively, each containing

FIGURE 5.14. Syllable sets from Phrases 3 and 4.

three syllables and features the tonal contour *shang-qu-shang* 上-去-上 according to the northern phonology of *Zhongyuan yinyun*.[20]

One notable difference between the two syllable sets is their opposite melodic motion: ascending-descending for the Phrase 3 set, and descending-ascending for Phrase 4 (Figure 5.14). Differences in melodic motion alone do not always indicate a contradiction in tone-and-pitch relation, however; if the linguistic tone of a syllable has already been implicated in the *qiangtou* 腔頭 (the "head" portion of a melodic segment), the remainder of the melody (*qiangfu* 腔腹 "body" and *qiangwei* 腔尾 "tail") may diverge from the corresponding tonal contour, allowing for a certain freedom in composition and performance (Wu, 1993). Besides, tone-and-pitch relationships depend not only on the melodic manifestation within individual syllables (intra-syllabic relationships) but also on the movement of pitches across adjacent syllables (inter-syllabic relationships). In order to determine the effects of intra- and inter-syllabic relationships on *kunqu* melodies, the two syllable sets are first compared using the "voice-leading" rules provided by Yang Yinliu (1983) and Wang Shoutai 王守泰 (1982) (Figure 5.15).

Upon comparison, while there are numerous cases of the two melodic segments conforming to the rules, there are also instances when the rules are not followed. Besides, there are discrepancies and even contradictions between Yang and Wang's rules, and sometimes neither captures particular melodic motions. Such findings should not come as a surprise: "regulations" in voice-leading are essentially summaries based on experience and observation. Rule violations are therefore not necessarily "wrong" and in a "composed" tradition like *kunqu*, aesthetic considerations may also take precedence over intelligibility or even tone-and-pitch relationships.[21]

In the case of Phrase 4, the melodic movement does seem to mostly comply with the language contour of 撇父母, as can be seen in the stepwise ascending motion for the *shang* tone in both 撇 and 母 (Figure 5.16). Even though the syllable 父 corresponds to only a single pitch, the falling *qu* tone is implied inter-syllabically by the descending motion from scale degree 3' (C or *mi*) in the higher-octave to 6 (F or *la*) and the "escape tone"-like downward leap from (higher octave) 1' to 5 which together, accentuate the ascending motion of 母 beginning at a lower register.

The music-language relationships in the Phrase 3 set (Figure 5.17) are more problematic. First, 有六七 does not constitute an intact semantic unit within the textual phrase. It is therefore unclear if typical rules for tone-and-pitch interaction are equally applicable in this case. Likewise, the character 有 is a padding syllable and could potentially

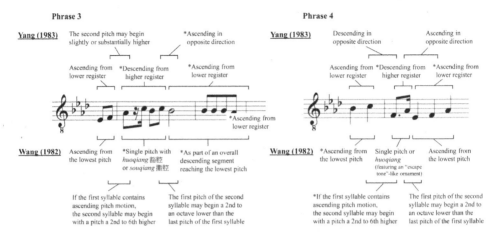

FIGURE 5.15. Voice-leading rules for "Feng ru song," Phrases 3 and 4.

Note: Rules derived (and significantly abbreviated) from Yang (1983) and Wang (1982). Only rules applicable to the two syllable sets are listed. Rules that contradict melodic motion are marked by asterisks (*).

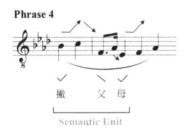

FIGURE 5.16. Tone-pitch relationships in Phrase 4 syllable set.

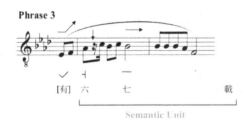

FIGURE 5.17. Tone-pitch relationships in Phrase 3 syllable set.

assume less structural significance both musically and textually. As for 六, although the southern glottal stop (marked by ┤) is implied by the presence of a pause, the melodic movement does not reflect the falling *qu* tone contour based on either *Zhongyuan yinyun* or Mandarin. Conversely, the syllable 七, which also contains a stop consonant/glottal stop in southern languages, does not receive a melodic pause. Instead, the melodic motion for 七 seems to suggest the low-level tone of Mandarin through its static motion, and not the falling-rising *shang* tone according to *Zhongyuan yinyun*.

The Phrase 3 syllable set thus illustrates some of the challenges in *kunqu* analysis when the exact linguistic standard being used is uncertain (even within the northern phonological system). Without additional information, it is difficult to ascertain whether the observed tone-pitch discrepancies are due to the adoption of non-northern phonologies, unintentional "mistakes," deliberate rule departures by musicians, or a combination of these factors. It is also possible that the different melodic manifestations are due to the sets being situated in rather different musical and syntactical environments.

The juxtaposition between the *shang-qu* and *qu-shang* tonal sequences in the Phrase 4 set reveals additional differences between music and language. As shown in Figure 5.18, despite slight variations, the tonal contour is relatively conserved for both the first and third syllables in 撇父母. In other words, the falling-rising shape of the *shang* tone is not subject to drastic changes (at least at a macroscopic level) with respect to its temporal placement within the textual phrase. There is thus a greater level of "time-independency" associated with tonal contours as individual linguistic units. Contrastingly, the arrangement of musical pitches is "temporally progressive." Even when accompanying syllables with the same linguistic tone, pitch order readily changes depending on the position within a melody and as a function of time, for example, as 2-to-3 for 撇 and 5-6-1' in the case of 母, with both maintaining the general ascending melodic motion required to realize the *shang* tone.

Overall, voice-leading rules as summarized by veteran practitioners are invaluable resources for understanding the stylistic features of *kunqu*. Yet these rules tend to be observational, descriptive, and even "prescriptive" and may not explain the tendencies and forces responsible for particular real-life tone-and-pitch interactions. When exploring some of the most subtle aspects of music-language relationships, one inevitably touches upon the realm of human perception and cognition. Current methods for analyzing *kunqu* may therefore be inadequate to fully assess the complexities underlying these

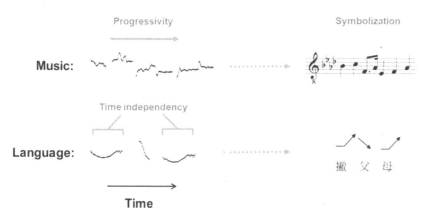

FIGURE 5.18. Temporal relationships in music and language, Phrase 4 syllable set.

phenomena, calling for the need to develop more "generative" or multidisciplinary analytical tools and approaches.

Melodic Relationships

The investigation thus far has been mostly concerned with the interfacing between music and language; the focus will now shift toward the various pitch and melodic relationships within the musical domain, while incorporating and expanding on some of the concepts introduced in the preceding sections. Regarding different *kunqu* arias that belong to the same vocal *qupai*, one reasonable expectation would be the presence of identical, or at least similar, and readily recognizable melodies. Yet, the synoptic comparison of Phrase 4 from historical and modern "Feng ru song" arias from different *kunqu* operas (Figure 5.19) illustrates the problematic nature of this assumption: whereas the beginning of these arias tends to display a higher level of melodic and

Figure 5.19. Melodic diversity and stability of "Feng ru song" arias, Phrase 4.

Note: The transcription from *Nanci dinglü* (a1) has been transposed an octave above the *Jiugong dacheng* notation (a2) to facilitate comparison. Examples a3–4 and b–d are based on Wang (1997).

rhythmic diversity, a certain cadential pattern can be observed toward the end of each phrase, consisting of a melodic descent from 2' or 3' to a characteristic penultimate pitch of 3 (the lowest point of the entire aria), before reaching a 5 finalis.

Such selective melodic consistency across different versions of the same vocal *qupai* has long perplexed *kunqu* theorists and musicians.[22] In fact, it was by noting the presence of common cadential patterns or formulas through the comparison of *gongche* 工尺 notations that Wang Jilie 王季烈, in 1923, designated the term *zhuqiang* 主腔 ("chief melodic characteristics"). The concept of *zhuqiang* was further developed by his son Wang Shoutai, who provided descriptive summaries of commonly occurring melodic segments in both *beiqu* and *nanqu*, a majority of which were also cadential patterns (Wang, 1982 and 1993). Despite the controversies regarding the existence of *zhuqiang* in recent years and various attempts at further defining the term (summarized in Picard and Lau, 2016), Figure 5.19 and similar analyses show that certain melodic commonalities do seem to exist. Therefore, instead of continuing with the *zhuqiang* debate, the main issues addressed in this section include: 1) how to characterize observed connections among melodies belonging to the same vocal *qupai*; 2) what are the driving forces behind the above melodic homogeneities and dissimilarities.

"Hidden Melodies" from the Past

An examination of Phrase 4 (female role) of "Feng ru song" from the opera, *Hongli ji* 紅梨記 (*The Tale of Red Pear Blossoms*), as transcribed from two of the earliest known collections of *kunqu* notation, *Nanci dinglü* 南詞定律 (Lu, Yang, et al., 1720) and the *Jiugong dacheng* compendium (Figure 5.19, lines a1 and a2), reveals a simpler melody compared to the contemporary version (Figure 5.19, line a3). Considering the relatively ornate and melismatic nature of *kunqu* melodies, especially in *nanqu*, this raises questions regarding the possibility of a gradual increase in the level of melodic embellishment in *kunqu* arias through time—and if so, whether the different versions of "Feng ru song" could be derived from a single, simpler tune from an earlier period, in a process analogous to the preservation and transformation of Tang and Song-dynasty music respectively in extant Japanese *Tōgaku* とうがく/唐楽 and Korean *Dangak* 당악/唐樂. According to the "Cambridge School" of historical music reconstruction (Picken, 1981a; Condit, 1981), such pieces of Chinese origin have slowed down substantially in tempo over the centuries in part due to incremental melodic stratification and rhythmic/metrical expansion. In this respect, Picken (1981b) has noted a greater pitch-to-character ratio in *kunqu* arias of the *nanqu* type as compared to that in northern-style *zaju* 雜劇 of the Yuan dynasty (based on the *beiqu* repertoire from the Qing-dynasty *Jiugong dacheng*), which could imply an increase in melodic "melismaticity" over the course of *kunqu* development.[23]

For this purpose, Phrase 3 of the *Hongli ji* aria is further investigated (Figure 5.20). As with Phrase 4, the two eighteenth-century notations from *Nanci dinglü* and *Jiugong dacheng*, which are themselves identical in this case, are also melodically less ornate

FIGURE 5.20. Historical and contemporary sources ("Feng ru song," Phrase 3, female role, from *Hongli ji*).

Note: *Gongche* notation (left) from *Jiugong dacheng* (image source: Internet Archive). The transcription of *Nanci dinglü* has been transposed an octave above the *Jiugong* notation to facilitate comparison.

compared to the modern version.[24] While there is an upward leap of a fourth at the end of Phrase 3 in the two early versions, which is rather unusual for *kunqu* cadences, the corresponding section in the modern version contains a stepwise ascending segment followed by a melodic descent, a more idiomatic treatment in *kunqu*.

One explanation for the above melodic difference is the fact that the two early notations are examples of the so-called *qing-gongpu* 清宮譜, which were meant as general melodic guides for amateur singing, and less detailed or nuanced compared to *xi-gongpu* 戲宮譜 notations intended for theatrical use (Lin, 2016). As such, amateur learners were likely expected to "fill in" the melodic gaps in their *qing-gongpu* notations using vocal elaborations taught by their masters via aural transmission.

Melodic consistency in "Fong ru song" can also be observed through the historical development of the "Sao song" aria. Despite differences in vocal embellishment, the three modern interpretations of Phrase 4 are remarkably similar to the *xi-gongpu* notations dated from the late-eighteenth and nineteenth centuries (Figure 5.21).

Significant conservativeness of *kunqu* melodies, at least pertaining to the illustrated examples, can therefore be traced back to the 1700s, establishing certain continuity across almost half of the history of *kunqu*—about four hundred years if calculated from the time of Wei Liangfu's standardization in the 1500s until the early 1900s. Relative structural stability of the aria can be further extended back to the late Ming dynasty based on the rather consistent placement of *ban* beats in earlier "notations" such as *Zengding nanjiugong qupu* 增訂南九宮曲譜 (Shen, 1594), which contains rhythmic markings but not *gongche* or pitch symbols. With melodic conservativeness applying to both the "varied" region and the cadential pattern of Phrase 4 in Figure 5.21, one could even speculate that melodies from different arias of the same *qupai* probably have existed in their current "diversified" form at least since the eighteenth century, adding to the likelihood that the melodies were significantly different from one another when they were first "composed."

Reductive analysis of the five versions of Phrase 4 also fails to reveal a "hidden melody" (Figure 5.22). The level of reduction is in fact limited by the presence of lyrics, as each syllable of the seven-character phrase ought to correspond to at least one musical note.

FIGURE 5.21. Historical sources and contemporary performances ("Feng ru song," Phrase 4).

Note: *Gongche* notations from (top left, a) *Nashuying qupu* (1792) and (top right, b) *Eyunge qupu* (Wang, 1893), from the Internet Archive. Interpretation by Wu Hongmai (c) adapted from Zhongguo (1997). The version by Ji Zhenhua (d) is transcribed from a 2010 live performance (credit: Kunqu Research and Promotion Project, The University Hong Kong). Chen Rui's version (e) is based on Figure 5.6. Actual initial performance pitches in (c) through (e) are indicated in brackets.

Moreover, the regular punctuation of *ban* beats at adjacent syllables 4, 6, and at the end of syllable 7 seems to indicate a relatively fixed occurrence of the melismatic segments at syllables 5 and 6, which is less likely the result of pure metrical expansion (Figure 5.23).[25]

While *kunqu* melodies may have indeed existed in a simpler, less ornate form during the Ming dynasty, based on the above analyses, any melodic or metrical expansion would have occurred to a lesser extent compared to the four- to eight-time augmentation of *Tōgaku* pieces spanning approximately twelve centuries (Nelson, 2008), or the potentially three- to six-fold expansion in the case of *Dangak* over eight hundred years (Condit, 1981). In contrast to the relative isolation of the two court traditions, *kunqu* had a totally different "ecology." While contributing to the regional divergence of *kunqu*, the continuing interactions with other operatic styles, languages, and dialects, as well as the theatrical and popular nature of the genre, might have also exerted certain "buffering" or "leveling" effects, which, along with unifying forces such as the *qupai* paradigm and aural

FIGURE 5.22. Reductive analysis of "Feng ru song" arias, Phrase 4.

Note: The five arias are derived from Figure 5.19 and are arranged in the same order for comparative purposes. Core pitches are derived with respect to the text while maximizing stepwise motions between adjacent pitches.

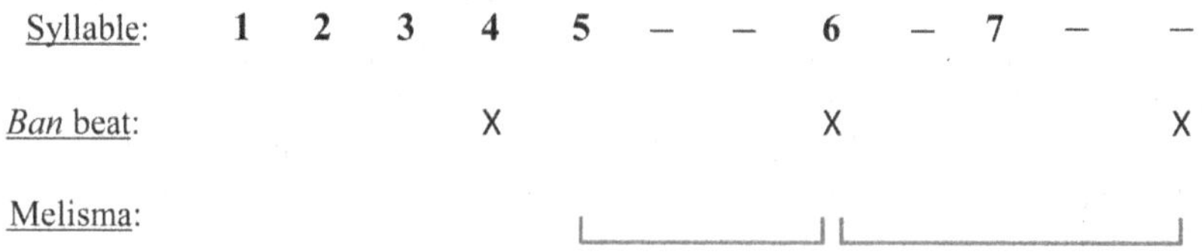

FIGURE 5.23. Typical placement of syllables, *ban*, and melisma in "Feng ru song," Phrase 4, from "Sao song."

transmission, prevented considerable "gigantism" from taking place. Such stabilizing forces, in addition to possible reworking or even recomposition of the arias during later periods, could also explain the stylistic unity among the five "Feng ru song" arias, despite the fact that some of the operatic texts were created close to three hundred years apart.[26]

Reductive Analytical Approaches

Figure 5.22 illustrated further challenges in analyzing *kunqu*. Compared to Western tonal (common practice) music, reductive and hierarchy-based analysis of pentatonic (and non-major/minor heptatonic) melodies often leads to ambiguities due to the presence of two "tonal" (or more precisely, "modal") centers (Day-O'Connell, 2009). In the case of "Feng ru song," the bi-modal emphasis on 5 (*sol*) and 1' (upper-octave *do*) gives rise to two pitch sets: {5, 6} and {1', 2', 3'} within the 5-6-1'-2'-3' *zhi* 徵-mode pentatonic pitch collection, typical of *nanqu* (as opposed to the heptatonic collection of 3-↑4-5-6-↓7-1'-2' in *beiqu*).[27] Although Figure 5.22 has revealed certain stepwise, descending skeletal patterns among the "Feng ru song" arias, the utility of such scale-like progressions is limited, as they provide little information regarding the tendency and progression between adjacent pitches, especially across the "gap" intervals of 6-1' and 3'-5'.

A two-voice reductive method is proposed to overcome the above difficulties. By acknowledging the presence of two modal centers (which are not necessarily of equal importance), a pentatonic melody can be perceived as a composite of two independent and concurrently occurring voices, each featuring mostly stepwise motions within the 6-5 and 3'-2'-1' sets (Figure 5.24).

The advantage of this two-voice approach is the ability to isolate and highlight melodic tendencies within each pitch set. At a fundamental level, reduction of Phrase 4 of the "Sao song" aria reveals an overarching progression of two "chords" involving the melodic motions 2'-to-1' and 6-to-5 (Figure 5.25). The result is an implied harmony that emphasizes the bi-modal centers 5 and 1'. The harmonic tension created by the tendency of the 2'-6 chord to resolve into the 1'-5 chord then generates a "tonal gradient," along which individual pitches progress while gravitating toward the two modal centers.[28]

Similar melodic and harmonic frameworks can also be deduced from Phrase 4 of the other "Feng ru song" arias (Figure 5.26). Under this approach, seemingly dissimilar pentatonic melodies, such as Figure 5.26.b (the "Sao song" aria) and Figure 5.26.c, can be interpreted as different "melodic excursions" into one of the two modal areas or "strata" while still conforming to the underlying melodic-harmonic structure. These background tendencies and the overall temporal-musical framework may in fact be defined as a type of *zhuqiang* in a very broad sense.

A comparison between the reduction of the melody and the text of Phrase 4 (Figure 5.27) further illustrates the differences between language and music in terms

FIGURE 5.24. First "Feng ru song" aria from "Sao song," Phrase 4, as a compound melody.

Note: The last two beats of Phrase 3 has been included, which seems to function both as a phrase ending of Phrase 3 (especially the first beat) and as an anacrusis/"pick-up" for Phrase 4; the pre-ultimate pitch 3 in the original melody has been treated as an elaboration of 6 in this representation.

Phrase 4

FIGURE 5.25. Two-voice reductive analysis of "Feng ru song," Phrase 4, from "Sao song."

Note: Neighboring elaboration of the same pitch indicated by the letter N. The letter P represents "passing" motion of structurally less important pitches connecting the two tonal areas.

of structural/syntactic organization and temporal progressivity. From a cognitive perspective, the melodic-harmonic tendencies of Phrase 4 can be said to be driven by anticipation for the resolution of the core pitches at the background level as discussed above. Such an overarching tendency is not observed in the case of the textual Phrase 4. Instead, the three semantic units (撇父母, 抛妻, and 不睬) could exist independently under various circumstances without eliciting a strong sense of incompleteness from readers or listeners. Certain temporal progressivity can still be observed, nonetheless, when the subject-less textual phrase is analyzed using simple, hierarchy-based "parsing" toward the "resolution" of the various parts of speech. For example, progressivity (indicated by the arrow sign) is generated by the anticipation of the verb 撇 ("to abandon") to "receive" a certain grammatical object as the "target" (父母 or "parents" in this case). The same temporal tendency also applies to the units 抛妻 and 不睬.

Despite these structural differences, interactions continue to occur between text and melody even at the background level. In particular, the melody can be divided according to the three semantic units of the textual phrase (Figure 5.27). While both pitch sets 3'-2'-1' and 5-6 are utilized in section "a," section "b" features only the 3'-2'-1' set, and section "c" focuses mostly on 5-6 as part of the descending cadential pattern. Such correspondence could in part be due to influences exerted by the textual phrase upon the melody by means of pitch selection. Most importantly, the syntactic disparities in Figure 5.27

KUNQU FROM ANALYTICAL PERSPECTIVES   87

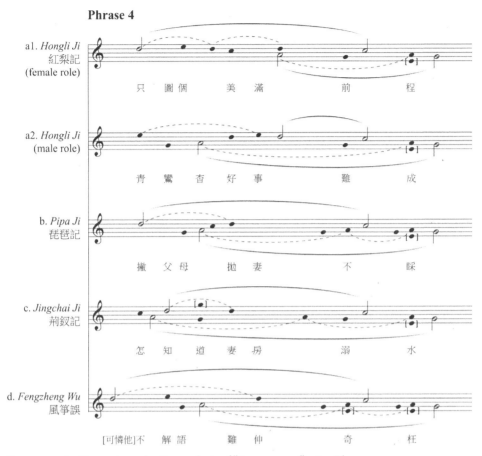

FIGURE 5.26. Two-voice reductive analysis of "Feng ru song" arias, Phrase 4.

reaffirm the fundamental differences between music and language as distinct temporal phenomena; the same conclusion as established in the sections on language-music interactions has therefore been reached but from an entirely different direction.

Kunqu *Composition Revisited*

Considering the current lack of evidence for the existence of a single melodic prototype, the relative diversity among different versions of "Feng ru song," and the conservativeness of individual "Feng ru song" arias since the 1700s, two conclusions regarding *kunqu* melodies can be made: 1) each version of the "Feng ru song" aria was likely "composed" independently; 2) more than one mode of composition would have been involved to create each version of the aria. There were likely key pitches, melodic segments, and cadential formulas that musicians could utilize and insert at particular time points of the *qupai* framework, either by convention or by following certain rules. Upon this rather restrictive form of "composition" musicians would then enjoy greater liberty in formulating musical materials which connect between the relatively fixed elements.

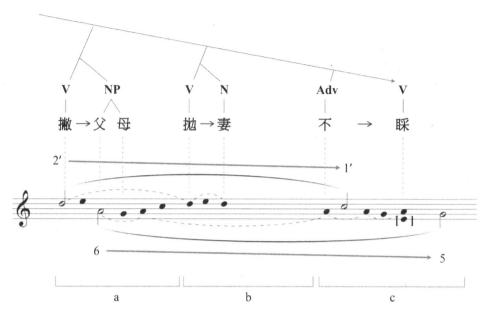

FIGURE 5.27. Structural organization and temporal progression ("Feng ru song," Phrase 4, from "Sao song").

Note: Arrow signs indicate cognitively driven semantic and pitch progression (V = verb; NP = noun phrase; N = noun; Adv = adverb).

This two-tier compositional approach would account for the "varied" versus "stable" melodic topology of "Feng ru song," with the fixed musical elements labeled as *zhuqiang* as originally endorsed by Wang Jilie and Wang Shoutai. The referencing of such *zhuqiang* segments as discrete structural elements, or what Lindy Li Mark (2001, 2013) refers to as "melodic motif memories" or "*leit motifs*," is in fact analogous to the referencing of an entire musical tune commonly observed in *qupai* practice.[29] In contrast, melodic and rhythmic diversities are introduced to the *qupai* template through not only language-music interactions but also the emphasis on alternative modal areas and by temporal expansion with the addition of padding syllables, as illustrated in Figure 5.28.

Several important forces are therefore at work in the "molding" of a *kunqu* melody (Figure 5.29). First, at an "intrinsic" and background level (which often operates beyond the conscious awareness of musicians and composers), there is the interaction between the textual/temporal-rhythmic and melodic-harmonic structures of the *qupai*. Specifically, embedded within the rhythmic-temporal framework created by textual phrasing and the punctuation of *ban* beats or rhyme syllables, the harmonic tension serves to guide a general sense of pitch tendency and idiomatic voice-leading. Respecting this underlying structure, active composition then occurs at a "cognitive" level through the insertion of *zhuqiang* segments and the surface-level adjustment of pitches to reflect and accommodate the linguistic tones of the lyrics.[30] Figure 5.29 thus illustrates not only an updated view of the interactions between the musical, linguistic, and textual domains presented in Figure 5.4 but also the integration of the textual, linguistic, rhythmic-temporal, and melodic-harmonic definitions of *qupai* into a unified whole.

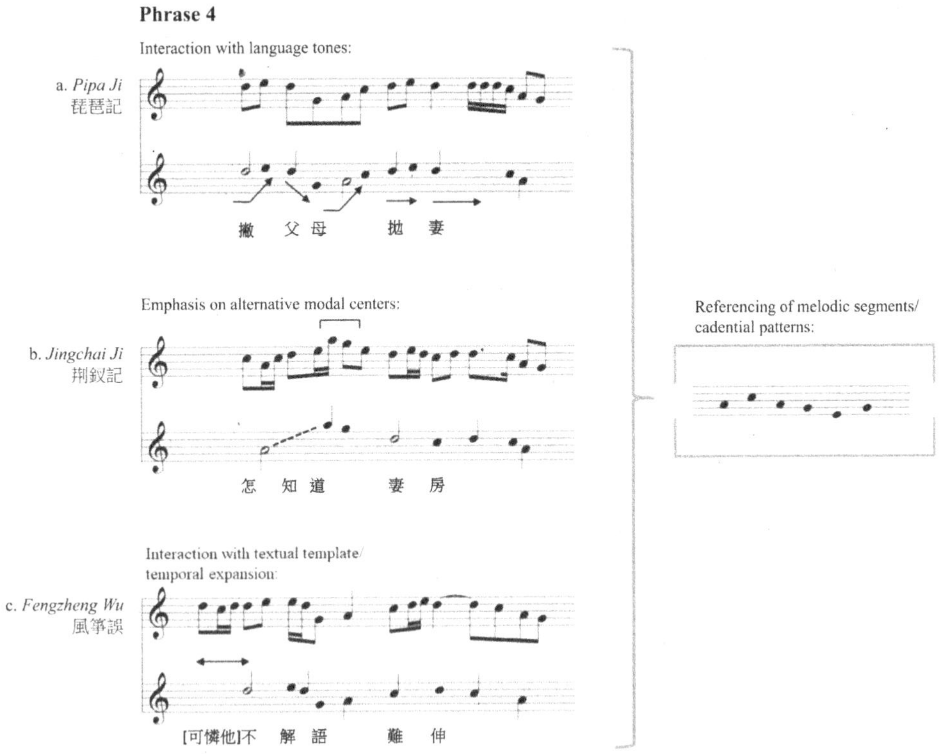

FIGURE 5.28. Melodic diversity and stability in various "Feng ru song" arias, Phrase 4.

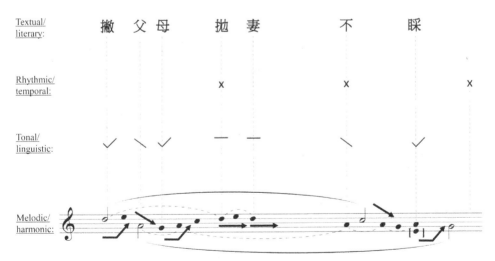

FIGURE 5.29. Multidomain interactions in the first "Feng ru song" aria, "Sao song," Phrase 4.

Finally, at a "collective" level, the resulting melody continues to develop and evolve through time and space, modified by musicians and performers via reinterpretation and re-creation, and subject to both stabilization and diversification forces. Figure 5.30 attempts to further highlight the multidomain complexities of the *kunqu* creative process and the *qupai* paradigm by incorporating elements from the various models examined in this chapter. While beyond the scope of the present discussion, the dichotomy between the rhythmic-temporal and melodic-harmonic *qupai* frameworks as separate yet closely intertwined domains—which is derived from traditional notions of *kunqu* composition as perceived by the literati, is in fact consistent with the "dual" processing of rhythm and melody within the brain according to latest neuroscientific research.[31]

The creation and transmission of vocal arias thus appears to be procedural, fragmental, and, in fact, somewhat artificial.[32] Yet, within this "patchy" network, the transfer of musical (and textual) materials still complies with the "didactical" nature of the *qupai* paradigm, while allowing for individual and collective inventions to occur. In comparison, modification of instrumental *qupai* is often applied to the entire tune in a more consistent and uniform fashion, through processes such as *jiahua* 加花 (melodic embellishment) and *banshi bianzou* 板式變奏 (beat-form variation) (Thrasher, 2016), as well as segmentation, repetition, and omission.

Figure 5.31 shows an instrumental *suona* 嗩吶 version of "Feng ru song" typically used in Beijing opera, which in essence represents a metrical reduction of the *kunqu* aria. In this case, the performer Wu Zhongxi 吳忠喜 elects to perform (and reference) only the first four phrases of the *qupai*. These phrases are then repeated as a single section.[33]

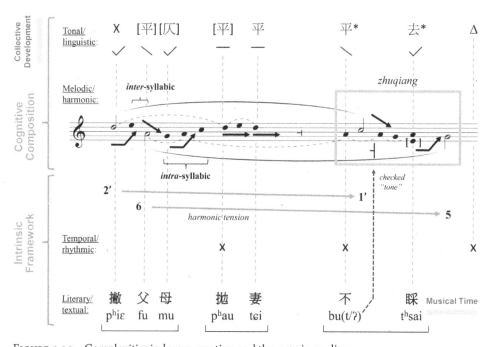

FIGURE 5.30. Complexities in *kunqu* creation and the *qupai* paradigm.

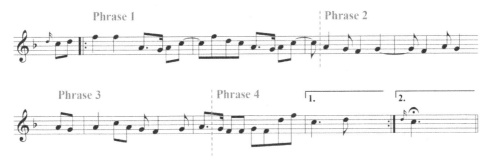

FIGURE 5.31. Instrumental "Feng ru song" for *suona*.

Such manipulation and disposition of melodic fragments as individual units can be viewed as yet another manifestation of the *qupai* paradigm, with the temporal framework of "Feng ru song" created by the textual and vocal *qupai* templates (the uneven *qu* poetry phrasing and remnants of language-music interactions) readily permeating throughout the instrumental counterpart.[34] Taking on a new life and assuming various functionalities in different regional settings, the instrumental "Feng ru song" nonetheless retains its ties with its vocal and textual roots, echoing its distant past.

Conclusion

One possible way to approach the *qupai* paradigm is to consider it as a sum of information transfer, not only between the musical, language/textual, and other cognitive domains but also across time, space, and cultures, as conceived, designed, and prescribed by the literati, musicians, and performers.[35] *Kunqu* thus allowed the literati to observe and interpret the world—through *qupai* as an "introspective lens."[36] As illustrated throughout this chapter, a tight cross-domain connection, especially between music and language, two innately different processes, while desirable, is not guaranteed. In the case of *kunqu*, music-language relationships are subject to further modulation by a myriad of factors, from the segmented three-part compositional model to individual and collective variabilities and creativities, as well as stylistic evolution and assimilation; the result is a system truly dynamic and complex.

As the process of standardization, globalization, and the *minyue* 民樂 ("modernized traditional music") movement continues to displace the niche of many unique traditions and genres in the twenty-first century (further discussed in Part III of this volume), the need to strike a subtle balance between conservation and innovation (and, for that matter, to distinguish between originality versus appropriation) has become ever more acute. Focusing on a single *qupai*, the current study is limited by materials obtained from individual performers with small sample sizes. It is hoped that future efforts will expand to systematically record, archive, and analyze both musical and linguistic materials collected from *kunqu* practitioners from different generations and regions, with the results (alongside the original field work) readily available to the public and researchers alike. Mostly employing comparative-reductive methodologies, this study also alludes to alternative approaches to analyzing *kunqu*, from historical investigation and prescriptive voice-leading, to musical set theory, and linguistic contour and syntactic analysis. It is only by embracing the fluidity and complexity of *kunqu* through multidisciplinary and integrative angles can one better elucidate the *kunqu* phenomenon.

Acknowledgments

The author would like to thank Drs. Alan Thrasher, Lindy Li Mark, and François Picard, as well as Rui Chen, Zhongxi Wu, Kathleen Zaragosa, David Badagnani, and Min Lin for their invaluable resources and suggestions for this chapter. The author would also like to acknowledge the Kunqu Research and Promotion Project (The Chinese University of Hong Kong), Dr. Wei Hua, Calvin Jiang, Angela Pietrobon, Lucia Park, Phoebe Chow, Juying Howe, Jirong Huang, and Weiting Su for their generous support for this research.

Glossary

ban 板, emphasized metrical beat
banshi bianzou 板式變奏, metrical variation
beiju 北劇, northern theater tradition
beikun 北崑, northern-style *kunqu*
beiqu 北曲, "northern songs"
Chao Yuen-Ren 趙元任, composer, linguist, and researcher (1892–1982)
Chen Rui 陳睿, *kunqu* performer (b. 1987)
chenzi 襯字, padding syllables
ci 詞, poetry with irregular phrasing, popular during the Song dynasty
Dangak 당악/唐樂, "Tang music," Korean court-music repertory
duanqiang 斷腔, melodic pause in singing
"Feng ru song" 風入松, "Wind Entering Through the Pines," *qupai* title
Gao Ming 高明, playwright (c. 1305–c. 1370)
gongche 工尺, notation using simple characters as pitch symbols
guanhua 官話, "official speech," *lingua franca*
jiahua 加花, melodic embellishment
Ji Kang 嵇康, Jin-dynasty musician (c. 223–c. 262)
kunqu 崑曲, traditional opera genre
Li Bai 李白, Tang poet (701–62)
minyue 民樂, modernized folk-music traditions
nankun 南崑, southern-style *kunqu*
nanqu 南曲, "southern songs"
nanxi 南戲, "southern drama," Yuan-dynasty theater genre
nianbai 念白, recitation of lyrics in theater
Pipa ji 琵琶記, *The Tale of the Lute*, drama

qiangfu 腔腹, "song body," central portion of a vocal melody
qiangtou 腔頭, "song head," opening portion of a vocal melody
qiangwei 腔尾, "song tail," closing portion of a vocal melody
qu 曲, flexible poetic format of the Yuan, Ming, and Qing dynasties
Qulü 曲律, *Rules for Singing* Qu *[Poetry]*, book by Wei Liangfu
qupai 曲牌, "labeled tune" to which new song texts could be fitted
sandu chuangzuo 三度創作, three-part compositional model used to create *kunqu* arias
"Sao song" 掃松, "Sweeping [Under] the Pines," act in *Pipa ji*
shengdiao 聲調, linguistic tones
shi 詩, equal-phrased poetry of Tang and earlier dynasties
sisheng 四聲, the four tones recognized in contemporary Standard Mandarin
tianci 填詞, "filling in text," process used in poetry writing
Tōgaku とうがく/唐楽/唐樂, "Tang music," Japanese court-music repertory
Wang Jilie 王季烈, *kunqu* scholar (1873–1952)
Wang Shoutai 王守泰, *kunqu* expert (1908–92)
Wei Liangfu 魏良輔, singer and codifier of *kunqu* opera (c. 1489–c. 1566)
wenren 文人, literatus, traditional scholar
Wu Zhongxi 吳忠喜, *suona* and *sheng* performer (b. 1973)
Yang Yinliu 楊蔭瀏, musicologist (1899–1984)
yinchang 吟唱, "musical recitation," used for various poetic forms
yunbai 韻白, recitation of lyrics in theater
Yu Zhenfei 俞振飛, *kunqu* performer (1902–93)
zaju 雜劇, northern-style operas, during the Yuan dynasty
zhiqu 製曲, "song creation," the process of creating lyrics or texts based on *qupai* templates
Zhongzhou yun 中州韻, "Rhymes of the central plains," phonology derived from phonological standards of the central Chinese region
zhuqiang 主腔, "chief melodic characteristics," concept used in analyzing *kunqu* music

Notes

1. This study complements and continues the investigation of the northern-style *qupai*, *Daodao ling* 叨叨令, in Picard and Lau (2016). Original recordings of selected musical examples from this chapter can be accessed at: www.youtube.com/channel/UCQ5OolsGAUczXzFjQ7BDaPg.
2. A term used by scholar Huang Jinpei 黃錦培 in the 1990s to describe the nature of *kunqu* creation (Alan Thrasher, personal communication, 2015).
3. Due to the relative lack of relevance in *kunqu* tone-and-pitch interactions, the *qingsheng* 輕聲 (fifth or "neutral" tone) in Standard Mandarin is not included in this discussion.
4. Yang Yinliu (1983) refers to the *ping-shang-qu-ru* 平-上-去-入 nomenclature as the "old tone system," which was "shifted" into the "new system" of *yinping-yangping-shang-qu* 陰平-陽平-上-去 in Mandarin phonology; see further Picard and Lau (2016).
5. Common in Middle Chinese (and earlier forms of Chinese), stop consonants have been preserved in southern languages such as Hokkien (Min 閩), Hakka (*Kejia* 客家), and Cantonese (Yue 粵).
6. See Picard and Lau (2016) and Thrasher (2016) for discussions regarding inter-*qupai* relationships such as suite-form construction in both vocal and instrumental music.

7. The two phrases may be translated as "freshness beneath the pines as wind enters; tranquility of dew permeates the grass."
8. *Pipa ji* details the tragic circumstances faced by Zhao Wuniang 趙五娘 while her husband, Cai Bojie 蔡伯喈, is away in the capital city. During the act, "Sao song," the character, Zhang Guangcai 張廣才, encounters Cai's porter, Li Wang 李旺, as he sweeps under the pines at the tombs of Cai's parents. In the first "Feng ru song" aria, Zhang expresses his disdain for Cai's negligence of filial duties (Figure 5.6), only to learn later from Li of Cai's own strenuous situation. The use of "Feng ru song" as the main vocal *qupai* throughout this act is likely an intentional reference to the theme of pine trees.
9. For a concise overview of the history of *kunqu* and its compositional process, see Li Mark (2013).
10. See Koo (2009) and Luo (2012) for the various attempts to define *Zhongzhou yun* throughout the development of *kunqu*.
11. Despite the two-dimensional representation, it should be stressed that the diversification and assimilation of *kunqu* are dynamic, three-dimensional processes, involving the musical and linguistic evolution of individual styles along the time axis, and the simultaneous dissemination across geographical regions.
12. All examples of the "Feng ru song" melody and recitation presented in the Music-Language Interactions in *Kunqu* section are based on demonstrations of the first "Feng ru song" aria from "Sao song," *Pipa Ji*, by Chen Rui, recorded in Nanjing, China, in December 2017. Chen Rui is a professional *kunqu* performer at the Jiangsu Kunqu Opera Theatre 江蘇省崑劇院 who specializes in the *laosheng* 老生 ("dignified older male") role.
13. The succession of pitches is somewhat obscured in the contour profile of the vocal melody due to the use of vibrato by the singer and to continual lip or mouth movements between the pitches.
14. Information provided by Chen Rui in this section is based on personal communication, April 2018.
15. Curiously, while the character 不 (*bu* in Mandarin pinyin) contains a glottal stop (transcribed as *beʔ*) in the northern-style example, it is not present in the southern version.
16. Disagreement continues regarding the exact relationship between the Yuan-dynasty *Zhongyuan yinyun* and the early Ming-dynasty *Hongwu zhengyun*, considering that they were compiled within a span of merely fifty-one years. While *Hongwu* could potentially represent the phonology of southern languages with the inclusion of the *ru* "tone" category, some speculate that such stop consonants or glottal stops continued to persist, at least to some extent, in Yuan-dynasty northern languages (Li, 2016).
17. Reconstruction of *Zhongyuan yinyun* by Ning (1985) is used as no comparable efforts have been identified for the restoration of *Hongwu zhengyun*, and since the similarity in tone categorization (as pertaining to Phrase 4) has been demonstrated in Figure 5.10.
18. Another important question to consider throughout this chapter is the potential limitations of using two-dimensional representations such as wave contours and symbols or notations to depict the temporal linearity of music and language.
19. One possible explanation is that repeated descending-ascending or "zigzag" melodic motions would likely be perceived as being unidiomatic and therefore be aesthetically rejected by musicians and performers.
20. The character *pie* 撇 can be uttered in either Tone 1 or 3 in Standard Mandarin. Chen Rui naturally used Tone 1 when recording for Figure 5.8, and was asked to adopt Tone 3 to

approximate *Zhongyuan yinyun* phonology in Figures 5.12, 5.13 and 5.18 to facilitate the comparison.
21. For example, even if the characters 父母 (*fùmǔ* in Mandarin pinyin, "father-mother") in Phrase 4 were musically rendered to convey the tonal contour of 浮木 (*fúmù*, "floating wood"), the wider context of the lyrics would likely prevent listeners from misunderstanding the term.
22. Li Mark (2013) emphasizes the subtle difference between "version" and "variation," an important concept that underlies the discussions in this section.
23. An inherent problem with equating *beiqǔ* pieces in *Jiugong dacheng* with Yuan-dynasty *zaju* is the close-to-four-hundred-year gap between the Yuan dynasty (thirteenth and fourteenth centuries) and the completion of *Jiugong* in 1746 (see Lau, 2016).
24. It is stated in the preface of *Suijin cipu* 碎金詞譜 (Xie, 1844) that *kunqu*-style music was purposely used to accompany classical *ci* poetry texts in the volume to enhance the "contemporary" appeal of the arias, thus further disputing the claim that Qing-dynasty *kunqu* notations have preserved highly intact melodies from earlier eras.
25. In contrast, syllables 1 to 4 are relatively syllabic even in the modern versions, each occupying only one to two beats.
26. As mentioned, *Pipa ji* originated as a *nanxi* drama from the Yuan dynasty, and *Jingchai ji* might also be of a similar origin; whereas *Hongli ji* was a product of the Ming-dynasty, *Fengzheng wu* was written by Li Yu 李漁 (1611–80) in 1653, almost three centuries after the creation of *Pipa ji* and closer to the compilation of *Nanci dinglü* and *Jiugong dacheng* in the 1700s.
27. The use of the term "modal center" in this chapter also serves to avoid unnecessary association with Western tonal music and distinguishes the musically focused discussions from those regarding the "tonal" nature of Chinese languages.
28. It should be emphasized that this "two-voice" approach is intended to serve as a "bookkeeping tool" (much like Schenkerian analysis) for the pentatonic pitch sets and for visualizing certain pitch or melodic tendencies that may not otherwise be apparent. This approach thus represents one of many possible ways to describe pentatonic music and does not necessarily reflect musical "reality"; after all, as discussed in Note 31, the human brain appears to process music in a very different way compared to typical (Western) analytical methods which often focus on the two-dimensional representation and symbolization of music, again, despite its linear and one-dimensional nature.
29. The recurrence of cadential *zhuqiang* patterns could potentially be explained by the more limited voice-leading options available for pentatonic pitch collections, and an emphasis on descending and stepwise motions toward particular destination pitches especially toward phrase endings, contributing to the formulaic and referential nature of such patterns.
30. Fixed melodic elements such as *zhuqiang* also serve to reinforce the overall temporal-melodic structure of the *qupai*.
31. Rhythm and melody appear to be perceived very differently by the brain; in the case of rhythm, simple and regular periodicities are generally processed automatically or subconsciously at the basal, subcortical levels, while the upper cortical area engages in more conscious processing and recognition of complex and irregular rhythmic patterns, essentially in a hierarchical fashion (Snyder and Large, 2005). In contrast, current understanding of the perception of melody and musical syntax is rather rudimentary and even "piecemeal," consisting mostly of the detection of various brain wave potentials occurring in a linear manner (Koelsch, 2011). One interesting speculation would be the prospect of a model with the perception of melody and syntax "embedded" within the hierarchical framework of rhythm perception.

32. The typical apprehension toward the nature of vocal *qupai* music seems to be rooted in a cognitive dissonance between the fluid and dynamic state of *kunqu*, and the traditional notion of using simple, unaltered tunes in *tianci* and song composition—a theoretical approach rarely observed in actual *kunqu* practice.
33. Figure 5.31 is transcribed from a demonstration by Wu Zhongxi (recorded in Coquitlam, Canada, in January 2018).
34. The instrumental "Feng ru song" has become widespread within the Chinese diaspora, and is frequently featured in celebratory and ceremonial contexts in Taiwanese *beiguan* 北管 ("northern pipe") music and *gezaixi* 歌仔戲 opera, subject to Western, popular, and even electronic transformations (Lu, 2003).
35. See Picard (2016) for examples of the transmission of the *qupai* tunes, *Chao tianzi* 朝天子 and *Liu yao jin* 柳搖金 to the West and for related documentations in European scholarship.
36. Aptly referred to as a principle of "the unlimited within the limited" by Wang Ying-fen (1992), the freedom of manipulating linguistic, literary, and musical elements as enjoyed by the literati and musicians within the (often self-imposed) boundaries of *qupai*, is in fact, not dissimilar to the microcosmic and introspective aesthetics of arranging rock-scapes, vegetation, and waterways within the enclosure of a Suzhou classical garden, where *kunqu* would have been performed.

References

Chao Yuen-Ren 趙元任. (1930). "ə sistim əv "toun-letəz" [A system of "tone-letters"]." *Le Maître Phonétique* 45: 24–27.

Condit, Jonathan. (1981). "Two Song-dynasty Chinese Tunes Preserved in Korea." In *Music and Tradition: Essays on Asian and Other Musics Presented to Laurence Picken*, edited by D. R. Widdess and R. F. Wolpert, 1–40. London: Cambridge University Press.

Day-O'Connell, Jeremy. (2009). "Debussy, Pentatonicism, and the Tonal Tradition." *Music Theory Spectrum* 31 (2): 255–261.

Gao Hang 高航. (2009). *"Jiugong dacheng nanbeici gongpu" shengdiao xunyi* 《九宮大成南北詞宮譜》聲調尋繹 [Inquiry into Linguistic Tones in the Compendium of Notations of Southern and Northern Songs and Lyrics in Nine Modes]. Tianjin: Tianjin guji chubanshe.

Gao Ming 高明. (n.d.). *Xinkan yuanben Cai Bojie Pipa ji* 新刊元本蔡伯喈琵琶記 [Reissued Yuan (c. 13th century) version of Cai Bojie's *Tale of Pipa*], edited by Lu Yi 陸貽. Qing-dynasty edition. Accessed August 29, 2021. https://archive.org/details/02111372.cn.

Koelsch, Stefan. (2011). "Toward a Neural Basis of Music Perception—A Review and Updated Model." *Frontiers in Psychology* 2, article no. 110. https://doi.org/10.3389/fpsyg.2011.00110

Koo Siu-sun 古兆申. (2009). *Changyan yayin lun kunqu* 長言雅音論崑曲 [Discussion of Kunqu through Long Essays and Refined Tunes]. Hong Kong: Cosmos Books Ltd.

Kunqu Research and Promotion Project, Chinese University of Hong Kong. (2010). *Saosong* 掃松 [Sweeping the Pines]. Video. Accessed July 28, 2018. http://cukunyue.blogspot.com.

Lau, Kar Lun A. 劉嘉麟. (2016). "History through *Qupai*: A Re-examination." In *Qupai in Chinese Music: Melodic Models in Form and Practice*, edited by Alan R. Thrasher, 17–50. New York: Routledge.

Li Huimian 李惠綿. (2008). "Cong yinyun xue jiaodu lunshu Wang Jide nanqu duqu lun zhi jiegou" "從音韻學角度論述王驥德南曲度曲論之結構" [An Analysis of the Structure and Formation of Wang Jide's *Theory of Duqu* in Southern Chinese Traditional Opera]. 戲劇研究 [Journal of Theater Studies] 1: 131–78.

Li Huimian 李惠綿. (2016). *Zhongyuan yinyun jianshi* 中原音韻箋釋 [Annotations of "Phonology of the Central Plains"]. Taipei: National Taiwan University Press.

Li Mark, Lindy 李林德. (2001). "Qupaiti yinyuezhong 'xuanlü muti jiyi' zhi shenmei zuoyong—yi 'Xuge' 'Zuihuayin' wei li" "曲牌體音樂中「旋律母題記憶」之審美作用—以「絮閣」「醉花陰」為例" [The Aesthetic Use of "Melodic Motif Memories in *Qupai*-based Music"—"Flocculent Pavilion" from "Indulgence in the Shades of Blossoms" as an Example]. 中國文哲研究通訊 [Newsletter of the Institute of Chinese Literature and Philosophy] 11 (1): 31–38.

Li Mark, Lindy 李林德. (2013). "From Page to Stage: Exploring Some Mysteries of *Kunqu* Music and Its Melodic Characteristics." *Chinoperl* 32 (1): 1–29.

Lin Chiayi 林佳儀. (2016). *Qupu bianding yu paitao bianqian* 曲譜編訂與牌套變遷 [Compilation of *Qu* Notations and the Changes and Development of *Qupai* Suites]. Taipei: Chengchi University Press.

Lu Shixiong 呂士雄, Yang Xu 楊緒, et al., eds. (1720). *Nanci dinglü* 南詞定律 [New Standards for Southern Arias].

Lu Yu-Hsiu 呂鈺秀. (2003). *Taiwan yinyue shi* 臺灣音樂史 [History of Taiwnese Music]. Taipei: Wunan Book Co., Ltd.

Luo Li-Rong 羅麗容. (2012). *Nanxi • Kunqu yu Taiwan xiqu* 南戲•崑劇與臺灣戲曲 [Nanxi • Kunqu and Taiwnese Operas]. Taipei: Shin Wen Feng Print Co.

Nelson, Steven G. (2008). "Court and Religious Music (1): History of *Gagaku* and *Shōmyō*." In *The Ashgate Research Companion to Japanese Music*, edited by Alison McQueen Tokita and David W. Hughes, 35–48. Aldershot: Ashgate Publishing.

Ning Jifu 寧繼福. (1985). *Zhongyuan yinyun biaogao* 中原音韻表稿 [Draft Tables of "Phonology of the Central Plains"]. Jilin: Jilin wenshi chubanshe.

Picard, François. (2016). "Crossing Stage, Crossing Countries, Crossing Times: Instrumental *Qupai* in European Scholarship." In *Qupai in Chinese Music: Melodic Models in Form and Practice*, edited by Alan R. Thrasher, 53–72. New York: Routledge.

Picard, François, and Kar Lun A. Lau. (2016). "*Qupai* in *Kunqu*: Text-music Issues." In *Qupai in Chinese Music: Melodic Models in Form and Practice Qupai in Chinese Music: Melodic Models in Form and Practice*, edited by Alan R. Thrasher, 119–54. New York: Routledge.

Picken, Laurence. (1981a). "Introduction." In *Music from the Tang Court: Transcribed from the Original Unpublished Sino-Japanese Manuscripts Together with a Survey of Relevant Historical Sources (Both Chinese and Japanese) and with Editorial Comments*, edited by Laurence E. R. Picken, et al., 5–14. London: Oxford University Press.

Picken, Laurence. (1981b). "The Musical Implications of Chinese Song-texts with Unequal Lines, and the Significance of Nonsense-syllables, with Special Reference to Art-songs of the Song Dynasty." *Musica Asiatica* 3: 53–78.

Qiao Jianzhong 喬建中. (1994). "Qupai lun" "曲牌論" [Discussions on *Qupai*]. *Yinyuexue wenji* 音樂學文集 [Collection of Articles in Musicology], 403–20. Ji'nan: Shandong youyi chubanshe.

Shen Jing 沈璟, ed. (1594). *Zengding nanjiugong qupu* 增訂南九宮曲譜 [Updated Southern *Qu* Notations in Nine Modes].

Shi Haiqing 石海青. (2007). *Kunqu Zhongzhou yun jiaocai* 崑曲中州韻教材 [Teaching Material for *Zhongzhou* Rhymes]. Taipei: Liren shuju.

Shibles, Warren A. (1994). "Chinese Romanization Systems: IPA Transliteration." *Sino-Platonic Papers* 52: 1–5.

Snyder, Joel S., and Edward W. Large. (2005). "Gamma-band Activity Reflects the Metric Structure of Rhythmic Tone Sequences." *Brain Research: Cognitive Brain Research* 24 (1): 117–26.

Thrasher, Alan R. (2016). "*Qupai* in Theory and Practice." In *Qupai in Chinese Music: Melodic Models in Form and Practice*, edited by Alan R. Thrasher, 3–16. New York: Routledge.

Wang Shoutai 王守泰. (1982). *Kunqu gelü* 崑曲格律 [Rules of *Kunqu*]. Yangzhou: Jiangsu renmin chubanshe.

Wang Shoutai 王守泰. (1997). *Kunqu qupai ji taoshu fanli ji: nantao* 崑曲曲牌及套數範例集: 南套 [Examples of *Kunqu Qupai* and Suite Form: Southern Suites]. Shanghai: Xuelin chubanshe.

Wang Xichun 王錫純, ed. (1893). *Eyunge qupu* 遏雲閣曲譜 [*Qu* Notations of the "*Eyun* Pavilion"], vol 2. Accessed July 28, 2018. https://archive.org/details/02111058.cn/v2.

Wang Ying-fen 王櫻芬 (1992). "The 'Mosaic Structure' of Nanguan Songs: An Application of Semiotic Analysis." *Yearbook for Traditional Music* 24: 24–51.

Wu Junda 武俊達. (1993). *Kunqu changqiang yanjiu* 崑曲唱腔研究 [Studies of *Kunqu* Vocal Style]. Beijing: Renmin yinyue chubanshe.

Xie Yuanhuai 謝元淮. (1844). *Sujin cipu* 碎金詞譜 [Fragmentary Gold *Ci* Scores].

Yang Yinliu 楊蔭瀏. (1983). "Yuyan yinyue xue chutan" "語言音樂學初探" [Initial Investigations into Linguistic Musicology]. *Yuyan yu yinyue* 語言與音樂 [Language and Music], 1–96. Beijing: Renmin yinyue chubanshe.

Ye Tang 葉堂, ed. (1792). *Nashuying qupu* 納書楹曲譜 [Timeless Collection of *Qu* Notations], vol 1. Accessed August 29, 2021. https://archive.org/details/02111036.cn.

Yu Zhenfei 俞振飛, ed. (1982). *Zhenfei qupu* 振飛曲譜 [Zhenfei's *Kunqu* Notations]. Shanghai: Shanghai wenyi chubanshe.

Yue Shaofeng 樂韶鳳, Song Lian 宋濂, et al. (1375). *Hongwu zhengyun* 洪武正韻 [Proper Phonology of the Hongwu Era].

Zhou Deqing 周德清. (1324). *Zhongyuan yinyun* 中原音韻 [Phonology of the Central Plains].

Zhou Xiangyu 周祥鈺, Jinsheng Zou 鄒金生, et al., eds. (1746). *Jiugong dacheng nanbeici gongpu* 九宮大成南北詞宮譜 [Compendium of Notations of Southern and Northern Arias and Lyrics in Nine Modes], vol. 3. Accessed August 29, 2021. https://archive.org/details/02110987.cn.

Zhongguo Minzu Minjian Qiyue Jicheng Bianji Weiyuanhui 中國民族民間器樂集成編輯委員會, eds. (1997). *Zhongguo xiqu yinyue jicheng: Jiangsu juan* 中國戲曲音樂集成: 江蘇卷 [Anthology of Chinese Operatic Music: Jiangsu Volume], vol 1. Beijing: China ISBN Center.

CHAPTER 6

WHY AND HOW DO CHINESE SING *SHIJING* SONGS?

JOSEPH S. C. LAM

THE CHINESE TRADITION OF CHANTING AND SINGING *SHIJING* SONGS

CONTEMPORARY Chinese advocates of historical culture and performing arts chant and sing many songs from the twenty-five-centuries-old *Shijing*詩經(*Classic of Poetry*), an anthology of 305 folk (*feng* 風), banquet (*ya* 雅), and state sacrificial (*song* 頌) songs of ancient China that Confucius (Kongzi 孔子, 551–479 BCE) compiled and used as a reference for his teaching of history and humanist ideals.[1] Allegedly, Confucius could sing every one of the songs he anthologized; he did not, however, bequeath any notated scores or detailed instructions for their performance.[2] Five centuries after Confucius's time, the *Shijing* was imperially canonized. In 136 BCE, the emperor Wu (156–87 BCE) of the Western Han dynasty promoted Confucianism as a state ideology and designated the anthology as one of five state classics, which subsequently became the *loci classici* of imperial Chinese culture and history. Since then, culture- and history-loving Chinese have been continuously studying the *Shijing*, producing a plethora of erudite treatises and personal records, promoting the songs as ancient music (*guyue* 古樂), ritual and proper music (*yayue* 雅樂), and traditional music. And during the same period, they have discontinuously been chanting and singing *Shijing* songs with either "preserved" or newly created tunes, with and without dances, and at secular and/or ritual sites. Since the 1930s, Chinese composers have been setting *Shijing* lyrics with music composed in Westernized music idioms and performed with piano and orchestral accompaniment.[3] Since the 1990s, globalized China has been actively reclaiming its historical and musical heritages; as a result, the tradition of *Shijing* singing has been invigorated, producing a new wave of "reconstructed" or new tunes sung with historically informed performance practices.[4]

Viewed from ethnomusicological perspectives oriented toward music as and in culture,[5] and seeing music as a form of social history and of the performance of desires and identities, Chinese people's singing of *Shijing* songs is a multifaceted and significant phenomenon in world music and music cultures. If its ethnographic, historical, and musical details reveal the ways Chinese remember, see, feel, and make sense of their past and present realities, its underlying principles are germane to international studies on world music that are being challenged by globalization and other contemporary forces. What, why, and how people sing is a fundamental question in music anthropology, ethnography, and history, a point that Anthony Seeger (2004) has eloquently made.[6] Why and how Chinese people sing *Shijing* songs is thus not only a question for Chinese music studies but also a topic for international ethnomusicology and musicology.

This chapter will survey the expressive and structural features of *Shijing* songs and trace historical developments of their performance and scholarly traditions,[7] pinpointing the songs' embodiment of cultural memories, historical narratives, nationalistic aesthetics and morals, discursive soundscapes, and creative-expressive models. This chapter posits that Chinese sing *Shijing* songs to objectively and subjectively perform and navigate their historical realities and expressive selves across changing times and places.

SHIJING SONGS AS TEXT, MUSIC, AND PERFORMANCE

Any critical reading of the *Shijing* would find that its songs have distinctive lyrics and musical features, typical examples of which can be found in the first song in the anthology, "Guanju" ("*Guanguan*, Cry the Ospreys"; #1) (all song titles appear with Chinese characters in this chapter's Appendix). Depicting courtship with a simple literary-musical structure, the song's lyrics comprise five stanzas of tetrasyllabic rhyming phrases built from expressive and repeated key concepts and words. As translated,[8] the lyrics of the song "Guanju" are:

> *Guan-guan*, cry the ospreys,
> On the islet in the river.
> The modest, retiring, virtuous, young lady:
> For our prince a good mate, she.
>
> Here long, there short, is the duckweed,
> To the left, to the right, borne about by the current.
> The modest, retiring, virtuous, young lady:
> Waking and sleeping, he sought her.

He sought her and found her not,
And waking and sleeping, he thought about her.
Long he thought: oh! long and anxiously;
On his side, on his back, he turned, and back again.

Here long, there short, is the duckweed;
On the left, on the right, we gather it.
The modest, retiring, virtuous, young lady:
With lutes, small and large, let us give her friendly welcome.

Here long, there short, is the duckweed;
On the left, on the right, we cook and present it.
The modest, retiring, virtuous, young lady:
With bells and drums let us show our delight in her.

As performed and heard music, the song exists in many versions. Each is a unique sonic object of historically transmitted or newly composed melodies, rhythms, textures, and timbres generated with contrasting performance practices and diverse musical instruments, a fact that the following notated examples of four versions attest (Figure 6.1).

Shijing Songs as Chinese Memory

The lyrics of "Guanju" and other *Shijing* songs tell much about ancient Chinese lives and society. Verifiable or not, the information constitutes memories of ancient China and projects ideals of Confucian living that have held currency since Confucius's time.[9] A good number of *Shijing* songs are romantic or even suggestive; many have become classical references for amorous desires and intimate relationships. For example, "Jianjia" ("Reeds and Rushes"; #129) evokes the unreachable beloved who lives somewhere upstream, while "Taoyao" ("Peach Tree"; #6) compares a beautiful bride with a desirably ripe fruit. As "Guanju" depicts, passionate men would actively look for their objects of desire, attracting and entertaining them with music and dance. And women were free to invite their lovers to meet them by the river, as "Zhenwei" ("Zhen and Wei Rivers"; #95) reports. "Yeyou sijun" ("Dead Antelope"; #23) tells that bold couples would have their trysts outdoors.

A number of *Shijing* songs comment on blissful marriages and faithful couples. Two with the most moving lyrics are "Lüyi" ("Green Robe"; #27) and "Gesheng" ("The Dolichos Grow"; #124), eulogies for beloved and deceased wives and husbands. But many affairs and marriages in ancient China do fall apart, just like those of their contemporary counterparts. "Gufeng" ("East Wind"; #35) is an abandoned woman's lament, and "Mang" ("Men"; #58) tells how a resentful woman disparages her fickle and heartless lover.

FIGURE 6.1. Four musical versions of "Guanju."

FIGURE 6.1A. "Guanju" as preserved in a thirteenth-century notated source and literally transcribed into staff notation (Pian, 2003: 165–66); notice the notational format of "one note for one word in the lyrics," which graphically establishes the syllabic style (*yizi yiqin*) of state sacrificial Chinese music and court performance.

FIGURE 6.1B. "Guanju" as preserved in an eighteenth-century *qin* (seven-string zither) score, and transcribed into staff notation (Wang, 1983: 69); notice the melismatic nature of the melody, an obvious result of idiomatic instrumental playing of the *qin*; the eighteenth century was also a time when melismatic *kunqu* opera arias were popularly sung.

FIGURE 6.1B. Continued

FIGURE 6.1C. "Guanju" as an art song with piano accompaniment (Chu, Xu, and Yu, 2007: 1–3); notice the creative blending of the syllabic style with piano playing and Western-style harmonies.

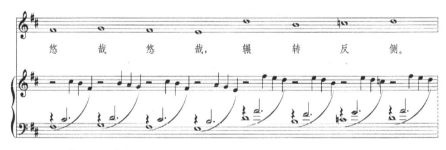

FIGURE 6.1C. Continued

FIGURE 6.1C. Continued

FIGURE 6.1D. "Guanju" as historical music from Southern Song China (1127–1279) and performed with a "reconstructed court orchestra" (Yang Bo et al., 2014: 47–57); notice the adjusted syllabic style of the music, which is performed on chime-bells, chime-stones, and other ancient musical instruments of "court orchestras."

FIGURE 6.1D. Continued

Many *Shijing* lyrics describe living within and without the family, the nexus of traditional Chinese society. For example, "Yanyan" ("Swallows"; #28) describes a royal wife's sisterly farewell to a concubine forced to leave. And "Changdi" ("Cherry Flowers"; #164) describes how brothers would gather to party, celebrating their male bonds. *Shijing* songs repeatedly make reference to filial piety, a cardinal virtue in Confucian China. "Kaifeng" ("Genial Wind"; #32), for instance, registers a son's memories of his nurturing mother. Similarly, "Lu'e" ("Long and Large Bushes"; #202) details a son remembering how his parents raised him and feeling regret about failing to take care of them in later life.

Many *Shijing* lyrics expose conflicts, inequalities, injustices, and other harsh realities that ancient Chinese confronted in their time, underscoring social-political problems that have plagued historical and contemporary China. "Xiaoxing" ("Starlets"; #21) and "Shiwei" ("Reduced"; #36), for example, tell of how officials abuse their lowly subordinates. Similarly, "Qifu" ("Minister of War"; #185) registers soldiers' grudges against their supervisors. "Xiangshu" ("Look at a Rat"; #52) exposes how the privileged appropriate the fruits of commoners' hard labor. "Beifeng" ("Cold Blows the North Wind"; #41) declares that the ruling classes are always concerned with maintaining the status quo and taking care of themselves. "Qiang youci" ("Tribulus Grows on the Wall"; #46) whispers about the incestuousness of those living in palaces. "Xiaomin" ("High Heaven"; #195) and "Xiaoming" ("Bright Heaven"; #207) openly critique abusive and irresponsible rulers. And in explicit terms, songs like "Chuju" ("Military Carriages"; #168), "Dongshan" ("March to East Hill"; #156), and "Caiwei" ("Gathering Thorn-ferns"; #167) describe battle scenes and warn of national decline and even collapse (Wang, 2015).

Shijing lyrics on filial piety and political-social tensions directly make reference to Chinese state worship of royal ancestors and deities with the grand music-ritual performance of state sacrifices. Forty *Shijing* lyrics are state sacrificial songs; all evoke imperial ideology, ritual liturgy, and musical grandeur in ancient Chinese courts. For example, "Haotian you chengming" ("Heaven Made Its Imperial Appointment"; #271) honors the king Cheng (*c.* 1055–1020 BCE), the second ruler of the Zhou dynasty, who allegedly developed China into a civilized land. The liturgies evoked in songs like "Wenwang" ("King Wen"; #235), "Qingmiao" ("Solemn Temple"; #266) and "Liezu" ("Meritorious Ancestors"; #302) are models for state sacrifices in subsequent dynasties. Performance practices and soundscapes reported in "Yougu" ("Blind Musicians"; #280) define the Chinese court tradition of performing state sacrificial music, with male singers and instrumentalists playing chime-bells, chime-stones, drums, and other ritual and musical instruments. Many key words and phrases in *Shijing* lyrics, such as *haotian* ("pure heaven") and *wojiang woxiang* ("we worship with offerings"), reappear exactly or with minor adjustments in state sacrificial songs of imperial China from the Han through the Qing dynasties.[10]

SHIJING SONGS AS CHINESE HISTORY

Shijing memories become verifiable history when their events, agents, and chronologies corroborate with archaeological objects and facts registered in seminal Chinese documents, such as the *Zuozhuan* 左傳 (*Commentary of Zuo*), *Guoyu* 國語 (*Discourses of the States*), and *Shiji* 史記 (*Records of the Grand Historian*).[11] An essay in the *Zuozhuan*, for example, tells of how Master Ji Zha 季札 responded to a performance of Zhou-dynasty court music that he witnessed in the state of Lu in the year 544 BCE.[12] The nobleman praised the harmonious tones, formal structures, and distinctive performance styles of the music he heard, heralding how Confucius approached music as a means of self-cultivation and governance and underscoring the indigenous music-court-humanist tradition that *Shijing* songs inherited, embodied, and bequeathed to Chinese posterity.

The historical nature of *Shijing* songs is most apparent in the state sacrificial songs that honor Shang and Zhou ancestors. "Xuanniao" ("Heaven Commissions the Black Swallow"; #303), for example, is a narrative on the origin and identity of the Shang clan, sung by descendants living in the state of Song. Even if the narrative song was newly composed when the state, a tributary to the Zhou and imperial court, was launched in the beginning of the Zhou dynasty (1046–256 BCE), and after the fall of the Shang dynasty (c. 1600–1046 BCE), the information in the song comprises historically organized memories and interpretations about Shang ancestors. Similarly significant as a historical text are the lyrics of "Bigong" ("The Ancestral Temple"; #300); as the longest poem in the *Shijing*, comprising 9 stanzas and 120 tetrasyllabic phrases, it tells of the origin of the Zhou people and the achievements of the king Xi of Lu, blending unverifiable legends with documented facts. As a ritual, political, and literary masterpiece, the lyrics of "Bigong" were much emulated in imperial China.

Just as the *Shijing* documents the past, it also creates it. In fact, its reception history since the Han dynasty offers a microcosm of Chinese intellectual, literary, and musical transformations during the past twenty or more centuries. Names of emperors, officials, and scholars involved in historical *Shijing* performance and scholarship constitute a who's who of Chinese biography and history. As mentioned above, the emperor Wu's canonization of the *Shijing* rendered it a seminal text, one that Chinese men had to master if they wanted to function as scholar-officials in imperial China. By the end of the Eastern Han period, authoritative commentaries by Zheng Xuan 鄭玄 (127–200) and other critics appeared (Zheng, 2013; Riegel, 1997; Kern, 2007). By the time of the Western and Eastern Jin dynasties (265–420), *Shijing* scholarship had become a cultural and intellectual exercise, one that nevertheless marginalized auditory dimensions of the songs examined. Memories about *Shijing* tunes and performance practices, nevertheless, lingered among scholars who had musical skills. To facilitate memorization and understanding of this classic, they read aloud or chanted the lyrics with simple melodic and rhythmic formulae—chanting or reading poetic texts aloud was, and still is, a common Chinese educational practice.[13]

Such a practice has probably helped sustain the tradition of *Shijing* singing, which has been declining since the beginning of the Jin period—some scholars have even lamented that by that time, *Shijing* music had been forgotten. Reconstructions or recreations of *Shijing* tunes and of their ways of being sung have also helped keep the tradition going. A critical development was Tang-period (618–907) efforts in reestablishing the communal drinking ritual (*xiang yinjiu li* 鄉飲酒禮) as a liturgically and musically standardized ceremony. This court action shaped historical developments of *Shijing* singing in post-Tang China.

The impetus that transformed the tradition was in all likelihood launched by Hu Yuan 胡瑗 (993–1059), a scholar-teacher and a music theorist who briefly participated in a court music reform in the early Song period (960–1127). Data on Hu's promotion of *Shijing* singing is sketchy, but it is clear that in the schools he directed, students sang the classical songs with instrumental music accompaniment (Zhang, 2009). A number of his students rose to prominent court positions; they probably shared their *Shijing* singing experiences with their court colleagues and subordinates, and thus directly or indirectly stimulated developments.

In the mid-Southern-Song period, Zhao Yansu 趙彥肅 (d. c. 1197), a relatively minor but not unknown scholar, had students sing *Shijing* songs in his studio with what he claimed were authentic melodies from the Kaiyuan period (713–41) of the Tang period (Zheng, 2004: 74–75). Zhao was an acquaintance of Zhu Xi 朱熹 (1130–1200), the great Neo-Confucianist and authority on *Shijing* exegesis, who obviously had access to Zhao's notated music for singing *Shijing* songs. Sometime after Zhu Xi's death, a notated score of *Zhao Yansu chuan fengya shiershipu* 趙彥肅傳風雅十二詩譜 (*Twelve* Shijing *Folk and Banquet Songs Transmitted by Zhao Yansu*; hereafter *Twelve Shijing Songs*) appeared in the Neo-Confucian's posthumously published *Yili jingchuan tongjie* 儀禮經傳通解 (*A General Survey of Ritual*).[14] The publication promptly became an authoritative source of *Shijing* songs (*shiyue* 詩樂), one that has promulgated the syllabic style for singing them.

As an authoritative commentator on the *Shijing*, Zhu thoroughly grasped the historical and musical importance of singing the classical songs.[15] He was, however, skeptical of the provenance of the *Twelve Shijing Songs*: they featured contemporaneous (i.e., twelfth century) use of modal pitches and ranges. He also doubted whether syllabic singing was the only way to perform *Shijing* songs; he knew that some historical musicians had sung melismatically. Zhu could not, however, dismiss Zhao's claim that the songs came from the Kaiyuan period of the Tang empire—the time when the singing of *Shijing* songs during communal drinking rituals had been reestablished. As an objective historian and investigative philosopher, Zhu chose to preserve Zhao Yansu's score, so that the music it contained could be discussed and perhaps performed by future scholars and musicians. With precise and insightful words, Zhu pinpointed fundamental issues in the songs' transmissions, structural features, and performance practices. As quoted in the *Songshi* (Tuo, 1973: 172.3339–.3341), Zhu Xi's seminal comment read:

> At the end of the Han dynasty, Du Kui taught four ancient songs: namely "Luming" ["Deer Calls"; #161], "Zhouyu" ["Hunters"; #25], "Fatan" ["Cutting Down Sandal Trees"; #112], and "Wenwang," the lyrics and tunes of which were all verifiably historical. Then, new lyrics were composed [in the Jin period (266–420)], and ancient [*Shijing* tunes] became obsolete. From the time when the communal drinking ritual was instituted in the Kaiyuan years, a list of twelve [*Shijing* songs for performance

during the ceremony] was established. No one [living now] has heard how [past] performance of the listed tunes sounded. The score [that I preserve here] allegedly preserves historical tunes from the period.

The sounds of ancient music vanished a long time ago. I have no idea how Tang musicians got the score and I cannot verify their conclusions. I believe that ancient music involved singing [*chang* 唱] and affective oral deliveries [*tan* 嘆]. [In their performance, solo] singers would begin musical phrases of the songs they perform, while the chorus would follow-up by singing refrain phrases. In addition to words proper in the lyrics, song texts would include repeated words [*diezi* 疊字] and [vocables sung with] ornamental tones [*sansheng* 散聲], which are expressively performed to communicate poetic messages and pleasures.

Transmission of [tunes and performance practices for singing] ancient songs stopped sometime during the Han and Jin dynasties. Thus, even though ancient [*Shijing*] song lyrics have been preserved, their [original tunes] are neither known nor reconstructable by generations of [post-Han and post-Jin] musicians. Should ancient songs be sung like the tunes notated in this [score transmitted by Zhao Yansu], which features the syllabic style of singing one word of the poetic text with one musical pitch, then every ancient [*Shijing*] song can be sung.

Also, Zhao's score features octave pitches in its modal melodies—this is unlikely an ancient practice. Since ancient [*Shijing*] music can hardly be investigated [without notated records], I preserve Zhao's score so that its [notated music] can be somehow [performed and] heard, and its [authenticity] can be verified by future music masters.

Zhu Xi's seminal comments shaped *Shijing* music discussions and performances in Yuan (1271–1368), Ming (1368–1644), and Qing (1644–1911) China. A representative result of developments during the turn of the Song and Yuan dynasties is Xiong Penglai's 熊朋來 (1246–1323) *Sepu* 瑟譜 (*Music for* Shijing *Songs with Se Zither Accompaniments*) (Pian, 2003: 188–231). It not only reproduces Zhao's scores but also presents Xiong's newly created tunes for singing thirty-one *Shijing* songs as syllabic and modal melodies.

Ming China inherited and advanced Southern Song practices of singing *Shijing* songs. The emperor Chengzu of the dynasty (1360–1424; r. 1403–24) promoted Zhu Xi's Neo-Confucianism by printing and distributing copies of Confucian classics (*Sishu wujing* 四書五經) that aspiring scholar-officials had to master to pass state examinations, the gateway for launching their court careers. Emperor Shizong (1507–67; r. 1521–67) helped advance the singing of *Shijing* songs when he extensively reformed court ritual and music for personal and political reasons (Lam, 1998: 75–98), generating vigorous discussions and writings about music during his reign. A representative publication is the *Shiyue tupu* 詩樂圖譜 (*Illustrated Scores of* Shijing *Songs*, 1536) by Lü Nan 呂柟 (1479-1542), which reproduces scores of the *Twelve Shijing Songs*, while other treatises argued that original melodies for singing the ancient songs are outlined by the linguistic tones of words in their lyrics (Lam, 1988: 661–703). In 1606, Zhu Zaiyu 朱載堉 (1536–1611), a Ming prince, presented his *Yuelü quanshu*

樂律全書 (*Complete Collection of Music Treatises*) to the imperial court. Compiling results of the prince's research projects since the 1560s, the collection includes the *Lülü zhengyi* 律呂正義 (*Essential Music Theories*) and *Xiangyin shiyuepu* 鄉飲詩樂譜 (*Music Scores for Singing* Shijing *Songs at the Communal Drinking Ritual*), two treatises that present traditional and newly created tunes for singing *Shijing* and other ritual lyrics (Zhu, 2000: 532–674).

Shijing songs were widely chanted or sung in late Ming China; many were heard in private or communal schools. A theatrical representation of such sixteenth-century educational-musical practice occurs in *Mudanting* 牡丹亭 (*The Peony Pavilion*, 1598) by Tang Xianzu 湯顯祖, which includes a scene on *Shijing* reading and chanting (Tang, 1994: 24–30). Some were even sung as art songs with *qin* accompaniment (Wang, 1983). When the Ming empire was collapsing, Wei Zhiyan 魏之炎, a merchant and musician from Fujian, fled to Japan about 1629 with his music, where he launched a Chinese-Japanese tradition of singing Chinese art and *Shijing* songs. His *Weishi yuepu* 魏氏樂譜 (*A Songbook of the Wei Family*) includes the notated music for eighteen *Shijing* songs (Qi, 2017: 932–74).

The Ming tradition of singing *Shijing* songs continued into Qing China, but the emperor Qianlong (1711–99; r. 1735–96) triggered a new development. In 1788, he declared Zhu Zaiyu's notated music and performance prescriptions for singing *Shijing* lyrics "inauthentic" and had the *Qinding Shijing yuepu* 欽定詩經樂譜 (*An Imperial Anthology of Notated Music for* Shijing *Songs*) compiled and published. It proclaimed a new repertory of tunes for singing of *Shijing* songs and stimulated their ritual and secular performance throughout Qing China. One example of secular performance that critically affected twentieth-century interpretations was Qiu Zhilu's 邱之稑 (1781–1848) rendition of "Guanju" as a song with *qin* 琴 accompaniment (Wu, 2003).

Early twentieth-century China, which actively embraced Western concert music, had *Shijing* lyrics sung as modern and nationalistic art songs. On September 18, 1938, Ying Shangneng 應尚能 (1902–73) composed "Wuyi" ("No Clothes?"; #133) to musically protest the ongoing Japanese invasion of China; it features a classical *Shijing* lyric with a Western-style melody and piano accompaniment (Zhou, 2003: 93–95). In socialist China of the mid-twentieth century, singing *Shijing* songs was dismissed as an antiquarian and elitist exercise; the *Twelve Shijing Songs* were discredited as musical fakes (Yang, 1980: 383–85), and their performance discouraged. Chinese and international musicians and scholars living and working outside mainland China, however, continued to study and sing the songs.[16] Since the 1990s, the Chinese tradition of singing the classical songs has been reviving, prompting the composition of many new vocal works accompanied by orchestras of Chinese and/or Western musical instruments. In the globalized China of the twenty-first century, many Chinese musicians who promote Chinese culture and history chant and/or sing *Shijing* songs with contrasting tunes and performance styles. Many also post audio-visual recordings of their performances online.[17]

Shijing Songs as Chinese Aesthetics and Morals

A driving force sustaining the centuries-long tradition of singing *Shijing* songs is aesthetic and moralistic in nature. The songs manifest Confucian ideals that permeated imperial and traditional China and are still relevant for Chinese living today. In traditional China, even the illiterate would utter aphorisms from the *Analects* (*Lunyu* 論語), such as "Is it not a joy to have friends come from afar?" or "A piece of rotten wood cannot be carved" (Lau, 1979: 1, 77).[18] Many contemporary Chinese musicians and audiences still grow up with explicit and implicit lessons in Confucian values. Even if they do not diligently read Confucian classics from top to bottom, they have learned of the Confucian promotion of proper music (*yayue*) and rejection of vernacular and/or licentious music (*suyue* 俗樂) (Lau, 1979: 146).

Historically informed Chinese musicians are familiar with Confucius's teachings on music as a means of self-cultivation and governance. As registered in the *Analects*, Confucius declared that "Guanju" was a piece of proper music, entertaining without being licentious, and that its finale made busy sounds filling the audience's ears (Lau, 1979: 70, 94). Confucius made it clear that sonically proper and expressive music was also morally enchanting. He confessed that after having witnessed a performance of *Shao* 韶 (music by the sage king Xun), he was so mesmerized that he forgot the exquisite taste of meat for three months (Lau, 1979: 87).

Whereas Confucius repeatedly promoted *Shijing* songs as examples of proper music, he did not specify how and why one should sing them. Clarifications, nevertheless, can be found in Han-dynasty documents like the "Maoshi daxu" 毛詩大序 ("Mao Preface to the *Shijing*") and the *Yueji* 樂記 (*Record of Music*), results of Han scholars' interpretations of Confucian classics (Ji, 1983: 104–6 and 69–82, respectively; Cook, 1995). Both classics declare that when people are touched by external forces and want to express what they have experienced and harbor in their heart-minds (*xin* 心), they utter words, creating poetry; when they find poetic words inadequate in revealing what they feel and want to tell, they chant or sing out their lyrics; when they find such oral deliveries insufficient, they dance and act out what they want to express.

By the end of the Han dynasty, an orthodox understanding of musical Confucianism had been established; from then on, it dominated Chinese scholarly discussions of music aesthetics and morals.[19] Its tenets can be sketched as follows:[20] People become benevolent gentlemen by studying poetry, practicing ritual, and expressing themselves with music. Studying *Shijing* lyrics, they learn no improper thoughts (*siwuxie* 思無邪) but rather historical facts, vocabulary, and rhetoric for effective speaking. Performing *Shijing* songs as ritual music, they acquire skills to interact with human beings and supernatural forces; when they perform music (*yue* 樂), they reveal what they harbor in their heart-minds. Since music is so revealing a performing art, only its *ya* 雅 ("proper and refined") compositions, such as the banquet and state sacrificial songs found in the *Shijing*, should be practiced; vernacular and licentious music (*suyue*), such as the folk songs from the states of Zheng (*Zhengsheng* 鄭聲) that the *Shijing* records, should be discouraged.

In addition to the broad tenets summarized above, orthodox musical Confucianism prescribes who could institute music and what its features and meanings are. The *Yueji*, for example, declares: only meritorious rulers could institute court and proper music; musical tones associatively correspond to cosmic elements and cardinal directions; people have distinctive types of music, the sounds of which reveal who they are and why their worlds flourish or collapse.

To substantiate their arguments on licentious and nation-toppling music, Chinese moralists would cite songs from the Zheng and Wei states that the *Shijing* anthologizes, arguing how they are or are not depraved, and demonstrating the role the classic plays in Chinese negotiations of morals and social-political communities. As argued by Zhu Xi (Chen, 2016: 9–10), Confucius compiled the *Shijing* as a reference on what music people should practice or reject; he included folk songs from the Zheng and Wei states to show what licentious music is, or might be, and how people should stay away from it (Yang Tianshi, 2019: 128–30; Mittag, 1993: 197–99, 203–5).

SHIJING SONGS AS SOUNDSCAPES

Confucian music aesthetics and morals are persuasive, but they are not the only reasons why Chinese sing *Shijing* songs. The songs are sung because their lyrics are musical and musically inspiring. *Shijing* songs describe a variety of sounds and soundscapes that would underscore, on the one hand, why and how early Chinese sang, danced, and played musical instruments to express their humanity and, on the other hand, inspire present-day Chinese to emulate or recreate their ancestors' musical works. Many *Shijing* lyrics describe natural and man-made sounds with repeated onomatopoeic words, such as "*guanguan*, cry the ospreys," "*youyou*, the deer call," "*huanghuang*, the chime-bells and chime-tones resonate," "*qiangqiang*, the mouth-organ and flute melodies flow," and "*dingding*, the tree-cutting axes hit."

Among natural sounds that ancient Chinese heard and emulated, bird songs are most thoroughly understood and purposefully interpreted. "Getan" ("Dolichos and Yellow Birds"; #2), for example, tells of how when a young wife heard a school of yellow birds singing on a shrub outside her house, she was reminded of happy times frolicking in her natal home and developed a yearning to see her parents and siblings; thus, she requested permission to visit them and made preparations for her travel. "Yanyan" depicts birds flying one after another, singing high and low tones, just like sisters sending a new bride on her way and bidding her a heartbreaking farewell. And "Xiongzhi" ("Male Pheasant"; #33) tells of how a lonely wife heard a male pheasant singing as it soared up and down in the sky; the view made her ask when her traveling husband would return. Men with tender feelings in their hearts also identified with bird songs. A lonely soldier asked why he could not sing like a yellow bird, showing filial gratitude to his mother with a pleasurable tune, as the lyrics of "Kaifeng" tell.

Shijing songs show how ancient Chinese listened to natural sounds and used what they heard to express mundane or lofty concerns in their lives. A comical dramatization of their sonic maneuvers appears in "Jiming" ("The Cock has Crowed"; #96): early in the morning, the wife heard the cock crowing, and she urged her husband to get up and go to work; he responded by declaring that he had only heard flies buzzing, and it was too early to get out of bed. In "Qingying" ("Blue Flies"; #219) too, the buzzing of flies is heard as an annoyance—it is compared to slanderous words that destroy trust between people and states. In contrast, "Heming" ("Crane Crows"; #184) claims that a lofty crane would call alone in the wildness, just like virtuous, talented, but unrecognized scholar-officials, who would only vocalize their aspirations to and by themselves.

With the same sophistication, ancient Chinese used natural and man- or machine-made sounds to evoke the harsh realities of warfare. For example, "Jigu" ("Drum Rolls"; #31) depicts a tired and lonely soldier's wish to go home while marching to the thunderous *tangtang* sounds of beating drums. "Caiqi" ("Gathering White Millet"; #178) projects a cacophonous soundscape of thunderous drums, ringing gongs and bells, and the squeaking wheels of the running chariots with which the Zhou army subdued Chu rebels.

Ancient Chinese made many expressive sounds themselves. Amorous men would sing to reach out to women whom they desired, as "Dongmen zhici" ("The Moat at the East Gate"; #139) reports. Virtuous men would sing by themselves and in huts they built in valleys and by streams, enjoying their independence and asserting their personal integrity, as recorded in "Kaopan" ("Hut by the Stream"; #56). Women would also sing; "Jiang yousi" ("The River has Branches"; #22) features an ignored wife lamenting her husband's taking of a new concubine. And they would make sounds to announce their presence; "Younü tongju" ("Lady in the Carriage"; #83) reports how a lady attracted a male admirer's attention by making her jade accessories tinkle. Much louder but equally effective is the singing and playing of drums and ceramic bowls by a female shaman commoner; her performance attracted many men to her audience, as "Wanqiu" ("Highland Wan"; #136) declares.

Music making served many social-political functions in ancient China. As a means of social interaction, it afforded time and place for people to efficaciously engage with one another, just as it does in contemporary China. "Juxia" ("Wedding Procession"; #218), for example, tells of how music and dance are performed at weddings. "Luming," the song that was regularly sung at communal drinking rituals during the Ming and Qing periods, provides a snapshot of the music making that was typical at banquets, where men consumed sumptuous food and wine; in between such acts, they made harmonious music and expressed friendship by beating drums, plucking zithers, and blowing mouth-organs. They sang and danced outdoors too; "Famu" ("Cutting Trees"; #165) reports on an outdoor-work-related party at which friends and clansmen gathered to chop down trees with axes, making *dingding* noises amid bird calls and other natural sounds. After work, they feasted, drank, danced, sang, played flutes, and beat drums together as brothers and uncles, sounding and sealing their homosocial camaraderie.

Drinking and music making at parties, however, would sometimes lead to awkward but revealing moments. "Youbi" ("Fat and Strong Horses"; #298) describes how citizens of the state of Lu would get drunk at harvest parties. And "Bin zhi chuyan" ("When Guests are Seated, the Banquet Begins"; #220) depicts how alcoholic and musical intoxication led to guests letting down their good manners and doing things that exposed who they really were. At the beginning of the banquet, the poem tells, all guests properly took their assigned seats, toasting one another courteously. Then as they continued to offer toasts to fellow guests, they began to get drunk and restless. As they started playing archery games, danced, played musical instruments, and frolicked in and around the banquet venue, they knocked down cups and dishes, made silly bodily gestures that mangled their party attire, and uttered inappropriate words. They showed their true colors in this commotion of acts, sounds, and sights.

This soundscape of unruly and uninhibited guests sharply contrasts with those found at court and ritual sites and occasions. As reported in "Julin" ("Approaching Chariots"; #126), "Tingliao" ("Torches Burning in the Courtyard"; #182), and "Caishu" ("Gathering Beans"; #222), ancient Chinese kings, noblemen, and officials traveled with musical processions. Bells hung on their chariots and banners announced their anticipated approaches. And as described in "Tonggong" ("Red Bows"; #175), when Zhou kings awarded meritorious nobles with gifts of red bows, the ceremony unfolded with the grand and orderly performance of banquet music. Rulers and generals manifested their might by making military and orderly sounds, which strikingly contrasted with the cacophony heard during battles. "Jugong" ("Chariots and Horses"; #179) states: when the king Xuan returned from his hunting or battle exercise, his approach was marked by orderly sounds of soldiers marching with chariots and horses; neither noisy and uncoordinated chattering nor other sounds were heard.

Sound defined state sacrifices in ancient China, all of which were performed with grand orchestras of chime-bells, chime-stones, and other court and ritual musical instruments. "Na" ("How Admirable!"; #301), for example, highlights the ways people of the state of Song honored their ancestors with the drum and flute music that accompanied grand dances by handsome men. Similar scenes are described in "Chuci" ("Tribulu"; #209) and "Futian" ("Bright and extensive fields"; #211), corroborating descriptions in the *Zhou li* 周禮 (*Rites of Zhou*) (Lin Yin, 1985). Zhou state sacrifices, their liturgies, and performance practices were most elaborate. The actions of offering sacrificial victims, wine, and dishes of grains and other foods were all performed with meticulously coordinated vocal and orchestral music.

Sound and humanity were inseparable in ancient China. Indeed, "Wenwang yousheng" ("King Wen's Voice"; #244) reports how a ruler's physical voice sonically indexes his personal presence and governmental reputation.[21] Similarly, "Zhonggu" ("Chime-bells and Drums"; #208) declares that the distinctively resonant sounds of chime-bells, drums, mouth-organs, zithers, and other instruments of state sacrificial orchestras made citizens living in imperfect times yearn for benevolent rulers and peaceful periods.

Shijing Songs as Creative Stimulus and Expressive Model

Many *Shijing* lyrics have inspired contemporary Chinese to sing the classical songs. For instance, the lyrics of "Yougu" not only detail the liturgically specified placement of musical instruments but also evoke the grand and harmonious sounds that Zhou-dynasty court and blind musicians made, sounds that historically informed musicians and cultural activists in contemporary China might hear or play themselves. In translation, the lyrics read:

> Blind musicians, blind musicians,
> Performing in the courtyards of Zhou temples.
> Playing chime-bells hung on frames with painted boards, wedged-edges, and feathered ornaments,
> Shaking small hand-held drums with swinging beaters, and hitting large and stand-alone drums [with sticks],
> And playing chime-stones, wooden crates (*zhu* 筑) and wooden tigers (*yu* 敔),
> The [musicians] make grand and articulated tunes.
> They also blow panpipes and flutes,
> Generating resonant tones,
> Which solemnly blend into harmonious echoes,
> Honoring meritorious ancestors who listen attentively.
> Guests invited to our sacrifice also observe respectfully,
> Listening to songs being sung stanza by stanza.

Echoing musical information that *Shijing* lyrics tell, Chinese historical documents offer many suggestions for composing and singing the classical songs in the present day. *Yueji*, for example, specifies seven patterns of ascending, descending, concave, convex, and zigzagging melodic contours (Lam, 1998: 90–92), all of which can be readily identified in the notated music preserved in Zhu Xi's *Twelve Shijing Songs*, Xiong Penglai's *Sepu*, and other historical *Shijing* scores.

Since Confucius's time, Chinese poets and musicians have been studying the *Shijing* as an exemplar for their own creative and expressive works. Tang and Song poetry, two esteemed genres of Chinese literature that are also chanted and sung, show many *Shijing* influences and references. "Lüyi" is clearly an inspiration, if not an actual model, for the celebrated *ci* 詞 song "Jiangchengzi" 江城子 ("To the Tune of River City'"), a heart-wrenching eulogy written by Su Shi 蘇軾 (1037–1101) for his deceased wife in early

1075 after a dream about her (Burton, 1994: 65). The poetic mise en scène and tender feelings in Su's simple poem echo those found in "Lüyi." Similarly, "Yangzhou man" 揚州慢 ("A Long Song on Yangzhou") by Jiang Kui 姜夔,[22] also a historically and literarily celebrated *ci* masterpiece, evokes images of a misunderstood and wandering man, images that "Shuli" ("Millet Fields"; #65) also depicts. Many favorite and meaningful words and phrases in traditional Chinese writings and even conversations come from *Shijing* lyrics. These aphorisms include, for example, *quishui yiren* ("the beloved") from "Jianjia," *xiaoxing* ("the concubine") from "Xiaoxing" and *rulü bobing* (navigating a dangerous situation like walking on thin ice) from "Xiaomin."

In addition to the poetic imagery contained within their lyrics, and the sounds of the classical texts read aloud, *Shijing* songs demonstrate a variety of literary-musical structural features that evoke specific composition-performance practices. These include, for example, stanza structures, phrase lengths and types, rhyme schemes, linguistic tones of words in the lyrics that suggest melodic progressions, and semantic divisions that suggest rhythms and accents. All can be objectively analyzed, codified, and emulated in reconstructive and/or recreated compositions and performances of the classical songs.

The fundamental challenge for the contemporary singing of *Shijing* songs is clear. No original tunes of the songs have been notationally preserved from Confucius's time. As described above, the earliest available and verifiable score of the music is the *Twelve Shijing Songs* printed between the years 1217 and 1222—approximately seventeen hundred years after Confucius's death. Furthermore, this score does not provide any detailed prescriptions on rhythmic and melodic interpretations of the notated music, a representational incompleteness that is prohibitive for positivist musicians but encouraging for musicians familiar with the dynamic interrelations between music and text.

The latter group of musicians argue that linguistic tones in *Shijing* lyrics suggest skeletal melodies for their singing. Chinese is a tonal language; to be linguistically correct and semantically communicative, Chinese words (especially in certain dialects) are uttered at appropriate pitch levels and with specified pitch movements, generating melodic movements that can be heard and interpreted as "inherent" tunes (Yang, 1983).[23] Such tunes become skeletal melodies when words of the lyrics are meaningfully divided into linguistic and rhyme units, and assigned rhythmic accents and values. For example, the last and rhyming word in a tetrasyllabic phrase in a *Shijing* text might appear on a downbeat, and/or it can be rhythmically extended (Xia, 1987). Skeletal melodies can promptly be organized into expressive music by skilled composers and/or singers.

They can begin their composition and/or performance processes by tracing the literary structures of *Shijing* songs that they want to sing. Ten distinctive formal patterns or performance procedures have been identified by Yang Yinliu 楊蔭瀏, the doyen of twentieth-century Chinese musicology (Yang, 1981: 57–61). Repetitive stanzas and phrases, Yang theorized, can be sung with the same tune or melodic phrase; lyrics with refrains or alternating phrases can be sung with two alternating tunes or melodic phrases; short musical preludes and/or codas can be added to introduce main phrases or melodic phrases in the songs.

The musical clues that *Shijing* lyrics suggest can be readily identified by examining their words and literary structures. To illustrate what the clues might reveal and how, heuristic "reconstructions/creations" of "melodies and rhythms" for singing three structurally and semantically contrasting songs will suffice;[24] due to space limitations, only the first song will be discussed with its full Chinese text, an English translation, and references to Chinese linguistic tones.[25] That song is "Taoyao," the lyrics of which comprise three repetitive stanzas of four tetrasyllabic phrases. The first and third phrases in each stanza are identical. The second phrases introduce two or three new words to develop the song's narrative. The fourth phrases differ from one another with changes of single words. As a result of this formal and repetitive structure in the lyrics, "Taoyao" can be readily sung with a through-composed tune, one that repeats for each of the three stanzas with a minimum of melodic adjustments. The tune has two parts or two sets of precedent and subsequent musical phrases. For convenience in discussing them, they are numbered P1, P2, P3, and P4. The lyrics of the song are as follows:

P1: *táo zhī yāo yāo* 桃之夭夭 (The peach tree is young and elegant),
P2: *zhuó zhuó qí huā* 灼灼其華 (Brilliant are its flowers).
P3: *zhī zǐ yú guī* 之子於歸 (This young lady is going to get married),
P4: *yí qí shì jiā* 宜其室家 (And will do well with her husband in her new home).

P1: *táo zhī yāo yāo* 桃之夭夭 (The peach tree is young and elegant),
P2: *yǒu fén qí shí* 有蕡其實 (Abundant will be its fruits).
P3: *zhī zǐ yú guī* 之子於歸 (This young lady is going to get married),
P4: *yí qí jiā shì* 宜其家室 (And will take good care of the house in her new home).

P1: *táo zhī yāo yāo* 桃之夭夭 (The peach tree is young and elegant),
P2: *qí yè zhēn zhēn* 其葉蓁蓁 (Luxuriant are its leaves)
P3: *zhī zǐ yú guī* 之子於歸 (This young lady is going to get married),
P4: *yí qí jiā rén* 宜其家人 (And will nurture well members in her new home).

Tones and rhythms for singing each stanza of the "Taoyao" can be derived from the linguistic tones of words in its lyrics—the melodic contour essentially follows the skeleton melody suggested by the linguistic word tones. Yet, if the song is rigidly sung as a syllabic melody, it progresses with many repeated tones.[26] If some flexibility is allowed, the tune can feature several concave and convex melodic contours. Thus, P1 begins with *mi* and ends with a slight rhythmic pause on the cadential tone of *sol*. P2 melodically moves between the *mi* and *sol* tones, ending with a rhythmically extended cadence. P3 has a relatively level progression of *sol*, except with a dip to *mi* on the third word of the phrase; P4 has a similar contour but it includes a sharp drop of pitch from *sol* to *do* on the third or fourth word of the phrase, before arriving at its final cadence. Should the melody be performed with some rhythmic variation, the semantic meanings and structure of the phrases demand that the fourth word of each phrase fall on a strong beat.

The auxiliary words *zhī*, *yú*, and *qī* should not be rhythmically stressed. To transform this skeleton tune into an expressive melody for a contemporary audience, ignoring the historical prescription of syllabic style completely, bent or heightened pitches, melodic ornaments, and rhythmic accents, syncopations, and fermatas can be applied to keywords in the lyrics. For example, the words *táo* (peach), *yúguī* (get married), and *jiāshì* (home, house) might be musically highlighted. And the rhyming final words of textual phrases such as *huā* (flower) and *jiā* (home, house) can be sung with modal tones and stretched rhythms.

Realizing the semantic content of "Taoyao," aged singers would perform the song in weddings and in the roles of parents or guardians, bestowing blessings on the young bride with a dignified voice. In traditional and morally conservative China, the song would not be sung by a young female vocalist—such a performance would draw sexualized attention to the singer's and the bride's womanly bodies.[27] Depending on whether the song is interpreted as a folk song or a banquet song for the elite, accompaniment can range from that of zither or lute to employing a full orchestra of chime-bells, drums, and other ancient and court musical instruments. To enhance their performance, singers might dance or have dancers perform illustrative choreography.

The same process of identifying and applying musical clues to reconstruct or recreate *Shijing* songs can be applied to "Nüyue jiming" ("A Couple's Morning Dialogue"; #82). The process, however, needs to address three specific problems that the song's unique structural and verbal features generate. First, "Nüyue jiming" has three stanzas: the first two have six tetrasyllabic phrases and the last stanza has six pentasyllabic phrases with a distinctive word sequence (2 + [1+2] words). To musically address this textural structure, stanzas one and two can be sung with a simple tune derived from linguistic tones and semantic units of 2 + 2 words; in contrast, stanza three might be sung to an adjusted version of the tune, accommodating the distinctive word sequence. Second, the word *zhī*, a conjunction, is repeated nine times in the third stanza. Thus, its melodic setting demands some melodic and rhythmic variation to avoid musical monotony. Third, the song presents a narrative text, one that unfolds as a dialogue between a loving couple; the gendered voices and timbres of the wife and the husband demand contrasting musical treatments. Should the song be sung as a folk song in rural China, it might take the form of a male/female duet—there are many such duets in Chinese folk songs, sung with or without theatrical dances.

"Siwen" ("Oh Accomplished Houji"; #275), a state sacrificial song about a deified Chinese ancestor, can similarly be reconstructed or recreated. Given the cultural, historical, and ritual meanings of the lyrics, and given its structural features (Cheng, 1985: 629–30), however, the process presents several musical challenges. Structurally, "Siwen" unfolds as a sequence of eight phrases with no repeated words; the first six of the phrases are tetrasyllabic and the last two are pentasyllabic. In other words, the lyrics demand to be sung with a developing through-composed tune, one that might not be mechanically derived from the linguistic tones of words in the lyrics. Furthermore, given the ritual nature of the song, they should be sung in the syllabic style, by a male chorus with orchestral accompaniment. As state sacrificial music, the performance needs to produce solemn and stately sounds, which can only be generated with the orchestrated striking of the chime-bells, chime-stones, drums, and other court and historical instruments. How the sounds communicate ritual and imperial meanings is a critical concern because semantic meanings of the sung words are lost with the syllabic and slow singing. And whether the song is expressively performed in the expansive outdoor courtyards of temples, in the cavernous ritual halls of palaces, or in contemporary concert auditoria, there are various practical considerations that cannot be ignored. How the performed sounds might evoke ancient and imperial China while entertaining contemporary audiences unfamiliar with Confucian ideals and practices is, for example, a challenge with no easy solutions. To be musically affective and intelligible, reconstructed or recreated performances of "Siwen" have to align with histories and imaginations about ancient imperial China that contemporary Chinese tell themselves and find relevant to their desires and needs.[28]

Concluding Remarks: Singing *Shijing* Songs to Express Chinese Heart-minds

Such a performance of "Siwen" might qualify as historically informed, but sonically it would be ahistorical. Even if what is sung is a historically authentic text, and even if its composition and performance reference documented data about the centuries-old tradition of singing *Shijing* songs, the sounds that are generated and heard in the present can hardly be what Confucius, Zhu Xi, or the emperor Qianlong would have witnessed in their particular circumstances. This reality underscores the question raised by this chapter: why and how have Chinese sung *Shijing* songs across different times and places? There are many answers to the question; one is that Chinese sing the songs differently and for diverse reasons. In fact, each performance by a specific group of musicians in historical and contemporary China is a story by itself. Each should be meticulously investigated with macro- and micro-approaches. The former broadly charts the story along the tradition's basic continuities and changes, while the latter exposes specific features of the story—what and how it tells of *Shijing* songs and their singers, their composition and performance practices, and evolving meanings.

Comprehensive understanding of the Chinese tradition of singing *Shijing* songs is musicologically relevant for the present international reclaiming of historical music throughout the world. It is critical to note that Chinese do not sing *Shijing* songs to factually bring back a musical reality that has long vanished with the passing of time. Pragmatically, they know that even if they harbor hopes of singing like Confucius did, they can only reclaim and restore some essence or sketches of the sage's songs and singing. They know that preserved texts and notated scores do not, and cannot, tell exactly how *Shijing* songs sounded in ancient China or how they can be authentically replayed in the present.[29] Just like Zhu Xi, most informed and pragmatic Chinese musicians only want to sing the songs to engage with an idealized version of their culture and their nation's past.[30]

Such an engagement is both factual and imaginative. As musicians study preserved historical sources and ethnographic evidence, they realize that the tradition of singing *Shijing* songs is like a long and evolving river (Huang, 1990: 3–4, 105–43). It offers a wealth of historical records about music compositions and performances, simultaneously informing them about the past and encouraging them to create in the present and for the future. It confirms that there is no one and definitive score for singing *Shijing* songs, be it the *Twelve Shijing Songs* or *Qinding Shijing yuepu*. No *Shijing* scores or verbal records can provide definitive answers to all questions about the tradition and its present and future performance and listening practices. In fact, the diversity of documented information and conflicting interpretations about *Shijing* music promote creative and relativist solutions—just as the wise and practical Zhu Xi postulated.

Such a Chinese approach to music of the past is distinctive, if not idiosyncratic, but it underscores Chinese aesthetics, memories, histories, practices, and values. As "Maoshi daxu" and *Yueji* declare, Chinese sing poetic words to genuinely and effectively express themselves. Subscribing to no positivist aesthetics and rigid research paradigms, creative Chinese musicians and cultural advocates sing *Shijing* songs not only as historically fixed and autonomous objects of sounds from the past but also as verbal, sonic, and kinetic representations of the realities, dreams, and emotions that they harbor in their present heart-minds, which they use to engage with ancestors of the past and with contemporaneous others. When they sing *Shijing* songs, they live as creative, cultivated, and expressive Chinese who possess histories. And when they post audio-visual recordings of their concerts online, they expand their musical worlds into cyberspace. Their historically informed or historically inspired *Shijing* songs musically invite their global partners to visit their Chinese worlds.

Appendix: *Shijing* Songs Cited

Beifeng 北風, "Coldly Blows the North Wind," #41
Bigong 閟宮, "The Ancestral Temple," #300
Bin zhi chuyan 賓之初筵, "When Guests are Seated," #220
Caiqi 采芑, "Gathering White Millet," #178
Caiwei 采薇, "Gathering Thorn-ferns," #167
Changdi 常棣, "Cherry Flowers," #164
Chuju 出車, "Military Carriages," #168
Dongmeng zhici 東門之池, "The Moat at the East Gate," #139
Dongshan 東山, "March to East Hill," #156
Famu 伐木, "Cutting Trees, #165
Futian 甫田, "Bright and Extensive Fields," #211
Gesheng 葛生, "The Dolichos Grow," #124

Getan 葛覃, "Dolichos and Yellow Birds," #2
Guanju 關雎, "*Guanguan*, Cry the Ospreys," #1
Gufeng 谷風, "East Wind," #35
Haotian you chengming 昊天有成命, "Heaven Made Its Imperial Appointment," #271
Heming 鶴鳴, "Crane Crows," #184
Jiang yousi 江有汜, "The River has Branches," #22
Jianjia 蒹葭, "Reeds and Rushes," #129
Jigu 擊鼓, "Drum Rolls," #31
Jiming 雞鳴, "The Cock has Crowed," #96
Jugong 車攻, "Chariots and Horses," #179
Julin 車鄰, "Approaching Chariots," #126
Juxia 車舝, "Wedding Procession," #218
Kaifeng 凱風, "Genial Wind," #32
Kaopan 考槃, "Hut by the Stream," #56
Liezu 列祖, "Meritorious Ancestors," #302
Lu'e 蓼莪, "Long and Large Bushes," #202
Luming 鹿鳴, "Deer Calls," #161
Lüyi 綠衣, "Green Robe," #27
Mang 氓, "Men," #58
Na 那, "How Admirable," #301
Nüyue jiming 女曰雞鳴, "A Couple's Morning Dialogue," #82
Qiang youci 牆有茨, "Tribulus Grows on the Wall," #46
Qifu 祈父, "Minister of War," #185
Qingmiao 清廟, "Solemn Temple," #266
Qingying 青蠅, "Blue Flies," #219
Shiwei 式微, "Reduced," #36
Shuli 黍離, "Millet Fields," #65
Siwen 思文, "Oh Accomplished Houji," #275
Taoyao 桃夭, "Peach Tree," #6
Tingliao 庭燎, "Torches Burning in the Courtyard," #182
Tonggong 彤弓, "Red Bows," #175
Wanqiu 宛丘, "Highland Wan," #136
Wenwang 文王, "King Wen," #235
Wenwang yousheng 文王有聲. "King Wen's Voice," #244
Wuyi 無衣, "No clothes," #133
Xiangshu 相鼠, "Look at a Rat," #52
Xiaoming 小明, "Bright Heaven," #207
Xiaomin 小旻, "High Heaven," #195
Xiaoxing 小星, "Starlets," #21
Xiongzhi 雄雉, "Male Pheasant," #33
Xuanniao 玄鳥, "Heaven Commissions Black Swallow," #303
Yanyan 燕燕, "Swallows," #28
Yeyou sijun 野有死麇, "Dead Antelope," #23

Youbi 有駜, "Fat and Strong Horses," #298
Yougu 有瞽, "Blind Musicians," #280
Younü tongju 有女同車, "Lady in the Carriage," #83
Zhenwei 溱洧, "Zhen and Wei Rivers," #95
Zhonggu 鐘鼓, "Chime-bells and Drums," #208
Zouyu 騶虞, "Hunters," #25

Glossary

chang 唱, sing
ci 詞, genre of classic poetry
diezi 疊字, repeated words
feng 風, folk songs of the *Shijing* anthology
Guoyu 國語, *Discourses of the States*
guyue 古樂, (ancient music) category for repertory thought to be inherited from antiquity
Hu Yuan 胡瑗, scholar, music-theorist, and court music reformer (993–1059)
Ji Zha 季札, Zhou-dynasty noble (c. 561–515 BCE)
Jiang Kui 姜夔, songwriter (1155–1221)
"Jiangchengzi" 江城子, "To the Tune of River City," *ci* poem written by Su Shi (1075)
Kongzi 孔子, Confucius (551–479 BCE)
Lülü zhengyi 律呂正義, *Essential Music Theories*, treatise by Zhu Zaiyu
Lü Nan 呂柟, compiler of sixteenth-century *Shijing* song collection
Lunyu 論語, *Analects* of Confucius
"Maoshi daxu" 毛詩大序, "Mao Preface to the *Shijing*," Han-dynasty document
Mudanting 牡丹亭, *The Peony Pavilion*, drama by Tang Xianzu
qin 琴, seven-stringed zither
Qinding Shijing yuepu 欽定詩經樂譜, *An Imperial Anthology of Notated Music for* Shijing *Songs*, treatise of 1788
Qiu Zhilu 邱之稑, creator of *Shijing* song "Guanju" with *qin* accompaniment (1781–1848)
sansheng 散聲, ornamental tones
Sepu 瑟譜, *Music for* Shijing *Songs with Se Zither Accompaniments*, by Xiong Penglai
Shao 韶, music by Sage King Xun that mesmerized Confucius
Shiji 史記, *Records of the Grand Historian*, by Sima Qian
Shijing 詩經, *Classic of Poetry*, or *Book of Songs*
shiyue 詩樂, music for the *Shijing*
Shiyue tupu 詩樂圖譜, *Illustrated Scores of* Shijing *Songs*, by Lü Nan (1536)
Sishu wujing 四書五經, *The Four Books and Five Classics*
siwuxie 思無邪, "no improper thoughts"
song 頌, state sacrificial songs in the *Shijing* anthology
Su Shi 蘇軾, poet (1037–1101)
suyue 俗樂, vernacular music
tan 嘆, affective oral deliveries
Tang Xianzu 湯顯祖, playwright (1550–1616)
Wei Zhiyan 魏之炎, musically inclined merchant (early seventeenth century)
Weishi yuepu 魏氏樂譜, *A Songbook of the Wei Family*, compiled by Wei Zhiyan (1629)

xiang yinjiu li 鄉飲酒禮, ritual of communal drinking in imperial China
Xiangyin shiyuepu 鄉飲詩樂譜, *Music Scores for Singing* Shijing *Songs at the Communal Drinking Ritual*, treatise by Zhu Zaiyu
xin 心, heart-mind
Xiong Penglai 熊朋來, compiler of the *Sepu* collection (1246–1323)
ya 雅, "proper and refined," banquet songs in the *Shijing* anthology
Yang Yinliu 楊蔭瀏, musicologist (1899–1984)
"Yangzhou man" 揚州慢, "A Long Song on Yangzhou," composition by Jiang Kui
yayue 雅樂, proper or refined music; music used in ritual
Yili jingquan tongjie 儀禮經傳通解, *A General Survey of Ritual*, posthumous publication by Zhu Xi
Ying Shangneng 應尚能, composer (1902–73)
yu 敔, tiger-shaped instrument sounded by running a stick across serrated ridged on its back
yue 樂, music
"Yueji" 樂記, *Record of Music*, Han-dynasty document on court ritual music
Yuelü quanshu 樂律全書, *Complete Collection of Music Treatises*, research collection made by Zhu Zaiyu (1606)
Zhao Yansu 趙彥肅, a Neo-Confucianist, whose students sang *Shijing* (d. *c.* 1197)
Zhao Yansu chuan fengya shiershipu 趙彥肅傳風雅十二詩譜, *Twelve* Shijing *Folk and Banquet Songs Transmitted by Zhao Yansu*
Zheng Xu 鄭玄, early critical commentator on the *Shijing* (127–200)
Zhengsheng 鄭聲, tunes of the Zheng state, considered to be vulgar music
Zhou li 周禮, *Rites of Zhou*, classic Confucian work (mid-second century BCE)
zhu 筑, rectangular wooden stringed instrument that is struck to make a sound
Zhu Xi 朱熹, Neo-Confucian scholar and calligrapher (1130–1200)
Zhu Zaiyu 朱載堉, court scholar (1536–1611)
Zuozhuan 左傳, *Commentary of Zuo*, ancient narrative history

Notes

1. For further readings on the *Shijing*, see Waley (1957), Gong (1995), Allen (1996), and Granet (2016).
2. For a richly illustrated volume in English on ancient Chinese musical culture, and in particular archaeological findings about chime-bells, chime-stones, and other instruments from the period, see So (2000); for an interpretation of *Shijing* songs performances in ancient China, see Major and So (2000: 31–32).
3. For a study on twentieth-century Chinese music compositions with *Shijing* lyrics or references, see Liang (2010). For scores of contemporary *Shijing* music compositions/arrangements for voice and piano accompaniment, see Chu, Xu, and Yu, eds. (2007) and Wang Sufen (2013).
4. For examples of these performances and compositions, see, for example, "Shijing Performed Small Elegant Airs: Huang-Huang Zhe Hua" https://www.youtube.com/watch?v=OP-uK_obT04; uploaded by Juni L. Yeung; last accessed on July 15, 2021; "HaHui Guanju" https://www.youtube.com/watch?v=9qgPOojbZYs; uploaded by Ha Hui on Jan 31, 2013; last accessed on July 15, 2021; "Musical Echoes and Reminiscences from Southern

Song Dynasty of Music China" https://www.youtube.com/watch?v=28B0jLQXWmk; uploaded by the Confucius Institute at the University of Michigan on April 25, 2017; last accessed on July 15, 2021; and "Guan Ju love song from Shi Jing with translated lyrics" https://www.youtube.com/watch?v=saUqqJ2nhIQ&list=PLttKSDUVGxpWL9R75cGuCjZRCzKRmJsv_ uploaded by Xu Yu on May 31, 2017; last accessed on July 15, 2021. For a scholarly report on the singing of *Shijing* songs as folk songs in Yunnan in the 1980s, see Li (1991).

5. This ethnomusicological reading of *Shijing* is theoretically informed by the following works: de Certeau (1984), Attali (1992), Small (1998), and DeNora (2000).
6. The theoretical and methodological template for this essay is Seeger's (2004) seminal thesis.
7. This examination of *Shijing* songs is based on the following Chinese and English editions: Cheng (1985), Cheng and Jiang (1991), Deng (2014), and Wang (2015); and Legge (1972) and Allen (1996). For convenient access to *Shijing* lyrics and related references, individual songs are written with standard Chinese titles, interpretive titles in English, and numerical tags that register the songs' order of appearance in the Mao version of the *Shijing*.
8. Unless noted, all English translations of *Shijing* songs presented in this essay are based on those by James Legge (1972) and http://www.shigeku.org/shiku/ws/zg/shijing.htm; adjustments and changes are made by the author to reflect current musicological readings.
9. For an informative and insightful study on *Shijing* songs as myth and history, see Schabert (1999). For a discussion on the ways Confucianism shapes contemporary China, see Tu, Hejtmanek, and Wachman (1992).
10. For a study on repeated use of keys words and phrases in the *Shijing* and Chinese culture, see Owen (2001).
11. For a detailed study on *Shijing* songs as history, see Sun (1996); for an English introduction to the historical sources, see (Wilkinson, 2000: 478–79 and 496).
12. For Chinese text of the essay, see "Ji Zha guanyue" 季札觀樂; http://so.gushiwen.org/shiwenv_4b65911cbd27.aspx; for a musicological study on the essay, see Yang Jiarong (2012).
13. For current studies on Chinese poetry chanting, see Chen Shaosong (1997), Lam (2010), and Ye (2014.)
14. For two authoritative musicological studies in English on the *Twelve Shijing Songs*, see Pian (2003) and Picken (1956).
15. For an insightful study on Zhu Xi's understanding of *Shijing* songs as culture and as music, see Mittag (1993).
16. For decades, Laurence E. R. Picken of England, for example, studied and published on *Shijing* songs (Picken, 1956, 1969, 1978).
17. See note 4; for an example of the singing of *Shijing* songs in current populist style: "Jigu," https://www.youtube.com/watch?v=TeXS804FSF8 uploaded by Satomiao on September 11, 2014; last accessed on July 15, 2021.
18. For an insightful discussion of vernacular use of classical citations in common speech in historical China, see He (2013: 43–53).
19. There is a substantive gap between Chinese music aesthetics as theory and as practice. History has recorded many Chinese music developments, such as the rise of secular and non-Han music in Tang China, that cannot be adequately explained with Confucian ideals on music as a means of cultivation and governance. That music reveals and communicates

human thoughts and emotions is, however, a Confucian argument that historical China fully explored.

20. This summary is based on my reading of Confucian classics and studies of Chinese music history. For further notes on musical Confucianism and its contemporary practices, see Lam (2002).
21. Early Chinese relied on sound and hearing in their daily activities; see DeWoskin (1982: 29–42).
22. For two transcriptions of the tune for singing Jiang's poem, see Yang and Yin (1979: 42–43) and Pian (2003: 105–6); for a cultural and literary discussion, see Shuen-fu Lin (1973: 72–82).
23. Chinese theories on interrelationships between music and text are complex; meaningful discussions can only proceed with reference to not only specific systems and/or dialects of pronunciation and intonation but also musical genres and performance practices. The theories and practices cannot be summarized in just a few sentences. Nevertheless, the most fundamental concept in the theories is the insight or ideal that linguistic tones have distinctive pitch levels and melodic progressions and contours, and thus they demand different melodic settings. For example, in contemporary Chinese (Putonghua) which was until the 1930s a northern, Beijing-based dialect, words of the first tone should be uttered with a relatively high tone or contour, which is heuristically described as *sol-sol*; words of the second tone, as *mi-sol*; words of the third tone as *re-dol-fa*; and words of the fourth tone, as *sol-do* (Yang, 1983: 4–7). If these word and melodic contours are applied to specific lyrics, such as those of "Taoyao," a simple and skeletal melody will result, and it can be transformed into a tune.
24. By "Chinese melodies and rhythms," I refer to pentatonic scales, modal cadences, rhythms, and formal structures that Chinese musicologists have theorized as representative of Chinese songs. For representative theories on Chinese folk-song structures, see Jiang (2004) and Du (2004: 128–56).
25. For convenience in the discussion here, Putonghua pronunciation will be applied to the lyrics of "Taoyao," a national practice nowadays. Nevertheless, many Chinese musicians and scholars attempt to read *Shijing* lyrics with ancient, medieval, or dialectic pronunciation systems. For example, some Hong Kong and Taiwanese singers have sung *Shijing* songs with Cantonese and Hakka pronunciations, arguing that their dialects have preserved many historical linguistic features. Responses to their performances are diverse.
26. If the words of the "Taoyao" are read with linguistic tones and contours of contemporary Chinese explained in the notes above, the reading generates the following skeleton melody for stanza 1: *mi-sol/sol-sol/sol-sol/sol-sol; mi-sol/mi-sol/mi-sol/sol-sol; sol-sol/re-do-fa/mi-sol/sol-sol; mi-sol/mi-sol/sol-do/sol-sol.*
27. "Taoyao" vividly manifests the problem of "no improper thoughts" in *Shijing* exegesis. As the song metaphorically compares a woman to a peach tree, it evokes associations between the fruit and a woman's body, both of which are to be "consumed" by men. The objectification of women as sex objects or reproductive tools is undeniable.
28. The 1978 rediscovery of the Marquis Yi chime-bells greatly stimulated Chinese scholarship on and performance of ancient music with chime-bells and chime-stones. For links to representative online audio-visual recordings of these performances, see note 3. For insightful studies on interrelationships among Chinese ancient music and musical culture, archaeology, historical studies, and contemporary performances practices, see Falkenhausen (2000).

29. Contemporary Chinese musicians and scholars are critically cognizant of the mix of historical facts and creative interpretations in their singing of *Shijing* songs. Very few would insist that their reconstructed songs are completely authentic; many would, however, argue that their works and performances are historically informed and have in one way or another captured the essence of the classical songs.
30. For a theory on Chinese uses of music to reminisce about the past in service of the present, see Lam (2019).

References

Allen, Joseph R., ed. (1996). *The Book of Songs*, translated by Arthur Waley and edited with additional translations by Joseph R. Allen. New York: Grove Press.

Attali, Jacques. (1992). *Noise: The Political Economy of Music*, translated by Brian Massumi. Minneapolis: University of Minnesota Press.

Certeau, Michel de. (1984). *The Practice of Everyday Life*, translated by Steven Rendall. Berkeley: University of California Press.

Chen Mingmin 陳名珉, ed. (2016). *Shijing: Zhu Xi jichu; Hong ziliang chushi zhangzhi; Chen Mingmin yuyi jianzhu zhengli* 詩經：朱熹集註；洪子良註釋章旨；陳名珉語翻譯箋註整理 [The *Shijing*, with Annotations by Zhu Xi, Hong Ziliang, and Chen Mingming]. Taipei: Shangzhou chuban.

Chen Shaosong 陳少松. (1997). *Gu shi-ci-wen yinsong yanjiu* 古詩詞文吟誦研究 [Studies on Chanting Historical Poetry and Prose]. Beijing: Xinhua shudian.

Cheng Junying 程俊英. (1985). *Shijing yizhu* 詩經譯注 [*Shijing* with Translations and Notes]. Shanghai: Guji chubanshe.

Cheng Junying 程俊英, and Jianyuan Jiang 蔣見元. (1991). *Shijing zhuxi* 詩經注析 [*Shijing*, with Analytical Comments]. Beijing: Zhonghua shuju.

Chu Shenghong 儲聲虹, Lang Xu 徐朗, and Dugang Yu 余篤剛, eds. (1997). *Zhongguo gudai gequ xuan/xiqu quyi changqiang xuan* 中國古代歌曲選／戲曲曲藝唱腔選 [Selected Ancient Chinese Songs/Selected Operatic Arias and Narrative Ballads], vol. 1. Beijing: Renmin yinyue chubanshe.

Cook, Scott. (1995). "'Yue Ji'—Record of Music: Introduction, Translation, Notes, and Commentary." *Asian Music* 26 (2): 1–96.

De Woskin, Kenneth J. (1982). *A Song for One or Two: Music and the Concept of Art in Early China*. Ann Arbor: Center for Chinese Studies, the University of Michigan.

Deng Qitong 鄧啟銅, annotated. (2014). *Shijing* 詩經 [*Shijing*]. Nanjing: Nanjing daxue chubanshe.

DeNora, Tina. (2000). *Music in Everyday Life*. Cambridge, UK: Cambridge University Press.

Du Yaxiong 杜亞雄. (2004). *Zhongguo chuantong yueli jiaochen* 中國傳統樂理教程 [A Textbook of Traditional Chinese Music Theory). Shanghai: Yinyue chubanshe.

Falkenhausen, Lothar von. (2000). "The Zeng Hou Yi Finds in the History of Chinese Music." In *Music in the Age of Confucius*, edited by Jenny F. So, 101–13. Washington DC: Smithsonian Institution, Freer Gallery of Art and Arthur M. Sackler Gallery.

Gong Daoyun 龔道雲. (1995). *Shijing di yinyuexing ji qi meixue yiyi* 詩經的音樂性及其美學意義 [The Musical Nature of the *Book of Songs* and Its Aesthetic Significance]. Singapore: Department of Chinese Studies.

Granet, Marcel. (2016). *Festivals and Songs of Ancient China*. Reprint. New York: Martino Fine Books.

He, Yuming. (2013). *Home and the World: Editing the "Glorious Ming" and Woodblock-Printed Books of the Sixteenth and Seventeenth Centuries.* Cambridge, MA: Harvard University Asia Center.

Huang Xiangpeng 黃翔鵬. (1990). *Chuantong shi yitiao heliu* 傳統是一條河流 [Tradition Flows Like a River]. Beijing: Renmin yinyue chubanshe.

Ji Liankang 吉聯抗, ed. (1983). *Zhonggguo gudai yuelun xuanji* 中國古代樂論選集 [A Selective Anthology of Ancient Chinese Music Aesthetics and Theory]. Beijing: Renmin yinyue chubanshe.

Jiang Mingdun 江明惇. (2004). *Hanzu minge gailun* 漢族民歌概論 [Introduction to Han Chinese Folksongs]. Reprint. Shanghai: Yinyue chubanshe.

Kern, Martin. (2007). "Beyond the 'Mao Odes': *Shijing* Reception in Early Medieval China." *Journal of the American Oriental Society* 127 (1): 131–42.

Lam, Joseph S. C. (1988). "Bibliographical Survey of Ming Musical Treatises." In "Creativity within Bounds: State Sacrificial Songs from the Ming Dynasty (1368–1644 A.D.)," 661–703. PhD diss., Harvard University.

Lam, Joseph S. C. (1998). *State Sacrifices and Music in Ming China.* New York: State University of New York Press.

Lam, Joseph S. C. (2002). "Musical Confucianism: The Case of 'Jikong yuewu.'" In *On Sacred Grounds: Culture, Society, Politics and the Formation of the Cult of Confucius*, edited by Thomas A. Wilson, 134–72. Cambridge, MA: Harvard University Asia Center.

Lam, Joseph S. C. 林萃青. (2019). "Huaigu yinyue lilun yu shijian de yi ge chubu ti'an" "懷古音樂理論與實踐的一個初步提案" [A Proposal on Music of Reminiscence: Theory and Practice]. *Yinyue yishu* 音樂藝術 [Art of Music] 154, no. 2: 6–29.

Lam, Lap. (2010). "Cultural Identity and Vocal Expression: The Southern School Tradition of Poetry Chanting in Contemporary Guangzhou." *Chinese Literature: Essays, Articles, Reviews (CLEAR)* 32: 23–52.

Lau, D. C., translator. (1979). *The Analects (Lunyü) Translated with an Introduction by D. C. Lau.* London: Penguin Books.

Legge, James. (1972). *The Book of Poetry.* In the *Chinese Classics*, vol. 4. Reprint, Taipei: Wenshi chubanshe.

Li Anming 李安明. (1991). "Shijing yinyue zhi wo jian—Shijing yinyue chutan zhi'er" "詩經音樂之我見—詩經音樂初探之二" [My Understanding of *Shijing* Music: Preliminary Studies on *Shijing* Music, #2]. *Minzu yishu yanjiu* 民族藝術研究 [Folk Arts Research], no. 4: 23–31.

Liang Zhiqiang 梁志鏘. (2010). *Shijing yu Chuci yinyue yanjiu* 詩經與楚辭音樂研究 [A Study on Music Compositions for *Shijing* and *Chuci* Lyrics]. Shanghai: Guji chubanshe.

Lin Shuen-fu. (1973). *The Transformation of the Chinese Lyrical Tradition: Chiang K'eui and Southern Sung Tz'u Poetry.* Princeton, NJ: Princeton University Press.

Lin Yin 林尹. (1985). *Zhouli jinzhu jinyi* 周禮今注今譯 [*Rites of Zhou*, with Annotation and Translation into Contemporary Chinese]. Beijing: Shumu wenxian chubanshe.

Major, S. John, and Jenny F. So. (2000). "Music in Late Bronze Age China." In *Music in the Age of Confucius*, edited by Jenny F. So, 13–34. Washington DC: Smithsonian Institution, Freer Gallery of Art and Arthur M. Sackler Gallery.

Mittag, Achim. (1993). "Change in *Shijing* Exegesis: Some Notes on the Rediscovery of the Musical Aspect of the "Odes" in the Song Period." *T'oung Pao* 2nd series, 79 (4/5): 197–224.

Owen, Stephen. (2001). "Reproduction in the *Shijing* (Classic of Poetry)." *Harvard Journal of Asiatic Studies* 61 (2): 287–315.

Pian, Rulan Chao. (2003). *Song Dynasty Musical Sources and Their Interpretation*. Reprint, Hong Kong: The Chinese University Press.

Picken, Laurence E. R. (1956). "Twelve Ritual Melodies of the Tang Dynasty." In *Studia Musicologica Bela Bartok Sacra*, edited by Benjamin Rajeczky and Lajos Vargyas, 147–73. Budapest: Aedes Academiae Scientiarum Hungariae, Budapest.

Picken, Laurence E. R. (1969). "The Musical Implications of Line-sharing in the *Book of Songs* (*Shih Ching*). *Journal of the American Oriental Society* 89 (2): 408–10.

Picken, Laurence E. R. (1978). "The Shapes of The Shi Jing Songs-texts and Their Musical Implications." *Musica Asiatica* 1: 85–109.

Qi Mingjing 漆明鏡. (2017). *Weishi yuepu: Lingyunge liuquan ben zongpu quanyi* 魏氏樂譜:淩雲閣六卷本總譜全譯 [A Songbook of the Wei Family: A Complete Transcription of the Orchestral Score Preserved in the *Lingyun'ge* Manuscript]. Guilin: Guangxi shifan daxue chubanshe.

Riegel, Jeffrey. (1997). "Eros, Introversion, and the Beginning of *Shijing* Commentary." *Harvard Journal of Asiatic Studies* 57 (1): 143–77.

Schabert, David. (1999). "Song and the Historical Imagination in Early China." *Harvard Journal of Asiatic Studies* 59 (2): 305–61.

Seeger, Anthony. (2004). *Why Suyá Sing: A Musical Anthropology of an Amazonian People*. Urbana: University of Illinois Press.

Small, Christopher Small. (1998). *Musicking: The Meaning of Performing and Listening*. Middletown, CT: Wesleyan University Press.

So, Jenny F. ed. *Music in the Age of Confucius*. Washington DC: Smithsonian Institution, Freer Gallery of Art and Arthur M. Sackler Gallery.

Sun Zuoyun 孫作雲. (1966). *Shijing yu Zhoudai shehui yanjiu* 詩經與周代社會研究 [The Research of the *Shijing* and Zhou Society]. Beijing: Zhonghua shuju.

Tang Xianzu 湯顯祖. (1994). *The Peony Pavilion: Mudanting*, translated by Cyril Birch. Boston: Cheng and Tsui.

Tu Weiming, Milan Hejtmanek, and Alan Wachman, eds. (1992). *The Confucian World Observed: A Contemporary Discussion of Confucian Humanism in East Asia*. Honolulu: University of Hawai'i Press.

Tuo Tuo 脫脫, ed. (1973). *Songshi* 宋史 [Song History]. Beijing: Zhonghua shuju.

Waley, Arthur, translator. (1957). *The Book of Songs*. New York: Grove Press.

Wang Di 王迪. (1983). *Qinge* 琴歌 [Qin Songs]. Beijing: Wenhua yishu chubanshe.

Wang Sufen 王蘇芬. (2013). *Zhongguo gudian shici gequ jiaocheng* 中國古典詩詞歌曲教程 [A Tutor for Singing Classical Chinese Poems/Songs]. 2 vols. Beijing: Xueyuan chubanshe.

Wang Xiumei 王秀梅. (2015). *Shijing* 詩經 [*Shijing*]. Beijing: Zhonghua shuju.

Watson, Burton. (1994). *Selected Poems of Su Tung-p'o*. Port Townsend, WA: Copper Canyon Press.

Wilkinson, Endymion. (2000). *Chinese History: A Manual*. Revised and enlarged edition. Cambridge, MA: Harvard University Asia Center.

Wu Wenguang 吳文光. (2003). "Qingdai Qiu Zhilu *Lüyin huikao* 'Guanju' qinpu shitan ji qi guanlian" "清代邱之稑律音匯考關雎琴譜試彈及其關聯" [A Reading of *Qin* Tablatures for 'Guanju' in Qiu Zhilu's *Lüyin huikao*]. *Zhejiang yishu zhiye xueyuan xuebao* 浙江藝術職業學院學報 [Journal of the Zhejiang Arts Specialist College], no. 3: 3–9.

Xia Ye 夏野. (1987). "Tangdai *Fengya Shier Shipu* di jiezou wenti" "唐代風雅十二詩譜的節奏問題" [The Issues of Rhythm in Interpreting the Notated Music of the *Twelve Shijing Songs*]. *Yinyue yanjiu* 音樂研究 [Music Research] 120, no. 4: 9–10.

Yang Bo 楊波 et al. (2014). "*Fengzi Shier Shipu* Yang Yinliu yipu 'Guanju'" "風雅十二詩譜楊蔭瀏譯譜關雎" ["Guanju" of the *Twelve Shijing Songs* Transcribed by Yang Yinliu]. *Yinyue chuangzuo* 音樂創作 [Musical Creation], no. 4: 47–57.

Yang Jiarong 楊佳蓉. (2012). "Zuochuan Ji Zha guanyue zhi neirong yu meixue tanxi" "左傳季札觀樂之內容與美學探析" [A Study on the Content and Aesthetics of "Ji Zha Listens to Music" in *Zuochuan*]. *Yu Da Academic Journal* 32: 29–49.

Yang Tianshi 楊天石. (2019). *Zhu Xi: Kongzi zhi hou diyi ru* 朱熹：孔子之後第一儒 [Zhu Xi: The Top Confucianist after Confucius). Beijing: Dongfang chubanshe.

Yang Yinliu 楊蔭瀏. (1981). *Zhongguo gudai yinyue shigao* 中國音樂史稿 [A Draft History of Chinese Music]. 2 vols. Beijing: Renmin yinyue chubanshe.

Yang Yinliu 楊蔭瀏. (1983). *Yuyan yu yinyue* 語言與音樂 [Language and Music]. Beijing: Renmin yinyue chubanshe.

Yang Yinliu 楊蔭瀏 and Yin Falu 陰法魯. (1979). *Song Jiang Baishi chuangzuo gequ yanjiu* 宋姜百石創作歌曲研究 [A Study on Jiang Baishi's Compositions of *Ci* Songs]. Reprint, Beijing: Renmin yinyue chubanshe.

Ye Jiaying 葉家瑩. (2014). *Gudian shige yinsong jiujiang* 古典詩歌吟誦九講 [Nine Lectures on Chanting Classical Poetry]. Guilin: Guanxi shifan daxue chubanshe.

Zhang Shujun 張樹俊. (2009). "Lun Hu Yuan de shehui pingjia yu lishi gongxian" "論胡瑗的社會評價與歷史貢獻" [On Hu Yuan's Social Reputation and Historical Contributions]. *Journal of Wuxi Institute of Commerce* 9 (3): 102–6.

Zheng Junhui 鄭俊暉. (2004). "Zhu Xi zhuzuo yinyue zhushu de wenxianxue yanjiu—yi zhuwengong wenji wei zhongxin" "朱熹著作音樂著述的文獻學研究—以朱文公文集為中心" [A Bibliographic Study on Zhu Xi's Musical Writings, A Case Study of Zhu Xi's Collected Works]. MA thesis, Fujian Normal University.

Zheng Xuan 鄭玄. (2013). *Maoshi zhushu* 毛詩注疏 [*Shijing*, Mao version, with Annotations and Commentaries]. Shanghai: Guji chubanshe.

Zhou Shuhua 周淑華 ed. (2003). *Ying Shangneng yinyue lunzhu ji zuopin xuanji* 應尚能音樂論著及作品選集 [A Selected Collection of Ying Shangneng's Musical Writings and Compositions]. Changchun: Jilin yinxiang chubanshe.

Zhu Zaiyu. (2000). *Yuelü quanshu* 樂律全書 [Complete Collection of Music Treatises]. Beijing tushuguan guji zhenben congkan, vol. 4. Reprint, Beijing: Shumu wenxian chubanshe.

CHAPTER 7

MUSIC HISTORY AND HISTORIOGRAPHY IN THE CHINESE CONTEXT

Hon-Lun Helan Yang

Introduction

A multiethnic nation with very diverse musical traditions from different geographic regions, China has a very long history of musical practices. Archaeological excavation of stone whistles (*xun* 壎) and bone flutes trace musical activities to the Neolithic period of seven to eight thousand years ago (see also Yang et al., 2005; Shen, 2008; and Fang et al., 2012), and bone oracles with inscriptions dated to four thousand years ago document the use of music and dance in rituals (Cheung, 1975). Writings about the origin and the social and educational values of music were recorded in works of historical literature such as the *Historical Records* (*Shiji*史記) (finished about 94 BCE), and literary writings such as the *Analects* (*Lunyu*論語) of Confucius (written probably after Confucius's death in 479 BCE) (see Kaufmann, 1976; Zhou, 2014; Li, 2016; and Yang, 2017) also provided information about musical practices of their respective times. Notwithstanding the presence of a rich set of indigenous historical records, China's musical development has always been open to outside influences. For instance, the dance music of the Tang dynasty (618–907) was imported from the Middle East. Indeed, China's encounters with the West have left a profound impact on the musical trajectory of the nation as well as that of its diasporas (see, for example, Yang and Saffle, 2017; Yang, Mikkonen, and Winzenburg, 2020).

We must not overlook the fact that societies in mainland China, Hong Kong, Taiwan, and those across Chinese diasporas worldwide have developed fluid musical cultures of their own over time. This renders the definition of Chinese music a challenge: What is Chinese music? Is Chinese music defined by where it originated or where it was or is practiced? Is it defined by instrumentation, ensemble, or format? Is Chinese music defined by the nationality of its creators, disregarding instrumentation, format, or ensemble? Or is it defined by the musical characteristics, thoughts, and institutions perceived as Chinese, disregarding the rest? Or is Chinese music defined by the people and locale by and in which it is consumed? Then, what is a Chinese context? Does it have to be a nation, a locale, or a concrete community? Or could it be a "habitus,"[1] a group of people's embodiments of some sort of common experience recognized as "Chinese"—as manifested in their forms of cultural capital, their discourses, artifacts, ingrained habits, skills, and dispositions? Even though the purpose of this chapter is not to propose a new definition of Chinese music, it does emphasize that how Chinese music has been defined over time is closely connected to how Chinese music histories were and are written, then and now, something that influences our contemporary perceptions and understanding of Chinese music. Therefore, I argue for the need to examine the historiography of Chinese music, asking questions about how sources and ideologies are intertwined in historians' narratives and how we as citizens of a place can safeguard our past through different forms of memory-keeping.

To understand history in general, and Chinese music history in particular, it is important to note that "past" and "present" are opposite concepts that are essential reference points in the writing of any work of history (Le Goff, 1992: xii). The word "history" is used in at least two quite different ways, one referring to incidents of the past and the other to written records of the past. While there is a clear distinction between the two, their relationship is intricate (Spalding and Parker, 2007: 1) as the actual past and the recorded past are two very different things. The former represents the so-called "objective past" whereas the latter is the "subjective past" reconstructed by historians in light of their own present (Liu, 2007).

There is no doubt that the chapters in this part of the volume illustrate the intricate connections between the past and present: how new research and new discourse shed light on past musical practices. Each of these chapters also invites readers to reflect on how history was written, generally known as historiography. Elusive in definition even for professional historians, historiography means many different things. For some, it means writing the past or the study of the methodology adopted by historians in writing the past. But for others, it also means the study of different schools of interpretation for a particular historical topic as well as the study of the history of history writing (see further, Cheng, 2012).

The current chapter's objectives are two-fold. First, it provides a brief introduction to different types of historical sources, explicating their usefulness and limitations for a better understanding of China's musical past. Second, it examines issues pertinent to Chinese music historiography, focusing on writings by scholars from China (the People's Republic of China, or PRC) and Hong Kong from the following three perspectives: 1) ideology, 2) discourse, and 3) memory. In the part on ideology, it unravels how recurring themes in Chinese music sources and histories are manifestations of cultural trends and dominant ideologies of the time. In the part on discourse, drawing on Michel Foucault's notion of discourse and power, it explores the differences in dominant discourse versus minority discourse. Informed by

Pierre Nora's discussion on memory and history (1989), the final part of the chapter examines how history and memory are not only entwined but also often in conflict; thus, it argues for the need for different forms and types of histories in keeping people's memories alive.

Sources

Historians reconstruct the past through different types of sources. The most common types include written literature, artifacts (musical instruments, murals, paintings, sculptures, etc.), and notations and tablatures. Written sources pertinent to Chinese music are abundant, and they are marked by their ancient roots, interconnectedness, and their vast numbers and diverse formats (Feng, 2007). Two of the earliest written sources on music offer an example—*Lü's Spring and Autumn Annals* (*Lüshi chunqiu* 呂氏春秋) and the "Record of Music" ("Yueji" 樂記); even though they stem from different periods (approximately one-hundred-fifty years apart), they both provide valuable information about music of the early Qin era. They interconnect in a number of ways, not least in that they both emphasize the social functions of music as a tool for moral education and emotional regulation (Wang, 2013). They both touch on the origin of music, regarding music as the manifestation of human emotions with the power to create harmony (*he*) at different levels and thus a subject that should be given importance in education (Xue, 2011). The musical domains they cover also share commonalities: both present instruments according to the materials from which they were made, a categorization later known as the "eight tones" (*bayin*/八音), and both discuss tuning, scales, and the naming of notes while also examining the importance of dance in ceremonies (Liu, 2016).

Aside from historical writings, archaeological findings also provide invaluable insights into the past (Huang, 1990). Taking the bells (*bianzhong* 編鐘) of Marquis Yi 曾侯乙 (c. 475–433 BCE), excavated in 1977, as an example, the set consists of sixty-five bells organized in three layers of eight groups each hung on rods, presumably played by multiple musicians at the same time. The properties of the bells reveal musical characteristics of the Eastern Zhou era (770–256 BCE) and also help verify descriptions in ancient sources.[2] The bells cover a melodic range of five octaves, showing the use of heptatonic scale structures and an overall twelve-note temperament. The accuracy with which they were tuned testifies to the fact that the tuning systems mentioned in ancient sources were not just theoretical but also reflected actual practice. Writings engraved on the bells also describe musical practices and theories of the period, and they are far more detailed than extant written sources (Wang, 2010). Aside from excavated instruments, other types of artifacts—figurines of musicians excavated from Western Han-dynasty tombs, cave sculptures and paintings from the Tang dynasty, and the portrayal of musical scenes in Song- and Ming-dynasty paintings—offer indispensable sources that augment information found in written records.[3]

The different types of music notation from different instrumental traditions are equally valuable, including the *qin* 琴 notations extant in music anthologies from the eighth century to modern times and the *gongche* 工尺 notation employed in numerous vocal and instrumental genres across different regions.[4] For instance, the scores of twenty-five *pipa* pieces copied in 933 CE onto the back of Buddhist scriptures that were hidden away in the Dunhuang grottoes until 1900 have fascinated Eastern and Western scholars.[5] These extant scores and the hundreds of music-related murals and reliefs found in the Dunhuang grottoes have left invaluable information about the musical entertainment of the royal court in the Tang dynasty.

Nonetheless, all sources have their limitations. Prehistoric records based on myths and legends cannot be treated as equivalent to historical facts. We must not read information in ancient historical records without a grain of salt, bearing in mind the possibility for errors in transmission or through subsequent misinterpretation. Most of all, as written records were largely official documents, they inevitably present the past in ways sanctioned by those in power. Archaeological materials also have their own limitations. For example, artifacts are unlikely to provide information about how the musical activities with which they were associated were executed back in history, let alone revealing how the music actually sounded. Lastly, even though the study of ethnic groups' musical practices can contribute to our understanding of the past, their practices in the present cannot be equated with the practices of the past: culture and cultural practices do not necessarily remain unchanged.

IDEOLOGY

An effective way to make sense of the large amount of written literature in Chinese music is to identify recurring themes. Jonathan Stock suggested four such themes after examining twelve sources from the Shang dynasty to the Republican era in his chapter on Chinese music history in the *Cambridge History of World Music* (2013). The first theme concerns interests in music's origins, even though how it was accounted for is quite distinct from source to source. The second pertains to the connections perceived between music and politics as manifested in the science of tuning, which as Stock points out, was often politically colored, presuming "an intimate connection between a nation's musical pitchscape and its political health" (2013: 399). The third notes the abundance of extant information on specialized musicians despite their low social status. The last theme is about historians embracing imported music from cultural contacts across China's national boundaries in writings not only in the twentieth century but also in earlier times.

Among these four recurring themes suggested by Stock, I would like to examine further how ideologies and practices were intertwined in historical writings and past musical activities. For instance, as mentioned in the "Record of Music," the ruler of the Zhou dynasty (1046–256 BCE) established the proprieties of music and rites. While rites (*li*禮) were used as a guide to regulate the behavior of the ruled subjects based on their hierarchies, music (*yue*樂) was deployed as a specific tool through which such a goal was accomplished (see Reference 37 I, entries 13 and 14 in Kaufmann, 1976: 34).

In ancient China, state ceremonies were large-scale events that involved many people and spanned months. These ceremonies continued from dynasty to dynasty, naturally with variations. There were very strict prescriptions about the formats of these rituals, such as the placement of the performers and their number and the instruments involved. In the Zhou dynasty, as mentioned in historical records, the performing forces for the emperor could be placed on all four sides of the ritual venue, whereas those performing for a marquis could occupy three sides and those serving government officials only two. Likewise, the emperor could use eight rows of eight performers each, whereas for a marquis there were six columns of six performers (see further, Yang, 1981, vol. 1: 13–14).

The presentation of state rituals became a site of power struggle in later dynasties. Joseph Lam's (1996) study of sources pertinent to the implementation of sericultural ceremonials in the Ming dynasty reveals many negotiations between the emperor Shizong and his ritual officials in the 1530s and 1540s regarding who was to be in charge of the ritual and how and where music performance should take place; such negotiations often led to political struggles between officials of different camps.

Even though state rituals became obsolete along with the fall of the Qing empire in 1911, music's connection with politics and governance has continued, a trait I examined in a number of writings (Yang, 2004; 2005; 2006; 2007). For instance, in the early twentieth century, the development of Western-style music, then known as "new music" (*xin yinyue*新音樂),[6] was seen as the embodiment of the new era that China finally embraced after the monarchy had come to an end. While Western singing was introduced to the school curriculum, the state-funded and Western-modeled National Conservatory of Music was founded in Shanghai in 1927 (see further, Yang, 2012). Though the school was significantly different from ancient music institutions set up by the state to train musicians in serving the dynastic rulers—such as the Dasiyue 大司樂 of the Zhou dynasty, the Yuefu 樂府 of the Han dynasty, and the Dayueshu 大樂署 of the Tang dynasty—the fact that musical training was still seen as an official institution of the government in the twentieth century testified to the continuity of a long tradition of music's close ties with politics in China. But unlike in earlier times, the state-funded National Conservatory in Shanghai was independent in its operation, and its students had no obligation to serve the government.

In the PRC, particularly during the first couple of decades of the nation's history, music was seen as a weapon for class struggle, and musicians had to follow an ideological mandate traceable to Mao Zedong's famous speech of 1942, "Talk at the Yan'an [Yenan] Forum on Art and Literature" (Mao, 1956). Mao proclaimed in the talk that:

> [R]evolutionary art and literature are the products of the brains of revolutionary artists and writers reflecting the life of the people.... We [communists] must take over all the artistic and literary legacy, critically assimilate from it whatever is beneficial to

us and hold it up as an example when we try to work over the artistic and literary raw material derived from the people's life of our own time and place. (Mao, 1956: 22–23)

Mao's talk, which was seen as a prime artistic directive for the PRC's cultural scene, naturally had a profound impact on the musical activities, creativities, and discourse in the years to come.

The song-and-dance epic *The East is Red* (*Dongfang hong* 東方紅, 1964) is a quintessential example of music propaganda in socialist China. Set in eight scenes with fifty-three different numbers of songs, dances, instrumental interludes, and melodramas, all threaded together by a narrative concerning the coming to power of the Chinese Communist Party from 1921 to 1949, the work eulogizes Mao Zedong's role in this occurrence. The creation and production of the work was said to have involved at least three thousand participants from different parts of the nation, including a choir of a thousand members accompanied by a large orchestra of Western and Chinese instruments (see further, Yang, 2016).

The East is Red is comparable to an ancient piece called *The Great Wu* (*Dawu* 大武) of the Western Zhou dynasty, which, as described in the "Record of Music," depicted the victory of the Zhou dynasty's founder, the emperor Wu, over the ruler of the Shang dynasty, an event that allegedly took place in or about 1046 BCE. Set in six sections of dances, *The Great Wu* was still performed in the period of Confucius's life (551–479 BCE), almost five hundred years after Wu came to power (Yang, 1981: 31–32). While both pieces were multisectional and involved a large number of performers, they both served the political function of glorifying the ruler and the state with dance and music. I emphasize here the fact that recurring themes in music history result from the ruling party's wish to make ideology and politics tangible through performance, a manifestation of the grand narrative that guided the historiography of the state, the ways that most histories were constructed by historians.

Recent histories of Chinese music were not spared from the impact of contemporary socio-political-cultural trends, and it is inevitable that ideological indoctrination was entwined with historical narratives, as is evident in the following examples. For instance, the *Chinese Music History* (*Zhongguo yinyue shi* 中國音樂史) of Wang Guangqi 王光祈 (1892–1936) (Wang, [1934] 2014) is a monograph that reflects the influence of Darwin's evolutionary theory as well as the new historicism of Wang's time. In 1902, the reformist intellectual Liang Qichao 梁啟超 (1873–1929) proposed the need for a new historiography and new histories that would reflect the evolution of the people, paving the way for Chinese historians to adopt the Western format of structuring historical narrative into chapters and sections in the early twentieth century (Chen, 2008). Such a new approach toward the writing of history was coupled with nationalism and evolutionism, as evident in the proliferation of Chinese music histories from the period, and it also resulted in the transformation of Chinese historiography in the twentieth century.

Educated in Germany and a supporter of these historiographic changes, Wang wrote *Chinese Music History* while in Berlin, with a preface dated 1931. He organized it around different topics, such as tuning, instruments, and ensemble music, each of which is examined from the perspective of evolution, tracing the subject matter's origin and overall development, and occasionally comparing it to parallels in the West. Influenced by the notion of evolution, Wang's narrative, along with those of many others of his time, saw Chinese music as backward for its lack of a well-developed notation system, its heavy emphasis on oral tradition, and the absence of harmonic complexity in its musical conceptions. Many intellectuals of the time advocated musical reforms by following Western models, something that has had a profound impact on musical development in China in the twentieth and twenty-first centuries.

Yang Yinliu 楊蔭瀏 (1899–1984)'s *A Draft History of Ancient Chinese Music* (*Zhongguo gudai yinyue shigao* 中國古代音樂史稿, 1981), a seminal work on ancient Chinese music history known for its meticulous research, is a case in point of the embodiment of a different kind of ideology: the Marxist historical materialism that reigned over China's cultural discourses after the founding of the Chinese communist state in 1949. For example, the volume's explanation of music's origin in labor is based on Frederick Engels's notion of labor being the most important aspect in mankind's evolutionary process, thereby deviating from the mythical discourses recorded in ancient Chinese sources, as Stock has pointed out (2013: 400–401).

A recurring grand narrative in Yang's volume is class struggle in music's evolution, taken by Yang as a guiding principle in his assessment of various musical practices. For example, the *liyue* 禮樂 system of the Zhou dynasty is taken by Yang as a clear articulation of the rulers' tactics: "[T]hey used music to propagate the legitimation of the class system; they established specific music institution to control musical activities; they introduced music education as a 'national curriculum' to educate the young, so as to strengthen their governance, using music to reinforce their dynastic governance" (1981: 30, translation by present author). While portraying the ruling class and the masses as one another's enemies, Yang emphasizes that the music used to serve the ruling class was created by the people (1981: 35), who were also being controlled by the music they performed (1981: 37). Most of all, Yang thought that later intellectuals who showed great interest in music of the Zhou dynasty overrated its importance, some merely using it as an excuse for conservatism in the hope of keeping folk culture at bay, which he thought was incompatible with a progressive historical reality (1981: 30).

Such skepticism toward dynastic musical practice is not at all present in another highly regarded volume from the 1970s—Cheung Sai-Bung (Zhang Shibin) 張世彬's *A Draft History of Chinese Music* (*Zhongguo yinyue shi lunshu gao* 中國音樂史論述稿, 1975), which represents a different historiographic tradition. The volume was published in Hong Kong, a British colony from 1842 to 1997, where Marxist ideologies had very limited resonance, and it is not a surprise that its narrative is much less ideologically colored. For example, instead of criticizing Zhou-dynasty musical practice as a form of political control, its author simply points out the music's educational values and such a value system's root in Confucian teaching. When discussing the three hundred or so poems in the *Book of Songs* (*Shijing* 詩經), unlike Yang, who regarded certain categories of songs as the products of the ruling class's appropriation of folk materials with inevitably twisted meanings (Yang, 1981: 47), Cheung instead focuses on these songs' formal structures, offering no sense of the class sensitivity so explicit in Yang's volume or other writings from the period of the 1950s to the 1980s.

Discourse

The close ties between ideology and history's grand narratives discussed above can also be understood as the power politics of "discourse," a concept proposed by the French philosopher Michel Foucault (1926–84) (Foucault, 1972). Discourse originally refers to any form of communication, both verbal and written. But when we start to ask questions about a discourse's nature, such as what subject matter the discourse is about, what boundaries a particular discourse sets up, and then what social function a discourse intends in terms of maintaining the status quo and safeguarding social values, the notion goes beyond just ordinary communication (Wang, 1994). Foucault came to such a realization after examining the intricate connections between discourse, language, knowledge, and power relations. He argued that discourse is a powerful tool in instigating action, and thus it has the power to "conquer."[7] As a result, discourse has often been deployed by those in power as a form of control (Hall, 2001).

Dynastic histories of the past are good examples of discourse as a form of control, in the sense that the perception of the past dynasties was constructed and reconstructed by state officials of later periods in a way that legitimized their rule. In the same vein, the "will" of the PRC government to impart a communist or socialist worldview to the masses is evident in music histories and writings from the period between the 1950s and the 1980s, as discussed above.

Another interesting case in point is evident in PRC scholars' writings about the former British colony of Hong Kong, following its reunification with China in 1997. As pointed out by the Hong Kong scholar Wong Wang-Chi (Wang Hongzhi) 王宏志 in his monograph *The Burden of History: A Historical Account of Hong Kong from Mainland China* (*Lishi de chenzhong: Cong Xianggang kan Zhongguo dalu de Xianggang lunshu* 歷史的沉重: 從香港看中國大陸的香港史論述, 2000), an array of PRC scholars published histories of Hong Kong in or about 1997, their narratives mostly following the model of "national discourse." Such narratives served the purpose of constructing a nationally endorsed collective memory of Hong Kong with profound political implications (Wong, 2000: 51–52). Wong noted four recurring themes in all these histories: 1) regarding Hong Kong's colonial past as a phase of "vicissitude" in China's history (Wong, 2000: 71–76); 2) downplaying Hong Kong's economic development from the 1950s to the 1980s (Wong, 2000: 76–88); 3) highlighting the colonial government's racist policies and managerial problems (Wong, 2000: 104–24); 4) emphasizing Hong Kong's roots in the mainland and the latter's contribution to Hong Kong's prosperity (Wong, 2000: 125–49).

Such recurring themes can also be found in discourse about Hong Kong's musical past in the volume *Hong Kong Composers: The 1930s to the 1990s* (*Xianggang zuoqujia: Sanshi zhi jiushi niandai* 香港作曲家: 三十至九十年代, 1999), a monograph written by the PRC scholar Liang Maochun 梁茂春. Focusing on composers of art music from the 1930s to the 1990s, the volume is structured in five chapters of varied lengths: in chapter 1, four pioneer composers (one white Russian and three mainland Chinese) comprise 15 percent of the volume; in chapter 2, seven Hong Kong composers of local origin account for 20 percent of the volume; in chapter 3, ten PRC composers who settled in Hong Kong account for 32 percent of the book's content; in chapter 4, two composers from overseas who became Hong Kong residents take up 4 percent of the text; and in chapter 5, seventeen local-born composers of two generations from the 1980s and the 1990s respectively account for only 29 percent of the volume.

Given that less than 50 percent of the volume's coverage concerns Hong Kong–born composers, any reader could easily gain the impression that: 1) Hong Kong's music education has failed to train local composers; 2) most of Hong Kong's successful composers migrated from China after gaining their education there; 3) composers from China have made a great contribution to Hong Kong's serious music scene; 4) the emergence and flourishing of a new generation of Hong Kong composers since the 1980s resulted from the impact of the migrant composers from mainland China.

Liang's discussion treated Hong Kong's contemporary music development as a branch of Lingnan (southern China) culture, claiming that its trajectory was strongly influenced by the development of "new music" in China in the 1930s and 1940s. Whether this is the case is up for debate. But in setting up such a narrative, Liang's volume communicates the message that Hong Kong culture is a part of its motherland's culture. Liang also repeatedly criticizes the Hong Kong British government for not spending resources on developing culture during its rule and condemns its failures in policy, as evidenced by a lack of success in producing world-renowned musicians or compositions. To reinforce such a narrative, the volume downplays the leaps that occurred in the 1970s and 1980s, such as the establishment of music departments in several of Hong Kong's universities, the founding of the Academy for the Performing Arts and the Music Office, the latter being a Hong Kong version of El Sistema, providing very-low-cost music training to youngsters. All these endeavors have collectively contributed to the rise of a thriving contemporary music scene in Hong Kong and the emergence of a new generation of composers and performers who have achieved international recognition. Lastly, Liang did not forget to fulfill the historical mission of his volume: he reminds Hong Kong composers of their lag in cultural roots and the need for them to write works that are more "profound in meaning" now that the city is no longer a colony (1999: 273–78).

Having been a colony for a century and a half, Hong Kong's past and present relationship with its ex-sovereign (the colonizer) and then its present sovereign (its motherland) is complex and ingrained with ambiguity and ambivalence. Hong Kong existed and is existing geopolitically at the margins of each, as though surviving and thriving in the crack between two hegemonic powers, neither of which has treated Hong Kong as a fully integral part. This is particularly the case after the 1970s when Hong Kong began to develop its own cultural identity, one that was distinct from that of the wider region of the PRC, as manifested most clearly in the colony's popular culture, such as its films and popular music that showcase a unique synergy of Eastern and Western elements marked by emblematic local twists. As a result, the postcolonial dilemma faced by Hong Kong is different from that of other ex-colonies such as India and South Africa. As pointed out by the cultural theorist Rey Chow, who originated from Hong Kong, the territory "does not have the privilege of an independence to which it can look forward. Between Britain and China, Hong Kong's postcoloniality is marked by a double impossibility—it will be as impossible to submit to Chinese nationalist/nativist repossession as it has been impossible to submit to British colonialism" (Chow, 1992: 153). Such a dilemma is most evident in Hong Kong's decolonization discourse, which, as Chow has noted, "is part of China's self-writing," and which "is definitely not self-writing for Hong Kong" since "the restoration of China's territorial propriety in and through Hong Kong does not amount to Hong Kong's repossession of its own cultural identity" (154).

It is perhaps with the above-articulated sense of self-awareness that a handful of Hong Kong scholars embarked on many forms of "self-writing" prior to 1997, thereby arguing, in Chow's words, "for the autonomy of a historiography by the 'natives' themselves" (Chow, 1992: 155). In this regard, the edited volume of Chu Sui-Bing (Zhu Ruibing 朱瑞冰), *An Introduction to the Development of Music in Hong Kong* (*Xianggang yinyue fazhan gailun* 香港音樂發展概論) (Chu, 1999), published in the same year as Liang's volume, is an example of such self-writing and offers a narrative distinct from Liang's. Rather than emphasizing Hong Kong's Chinese lineage, the volume highlights complexities and multiplicities in the city's musical development. Chu, a native of Hong Kong, articulated in the editorial preface that "Hong Kong has a lot of music. So, it was quite a challenge to formulate the volume's content and scope" (1999: v). Compared to Liang's volume, which focuses exclusively on art-music composers and their works, Chu's volume covers a much broader scope. Aside from chapter 3 written by Liang, which summarizes information from his own volume, Chan Wing-Wah's chapter 4 highlights Hong Kong's contemporary music scene after the 1980s, thus filling in an omission in Liang's study. Other aspects of Hong Kong music are covered in the rest of the volume, namely on early and recent music education written by Liu Ching-Chih (Liu Jingzhi) and Lam Ching-Wah (Lin Qinghua) in chapter 1 and chapter 4 respectively, important musical activities in the city by Chow Fan-Fu 周凡夫 in chapter 2, Chinese music by Yu Siu-Wah (Yu Shaohua) 余少華 in chapter 6, musical transmission by Lai Kin (Li Jian) in chapter 8, and popular music and copyright issues by Paul Leung (Liang Bao'er) in chapters 7 and 9.

Since seven of the eight contributors to Chu's volume were Hong Kong scholars, they consciously or unconsciously chose to emphasize phases of Hong Kong's musical development distinct from those chosen by Liang. For instance, Liu's study reveals early musical activities by Western settlers, and Yu's study points out the unique trajectory taken by Chinese music in this colonial setting. With much more room devoted to different kinds of musical practices as well as musical development after the 1970s, a different meta-narrative emerges from the volume, with the theme of localization infiltrating most of the discussions. As Chow Fan-Fu points out, "with the new generation of [Hong Kong people] born after World War II, the mentality of society as a whole changed. This new generation began to recognize Hong Kong as their home and looked for a cultural life founded upon their identification with Hong Kong, resulting in the localization of musical forms that clearly demonstrated so-called Hong Kong characteristics" (Chow, 1999: 32).

Yu Siu-Wah also articulates a similar view in his own chapter. Regarding the development of Chinese music in Hong Kong, Yu writes of:

> . . . a process of continuous integration of musical elements of the North and South and also of the East and West, resulting in a hybrid tradition that is full of innovations. In the face of industrialization, urbanization, capitalization, and commercialization, traditional Chinese instrumental music and operatic genres that were introduced to Hong Kong after 1949 have to constantly re-position and update themselves in response to the changes of the society and of the demand of the market. Such transformation was inevitable for these genres to survive and to find a way to continue in their own carved out space, resulting in local features that distinguish them from similar genres in the PRC (Yu, 1999: 324, translation by the present author).

Yu reiterates similar views in his later volume *Out of Chaos and Coincidence: Hong Kong's Music Cultures* (*Le zai diancuo zhong: Xianggang yasu yinyue wenhua* 樂在顛錯中—香港雅俗音樂文化, 2001). Yu points out that Hong Kong's musical culture, both serious and popular, originated mainly from mainland China, but that source does not fully determine its present shape:

> However, after more than a century of political, economic, social, and cultural separation, Hong Kong's music culture has evolved into an individual form different from its motherland's. If we look at examples of Hong Kong's musical culture from the PRC's perspective, they would be considered deviants of the "original" that are full of distortions and variations, which are precisely their characteristics (Yu, 2001: inside cover page, translation by the present author).

While it is not possible for Hong Kong to achieve political autonomy, and while self-writing can be treated as a collective effort to keep memories alive, as a construction of its own historiography, self-writing is also a form of power negotiation and symbolic resistance. Such discourse, known in the West as "minority discourse," has accumulated considerable supporters (see further, JanMohamed and Lloyd, 1987). In Hong Kong's context, these self-writing discourses reposition the relationship of the center and the periphery, putting the minority and the marginalized onto center stage, presumably with the hope of asserting influence on the existing or established power structure, making the impossible possible for the future. But such efforts in self-writing are usually entwined with a web of intentions and aspirations from different parties involved in the process, and the resulting discourse(s) can become diverse in nature and fluid in function, showcasing negotiations at many different levels, as will be discussed below (and also as exemplified further in Chou, 2017).

Memory

Memory is an individual's relationship to the past, stored in the hippocampus of the brain. Many scholars and historians have pointed out the interconnectedness of the two. Memories would be fragmented without the historian to put them into a coherent narrative. Likewise, without the existence of various forms of memories, there would be nothing to relate in history. But scholars such as Maurice Halbwachs and Pierre Nora, and some of their followers, were suspicious of history. While seeing memory and history as in conflict, they placed high currency on memory despite its ever-changing nature and vulnerability to manipulation. Nora points out, in his work "Between Memory and History: Les Lieux de Mémoire," that "[m]emory is a perpetually actual phenomenon, a bond tying us to the eternal present" whereas "[h]istory . . . is the reconstruction, always problematic and incomplete, of what is no longer" (1989: 8). The terror of history, to Nora, is that it generally represents the past in a way to legitimate the future, whereas memory's function is to serve the individual concerned and is thus more multifaceted and democratic. History, as the representation of the past, inevitably conveys "an integrated, dictatorial memory—un-self-conscious, commanding, all-powerful, spontaneously actualizing" (Nora, 1989: 8). This is all the more so in authoritative states that monitor discourses carefully for the sake of self-justification.

A case in point is provided by three recent histories by PRC scholars on the model operas (*yangbanxi* 樣板戲) of the Cultural Revolution,[8] namely: Shi Yonggang 師永剛 and Zhang Fan 張凡's *A Historical Record of Model Opera* (*Yangbanxi shiji* 樣板戲史記, 2009); *A Compositional History of the Ballet "The White-Haired Girl"* (*Balei wuju Baimaonü chuangzuo shihua* 芭蕾舞劇"白毛女"創作史話, 2010) by Yang Jie 楊潔; and Li Song 李松's *A Historical Chronicle of the Model Operas* ("*Yangbanxi*" *biannian shi* "樣板戲"編年史, 2011–12). The authors of these three monographs show a clear sense of historical awareness, as evident in their volume titles as well as in their conscious use of primary sources, newspaper articles, memoirs, and archival records and documents. Even though none of these authors is a professional historian, nor were they all equally trained in historiographic discourse, they share one trait in common: they belong to the post–Cultural Revolution generation. Not having experienced the event firsthand presumably allows these authors to interpret their sources and the event more objectively. These authors also show a sense of mission to keep memories alive. What they have accomplished is a conscious attempt to bridge the past and present, safeguarding the past for future generations, so to say. But these three works also show that Nora's concern over history's function of serving a state-sanctioned narrative is well grounded.

I note three common features among these three monographs. The first is the notion that the model operas had a prior history before they were adapted to become propaganda works of the Gang of Four (*siren bang* 四人幫).[9] The second pertains to a general assumption that all model operas were of high artistic quality as they were collectively created by the best talents in the country at the time. The third emphasizes the model operas' positive reception then as well as now. Uncovering the early history of the model operas is, in a way, to separate the genre from Jiang Qing and the Gang of Four, often simplistically rendered as the primary perpetrators of the Cultural Revolution. Meanwhile, the second and third themes, which affirm the aesthetic values of the model operas and recover their respective reception histories, are mutually constructive and, to an extent, self-validating for the authors as well as for readers.

These common themes are realized at different levels and through different means, namely research approach, study scope, narrative structure, and selection and presentation of data, not to mention the assessment of the model operas concerned. For example, the chosen scope of each of these three monographs indeed puts a heavy emphasis on the prehistory of the genre. For instance, the first volume of Li's *Historical Chronicle* traces the genre to opera reforms in the Yan'an period of the 1930s and covers only the period up to 1966, the year the nomenclature "model opera" came into use. Similarly, Yang's *Compositional History* also sets aside the first three chapters to trace the early history of the work, which originated as a folk tale, then an opera, and then also a movie, before it was turned into a model ballet. Shi and Zhang's *Historical Record* begins with a chapter (entitled "Prequel") on Beijing opera. By treating model opera as the product of operatic reforms of the 1950s, the book's narrative downplays the political aspiration and the propagandist intention of these works.

In fact, the scope of a monograph or a history, what to cover or leave out, is inherently tied to power structures in a society, particularly in an autocratic society. It is thus interesting to note what is not covered or what is lightly covered in these writings. Perhaps not coincidentally, the shortest chapter in Yang's *Compositional History* concerns the Cultural Revolution. Entitled "One Wave and Three Setbacks," the chapter is only nine pages in length, of which only four pages are devoted to discussing what the work went through during the first stage of the Cultural Revolution, between 1966 and 1967. A reader cannot be sure if the rationale behind such a treatment is a result of censorship or of the author's lack of information. But apparently, the memory represented in this volume is fragmented, rendering that part of the past almost nonexistent for the generation whose memories are based upon such a history.

Yang's *Compositional History* is an official history. Commissioned by the Shanghai Ballet School to mark its fiftieth anniversary in 2010, its narrative is somewhat dominated by the memory of the choreographer Hu Rongrong 胡蓉蓉, the initiator of the project. Many of her memories, including her interviews with Yang as well as her account of the creative process of the *White-haired Girl* are deeply embedded in the narrative. To make a point about the nature of historical bias, I note that the reminiscence of the original principal dancer of the role of the white-haired girl, Shi Zhongqin 石鐘琴, is not present in Yang's volume. During a TV program, Shi talked about her memories of the work: how the role changed her life, alleviating her doomed fate of coming from a capitalistic family, and how human resources were wasted toward improving the work.[10] It is easy to imagine that the message communicated by Shi through such reminiscences would not be in tune with the meta-narrative of the present volume. Perhaps most important of all, the question at hand is how these different types of memories shape the next generation's understanding of the past.

It is thus not a surprise that histories of model operas published in the PRC mostly follow the common themes mentioned above, forming a grand narrative in studies of the genre that have begun to proliferate in the past few years.[11] Though the PRC has embraced a market economy and become an economic superpower, its attitude toward historiography and discourse has yet to match any progressive character that may be presumed by the nation's economic development. That is, its sense of the past is still guided by what is known as the "monologic historical explanation"—that is, an orthodox view imposed upon the historical narrative (Watson, 1994: 2). The common themes in the histories of the model operas identified above are a case in point of the production of history taken as tremendously significant, politically, ideologically, and morally, and as a means of political legitimization.

In this context, it is particularly striking that Li's *A Historical Chronicle of the Model Operas*, breaks away from the state-sanctioned narrative by letting primary sources speak for themselves. According to Li, a historian rather than a music scholar,[12] his choice of the chronicle format is to ensure that "the polyphonic, multiple voices of history can be heard" (2011, vol. 1: 12). Memory is like a laboratory to him, one in which the individual is forced to reinvent himself/herself as well as to get to know himself/herself; presenting raw historical data like contrasting instrumental lines in a polyphonic symphony is a way to overcome any individual's subjectivity and onesidedness.

In the PRC, the Cultural Revolution is still considered a very sensitive topic by the government, and thus any pertinent discourse has to follow a government-sanctioned narrative and must be scrutinized. If one searches for entries on the Cultural Revolution in Baidu, China's online encyclopedia, one will note that those entries are locked and allow no changes. In Li's volume, the presentation of documents hitherto unfamiliar to his readers—containing multiple views deviating from the established interpretation of the Cultural Revolution—explains why it was first not published in the PRC but instead in Taiwan by a non-academic publisher, even though the work is groundbreaking and of great value to the future generation of researchers; it was then published in the PRC a year later (in 2012) as a single volume work. In a way, it is possible to interpret Li's chronicle as a form of resistance through memory-keeping: his will to let multiple voices replace the state-sanctioned monolithic narrative as a way to safeguard the past. The memories of model opera, indeed, are in urgent need for preservation, be it in the form of oral history or via an array of other means. Only when as many different fields of memory as possible are preserved will historians of the genre be able to present the past with as much accuracy as possible.

To the French historian Pierre Nora, memory is ever disappearing, and thus we need to establish "lieux de mémoire" to safeguard the past. Lieux de mémoire—fields of memory—can be material, symbolic, and functional. For example, archives and museums are places for preservation and presentation of material memories; memorials and commemorations are sites of symbolic memories; and the writing of histories and educating the next generation in the classroom are places where functional memory is activated. Naturally, only with the desire to remember will these fields of memory become meaningful, thereby safeguarding history for generations to come (Nora, 1989: 19). In other words, it is perhaps not history but rather fields of memory that are crucial for any group of people who seek to keep their past alive.

Conclusion

It is timely to revisit issues pertinent to the study of Chinese music history and historiography. Chinese music has a long history, as recorded in different types of sources—historical writings, archaeological findings, and music notations, to name just some. While many of these sources were interconnected, with their narratives supporting each other and becoming valuable in the study of Chinese music, they provided very little information about how music in ancient times sounded. The coming to light of early manuscripts with music notations did provide glimpses into the musical sounds of the past, but, due to the lack of a thorough understanding of these notations, the authenticity of the reconstruction and reproduction of music from these manuscripts is somewhat questionable.

In this regard, even though Chinese music has a long history, the sonic features of current musical practices are continuously changing as they are passed down through oral transmission; this is music of living traditions. In China—just as elsewhere, undoubtedly—ideologies, histories, and music have been intertwined, and geopolitics have shaped and will continue to shape historical narratives. Most of all, this chapter advocates safeguarding different forms of memory-keeping in music and challenging biases produced in written histories, as they tend to reflect the narratives of the victor, the powerful, and the dogmatic—those who have access to the privilege of discourse. Readers of this volume and other works are thus reminded to approach any utterance and discourse with skeptical eyes.

Glossary

bayin 八音, "eight tones," classification system for musical instruments
bianzhong 編鐘, bells
Cheung Sai-Bung (Zhang Shibin) 張世彬, music scholar (twentieth century)
Chow Fan-Fu (Zhou Fanfu) 周凡夫, music scholar (contemporary)
Chu Sui-Bing (Zhu Ruibing) 朱瑞冰, music scholar (contemporary)
Dasiyue 大司樂, Zhou-dynasty court training school for musicians
Dawu 大武, The Great Wu, ancient piece of the Western Zhou dynasty
Dayueshu 大樂署, Tang-dynasty court training school for musicians
Dongfang hong 東方紅, The East is Red, 1964 song-and-dance epic which was made into a film in 1965

gongche 工尺, notation using simple symbols to depict scale steps and some metrical information

Hu Rongrong 胡蓉蓉, choreographer (b. 1929)

jianzipu 減字譜, tablature notation for *qin*

jiuyue 旧樂, "old music," early-twentieth-century designation for traditional music

li 禮, rites

Li Jinhui 黎錦暉, composer of Shanghai popular music (1891–1967)

Li Song 李松, historian (contemporary)

Liang Maochun 梁茂春, music historian (b. 1940)

Liang Qichao 梁啟超, reformist intellectual (1873–1929)

liyue 禮樂, system of rites and music that supported the maintenance of dynastic society

Lunyu 論語, *Analects* (probably written after Confucius's death in 479 BCE)

Lü Ji 呂驥, leading leftist musician (1909–2002)

Lüshi chunqiu 呂氏春秋, *Lü's Spring and Autumn Annals* (c. 239 BCE)

qin 琴, zither

Shi Yonggang 師永剛, writer on Cultural Revolution art works (contemporary)

Shi Zhongqin 石鐘琴, original principal dancer in the ballet, *White-haired Girl* (*Baimaonü*, 白毛女) (b. 1945)

Shiji 史記, *Historical Records* (finished c. 94 BCE)

Shijing 詩經, *Book of Songs*

siren bang 四人幫, "Gang of Four," political faction that became significant during the Cultural Revolution (1966–76)

Wang Guangqi 王光祈, music scholar (1892–1936)

Wong Wang-Chi (Wang Hongzhi) 王宏志, historian (contemporary)

xin yinyue 新音樂, "new music," early-twentieth-century term for non-indigenous musical genres, including Western art and popular music

xun 塤, stone whistle or ocarina

Yang Jie 楊潔, performance studies scholar (contemporary)

Yang Yinliu 楊蔭瀏, musicologist (1899–1984)

yangbanxi 樣板戲, model operas of the Cultural Revolution period

Yu Siu-Wah (Yu Shaohua) 余少華, music scholar (contemporary)

yue 樂, music

Yuefu 樂府, Han-dynasty training school for musicians

"Yueji" 樂記, "Record of Music"; or "Yueshu" 樂書, "Book of Music," part of the *Shiji*

Zeng Hou Yi 曾侯乙, Marquis Yi (c. 475–433 BCE)

Zhang Fan 張凡, writer on Cultural Revolution art works (contemporary)

Notes

1. The notion of habitus is borrowed from Pierre Bourdieu and is one of his most frequently referenced social theories. For his development of the concept, see 1977: 159–97 and 2000: 131–46, 208–37.
2. For more information on the bells written in English, see von Falkenhausen 1993.
3. Yang's volumes (1981) feature photos of these artifacts in the appendix, with better quality illustrations in Liu and Yuan, 2008. According to Yu Hui, the editor of this volume, Yang's volumes were completed decades ago, prior to the founding of the PRC, and Yang's narrative was also indebted to Darwinism.

4. *Qin* music is recorded through tablature notation. The ancient type used written words to describe what and how to play on the instrument whereas the modified type used a shorthand form of words known as *jianzipu* 減字譜. *Gongche* notation uses Chinese characters to represent the seven pitches of the diatonic scale, such that *gong* 工 refers to *do*, *che* 尺 to *re*, etc.
5. The scrolls were taken from Dunhuang by the French sinologist Paul Pelliot in 1908. They were deposited in the Bibliothèque Nationale de France (catalogued as P3808, P3539, and P3719); see further, Chen, 1991.
6. The term "new music," in addition to denoting the practice of Western music, was used variably in Republican China. For instance, in 1931, the songwriter Li Jinhui 黎錦輝 (1891–1967) created the first musical drama in a Western pop-song style, and in the preface to the publication of his one-act drama *Three Butterflies*, he referred to his endeavor as "new music" that would improve and construct China. In 1936, the leftist musician Lü Ji 呂驥 (1909–2002) defined "new music" as a weapon to win the masses. Chinese musicians then looked at all sorts of musical endeavors as "new music" as long as they did not involve traditional music, which was called *jiuyue* 旧樂 ("old music"); see Ming, 2012.
7. Foucault discusses the formation and the consequences of discourse in great detail in *The Archaeology of Knowledge* (1969) and also *The Discourse on Language* (1971). He explicates how language and knowledge are based on established discourses to regulate, impart, and continue normative ways of thinking and practices that often are entwined with power. These two writings were translated and published together in a single volume in 1972.
8. The model operas formed a genre of largely Beijing operas as well as a couple of ballets and cantatas, which grew from eight to about two dozen works closely entwined with the infamous Cultural Revolution (1966–76), a decade-long period of political and social chaos that brought atrocity to millions of Chinese. Intended as artistic models of socialist propaganda for other PRC cultural workers to follow, the model operas also underlined contemporaneous music reform initiatives, namely: 1) renovating traditional Beijing opera to suit China's modern audience, 2) synthesizing Western musical influences into traditional Chinese music, and 3) modifying Western artistic forms to serve a larger Chinese audience.
9. The Gang of Four was a political faction of communist officials—Jiang Qing (Mao's wife), Zhang Chunqiao, Yao Wenyuan, and Wong Hongwen—who played significant roles in the Cultural Revolution.
10. "The Covenant of Culture: Life *en pointe*—an interview with ballerina Zhongqin Shi" (Wenhua zhi yue: Zujian shang de rensheng. Zhuangang baleiwu yanyuan Shi Zhongqin) posted on the following URL: http://video.tudou.com/v/XMjYwOTI1ODcoOA==.html?spm=a2h0k.8191414.0.0&from=s1.8-1-1.2&f=50994822, accessed September 7, 2019.
11. There is a growing number of studies and memoirs published on this topic. A search for the term *yangbanxi* in the PRC's Academic Journal Database shows that roughly half of the four hundred articles pertinent to the topic were written in the past decade. However, the ubiquity with which printed articles, also known as paper memories, are accessible online means that they run the danger of representing only sanctioned memories, particularly when censorship is strictly observed by the state. Other memory-keeping sites include a museum built in Tashan Park, Shantou, in 1996, which opened to the public in 2005 but closed in 2016. Private museums of Cultural Revolution artifacts are found in Shanghai, Guangzhou, Chengdu, and other places. For instance, I once visited the Shanghai Propaganda Poster Art Centre, which was located in the basement of a

residential building. There is also a virtual museum providing information pertinent to the Cultural Revolution in both Chinese and English (http://www.cnd.org/CR/english/), accessed September 7, 2019.

12. I am indebted to Yu Hui, the editor of this volume, for drawing my attention to this fact. Li is currently a professor at Wuhan University.

REFERENCES

Bourdieu, Pierre. (1977). *Outline of a Theory of Practice*. Translated by Richard Nice. Cambridge, UK: Cambridge University Press.

Bourdieu, Pierre. (2000). *Pascalian Meditations*. Translated by Richard Nice. Stanford, CA: Stanford University Press.

Chen Yingshi. (1991). "A Report on Chinese Research into the Dunhuang Music Manuscripts." Translated by Coralie Rockwell. *Musica Asiatica* 6: 61–72.

Chen Yong 陳永. (2008). "Jindai 'Zhongguo yinyue shixue' zhi xingcheng ji qi tedian" "近代'中國音樂史學'之形成及其特點" [The Formation and Characteristics of Contemporary "Chinese Music Historiography"]. *Huangzhong: Wuhan yinyue xueyuan xuebao*黃鐘: 武漢音樂學院學報 [Yellow Bellow: The Journal of the Wuhan Conservatory of Music], no. 4: 99–108.

Cheng, Eileen Ka-May. (2012). *Historiography: An Introductory Guide*. New York: Continuum International Publishing Group.

Cheung Sai-Bung [Zhang Shibin] 張世彬. (1975). *Zhongguo yinyue shi lunshu gao* 中國音樂史論述稿 [A Draft History of Chinese Music]. Hong Kong: Youlian chubanshe.

Chou Kwong Chun [Zhou Guangzhen] 周光蓁. (2017). *Xianggang yinyue de qianshi jinsheng: Xianggang zaoqi yinyue fazhan licheng (1930s–1950s)* 香港音樂的前世今生: 香港早期音樂發展歷程 *(1930s–1950s)* [The Past and Present of Hong Kong Music: The Development of Early Hong Kong Music (1930s–1950s)]. Hong Kong: Joint-Publishing (H.K.) Co. Ltd.

Chow Fan Fu [Zhou Fanfu] 周凡夫. (1999). "Ben shiji de xianggang yinyue yanchu huodong" "本世紀的香港音樂演出活動" [Hong Kong's Music Activities in This Century]. In *Xianggang yinyue fazhan gailun* 香港音樂發展概論 [Introduction to Music Development in Hong Kong], edited by Zhu Ruibing 朱瑞冰, 29–127. Hong Kong: Joint-Publishing (H.K.) Co. Ltd.

Chow, Rey. (1992). "Between Colonizers: Hong Kong's Postcolonial Self-Writing in the 1990s." *Diaspora* 2 (2): 151–70.

Chu Sui Bing [Zhu Ruibing] 朱瑞冰, ed. (1999). *Xianggang yinyue fazhan gailun*香港音樂發展概論 [An Introduction to the Development of Music in Hong Kong]. Hong Kong: Joint-Publishing (H.K.) Co. Ltd.

Falkenhausen, Lothar von. (1993). *Suspended Music: Chime-Bells in the Culture of Bronze Age China*. Berkeley: University of California Press.

Fang Xiaoyang 方曉陽, et al. (2012). "Jiahu gudi de jingjue fuyuan yanjiu" "賈湖骨笛的精確復原研究" [The Research of the Precise Restoration of the Jiahu Bone Flutes]. *Zhongguo yinyuexue* 中國音樂學 [Chinese musicology], no. 2: 100–105.

Feng Wenci 馮文慈. (2007). "Zhongguo gudai yinyue wenxian mulu gaiyao (shang)" "中國古代音樂文獻目錄概要(上)" [An Annotation of Ancient Chinese Music Sources (Part 1)]. *Zhongyang yinyue xueyuan xuebao* 中央音樂學院學報 [Journal of the Central Conservatory of Music], no. 3: 87–96.

Foucault, Michel. (1972). *The Archaeology of Knowledge and The Discourse on Language*. Translated by A. M. Sheridan Smith. New York: Pantheon Books.

Hall, Stuart. (2001). "Foucault: Power, Knowledge and Discourse." In *Discourse Theory and Practice: A Reader*, edited by Margaret Wetherell, Stephanie Taylor, and Simeon J. Yates, 72–81. London: Sage Publications.

Huang Xiangpeng 黃翔鵬. (1990). *Chuantong shi yitiao heliu* 傳統是一條河流 [Tradition is a River]. Beijing: Renmin yinyue chubanshe.

JanMohamed, Abdul, and David Lloyd. (1987). "Introduction: Toward a Theory of Minority Discourse." *Cultural Critique* 6: 5–12.

Kaufmann, Walter. (1976). *Musical References in the Chinese Classics*. Michigan: Information Coordinators, Inc.

Lam, Joseph. (1996). "Ritual and Musical Politics in the Court of Ming Shizong." In *Harmony and Counterpoint*, edited by Bell Yung, Evelyn S. Rawski, and Rubie S. Watson, 35–53. Stanford, CA: Stanford University Press.

Le Goff, Jacques. (1992). *History and Memory*. Translated by Steven Rendall and Elizabeth Claman. New York: Columbia University Press.

Li Keping 李科平. (2016). "Qianxi *Shiji: Yueshu* de yue lun sixiang" "淺析《史記·樂書》的樂論思想" [An Analysis of the Music Discourse in *The Book on Music* in the *Historical Records*]. *Weinan shifan xueyuan xuebao* 渭南師範學院學報 [Journal of Weinan Normal University] 13: 89–93.

Li Song 李松. (2011–12). *"Yangbanxi" biannianshi* "樣板戲"編年史 [A Historical Chronicle of the "Model Operas"]. Taipei: Xiuwei zixun keji gufen youxian gongsi.

Liang Maochun 梁茂春. (1999). *Xianggang zuoqujia: Sanshi zhi jiushi niandai* 香港作曲家: 三十至九十年代 [Hong Kong Composers: 1930s to 1990s]. Hong Kong: Joint-Publishing (H.K.) Co. Ltd.

Liu Dongsheng 劉東升 and Yuan Quanyou 袁荃猷. (2008). *Zhongguo yinyue shi tujian (xiudingban)* 中國音樂史圖鑒 (修訂版) [An Illustrated History of Chinese Music, revised edition]. Beijing: Renmin yinyue chubanshe.

Liu Shun 劉順. (2007). "Zhongguo yinyue shixue yanjiu de xianzhuang yu fangfa" "中國音樂史學研究的現狀與方法" [On the Situation and Approach of Studies in Chinese Music History]. *Yishu baijia* 藝術百家 [A Hundred Schools of Art], no. 2, 86–88.

Liu Yutong 劉宇統. (2016). "'*Lüshi chunqiu*' he '*Yueji*' zhong de yinyue shuyu bijiao" "《呂氏春秋》和《樂記》中的音樂術語比較" [A Comparison of the Musical Terms in *Lü's Spring and Autumn Annals* and the *Record of Music*]. *Dangdai yinyue* 當代音樂 [Contemporary Music] no. 10: 1–4.

Mao Tse-tung [Mao Zedong]. (1956). *Talks at the Yenan Forum on Art and Literature*. Peking: Foreign Languages Press.

Ming Yan 明言. (2012). *Zhongguo xin yinyue* 中國新音樂 [Chinese New Music]. Beijing: Renmin yinyue chubanshe.

Nora, Pierre. (1989). "Between Memory and History: Les Lieux de Mémoire." *Representations* 26: 7–24.

Shen Leiqiang 沈雷強. (2008). "Tanjiu xun de lishi fazhan guiji" "探究塤的歷史發展軌跡" [On the Historical Development of the *Xun*]. *Yishu baijia* 藝術百家 [A Hundred Schools of Art], no. 1: 177–78.

Shi Yonggang 師永剛 and Zhang Fan 張凡. (2009). *Yangbanxi shiji* 樣板戲史記 [A Historical Record of the Model Operas]. Beijing: Zuojia chubanshe.

Spalding, Roger, and Christopher Parker. (2007). *Historiography: An Introduction.* Manchester, IN: Manchester University Press.

Stock, Jonathan. (2013). "Four Recurring Themes in Histories of Chinese Music." In *The Cambridge History of World Music*, edited by Philip V. Bohlman, 397–415. Cambridge, UK: Cambridge University Press.

Wang Ding 王汀. (2013). "Yinyue shehui gongyong zhi dangyi: yi *Yueji* he *Lüshi chunqiu* weili" "音樂社會功用之芻議：以《樂記》和《呂氏春秋》為例" [Discussing Music's Social Function: Taking the *Record of Music* and *Lü's Spring and Autumn Annals* as Examples]. *Jilin guangbo dianshi daxue xuebao* 吉林廣播電視大學 [Journal of Jilin Radio and TV University], no. 6: 75–76.

Wang Fengzhen 王逢振. (1994). "Shenme shi 'discourse'? Yige bu keyi shuo you yao shuo de wenti" "什麼是'discourse'? 一個不可以說又要說的問題" [What is Discourse? An Untouchable Issue that Needs to be Addressed]. *Wenyi lilun yu piping* 文藝理論與批評 [Theory and Criticism of Literature and Art], no. 2: 130–35.

Wang Guangqi 王光祈. ([1934] 2014). *Zhongguo yinyue shi* 中國音樂史. [Chinese Music History]. Shanghai: Zhonghua shuju. Reprint, Shanghai: Sanlian shudian, 2014.

Wang Zichu 王子初. (2010). "Lun Zhongguo yinyue shiliao xitong de chonggou" "論中國音樂史料系統的重構" [On the Reconstruction of Chinese Music Historical Sources]. *Xinghai yinyue xueyuan xuebao* 星海音樂學院學報 [Journal of the Xinghai Music Conservatory], no. 4: 23–32.

Watson, Rubie S. (1994), "Memory, History, and Opposition under State Socialism: An Introduction." In *Memory, History, and Opposition under State Socialism*, edited by Rubie S. Watson, 1–20. Santa Fe, NM: School of American Research Press.

Wong Wang-Chi [Wang Hongzhi] 王宏志. (2000). *Lishi de chenzhong: cong Xianggang kan Zhongguo dalu de Xianggang lunshu* 歷史的沉重：從香港看中國大陸的香港史論述 [The Burden of History: A Historical Account of Hong Kong from Mainland China]. Hong Kong: Oxford University Press.

Xue Yongwu 薛永武. (2011). "Lun *Lüshi chunqiu* yu *Yueji* yinyue meixue de qutong" "論《呂氏春秋》與《樂記》音樂美學思想的趨同" [On the Convergence of Music Aesthetics in *Lü's Spring and Autumn Annals* and the *Record of Music*]. *Shandong daxue xuebao: Zhexue shehuikexue ban* 山東大學學報哲學社會科學版 [Journal of Shandong University: Philosophy and Social Sciences Edition], no. 6: 121–125.

Yang Dongju 楊冬菊. (2017). "*Shiji* suo ji ge jieceng renwu de yueqi yanzou" "《史記》所記各階層人物的樂器演奏" [Musical Instrument Performance of People from All Social Levels as Recorded in *The Record of Historian*]. *Weinan shifan xueyuan xuebao* 渭南師範學院學報 [Journal of Weinan Normal University] 21: 87–92.

Yang, Hon-Lun. (2004). "Socialist Realism and Chinese Music." In *Socialist Realism and Music*, edited by Mikuláš Bek, Geoffrey Chew, and Petr Macek, 135–44. Prague: Koniasch Latin Press.

Yang, Hon-Lun. (2005). "The Making of a National Musical Icon: Xian Xinghai and his Yellow River Cantata." In *Music, Power, and Politics*, edited by Annie Randall, 87–111. New York: Routledge.

Yang, Hon-Lun. (2006). "People's Music in the People's Republic of China: A Semiotic Reading of Socialist Musical Culture from the mid to late 1950s." In *Music, Meaning and Media*, edited by Erkki Pekkilä, David Neumeyer, and Richard Littlefield, 195–208. Imatra: International Semiotics Institute.

Yang, Hon-Lun. (2007). "Power, Politics, and Musical Commemoration: Western Musical Figures in the People's Republic of China." *Music and Politics* 2 (July). (https://quod.lib.umich.edu/m/mp/9460447.0001.205?view=text;rgn=main).

Yang, Hon-Lun. (2012). "The Shanghai Conservatory, Chinese Musical Life, and the Russian Diaspora: 1927–1949." *Twentieth-Century China* 37 (1): 73–95.

Yang, Hon-Lun. (2016). "Unravelling *The East is Red*: Socialist Music and Politics in the People's Republic of China." In *Composing for the State: Music in Twentieth-Century Dictatorships*, edited by Esteban Buch, Igor Contreras Zubillaga, and Manuel Deniz Silva, 51–68. New York: Routledge.

Yang, Hon-Lun, and Michael Saffle, eds. (2017). *China and the West, Music, Representation, and Reception*. Ann Arbor: University of Michigan Press.

Yang, Hon-Lun, Simo Mikkonen, and John Winzenburg. (2020). *Networking the Russian Diaspora: Russian Musicians and Musical Activities in Interwar Shanghai*. Honolulu: University of Hawai'i Press.

Yang Jie 楊潔. (2010). *Balei wuju "Baimaonü" chuangzuo shihua* 芭蕾舞劇白毛女創作史話 [A Compositional History of the Ballet "The White-Haired Girl"]. Shanghai: Shanghai yinyue chubanshe.

Yang, X.-Y., et al. (2005). "TL and IRSL Dating of Jiahu Relics and Sediments: Clue of 7th Millennium BC Civilization in Central China." *Journal of Archaeological Science* 32 (7): 1045–51.

Yang Yinliu 楊蔭瀏. (1981). *Zhongguo gudai yinyue shigao* 中國古代音樂史稿 [A Draft History of Ancient Chinese Music]. Beijing: Renmin yinyue chubanshe.

Yu Siu Wah [Yu Shaohua] 余少華. (1999). "Xianggang de Zhongguo yinyue" "香港的中國音樂" [Chinese Music in Hong Kong]. In *Xianggang yinyue fazhan gailun* 香港音樂發展概論 [Introduction to Music Development in Hong Kong], edited by Zhu Ruibing 朱瑞冰, 261–360. Hong Kong: Joint-Publishing (H.K.) Co. Ltd.

Yu Siu Wah [Yu Shaohua] 余少華. (2001). *Le zai diancuo zhong: Xianggang yasu yinyue wenhua* 樂在顛錯中—香港雅俗音樂文化 [Out of Chaos and Coincidence: Hong Kong's Music Cultures]. Hong Kong: Oxford University Press.

Zhou Jian 周劍. (2014). "Shiji zhong de yinyue sixiang jiedu" "史記中的音樂思想解讀" [Reading the Musical Ideas in *The Record of the Historian*]. *Zhonggong Ji'nan shiwei dangxiao xuebao* 中共濟南市委黨校學報 [Journal of the Ji'nan City Chinese Communist Party Municipal Committee School], no. 1: 63–66.

CHAPTER 8

CHINESE MUSIC MODERNITIES

FREDERICK LAU

INTRODUCTION

The concept of modernity began to emerge in China in the late nineteenth century as a consequence of, and reaction to, a series of catastrophic defeats China suffered at the hands of foreign powers. Its emergence was part of efforts to resolve the political crises that had gripped the nation since the mid-nineteenth century. In China, modernity became a euphemism for catching up with Western countries. This idea, initially spearheaded by an open-minded Qing official named Li Hongzhang 李鴻章 (1823–1901), was first adopted to reform the Chinese army according to Western standards and to strengthen China's military power. The movement to absorb Western ideas soon spread to other domains of Chinese society. In addition to introducing Western knowledge to Chinese intellectuals through translations of seminal works, such as Thomas Huxley's *Evolution and Ethics*, John Stuart Mill's *A System of Logic*, Herbert Spencer's *A Study of Sociology*, and others, the Qing government began to send students to study abroad, expediting the transfer of knowledge from the West to China.

From the start, China's push to become modern was inseparable from the process of nation-building and enhancing traditional knowledge with that of the West. Armed with new awareness of Western culture through translated works and those brought back by students returning from Japan, Germany, the United States, and Great Britain, Chinese intellectuals began to propose a series of changes to traditional Chinese learning and knowledge acquisition. However, opinions regarding what Western knowledge and practices to adopt, and how, were diverse and hotly debated. Although the English word "modern," and its French counterpart *moderne*, was first translated into Chinese as *modeng* 摩登, a phonetic equivalent of the European words, in cosmopolitan Shanghai about the 1920s (Lee, 1999: 5), an appetite for novelty and things Western permeated the intellectual and creative psyche of the nation long before the neologism became fashionable in the Chinese language.

Since its introduction in twentieth-century China, the modern—*modeng* or *xiandai* 现代, in current Chinese usage—has become part of the cultural zeitgeist. One common view among early modernists was that China's past was a hindrance to the nation's progress and development, and they believed that traditional learning and knowledge needed to be reformed. This view, stemming from a linear progressive view of history, construed the past as ancient, antiquated, traditional, backward, and passé (Duara, 1995: 17; Shih, 2012: 20). Given the diverse interpretations of the concept of the modern, there were multiple ways of realizing modernity even within the same genre, field, or context. This is evidenced by the many fascinating studies tracing China's road to modernity in multiple fields of study, including mathematics (Bréard, 2019), medicine (Lei, 2014), literature (Huters, 2005), translation (Liu, 1995), culture (Lee, 1999), and music (Jones, 2001). Chinese expressions of modernity were not wholesale mimicry of all things modern in the West; rather, they comprised indigenous practices set against the backdrop of China's historical context and sociopolitical climate.

The question of modernizing music is a complicated one given Chinese music's diverse roles in imperial settings, literati circles, and regional cultures. As Chinese music has for a long time been associated with governance, morality, Confucianist ethics, and literati, its functions, meanings, and practices were incompatible with those of Western music. There were no easy solutions to bringing Chinese music in line with Western music. To reform Chinese music required changing not only the production of music but also, more importantly, the infrastructure that underscored musical practices and conceptions. A few questions will help us to get a better understanding of the formation of a modern Chinese musical culture: What is the quality of being modern in Chinese music? Which elements made Chinese music modern? How do we discuss modernity in Chinese music?

Before tackling these key issues, it is crucial to recall that the central narrative of China in the early twentieth century was about building a strong nation and advancing society in the face of political turbulence. Following this narrative, the Qing dynasty crumbled because of its weak military, and its traditional elite literati education was blamed for its inability to produce what it took to stand up to foreign aggression and invasions. This national crisis forced Chinese intellectuals to question the effectiveness of traditional learning and past practices and to advocate the adoption of Western sciences and knowledge. From the start, the discussion was tightly intertwined with, indeed inseparable from, the modernist discourse. This thinking generated a profound impact on Chinese society and culture and became an impetus for reform in all social domains. Chinese music modernity was born out of this ideological disjuncture, where the old and the new worldviews were clashing, all against a political backdrop that was teetering on the edge of disintegration.

The first public argument for using Western music to improve Chinese music was presented in 1903 during the final years of the Qing dynasty. The Chinese scholar Fei Shi 匪石 wrote an article entitled "Thoughts about Developing Chinese Music"

("Zhongguo yinyue gailiangshuo" 中國音樂改良說) published in the journal *The Tide of Zhejiang* (*Zhejiang chao* 浙江潮) (Wang and Hu, 2006: 74). To support his argument, Fei Shi points out four basic problems that had hampered the development and progress of Chinese music. In his opinion, Chinese music: 1) Is not for the general public; 2) Does not possess an ambitious and progressive spirit and tends to be decadent and vulgar; 3) Does not rely on mechanical means for tone production and is a waste of human energy; 4) Has no systematic music education and pedagogy. Using Western music as his basis of comparison, Fei Shi concludes that Western music can be used to improve Chinese music, with the former helping to cultivate an ambitious and progressive spirit while fostering a unified resolve for all Chinese citizens.

Shortly after Fei Shi's proclamation, a student who had studied in Japan, Zeng Zhimin 曾志忞 (1879–1929), made a similar point. In 1904, Zeng states that the only way to develop China's music education is to go outside China and learn from more advanced countries (Wang and Hu, 2006: 75). The message that only by learning from the West could Chinese music be improved was made abundantly clear by these music scholars, and it spread rapidly across the nation. Their call not only involved advocating the adoption of elements of Western music—such as scales, instruments, measurement, rhythm, and theoretical systems—but also established the necessary conditions for relying on Western music aesthetics, preferences, theoretical underpinnings, practices, and sonic sensibility as tools for improving Chinese music.

In this chapter, I view modernity as a condition, dynamic process, and indigenous practice of musical transformation rather than a teleology with a goal and point of arrival (Wade, 2013). As a practice subjected to the push and pull of historical conditions and dynamics of contexts, modernity in Chinese music is an ongoing project that is shaped by constantly shifting sociocultural terrains and premises. To understand the ways in which China constructs its musical modernity, I focus on five foundational moments of modernist formation. These moments were groundbreaking because they produced long-lasting effects on Chinese music, and what we now know as Chinese music owes much to these initial modernist endeavors. Although they happened independently, they reinforced each other in subtle ways. These interrelated moments began roughly at the beginning of the twentieth century, and while their concerns may have been different, the spirit behind them can be traced back to these early moments. Even at the time of writing this chapter, the rhetoric of being modern is alive and well in music circles across the nation.

The Genre of *Xuetang Yuege* School Song

The first and perhaps the most momentous modernist turn in Chinese music was the creation of a new genre of song in the 1900s called *xuetang yuege* 学堂乐歌 (literally, "school song"). This genre of songs departed drastically from traditional Chinese vocal music and sound, as it was derived from Western verse-and-refrain song form, with melodies and accompaniment written in diatonic scales and with common-practice harmony. These songs were easy to sing and learn. Most of them consisted of simple melodies and lyrics that were easy to remember and understand. The themes of these songs invariably centered on promoting nation-building, patriotism, courage, strength, civic duty, and standing up to bullies—all inspired by the prevalent sociopolitical sentiments of the time.

School songs were created to cater to the increasing number of music classes that were implemented as part of the new public education system. Traditionally, Chinese education was provided by teachers in private schools (*sishu* 私塾). The educational goal in these private schools focused exclusively on the study of major classical texts, such as the "four books" and "five classics," and in preparing students for the imperial examination. Music was never a subject covered in traditional education. In 1905, the long history of Confucianist education and imperial examination came to an abrupt end and was replaced by a new type of education system adopted from the West.

This new education emphasized the training of the whole person, not only the mind but also the body and soul through a combination of humanities, sciences, and artistic subjects. Music, a field missing from traditional classical training, was one of several introduced as part of the new school curriculum. School songs were in great demand because of the increasing number of modern schools established across the nation. Most of these songs were composed in the early 1900s and widely adopted in music classes. Singing collectively became common practice for students of the time, and it offered them a new way of expressing themselves in public and in groups.

Through school songs, a new musical style and singing technique began to be popularized throughout China. In fact, these early songs built a foundation for the creation and popularity of mass songs and revolutionary songs in later years. School songs also offered an opportunity for the average Chinese person to come into contact with Western-style melodies and instruments such as the piano, harmonica, accordion, and pedal-pump organ. The incorporation of these instruments brought unprecedented additions to the Chinese musical life and cemented the centrality of songs and public singing in Chinese society.

Early school-song composers borrowed melodies from Japan, the United States, France, and other European countries, since many of them were students in these countries. Numerous early examples of these new songs were created by fitting new lyrics to borrowed melodies. The process was similar to the traditional text-setting *tianci* (填詞) method of adding new lyrics to existing labeled-tune *qupai* (曲牌) in operatic and narrative genres. A *qupai* is essentially a short piece of music that has a fixed melody, mode, rhythm, and title or label. Since Chinese is a tonal language, the skill of lyricists is judged by how effectively the linguistic tones of the new lyrics are aligned with the tones of the melody so as not to undermine the integrity of textual meaning. The art of text-setting, therefore, requires knowledge of both language and music, and early school-song writers demonstrated compositional skills and knowledge of traditional Chinese culture through their work. Later *xuetang yuege* composers began to assert their musical competency and identity by composing new melodies or making use of indigenous musical materials and local folk songs as the basis of their songs.

Characteristic features of school songs are that the melodies are short and simple and the lyrics are made up of uncomplicated words that are easy to sing, memorize, and understand. The songs were sung in unison and rarely in harmony or multiple parts. For example, the lyrics of the song "Bamboo Horse" ("Zhuma" 竹馬) composed by Shen Xingong 沈心工 (1870–1947) comprise four short, simple phrases, and the melody makes use of just five pitches arranged in conjunct motion and in duple meter (Qian, 2001: 38–39).

The whole song is made up of four four-measure phrases, each consisting of two sub-phrases. My translation of the text goes as follows: "The little child has high ambitions. He wants to contribute to the country. He holds the bamboo horse between his legs as if he was riding a real horse. He is so happy that he hops around." The text relies on simple, vernacular language, and its implied meaning aims to instill patriotic sentiments in children. Even though the song is about the playfulness of a boy, the theme of serving the country and being patriotic is strongly suggested. "Bamboo Horse" is representative of many school songs in terms of its musical and lyrical constructions.

Among the early promoters of school songs were music educators who themselves received education in Japan, such as Shen Xingong, Li Shutong 李叔同 (1880–1942), and Zeng Zhimin. Shen was considered the father of *xuetang yuege*, and his idea of using Western music to help China was undoubtedly related to his overseas experience. Born in Shanghai and subsequently educated at a teacher-training college, in 1902 he went to study music in Tokyo and returned in 1903 to China, where he began teaching. He was inspired by music education in Japanese schools and the power of songs and singing for improving people's lives and as political propaganda in post-Meiji Japan. For Shen, singing could generate enthusiasm and arouse deep nationalistic sentiments about the spirit of China. His experience motivated him to organize Chinese students in Japan to set up a "music workshop" where they would learn the techniques for writing school songs from Japanese teachers. The songs crafted from these workshops featured a wide range of timely topics that were easily digestible for children. Shen is also credited with using the newly popular vernacular language, *baihua* 白話, in lyrics. The use of simple *baihua* language became a hallmark of school songs and signified a modernist turn in education for children.

Shen is credited with composing the first school song in 1902 when he was in Japan and with writing the first larger set, entitled *A Collection of School Songs* (*Xuexiao gechangji* 學校歌唱集), in 1904 after he returned to China. His first song is entitled "Men Need to Have High Ambition" ("Naner zhiqi gao" 男兒志氣高) (Qian, 2001: 137). The song is twenty-four measures in length, comprising a simple four-measure phrase repeated six times. The rhythm is uniform and made up mostly of eighth notes, and the implied harmony of the phrase is I-V-I. The title unambiguously reveals the message of the song, with the lyrics encouraging boys to be courageous and healthy for fighting China's enemies—clearly in relation to wider concerns about nation-building and avenging national humiliation. The song was later renamed "Physical Exercise" ("Ticao" 體操) and "Military Drill" ("Juncao" 軍操).

According to Republican official records and scholar Qian Renkang's assessment, Shen was one of those early music educators who advocated singing classes in Chinese primary schools (Qian, 2001). Subsequently, he published three volumes of the *Collection of School Songs*, six volumes of the *Revised Edition of Collection of School Songs* (*Chongbian xuexiao gechangji* 重編學校歌唱集, 1912a), and *Volume of Republic Songs* (*Minguo gechangeji* 民國歌唱集, 1912b). He was a prolific composer, writing over 185 songs in his lifetime. He also translated and published the 1905 *Instruction Book for Primary School Singing* (*Xiaoxue gechang jiaoxuefa* 小學歌唱教學法), which was widely circulated as an important text for promoting the genre. Judging from Shen's publications, his contribution to promoting school songs, and by extension Western music, was remarkable and long-lasting.

The birth of *xuetang yuege* opened the first modernist chapter for Chinese music by altering China's soundscape and musical practices, introducing students to a form of Western music through singing. Generations of children grew up singing this type of song as an important part of their education; the tradition popularized and democratized participation in music. For many youths of the time, the practice of group singing highlighted the power of song in generating collective sentiments during political rallies, marches, and large gatherings. It laid the foundation for a new tradition of songwriting and singing. Many later Chinese vocal genres—such as art songs, mass songs, protest songs, anti-Japanese songs, and revolutionary songs—owed their development to *xuetang yuege*.

Institutions and Music Education

Following the creation of *xuetang yuege*, another significant modernist turn in Chinese music came with the establishment of professional training grounds such as music institutes and conservatories. The ethnomusicologist Bruno Nettl remarks that when cultures adopt Western music, setting up new Western-style music institutes is often considered an important step to "improving" the country's music (Nettl, 1985). The Chinese situation is no exception.

Chinese students who studied music abroad had long concluded that the reason for Chinese music's stagnation was that China had no systematic music education (Wang and Hu, 2006: 80). This was emphatically stated, for instance, by Fei Shi, who put China's musical backwardness down to this lack of formal music education (Wang and Hu, 2006: 74). His assessment echoed the main sentiment associated with the Self-Strengthening Movement (Ziqiang yundong, 自強運動) from 1861 to 1895, which attributed China's wider poverty and weakness to its backward education. The Qing government was aware of the situation and tried to remedy it by introducing education reform and music classes in its newly instituted school system. But these steps were too superficial to be effective (Wang and Hu, 2006: 76). A formal modern-music education was not implemented until the 1920s.

In the past, Chinese music was passed down through oral transmission and from teacher to student in private settings; there were no formal music schools or institutions. Instruction methods varied from region to region and from teacher to teacher, and there was no consensus among them (Liang, 1985; Jones, 1995). Although court music departments existed during the Han and Tang dynasties, they only trained musicians for court performances and entertainment and were not for the general public or commoners. No general musical training was offered for others, inside or outside the imperial palace. The overseas musical experiences of Chinese who studied abroad convinced them that China needed to catch up with the West and to develop systematic, nationwide music education. Equipped with the newly adopted principle that music and the arts were crucial for training China's youth, music scholars began to construct new music institutions using Western music schools as a model.

Two seminal music institutes set in motion a new way of training musicians and provided music pedagogy for both Chinese and Western music and instruments. The Peking University Music Research Association and the National Music Conservatory established in Shanghai were among the earliest music institutes in China. Their influence was remarkable and long-lasting. What they achieved greatly expedited the modernization process of Chinese music.

Peking University Music Research Association

The Peking University Music Research Association (Beijing daxue yinyue yanjiuhui 北京大學音樂研究會) was founded in 1916 when the Western-trained intellectual Cai Yuanpei 蔡元培 (1868–1940) became the president of Peking University. It was the first Western-style university to include music as part of modern education. Cai established the Peking University Music Group, later changing its name to the Peking University Institute of Music Transmission and Learning (Beijing daxue yinyue chuanxisuo 北京大學音樂傳習所), to provide students with formal music training. This was perhaps the first attempt to provide modern music education by offering classes on Western music theory and musical practice in a formal educational setting.

As director of the music association, Cai went on to reorganize it into distinct music research and training institutes. He set up five different types of classes, focusing respectively on the piano, violin, *guqin* 古琴, *pipa* 琵琶, and the elite operatic genre *kunqu* 崑曲. In 1919, Cai also enlisted the help of the German-trained musician and composer Xiao Youmei 蕭友梅 (1884–1940), further strengthening the organization in its capacity to provide training in composition, music theory, harmony, music history, and music research. In 1922, the Chinese instrumentalist and educator Liu Tianhua 劉天華

(1895–1932), along with others who taught *pipa*, *erhu* 二胡, and *guqin*, was employed by Peking University to train students in these traditional instruments. The structure of the institute was visionary in that it not only aimed to train students in Western music, theory, and practice but also established a precedent for teaching and preservation of traditional Chinese music.

Of all the institute's teachers of Chinese music, Liu Tianhua is perhaps the most influential. Although trained as a traditional instrumentalist, Liu's idea of music and training was far from traditional. He disagreed with Western notions of art for art's sake and the autonomy of music, and he advocated music as being closely related to the life of society and carrying important social functions. For Liu, music is an art that can inspire and uplift people and awaken the nation. He did not rigidly stick to tradition but instead explored innovative ways to develop music according to the intellectual climate of the time. For example, he published books from his own collection of music, and he wrote exercises and etudes, in the style of violin-exercise books, for systematically training *erhu* players. He insisted that only through systematic and scientific methods could Chinese music be improved. In this sense, Liu's artistic endeavor was closely related to and inspired by the May Fourth New Cultural Movement (五四新文化運動), in which progress, scientific thought, and democracy were the main driving intellectual forces.

During the same period, the government of the Republic implemented compulsory music and singing classes in primary schools throughout the country as part of the new education system. Formal music education in Chinese schools began to take shape in the 1920s. But, due to the civil war and infighting among warlords in northern China, all music departments were assessed as being harmful to society and a waste of state money, and they were suspended in 1922. After six years, Xiao Youmei and Liu Tianhua had to disband the Music Research Association, changing its name to the Institute of Music Transmission and Learning to make it officially a part of Peking University. The newly christened Institute had blazed a new trail for music education in China. The backbone of the school was the tenets of the May Fourth New Cultural Movement. Therefore, the Institute itself reflected the spirit of the nation and of scientific progress. At the same time, it advocated and practiced the idea that music should be popularized and available to most people. The Peking University Music Association was a pioneer in not only passing down musical skills to the future generation but also bringing awareness and legitimacy to the study of music as a respectable subject in modern higher education.

National Academy of Music

The closing of all music classes by the government of the northern warlords put a damper on modern music education in China. Although the momentum for setting up modern music education was temporarily put on hold in the early 1920s, it also strengthened the resolve of Cai Yuanpei and Xiao Youmei to continue the work they had begun at Peking University (Liu, 2009: 99). With the support of Cai Yuanpei, Xiao Youmei proposed that the Republican government establish a national academy of music in Shanghai. More ambitious and expensive in structure and organization than the Peking University Institute of Music Transmission and Learning, the National Academy of Music (Guoli yinyue zhuanke xuexiao 國立音樂專科學校) was ultimately founded in November 1927. Influenced by his musical training in Germany, where he received a PhD from the University of Leipzig, Xiao Youmei modeled the National Academy on the format of German music conservatories, with slight modifications to include training in Chinese music. The curriculum featured music theory and composition, keyboard skills, orchestral instruments, and Chinese music. To promote music education in China further, the Academy also created courses for the training of teachers at different levels.

One of Xiao's methods for modernizing Chinese music education was the hiring of Western musicians as teachers. As a metropolis in the early twentieth century, Shanghai had attracted many foreign musicians in classical and popular music. Yang, Mikkonen, and Winzenburg (2020) describe a vibrant music scene in which Russian musicians and teachers were working particularly actively, contributing much to musical life in China. According to these authors, Russians began to settle in China after the October Revolution in 1919, especially in the cities of Harbin and Shanghai. As enclaves formed in these places, music became a way to "provide cohesion to Russian communities abroad" (Yang, Mikkonen, and Winzenburg, 2020: 11). They argue also that "music let Russian emigres reach out to other communities, and they have left an impact on Chinese musical development" (Ibid.).

Xiao was able to take advantage of the large number of foreign musicians in Shanghai by hiring some of them as teachers for the Academy. Among them were Boris Zakharov (1887–1943), Vladimir Shushilin (1894–1978), Zinaida Pribikova, Sergei Asakoff, Boris Lazarev, Alexander Tcherepnin (1899–1977), and Arrigo Foa (1900–81). Of the forty-two music faculty members, over half were foreign teachers (Kraus, 1989: 5; Liu, 2009: 92). This established a firm foundation for the learning of Western music in China. In fact, many graduates of the conservatory went on to have distinguished careers in music and became prominent musicians of twentieth-century China. The composers He Luting 賀綠汀 (1903–99), Ding Shande 丁善德 (1911–95), and Lin Shengxi 林聲翕 (1914–91) taught many composers of the next generation of musicians. They also established new compositional styles through combining Chinese elements with Western techniques. During the anti-Japanese war in China, the Academy was no longer able to operate in Shanghai. It retreated to western China, to the city of Chongqing, remaining there until the end of the war in 1945.

The history of these two music academies reflected the determination of China's early music education to modernize and professionalize. The establishment of the National Academy of Music was monumental because it was the model on which other conservatories would be based after 1949. Although Xiao Youmei's and Liu Tianhua's efforts to build a new music institution at Peking University were complicated by the political situation of the time, their vision and attempts to methodically train students in performance and research turned music from being not only a communal and participatory endeavor but also a professional and presentational one. This shift forever altered the status of music and musicians in China.

THE FIELD OF COMPOSITION

The third modernist turn in Chinese music was the adoption of Western-style composition and techniques and the creation of the field of composition, never before recognized as a discipline in its own right (Yung, 1994; Liang, 1985: 21). In the West, the role and function of performer and composer diverged as music began to enter the market economy of the eighteenth century. From the Enlightenment period, European composers began to gain social prestige and acceptance as the idea of musical authorship and individualism became recognized and valorized. Composing became a respectable social and commercial profession. Composers were acclaimed for their artistic talent and superhuman-like ability to create something sublime, with figures like Mozart, Beethoven, Brahms, and Wagner especially revered for their creativity. But in Chinese music culture, little attention was paid to composers. Instead, pieces are attributed to tradition or the region whence the music originated. Composing new pieces was neither valued nor a common endeavor among musicians, and many older scores or music manuscripts rarely identified the composer; the idea of the composer was simply not as prominent as the title or sentiment of the composition. Pieces are often known as "old or ancient pieces" (*guqu*) or "traditional pieces" (*chuantong qumu*), with the distinct identity of the composer or composition less important than the performer who brings it to life.

The contemporary scholars David Liang and Bell Yung have noted that the division between performer, composer, and audience in traditional Chinese music contexts is often not clearly delineated and that these roles frequently overlap (Yung, 1994: 55; Liang, 1985: 13). Unlike performers of Western music, traditional Chinese music performers were expected to perform their own renditions of a piece by adding notes, ornaments, or altering the melodies during performance. According to Liang and Yung, this form of on-the-spot creation, akin to what jazz musicians do when they improvise, is essentially a form of composing.

A word on Chinese performance practice is in order here. Unlike Western classical music, which usually contains multiple parts or lines, traditional Chinese music often only consists of a single skeleton melody that is played by all instruments. Performers are expected to alter the melody and insert something new into the skeleton melody during a performance. In other words, a musical piece exists not as a fixed product in the score but rather as a basis for a performer to exercise creativity when performing. The piece is only fully realized when it is interpreted and performed by the performer. Although common in most Chinese genres, this practice of improvisation—that is, adding ornaments or changing the notes of a piece during a performance—goes against the practice of most Western classical-music performers, who must adhere to the score without altering any notes.

To further illustrate the finer points concerning Chinese performers, it is worth briefly examining the playing of the seven-string plucked zither *guqin* and regional ensemble music. Abbreviated character notation (*jianzipu* 減字譜) is a form of prescriptive notation that gives instructions on how to produce the designated notes and effect without indicating rhythm and duration. A performer is required to determine the length of notes, melodies, the duration of phrases and pauses, and overall dynamics. Bell Yung considers this a process of re-creation that relies on the literary ability and technique of the performer (Yung, 1984, 1994). Likewise, in regional-ensemble music playing, skilled performers are expected to embellish the skeleton melody and musical phrases by adding or subtracting notes or adding ornaments, in a process called *jiahua* 加花 (literally, "adding flowers") (Jones, 1995; Witzleben, 1995). While there might be some differences between secular music and intellectual music, such as art songs composed by Jiang Kui 姜夔 (1155–1221) of the Song dynasty, the *jiahua* process bestows upon performers great creative authority. A performer's ability is recognized not for executing the notes in the score but rather for improvising and embellishing the skeleton melody. This process is prevalent in all regional instrumental, vocal, and operatic genres.

This characteristic performance practice, which gives regional music its specific sonic qualities, contrasts greatly with the notion of composing and performing in the West, where a classical performer's role is to faithfully render the composed piece or score in sound during a performance. In Western music, a performer's creative input is limited to such areas as tempo, dynamics, and micro-level rhythmic freedom (tempo rubato). Except for the occasional cadenza, there is no departure from and addition to the composed music in terms of notes or ornaments. With this comparison in mind, it is easy to understand why the famous scholar Liang Qichao, who promoted the reform of Chinese culture in 1900 during his period of study in Japan, remarked that it was a shame no one in China could write new music (Wang and Hu, 2006: 71). Liang's judgement reflected his preference for Western-style composition and his negative views of Chinese music. Obviously, he was unable to see traditional practice as creative or as a form of composition, and his definitions of composition, talent, and genius narrowly adhered to the standards of Western practice. Nonetheless, heeding his call for the development of composition as a field, many Chinese musicians and educators took up the composition of works intended to contribute to China's new music. This trend was also replicated in the 1960s when various performers of traditional music also became composers.

Composers: Individualism Established

Communalism and relationships are at the heart of Confucianism. In traditional society, individuals were not divorced from their contexts but were instead subsumed under the umbrella of a larger collective social order. This underpins the often-heard distinction that Chinese society is based on collectivism while individualism is the foundation of Western culture. The creation of the field of composition in China introduced the concept of post-Enlightenment individualism and the idea of composers being autonomous and authoritative. As new genres of music modeled on Western styles were being introduced in China, the demand for new compositions skyrocketed, beginning with the *xuetang yuege*. Many proponents of this genre were trained in fields other than music composition, but they saw it as their responsibility to compose new songs catering to demand. As more new musical genres were created, the category of composer became a permanent addition to the field of Chinese music.

Here I focus on three composers and their accomplishments. Among other composers such as Tan Xiaolin 譚小麟 (1911–48), Nie Er 聶耳 (1912–35), and Xian Xinghai 冼星海 (1905–45) (Wang, 1988; Qian, 2004; Wang and Hu, 2006), their emergence marked the beginning of individual attempts at exercising creativity and personal aspirations through new music compositions. In addition to declaring a composer's status and authority in musical production, their unique approaches stressed scientific precision over oral tradition and improvisation in performance. While their compositional styles and approaches are different from each other, each composer clearly articulated his autonomy, aesthetic preference, and individuality. Their collective activities and effort, perhaps a direct answer to Liang Qichao's remarks, established a way for composers to express their creativity with unique voices and compositional techniques in response to their immediate environments.

The first composer is Zhao Yuanren 趙元任 (1892–1992, also known as Yuen Ren Chao). Zhao was born in Tianjin, and he studied in China before earning degrees from Cornell University and Harvard University. He was trained as a linguist and taught at the University of California, Berkeley, from 1947 to 1960. An avid translator of various language texts into Chinese, Zhao was a pioneer in systematizing the learning and teaching of Mandarin through his romanization method. As an intellectual of the May Fourth generation, Zhao was a strong supporter of the New Cultural Movement in China and was a modernist in language as well as music. Like his contemporary Hu Shih 胡適 (1891–1962), Zhao was a proponent of the vernacular *baihua* language that he used in his lyrics. His interests in language and music prompted him to explore different forms of expression through songs.

Zhao was also a strong enthusiast of the German art-song tradition in China. In 1928, he published a collection containing fourteen of his original solo songs. In the introduction, Zhao explained that his songs were inspired by the German Lieder of Schubert and Schumann. He composed them for people who had developed a taste for Western art songs and for educating high-school students (Wang and Hu, 2006: 91), the intention being to create a kind of Chinese art song, which he envisioned as a new genre and cultural icon of modern China. His hugely famous solo song "How Can I Not Keep Thinking of Her?" ("Jiaowo ruhe buxiang ta" 教我如何不想她) was remarkable in terms of expression. Aside from his creative use of harmonic progression, modulation, and different rhythmic configurations in the vocal line and piano accompaniment, he also skillfully brought the idea of romantic love into the lyrics. Marriage for love, as opposed to traditional arranged marriage, was a new social phenomenon after the May Fourth movement, and it was gaining traction in China at the time. Although this song was written almost a century ago, it continues to be popular in most Chinese-speaking communities in Asia and North America (Liu, 2009: 141).

Huang Zi 黃自 (1904–38) was born in Shanghai, where he undertook modern school education and training in school songs and early music education. In 1924, Huang went to study in the United States, first at Oberlin College and then at Yale University, where he focused on Western music and composition. While at Yale, he composed an overture called *In Memoriam*, which is believed to be the first large-scale orchestral work by a Chinese composer. The piece was greeted with the approval of Huang's composition teacher, David Stanley Smith (1877–1949), and it was equally well received by a US audience when it was performed by the New Haven Symphony in a public concert the same year. The piece was written in the musical language of the late Romantic style, with little reference to Chinese music. Prior to Huang's American success, no Chinese musicians had achieved such recognition.

Huang returned to China in 1929 and began to develop a personal style as he composed some of his best-known songs. He also taught at the University of Shanghai, the National Music College, and other music schools. In 1935, he established the Shanghai Orchestra, the first all-Chinese orchestra. Some of his students, including He Luting, Ding Shande, Lin Shengxi, and Liu Xue'an 劉雪庵 (1905–85), became influential composers and greatly expanded the field of composition in China. Despite the success of Huang's orchestral work in the United States, he is best known in China for his vocal works, including "Philosophical Song" ("Tianlunge" 天倫歌, 1935); *Plum Blossoms in the Snow* (*Taxue xunmei* 踏雪尋梅, 1933), a large cantata based on the poem "A Song of Immortal Regret" ("Chang hen ge" 長恨歌) by the renowned Tang-dynasty poet Bai Juyi 白居易 (772–846); "Flower in the Mist" ("Huafeihua" 花非花, 1935); "Lotus Song" ("Cailianyao" 採蓮謠, 1935); and "Ability" ("Benshi" 本事, 1930). Each has become canonic in the repertory of Chinese vocal tradition.

Xiao Youmei was a musicologist, educator, and composer. Xiao's contribution to the field of music was extensive and far reaching. While he is frequently cited as having established the first music conservatory in China and having contributed to the development of China's music education, he was also a prolific writer and composer. He wrote 102 choral works, including solo, two-part, three-part, and four-part choral pieces. In addition, he composed three piano solos, one string quartet, and two instrumental pieces.

While Xiao's musical idiom mostly adopted the diatonic harmonic style of nineteenth-century Europe, he paid particular attention to lyrics and how to fit them to melody. One of the most remarkable achievements of his musical output was his contribution to the genre of *xuetang yuege*. With his five volumes of school songs, he played an important role in establishing the genre, much like Shen Xingong and Zhao Yuanren. On the one hand, as Xiao was one of the pioneers of Chinese music, his musical style could be described as transitional and experimental in its fusing of Chinese and European music through his individual musical expression. On the other hand, his music has also been criticized by a recent scholar for lacking in structure, climax, and modulation compared to standard European musical practice (Liu, 2009: 105). But perhaps Xiao's intentions have been misunderstood. In his music, we hear a unique individual voice and compositional technique that captured the spirit of his time, evidence of liberated movement rather than of a composer with deficient training in Western music. Even so, his contribution to modern Chinese music lies not so much in what and how he wrote but rather in his attempt to open up a space to allow for individual musical expression during a period when traditional values and habits clashed with new ones.

The contributions of these three composers firmly instituted the field of composition in China, and their impacts were far reaching. While Shen Xingong's school songs instigated the tradition of singing and composing in Western styles, Huang, Zhao, and Xiao perfected the art of composition through their orchestral output and song writing. As these figures raised Chinese music writing to a level comparable to that of their Western counterparts, they created the field of composition for modern Chinese music. By writing music that clearly demonstrated not only their mastery of the languages of the Western art tradition and Chinese musical culture but also their individual artistry, they opened the door for later composers to explore their own stylistic preferences. Zhao's art songs transformed the practice of writing *xuetang yuege* by infusing his songs with artistic sensibility and complexity, bringing intricate piano accompaniment and complicated harmony into most of them. His *Collection of New Songs and Poetry* (*Xin shige ji* 新詩歌集, 1928), containing fourteen of his original compositions, is a leading example of how he illustrated his artistry as a composer. Along with other composers of their time, Huang, Zhao, and Xiao forged a new path and developed a new arena for the aspiring composers and composition students who came after them.

Commodifying Music and the Making of Chinese Pop

The adoption of Western classical music in China substantially altered the way music was perceived, produced, and consumed. While music performed important functions in traditional Chinese society, new social formations in the early twentieth century necessitated new modes of consuming and listening to music. Through sound recordings, live concerts, and films, the essence of Chinese music was altered so that it became a commodity, a status symbol of the bourgeoise, and an object of exchange across the nation.

If the modern age is defined by significant developments in science and technology, Chinese music entered the modern age when it began to adopt Western recording technologies. This major technological thrust greatly altered the way Chinese music was transmitted. It also laid the groundwork for developing China's music-recording industry. For the first time in history, Chinese music entered a new mode of existence—one that presented a stark contrast to its previous status, of being tied to social functions and defined by traditional Confucianist values that saw music as part of the education of scholars.

When Thomas Edison invented the phonograph, a device for the mechanical recording and reproduction of sound, he could not have been thinking of the impacts it would have on Chinese music. The American recording engineer Fred Gaisberg went to China in 1903 in search of Chinese music for the growing record industry, under the sponsorship of the Victor Talking Machine Company. The traditional Chinese music he selected set in motion a chain of unexpected consequences that included the popularization of certain regional genres and famous performers across the nation, and it set the stage for launching China's entertainment and popular-music businesses. For example, the early French record companies focused mainly on Peking opera before branching out into other regional and popular music genres. Most of these companies began with recording traditional music but later expanded to become promotors of Chinese popular music, especially film music and Mandarin pop songs called "songs of the time" or "songs of the epoch" (*shidaiqu* 時代曲). Among the famous recording companies involved were: the Gramophone Company (in the UK); Victor, Columbia, and Zonophone (in the US); Pathé (in France); and Odeon and Beka (in Germany) (Ge, 2009).

The arrival of the recording industry soon gave birth to China's popular music. *Shidaiqu* was a type of song that combined jazz and Chinese folk songs, with Chinese lyrics sung in Mandarin, a language that was originally the dialect of Beijing but was later to become the national language for modern and educated Chinese. The key person responsible for the development of this type of music was Li Jinhui 黎錦暉 (1891–1967), a pop-song composer and writer from Shanghai who was also known as a father of children's literature and childhood music education. Li began his career writing books promoting Mandarin Chinese for children, and he later branched out into composing children's songs and musical theater for young learners. At the same time, he was also active in Shanghai's pop music and dance hall scenes. Li's principal conviction concerned the importance of creating music for the average urban city dweller, and it was with this mindset that he founded the Bright Moon Song and Dance Troupe (Mingyue gewutuan 明月歌舞團), the first Chinese song-and-dance troupe to feature all-female performers. He also began to train young female singers, including his daughter Li Minghui 黎明暉 (1909–2003), who purportedly sang the first *shidaiqu* written by her father.

The song "Drizzle" ("Maomao yu" 毛毛雨), is a prime example of the musical fusion of jazz and Chinese folk elements. The song had a pentatonic melody and a vocal style similar to the high-pitched singing of Peking opera. This was accompanied by a late-1920s big band, the beginning of a trend in *shidaiqu* of using big-band accompaniment for Chinese melodies and singing styles. Li Jinhui was also responsible for training some of the most famous female singers of the time, including Wang Renmei 王人美 (1914–87) and Zhou Xuan 周璇 (1920–57). This early style of Chinese pop incorporated various popular Western music genres, such as Latin dance, producing a type of music that contained both Chinese and Western elements. Some *shidaiqu* were composed in the traditional Chinese idiom but followed a Western principle of composition, while others were formed largely in a Western style but were accompanied by traditional Chinese or Western instrumentation.

Chinese pop music was intrinsic to the development of China's film music, which has a shorter history than that of Chinese pop music. Although silent film was introduced in China in 1896, the first sound film in the country did not come along until *Sing-Song Girl Red Peony* (*Ge'nü hongmudan* 歌女紅牡丹) of 1931. As a way to boost film circulation and popularity, the film industry utilized the popularity of Chinese pop songs to their advantage. In 1931, the Lianhua Film Studio (Lianhua yingye gongsi 聯華影業公司) annexed the Bright Moon Song and Dance Troupe to secure an in-house supplier of Chinese-language screen songs and dance numbers for its talking pictures. Zhou Xuan's famous song "Shanghai Night" ("Ye Shanghai" 夜上海) originated in the movie *An All-Consuming Love* (*Chang xiangsi* 長相思, 1947); the songs "The Wandering Songstress" ("Tianya ge'nü" 天涯歌女) and "Four Seasons Song" ("Siji ge" 四季歌) were both penned by the famous Chinese composer He Luting for the movie *Street Angel* (*Malu tianshi* 馬路天使, 1937); meanwhile, the song "Blooming Flowers and the Full Moon" ("Yueyuan huahao" 月圓花好) was produced for the movie *Story of the Western Chamber* (*Xi xiang ji* 西廂記, 1940). Each genre benefited from the popularity of the other when combined.

In tandem, the recorded and film-music industries created a new platform for music composition and creativity. Many composers and scriptwriters such as Li Jinhui, He Luting, Tian Han 田漢 (1898–1968), and Nie Er, who were writing Western-style Chinese music, were active in the popular entertainment arena. Their contributions to these fields cemented unique characteristics of mixing Western and Chinese music for China's modern music industry during the first half of the twentieth century. The rise of recorded music in the early 1900s, closely linked to the music industries in Europe and the United States, laid the foundation for the burgeoning of the recorded music industry in China from the 1950s onward.

Conclusion

Since my aim in this chapter was to highlight multiple expressions of modernity, I have identified five significant moments for modernity's formation in Chinese musical contexts. Each moment stemmed from specific agendas and rationales, and the music produced in each formed a unique interpretation and expression of modernity. Although these moments arose at different times in the first half of the twentieth century, they intertwined in subtle ways while being informed by larger social contexts and elements of the cultural ethos of the period. As a response to the specific social environment, each moment often appeared as individual rationalized and authoritative formations of development and progress in the name of modernity (Comaroff and Comaroff, 1993: xxx). Rather than pointing to a single incident or a particular event that created China's modern music, my intention is to show how cumulative energies and dynamics of a shifting society shaped the trajectories of the people modernizing Chinese music according to how they defined and expressed the concept in music and behavior.

Learning about these moments is valuable in understanding the shifting foundations of Chinese music and what drove individuals like the intellectual Fei Shi to push for Chinese music modernization at the very beginning of the twentieth century. The process of modernization is sometimes seen as synonymous with Westernization in ethnomusicology (Kartomi, 1981; Nettl, 2005). In Bruno Nettl's terminology, Westernization is the extreme case of modernization, entailing "the substitution of central features of Western music for their non-Western analogs, often with the sacrifice of essential facets of the tradition" (1985: 20). The Chinese case reveals a different scenario, and it would be erroneous to equate the two processes.

To equate Westernization with modernization inadvertently renders local musicians passive. The five moments outlined in this chapter reveal the considerable agency involved in adapting Western musical practices. In the case of *xuetang yuege*, the use of vernacular Chinese in lyrics and selected Chinese folksongs as melodies is result of a process of domestication involving the active participation of local musicians. School songs were composed with students of the new education system in mind, and their themes and lyrics were deliberately chosen. In the field of composition, composers began to experiment with the techniques of mixing Chinese musical elements with Western harmonic practices, thereby asserting their individual identities. New compositional styles created by early composers not only established the field of Chinese composition but also inadvertently heralded the style of intercultural composition, long before the style came into vogue in more recent years.

The personal visions of modernity held by the important figures discussed in this chapter produced specific materials that helped realize China's ambitions to be modern. Over time, the actions of these people have helped generate a larger picture of musical modernity and produced lasting effects on the nation. The musical modernizing project is notable for its multiple dimensions; outlined above are five significant modernist moments that set the project in motion. These moments are cumulative in effect because of their overlaps. This makes the achievements of each moment historic in nature and historical in scope.

To fully understand musical modernity in China, it should be viewed from insiders' perspectives and with particular reference to context (see for example, Lau, 2007). Although modernity is a global phenomenon, its impacts are never universal, with receptions changing according to time and place. Lisa Rofel reports exchanges on the subject with people from all walks of life in 1990s China, finding that they continue to hold strong views on modernization, development, the West, backwardness, and progress (Rofel, 1999: xi). These keywords have been around since the turn of the twentieth century, but their contemporary relevance indicates that the pursuit of modernity, whether at the national or personal level, is far from complete. Only time will tell what modernity will mean in the future of China's ever-changing sociopolitical conditions.

Glossary

baihua 白話, writing based on vernacular speech
Beijing daxue yinyue yanjiuhui 北京大學音樂研究會, Peking University Music Research Association, founded in 1916 and later renamed Beijing daxue yinyue chuanxisuo 北京大學音樂傳習所, Peking University Institute of Music Transmission and Learning
"Benshi" 本事, "Ability," 1930 song by Huang Zi
Cai Yuanpei 蔡元培, president of Peking University (1868–1940)
"Cailianyao" 採蓮謠, "Lotus Song," 1935 song by Huang Zi
Chang xiangsi 長相思, *An All-Consuming Love*, 1947 film directed by He Shaochang 何兆璋
Ding Shande 丁善德, composer (1911–95)
erhu 二胡, two-stringed fiddle
Fei Shi 匪石, scholar (1884–1959)
Ge'nü hongmudan 歌女紅牡丹, *Sing-Song Girl Red Peony*, first Chinese sound film (1931)
guqin 古琴, zither
Guoli yinyue zhuanke xuexiao 國立音樂專科學校, National Academy of Music, founded 1927
He Luting 賀綠汀, composer (1903–1999)
Hu Shih 胡適 (or Hu Shi), language reformer and diplomat (1891–1962)
"Huafeihua" 花非花 "Flower in the Mist," 1935 song by Huang Zi
Huang Zi 黃自, composer (1904–1938)
jiahua 加花, "adding flowers," practice of adding musical ornamentation
jianzipu 減字譜, abbreviated character notation for *guqin*
Jiang Kui 姜夔, songwriter (1155–1221)
"Jiaowo ruhe buxiang ta" 教我如何不想她, "How Can I Not Keep Thinking of Her?," song by Zhao Yuanren
kunqu 崑曲, traditional opera genre
Li Hongzhang 李鴻章, Qing-dynasty general and politician (1823–1901)
Li Shutong 李叔同, composer, painter, and Buddhist monk (1880–1942)
Li Jinhui 黎錦暉, composer and educational writer (1891–1967)
Li Minghui 黎明暉, singer and film actress (1909–2003)
Lianhua yingye gongsi 聯華影業公司, Lianhua [United China] Film Studio
Lin Shengyi 林聲翕, composer (1914–1991)
Liu Tianhua 劉天華, composer, instrumentalist, and music reformer (1895–1932)
Liu Xue'an 劉雪庵, composer (1905–1985)
Malu tianshi 馬路天使, *Street Angel*, 1937 film
"Maomao yu" 毛毛雨, "Drizzle," 1927 song by Li Jinhui
Mingyue gewutuan 明月歌舞團, Bright Moon Song and Dance Troupe, formed by Li Jinhui (c. 1927)
modeng 摩登, 1920s Chinese term for "modern"
"Naner zhiqi gao" 男兒志氣高, "Men Need to Have High Ambition," song by Shen Xingong (1902), later renamed "Ticao" 體操 ("Physical Exercise") and "Juncao" 軍操 ("Military Drill")
Nie Er 聶耳, composer (1912–1935)

pipa 琵琶, lute
qupai 曲牌, "labeled tune," a short tune that can be reused with different sets of lyrics
Shen Xingong 沈心工, composer (1870–1947)
shidaiqu 時代曲, "songs of the epoch," 1920s genre that combined jazz with Chinese folk song
"Siji ge" 四季歌, "Four Seasons Song," 1937 song by He Luting
sishu 私塾, private schools
Taxue xunmei 踏雪尋梅, *Plum Blossoms in the Snow*, 1933 cantata by Huang Zi, based on the poem, "A Song of Immortal Regret" (Chang hen ge 長恨歌) by Bai Juyi 白居易
Tan Xiaolin 譚小麟, composer (1911–48)
Tian Han 田漢, playwright and lyricist (1898–1968)
"Tianlun ge" 天倫歌 "Philosophical Song," 1935 song by Huang Zi
"Tianya genü" 天涯歌女, "The Wandering Songstress," 1937 song by He Luting
tianci 填詞, process through which a new text is set to an existing melody
Wang Renmei 王人美, singer (1914–1987)
Wusi xin wenhua yundong 五四新文化運動, May Fourth New Cultural Movement
Xi xiang ji 西廂記, *Story of the Western Chamber*, film (1940)
Xian Xinghai 冼星海, composer (1905–45)
xiandai 現代, present-day Chinese term for "modern"
Xiao Youmei 蕭友梅, music educator and composer (1884–1940)
xuetang yuege 学堂乐歌, genre of school songs
"Ye Shanghai" 夜上海, "Shanghai Night," film song popularized by Zhou Xuan
"Yueyuan huahao" 月圓花好, "Blooming Flowers and the Full Moon," film song popularized by Zhou Xuan
Zeng Zhimin 曾志忞, music reformer (1879–1929)
Zhao Yuanren 趙元任, linguistic and song-writer (1892–1992)
Zhou Xuan 周璇, singer (1920–1957)
"Zhuma" 竹馬, "Bamboo Horse," song by Shen Xingong
Ziqiang yundong 自強運動, Self-Strengthening Movement (1861–1995)

References

Bréard, Andrea. (2019). *Nine Chapters on Mathematical Modernity: Essays on the Global Historical Entanglements of the Science of Numbers in China*. Cham: Springer.

Chang xiangsi 長相思 [An All-Consuming Love], Directed by He Shaochang. Shanghai Huaxing yingbian gongsi [Shanghai Chinese Star Film Company], 1947.

Comaroff, Jean, and John Comaroff, eds. (1993). *Modernity and Its Malcontents: Ritual and Power in Postcolonial Africa*. Chicago: University of Chicago Press.

Duara, Prasenjit. (1995). *Rescuing History from the Nation: Questioning Narratives of Modern China*. Chicago: University of Chicago Press.

Ge Tao 葛濤. (2009). *Changpian yu jindai Shanghai shehui shenghuo* 唱片與近代上海社會生活 [Records and Social Life of Recent Shanghai]. Shanghai: Shanghai cishu chubanshe.

Huters, Theodore. (2005). *Bringing the World Home: Appropriating the West in Late Qing and Early Republican China*. Honolulu: University of Hawai'i Press.

Jones, Andrew F. (2001). *Yellow Music: Media Culture and Colonial Modernity in the Chinese Jazz Age*. Durham, NC: Duke University Press.

Jones, Stephen. (1995). *Folk Music of China: Living Instrumental Traditions*. Oxford: Oxford University Press.

Kartomi, Margaret. (1981). "The Processes and Results of Musical Culture Contact: A Discussion of Terminology and Concepts." *Ethnomusicology* 25 (2): 227–50.

Kraus, Richard. (1989). *Pianos and Politics in China: Middle-Class Ambitions and the Struggle over Western Music*. New York: Oxford University Press.

Lau, Frederick. (2007). "Context, Agency and Chineseness: The Music of Law Wing Fai." *Contemporary Music Review* 26 (5/6): 585–603.

Lee, Leo Ou-fan. (1999). *Shanghai Modern: The Flowering of a New Urban Culture in China, 1930–1945*. Cambridge, MA: Harvard University Press.

Lei, Xianglin. (2014). *Neither Donkey nor Horse: Medicine in the Struggle over China's Modernity*. Chicago: University of Chicago Press.

Liang, Ming-Yüeh. (1985). *Music of the Billion: An Introduction to Chinese Musical Culture*. New York: Heinrichshofen Verlag.

Liu Ching-chih 劉靖之, ed. (2009). *Zhongguo xin yinyue shilun* 中國新音樂史論 [A Critical History of New Music in China]. Hong Kong: The Chinese University Press.

Liu, Lydia H. (1995). *Translingual Practice: Literature, National Culture, and Translated Modernity—China, 1900–1937*. Stanford, CA: Stanford University Press.

Malu tianshi 馬路天使. (1937). [*Street Angel*]. Directed by Yuan Muzhi, Mingxing yingbian gongsi, [Mingxing Film Company].

Nettl, Bruno. (1985). *The Western Impact on World Music: Change, Adaptation, and Survival*. New York: Schirmer Books.

Nettl, Bruno. (2005). *The Study of Ethnomusicology: Thirty-One Issues and Concepts*. Urbana: University of Illinois Press.

Qian Renkang 錢仁康. (2001). *Xuetang yuege kaoyuan* 學堂樂歌考源 [On the Origins of Xuetang Yuege]. Shanghai: Shanghai yinyue chubanshe.

Qian Renping 钱仁平. (2004). "Tan Xiaolin yanjiu zhi yanjiu (shang)" "譚小麟研究之研究(上)" [On the Research of Tan Xiaolin (Part I)]. *Huangzhong: Wuhan yinyue xueyuan xuebao* 黄钟: 武汉音乐学院学报 [Yellow Bell: Journal of the Wuhan Conservatory of Music], no. 2: 28–33.

Rofel, Lisa. (1999). *Other Modernities: Gendered Yearnings in China after Socialism*. Berkeley: University of California Press.

Shen Xingong 沈心工. (1904). *Xuexiao gechangji* 學校歌唱集 [A Collection of School Songs]. Shanghai: Wenming Shuju.

Shen Xingong 沈心工. (1905). *Xiaoxue gechang jiaoxuefa Instruction* 小學歌唱教學法 [Instruction Book for Primary School Singing]. Shanghai: Wenming Shuju.

Shen Xingong 沈心工. (1912a). *Chongbian xuexiao gechangji* 重編學校歌唱集 [Revised Edition of Collection of School Songs]. Shanghai: Wenming Shuju.

Shen Xingong 沈心工. (1912b). *Minguo gechangeji* 民國歌唱集 [Volume of Republic Songs]. Shanghai: Shangwu yinshuguan.

Shih, Chih-yu. (2012). *Civilization, Nation and Modernity in East Asia*. New York: Routledge.

Wade, Bonnie. (2013). *Composing Japanese Musical Modernity*. Chicago: University of Chicago Press.

Wang Yuhe 汪毓和. (1988). "Tan Xiaolin ji qi yinyue chuangzuo" "譚小麟及其音樂創作" [Tan Xiaolin and His Musical Creation]. *Zhongyang yinyue xueyuan xuebao* 中央音樂學院學報 [Journal of the Central Conservatory of Music], Issue no 3: 68–71.

Wang Yuhe 汪毓和 and Hu Tianhong 胡天虹, eds. (2006). *Zhongguo jin xiandai yinyueshi: 1901–1949* 中國近現代音樂史: 1901–1949 [Modern History of Chinese Music: 1901–1949]. Beijing: Renmin yinyue chubanshe.

Witzleben, Lawrence. (1995). *"Silk and Bamboo" Music in Shanghai: The Jiangnan Sizhu Instrumental Ensemble Tradition*. Kent, OH: Kent State University Press.

Xi xiang ji 西廂記. (1940).[*Story of the Western Chamber*]. Directed by Zhang Shichuan. Shanghai Guogying gongsi [Shanghai Guoying film company].

Yang, Hon-Lun Helan, Simo Mikkonen, and John Winzenburg. (2020). *Networking the Russian Diaspora: Russian Musicians and Musical Activities in Interwar Shanghai*. Honolulu: University of Hawai'i Press.

Yung, Bell. (1984). "Choreographic and Kinesthetic Elements in Performance on the Chinese Seven-String Zither." *Ethnomusicology* 28 (3): 505–17.

Yung, Bell. 1994. "Not Notating the Notatable: Reëvaluating the Guqin Notational System." In *Themes and Variations: Writings on Music in Honor of Rulan Chao Pian*, edited by Bell Yung and Joseph S. C. Lam, 45–58. Cambridge, MA: Department of Music, Harvard University; Hong Kong: The Chinese University Press.

Zhao Yuanren 趙元任. (1928). *Xin shige ji* 新詩歌集 [A New Collection of Songs]. Shanghai: Shanghai shangwu yinshuguan.

PART II

MUSIC GENRES AND PRACTICES IN EVOLVING CONTEXTS

CHAPTER 9

TRADITIONAL INSTRUMENTS AND HETEROPHONIC PRACTICE

ALAN R. THRASHER

Introduction

Musical instruments in popular usage today emerged soon after the end of the Zhou dynasty (c. eleventh century BCE–256 BCE). With the founding of the Han dynasty (206 BCE–220 CE), continuing into the eclectic Tang period (618–907) and beyond, many instruments from India and central Asia were introduced into China with the flow of Buddhism. Imported instruments arrived in several waves. Among the first to be introduced were the *pipa* 琵琶 lute, *konghou* 箜篌 harp, *di* 笛 transverse flute, *bili* 篳篥 reed-pipe, metal horns, and small percussion types. Well described in the *Tongdian* 通典 (*Survey of Institutions*, 801), *Yueshu* 樂書 (*Music Book, c.* 1100), and other sources, these instruments are also pictured in artwork found in the earlier Dunhuang and Yungang caves from the fourth century CE onward, and again in the important Wang Jian reliefs of the early tenth century.[1] Instruments imported after this period include the *sanxian* 三弦 long-necked lute, *yangqin* 楊琴 dulcimer, *suona* 嗩吶 shawm-type, and *huqin* 胡琴 bowed string types, mostly introduced from western Asian sources.

The following is an overview of the most significant common-practice Han Chinese instruments, together with an examination of their interaction within selected regional ensembles. The older, historic court ritual instruments will not be included in this overview. Most common-practice instruments have been well introduced in English and Chinese publications.[2] Their heterophonic interactions within ensembles, however, have received sparse attention, so I propose to introduce this performance concept first, after which the instruments will be better understood in perspective.

Heterophonic Performance Practice

Heterophony in Chinese music is locally known as *zhisheng ti* 織聲體 ("weaving sound form") or *zhisheng fuyin* 支聲複音 ("compound sounds"), not to be confused with the Western concept of polyphony (*fudiao yinyue* 複調音樂).[3] When viewed in comparison with Western textures and harmonic complexities, Chinese heterophony is sometimes assumed to be a rather simple system. As a result, it has not been treated critically in either Chinese or Western scholarship.[4] In practice, however, Chinese heterophony is a system of great sophistication, in which all musicians perform the same basic melody with simultaneous "variations" suitable to instrumental idioms and, importantly, in accordance with well-established interactive principles relating to musical texture.[5]

Traditional performance practice is governed by a number of guiding principles, or *guilü* 規律, essentially meaning "regular patterns" or, as one musician explained, "inner rules." Some "inner rules" are strictly followed (such as heterogeneous ensemble makeup, moderation of expression, and maintenance of unisons on strong beats); other principles allow for invention. First to be considered are idiomatic practices. The sound ideal in *sizhu* 絲竹 ("silk-bamboo") and other types of music requires heterogeneous distribution of instruments—that is, instruments of mixed timbres together in one ensemble (unlike, say, those in a string quartet). One instrument per part is the norm. Associated with each instrument type are specific idiomatic techniques which distinguish that particular instrument from the others. For example, on flutes, various finger articulations, trills, and fast passage work can be played with ease. *Sheng* 笙 mouth-organ techniques are minimal, but their performance in parallel fifths is distinctive. Most characteristic of the *erhu* 二胡 two-stringed fiddle are legato phrasing and string inflections, especially *huayin* 滑音 (portamentos) of varying types. The *pipa* lute and other plucked string instruments are performed with active finger articulations, notably finger rolls, pitch reiterations (or tremolos) on notes of longer duration, and octave duplications on after-beats. When these instruments are performed together, their combined idiomatic techniques—while not technically part of the variation process—form an essential part of the heterophonic texture.

Performance variation is known as *bianzou* 變奏. It is generally understood that musicians retain in their memories a basic skeleton of each piece of music (including melodic shape and beat structure). This is known as the *zhudiao* 主調 ("main melody") or, in academic circles, *guganyin* 骨幹音 ("melodic skeleton"). The "melodic skeleton" becomes the foundation upon which variations are created, notably by substituting pitches, adding melodic interpolations, and interacting with others in the ensemble.[6]

At the root of ensemble interaction is the variation principle known as *fanjian fa* 繁簡法 ("complex-simple"), in reference to the division of a melody into simultaneous variations of greater and lesser complexity. In practice, musicians say that the textural ideal should be *shangfan xiajian* 上繁下簡 ("complex above, simple below"), meaning that the higher-pitched instruments dominate with active melodic realizations and lower-pitched instruments support in more basic ways—often by simply sketching the melody. The resultant effect is one of contrast between "complex" and "simple" (or active and passive) forms of the same melody performed simultaneously.[7] This interactive practice is widespread in China. Some musicians see this dynamic as a manifestation of *yin-yang* 陰陽 philosophy, in which passive and active melodic realizations are mutually complementary, as the forces of *yin* and *yang* are harmonious.

With this understanding of basic performance practice, the common-practice instruments will be briefly overviewed in this chapter's subsequent sections, as classified within four categories by musicologist Hu Dengtiao (1982) and his late-twentieth-century colleagues. Following the introduction of each category, the heterophonic practices of three Chinese regions will be explored.

PLUCKED STRING INSTRUMENTS (*TANBO YUEQI* 彈撥樂器)

Indigenous plucked string instruments are almost entirely zither types used in ritual performances and, in the case of the *zheng* 箏 zither, in traditions outside of the court rituals. Most significant among the newer string instruments to emerge during the Han period are the *pipa* and *ruan* 阮 lutes and their variants. The *sanxian* lute and *yangqin* dulcimer (with struck strings) would be introduced into China nearly one thousand years later.[8]

The *zheng* is one of the historic, traditional zithers. It has a rectangular sound box of wood, with chess-piece-shaped bridges on a diagonal line, and variable numbers of strings—formerly of silk, subsequently of copper and nylon-wrapped steel in the twentieth century. The instrument's name was mentioned in both Zhou and Han sources as being onomatopoeic, based upon the sound of its strings: "*zheng-zheng*." The *zheng* is well represented in Tang- and Song-period art, showing it to be an important instrument in palace entertainment music. Zithers with thirteen, fourteen, and sixteen strings survived into the mid-twentieth century; larger *zheng* with eighteen, twenty-one, and twenty-three strings emerged during the late twentieth century. While generally considered a popular instrument in China today, among performers in the regional *zheng* schools—Chaozhou and Hakka in Guangdong province, and Henan and Shandong in central China—the *zheng* is considered a classical instrument.[9]

One of the first instruments to be introduced from India or central Asia is the *pipa* 琵琶 lute, which is well documented from the Qin and Han periods onward. Its image is found in the pre-Tang Dunhuang cave paintings and many carved reliefs. The name *pipa* is traditionally explained as being onomatopoeic, based upon its plucking technique: "*pi*" a forward finger stroke, "*pa*" a backward stroke. *Pipa* was initially a generic name for different varieties of plucked lutes, of which the bent-necked *pipa* with pear-shaped body and four strings (*quxiang pipa* 曲項琵琶) became dominant. Within a few centuries of its appearance, the bent-necked *pipa* (which at that time was held in a horizontal position and plucked with a large plectrum) became fashionable in court entertainment ensembles. The contemporary *pipa*, with an elaborately decorated curved peg box, emerged during the Ming-Qing period (1368–1911) from the bent-necked *pipa*. The strings are traditionally plucked with the performer's fingernails, though today usually with taped synthetic fingernails. The *pipa* has a large, virtuosic solo repertoire,[10] and it is considered one of the indispensable instruments employed in the "silk-bamboo" ensembles throughout China and Taiwan, notably in Fujian *nanyin* 南音 (also known as *nanguan* 南管) and Jiangnan *sizhu* 江南絲竹, as well as in accompaniment of Suzhou *tanci* 彈詞 narrative song.[11]

The *ruan* lute has a large, round resonating chamber covered with a soundboard of *wutong* wood, a fretted neck, and four strings attached to laterally inserted tuning pegs. The instrument is believed to have emerged on Chinese soil. Initially called *qin pipa* 秦琵琶 ("Qin-kingdom *pipa*") and by other names during the Han dynasty, this lute was used in Tang-period entertainment music, but its popularity faded over time and it survived marginally into the twentieth century. With the emergence of the concert-hall tradition during the mid-twentieth century, the *ruan* was revived and constructed in families, the tenor-range *zhongruan* 中阮 and bass-range *daruan* 大阮 becoming especially common.

Several other lute types are similar in construction to the *ruan*, possibly emerging from it—notably the *yueqin* 月琴 and *qinqin* 秦琴. The *yueqin* ("moon lute") also has a large round resonating chamber and lateral tuning pegs, but its fretted neck is short (*c.* 60 cm). On traditional instruments, its four strings are distributed in double courses and tuned a fifth apart. The *yueqin* is primarily an opera instrument, used together with the bowed *jinghu* 京胡 in Beijing opera. The *qinqin* ("Qin-kingdom lute"), on the other hand, has a smaller resonating chamber in a "plum blossom" shaped frame and a long fretted neck (*c.* 90 cm). Traditionally, the *qinqin* is strung with only two or three strings. It is primarily performed in Chaozhou and Cantonese music and opera of South China.

Imported into China after the Tang dynasty, the *sanxian* 三弦 (literally, "three string") was an adaptation of a central Asian three-stringed lute, possibly the *setar* or *tanbur*, with which it shares important structural features. The *sanxian* is constructed of a long fretless neck of redwood or other hardwood, its lower end passing through a small square sound chamber, which is covered on both sides with snakeskin (usually python), producing a banjo-like tone. Strings, commonly silk or nylon, are plucked using fingernails or a small plectrum. Sizes differ according to region, the most commonly seen being the "small *sanxian*" with a neck of about 95 centimeters, used in Jiangnan *sizhu* ensembles and *kunqu* 崑曲 opera.

One of the last of the string instruments to be introduced during the late imperial period is the *yangqin* 楊琴, a trapezoidal dulcimer with seven or more courses of metal strings, struck with two slender beaters. The *yangqin* is an adaptation of the Persian *santur*, which was introduced to coastal Guangdong province late in the Ming dynasty (1368–1644) and later accepted into the local Cantonese and Chaozhou music ensembles—where today it is of central importance. Subsequently, the *yangqin* was brought into Jiangnan *sizhu* ensembles, the accompaniment of narrative song and other traditions. On the oldest instruments, two rows of chess-piece-shaped bridges line the central area of the soundboard, each row with seven or eight bridges dividing the strings in a two-to-three relationship, providing intervals of fifths (e.g., *sol–re, la–mi*, etc.). Strings of copper (now of steel) run from fixed pins on one side of the frame, across separate bridges to tuning pegs on the opposite side of the frame. Since the late twentieth century, there have been many changes on the *yangqin*, which now has four or five rows of bridges, ten to fourteen courses of strings, and "quick-change" mechanisms to facilitate fine tuning and greater chromaticism.

Plucked Strings in Ensemble

The place of plucked string instruments—notably *pipa, sanxian*, and *zheng*—as the foundation of Chinese chamber ensembles had become well established by the Ming dynasty. In northern China, repertoire based upon this instrumentation was known as *xiansuo* 弦索 ("strings"). Indeed, thirteen *xiansuo* instrumental suites, notated in *gongche* 工尺 notation in the 1814 collection *Xiansuo beikao* 弦索備考, were already in performance during that period. In this source, four stringed instrumental parts are notated in heterophonic detail: *pipa, sanxian, zheng*, and *huqin*.[12] *Xiansuo* music is still performed in Shandong and Henan provinces, and its influence on the conservative traditions of southern China over the years has been profound. For example, Chaozhou chamber music of coastal Guangdong province, known as *xianshi* 弦詩 ("string poem") or *xianyue* 弦樂 ("string music"), is based upon the *xiansuo* instruments *pipa, sanxian*, and *zheng*—which the Chaozhou refer to as *santan* 三彈 ("three plucked"). As in northern *xiansuo*, bowed instruments and sometimes flutes may be added.

A brief excerpt from the Chaozhou classic suite *Hanya xishui* 寒鴉戲水 is notated in Figure 9.1. The *pipa, sanxian*, and *zheng* realizations of this melody are closely related, their differences being mostly idiomatic. Note that the ornamented *pipa* and *sanxian* parts (both with tremolo lead-in notes) are one octave apart. Within

FIGURE 9.1. Chaozhou *xianyue, Hanya Xishui*, reflecting moderate heterophonic interaction among the four instruments. (Excerpt from 1986 field tape.)

this ensemble context the *zheng* player is essentially performing a bass line, merely sketching the melody rather than embellishing it highly, as would be expected in solo performance. The *erxian* 二弦 bowed fiddle realization is only slightly varied, though more melismatic than that of the plucked strings, with other idiomatic variations as well. That these heterophonic realizations are stylistically close is due to the social makeup of the ensemble, all instruments being played by members of one family.[13]

Wind Instruments (*Chuiguan Yueqi* 吹管樂器)

Most wind instruments employed in the old ritual ceremonies retained their status as specifically court instruments. But two instruments, the *xiao* 簫 vertical flute and *sheng* 笙 mouth-organ, were also accepted into common-practice music making. Both are important instruments still used in ensemble music, the *xiao* mostly in Jiangnan and southern ensembles, also with *qin* 琴 and *zheng*, and the *sheng* mostly in northern ensembles. Principal among the new wind instruments to emerge during the Han period are transverse flutes and reed-pipes.

The flute today known as *xiao* is a vertical flute, with a notch at the blowing end (to facilitate tone production), five frontal finger holes, and one thumbhole. Several types exist, the most common being the long *zizhu xiao* 紫竹簫 ("purple bamboo *xiao*") and the shorter *dongxiao* 洞簫 of Fujian province and Taiwan, also known as *chiba* 尺八 ("1.8 [Chinese] feet").[14] The *zizhu xiao*, constructed from *zizhu* 紫竹 ("purple bamboo"), is a slender instrument with several long internodal sections and a U-shaped notch carved through the uppermost node. The *dongxiao*, by contrast, is constructed from *shizhu* 石竹 ("stone bamboo") or other thick species, with relatively short internodal sections and a U- or V-shaped notch at the top end, which is completely open. Clearly one of the most venerated of Chinese instruments, the *xiao* has an extended history in both ritual and common-practice music dating from the Zhou dynasty.[15]

The *sheng* is constructed of a cup-shaped wind-chest of wood or metal, into which seventeen or more bamboo pipes are inserted. The pipes are fitted with free-beating reeds near their bottom ends. Free-reeds vibrate when a performer closes a finger hole and blows through the blowpipe. The pipes' top ends are cut in graded lengths with a double-wing-shaped profile, believed to represent the mythical phoenix.[16] The *sheng* is mostly associated with the *sheng-guan* 笙管 ritual ensembles of northern China where, from Beijing (and neighboring regions) to Xi'an in the northwest, it is performed together with other wind and percussion instruments. It is also performed with *suona* in Shandong province and included in *chuida* 吹打 and *sizhu* ensembles of southern Jiangsu province and Shanghai, but it is rarely used in the string-based ensembles of southern China.

The *dizi* 笛子 transverse flute is constructed from varying species of bamboo, such as purple bamboo and *jianzhu* 箭竹 ("arrow bamboo"). Distributed along the upper surface of the flute are a blow-hole, a membrane hole, and six finger holes. Two types of *dizi* are historically differentiated: *qudi* 曲笛, the prevailing southern type; and the short *bangdi* 梆笛, the prevailing northern type.[17] Initially known as *hengdi* 橫笛 ("transverse flute") and by other names, the *dizi* is believed to have been introduced from central Asia (Xiyu 西域) early in the Han period. Employed in Tang-dynasty court entertainment ensembles, *hengdi* flutes (then without vibrating membranes) were included in ensembles together with *bili* and *sheng*, as they are today in Xi'an *guyue* 西安鼓樂 and Japanese *gagaku* 雅樂. During the Ming dynasty the *qudi*, with membrane, became the lead accompanying instrument in *kunqu* opera and subsequently in Shanghai-region instrumental ensembles. The *bangdi* was similarly employed in Hebei *bangzi* 河北梆子 opera and Buddhist ritual music of northern China. Today, *qudi* and *bangdi* are both important solo instruments and are used in the concert-hall repertoire.

The *guanzi* 管子 is a reed-pipe of bamboo or wood, with a large double reed inserted in the top end but without a bell at the bottom. The tube itself is short (*c.* 18–24 cm long), and it has seven frontal finger holes and one dorsal thumbhole. Due to its cylindrical bore and extended distribution of finger holes, it has a basic range of one octave and a fourth, above which several higher pitches can be obtained by overblowing.[18] Initially called *bili* 篳篥, the *guanzi* most likely emerged from a central Asian instrument. During the Sui and Tang dynasties, the *bili* assumed a lead position in court entertainment ensembles. Following a decline of usage in later court music, the reed-pipe became popular within Buddhist ritual music such as the Beijing-region *jingyue* 京樂 and Xi'an *guyue*, performed together with *dizi*, *sheng*, and *yunluo* 雲鑼 ("cloud gongs").

The *suona* 嗩吶 is a shawm type, typically constructed from a species of redwood or other hardwood, with seven frontal finger holes and one thumbhole. Its bore is conical and its exterior slightly scalloped in profile. At the top, a small double reed is attached to a metal staple; at the bottom, a large flaring metal bell is suspended by friction. Sizes vary according to region and function. The *suona* was introduced into China from central or western Asia, possibly as early as the thirteenth century, its name a transliteration of the Arabic *zurna* or central Asian *surnai*. Indeed, this instrument is strikingly similar to the *suernai* still played by the Uighur people of northwestern China (Liu et al., 1987: 296). By the Ming period, the *suona* was already established on the central plain of northern China, after which a large solo repertoire emerged during the twentieth century. Today, it is widely played during village wedding and funeral processions, as well as in traditional opera ensembles to announce auspicious moments.[19]

Wind Instruments in Ensemble

Chinese wind instruments traditionally are most prominent in the "silk-bamboo" genres of Jiangsu and Fujian provinces, and in the "blowing-hitting" genres of Hebei and Shaanxi provinces (and across northern China). Wind instruments are only occasionally included in the Chaozhou and Cantonese traditions of Guangdong province, where stringed instruments are predominant. Among the most important winds in southern Jiangsu (the Shanghai region) are *dizi* and *sheng*. These instruments are played together in accompaniment of *kunqu* opera (see Chapter 5), in which the *dizi* plays a lead role, doubling the melody in support of the vocalist. They are also played together in the chamber tradition of Jiangnan *sizhu* and in Su'nan *chuida* 蘇南吹打 as well (see Chapter 10 for background of *sizhu*). As seen in Figure 9.2, an excerpt from the classic *Zhonghua liuban* 中花六板, these two wind instruments perform heterophonic variations of the melody according to their idiomatic and other characteristics. Here, the *dizi* player assumes a leading role, though one of interacting with the other musicians. Of the three measures shown in the example, the *dizi* player performs actively in the first measure (using finger articulations) and again in the third measure with increased rhythmic density (compared with the *sheng* and alto-pitched fiddle, *zhonghu* 中胡). In the second measure, the *pipa* is more active. The *sheng* is basically a supporting instrument, the player performing the same melody in mostly even rhythmic values and in idiomatic open fifths—essentially an indigenous harmonic system. Also shown are simultaneous variations performed on *zhonghu*, which sketches the skeletal melody with minimal embellishment. Thus, in Jiangnan *sizhu*, musicians perform the same basic melodic skeleton according to their instruments' idiomatic characteristics and in "complex-simple" interaction with each other.[20]

FIGURE 9.2. Jiangnan *sizhu*, *Zhonghua Liuban*, showing an active heterophonic texture based upon differing idiomatic techniques and ensemble interaction. (Excerpt from 1989 field tape.)

The wind-string relationship is particularly interesting in Fujian *nanyin* ("southern tones"), which in Taiwan is called *nanguan* ("southern winds"), but in the Quanzhou region of Fujian province is historically known by its string-based name, *xianguan* 弦管 ("strings and winds").[21] The *nanyin* instrumentation is fixed at five instruments: *pipa*, *sanxian*, *dongxiao* (end-blown flute), *erxian*, and *paiban* 拍板 (clapper). The *zheng* zither, standard in Chaozhou and other *xiansuo* ensembles, is not included. The *pipa* and *sanxian* function as root instruments—in that they perform melodies

FIGURE 9.3. Fujian *nanyin* suite, *Bazhan Wu*, heterophonic excerpt from metered Section 1, showing a minimally ornamented *pipa* realization of the skeletal melody and a highly ornamented *dongxiao* realization. (Excerpt from 1979 field tape.)

strictly without embellishment—and the *dongxiao* and *erxian* are essentially coloring instruments. This relationship can be seen in a brief excerpt from the suite *Bazhan wu* 八展舞 (Figure 9.3). While the skeletal melody is performed on *pipa* (as notated in the old notations), wide-ranging freedom is given to the *dongxiao* to embellish. Thus, the plucked strings provide a sense of melodic stability, allowing the flute (and *erxian*) to add movement—a relationship local musicians suggest to be a manifestation of *yin* and *yang*. Most of the flute ornaments (such as upper and lower finger articulations) are idiomatic to the instrument, but a good *dongxiao* performer will take greater liberties, embellishing quite freely. These ornaments—the heart of *nanyin* music—can change with each performance.

PERCUSSION INSTRUMENTS (*DAJI YUEQI* 打擊樂器)

Chinese percussion instruments in common practice are of extraordinary diversity, encompassing at least a dozen drum types, clappers and woodblocks of different subtypes; bells, cymbals, and gongs are of equal diversity. The most common types are surveyed below, with emphasis on acoustical characteristics and ensemble relationships.

The oldest drums documented in China had barrel-shaped shells, with drumheads tacked to the shell at both ends. Most notable of the medium-size drums in common practice is the *tanggu* 堂鼓 ("hall drum") of between 20 and 30 centimeters in diameter, suspended in a stand and used in Beijing opera and percussion ensembles such as Su'nan *chuida*.[22] One drum of a different shape, used in *kunqu* opera and Jiangnan *sizhu* is the *diangu* 點鼓 ("point drum"), a smaller, flat frame drum of about 18 centimeters in diameter, with a thick wooden shell tapered toward the outer perimeter. The primary drum employed in Beijing opera accompaniment, and also in Su'nan *chuida*, is the *bangu* 板鼓 or *danpigu* 單皮鼓 ("single-skin drum"), consisting of a frame of thick hardwood wedges glued together in a circle of about 25 centimeters in diameter, covered on the top end only with pig- or cow-hide.

Clappers and woodblocks are primarily time-marking instruments. The oldest type of clapper in contemporary usage, the *paiban*, is constructed of five plaques of resonant hardwood (*c.* 25 cm in length) bound together with a connecting cord through their top ends. As employed in Fujian *nanyin* or *nanguan*, this instrument is held in both hands and "clapped" together on primary beats. A later variant is the three-plaque *paiban*, employed in Beijing opera, Jiangnan *sizhu*, and other genres. This clapper is held in the left hand only (suspended over the thumb) and swung to bring the plaques together, leaving the right hand free to strike a *diangu* or woodblock in alternation.

Woodblock types, such as *muyu* 木魚 ("wooden fish") and *nanbangzi* 南梆子 ("southern *bangzi*"), are used in Cantonese music, less often in other *sizhu* genres. The *muyu*, described in the Ming dynasty *Sancai tuhui* 三才圖會 (1609), is one of the oldest. It is most commonly constructed of mulberry or camphor wood, with a hollow interior resonating chamber and an exterior elaborately carved in a rounded abstraction of a fish. In the Buddhist context, the *muyu* is struck with a beater, in accompaniment of chant. The woodblock known as *nanbangzi*, essentially a *muyu* in rectangular form, similarly has a lateral slit on one side and an internal resonating cavity.[23]

Small *ling* 鈴 (bells) and *bo* 鈸 (cymbals), while morphologically different idiophones, are not always clearly differentiated in historical Chinese sources or by artists in cave reliefs. Pairs of small bells, *pengling* 碰鈴 ("colliding bells"), depicted in cave art of the fifth and sixth centuries and resembling Indian bells, are small hand-held clapper-less bells (*c.* 5–6 cm in diameter). Hemispheric in shape, these are made of a brass alloy and attached together with a cord through holes in their crowns. Pairs of small cymbals, historically known as *tongbo* 銅鈸 ("copper [alloy] cymbals"), are described in pre-Tang literature and depicted in earlier cave art, suggesting they were also introduced from India. Cymbals in use today are of various sizes, shapes, and regional names. The medium-size *jingbo* 京鈸 ("capital cymbals"), used in Beijing opera, measure between 15 and 20 centimeters in diameter. These and related cymbals of the *bo* type, have a large raised central bulb through which a strip of cloth or cord is tied for holding.[24]

Luo 鑼 (gongs) differ from bells and cymbals in that their area of greatest resonance is at their centers, not at their rims. Most Chinese gongs are made from an alloy of copper and tin (*xiangtong* 響銅, "resonant bronze"), hammered into various dish-shaped or basin-shaped structures. Gongs are described in the *Tongdian* as being "like large copper plates." Gong-type instruments may have originated in what is now south-central China, a region heavily populated by non-Han minority peoples, and in northern areas of Southeast Asia. Basin-shaped gongs, with tuned pitches, exist alone or in sets. In northern China, basin-shaped gongs known as *dangdang* 鐺鐺 (*c.* 15 cm in diameter, mounted in hand-held L-shaped frames) are depicted in sixteenth-century imperial processions and still employed in the villages of Hebei province. Other sets of basin-shaped gongs contain varying numbers of gongs in frames, the northern ten-gong *yunluo* being most common. *Yunluo* 雲鑼 are brass gongs with flat faces, narrow shoulders, and thin flanges extending outward; ten or more gongs are suspended in a single frame. These gongs are all of the same diameter (*c.* 8–9 cm) but of varying thickness—with thicker dimensions sounding higher pitches and thinner dimensions lower ones. The instrument typically has a diatonic range of a tenth and is played melodically. The *yunluo* is shown in Song- and Yuan-dynasty art, but it may have existed earlier. By the late imperial period it had become an essential ensemble instrument (together with *dizi*, *guanzi*, and *sheng*) in northern Buddhist ritual ensembles and in Xi'an *guyue*. Other basin-shaped gongs are found in regional areas.[25]

Dish-shaped gongs, used in Beijing opera and other opera traditions, are different in that their surface shapes are convex, with a flattened central striking area and relatively narrow shoulders. Their most distinctive acoustical feature, based upon metal thickness, is that their pitches change after being struck. For large gongs (*c.* 30 cm in diameter), generally known as *daluo* 大鑼 ("large gong"), centers are thicker than shoulders and rims, causing their pitches to descend; for small gongs (*c.* 22 cm in diameter), known as *xiaoluo* 小鑼 ("small gong") or *shouluo* 手鑼 ("hand gong"), centers are thinner than shoulders and rims, causing their pitches to ascend. These gongs, essential to Beijing opera, are performed together.[26]

Percussion in Ensemble

Most *sizhu*-type chamber ensembles employ time-marking *paiban* clappers, but differences abound. In Jiangnan *sizhu*, the three-plaque *paiban* is sounded on strong beats, with after-beats and rhythmic patterns played on a small woodblock (*nanbangzi*) or thin drum (*diangu*). In Cantonese music, strong beats are marked on *nanbangzi* or *muyu*, with other rhythmic patterns played on bells or very small woodblocks. In Fujian *nanyin*, the first beat of every metric cycle is marked on the five-plaque *paiban*, without other rhythmic patterns, except when four very small percussion instruments are added at the end of some suites for special effects (see notes 23 and 25). In Chaozhou *xianshi*, most ensembles consist of string instruments only, often without percussion of any type.

In *chuida* and related ensemble types, textures are dominated by larger percussion instruments. For example, in Su'nan *chuida*, *suona* melodies may be accompanied by up to five or six percussion instruments, typically with initial beats of four-beat metric cycles marked by *xiaobo* 小鈸 cymbals, fixed eighth-note after-beat patterns played on *xiaoluo* small gongs, and improvisatory eighth- and sixteenth-note patterns performed on *tonggu* 同鼓 or *tanggu* barrel drums. In addition, *daluo* large gongs are used occasionally for strong beat emphasis. *Chuida* melodies played on *dizi* flute tend to be accompanied by lighter percussion, such as *muyu*, *pengling*, *diangu*, and small gongs.[27]

In accompaniment of Xi'an *guyue*, stable quarter-note beats in four-beat metric cycles are maintained on medium-size *bo* cymbals for initial beats and small-size *bo* for beats two, three, and four. Over that base, repeating eighth-note and sixteenth-note syncopated patterns are played on the small basin-shaped gong *dangdang*, and other improvised rhythmic patterns are performed on the *zhangu* 戰鼓 or other large drums. Specific relationships among percussion instruments differ from one region to another, but lively drum patterns over stable beats (on cymbals or gongs) are common in most textures.

Bowed String Instruments (*Laxian Yueqi* 拉弦樂器)

The history of bowed instruments in China stretches back to the tenth century or earlier, when strings were scraped with a strip of bamboo rather than bowed with horsehair. The early ancestor of Chinese bowed strings is believed to be the *xiqin* 奚琴. The Xi were a northern tribal culture known for playing this instrument. According to an account by Chen Yang 陳暘 in his *Yueshu* (c. 1100), the *xiqin* had a neck of bamboo mounted in a bulbous tubular sound box that was covered on one end by a soundboard of thin wood. Unlike the present-day *erhu*, the two silk strings of the *xiqin* were set in vibration with a strip of bamboo and its tuning pegs were inserted into the front of the peg box. An important surviving example of this form is found in southern Fujian province, where a bowed instrument of very similar shape, the Minnan *erxian* 二弦, is still played in Fujian *nanyin*. Horsehair bows are first mentioned during the Song dynasty (960–1279), the *mawei huqin* 馬尾胡琴 ("horsetail fiddle") cited in poetry.[28] Due to their documented origin among northern ethnic minorities, bowed string instruments in China as a group were subsequently called *huqin* ("instrument of the Hu people" or "barbarian *qin*"). Different regional types emerged during the late imperial period. Two basic types may be distinguished, based upon the material used for the soundboard and the position of the tuning pegs: *erhu* and *banhu*.

Most recent of all *huqin* types, the *erhu* 二胡 has a long round neck of hardwood, with two tuning pegs dorsally mounted in the peg box at the upper end. The lower end is inserted into a sound box, which may be either hexagonal or octagonal in shape (rarely tubular), a piece of glued python skin (*mangpi* 蟒皮) serving as a soundboard. Two steel strings are tuned a fifth apart (d^1–a^1). The most distinguishing characteristic of Chinese bowed instruments is the position of the bow, the hair of which is inserted between the two strings and rosined on both sides. While the *erhu* is now the most popular and widespread type of bowed string instruments, there are related members of the *erhu* family, including: *gaohu* 高胡 ("high-pitched *hu*"), a specifically Cantonese instrument with a small round sound box and strings tuned a fourth higher than the *erhu*, usually g^1–d^2; and *zhonghu* 中胡 ("middle-pitched *hu*"), a slightly larger *erhu*, its strings tuned a fourth or fifth lower than the *erhu*, either g–d^1 or a–e^1.

More distant types, also with snakeskin soundboards, are high-pitched instruments employed in opera accompaniment. Best known is the Beijing opera *jinghu* 京胡, with its short neck and small sound box (both of bamboo) and strings of twisted silk. Related instruments exist in the various Chinese regions.[29] In southern China, the high-pitched Chaozhou fiddle is known as *erxian* 二弦 ("two string"). In northern China, the snakeskin-covered *sihu* 四胡 ("four-string *hu*"), documented in eighteenth-century sources, is different in that it has four strings, requiring a specially designed bow with two strands of bow hair to engage the strings for extra projection. In the later Qing dynasty, the *sihu* was played by both Mongolian and northern Han Chinese musicians.

Huqin types with wooden soundboards are of differing regional designs. The northern *banhu* 板胡 (literally, "board *hu*") is a high-pitched instrument with laterally mounted tuning pegs (i.e., both mounted through the same side of the peg box), used in accompaniment of *bangzi* 梆子 opera. Distantly related is the older *tiqin* 提琴 ("hand-held *qin*"), with its long neck and laterally inserted tuning pegs (similar to the smaller *banhu*). The *tiqin*, historically, was used in *kunqu* opera accompaniment. In southern China, the *yehu* 椰胡 ("coconut *hu*"), with a neck of moderate length and dorsal tuning pegs, is used in both Chaozhou and Cantonese music as a mid-range melody instrument. On all, the sound boxes are constructed from halved coconut shells, covered with a thin soundboard of *wutong* 梧桐 wood. As noted above, the Minnan *erxian* has a similar wooden soundboard, covering a relatively large resonator of carved wood, and frontally inserted pegs.

Bowed Strings in Ensemble

Bowed string instruments in the southern chamber ensembles have been assigned varying functions. The Minnan *erxian* in Fujian *nanyin* or *nanguan* appears to be one of the earliest types in present-day usage. Yet, its role in *nanyin* is one of support for the *dongxiao* flute. (This relationship is discussed above, in the "Wind Instruments" section.) In neighboring Chaozhou *xianshi* music, their thin-bodied *erxian* typically assumes a leading role. A brief excerpt of a Chaozhou *erxian* realization can be seen in Figure 9.1. Here, plucked string instruments dominate the ensemble. The Chaozhou *erxian* penetrates the texture with its high strident tonal quality and melismatic variations.

The Cantonese *gaohu* is similarly considered a lead instrument. When the Cantonese instrumental ensemble emerged during the late nineteenth century, local melodies and southern equivalents of Beijing opera instruments dominated the ensemble. A fundamental shift occurred about 1930, when the *gaohu* was invented. With its steel strings and penetrating volume, it became the lead instrument in the Cantonese ensemble, supported by the *yangqin*, *zhonghu*, *qinqin* (from Chaozhou music), and *daruan*. The *erhu*, another twentieth-century invention, is closely associated with the Shanghai region. As employed in Jiangnan *sizhu*, the *erhu* typically assumes a dominant melodic role, together with the *dizi*. The *zhonghu* functions as a supporting instrument. As seen in Figure 9.2, the *zhonghu*, with its lower range, usually performs a less active role (compared with *dizi* or *pipa*), remaining close to the melodic skeleton.

The Heterophonic Ideal

The Chinese system of heterophony, therefore, is the result of not one but several types of variation and performance practice—notably the "complex-simple principle," as well as idiomatic realizations and interpretive practices. These types function together as an organic whole to form the traditional sonic ideal. Of course, traditional Chinese music is still highly regional, and musicians in some conservative cultures (such as the Chaozhou and Hakka) tend to perform with moderate embellishment, while musicians in urban regions (Shanghai, Taipei and Hong Kong) tend to perform more freely and sometimes now with actual polyphonic imitation.

The essential element in performance, and one that gives Chinese chamber music its richness, is the spontaneity with which such decisions are made. Good performers, playing without notation but with a thorough understanding of local performance principles, improvise these variations, which are different for every performance. For these performers, "variation" is the lifeblood of their music and one of the primary determinants of good performance style.

Glossary

bangu 板鼓, drum of thick hardwood wedges covered by a skin, also called *danpigu* 單皮鼓 ("single-skin drum")
banhu 板胡, two-stringed fiddle with a wooden soundboard and laterally-inserted pegs
bangdi 梆笛, short transverse-flute type prevailing in northern China
bangzi 梆子, traditional opera genre
Bazhan Wu 八展舞, *Eight Exhibitions of the Dance*, Fujian *nanyin* suite
bili 篳篥, reed-pipe, subsequently called *guanzi* 管子
bianzou 變奏, performance "variation"
bo 鈸, cymbal type with a large raised central bulb, of different sizes
Chaozhou *daluogu* 潮州大鑼鼓, genre of traditional music from Chaozhou region,
Chen Tianguo 陳天國, Chaozhou music performer and scholar
chuida 吹打, "blowing-hitting," wind-and-percussion ensemble genres
chuiguan yueqi 吹管樂器, contemporary category of wind instruments
daluo 大鑼, "large gong"
daruan 大阮, bass-range *ruan* lute
daji yueqi 打擊樂器, contemporary category of percussion instruments
dangdang 鐺鐺, small basin-shaped gong
di 笛, transverse flute, commonly known as *dizi* 笛子
diangu 點鼓, "point drum," small frame drum
dongxiao 洞簫, vertical flute of Fujian province and Taiwan, also known as *chiba* 尺八
erhu 二胡, two-stringed fiddle, now dominant in concert-hall traditions
erxian 二弦, two-stringed fiddle, of three regional types
fanjian fa 繁簡法, "complex-simple principle," interactive principle in performance
fudiao yinyue 複調音樂, Western-style polyphonic music
Fujian *nanyin* 福建南音, classic ensemble music in southern Fujian province, known in Taiwan as *nanguan* 南管
gagaku 雅樂, Japanese court music, analogous to Chinese *yayue*
gaohu 高胡, "high-pitched *hu*," Cantonese two-stringed fiddle
gongche 工尺, notation system using simple characters to represent melodic pitches and aspects of meter and rhythm

guganyin 骨幹音, "melodic skeleton," shared melodic outline underlying heterophonic ensemble performance

guanzi 管子, reed-pipe of bamboo or wood, with a large double reed

guilü 規律, "regular patterns," basic principles governing traditional performance

Hanya xishui 寒鴉戲水, *Winter Ravens Playing in the Water*, classic suite in Chaozhou music

Hebei *bangzi* 河北梆子, traditional opera genre

hengdi 橫笛, historical designation for transverse flute

huqin 胡琴, general name for bowed string instruments

huayin 滑音, portamento, technique on bowed strings and other instruments

jiahua 加花, "adding flowers," interpolations added to a melody

jianzhu 箭竹, "arrow bamboo," used in flute construction

Jiangnan *sizhu* 江南絲竹, "silk-bamboo" chamber music from the Jiangnan region

jiezi 借字, "borrowed notes," variation through substitution of pitches

jingbo 京鈸, "capital cymbals," medium-size cymbals used in Beijing opera

jing erhu 京二胡, type of *erhu* used in Beijing opera

jinghu 京胡, small two-stringed fiddle used in Beijing opera

jingyue 京樂, Buddhist ritual music of the Beijing region

konghou 箜篌, historic harp type

kunqu 崑曲, genre of classical opera

laxian yueqi 拉弦樂器, contemporary category of bowed string instruments

ling 鈴, small bell

liuye qin 柳葉琴, "willow-leaf *qin*," three- or four-string miniature *pipa*, also called *liuqin* 柳琴

luo 鑼, gong, a general term for different gong types

mawei huqin 馬尾胡琴, "horsetail fiddle", historic type of two-string fiddle

mangpi 蟒皮, python-skin soundboard on the *erhu*

muyu 木魚, "wooden fish," woodblock in abstracted shape of a fish

nanbangzi 南梆子, rectangular woodblock used in Cantonese music

nanyin 南音, traditional music from Fujian, known in Taiwan as *nanguan* 南管

nao 鐃, large cymbals, hand-held on a small central knob

paiban 拍板, wooden clapper of three or five plaques

pengling 碰鈴, "colliding bells," paired small clapper-less bells

pipa 琵琶, four-stringed lute

qin 琴, seven-stringed zither

qin pipa 秦琵琶, "Qin [kingdom] *pipa*," archaic designation for *ruan* lute

qinqin 秦琴, "Qin [kingdom] lute," long-necked lute

qudi 曲笛, southern type of transverse flute

quxiang pipa 曲項琵琶, bent-neck type of *pipa*

ruan 阮, lute with large round sound chamber

Sancai tuhui 三才圖會, encyclopedia compiled by Wang Qi and Wang Siyi (published 1609)

santan 三彈, "three plucked," designation in Chaozhou music for the ensemble's core stringed instruments: *pipa*, *sanxian*, and *zheng*

sanxian 三弦, long-necked fretless three-stringed lute

shangfan xiajian 上繁下簡, "complex above, simple below," textural ideal in instrumental ensemble performance

shenbo 深波, "deep slope," large gong used in Chaozhou music

sheng 笙, mouth-organ, traditionally with 17 pipes

sheng-guan 笙管, designation for ritual ensembles of northern China

shizhu 石竹, "stone bamboo," thick species of bamboo used in *dongxiao* construction
sibao 四寶, "four treasures," two pairs of short wooden plaques, shaken in performance
sihu 四胡, four-stringed fiddle of northern China
sizhu 絲竹, "silk-bamboo," traditional chamber music genre of the Jiangnan region
Su jia ban 蘇家班, "Su Family Ensemble", Chaozhou music group
Su'nan *chuida* 蘇南吹打, wind-and-percussion ensemble from southern Jiangsu
suona 嗩吶, shawm type, with small double reed
tanbo yueqi 彈撥樂器, contemporary category of plucked string instruments
tanci 彈詞, narrative song tradition from Suzhou
tanggu 堂鼓, "hall drum," medium-size suspended drum
tiqin 提琴, "hand-held *qin*," long-necked historical fiddle
tongbo 銅鈸, "copper [alloy] cymbals," historic term for paired small cymbals
Tongdian 通典, *Survey of Institutions,* compiled by Du You 杜佑 (801)
tonggu 同鼓, moderately large barrel drum
wenluo 文鑼, "civil gong," very large dish-shaped gong
wutong 梧桐, paulownia wood used in musical instrument construction
Xi'an *guyue* 西安鼓樂, traditional ensemble music in the Xi'an region
xiqin 奚琴, ancestor of Chinese bowed string instruments
xianguan 弦管, "strings and winds," historical name in the Quanzhou area for *nanyin* music
xiansuo 弦索, "strings," chamber ensemble repertoire in northern China
xianshi 弦詩, "string poem," Chaozhou chamber music of coastal Guangdong province, also known as *xianyue* 弦樂 ("string music")
Xiansuo beikao 弦索備考, *Xiansuo Music in Reference,* detailed music score (1814)
xiangtong 響銅, alloy of copper and tin used in gong construction
xiangzhan 響盞, "resonating cup," small gong
xiao 簫, vertical flute, commonly made from "purple bamboo"
xiaobo 小鈸, "small cymbals"
xiaoluo 小鑼, "small gong," also known as *shouluo* 手鑼 ("hand gong")
yangqin 揚琴, trapezoidal dulcimer, with seven or more courses of metal strings
yehu 椰胡, "coconut *hu*," two-stringed fiddle with a coconut resonator
yin-yang 陰陽, field of philosophical thought and aesthetic practice
yueqin 月琴, short-necked lute, used in Beijing opera ensembles
yunluo 雲鑼, "cloud gongs," played as a set suspended in a frame
Yueshu 樂書, *Music Book,* compiled by Chen Yang 陳暘 (c. 1100)
zhangu 戰鼓, medium-large drum
zheng 箏, zither with moveable bridges and sixteen or more strings
zhisheng ti 織聲體, "weaving sound form," heterophonic principle of ensemble interaction, also known as *zhisheng fuyin* 支聲複音 ("compound sounds")
Zhonghua liuban 中花六板, *Moderately-embellished Six-beat,* classic ensemble piece in the Jiangnan *sizhu* repertoire
zhonghu 中胡, alto-range fiddle
zhongruan 中阮, tenor-range *ruan* lute
zhudiao 主調, "main melody," the melodic basis for creation of variations
zhuihu 墜胡, two-stringed fiddle used in narrative song accompaniment
zizhu 紫竹, "purple bamboo," used in flute construction
zizhu xiao 紫竹簫, "purple bamboo *xiao*"

Notes

1. For a comprehensive English-language review of instruments pictured at Dunhuang, see Zheng, 1993.
2. See the "East Asia" volume of *The Garland Encyclopedia of World Music* (2002); *The Grove Dictionary of Musical Instruments*, 2nd ed. (Oxford, 2014); and the Chinese-language sources *Zhongguo yueqi tujian* 中國樂器圖鑒 (Liu et al., 1992) and the journal *Yueqi* 樂器 [Musical Instruments].
3. *Zhisheng fuyin* can be literally translated as "branched voices and compound sounds," with "voices" meaning musical lines moving as branches. *Zhisheng ti* more exactly suggests a texture of "weaving voices or musical lines." These terms, in traditional usage, are not employed to identify polyphonic textures.
4. Gao Houyong (1981: 97ff) was probably the first to differentiate among several types of performance "variation" employed in Jiangnan *sizhu*, but he did not extend his discussion into other areas of heterophonic performance. His observations are summarized in Thrasher, 1993: 10ff.
5. The Chinese pentatonic structure, with its consonant major seconds and minor thirds and its absence of harmonic foundation, permits a wide degree of latitude for pitch substitution—an essential feature of the variation process. In music systems from other parts of the world, such as those based upon homophonic texture and heptatonic scale organization, the flexibility to perform concurrent variations by all or most musicians would necessarily be more restricted because of the functional separation between melody and accompaniment and the strength of the harmonic underpinnings (which limit the choice of substitute pitches). The Chinese multivoiced heterophonic and pentatonic systems allow performers the flexibility to contribute in different and varied ways.
6. The substitution of pitches is commonly known as *jiezi* 借字 ("borrowed notes"); adding interpolations to a melody is known as *jiahua* 加花 ("adding flowers"). For background on these concepts, see Thrasher, 2008: 81ff.
7. Roles of melodic leadership and support are considered essential to the texture. For example, in Jiangnan *sizhu* music, the *dizi* and *erhu* typically assume the role of lead instruments, though the plucked or struck string instruments *pipa* and *yangqin* are often melodically active as well. Supporting the *erhu* with a more basic melodic line is the *zhonghu*. Supporting the *pipa* and *yangqin* are lower-pitched lutes such as *sanxian* and/or *zhongruan*. For further information on Jiangnan heterophonic practice, see Witzleben, 1995: 89ff, and Thrasher, 1993: 4–20.
8. For information about plucked string instruments that were introduced into China but later disappeared, such as harps and other types, see Liu et al., 1992: 174–77, 226–27.
9. For an English-language summary of *zheng* schools and techniques, see the "Zheng" entry in *The Grove Dictionary of Musical Instruments*, 2nd ed. (Oxford, 2014); for illustrations, history, and contemporary developments, see Liu et al., 1992: 200ff.
10. For examination of the *pipa* repertoire, its performers, and its globalization, see Chapter 16.
11. The *liuye qin* 柳葉琴 ("willow leaf" *qin*, or simply *liuqin* 柳琴) is a three- or four-string miniature *pipa*, employed in local opera traditions of eastern China and in concert-hall ensembles (see Liu et al., 1992: 222).
12. For a transnotation of this extraordinary manuscript, see Cao and Jian (1955). A brief excerpt from one suite is transnotated and discussed in Zhongguo, 1984: 505.

13. This excerpt is transcribed from a 1986 recording of the famous Su Family Ensemble 蘇家班 (Su jia ban), led by the musician and scholar, Chen Tianguo 陳天國. This entire suite can be heard on the CD "Sizhu Chamber Music of South China" (Pan Records, 1994). For another realization of the same suite, see Chen, Su, et al., 2001: 51ff.
14. A more recent *xiao* variant designed to perform with *qin* zither has seven frontal finger holes and one thumbhole. It is simply a redesigned, very slender *zizhu xiao*.
15. For greater detail on *xiao* types and history, see the "xiao" entry in *The Grove Dictionary of Musical Instruments*, 2nd ed. (Oxford, 2014).
16. For an acoustical examination of the free reed and matching pipe system, see the "sheng" entry in *The Grove Dictionary of Musical Instruments*, 2nd ed. (Oxford, 2014).
17. The *qudi* is typically pitched in a^1 (all holes covered); short *bangdi* flutes are pitched in d^2, c^2, or e^2 (all holes covered).
18. Because the bore of this double-reed instrument is cylindrical, the *guanzi* sounds one octave lower than a tube of that length with a flute mouthpiece. Thus, it overblows at the twelfth rather than the octave, and it requires unusual fingering positions and breath pressure in mid-range. For details, see the "Guanzi" entry in *The Grove Dictionary of Musical Instruments*, 2nd ed. (Oxford, 2014).
19. For more on the *suona* in performance context, see Jones, 1995: 157–80, 312ff. Other wind instruments are used in Buddhist and Daoist rituals but not usually in *sizhu* or *chuida* ensembles.
20. Meter (or beat position) is another factor. My analysis has shown that the main thrust of creativity in *sizhu* music occurs over beats 2 and 4 (and selected after-beats), the skeletal pitches on beats 1 and 3 remaining mostly unchanged. In Figure 9.2, the four melodic realizations converge on beat 1, allowing greater creativity on the other beats. Thus, it is apparent that awareness of beat position is an underlying factor in Chinese heterophonic creativity as well.
21. It must also be noted that sections of the *nanyin* or *nanguan* repertoire are clearly related to, even derived from, the northern *xiansuo* tradition, discussed earlier. For details, see Lü, 2011: 141–43, and Thrasher, 2016: 180ff.
22. For other barrel-shaped drums similar to *tanggu*, such as the larger *tonggu* (used in Su'nan *chuida*) and the shorter *zhangu* (used in Xi'an *guyue*), see Liu et al., 1992: 18ff.
23. An especially distinctive instrument is the *sibao* 四寶 ("four treasures") employed in Fujian *nanyin*: four short plaques of bamboo or hardwood that are held (two in each hand) and shaken. Other clappers, woodblocks, and metal idiophones known to Moule during the early twentieth century are examined in his study of 1908: 12ff.
24. A second type, known as *nao* 鐃, is generally larger and constructed of thinner metal, with a very slightly upturned rim and a small central bulb, which is held directly. Both types are used in regional *chuida* and other percussion genres, opera ensembles, and in modern Chinese orchestras.
25. Smallest of the basin-shaped gongs is the *xiangzhan* 響盞 ("resonating cup"), a very small gong (c. 6 cm in diameter) suspended in a basket. It is struck with a thin unpadded beater in Fujian *nanyin*. Large basin-shaped gongs with flat surfaces and wide shoulders are found in Chaozhou music, notably the Chaozhou *shenbo* 深波 (literally, "deep slope," c. 60–80 cm in diameter).

26. Other gong types include knobbed gongs, such as those used in Chaozhou *daluogu* 潮州大鑼鼓, but these are rarely used in other ensemble music. Very large dish-shaped gongs with narrow shoulders or no shoulders, known as *wenluo* 文鑼 ("civil gong"), are found in Cantonese opera ensembles and Chinese orchestras. These gongs are suspended in standing frames and struck with padded beaters.
27. For more on percussion patterns in Su'nan *chuida*, see Jiangsu Juan Bianwei, 1998: 97ff.
28. For further information on the history of Chinese bowed strings, see Stock, 1993. For illustrations of the many types, see Liu et al., 1992: 236ff.
29. In Beijing opera, a slightly smaller *erhu* is called *jing erhu* 京二胡. In Shandong province, an unusual *erhu* type used in narrative song accompaniment is the *zhuihu* 墜胡, its two tuning pegs laterally mounted—one on the left side and one on the right. These instruments all have glued snakeskins serving as soundboards. For related instruments, see Liu et al., 1992: 242ff.

REFERENCES

Cao Anhe 曹安和 and Jian Qihua 簡其華, eds. (1955). *Xiansuo shisan tao* 弦索十三套 [String Music in Thirteen Suites]. 3 vols. Beijing: Yinyue chubanshe.

Chen Tianguo 陳天國, Su Miaozheng 蘇妙箏, et al., eds. (2001). *Chaozhou xianshi quanji* 潮州弦詩全集 [Complete Collection of Chaozhou String-poem Music]. Guangzhou: Huacheng chubanshe.

Gao Houyong 高厚永. (1981). *Minzu qiyue gailun* 民族器樂概論 [Outline of National Instrumental Music]. Nanjing: Jiangsu renmin chubanshe.

Hu Dengtiao 胡登跳. (1982). *Minzu guanxian yuefa* 民族管弦樂法 [Method for National Musical Instruments]. Shanghai: Shanghai wenyi chubanshe.

Jiangsu Juan Bianwei 江蘇卷編委, ed. (1998). *Zhongguo minzu minjian qiyuequ jicheng: Jiangsu juan* 中國民族民間器樂曲集成：江蘇卷 [Anthology of Chinese Instrumental Music: Jiangsu Volume], vol. 1. Beijing: Zhongguo ISBN Zhongxin.

Jones, Stephen. (1995). *Folk Music of China: Living Instrumental Traditions*. Oxford: Clarendon Press.

Liu Dongsheng 劉東昇 et al., eds. (1987). *Zhongguo yueqi tuzhi* 中國樂器圖誌 [Pictorial Record of Chinese Musical Instruments]. Beijing: Qinggongye chubanshe.

Liu Dongsheng 劉東昇 et al., eds. (1992). *Zhongguo yueqi tujian* 中國樂器圖鑒 [Pictorial Guide to Chinese Musical Instruments]. Ji'nan: Shandong jiaoyu chubanshe.

Lü Chui-kuan 呂錘寬. (2011). *Nanguan yinyue* 南管音樂 [Nanguan Music]. Taichung: Chenxing chuban.

Moule, A. C. (1908). "A List of the Musical and Other Sound-Producing Instruments of the Chinese." *Journal of the Royal Asiatic Society, North China Branch* 39: 1–160.

Stock, Jonathan P. J. (1993). "A Historical Account of the Chinese Two-stringed Fiddle *Erhu*." *Galpin Society Journal* 46: 83–113.

Thrasher, Alan R. (1993). "*Bianzou*: Performance Variation Techniques in Jiangnan *Sizhu*" *CHIME Journal* 6: 4–20.

Thrasher, Alan R. (2008). *Sizhu Instrumental Music of South China: Ethos, Theory and Practice*. Leiden: Brill.

Thrasher, Alan R., ed. (2016). *Qupai in Chinese Music: Melodic Models in Form and Practice.* New York: Routledge.

Witzleben, J. Lawrence. (1995). *"Silk and Bamboo" Music in Shanghai.* Kent, OH: Kent State University Press.

Zheng Ruzhong. (1993). "Musical Instruments in the Wall Paintings of Dunhuang." Translated by Antoinet Schimmelpenninck. *CHIME Journal* 7: 4–56.

Zhongguo Yinyue Yanjiusuo, ed. (1984). *Zhongguo yinyue cidian* 中國音樂辭典 [Dictionary of Chinese Music]. Beijing: Renmin yinyue chubanshe.

CHAPTER 10

JIANGNAN *SIZHU* IN THE GREATER SUZHOU AREA

Repertoire, Revitalization, and Sustainability

MERCEDES M. DUJUNCO

Introduction

Sɪzнu (絲竹, "silk and bamboo") presently refers to the music of ensembles composed of relatively soft-sounding string and wind bamboo instruments, accompanied by small percussion instruments, if any. The characters for *si* (絲) and *zhu* (竹) first appeared in the *Zhou Rites* (周禮, c. 2nd BCE), as part of the eight categories in the ancient Chinese instrument classification system called *bayin* (八音, literally, "eight sounds"), in which instruments are categorized according to a salient material used in their construction. *Si* generally referred to instruments made with silk strings and *zhu* to wind instruments made of bamboo, for the most part.

Jiangnan *sizhu* (江南絲竹) is arguably the best known among China's various regional *sizhu* traditions, most of which are based in southeastern China. There is governmental support for Jiangnan *sizhu*, and the area, particularly the city of Shanghai, is easier to access than most of the locales of other regional *sizhu* music. As such, most studies about *sizhu* deal with Jiangnan *sizhu*, and indeed most studies of Jiangnan *sizhu* focus on this music as it has been performed in Shanghai.[1]

Actually, the area in which Jiangnan *sizhu* has historically been performed at the grassroots level goes farther than Shanghai, to include cities, towns, and villages in both Jiangsu and Zhejiang provinces and, to a lesser extent, in Anhui province as well. Although not as much written about, Jiangnan *sizhu* continues to be performed in these places and, in fact, is thriving there. As Stephen Jones has written in his book, *Folk Music of China: Living Instrumental Traditions*:

> The present music [of Jiangnan *sizhu*] evolved mainly in the changing environment of a newly prosperous cosmopolitan city early in the twentieth century. . . . However, the Shanghai silk-and-bamboo music has remained much more traditional. The very ease of access to current urban practice makes it appear less urgent to pursue the traditional rural repertory from which it derives; in the long term, however, I hope the Shanghai music will be seen in this larger context, for the older layer in the villages is still there to be sought. The current Jiangnan silk-and-bamboo repertory can only be traced firmly back to the nineteenth century. It has become standardized, and limited, since the 1940s, but was formerly more varied. (Jones, 1995: 271–72)

In this chapter, I report on Jiangnan *sizhu* as I had found it performed in the county-level city of Taicang and in a village on the outskirts of Suzhou, both in Jiangsu province, during two separate visits in 2014 and in 2016. In the process, I show how this regional *sizhu* tradition has a much broader repertoire than the *badaqu* (八大曲, "eight great pieces") routinely performed in Jiangnan *sizhu* music clubs in Shanghai and how those other pieces have been reintroduced into the repertoire of Jiangnan *sizhu* musicians in Taicang, thus offering alternatives and disrupting the prevalence of the *badaqu*, even if only in Taicang. I also show that the setting in which Jiangnan *sizhu* is performed goes beyond the confines of music clubs exclusively devoted to performance of the genre, thereby also clarifying the different kinds of contexts and performers of this type of music beyond those already described by J. Lawrence Witzleben (1995) and several other Jiangnan *sizhu* scholars.

Locating Jiangnan in Jiangnan *Sizhu*

The region in eastern China that is immediately to the south of the middle and lower reaches of the Yangzi (Changjiang) river is often referred to as Jiangnan. From ancient times until now, Jiangnan has been a constantly changing and flexible regional concept. Like Lingnan ("south of the Nanling mountain range"), Zhongyuan ("central plains"), and Xiyu ("western regions"), it indicates an area rather than a specific location with a definite boundary. During the Tang period, what was known as Jiangnan was a huge expanse that included all of present-day Zhejiang, Jiangxi, Hunan, and Fujian, and the southern parts of Jiangsu and Anhui provinces. Beginning in the Ming period and until the early Qing, the land north of the Huai river and south of the Yangzi—which correspond to present-day Shanghai and the provinces of Jiangsu and Anhui—formally became Jiangnan province, with Jiangning (present-day Nanjing) as its capital. During the eras of the Kangxi (1654–1722) and Qianlong (1736–95) emperors of the Qing, Jiangnan province was divided into the provinces of Jiangsu and Anhui and ceased to exist as an administrative entity in its own right. Today, the term "Jiangnan" geographically encompasses the city of Shanghai, the southern part of Jiangsu, the entire Zhejiang province, the southeastern part of Anhui province, and the northern part of Jiangxi and Fujian provinces.

Aside from simply indicating a geographical area, however, Jiangnan is also a symbol of economic plenty. It has consistently been regarded as one of the most prosperous regions in China, with superior natural conditions, abundant natural resources, and a highly developed commodity production in a wide range of industries. After the Qing period, the notion of Jiangnan as a distinct economically rich and highly productive region superseded its geographical definition. Consequently, less wealthy areas such as those parts of Anhui, Jiangxi, and Fujian provinces, which had historically been regarded as part of Jiangnan from a geographical perspective, came to be excluded.

Perhaps more significantly, Jiangnan is also a cultural region, one which has always conjured up images of scenic water towns and villages, people of outstanding talent in the arts and letters, as well as beautiful women. From a cultural standpoint, Jiangnan encompasses the so-called Jiang-Zhe[2] area and part of Anhui province, all of which are seen as sharing many cultural similarities (see Figure 10.1). In fact, the region is not entirely linguistically homogeneous; although Yangzi Mandarin and Wu dialects are widely spoken, the dialects often take local variants that are not well understood outside each specific area of use.

FIGURE 10.1. Map showing the extents of the Jiangnan region from different perspectives.
(Image courtesy of Seasons in the Sun, from Wikimedia Commons,
https://commons.wikimedia.org/wiki/File:Jiangnan.png.)

In terms of music, there is also some disagreement among scholars who have written on the music traditions found in this region as to the exact places covered by the Jiangnan designation, but most include the southern part of Jiangsu province, the western part of Zhejiang province, and Shanghai (Qi, 2009: 10–14). Interestingly, most of the traditional music and opera genres found regularly performed therein are related and thus share many stylistic traits. The Jiangnan musical area is home to: *kunqu* (崑曲) opera and numerous related but lesser-known local operas sung in one or the other of the various Wu dialects; Wu folk songs (Wu *ge*, 吳歌); *pingtan* (評彈) sung storytelling accompanied by the *pipa* (琵琶) and *sanxian* (三弦) plucked lutes; *shifan luogu* (十番鑼鼓) gong-and-drum music and Su'nan *chuida* (蘇南吹打) wind-and-percussion ensemble music; and, most relevant to this chapter, the string-and-wind instrumental ensemble music now known as Jiangnan *sizhu*.

Jiangnan *sizhu* is a form of folk-instrumental ensemble music that has evolved and developed since the Ming and Qing periods out of an assortment of string-and-wind instrumental ensembles found in the Jiangnan region. At present, it is most commonly performed in the southern part of Jiangsu province, the northern part of Zhejiang province, and the city of Shanghai, an area that corresponds to the Yangzi river delta.[3] Before it was called Jiangnan *sizhu*, a name coined in the 1950s by a group of musicians in Shanghai, this string-and-wind ensemble music was known by different names in the various localities where it was often performed. In Shanghai and its environs, it was simply called *sizhu*, *guoyue* (國樂), or *qingyin* (清音) (see Li, 1993: 3). In the rural peripheries of Suzhou in Jiangsu province, it was called *shi'erxi* (十二細) or *xibapai* (細八派) (see Zheng, 1994: 877). A couple of other names are *xiyue* (細樂) and *shifan xiyue* (十番細樂).

Regardless of its name in different parts of the Yangzi river delta, an independent, standalone instrumental ensemble tradition performed on bowed and plucked stringed instruments, bamboo flutes, and reed mouth organs performed in a style distinct to this region did not come into fruition all at once but, rather, developed over a long period of time. Two theories are advanced by many scholars with regard to the origins and formation of the instrumental ensemble of Jiangnan *sizhu*. The first suggests that Jiangnan *sizhu* came out of the reformed *xiansuo* (弦索) instrumental ensemble section that accompanied *kunqu* opera, whose music had developed from *kunqiang* (崑腔), melodies popular in the city of Kunshan in southeastern Jiangsu (Qi, 2009: 25–28). In the mid-sixteenth century, Wei Liangfu (魏良輔), a musician from Taicang, instigated changes not only in the music and style of the dramatic singing of southern tunes (*nanqu*, 南曲) but also in the instrumentation of the accompanying ensemble. He and his son-in-law, Zhang Yetang (張野塘), reportedly borrowed the instrumentation of the *xiansuo* string ensemble music of northern China and employed it in the performance of southern tunes. The result has been termed *Wuzhong xiansuo* (吳種弦索, "string ensemble of the Wu [region]"), comprising *di* (笛) transverse bamboo flute; *xiao* (簫) end-blown bamboo flute; *sheng* (笙) reed mouth organ; *xianziqin* (弦子琴) and *tiqin* (提琴) bowed lutes; and *pipa*, *sanxian*, and *yueqin* (月琴) plucked lutes; with a small drum and a wooden clapper to provide percussive accompaniment. The replacement of the big *sanxian* in the former accompanying ensemble by a smaller *sanxian* and the addition of the *xiao* made for a softer and mellower sound—not unlike that of Jiangnan *sizhu*. Of course, similarity in instrumentation alone does not prove origin, although it might point to a similarity in sound and musical style and therefore a relationship between the two genres. However, a comparison of the music of *kunqu* and Jiangnan *sizhu* reveals that they have very few pieces in common and therefore this theory is inconclusive (Qi, 2009: 25–28).

Another oft-cited origin theory for Jiangnan *sizhu* suggests that it grew out of the melodic sections performed by wind and string instruments in alternation with the percussive sections of *shifan luogu*, a form of gong-and-drum ensemble music prevalent in the Jiangnan region since the Ming period. The instrumentation of the wind and string ensemble is basically the same as that of the above-mentioned *Wuzhong xiansuo* used in *kunqu*. *Shifan luogu* is divided into *cu* (粗, rough) and *xi* (细, fine) types. In the former, the melodic sections are led by the *suona* (嗩吶) double-reed wind instrument, while in the latter they are led by the *di* bamboo flute, which results in a finer sound. During the mid-1800s, *Luogu sihe* (鑼鼓四合, *Gongs and Drums Four Unified*), a suite of pieces in the *shifan luogu* repertoire, was popular among amateur performers of this type of gong-and-drum ensemble in the western suburbs of Shanghai. It is said that the first group of Jiangnan *sizhu* pieces were drawn from the *sizhu* melodic sections of *Luogu sihe*, although there are no adequate written sources to absolutely attest to this.[4]

Meanwhile, the musicologist Wu Guodong (伍國棟) takes a more cautious, overarching approach, not designating any specific genre in any particular place or performed by any particular group as the point of origin of Jiangnan *sizhu*, preferring instead to bring up known antecedents during its formative phase. He uses the term "matrix" to refer to the various *sizhu*, *xiyue*, and *qingyue* wind-and-string instrumental ensembles that circulated widely in the Jiangnan region during the Ming and Qing periods and that a group of literati—deeply nourished by Wu culture—further modified, embellished, and shaped. These ensembles, Wu says, can be traced back to the *xiyue*, *qingyue*, and other small instrumental ensembles of the Song period, and even further to the *qingshangyue* (清商樂) ensemble during the Eastern Jin (266–420 CE) and Northern and Southern Dynasties (420–589 CE) period that featured a conglomeration of string and wind instruments. Wu argues that it is this matrix that musicians in Shanghai in the 1920s drew from, performing their silk-and-bamboo ensemble music within the context of literati gatherings (*yaji*, 雅集) and, in the 1950s, renaming it Jiangnan *sizhu* (Wu, 2010: 74).

By then, a core ensemble included a *di* bamboo flute, an *erhu* (二胡) bowed fiddle, a *pipa*, and a *yangqin* (扬琴) dulcimer. Supporting instruments included *xiao*, *sheng*, and *sanxian*, *ruan* (阮) lute, and/or *yueqin*, as well as small percussion instruments such as a *paiban* (拍板) clapper, woodblocks, and a small drum called *huaigu* (怀鼓). The size of the ensemble varies, depending on the availability of instruments and performers to play them, although nowadays the above-mentioned instruments are regarded as mainstays of a complete Jiangnan *sizhu* ensemble. On the whole, instruments are added as desired and a performing group can number from three to seven or eight people.

When performing indoors as a stationary music ensemble, Jiangnan *sizhu* musicians are often seated around a long rectangular table. This is especially the case during music sessions in music clubs (*yueshe*, 樂社) devoted to the performance of this type of music, with the *yangqin* dulcimer player at one end and the percussionist, if there is one, at the other.

Despite the wide geographical area covered by the term "Jiangnan" and the broad expanse of the Yangzi river delta wherein Jiangnan *sizhu* can be found performed today, as already noted, written studies on the genre have mostly focused on its performance in music clubs devoted to this music in and around the city of Shanghai. Of the English-language studies on Jiangnan *sizhu*, the first comprehensive ethnomusicological monograph on this Chinese regional string-and-wind ensemble music tradition was J. Lawrence Witzleben's, *"Silk and Bamboo" Music in Shanghai: The Jiangnan Sizhu Instrumental Ensemble Tradition* (1995). Based on fieldwork from 1981 to 1985, Witzleben studied members of nine music clubs, who met every week in Shanghai to perform for pleasure and recreation. His writing seems to have established Jiangnan *sizhu* as typically occurring indoors, not unlike chamber music in the Western art-music tradition, often in the context of music clubs, and, sometimes, in the context of tea houses (see Witzleben, 1995: 23–36; and Witzleben, 1987).

Jiangnan *sizhu*, however, is also performed in the rural outskirts of Shanghai and in rural areas of southern Jiangsu and western Zhejiang, and it continues to flourish in those locations.[5] In addition, Jiangnan *sizhu* is also performed in settings other than those of indoor tea houses and music clubs.[6] It is performed in connection with calendrical, life-cycle, and religious rituals (Jones, 1995: 250; Chow-Morris, 2010), many of which take place outdoors, as well as in connection with *kunqu* and regional opera forms (see Stock, 2002). This is particularly the case in rural areas, where there is greater observance of traditional festivals, thus probably accounting for the tendency of rural Jiangnan *sizhu* traditions to be louder and more boisterous than their urban counterparts, making use of gongs, cymbals, and other percussion instruments used in Daoist *shifan* gong-and-drum music in concert and in alternation with subdued-sounding wind and stringed instruments (see Jones, 1995: 271). These and other features distinguish rural Jiangnan *sizhu* practices from those of the Shanghai music clubs and were evident in performances of Jiangnan *sizhu* I witnessed in Taicang and in Tianchi village on the outskirts of Suzhou during visits in 2014 and 2016 respectively.

Jiangnan *Sizhu* in Taicang: New Lives for Old Tunes

Taicang is a county-level city located south of the Yangzi river estuary, bordered by Shanghai to the south and Kunshan to the southwest. Together with the latter, it falls under the jurisdiction of Suzhou, whose city proper is 53 kilometers further southwest (see Figure 10.2). Taicang is reportedly often referred to as the *sizhu zhi xiang* (絲竹之鄉, "hometown of silk and bamboo [music]"), because of its great number of Jiangnan *sizhu* musicians and music clubs, which comprised almost half the total number of those in the whole administrative area of Suzhou in 1997 (Ma et al., 1999: 5). In his book about Taicang's Jiangnan *sizhu* music scene, the Taicang native and local music historian, Gao Xuefeng (高雪峰), goes so far as to say that Jiangnan *sizhu* originated in his hometown during the reigns of the Ming-dynasty Jiaqing (1521–67) and Longqing (1567–72) emperors (Gao, 2010: 24). As mentioned above, Taicang was the hometown of Wei Liangfu, and his reforms in the mid-sixteenth century resulted in the emergence of *kunqu* opera, which then acted as a progenitor of many later regional opera forms in the Jiangnan area. Gao thus suggests that the origin of Jiangnan *sizhu* is tied to that of *kunqu*.

In 2004, a compact-disc recording called *Taicang Jiangnan sizhu shidaqu* (太倉江南絲竹十大曲, *Ten Great Pieces of Jiangnan* Sizhu *in Taicang*; Taicang, 2003) was given to me by one of the musicians who had performed on it. This alerted me to Taicang and a larger repertoire of Jiangnan *sizhu* pieces performed there other than the so-called *badaqu* played in most music clubs in Shanghai.[7] It contained ten pieces that I had not come across before, all rendered in the style of Jiangnan *sizhu*. Gao Xuefeng wrote that aside from *Sanliu* (三六, *Three-Six*), *Xingjie*, and other pieces commonly considered part of the "eight great pieces," others that have been popular and often been performed in Taicang include *Wuyeti* (烏夜啼, *Crows Crying at Night*), *Huaihuang* (槐黃, *Yellow Chinese Scholar Tree*), *Chunhua qiuyue* (春花秋月, *Spring Flowers and Autumn Moon*), and *Taizi qiche* (太子騎車, *The Crown Prince Rides the Carriage*), among many others native to the region and strong in regional flavor (Gao, 2010: 24). The first three of these latter four pieces are featured in the recording.

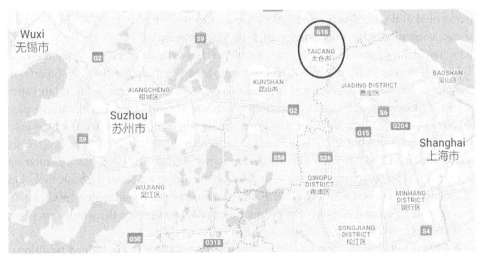

FIGURE 10.2. Area of Jiangsu province showing the Suzhou metropolitan area, which includes the county-level cities of Taicang (encircled) and Kunshan in relation to Shanghai.

Witzleben has explained the pleasure derived by Jiangnan *sizhu* aficionados in Shanghai who repeatedly perform an extremely small body of music. He attributes it to their appreciation of subtle changes and nuances in the interpretation of the same handful of pieces by different performers or even by the same performer on different occasions (Witzleben, 1995: 26). Even though this intensity of focus is to be admired, the small and limited repertoire and the requisite possession of the necessary sensibility to detect and appreciate such subtle nuances are not helping Jiangnan *sizhu* music clubs in Shanghai attract more and younger players and so ensure the continuity of the tradition. The average age of musicians in the Shanghai music clubs that I visited was about sixty-five. During my visits to a couple of the music clubs there in 2012 and 2013, I even noticed a decline in the quality of the playing of even the most often performed *badaqu* pieces—*Zhonghua liuban* and *Huanle ge*—because groups had lost one or two of their older and musically skillful members. For this reason, I regard Jiangnan *sizhu* to be the most precarious in terms of survival among the various *sizhu* music traditions I have encountered.[8] It was therefore with a lot of excitement and optimism that I welcomed the news about the more expanded repertoire of Jiangnan *sizhu* musicians in Taicang because it meant that the complete decline of this music tradition could possibly be mitigated.

According to Gao Xuefeng, old local folk musicians recollected 135 named Jiangnan *sizhu* pieces that had formerly circulated and been performed in Taicang. The origins of these pieces varied, including folk instrumental tunes from various parts of the Jiangnan area, folk songs and ditties, "labeled tunes" (*qupai*, 曲牌) from regional operas, ancient melodies, as well as folk melodies from outside the Jiangnan area (for example, Chaozhou, Kejia, and Cantonese folk tunes) (Gao, 2010: 62–63).

I finally had an opportunity to visit Taicang on two field trips in March and April 2014 to learn more about the ten pieces on the CD and discover whether they were really part of the active repertoire of the Jiangnan *sizhu* musicians there or had just been performed and recorded for archival purposes. On my initial trip, I was able to make the acquaintance of the music historian, Gao Xuefeng, who led people from the Taicang Jiangnan Sizhu Research Office in welcoming me. Gao had arranged beforehand for the Taicang Jiangnan Sizhu Ensemble, whose members are featured on the CD, to perform five pieces for me, including some from the recording. In between renditions and after the whole performance, I asked questions regarding the repertoire and about the production of the CD. Mr. Gao and the ensemble performers enthusiastically answered my questions, and Mr. Gao referred me to his book on Jiangnan *sizhu* in Taicang (Gao, 2010), which he had handed to me earlier upon my arrival. The book has a chapter on "the ten great pieces of Jiangnan *sizhu* in Taicang," including scores of the basic melodies of the pieces in cipher notation. He also directed me to a published review by Gu Lijian that gave details about not only the production of the CD but also the whole process of reviving those ten pieces prior to recording them (Gu, 2003).

It turned out that the ten Jiangnan *sizhu* pieces on the CD are indeed traditional *sizhu* melodies that used to be performed by Taicang musicians. They had been chosen out of the twenty-four melodies included in a published collection (Ma et al., 1999).[9]

They were then edited and arranged, and some of the titles were revised, apparently to straighten out names that seemed wrong and did not aptly reflect the mood of the pieces or to make them easier to utter and recall. For example, *Chunyue qiuhua* (春月秋花, *Spring Moon and Autumn Flowers*) became *Chunhua qiuyue* (春花秋月, *Spring Flowers and Autumn Moon*); the first character in *Huaihuang* (淮黄), which refers to the Huai river, was changed to a homonym (槐), which refers to the wood of the *Sophora japonica* tree, also known as "the Chinese scholar tree." And for each of the ten pieces of music on the CD, a text description was written with a summary of its origin, a brief analysis of its structure, or appropriate vocabulary to aptly describe its mood (Gu, 2003). In short, the project was a large and deliberate effort on the part of the Taicang City Cultural Bureau (Taicangshi Wenhuaguan, 太倉市文化館), which raised the funds to resurrect and reintroduce some of the old traditional melodies that used to be performed by Taicang Jiangnan *sizhu* musicians "in the old days." This revitalization project was carried out from the mid-1990s through the early 2000s.

Central to the project was one person—the composer Zhang Xiaofeng (張曉峰), a Taicang native who returned to his hometown in 1994 upon retirement as a resident composer of the Shanghai Opera House. I had a chance to meet and interview him during my initial field trip. He had been commissioned to take charge of the endeavor, from the selection of the pieces, through their arrangement and reworking into Jiangnan *sizhu*, and including the supervision of their performance for the recording. He used the traditional Jiangnan *sizhu* technique of melodic variation as well as a melodic augmentation process known as *fangman jiahua* (放慢加花, "slowing the tempo and adding flowers"). *Fangman* refers to the doubling of the meter of each measure of the piece, which lengthens the duration of each beat, thus slowing down the overall tempo. Meanwhile, melodic interpolations are inserted according to the idiomatic techniques of each instrument—referred to in colloquial Chinese as *jiahua*. The result is the sounding of different timbres and pitches that are sometimes dissonant but resolve and achieve consonance at points wherein all the instruments simultaneously sound the same structural tones of the basic melody or *qupai*. The mostly conjunct melodic fillers make for a smooth and continuous flow of musical sound until the final sections of a piece, when the unornamented basic melody is often played at a fast tempo. In a well-blended ensemble performance, instrumental parts are integrated seamlessly, without any one part sounding too prominently or particularly virtuosic—a characteristic that scholars writing on Jiangnan *sizhu* have remarked upon as being reflective of a communal ethos and the Confucian virtues of moderation, balance, and refined simplicity (Thrasher, 2008: 163–70; Witzleben, 1987: 247–48; Witzleben, 1995: 118–25; Jones, 1995: 280–81).

In listening to the CD recording, one does not get the sense that the pieces have been arranged or recomposed, even though this was indeed the case. Instead, one gets the impression of simply listening to one of those souvenir Jiangnan *sizhu* recordings that music clubs like to produce to give to fellow Jiangnan *sizhu* enthusiasts, most of whom are members of other music clubs; the only difference is that the playing on this CD recording was excellent throughout and the production very professional. The reason for this impression of authenticity is the use of the technique of adding melodic fillers in between the structural tones of the melodies. Melodic variation is something that Jiangnan *sizhu* musicians execute often intuitively, such that it seems natural. Zhang Xiaofeng's written arrangement (Zhang, 2003) thus served more as a guide or a blueprint for musicians well-versed in the technique. Meanwhile, players who are learning Jiangnan *sizhu* could use the arrangements as actual scores to follow and perform note for note until they have internalized the melodies and grasped how to vary them according to the idioms of their individual instruments.

In three of the music clubs that I visited in Taicang, I observed musicians with cipher notation copies of the published music score for the ten recorded pieces. I also heard four of the pieces performed during the course of my two visits, with many of the musicians playing without scores in front of them. With both notations of the pieces and the audio CD released,[10] Jiangnan *sizhu* musicians in Taicang could learn the ten pieces by score reading, by rote from other musicians, or by themselves through listening to the CD. Over the course of twelve years, from the issue of these sources until my visits in 2014, it was apparent to me that many musicians had internalized the pieces and were already intuitively varying the melodies according to the idiomatic techniques of their respective instruments. That signaled to me that the pieces have been reabsorbed into the repertoire of these Jiangnan *sizhu* music clubs in Taicang. Even though a top-down approach was initially employed, the musicians seem to have accepted these pieces.

At this point, a question begging to be answered is that of how to regard this whole scenario. My initial idealistic notion that the pieces in the recording had been circulating naturally at the grassroots level among Jiangnan *sizhu* musicians in Taicang had proven to be a misconception and was eliminated as I discovered the facts behind the scenes, during fieldwork. However, just because the repertoire turned out to have been the product of government intervention did not inherently make the pieces any less authentic or mean that they lacked a Jiangnan regional aesthetic sensibility. This sensibility, rooted in the communal ethos and values of balance, moderation, and refined simplicity mentioned earlier, is expressed in the musical interaction needed to give rise to the heterophonic texture brought about by each musician "adding flowers" between the structural tones of a basic melody. Such creative interaction is often explained by traditional musicians using the aphorism, *ni fan, wo jian; wo fan, ni jian* (你繁, 我簡; 我繁, 你簡, "When you play ornately, I play simply; when I play ornately, you play simply").[11] According to them, they are not simply playing together (*heyue*, 合樂, in colloquial terms); rather, they are engaging in a dialogue (colloquially referred to as *daduizi*, 打對子). In Shanghai, according to the ethnomusicologist Li Ya (2018), and further expounded by Xiao Mei (2021), musicians with different instruments engage with each other musically in what is referred to in Shanghainese dialect as *ghak* (掱). More aphorisms used by insiders to the musical tradition further explain these interactions: "You come, I go; you go high, I go low; you advance, I retreat," and so forth. The result is a tightly knit and mutually reactive musical symbiosis, one graphically suggested by the complex Chinese character used for *ghak*, which consists of the character for "hand" (手) written twice with the character for "unity" (合) sandwiched between them.

The composer Zhang Xiaofeng is clearly well-versed in the musical style of Jiangnan *sizhu*, having played in music clubs devoted to the performance of the genre in Taicang in his younger years (Zhang Xiaofeng, personal communication, March 21, 2014). To a certain extent, the "ten great pieces" could be regarded as *xin* Jiangnan *sizhu* (新江南絲竹, "new Jiangnan silk and bamboo [music]") in that they were deliberately arranged, or perhaps "recomposed." Yet, at the same time, they are different from the works of Gu Guanren (顧冠仁), Zhou Chenglong (周成龍), Peng Zhengyuan (彭正元), and other composers of music that has been called *xin* Jiangnan *sizhu*—music whose melodies are in the style of the Jiangnan region but orchestrated in the manner of Western music, employing harmonies and musical structures patterned after those of Western art-music genres (Wu, 2015). Such compositions are clearly meant to be performed as *minyue* (民樂) by professional or conservatory-trained musicians.[12] In contrast, Zhang Xiaofeng largely employed traditional Jiangnan *sizhu* techniques of adding melodic interpolations to the ten melodies in the idiom of each of the instruments in the Jiangnan *sizhu* ensemble. Harmonizations are practically nonexistent, and the musical structure follows a theme and variations form (see Figures 10.3a and 10.3b). As a result, the ten pieces can easily be learned and performed by traditional Jiangnan *sizhu* musicians in the community—indeed this was the main intent behind their creation (Gao Xuefeng and Zhang Xiaofeng, personal communication, March 21, 2014).

(a)

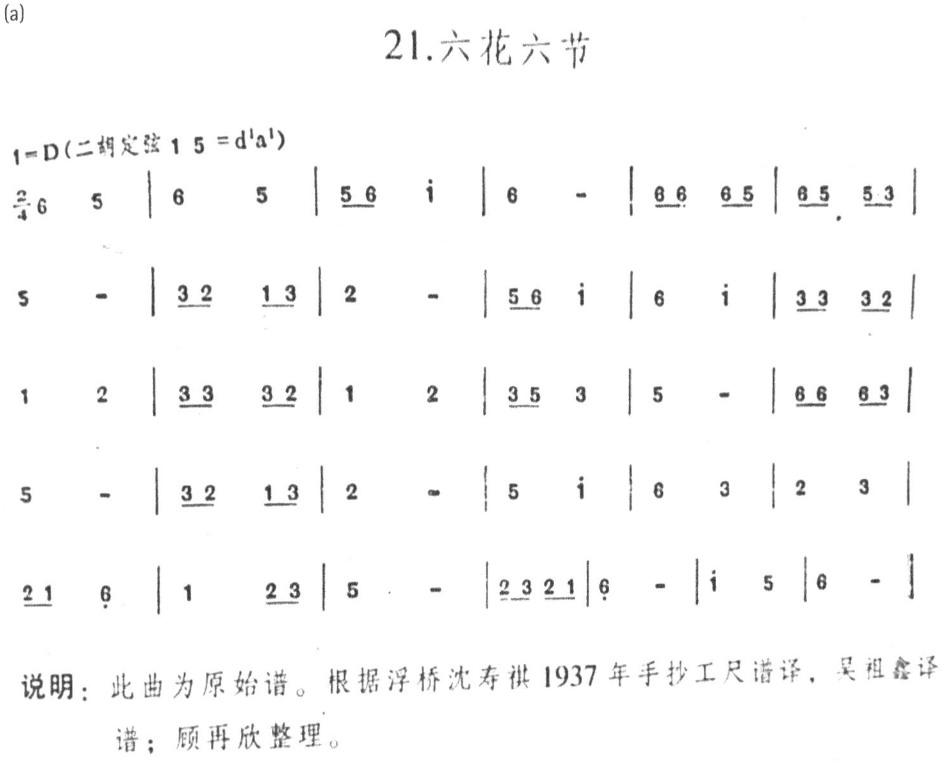

21. 六花六节

FIGURES 10.3. (a–b) Two versions of *Liuhua liujie*.
Note: (a) *Qupai* of *Liuhua liujie*, from the 1937 handwritten score of Shen Shouqi of Fuqiao village, Taicang (Gao, 2010: 91).
(b) First thirty-two measures of *Liuhua liujie*, arranged by Zhang Xiaofeng (2003: 44–46).

FIGURE 10.3. Continued

FIGURE 10.3. Continued

Interconnections with Regional Opera Music

Taicang is historically not only a center of Jiangnan music and culture but also a place of great affluence. Wealthy families settled there and many were patrons of music, theater, and art. Some had their own troupes of house musicians and performers of *kunqu*. The family of the Taicang resident Wang Xijue (王錫爵, 1534–1611), for example, was notable for maintaining a group of musicians who gave private performances of *kunqu* and instrumental music to entertain Wang family members and their guests. This clan's practice of keeping a private band of musicians continued through four generations of the Wang lineage, from 1594 to 1681. Among those who served as music director to the clan's house musicians was Zhang Yetang, the son-in-law and collaborator of Wei Liangfu, who was discussed above (Gao, 2010: 32–39).

The inter-genre relationship between Jiangnan *sizhu*, *kunqu*, *shifan*, and, to a lesser extent, *huju* (滬劇, "Shanghai opera") has been discussed by scholars writing about music of the Jiangnan region.[13] As mentioned earlier, whether or not Jiangnan *sizhu* evolved from the music of *kunqu* or from the *sizhu* sections of *shifan* gong-and-drum music is inconclusive. However, they certainly have very close stylistic connections.

In both Jiangnan *sizhu* and the instrumental ensemble accompanying the singing of *kunqu*, the instrument that often takes the lead (*lingzou*, 領奏), playing the first few bars of a melody and beginning the performance of a piece, is the *di* bamboo flute. The texture of the ensemble playing in both genres is heterophonic; each instrumentalist plays the same basic melody (*qupai*) as the others but does so in a way idiomatic to his/her instrument. Thus, for example, while the *di* player performs the *qupai* with flutter-tonguing, trills, grace notes, and other ornaments characteristic of the instrument, the *erhu* player performs more long-held notes with vibratos and ornamental glides typical of bowed instruments. Meanwhile, plucked lutes such as the *pipa*, *sanxian*, *yueqin*, or *ruan* perform the basic melody with upward and downward glides on particular tones, and they play rolls (*lunzi*, 輪子) of repeated notes that fill the spaces between the longer-held notes and pauses of the other instruments.[14] The result is a smooth and continuous flow of musical sound, so much so that where a melodic phrase ends and where another one begins is often not easily distinguishable.

The relatively similar instrumentation,[15] melodic style, and techniques of ornamentation and variation give *sizhu* music a shared sonic profile in spite of different repertoires, functions, and placement of this repertoire within the region's various operatic genres. In *kunqu*, the *sizhu* music not only serves as accompaniment to the singing but also figures as an overture prior to the opera's opening scene and as instrumental passages that accompany onstage action. In *huju*, especially as it existed during the 1950s and 1960s, the *sizhu* portions mainly served as preludes to the singing of folk songs that made up some of this opera's vocal music.

The music historian Gao Xuefeng writes that during the Ming and Qing dynasties, Taicang had a lively music scene, with many *tangming* (堂名) musicians who performed *kunqu* as well as *sizhu* music (Gao, 2010: 24). *Tangming* (literally, "hall name") referred to groups of instrumentalists and vocalists who performed for weddings and funerals and were treated as professionals and compensated for their performances. They often wore colored clothing and did not mix with guests during the banquets attached to these occasions. They performed traditional pieces in the *sizhu* repertoire as well as un-staged excerpts from *kunqu* and *huju* opera. Daoist priests who performed funeral rituals and the *shifan* wind-and-percussion music that accompanied them were sometimes also included in the designation of *tangming*.[16] In a tabulation in Gao Xuefeng's book (2010: 40–43), however, they are clearly identified as *daoshi* (道士). Of the thirty-eight groups performing *sizhu* professionally in Taicang during the Ming and Qing periods listed in Gao's table, twenty-three were *tangming*,[17] ten were groups of Daoist priests, and the rest were *kunqu* training groups (*peixunban*, 培训班).[18]

Musical versatility as a characteristic of Taicang musicians seems to have continued into contemporary times. During fieldwork in 2014 I observed that ensemble musicians who provided the instrumental accompaniment for the singing of *kunqu* and *huju* also typically performed Jiangnan *sizhu* and vice versa, often moving seamlessly from one genre to the other in the course of a music session. The general similarity in style of the *sizhu* parts in these genres easily lends itself to this phenomenon, especially with regard to *kunqu* and Jiangnan *sizhu*.

During my two-day field trip to Taicang in April 2014, I visited several music groups. According to Gao Xuefeng, in 2010, Taicang had about thirty-two formally registered music groups and countless others whose members met and gathered in private homes and clubhouses to perform music together in a more ad hoc and informal way.[19] Granted, the music groups I had visited were chosen for me by the Taicang Cultural Bureau, thus allowing me to see only part of the whole picture. But even so, one could not help but notice that almost all of them performed not only Jiangnan *sizhu* but also *huju*, and one club in particular also performed *kunqu*. Of the nine music groups I visited, which included a Daoist music group, only three solely performed *sizhu* music.

When I arrived at what I was told was a typical evening music session of the Taicangshi Loudong Kunqu Tangmingshe (太倉市婁東崑曲堂名社), their instrumentalists were accompanying a solo excerpt from the famous *kunqu* opera *Mudanting* (牡丹亭, *The Peony Pavilion*). This was followed by two duets from the same opera. They then proceeded to perform *Liuhua liujie* (六花六節, *Six Flowers, Six Festivals*), one of the revived "ten great pieces." This was followed by *Zizhu diao* (紫竹調, *Purple Bamboo Melody*), a folk ditty widespread in the Wu dialect areas (southern Jiangsu, Shanghai, most of Zhejiang and southern Anhui) and often heard in performances of *huju*; *Molihua* (茉莉花, *Jasmine Flower*), another popular folk song that is widely performed in the Jiangnan region; and, finally, two more—namely, *Chunhua qiuyue* and *Wuyeti*— from the revived "ten great pieces." All the instrumentalists performed without scores in front of them, unlike many of those in the other music groups I visited. Their ensemble playing was smooth and their coordination seamless. This could only come from performing together regularly over a sustained period. As the group's name indicates, it consisted of musicians who are present-day equivalents of pre-1949 *tangming* musicians. They often performed for monetary compensation at weddings, birthdays, and other "red and happy" occasions (*hongxishi*, 紅喜事), such as the inauguration of businesses and commemorations of joyous events, singing *kunqu* excerpts, and playing Jiangnan *sizhu*. It was no wonder, then, that their ensemble playing had polish.

Of the nine Taicang music groups I visited during the same field trip, five of them typically perform both *huju* excerpts and Jiangnan *sizhu* as a matter of course.[20] Most of these five groups referred to their gatherings as *huju shalong* (滬劇沙龍, "*huju* salons"), indicating that these assemblies were for the purpose of exhibiting showmanship in the singing of *huju* in the manner of Western salon concerts. They attract *huju* connoisseurs, for whom these gatherings represent a chance to sing without the social stigma suffered by professional opera actors.[21] They serve as training grounds where these amateur *huju* connoisseurs can improve their singing through performance in front of other opera enthusiasts and, sometimes, an invited expert—a respected professional *huju* singer-actor.

During my visit to the *huju* salon of one of these music groups—the Donghong Yishutuan (東紅藝術團, Donghong Arts Troupe; formerly called Donghong Sizhushe, 東紅絲竹社, Donghong Silk and Bamboo Music Club)—in April 2014, five female members were singing a *huju* excerpt that involved some choreographed dance-like movements. They were accompanied by a *sizhu* ensemble, led by a *shenhu* (see Figure 10.4). Afterward, the ensemble performed *Liuhua liujie*, one of the "ten great pieces," and a piece composed by one of their members, Gu Feiyun (顧飛雲), in the "new Jiangnan

FIGURE 10.4. *Sizhu* instrumentalists of the Donghong Yishutuan performing one of the revived "Ten Great Pieces" of Jiangnan *sizhu*.

sizhu" style. They then went back to accompanying two female members singing a *huju* excerpt to the tune of the folk ditty *Zizhu diao* that, as mentioned above, had been performed by the Taicangshi Loudong Kunqu Tangmingshe as a Jiangnan *sizhu* piece. This was followed by another *huju* excerpt sung by a female member who also plays the *zheng* 筝 zither whenever the ensemble performs Jiangnan *sizhu* pieces. Despite holding a weekly *huju* salon during which the group mostly performs various *huju* excerpts, the leader of the Donghong Yishutuan informed me that performing Jiangnan *sizhu* was the main emphasis of their group, as could be gleaned from their previous name.

One might wonder at these music groups' practice of performing *huju* or *kunqu* opera excerpts alongside Jiangnan *sizhu* music in their sessions. For professional groups such as the Taicangshi Loudong Kunqu Tangmingshe, it makes practical sense because the combined repertoires of the two genres allow them to offer their audience a wider variety and a larger body of music to listen to, thus making hiring them more cost-effective. As for the five music groups performing both *huju* excerpts and Jiangnan *sizhu* that I visited, they do so in an amateur capacity; that is, their members perform mainly for their own enjoyment and recreation. They also occasionally perform in contexts such as birthdays, weddings, and other happy occasions at the invitation of the hosts, with whom they would likely already share familiarity. It has therefore also been helpful for them to be able to perform un-staged opera excerpts as well as instrumental music such as Jiangnan *sizhu*. These performers do not receive monetary compensation but are instead treated as guests by the hosts. They mix with other guests during the banquets and often perform even after the feasting is over. In the first chapter of a book offering a socio-historical background of Jiangnan *sizhu*, the musicologist Ruan Hong wrote that musicians similar to those just described were referred to as *qingkechuan* (清客串)

before 1949 (Ruan, 2008: 6–7).[22] They were the antithesis of *tangming*. However, the practice of performing *kunqu* or *huju* opera excerpts alongside Jiangnan *sizhu* by these Taicang music groups, whether professional or amateur, seems to encourage the continued performance of the latter genre and thus aid in its continued vitality.

Meanwhile, the two remaining music groups that I visited during my second field trip to Taicang in 2014 solely perform Jiangnan *sizhu* and do so in a non-professional capacity. They are no different from most of the music clubs in Shanghai that are exclusively devoted to the performance of Jiangnan *sizhu* and whose dwindling membership and repertoire put the genre's continued long-term existence in doubt.

INTERCONNECTIONS WITH *SHIFAN* MUSIC

Un-staged *kunqu* and *huju* opera excerpts have not been the only genres to prop up Jiangnan *sizhu* and enable it to retain relevance through continued performance. *Shifan gu* (十番鼓, "*shifan* drum music") and *shifan luogu*, hereafter collectively referred to as *shifan* music, themselves contain portions of *sizhu* music—that is, melodic sections performed by traditional stringed and wind instruments. So, groups that perform *shifan* music almost always also perform Jiangnan *sizhu*; it is certainly not a stretch for them to do so.

Shifan gu and *shifan luogu* are two types of ensembles composed of strings, winds, and percussion. The term *shifan* literally means "ten times" or "multiple variations," pointing to the variety of instruments that make up these two ensembles, both of which also fall under the more general name *chuida* 吹打 (literally, "blowing and striking"). The main melodic instruments of both include the *di*, other wind instruments such as *sheng, xiao*, and sometimes a small *suona*, and plucked and bowed stringed instruments such as *pipa, ruan, sanxian*, and *erhu*—instrumentation basically very similar to that of Jiangnan *sizhu* and the *sizhu* ensemble that accompanies *kunqu*, save for the *suona*. As for the percussion instruments, two types of drums figure in *shifan gu*, while an array of other percussion instruments such as gongs and cymbals are included in *shifan luogu* in addition to the drums (Jones, 1995: 256–59).

The *shifan luogu* repertory can be divided into two types: 1) pure percussion pieces and 2) suites for melodic and percussion instruments. In the latter, melodic sections performed by the melodic instruments enumerated in the previous paragraph may consist of entirely independent melodic movements, may interact and alternate phrases with the percussion instruments, or may consist of a solo *di* alternating phrases with the percussion instruments (Jones, 1995: 264–66). It is in these melodic sections that *shifan* music shows similarities with Jiangnan *sizhu* and the *sizhu* music that accompanies *kunqu*.[23]

The music groups performing *shifan* music have historically been *tangming* or Daoist priests, who also normally played in exchange for money. Even today, those who perform this type of music are Daoist priests and present-day equivalents of *tangming*.

The association of *tangming* with *shifan* music, however, was not a given, as were the other labels for musicians based on their acceptance or non-acceptance of payment for the performance of such music or that of *kunqu*. In other words, the assignment of the classificatory labels such as *tangming* or *qingkechuan* were by no means absolute and could change depending on the context, as with the music performed by music groups assigned these labels. Even today, there may be occasions when professional musicians who are modern-day equivalents of *tangming* and typically perform *kunqu*, *sizhu*, *huju*, or *shifan* with financial remuneration might do so for free.

This insight came to me during a field trip in March 2016 to a village called Tianchi in the Suzhou countryside, where I had gone with a colleague to observe a wedding. When we arrived at the house of the groom's parents, an ensemble had already been performing music for some time; they were playing Jiangnan *sizhu*. In one corner of the large living room of the house, there was a table with musicians sitting around it, performing music; on the table lay instruments that were not being used at that time, containers of tea, and ashtrays—a typical set-up during music sessions in Jiangnan *sizhu* music clubs (see Figure 10.5).

The *Gujia Yinyueban* (顧家音樂班, Gu Family Music Troupe), headed by Gu Zaixin (顧再欣), is a professional group of musicians based in Mudu township, Suzhou. They mainly perform *shifan luogu* music but play Jiangnan *sizhu* as well, as was the case that morning in March 2016.[24] As guests arrived, they played well-known tunes such as *Suzhou mei* (蘇州美, *Beautiful Suzhou*), a *pingtan* piece; *Zizhu diao*; and the melody of a "new Jiangnan *sizhu*" piece, *Sudi manbu* (蘇堤漫步, *Strolling Along the Suzhou River*), by Gu Guanren. This was followed by a duet by a male and female singer from the group,

FIGURE 10.5. Gu Family Music Troupe (Gujia Yinyue Ban) performing Jiangnan *sizhu* at a wedding in Tianchi village, Suzhou.

who sang a *huju* excerpt, and then some dancing by a couple to a Chinese pop recording played from a laptop, amplified with a microphone, and broadcast through two large speakers. After a break of about two hours for lunch—a small feast partaken by all, including the musicians—the group resumed playing music. This time, they performed a couple of pieces from the Jiangnan *sizhu badaqu*, namely *Sanliu* and *Huanle ge*. These were followed by two short *shifan luogu* pieces to accompany a ritual, wherein the parents of the groom faced the ancestral altar in the center hall of the house, opposite the main doorway, and kowtowed. The first *shifan luogu* piece was of the *cu* type accompanied by two small *suona*, a pair of cymbals, and a frame drum on a stand. In the second, the two *suona* were replaced by two *di* accompanied by a pair of cymbals, a clapper, and a struck woodblock.

The bowing to the ancestors, accompanied by *shifan luogu* performed by the musicians while seated, signaled the beginning of the wedding proper. Right after this ritual, the musicians picked up their instruments, including a collapsible signaling trumpet (*haotong*, 號筒). With this instrument, together with two *suona*, a pair of cymbals, and a frame drum (*bangu*, 板鼓) held by the frame and beaten with a stick, the musicians led a procession out the door and gate of the property to fetch the bride (see Figure 10.6). Firecrackers exploded in the courtyard, adding to the loud and festive soundscape. Bringing up the rear of the wedding procession were the *sizhu* musicians, playing two *di*, an *erhu*, *pipa*, *ruan*, and a couple of small percussion instruments—a woodblock and a pair of bells (*pengling*, 碰鈴). The procession moved through narrow lanes in between houses and out on the road for about fifteen minutes until it came to a stop at a small intersection where a convoy of about ten black Audi sedans also stopped.

FIGURE 10.6. Gu Family Music Troupe leading the wedding procession from the groom's house to fetch the bride. (Instruments used are two *suona*, cymbals, gong, drum, and *haotong*)

Out of the first of these cars stepped the groom, who then went around to the other side and helped his bride alight. Apparently, the groom had gone together with a retinue of groomsmen earlier to the house of the bride to fetch her and her bridal party. Now they all got out of the cars and joined the wedding procession on foot back to the groom's house, where the formal wedding ceremony was to take place. Throughout these activities, the ensemble of musicians performed "scattered pieces" (*sanqu*, 散曲) of *shifan xiluogu* (十番細鑼鼓, *shifan luogu* music of the "fine" variety), with the *sizhu* melodic section, including a small *suona*, playing simultaneously and in alternation with the rhythmic percussion section.[25]

Back at the groom's house, the wedding party led by the ensemble of musicians performing *shifan xiluogu* made a grand entrance, and the wedding ritual proper began, with the bride and groom facing the altar in the center hall, bowing, and paying their respects to the ancestors (as represented by the ancestral banners on the altar) and to both sets of parents and older male siblings, all of whom stood on the other side of the altar facing the couple. Right after this, a new round of firecrackers was set off in the courtyard to announce that the couple were now husband and wife, and the musicians played fast-tempo folk tunes in a Jiangnan *sizhu* style, as they had done that morning. This time, however, they were all standing, mixed within the crowd of guests who were standing or milling about in the center hall near the altar and outside in the courtyard. If not for the absence of gong and drum accompaniment, one would have thought the musicians were still performing *shifan* music, not Jiangnan *sizhu*. The excitement in the whole place was palpable and increased to a fever pitch, aided by the sound of the music and the exploding firecrackers outside.

A sumptuous banquet followed. Round tables were set up in all areas of the house and in the front courtyard. Dishes piled high with food made their way to each table from the outdoor kitchen at the back of the house. The musicians occupied three round tables on one side of the center hall inside the house—a sure sign that they were being treated as guests by the host, not as paid entertainers. The reason for this deviation from the norm became clear when it was revealed to me that the groom happened to be the troupe leader Gu Zaixin's grandnephew and a *di* player himself. The troupe members had offered their services for free as a present to the newlyweds and as an expression of their camaraderie with the Gu family. Their close relationship became even more pronounced after the dinner banquet, when they again picked up their instruments and began performing. Paid musicians would have stopped performing long before then.

By this time, the mood of the event had become one of playful conviviality. With stomachs full and inhibitions down, helped by the liquor and wine consumed at the dinner banquet, the musicians and several guests and friends of the groom participated in a musical jam session, performing one piece after another led by the *di*. The audience, made up of the other guests, knowing that they were being given a treat, egged them on, with their mobile-phone cameras all raised to capture the impromptu performances on video. Then, at about nine o'clock, Gu Zaixin gathered all the members of his troupe around the table once again. He had been tuning a big *bangu* by pouring water on both sides of the drumhead. Finally satisfied with its sound, he took the microphone after the previous piece came to an end and announced that his troupe would perform *Jiangjun ling* (將軍令, *General's Orders*), a *chuida* piece used as an overture in many operas, including the *kunqu* opera of the same title. It opened with rhythms struck on the *bangu*, followed by alternating calls on two *haotong*, before the stately melody was played by two *suona*, rhythmically punctuated by two pairs of cymbals, a small hand-held gong, and a pair of struck bells. It was a relatively long piece (more than six minutes), very loud and martial in style, and quite fitting as the piece of music to close a festive day. From Jiangnan *sizhu* to *shifan luogu* and back to Jiangnan *sizhu* and then *shifan luogu* again and ending with a Su'nan *chuida* piece, the wedding afforded a chance to witness the impressive range of performance repertoire of the Gu Family Music Troupe and the relatively seamless way in which they went back and forth between the two genres during an actual performance event.

Conclusion: Keys to Musical Sustainability

Stephen Jones alludes to the evolution of Jiangnan *sizhu* from the *shifan* genres being a result both of the reduction of their percussion section to only the woodblock and clappers and of the retention mainly of their *sizhu* melodic sections. He points to a parallel in the transformation from *shifan* music to Jiangnan *sizhu* with the music's transition from rural to urban settings that, in turn, paralleled a transition from a ceremonial to a secular function (Jones, 1995: 250). The transformation of the music's function from ritual to secular effected a change in its volume and performance venue as well. In contrast to loud and boisterous *shifan* music, Jiangnan *sizhu* is softer and more refined; in contrast to the former's largely outdoor performance venue, Jiangnan *sizhu* is mainly performed indoors. Without the ceremonial and ritual contexts of *shifan* music and regional operas, Jiangnan *sizhu* in Shanghai can be said to have become basically unmoored. Its only remaining raison d'etre is the self-entertainment of enthusiasts who patronize and perform it in music clubs devoted to the genre. Meanwhile, since the initiation of the economic reforms in the late 1970s and particularly since the early 1990s, Shanghai has rapidly transformed into a First World city and re-emerged as a hub for international trade and finance as well as a center of cosmopolitan art and culture. Competition from the seemingly infinite and dazzling array of forms of entertainment, musical and otherwise, and the demands of modern city life have made it even less likely for most people, let alone young ones, to gravitate to Jiangnan *sizhu*. Given its small repertory, traditional aesthetics, and stylistic characteristics, picking up this form of music requires a definite investment of time and effort, something that not very many people can afford or are willing to give. Consequently, the number of people in Shanghai who perform Jiangnan *sizhu* has been in decline and, with their decrease in number, the continued existence of this regional *sizhu* music tradition is uncertain.

Yet, although Jiangnan *sizhu* has long been closely identified with Shanghai, that city became a center of music only in the late nineteenth century. Well before then, regional music such as *kunqu* and the *shifan* music genres from which Jiangnan *sizhu* derives many influences had long flourished in other major cities of Jiangnan (Nanjing, Suzhou, Yangzhou, Wuxi, and Hangzhou) as well as in the surrounding rural towns and villages. In such locales, the roots for Jiangnan *sizhu* are not only more deeply embedded but also presently show a wider range of performance contexts. Encounters with Jiangnan *sizhu* in two areas of Jiangsu province—one in Taicang and another in Tianchi village on the outskirts of Suzhou—presented a picture quite different from that seen in Shanghai. In these settings, I found Jiangnan *sizhu* performed in the context of music clubs for recreation by amateurs and professional musicians as well as during practice sessions for and actual performance events in celebration of happy occasions such as weddings. In the former instance, Jiangnan *sizhu* was performed alongside local opera excerpts (*kunqu* or *huju*); in the latter, it occurred alongside *shifan luogu*. Both of these other music genres are often performed as part of rituals or ceremonies, with *shifan luogu* often played by professional musicians during both joyous as well as solemn occasions. Outside of music clubs, *kunqu* or *huju* excerpts are sung during celebratory occasions such as birthdays, weddings, the openings of new businesses, and temple fairs (Gao Xuefeng, personal communication, April 27, 2014). Such rituals and celebrations remain integral to the observance of important calendrical, life-cycle, and religious events, and, for the people in both Taicang and Tianchi village, ensure the continued and robust existence of these music genres and, ergo, Jiangnan *sizhu*.

Annexing the performance of Jiangnan *sizhu* to the practice of singing excerpts of *kunqu* or *huju* within the setting of the music clubs has been a prudent decision on the part of members of many music clubs in Taicang. Doing so has certainly led to more performances than would otherwise have been possible. Another source of hope and optimism for the sustainability of Jiangnan *sizhu* in Taicang has been the reintroduction of ten old tunes that used to be performed as Jiangnan *sizhu* in and around the area before 1949. Under the aegis of the local cultural bureau, ten tunes recalled by some of Taicang's older musicians were then arranged by the local composer Zhang Xiaofeng into Jiangnan *sizhu* and recorded on compact discs, with their scores also published and distributed to music clubs in the area, allowing musicians to absorb this music into their active repertoire.

The project emerged from a systematic list of six goals and objectives that comprised "the long-term protection mechanism for the sustainable development of Jiangnan *sizhu*" in Taicang, namely: (1) protection and utilization; (2) transmission and innovation; (3) popularization and improvement; (4) promotion of activities and teamwork; (5) production of new works and talents; and (6) creation of atmosphere internally and expansion of external publicity (Gao, 2010: 208–15). My fieldwork observations suggest that the project had successfully realized everything it had set out to achieve. Indeed, that all this happened before the founding of the Intangible Cultural Heritage Program of China's Ministry of Culture in 2005 is impressive.[26] It suggests that traditional music at the grassroots can be sustained with the right kind and amount of help from governmental units, in consultation with and under supervision from people with a broad and deep knowledge of the local music culture, and with the cooperation of the local music community. With modifications to accommodate differences in the circumstances of various areas where Jiangnan *sizhu* can still be found, the said project could serve as a blueprint for promoting the sustainable development of this music tradition in other areas of Jiangnan and perhaps for other music traditions as well.

Glossary

badaqu 八大曲, "eight great pieces," core repertoire of traditional Jiangnan *sizhu*

bayin 八音, "eight sounds," ancient Chinese instrument-classification system that groups instruments by a salient material in their construction: silk (*si*, 絲), bamboo (*zhu*, 竹), stone (*shi*, 石), wood (*mu*, 木), earth (*tu*, 土), metal (*jin*, 金), leather (*ge*, 革), and gourd (*pao*, 匏)

bangu 板鼓, frame drum often used in *shifan luogu*

Chaozhou *xianshi* 潮州弦詩, *sizhu* genre from Guangdong and Fujian provinces

chuida 吹打, "blowing and striking," category of loud wind-and-percussion ensembles typically performed outdoors

Chunhua qiuyue 春花秋月, *Spring Flowers and Autumn Moon*, revived Jiangnan *sizhu* piece in Taicang (formerly *Chunyue qiuhua* 春月秋花, *Spring Moon and Autumn Flowers*)

cu 粗, "rough," categorization for ensembles including loud aerophones (such as *suona*) and large, loud percussion

daduizi 打對子, "engaging in dialogue," musical interaction in performance

daoshi 道士, Daoist priests

di 笛, transverse bamboo flute

Donghong Yishutuan 東紅藝術團, Donghong Arts Troupe, music club in Taicang that performs *huju* excerpts and Jiangnan *sizhu* (formerly Donghong Sizhushe 東紅絲竹社, Donghong Silk and Bamboo Club)

erhu 二胡, two-stringed spiked bowed lute with hexagonal-shaped soundbox

fangman jiahua 放慢加花, "slowing the tempo and adding flowers," term used by Jiangnan *sizhu* musicians for process of melodic augmentation

Fujian *nanguan* 福建南管, *sizhu* genre from Fujian province

Gao Xuefeng 高雪峰, music historian and author of a book about Jiangnan *sizhu* in Taicang; one of the present author's main research interviewees

ghak (or *ge*) 搿, "hug," term in Shanghai dialect for interactive performance

Gu Feiyun 顧飛雲, composer and member of the Donghong Yishu Yuetuan

Gu Guanren 顧冠仁, composer of *xin* Jiangnan *sizhu* (b. 1942)

Gu Zaixin 顧再欣, head of the Gu Family Music Troupe

Gujia Yinyueban 顧家音樂班, professional music group specializing in *chuida* music

Guangdong *yinyue* 廣東音樂, *sizhu* genre from Guangdong province

guoyue 國樂, name in Shanghai for Jiangnan *sizhu* before 1950s, also used for music composed for traditional Chinese instruments employing harmony and other Western compositional techniques

haotong 號筒, collapsible trumpet used for signaling before *chuida* music starts

heyue 合樂, colloquial term for "playing music together"

hongxishi 紅喜事, happy, festive occasions often marked by red-colored clothing, paper cuttings, and decorations

huju 滬劇, traditional opera genre of Shanghai region

huju shalong 滬劇沙龍, musical salon or gathering for singing *huju* excerpts

huaigu 懷鼓, small barrel drum used in *kunqu* opera and in Jiangnan *sizhu*

Huaihuang 槐黃, *Yellow Chinese Scholar Tree*, folk melody arranged in Jiangnan *sizhu* format in Taicang

Huanle ge 歡樂歌, *Song of Happiness*, one of the "eight great pieces" that form the core repertoire of Jiangnan *sizhu*

Jiangjun ling 將軍令, *General's Orders*, standard *chuida* piece often performed as an overture in many regional opera forms

Jiangnan *sizhu* 江南絲竹, string-and-wind ensemble music indigenous to the south of the middle and lower reaches of the Yangzi river

Kejia *handiao* 客家漢調, *sizhu* genre from Hakka areas in Guangdong province

kunqiang 崑腔, melodies popular in the city of Kunshan, Jiangsu

kunqu 崑曲, classical opera genre developed in and around Kunshan, Jiangsu

Lao liuban 老六板, *Old Six-Beat*, composition that some deem one of the core "eight great pieces" of Jiangnan *sizhu*

Lao sanliu 老三六, *Old Three-Six*, composition that some deem one of the core "eight great pieces" of Jiangnan *sizhu*

lingzou 領奏, lead instrument in an ensemble

Liuhua liujie 六花六節, *Six Flowers, Six Festivals*, one among ten pieces revived by the Taicang Cultural Bureau

lunzi 輪子, "rolls," performance technique on *pipa* and other lutes

Luogu sihe 鑼鼓四合, *Gongs and Drums Four Unified*, title of suite in *shifan luogu* repertoire, which may be the origin of the earliest Jiangnan *sizhu* pieces

Man liuban 慢六板, *Slow Six-Beat*, one of the "eight great pieces" that form the core repertoire of Jiangnan *sizhu*

Man sanliu 慢三六, *Slow Three-Six*, one of the "eight great pieces" that form the core repertoire of Jiangnan *sizhu*

minyue 民樂, "people's music," term in mainland China for music composed for Chinese musical instruments that features traditional elements combined with Western compositional techniques and forms

Molihua 茉莉花, *Jasmine Flower*, folk song from Jiangnan

Mudanting 牡丹亭, *The Peony Pavilion*, well-known *kunqu* drama by Tang Xianzu (1598)

nanqu 南曲, "southern tunes," melodies and melodic styles originating in southern China

nanyin 南音, *sizhu* genre from southern Fujian that also includes the singing of verses in the local dialect

ni fan, wo jian; wo fan, ni jian 你繁, 我簡; 我繁, 你簡, "When you play ornately, I play simply; when I play ornately, you play simply," aphorism used to describe the creative interaction that produces the characteristic heterophonic texture of Jiangnan *sizhu*

paiban 拍版, clapper made of two wooden slabs, usually ebony, strung together with a ribbon of cloth

peixunban 培訓班, training class

Peng Zhengyuan 彭正元, composer of *xin* Jiangnan *sizhu* (b. 1944) *pengling* 碰鈴, pair of small bells without clappers, struck together to mark the secondary strong beats of each measure of a *qupai*

pingtan 評彈, sung narrative tradition native to Suzhou

pipa 琵琶, four-stringed plucked lute with pear-shaped body and short, fretted neck

pingtan 評彈, sung story-telling genre

qingkechuan 清客串, traditional musicians in Jiangnan before 1949 who performed opera excerpts and instrumental music voluntarily at social events

qingshangyue 清商樂, string-and-wind ensemble of the Eastern Jin and Northern and Southern Dynasties period (317–587)

qingyin 清音, historical name for string-and-wind ensemble music in Shanghai

qupai 曲牌, "labeled tune," pre-existent melodies found in various regional forms with a certain number of measures or beats and notes per phrase that formerly corresponded to characters or syllables in a line of poetry

ruan 阮, four-stringed plucked lute with a round resonator and a long fretted neck

Sanliu 三六, Three-Six, one of the "eight great pieces" that form the core repertoire of Jiangnan *sizhu*

sanqu 散曲, "scattered tunes," stand-alone melodies in *shifan* music

sanxian 三弦, three-stringed lute without frets

shenhu 申胡, also known as *zhuhu*, two-stringed fiddle used as lead instrument in *huju*

sheng 笙, mouth organ

shi'erxi 十二細, historical name for Jiangnan *sizhu* in Jiangsu

shifan gu 十番鼓, outdoor ensemble composed mostly of drums and other percussion

shifan luogu 十番鑼鼓, outdoor and indoor ensemble tradition from Jiangnan comprising percussion, wind, and stringed instruments

shifan xiluogu 十番細鑼鼓, *shifan luogu* music of the "fine" variety

shifan xiyue 十番細樂, historical name in Jiangsu for Jiangnan *sizhu*

Sihe ruyi 四合如意 (sometimes simply *Sihe*), Four Unified as Intended, one of the "eight great pieces" that form the core repertoire of Jiangnan *sizhu*

sizhu 絲竹, "silk and bamboo," ensemble comprising plucked and bowed traditional stringed instruments and wind instruments wholly or partially made of bamboo, also the music performed by this group

sizhu zhi xiang 絲竹之鄉, "hometown of silk and bamboo," designation Taicang cultural officials apply to Jiangnan *sizhu* within their city

Sudi manbu 蘇堤漫步, Strolling Along the Suzhou River, a "new Jiangnan *sizhu*" composition by Gu Guanren

Su'nan chuida 蘇南吹打, "blowing-and-hitting [ensemble] music of southern Jiangsu," a category of wind-and-percussion music found in southern Jiangsu that is dominated by the wind instruments led by the *suona*

Suzhou mei 蘇州美, Beautiful Suzhou; relatively recent Suzhou *pingtan* piece whose instrumental accompaniment makes use of Jiangnan *sizhu* techniques

suona 嗩吶, double-reed aerophone with a flaring bell

Taicangshi Loudong Kunqu Tangmingshe 太倉市婁東崑曲堂名社, music club in Taicang

Taicangshi Wenhuguan 太倉市文化館, Taicang City Cultural Center, local cultural bureau of the city of Taicang

Taizi qiche 太子騎車, The Crown Prince Rides the Carriage, piece played in Jiangnan *sizhu* format in Taicang *tangming* 堂名, musicians who perform *kunqu*, other regional types of opera, or folk instrumental music mainly for monetary gain

tiqin 提琴, two-stringed bowed lute

Wang Agen 王阿根, *huju* singer active in Taicang (first half of the twentieth century)

Wang Xijue 王錫爵, wealthy Taicang resident and music patron (1534–1611)

Wei Liangfu 魏良輔, Taicang native who reformed the singing and instrumental accompaniment of *kunqu* opera (c. 1489–c. 1566)

Wu ge 吳歌, general term for folk songs sung in Wu dialects

Wuyeti 烏夜啼, *Crows Crying at Night*, popular Jiangnan *sizhu* piece in Taicang

Wuzhong *xiansuo* 吳種弦索, "string ensemble of the Wu dialect region," ensemble developed by Wei Liangfu and Zhang Yetang to accompany *kunqu* opera

xi 細, "fine," categorization for ensembles with a refined overall sound

xibapai 細八派, "refined group of eight," historical term in Suzhou for Jiangnan *sizhu*

xiyue 細樂, "refined music," historical term in Suzhou for Jiangnan *sizhu*

xiansuo 弦索, name for string ensemble that accompanies local opera

xianziqin 弦子琴, two-stringed bowed lute that characteristically accompanies certain northern opera styles, including Henan opera

xiao 簫, end-blown bamboo flute

xin Jiangnan *sizhu* 新江南絲竹, "new Jiangnan *sizhu*," music using melodies typical of the Jiangnan region and traditional instruments, harmonized, structured, and orchestrated in the manner of Western art music

Xingjie 行街, *Walking Along on the Streets*, one of the "eight great pieces" that form the core repertoire of Jiangnan *sizhu*

yaji 雅集, "elegant gathering," gathering of learned men (and women) who are connoisseurs of classical music genres, such as *qin* zither and *kunqu*, extended to classicized folk-music genres, such as Jiangnan *sizhu*

yangqin 扬琴, trapezoid hammered dulcimer

yueqin 月琴, four-stringed plucked lute with a short neck and a large round resonator

yueshe 樂社, music club or association formed to regularly perform a particular genre, mostly for self-recreation

Yunqing 雲慶, *Cloud Celebration*, one of the "eight great pieces" that form the core repertoire of Jiangnan *sizhu*

Zhang Xiaofeng 張曉峰, composer and *sizhu* revivalist from Taicang (b. 1931)

Zhang Yetang 張野塘, son-in-law of Wei Liangfu and his collaborator in reform of *kunqu* (sixteenth century)

zheng 箏, board zither, with eighteen to twenty-one strings

Zhonghua liuban 中花六板, *Middle Flower Six-Beat*, one of the "eight great pieces" that form the core repertoire of Jiangnan *sizhu*

Zhou Chenglong 周成龍, composer of *xin* Jiangnan *sizhu* (b. 1946)

zhuhu 主胡, "main *hu*," lead accompaniment instrument in *huju*

Zizhu diao 紫竹調, *Purple Bamboo Melody*, folk tune from Wuxi, often performed in Jiangnan *sizhu*

Notes

1. Examples include: Witzleben, 1987, 1995; Thrasher, 2008; Qi, 2009; Chow-Morris, 2010; Wu, 2010; Li, 2018.

2. This is an abbreviated name often used when referring to both Jiangsu and Zhejiang provinces.
3. Wu Guodong (2010) refers to this as the Lake Tai Rim Area, a narrower sense of Jiangnan than those in which the name is understood from a geographic, an economic, and/or a broader cultural perspective.
4. See Ruan, 2008: 2; and Qi, 2009: 28–30. Jones remarks that *shifan luogu* is related to *kunqu* vocal and instrumental music in terms of instrumentation, in that both have *di* flute, *sanxian* plucked lute, and a small drum or woodblock and clappers. Moreover, its instrumental music was often "used as an adjunct to *kunqu*, as overture or at transitional points." However, he makes it clear that *Jiangnan sizhu* repertories "owe little to *kunqu*" (Jones, 1995: 248).
5. Qi (2009) devotes a whole chapter of her monograph to depicting Jiangnan *sizhu* performed by music clubs in the rural county of Nanhui, whose northwest corner adjoins Shanghai.
6. In her article on the influences of Daoism on *Jiangnan sizhu*, Chow-Morris questions what she refers to as "the sanitized secular historiographies of Jiangnan *sizhu* widely propagated by Chinese performers and historians and Western academics alike who have . . . largely portrayed the genre as 'secular teahouse music' or described the music in positivistic terms" (2010: 60).
7. Different opinions remain as to what comprise the "eight great pieces," reflecting variety in what gets played in different *Jiangnan sizhu* music clubs and among different groups of musicians. For example, two versions list seven of the same pieces—*Man liuban* (慢六板, Slow Six-Beat), *Zhonghua liuban* (中花六板, Middle Flower Six-Beat), *Man sanliu* (慢三六, Slow Three-Six), *Sihe* (四合, Four Unified), *Xingjie* (行街, Walking Along the Streets), *Yunqing* (雲慶, Cloud Celebration) and *Huanle ge* (歡樂歌, Song of Happiness)—but diverge with regard to the eighth piece; one lists it as being *Lao liuban* (老六板, Old Six-Beat) while the other lists it as *Lao sanliu* (老三六, Old Three-Six) (Gao, 1981: 175–76). Some of these pieces are also known under abbreviated or variant titles.
8. Aside from Jiangnan *sizhu*, these include Chaozhou *xianshi* (潮州弦诗), Kejia *handiao* (客家漢調), Fujian *nanyin* (福建南音), and Guangdong *yinyue* (廣東音樂).
9. These twenty-four pieces with score notations were, in turn, part of a repertoire of 135 pieces that older Taicang musicians recalled performing during the early and middle part of the twentieth century.
10. Gao Xuefeng, personal communication, March 21, 2014.
11. Thrasher (2008: 157–62) refers to this as an interactive type of melodic variation, the two other types being idiomatic (the one that makes use of the technique of "adding flowers") and interpretive. (See also Chapter 9 in this volume.)
12. Also known as *guoyue* (國樂, "national music"). *Minyue* and *guoyue* both refer to music composed for Chinese musical instruments, often an extension of Chinese traditional music, except that it makes use of harmony, equal temperament, and other Western compositional techniques. Zhang Xiaofeng has also composed eight new pieces that are in the *xin Jiangnan sizhu* vein.
13. Examples include Jones, 1995: 248; Witzleben, 1995: 16–22; Stock, 2002; Zheng, 2005; and Qi, 2009: 43–76.
14. See Thrasher, 2008: 153–57 for discussion of the idiomatic techniques characteristic of the main Jiangnan *sizhu* instruments.
15. In *huju*, the lead instrument is not the *di* bamboo flute but rather a loud and rather raucous-sounding two-stringed spike fiddle called *zhuhu* (主胡, "main fiddle"; in Taicang, often referred to as the *shenhu* 申胡) (Stock, 2003: 255), leading one to overlook their remaining similarities. Moreover, present-day performances of this regional

opera, especially in Shanghai, often make use of a large Chinese orchestra, which includes some Western instruments (Witzleben, 1995: 17). In Taicang, however, the use of smaller ensembles mostly of Chinese instruments resembling a typical *Jiangnan sizhu* ensemble remains, save for the *zhuhu* serving as the lead instrument.

16. See Suzhoushi, n.d.; Jones, 1995: 251; Witzleben, 1995: 9–10; and Ruan, 2008: 6–7.
17. This number includes *tangming* who performed in Beijing opera and *kunqu*. In the table, this detail was specified, thus implying that the term *tangming* was used therein to refer to instrumentalists.
18. Jones (1995: 251) remarks that these groups or organizations became the training ground for many later *kunqu* performers.
19. See Gao, 2010: 95–130. At the time of writing, however, there are almost fifty registered music groups in Taicang (Gao Xuefeng, personal communication, December 24, 2020).
20. Gao Xuefeng shared with me that *huju*, which is essentially Shanghai's local opera and is sung in the Shanghainese dialect, is popular in Taicang. A reason for this is the geographic proximity with Shanghai, whose Baoshan and Jiading districts share a border with Taicang. The famous *huju* actor-singer, Wang Agen (王阿根) often performed in Taicang during the first half of the twentieth century and registered his troupe there after the founding of the People's Republic (Gao Xuefeng, personal communication, December 23, 2020).
21. In Chinese culture, professional actors and opera performers have historically occupied the lowest social rungs because they provided entertainment for monetary gain on the same level as prostitutes, "sing-song girls," and funeral ritualists, who are all deemed to be "polluted." In some Chinese regional cultures, opera performers also perform funeral rituals and become doubly stigmatized (Dujunco, 2010).
22. Qi also notes that *qingkechuan* were often from the higher classes and performed *kunqu* and *sizhu* music without monetary gain. This amateur aspect of the *qingkechuan* influenced performers of *kunqu* and Jiangnan *sizhu* musicians, who met in *yaji* performing mainly for their personal artistic cultivation and entertainment (2009: 20–23).
23. Yang Yinliu reportedly discovered that many *shifan luogu* melodies are actually adaptations of *kunqu* melodies (Jones, 1995: 265), thus lending more credence to the close connection between the melodic sections in *shifan luogu* and *kunqu*.
24. See Xiao (2017) for the musical background of Gu Zaixin and his troupe.
25. *Chuida* music, under which the *shifan* genres are often subsumed, can be performed either while sitting and stationary in one place or while walking in procession; seated performances typically comprise whole suites of melodic and percussion movements, while processional performance relies upon "scattered pieces" (Gao, 1981: 24).
26. China's Intangible Cultural Heritage Program was established in 2005 under the Ministry of Culture and the Office of the Ministry Level Joint Conference "to undertake the work of making guidelines and policies for Chinese intangible cultural protection, and to examine, approve, and coordinate protection programs for Chinese intangible cultural heritage." See https://www.culturalheritagechina.org.

References

Chow-Morris, Kim. (2010). "Going with the Flow: Embracing the Tao of China's *Jiangnan Sizhu*," *Asian Music* 41 (2): 59–87.

Dujunco, Mercedes M. 呂梅絲. (2010). "Taiguo, Malaixiya, Xinjiapo Chaozhou gongdeban sangzang yishizhong 'Xuepen' de zhanxian ji qi shehui he lishi yinsu de kaolü" "泰國、馬來西亞、新加坡潮州功德班喪葬儀式中'血盆'的展現及其社會和歷史因素的考慮" [The Performance of *Xuepen* by Chaozhou *Gongde* Troupes in Thailand, Malaysia and Singapore: Some Social and Historical Considerations]. *Dayin* 大音 3: 28–59.

Gao Houyong 高厚永. (1981). *Minzu qiyue gailun* 民族器樂概論 [Outline of Chinese Instrumental Music]. Nanjing: Jiangsu renmin chubanshe.

Gao Xuefeng 高雪峰. (2010). *Jiangnan Sizhu* 江南絲竹 [Jiangnan Silk and Bamboo]. Hangzhou: Xileng yinshe chubanshe.

Gu Lijian 顧禮儉. (2003). "Chuancheng minjian yinyue de xin chuangzuo—he CD *Taicang Jiangnan sizhu shidaqu chuban*" 傳承民間音樂的新創作——贺CD《太倉江南絲竹十大曲》出版 [Imparting New Works of Folk – Saluting the Publication of the CD, *Ten Great Pieces of Taicang Jiangnan Sizhu*] *Renmin Yinyue* 人民音乐 [People's Music], no. 4: 57–58.

Jones, Stephen. (1995). *Folk Music of China: Living Instrumental Traditions*. Oxford: Clarendon Press.

Li Minxiong 李民雄. (1993). "Shanghai shi minzu minjian qiyuequ zongshu" "上海民族民間器樂曲綜述" [A Summary of Shanghai's National Folk Instrumental Music]. In *Zhongguo minzu minjian qiyuequ jicheng: Shanghai juan* 中國民族民間器樂曲集成: 上海卷 [China National Folk Instrumental Music Collection: Shanghai Volume], edited by Li Minxiong 李民雄 et al., 1: 1–18. Beijing: Renmin yinyue chubanshe.

Li Ya 李亚. (2018). "Jiangnan sizhu de 'heyue' chuantong jiqi wenhua chanshi" "江南丝竹的'合乐'传统及其文化阐释" [An Explanation of the Tradition and Culture of 'Ensemble-playing' in Jiangnan *Sizhu*]. *Yinyue Yanjiu* 音乐研究 [Music Research], September Issue, no. 5: 84–92.

Ma Bingyan 馬炳炎 et al., eds. (1999). *Suzhou minjian qiyuequ jicheng* 蘇州民間器樂曲集成 [Suzhou Folk Instrumental Music Collection]. Suzhou: Guwuxuan chubanshe.

Qi, Kun 齐琨. (2009). *Jiangnan sizhu* 江南丝竹 [Jiangnan Silk and Bamboo]. Hangzhou: Zhejiang renmin chubanshe.

Ruan Hong 阮弘. (2008). *Guoyue yu dushi: Jiangnan sihu yu Guangdong yinyue zai Shanghai* 國樂與都市—江南絲竹與廣東音樂在上海 [National Music and the City: Jiangnan *Sizhu* and Guangdong *Yinyue* in Shanghai]. Shanghai: Shanghai wenhua chubanshe.

Stock, Jonathan P. J. (2002). "Huju." In *The Garland Encyclopedia of World Music, Vol. 7, East Asia: China, Japan, and Korea*, edited by Robert C. Provine, Yoshiko Tokumaru, and J. Lawrence Witzleben, 297–301. New York: Routledge.

Stock, Jonathan P. J. (2003). *Huju: Traditional Opera in Modern Shanghai*. Oxford: Oxford University Press.

Suzhoushi Wenhuaju Xiquzhi Bianjibao 苏州市文化局戏曲志编辑报. (n.d.). "Tangming ziliao huibian, shang yu xiace." "堂名资料汇编，上与下册" [A Collection of Materials on *Tangming*, Volumes 1 and 2]. Unpublished manuscript.

Taicang. (2003). *Taicang Jiangnan sizhu shidaqu* 太倉江南絲竹十大曲 [Ten Great Pieces of Taicang Jiangnan Sizhu]. Audio compact disc ISRCCN-#11-02-336-00/A.T6. Nanjing: Jiangsu yinxiang chubanshe,

Thrasher, Alan. (2008). *Sizhu Instrumental Music of South China: Ethos, Theory and Practice*. Leiden: Brill.

Witzleben, J. Lawrence. (1987). "*Jiangnan Sizhu* Music Clubs in Shanghai: Context, Concept, and Identity." *Ethnomusicology* 31 (2): 240–60.

Witzleben, J. Lawrence. (1995). *"Silk and Bamboo" Music in Shanghai: The Jiangnan Sizhu Instrumental Ensemble Tradition.* Kent, OH: Kent State University Press.

Wu Guodong 伍國棟. (2010). *Jiangnan Sizhu: Yuezhong wenhua yu yuezhong xingtai de zonghe yanjiu* 江南絲竹—樂種文化與樂種形態的綜合研究 [Jiangnan Silk and Bamboo: The Integration of Music Culture and Musical Form]. Beijing: Renmin yinyue chubanshe.

Wu Guodong 伍國棟. (2015). "Bu wan sizhu bu jieyuan—Gu Guanren xin Jiangnan sizhu yinyue zuopin shangxi you gan" "不玩絲竹不結緣——顧冠仁新江南絲竹音樂作品賞析有感" [No Playing, No Bonding: Appreciating Gu Guanren's New Jiangnan *Sizhu* Compositions]. *Nanjing yishu xueyuan xuebao* 南京藝術學院學報 [Journal of the Nanjing Arts Institute], no. 1: 5–7.

Xiao Mei 萧梅. (2021). *Tianye de huisheng* 田野的回声 [Echoes of Fieldwork]. Xiao Mei WeChat video channel, September 22, 2021. Accessed September 23, 2021.

Xiao Yuan 簫園. (2017). "Chuancheng Mudu 'Haoshengyin' Gu Zaixin jiangshu shifan jiyi" "傳承木瀆'好聲音'顧再新講述十番記憶" [Account of the Recollections of *Shifan* by Gu Zaixin, the Transmitter of "The Voice" of Mudu]. http://mp.weixin.qq.com/s/pA2v0JkfzzPrjm6a6FLOsQ. Accessed December 23, 2020.

Zhang Xiaofeng 張曉峰. (2003). *Taicang Jiangnan sizhu shidaqu* 太倉江南絲竹十大曲 [Ten Pieces of Taicang Silk and Bamboo Music]. Shanghai: Shanghai yinyue xueyuan chubanshe.

Zheng Hua 郑桦. (1994). "Jiangnan sizhu shulüe" "江南絲竹述" [A Brief Introduction to Jiangnan *Sizhu*]. In *Zhongguo minzu minjian qiyuequ jicheng: Jiangsu juan* 中國民族民間器樂曲集成: 江蘇卷 [China National Folk Instrumental Music Collection: Jiangsu Volume], edited by Zheng Hua 郑桦 et al., 2: 877–85. Beijing: Renmin yinyue chubanshe.

Zheng Lei 郑雷. (2005). *Kunqu* 昆曲 [Kun Drama]. Hangzhou: Zhejiang renmin chubanshe.

CHAPTER 11

SOCIAL CHANGE AND THE MAINTENANCE OF MUSICAL TRADITION AMONG THE WESTERN YUGURS

DU YAXIONG

INTRODUCTION

DURING the past forty years, China's economy has undergone tremendous changes. At the end of the 1970s, China was a poor and economically underdeveloped country. In 1976, after the end of the Cultural Revolution, it began to "reform and open up," and from 1980, its economy underwent rapid growth, at a rate of more than 10 percent annually. In 2004, China's gross domestic product (GDP) was the seventh highest in the world, and in 2007, it surpassed Germany's, taking third place. In 2011, it replaced Japan in second position, and by 2016, China contributed 1.2 percent to global GDP growth, exceeding the 0.8 percent growth of the United States, the European Union, and Japan combined (Polyak, 2017).

In the meantime, political lives in Chinese society, and the wider lives of the Chinese people, have also undergone profound changes. During the Second World War, Mao Zedong wrote: "a certain culture (as a culture of ideology) is a reflection of a certain society's politics and economics" (Mao, 1968: 624). According to his point of view, political and economic change inevitably lead to cultural change. At present, since the onset of rapid economic development, increasingly frequent international exchanges and shifts in production and lifestyles have resulted in the loss of a great many Chinese traditions. Consequently, China's traditional music also faces serious challenges (Du, 2012: 3).

All of China's fifty-six ethnic groups possess long and colorful musical traditions. At this time, there is great international interest in the current situation of China's ethnic-minority music and how it has been influenced by the dramatic economic, political, and social changes of the past forty years. Historically each group had its own definitions of "music," so these questions now arise: Have their ideas changed? Will these traditions fade with continuous development in economics, politics, and lifestyle? Have new varieties of music arisen? If so, then what are these new varieties?

The Yugurs (裕固族) are a small ethnic group in China, with a population of about 14,000. They live in the Sunan Yugur Autonomous County, within the administrative boundaries of Zhangye city, and in Huangnibao Autonomous District in Jiuquan city, both in Gansu province in northwestern China. Among the fifty-six ethnic groups, the Yugur is the only one with two languages. A Turkic language (called Western Yugur) is spoken by the Yugurs living in the western part of this area, and a Mongolic language (termed Eastern Yugur) is spoken by those living further east in Gansu.[1]

As an ethnomusicologist, I have been collecting, studying, and researching Yugur folk songs for more than fifty years, beginning in 1964. In 1985, I contributed the Yugur section of the *Zhongguo minjian gequ jicheng: Gansu juan*中國民間歌曲集成・甘肅卷 (*Anthology of Folk Songs of China's Peoples: Gansu Volume*) (Du, 1985b). In 2005, my proposal for Yugur folk songs to be included on the list of China's National Intangible Cultural Heritage items was approved. Meanwhile, as a composer, I am particularly interested in Yugur musical needs, trying to understand what kinds of songs these people enjoy singing and what kinds can be popularized. Of the numerous Yugur songs I have composed, some have become quite popular among the Yugurs. In this chapter, I will discuss issues concerning the history and the changing lifestyles of the Yugurs and how these have affected their folk songs.

An ethnic group can be defined as a community of people sharing a history; to understand the current situation for an ethnic group, first we have to understand its history. Folk songs are made by the people, and the songs are the reflection of the people's lives, so understanding these folk songs requires understanding the lives of the people who have created them. In this chapter, I will only discuss the situation in the area where the Western Yugur language is spoken, concentrating on Minghua district, Zhangye, since it is an area of Yugur agglomeration. The chapter has four parts: 1) Yugur history and people's lives; 2) original folk songs; 3) today's lifestyles; 4) the current situation for folk songs.

Brief History of the Yugur and Their Lifestyles Before Reform and "Open Door" Policy

The Yugurs have a very long history. This ethnic group and the ten million Uyghurs living in the Xinjiang Autonomous Region of China are both descendants of the Uyghur khaganate (Huihu 回鶻), a massive kingdom on the Mongolian plateau in the eighth century. The origin of these people can then be traced back to the Dingling (丁零), who lived on the southern shores of Lake Baikal during the Han dynasty (206 BCE–220 CE), and the Chile (敕勒), who led a nomadic life in the northern steppes during the Northern and Southern dynasties (420–581 CE). According to historical records of the Northern Wei dynasty (386–534), the ancestors of the Chile were Huns (Xiongnu 匈奴).

Records of the Tang dynasty (618–907) say that, in the year 840, Uyghurs from the khaganate—suffering from severe snowstorms, internal feuding within the ruling class, and attacks from the Kirghiz—migrated from the Mongolian plateau to today's Gansu and Xinjiang (Feng, 1958: 744). They moved westward in separate groups. One group migrated to Guazhou in Ganzhou (today's Zhangye) and to Liangzhou (today's Wuwei) in the Hexi Corridor, which later came under the rule of the Tibetan kingdom. They were called the Hexi Uyghurs. Later, they captured the city of Ganzhou and set up their own kingdom, hence gaining the appellation the Ganzhou Uyghurs.

In the mid-eleventh century, the Western Xia kingdom conquered Ganzhou and toppled the previous regime. The Hexi Uyghurs then moved to pastoral areas outside of today's Jiayuguan Pass. From the middle of the eleventh to the fourteenth century, they lived around Dunhuang in western Gansu and Hami in eastern Xinjiang. It is believed that during that time, some Mongolian-speaking tribes came to this area, and the Uyghurs assimilated the Mongolian tribes over a long period of coexistence, developing into the community that is the present-day Yugurs. About the year 1368, they moved back to the Hexi Corridor (Li, 1983: 9).

The Russian scholar Sergey Malov classifies the dozens of Turkic languages into four groups: remote, ancient, modern, and contemporary. This classification depends on the proportion of ancient linguistic elements present in each group. According to Malov, the language of the Western Yugurs belongs to the first, the remote Turkic language group. He also pointed out that the language of the Western Yugurs is closely related to ancient Uyghur and ancient Turkic (Malov, 1952). According to the Chinese scholars Chen Zongzhen and Lei Xuanchun, quite a number of ancient Turkic linguistic characteristics can be found in the Western Yugur language (Chen and Lei, 1985: 50).

Traditionally, the Yugurs were herdsmen. They lived in yurts made of yak-hair felt, the floors covered with logs. The rectangular yurt is about five meters long, three meters wide, and two meters high, coming to a point at the top. Like many nomadic nationalities, Yugurs are very hospitable to guests. Although the Yugurs have no writing system, they have a very rich oral tradition of legends, folk tales, proverbs, and ballads.

Before the 1950s, there were two types of kinship system: the matrilineal and the patrilineal. The matrilineal form might have been a remnant of the ancient matriarchal social system, but today the patrilineal dominates. Yugurs follow Lamaist Buddhism and at the same time practice the ancient worship of Khan Tenger (Heavenly Khan). Some scholars think that this older religion is possibly a legacy of shamanism (Ma, 1989: 132).

Traditionally, Yugurs lived in a tribal system; several clans formed a tribe, and a union had ten tribes. Each tribe had its own Lamaist monastery and a *mani* pole for worshipping Khan Tenger. The people living in Minghua belong to the Helongro tribe.

Although today the tribal system has weakened, the Yugurs are still aware of the system, and people of each clan share the same family name.

Thus, we see that the Yugurs have retained many ancient traditions: they speak an ancient Turkic language, they believe in shamanism and Buddhism, and some are still nomadic herders organized into tribal units, with patrilineal and matrilineal family systems. The question is: does Yugur music culture also have ancient characteristics?

THE YUGUR FOLK SONG TRADITION

Before the 1960s, the Yugurs did not dance and did not have their own special musical instruments, folk song being their only genre of traditional music. There is no word for "music" in the Yugur language. Only the word *jer* meaning "song" exists in Western Yugur. However, the meaning of *jer* does not completely cover the English definition of "song." One meaning of *jer* is "rhymed poetry," either sung or recited as prose. For example, the *jodatsko*, a long rhyming poem performed at a wedding ceremony, is a *jer*, though it has no melody. It is recited by two people in a loud, high-pitched tone. If the text does not rhyme, even if it has a melody, it cannot be called *jer* but rather *dimi* ("speech"). For example, when Yugurs used to make felt, they needed to sing out numbers to remember how many times they had pushed the wool. This work song is called "counting," not *jer*, even though it has a melody.

In ancient Chinese, there are also no distinct terms for poetry and song. Traditionally, a poem must be sung; in other words, a poem is a song, and a song is a poem. On the one hand, the Yugur classification of song and poetry belongs to this tradition. On the other hand, *jer* only includes songs sung between people to communicate and convey information, not those sung for livestock, spirits, or God. Therefore, shamanic songs or nursing-baby-animal songs (which will be discussed later) are not considered *jer*. Yugurs also categorize songs according to who composed them. They call their own folk songs *yugur jer*, and if a song was composed by a single composer, it is simply *jer*, not *yugur jer*. *Yugur jer* includes historical songs, story songs, ceremonial and ritual songs, work songs, and children's songs.

The most important historical song is "Xizhihazhi" 西支哈至 ("Song on the Road"). According to legend, Xizhihazhi was the name of the area from which the Yugurs' ancestors migrated to the Hexi Corridor in the fourteenth century. It is also believed that the Yugur ancestors composed "Song on the Road" during this migration. This song recounts whence the Yugur ancestors came and the date of their arrival.

> After we listened to the song of the elders,
> We all know that our ancestors came from the west.
> Ancestors walked toward the direction of the rising sun,
> Arriving here in the first year of the reign of Emperor Zhu Yuanzhang.

The "Song on the Road" continues, describing the topography of the areas the Yugurs passed through while moving eastward.

> After they walked for a long time in the Gobi Desert,
> They passed the thousand Buddha grottoes at Dunhuang.
> Then they visited the ten thousand Buddhas grottoes at Anxi,
> Finally arriving at a place where the ancestors founded a kingdom a thousand years ago.

Yugurs believe that the "ancestors' kingdom" refers to the Ganzhou Uyghur khaganate established during the ninth century.

There are a lot of story songs, the texts mostly describing past events or the miserable lives of women who were sold into marriage, such as in the song "Yadang Girl." Story songs also include those that recount myths, as found in "The Bee Girl" and "Song of the Rabbit."

The ritual songs can be divided into three categories: hair-cutting songs, wedding songs, and funeral songs or lamentations. According to Yugur custom, a child's hair is cut for the first time at age three. At this time, there is a hair-cutting ceremony, at which time relatives, friends, and neighbors are invited to give the child gifts or money. When the ceremony begins, the child's uncle (his or her mother's brother) cuts the first lock of the child's hair, and then the other relatives and friends also snip off small locks. At the same time, the child's aunts sing hair-cutting songs to congratulate the child. The ritual signifies the beginning of a person's life. It is such an important event that it is usually celebrated for three days. On the first day, they kill sheep and cattle and prepare food; on the second day, the formal ceremony is held; on the third, the parents hold a farewell party to thank guests for attending.

A traditional wedding is conducted on two separate days. It takes place at the bride's home on the first day and at the groom's, on a larger scale, the next day. The wedding begins at the bride's home in the very early morning before sunrise. The first step of the ceremony is to arrange the bride's hair into a women's knot. While a woman combs the bride's hair, the brother of the bride's mother sings a song-type called *aloi*, telling her that her childhood is now over and that she has become an adult. Then, after the bride's family has held a party, she leaves her home for the groom's place. Before she leaves, she and her uncle sing songs called *gez jer* ("girl's songs"). The uncle tells the bride that at her husband's home she should be a good wife and agreeable daughter-in-law. At this point the bride sings a sad farewell song to her family.

After the bride and her procession arrive at the groom's home, they are served mutton and liquor, and the wedding ceremony takes place that night. At first, a rite is performed by two singers, one holding a sheep's legs between the knees and ankles, and the other holding a piece of white silk called *hada*, which is used as a greeting gift among Yugurs. They perform a *jodatsko*, in which the text explains the reasons behind the Yugur marriage customs. After the singers perform this *jodatsko*, they invite the bride into the yurt.

Accompanied by a bridesmaid, the bride walks toward the yurt between two bonfires, and at the same time the groom, holding a miniature bow, shoots three harmless arrows at the bride. The groom then breaks the bow and arrows and throws them into the fire.

When the bride enters the yurt, she bows to her mother-in-law and gives her a gift. Then the bridal couple goes around to each guest, bowing to them and filling their cups with liquor. After the ceremony, the wedding celebration begins. While people eat and drink, they also sing songs. In these songs, the bride's relatives ask the mother-in-law to take good care of her, and the relatives of the groom sing songs in praise of their family and tell the bride's family not to worry. At the party, there is other singing too, sometimes of mutual congratulation and sometimes of funny or teasing songs to enliven the atmosphere.

After a person dies, the family sings dirges or laments to mourn the dead, and they also invite lamas to hold a ceremony to release the soul from purgatory. The funeral songs are grouped into two parts: one part, sung by the attendees, is similar to sobbing or lamenting; the other part is a solo sung by a family member. Generally, the content of the songs is a memorial to the dead.

Yugurs have many different kinds of work song. Among these, the most important are pastoral songs, felt-making songs, hay-cutting songs, and nursing-baby-animal songs. Although Yugurs do not think of all of these songs as *jer*, they occupy a very important position among their folk song because of their quantity. Yugur livestock is made up of cattle, camels, horses, sheep, and goats. They sing different songs for herding different animals, so there are sheep-grazing songs, cattle-grazing songs, and horse-grazing songs. The lyrics of the pastoral songs are mostly improvised, and the melodic range is quite wide. When Yugurs make felt blankets, they also sing work songs: several people line up, kneeling in the grass, and while they roll the felt in unison, they sing. The purpose of the singing is to unify their movements and keep count of the quantity of rolls through the externalizing of the numbers. When autumn comes and the grass becomes yellow, the herdsmen have to cut it as winter fodder for the livestock. The hay-cutting song is sung while performing this work.

Nursing-baby-animal songs are sung when dams refuse to nurse their calves. Yugurs believe that animals have the ability to feel music. Through the many thousands of years of animal herding, they have discovered that different kinds of livestock respond to different kinds of songs. The texts of these songs often scold or encourage the mother animal.

> Why don't you even look at your baby; don't you have eyes?
> Why don't you pay attention to the baby; aren't you ashamed?
> You don't recognize your lamb; is there another mother like you?
> You do not feed the lamb; do you want to starve it?
> The lamb is calling for its mother; it wishes you to nurse it.
> If you give it milk, I will give you some good hay to eat.
> If you feed the lamb, you will be my good sheep.

These songs feature various meaningless words, depending on the type of livestock. For example, the syllable *toi* is used to nurse a lamb, *gij* to nurse a kid, and when cajoling a cow into nursing her calf, a herdsman may sing songs containing the syllable *xie*. The melodies also vary according to the type of animal. The songs for cows and songs for ewes are the most distinctive. When singing for ewes, the herdsman also strokes the back of the animal. The melodic range of the song for a ewe is narrow; the rhythm is fine and very regular. In contrast, the range of the song for a cow is wide and undulating, and the rhythm is freer and more flexible.

Children's songs have two categories: lullabies and toddling or learning-to-walk songs. The Yugur lullaby has a special meaningless word, *beli*, and the learning-to-walk song is very particular. When children begin learning to walk, Yugur adults take their hands and sing toddling songs to them. Yugur people think toddling songs can help children learn quicker to walk. The rhythm of toddling songs is clear and the speed is moderate so that the children can set their feet to the pace. At the beginning, only adults sing the toddling songs, but after a while the children learn to sing them too.

The Yugur folk-song lyrics preserve the ancient Turkic poetry style. This is characterized by each stanza having four lines, with a rhyme form of AAAB (Du, 1985a: 20). According to their rhythmic characteristics, Yugur folk songs can be divided into two basic genres: the long tune and the short tune. The melodic range of the long tune is very wide. Big skips often occur, and melodies have steps of greater than an octave. Sometimes, the long tune uses free rhythm. But even when the rhythm is not free, this does not imply there is always a regular pulse. The high notes are often greatly extended, with singers showing their skill by sustaining them for as long as possible. Only a very skilled singer can sing this kind of song. The long-tune category includes historical songs, wedding songs, story songs, pastoral songs, and some shamanic songs. The melodic range of the short tune is narrower than that of the long tune. The short tune has almost no long notes, the beats are regular, and the melodies are easy to sing. The short-tune category includes work songs and children's songs.

Different melodies have different styles, but the form of Yugur folk songs is always very similar: all melodies comprise two phrases. When singers sing a song, its melody is repeated until the text is finished. Some melodies have a prelude before the first phrase, and singers use the meaningless words *a luo* or *ey*. Usually, the prelude begins from the lowest note and rises to highest note of the melody. Its function is to arouse the audience's attention and lead into the texts.

Almost all melodies use the tonal pentatonic scale, which is widespread in China. There are five tones in the scale, which Chinese music theory labels *gong* 宫, *shang* 商, *jue* 角, *zhi* 徵, and *yu* 羽, equivalent to *do*, *re*, *mi*, *sol*, and *la* in European music. Each tone can act as the tonic, so the pentatonic scale can form five different modes, which are correspondingly called *gong*, *shang*, *jue*, *zhi*, and *yu*. I collected ninety-four Western Yugur folk songs when I lived in the area from 1968 to 1978. There are fifty-six *yu* melodies among my collection, a mode that accounts for 59.57 percent of the total number of pieces collected. In this sample, the order of prevalence for the other modes is *shang* (nineteen melodies, 20.21 percent), *zhi* (ten melodies, 10.63 percent), *gong* (six melodies, 6.38 percent), and *jue* (three melodies, 3.19 percent). *Yu* is the most important mode of Western Yugur folk songs, and many of its melodies employ a downward quint-shift—that is, the second half of the melody is, by and large, identical to the first half but repeated a fifth lower. Marking the melodic lines with capital letters, the form of the melodic structure would be A5 Av (with "v" representing minor melodic divergences or variations) (Du, 1982).

According to the work of Zoltán Kodály (1971: 18), Hungarian folk songs also have these two characteristics. There are parallel melodies in Western Yugur and Hungarian folk songs. Among the ninety-four Western Yugur folk songs I collected, fifteen songs (accounting for 15.9 percent of the total) show similarities in scale, mode, and melodic structure to Hungarian folk songs (Du, 1992: 32). In 1989, Aerang Yinxing Jis, a famous Western Yugur singer visited Hungary, and the Yugur folk songs that she sang in Budapest were very similar to Hungarian folk songs. Many Hungarians listened to her songs and became very interested in the folk songs of the Western Yugurs. The lyrics of Hungarian and Yugur folk songs also have similar structures. One singular feature is the meaningless word *beli* in Hungarian lullabies, which is the exact same word used in Yugur lullabies, as mentioned above.

These similarities between Western Yugur and Hungarian folk songs call for more detailed study. They show that both belong to musical traditions that have been alive for thousands of years. Since Western Yugurs are descendants of ancient Turkic-speaking people, the similarity between Hungarian folk songs and Yugur folk songs would strongly suggest that the ancestors of the Hungarians can trace back their musical style to the Turkic peoples of Asia and an ancient homeland. The Western Yugurs, too, retain a very old Turkic musical tradition (Du, 1992), another feature of their ancient cultural inheritance.

Folk song is an art form that combines language (words) with music (tunes). According to Malov's research, mentioned above, several ancient linguistic elements are preserved in the Western Yugur language. My own findings suggest that, since Yugurs have kept their ancient language, nomadic lifestyle, tribal system, oral folklore, and a link to Hungarian folk songs, it is reasonable to suppose that their folk songs have also retained many ancient tunes and musical elements of their ancestors, the Dingling and the Huns.

Changes in Yugur Lifestyles

Before 1980, almost all Yugurs were nomads; animal husbandry was their main economic source. Their lifestyles, production, and supplies depended on livestock, and their means of transportation were the camel and the horse. At present, however, there are two reasons why this way of life has completely shifted. The first is alteration to natural conditions, and the second is social change.

First, because of global warming, the snowline of the Qilian mountain has risen, with grassland degradation resulting from severe water shortage. For this reason, animals have not had enough food, and they have not been able to provide a livelihood for the people. Yugurs have had to seek a new way of life. In addition, in the process of economic development, the nomadic lifestyle could no longer provide for all needs. People had to settle down in order to satisfy growing demands in all aspects of production and life. Therefore, during the final decade of the past century, increasing numbers of Yugurs abandoned nomadism and turned to agriculture. They had to give up their familiar lifestyles and adapt to environmental and economic changes.

To enable the Yugurs to develop agriculture, the government established a resettlement area and named it a "development zone." Yugurs were moved from the grasslands to this new development zone, solving the serious water-shortage problem. For example, at the newly settled Shuanghaizi village in Minghua, the herdsmen dug a 150-meter-deep well with the help of the government, and they built a 20-cubic-meter-capacity water tower. In the Hexi Corridor, winds are powerful. To develop agriculture, Yugurs had to build windbreaks and then learn the technologies of cultivation. In the early stages of relocation, the herdsmen had no such experience, and the survival rate of trees and species planted was very low. But after repeated experiments, they were eventually more successful. At present, there are a great many trees used for windbreaks in the development zone, and Yugurs successfully grow crops, including tomatoes, watermelons, corn, and wheat. In addition to agricultural production, some people breed cattle and sheep, open small shops, and transport goods. Others go to the surrounding counties and cities to make a living. At present, 80.9 percent of the people in this village are farmers, 6.5 percent are engaged in animal breeding, 4.3 percent have moved to other cities to make a living, and 4.3 percent are engaged in business.

Today in the Minghua area, 90 percent of the Yugurs have become farmers; they have gradually adapted to this lifestyle, having experienced the most dramatic social transformation in their history. But there are also some herdsmen who are not accustomed to this way of life. Yarji, born in 1972, is a friend and informant. She is an excellent folk singer and herdsman who grew up herding goats. In 1980, she participated in the National Minorities' Music and Dance Festival held in Beijing and won a prize singing Yugur folk songs. Until 1999, she lived in Lianhua township, Sunan county, and then she moved to the development zone and engaged in agriculture. In 2005 she told me that after relocation, farming became more labor-intensive than her original grazing at home, although the economic return was much higher. However, her two sons did not adapt to the life there. One of them moved back home, and the other moved to the nearby Jiayuguan city and opened a snack shop. In 2017, she moved to Jiayuguan to live with her youngest son, and the house and the land she owns in the development zone was rented to a Han farmer.

The change in the mode of production has brought great transformation to the Yugurs. It is manifest in different aspects, such as living conditions, eating habits, clothing culture, transportation, communication, and education, to name but a few. After settling down, all Yugurs live in houses built by unified planning authorities. Now the average living area for a family is about 120 square meters, each house having a living room, bedrooms, kitchen, and bathroom. Many of the houses have wooden floors and heating, and living conditions are, by modern standards, higher than those in small 20-square-meter tents. In the past, the staple foods for Yugurs were meat, dairy products, and milk-tea. At present, their diets consist mainly of rice, flour, vegetables, and fruit.

In the past, being engaged with animal husbandry, Yugurs' main means of transportation was horses, which earned them the name "the nation on horseback," and they also used yaks and camels for transporting goods far and near. From the beginning of the twenty-first century, motorcycles and cars have replaced horses and camels. To communicate, people previously sent written mail to each other, and because the Yugurs do not have their own writing system, they wrote in Chinese. At present, almost everyone has a mobile phone.

The Yugur have beautiful folk costumes with distinctive ethnic characteristics. Both men and women previously wore long gowns, which are not suitable for agricultural activities and labor. At present, they generally wear the Western-style clothing of the Han instead of their ethnic costumes, which today are mostly seen only at ceremonies or on stage.

Another important change has taken place in the area of education. Before they moved to the development zone, teachers on horseback traveled from tent to tent to teach students for several hours a week. They called this "the school on horseback." Of course, this method made it difficult to ensure the quality and speed of education. After the Yugurs settled down, new schools were built, and now all children attend school regularly. According to statistics for 2000, the Yugur nationality has the highest level of education in Gansu province. Proportionately, there are many more doctors, professors, experts, and intellectuals among the Yugurs today, when compared to many other minorities in China (He, 2011).

To sum up, between the twentieth and the twenty-first centuries, Yugurs experienced the most dramatic change in their history, greater even than in their migrations of the ninth and the fourteenth centuries. After such a change in economics and lifestyle, can they preserve the cultural traditions that they had kept for more than a thousand years? Can they preserve their even older folk-song tradition? These questions are not only for Yugurs but also for ethnomusicologists interested in Yugur folk songs.

THE CHANGING FOLK SONGS

With the modes of production and people's lifestyles undergoing such alterations, it is not surprising to find that Yugur folk songs have also changed. First, the concept of folk song shifted; some traditional folk songs disappeared, and compositions called "new folk songs" have been created, all while Yugurs are trying hard to guard and transmit their folk-song heritage.

As I noted above, there is no word for "folk songs" in the Yugur language. To denote this, Yugurs add the name of the ethnic group before the word *jer*. For instance, there is *yugur jer* for Yugur folk song, *mongol jer* for Mongolian folk song, or *sart jer* for the folk songs of the Hui nationality. For other songs, they use the general term *jer*. Prior to the 1980s, if the texts had no rhyme or the song was not sung for people but rather for animals or spirits, it could not be called *jer*. At present, the Yugur definition of folk song has altered. Now they consider nursing-baby-animal songs to be "folk songs." Some poems that have no melodies but used to be considered folk songs—such as the *jodatsko* performed at weddings—are no longer called "folk songs."

Before 1974, when Sunan county set up a song-and-dance ensemble, there were almost no professional Yugur musicians and singers. By the 1980s, many had become professional musicians and a lot of them wrote songs, while composers of other nationalities have also written Yugur songs. These songs use the lyrics of Yugur folk songs, and others, such as "Xizhihazhi" composed by a Tibetan composer, Cairang Danzeng, are written in the style of Yugur folk songs. Some contain lyrics written by Yugur poets and music by Han composers, including a piece called "I am a Yugur Shepherd," with text by He Jixin 賀繼新, music by Liu Tingxin 柳廷信. Though Yugurs know that these songs were created by composers, they call them "new folk songs." In 2004, when the Yugur singers Sar Tala and Nor Jis sang my composition "For a Wonderful Future" on CCTV, they announced to the audience that this was a "new Yugur folk song" composed by Du Yaxiong (Figure 11.1). Another typical case occurred in 2016, when Gansu Audio and Video Company was making a documentary on Yugur folk songs. Many Yugur singers asked the editors to record their "new folk songs" on the basis that otherwise the data in the film would not be complete. The company eventually agreed and added several "new folk songs" to the production.

Another change is that Yugurs now think of nursing-baby-animal songs not only as *jer* but also as pieces that can be sung to entertain people. At the national minority

FIGURE 11.1. Yugur singers with researcher Du Yaxiong (standing, third from right).

festival held in October 1980, Aerang Yinxing Jis, a professional Yugur folk singer, performed a nursing-baby-animal song on stage. The original song is slow, but she sang it in a joyful allegro. With that, there is evidence that Yugur conceptualizations have changed. In 2005, I continued my field work among the Yugurs. While I was recording more nursing-baby-animal songs, I used the traditional terms "speech" and "speaker," but the singers corrected me, asking me to use the terms "song" and "singer" instead. Another example is that Yugurs used to think of the *jodatsko* performed at a wedding as a "song," but now they call it a "poem." This is another very dramatic change in song categorization.

As Yugur concepts of folk song changed, some traditional folk songs were also lost. Three reasons had impact in tandem: 1) economies and lifestyles changed; 2) singers forgot the songs; 3) the songs were not passed on before the older generation of singers was lost. When the Yugurs settled and gave up nomadism, this greatly altered their working practices, and the songs of the past were no longer sung. Today, no one grazes animals or gathers hay, so no one sings herding and hay-cutting songs. Although some Yugurs keep animals, when the mother animal fails to recognize its young, the calves and lambs get a bottle of milk; the Yugurs do not sing a nursing-baby-animal song. The environment in the development zone is also different from that of the grasslands. Nowadays, every Yugur family has a TV that can receive more than forty channels from all over China, including Hong Kong, and watching TV has become one of the main forms of entertainment. Today, only a few people sing folk songs.

An Xiuzhen (安秀珍), born in 1945, was a very good singer. Before 1985, I collected many folk songs from her. In 2005, when I visited her again, she could not sing any songs at all. She said she had not sung for twenty years and had forgotten all the songs that she had sung in the past. Another important informant of mine, Enqing Zhuoma 恩情卓瑪 (1910–88) was a very famous singer, too. In the 1960s and 1970s, I recorded some of the many songs she sang. But during a period of fieldwork in 1985, I had no time to visit her to record more songs. Since nobody learned songs from her, all of her songs were lost when she died.

But while traditional folk songs disappeared, some composers and Yugur singers have created new ones. The most prevalent content for these new songs concerns the beautiful grassland and the nomadic life, with feelings of nostalgia for the past. An example is Aerang Yinxing Jis's composition "Danggena" ("It is Beautiful," 2003):

> The sky in the Yugur grassland is beautiful,
> The earth on the Yugur grassland is beautiful.
> When the smoke rises from the tents, shepherds are returning,
> This is the Yugur grassland in my heart.
> The water and the mountains of the Yugur grassland are beautiful,
> Yugur stories are in my memory.
> The lamb is chasing her mother outside the tent,
> This is the Yugur grassland in my heart.
> The people in the Yugur grassland are beautiful,

> To be a Yugur I never regret.
> My mother and father in the tent are smiling,
> This is the Yugur grassland in my heart.

Another representative work is "The Yugur Grassland Disappeared" composed by Nor Jis, another professional Yugur singer. This composition sings of the sadness of Yugur people at losing the grassland. During China's urbanization, increasing numbers of young and middle-aged people left their homes and went to cities to make a living. In many families, only the elderly and children live at home. In 2007, Nor Jis worried about the future of her ethnic group.

> The Yugurs' grassland has gone,
> When the grass is yellow, nobody mows it.
> All the horses and the camels were sold,
> The bird and the swallow also flew away.
> The girls traveled far away,
> The lads moved and ran away.
> Only the old men and women stayed,
> The children with their hearts flew away.
> The stories are forgotten,
> The language is not spoken.
> When mom and dad die,
> Are there still any Yugur souls remaining?
> I am a Yugur singer, and when I sing this song,
> My heart aches.

Almost all the lyrics of "new folk songs" are written in Chinese and then translated into the Western Yugur language by Yugur singers. The melodies try to absorb the musical elements of Yugur folk song, but the range is much wider and the songs are usually much longer than the traditional folk songs.

In 2006, the Culture Ministry of the Chinese government declared Yugur folk song an item of National Intangible Cultural Heritage. Since then, Yugurs have spared no effort to protect and transmit their folk songs. Outstanding achievements are folk-song collections on CDs and DVDs, the teaching of folk song at schools, and the efforts to invent a Yugur writing system to record and restore the old customs. After Yugur folk songs became recognized as National Intangible Cultural Heritage, the county government's office of cultural affairs published a list of artists called the "guardians of tradition," bidding them to work toward keeping and transmitting the traditional folk songs. Also, anthropologists, ethnologists, and ethnomusicologists go to Sunan county to collect folk songs, and usually they pay the singers. This encourages singers to seek out among the Yugurs folk songs that they have not heard before, so they can sell them to the scholars the next time these experts visit. This has resulted in the reappearance of some old folk songs, such as "Bird Song," "Twelve Chinese Zodiacs," and "Song of the Seasons."

Since the end of the twentieth century, the rapid development of digital information technology has changed how tradition can be preserved. The Sunan County Cultural Bureau has visited many singers, recorded folk songs, and published audio discs as well as issuing a number of DVDs. These audio-visual materials are used not only for studying, transmitting, and appreciating the music but also for providing valuable data to the fields of anthropology, ethnology, culture, history, and musicology.

During the Spring and Autumn period in China (770–476 BCE), just like today, ancient folk songs were gradually losing ground because of changes in lifestyle. Confucius (551–479 BCE), noticing the situation, began to compile and teach folk songs at his school. Confucius's practices of folk-song preservation through education have given the Yugurs great inspiration. At present, some schools in Sunan county are teaching Yugur folk songs. Most schools teach the historical songs; thus, this kind of song is much better preserved than others.

Yugurs have their own language but not their own writing system, which in today's fast-changing world makes the transmission of folk songs very difficult. From the beginning of the twenty-first century, some Yugur writers and singers began to use the Latin alphabet for the Yugur language. This approach has gradually matured, and on January 14, 2018, experts held a conference at the Minzu University of China in Beijing, a school designated for ethnic minorities, to discuss details of the Yugur spelling system, which hopefully can be put into practice in the near future.

Many Yugur folk songs are linked with folklore, and if those customs cannot be saved, the folk songs are also doomed to oblivion. People are currently engaged in various efforts to keep alive the customs regarding hair-cutting and ceremonies so that the folk songs linked to these practices can be maintained. One example is in connection to the traditional wedding. I know a young couple, Mr. Zhang Wen 張文 and Miss Tuo Likun 妥麗坤. When they decided to marry, they wanted to hold their wedding as soon as possible. They both live in Lanzhou, the capital of Gansu province, but they at once traveled nearly a thousand kilometers by train and bus back to their home village in Sunan county. Lanzhou is a large city with 4.4 million people, and Mr. Zhang and Miss Tuo have a lot of friends there. There are also many wedding companies in Lanzhou that plan and arrange elaborate events—a big business that is very popular with young people in China today. However, this Yugur couple did not want to hold such a wedding in Lanzhou, opting instead for a traditional Yugur one. They preferred this route even though they did not follow their parents into occupations as nomadic herdsmen, which their ancestors had been for thousands of years.

Today it is quite an involved process to hold a traditional wedding because of the elaborate preparations needed. First, the traditional costumes, not only for the couple but also for their parents and some other relatives, must be hand-made. Second, temporary tents have to be erected for various parts of the ceremony. Third, an integral part of the wedding are the several folk singers who sing traditional folk songs at each step. We can imagine the cost of such nuptials. Why, then, do some Yugurs spend so much money and give themselves so much trouble to have a traditional wedding? Because they want to hold on to Yugur traditional customs.

Conclusion

As noted at the beginning of the chapter, Mao believed that culture is a reflection of economics and politics and that the construction of a new economy and new politics inevitably produces and builds a new culture (Mao, 1968: 656). However, the construction of a new culture cannot "fall from the sky"; it must, at least in part, be based on the old culture. Rather, we can say that culture—which includes economics and politics—perpetually metamorphoses. Every part of culture influences the other, and this can be seen in daily life, especially today with the proliferation of information technology.

Throughout human history, it is also not difficult to see that technology and art have developed along different lines. The progress of technology is achieved by substitution: the new tends to replace the old. Thus, the tractor has replaced the hoe, and the computer has replaced the typewriter, to mention but two examples. However, the development of literature and art depends more upon augmentation than replacement. Contemporary English literature does not replace Shakespeare, and new Chinese poems do not replace the *Shijing* 詩經 (*Book of Songs*).

Ethnic groups have to strive to maintain their linguistic, musical, and artistic traditions in order to survive. If a facet of cultural heritage cannot be effectively preserved, it may lose its spiritual home. Moreover, with such a loss, no substrate is left for further innovation and development. Chinese history also tells us that the culture of an ethnic group is the fundamental condition for the survival of the group. Some ethnic groups, such as the Huns or the Xianbei (鮮卑), have disappeared because they did not or could not keep their traditions. At present, in the process of globalization, with rapid economic development and the frequency of exchanges between nations, many traditional cultures are in danger of extinction. The Yugur people have realized that only by preserving their cultural tradition can they survive as an ethnic unit. Failing this, they are in danger of being subsumed into a more dominant one, as so many others have before.

Music is an important cultural feature of every nation. But it is a more conservative cultural form than language. For instance, African Americans have not spoken African languages for hundreds of years, but even today their music has retained significant features of African music. If an ethnic group wants to survive as a unit, it is imperative that it preserve its own traditional music. A Yugur folk song says: "If I forget my home, I won't forget my native language. If I forget my language, I won't forget my native song."

In Chinese literature, the term "music" (*yue* 樂) appeared for the first time in *Lüshi chunqiu* 呂氏春秋 (*Lü's Spring and Autumn Annals*), a history book edited by Lü Buwei 呂不韋 during the Warring States period (476–221 BCE). The author considers the origin of music to be linked to measurements and the *yin-yang* 陰陽 theory as explained in the *Yijing* 易經 (*Book of Changes*), one of the thirteen Confucian classics. In the chapter entitled "Dayue" 大樂 ("Great Music"), we read:

The origin of music can be traced as far as the remote ages. It came from the concept of measurements, originating from the *taiyi* [太乙]. *Taiyi*, the primeval essence, gave birth to bi-direction, *liangyi* [兩儀], from which emerged *yin* and *yang*. *Yin* and *yang* interact from below and above, and thus music contains harmonious proportions of *yin* and *yang* (Zhongguo yishu yanjiuyuan yinyue yanjiusuo, 1983: 35).

The *Yijing* is a book of divination based on profound philosophy from the distant past, and it does not emerge from Yugur culture, but it nevertheless provides a clue as to how we might interpret the various relationships at stake in the maintenance of their musical culture today. According to Zheng Xuan 鄭玄 (127–200 CE), a famous Confucian scholar of the Eastern Han dynasty (25–220 CE), the meaning of *yi* 易 is at once "change" (*bianyi* 變易), "simplicity" (*jianyi* 簡易), and "invariability" (*buyi* 不易) (Qiu, 1993: 3). From this perspective, even when the effects of economic and political changes are profound, an ethnic group must maintain the characteristics of its own musical culture unchanged, otherwise it will disappear. The Yugurs have aptly been seeking musical-culture stability through various simple means during the past forty years, the era of greatest change in their history. Their survival as a distinct ethnic population may depend upon their success in this task.

Glossary

[Y] denotes an entry in Western Yugur language

a luo [Y], meaningless syllable used when performing the prelude to a song
Aerang Yinxing Jis [Y], professional Yugur folk singer and songwriter (contemporary)
aloi [Y], wedding ceremonial song
An Xiuzhen 安秀珍, singer (b. 1945)
beli [Y], meaningless syllable used in Yugur lullabies (also used in Hungarian songs)
bianyi 變易, change
buyi 不易, invariability
Chile 敕勒, nomadic people in the northern steppes during the Northern and Southern dynasties (420–581 CE)
"Dayue" 大樂, "Great Music", chapter of the *Lüshi chunqiu*
"Danggena" [Y], "It is Beautiful," song (2003)
dimi [Y], speech
Dingling 丁零, people from the southern shores of Lake Baikal during the Han dynasty (206 BCE–220 CE)
Enqing Zhuoma 恩情卓瑪, singer (1910–88)
ey [Y], meaningless syllable used when performing the prelude to a song
gez jer [Y], "girl's songs," wedding ceremonial song type
gij [Y], meaningless syllable used in songs for nursing a kid
gong 宮, first pentatonic tone in Chinese music theory (*do*)
hada [Y], piece of white silk used as a greeting gift among Yugurs
He Jixin 賀繼新, lyricist for new Yugur folk songs (contemporary)
Huihu 回鶻, ancestors of the Yugur, residing on the Mongolian plateau (eighth century)
jianyi 簡易, simplicity

jer [Y], rhymed song or poetic recitation on certain topics
jodatsko [Y], wedding recitation performed in rhyme by two people
jue 角, third pentatonic tone in Chinese music theory (*mi*)
liangyi 兩儀, bi-directional concept from ancient philosophy that led to *yin* and *yang*
Liu Tingxin 柳廷信, composer of new Yugur folk songs (contemporary)
Lüshi chunqiu 呂氏春秋, *Lü's Spring and Autumn Annals*, book edited by Lü Buwei 呂不韋 (c. 239 BCE)
Nor Jis [Y], Yugur singer and songwriter (contemporary)
Sar Tala [Y], Yugur singer (contemporary)
shang 商, second pentatonic tone in Chinese music theory (*re*)
Shijing 詩經, song collection compiled by Confucius (551–479 BCE)
taiyi 太乙, primeval essence
toi [Y], meaningless syllable used in songs for nursing a lamb
"Xizhihazhi" 西支哈至, "Song on the Road", song in Yugur style by Tibetan composer Cairang Danzeng (contemporary)
Xianbei 鮮卑, historical ethnic group
xie [Y], meaningless syllable used in songs cajoling a cow into nursing her calf
Xiongnu 匈奴, Huns, ancestors of the Chile people and other populations
Yijing 易經, *Book of Changes*, one of the thirteen Confucian classics
yin-yang 陰陽, theory explained in the *Yijing*
yu 羽, fifth pentatonic tone in Chinese music theory (*la*)
Yugur 裕固族, ethnic minority population in Gansu province
yue 樂, music
Zheng Xuan 鄭玄, Confucian scholar (127–200 CE)
zhi 徵, fourth pentatonic tone in Chinese music theory (*sol*)

Note

1. Since there is not yet an established means of writing Western Yugur, I use English translations to represent song titles and lyrics in this chapter.

References

Chen Zongzhen 陳宗振 and Lei Xuanchun 雷選春. (1985). *Xibu yuguyu jianzhi* 西部裕固語簡志 [A Short Description of the Western Yugur Language]. Beijing: Minzu chubanshe.
Du Yaxiong 杜亞雄. (1982). "Yuguzu xibu min'ge jiqi youguan min'ge zhibijiao yanjiu" "裕固族西部民歌及其有關民歌之比較研究" [Comparative Research Between Western Yugur Folksong and Related Folksongs]. *Zhongguo yinyue* 中國音樂 [Chinese Music], no. 4: 26–30.
Du Yaxiong 杜亞雄. (1985a). *Comparative Research of Chinese Folk Songs and Hungarian Folk Songs*. Buenos Aires: Ősi Gyökér.
Du Yaxiong 杜亞雄. (1985b). "Yuguzu minge" "裕固族民歌" [Yugur Folksong]. In *Zhongguo minjian gequ jicheng: Gansu juan* 中國民間歌曲集成・甘肅卷, edited by Zhongguo Minjian Gequ Jicheng Quanguo Bianji Weiyuanhui 中國民間歌曲集成全國編輯委員會, 769–74. Beijing: Renmin yinyue chubanshe.

Du Yaxiong 杜亞雄. (1992). "The Ancient Quint-Construction in Hungarian Folksongs." *Chinese Music* 15 (2): 24–33.

Du Yaxiong 杜亞雄. (2012). *Lingting Zhongguo: Wushiliuge minzu de minjian yinyue yichan* 聆聽中國：五十六個民族的民間音樂遺產 [Listening to China: The Music Heritage of China's Fifty-Six Nationalities]. Nanjing: Jiangsu wenyi chubanshe.

Feng Jiasheng 馮家升. (1958). *Weiwuer zu shiliao jianbian* 維吾爾族史料簡編 [Selected Historic Materials on the Uyghur Nationality]. Beijing: Minzu chubanshe.

He Weiguang. 賀衛光. (2011). *Yugu zu xiandai shehui yanjiu* 裕固族現代社會研究 [A Study on the Contemporary Society of the Yugurs]. Beijing: Minzu chubanshe.

Kodály, Zoltán. (1971). *A Magyar Népzene*. Budapest: Zeneműkiadó.

Li Yutang 李玉堂, ed. (1983). *Yugu zu jianzhi* 裕固族簡史 [A Brief History of the Yugur Nationality]. Lanzhou: Gansu renmin chubanshe.

Ma Yin, ed. (1989). *China's Minority Nationalities*. Beijing: Foreign Languages Press.

Malov, Sergey. (1952). "Древние и новые тюркские языки" [Ancient and Modern Turkish Languages]. *Известия АН СССР. Отделение литературы и языка* [Science Bulletin of the Academy of the USSR] 11 (2): 135–43.

Mao Zedong 毛澤東 (1968). *Mao Zedong xuanji* 毛澤東選集 *The Selected Works of Mao Zedong*. Beijing: Renmin chubanshe.

Polyak, Eszter. (2017). "Structural Transformation of the Chinese Economy" http://www.geopolitika.hu/en/2017/03/20/structural-transformation-of-the-chinese-economy/, accessed November 9, 2021.

Qiu Yin 邱吟, ed. (1993). *Zhou yi* 周易 [Yijing]. Changsha: Hunan renmin chubanshe.

Zhongguo yishu yanjiuyuan yinyue yanjiusuo 中國藝術研究院音樂研究所音研所, ed. (1983). *Zhongguo gudai yuelun xuanji* 國古代樂論選集 [Selected Musicological Papers of Ancient China]. Beijing: Renmin yinyue chubanshe.

CHAPTER 12

THE MAKING OF A MUSIC COMMUNITY AS A MANIFESTATION OF NATIONALISM

The Jinyu Qinshe Society in 1930s China

YU HUI

Cultural Radicalism Vs. Musical Conservatism

ONCE defined as "the hermeneutical science of human musical behavior" (Merriam, 1977: 198), ethnomusicology has long focused on the processes of music making across various nations and as born out of different motivations. The musical nationalism reflected in the *guqin* 古琴 seven-stringed zither activities of the Jinyu Qinshe 今虞琴社 (*Guqin* Society of Today's Yushan 虞山 School) community reveals a particularly fascinating set of human musical behaviors in China to which not enough attention has been paid. We can approach these behaviors through reference to Benedict Anderson's defining of the core concept of the nation through the term "imagined community," which emphasizes the nation's intrinsic foundations in shared cultural identity. Anderson asserts that cultural artifacts contribute to expressing nationalism among a specific group of people, and nationality, nation-ness, and nationalism "are cultural artifacts of a particular kind" (Anderson, 2006: 4).

The Han Chinese have traditionally called themselves the descendants of the Yan Emperor and the Yellow Emperor, and it is to the time of the latter that the creation of the musical instrument the *guqin* is attributed. Sima Qian 司馬遷, the famous historian of the Han dynasty (202 BCE–220 CE), "imagined" the founding myth involving the Yellow Emperor, who was said to have reigned over the middle and upper reaches of northern China's Yellow river two thousand years prior. In doing so, he "implicitly vindicated Chinese ethnic homogeneity" (Chong, 2018: 107).

After the Manchurian Qing dynasty had been weakened by the Taiping and Boxer rebellions domestically and by the humiliation of wars with foreign powers[1], the monarchic social system in operation for thousands of years was finally overthrown by the 1911 revolution led by Sun Yat-sen 孫逸仙. The early twentieth century saw significant transformations in many aspects of Chinese social life. Under the heavy influence of Western culture and intellectuals began to debate visions for the nation's future, Westernization, modernization, and nationalism have become intertwined in China's intellectual history.

The subsequent establishment of the Republic of China did not prevent the Western powers from further penetrating China's political, economic, and cultural life, and this fanned the flames of radical sentiments and disillusionment with traditional Chinese culture among young intellectuals, many of them foreign-educated. They believed that Confucian values were responsible for the nation's weakness, and called for the rejection of traditional values in favor of Western ones as a means to prevent China from slipping into deep decay and backwardness. Labeling their stance anti-imperialist and anti-feudalist, the New Culture Movement (Xin wenhua yundong 新文化運動) and May Fourth Movement (Wu-Si yundong 五四運動)—led by Cai Yuanpei蔡元培 (1868-1940), Chen Duxiu 陳獨秀 (1879-1942), Hu Shi 胡適 (1891-1962), and others—erupted into criticism of classical Chinese culture and promoted a replacement based upon Western democracy and science. As a result, Western arts, including literature, drama, and music, were endorsed, and Chinese traditional arts were denigrated. In one article, Hu Shi lamented that China was inferior not only in material matters and political systems but also in morality, knowledge, literature, music, arts, and physical conditioning: "[A]dmit you are wrong, and only then can you learn from others wholeheartedly! Don't be afraid to imitate [the West] . . . and don't be afraid to lose our national culture . . . . Your duty is to be progressive, not to conserve" (Hu, 1998: 515).

From the 1930s, the arrival of Western migrants, most of them refugees from Europe escaping the Soviet Revolution and Nazi Germany, made Shanghai one of the most Westernized financial hubs in Asia, and the Shanghai municipal symphony orchestra became one of the earliest and best examples on the whole continent, partly through employing world-class musicians fleeing from Europe. The jazz scene in Shanghai also attracted members of the elite class, such as the Song sisters, to frequent its clubs, and world-class jazz musicians like Buck Clayton came from the United States to earn a living (Yu, 2017). The changing urban culture and music landscape reflected many Western ideas, transforming the city of Shanghai into a "means of passage to modernity and beyond" (Fung, 2010: 6).

In the meantime, many conservative intellectuals still believed that the West had subjugated nature and conquered the environment but that it had yet to improve community life and achieve spirituality. Liang Shuming 梁漱溟 (1893-1988) coined the term "Easternization" and sought to remedy global issues with solutions derived from the Chinese and Indian cultures. Liang even anticipated a reverse process of assimilation as he believed the West had quite as much to learn from China as China did from the West. He saw that both East and West were changing: China, driven by the imperatives of national survival, was turning to observe matters abroad and to learn about democracy, individualism, as well as functional and structural differentiation; in the West, thinkers such as Henri Bergson (1859–1941), Rudolph Eucken (1846–1926), Bertrand Russell (1872–1970), and John Dewey (1859–1952) were expressing a need to turn to moral institutions, to study inner lives and develop a stronger culture of rites and music in search of an antidote to crass materialism (Liang, 1989: 401–7).

Guqin music was valued as a symbol of traditional Chinese culture by many conservatives in traditional culture, and guqin playing was considered an activity for the player's meditation purposes only. It closely embodied a classical Chinese way of life. However, the social changes of the early twentieth century altered the cultural environs that nurtured the traditional guqin culture in the following aspects:

First, the shuffling of social hierarchies caused the disappearance of the traditional literati class—the shi 仕—with whom the guqin had been associated for millennia. In traditional society, to play the guqin, one had to be educated enough to read the Chinese characters of which guqin tablature comprised. This requirement limited access to the instrument to a class of literate people. Many of them were educated with a life goal of pursuing official posts through the imperial exams and the study of the Chinese classics. According to statistics from the 1950s, only about 20 percent of the Chinese population could read (Li, 1991), so the guqin was traditionally only for the most privileged social classes. However, the abrupt abandonment of the imperial exam system in 1905 disrupted the life purpose of the entire shi class. The disintegration of the Qing dynasty in 1911 contributed further to the gradual desolation of guqin music—as one article in the Jinyu qinkan 今虞琴刊 (Journal of the Jinyu Guqin Society)[2] mentioned, "recruiting members is challenging because guqin studies are not popular in current times" (Jinyu Qinshe, 2018: 288). According to a survey published in Jinyu qinkan, there were only 224 guqin players in the country in 1937 when the journal was published, and this included beginners and people who had recently passed away (Jinyu Qinshe, 2018: 235–53).

Second, the impact of Western culture on Chinese life marginalized the traditional arts. When Western music and music-education systems were introduced and began to prevail in China, particularly in Shanghai, one of the most Westernized areas, the position of traditional music and other performing arts was gradually challenged. The leaders of the New Culture Movement strongly attacked the traditional Chinese arts in their flagship platform, the journal Xin qingnian 新青年 (New Youth), which published a special issue discussing the reform of old forms of drama (jiuju 舊劇, "old Chinese opera"). In this issue, Hu Shi and Fu Sinian 傅斯年 (1896–1950) heavily criticized Chinese opera as outdated and in need of replacement by new forms and Western styles. Hu argued that a new era and new culture necessitated arts that had contemporary relevance (Hu, 1918). Although an opposing opinion was also published, it was attacked by Fu Sinian in the same issue with a ferocity rare for academic debates (Fu, 1918a; Fu, 1918b).

The value of guqin music was not recognized by intellectuals either. According to the legendary guqin practitioner Zha Fuxi (查阜西, 1895–1976),[3] Zha once asked

Cai Yuanpei if he was still interested in advocating *guqin* music, the latter having invited *guqin* players to teach at Peking University's Institute of Music Learning and Transmission while he was the president of the university. Cai replied, "We have tried, but Chinese music does not work, and Western music has been proven to work" (Huang et al., 1995: 515). When Zha proposed to Hu Shi to rejuvenate *guqin* music, Hu replied, "*guqin* (only) has its place in the history of arts," and even Zhao Yuanren 趙元任 said that "good *guqin* music pieces can [only] be material for musicological studies" (Huang et al., 1995: 515). As *guqin* music continued to lose popularity, it was even excluded from the curriculum at the newly established National Music Institute founded by Cai Yuanpei, despite the effort made by Zha to push it into the first higher-music-learning institution in the country (Huang et al., 1995: 14).

Under these circumstances, many traditional *guqin* practitioners with shared ideologies, faith, lifestyles, artistic tastes, and recreational pastimes felt the urge to revive the instrument's musical heritage; they began to organize clubs and societies around the country. The Jinyu Qinshe in the Yangtze river delta area of Suzhou and Shanghai—one of the areas most affected by Western culture—became the most significant and influential among them in twentieth-century China. The Society worked to promote the *guqin* music tradition by uniting the shrinking population of *guqin* players into a unique music community, maintaining regular activities including *yaji* 雅集 ("elegant gatherings") and publishing the *Jinyu qinkan* for about a year, between 1936 and 1937, until the outbreak of the Second Sino-Japanese War with the Battle of Shanghai. Although remaining members in Shanghai continued activities on a smaller scale until the establishment of the People's Republic of China (PRC) in 1949 (Zhang, 2005), the legacy of the Jinyu Qinshe was mainly established between 1936 and 1937 and almost all of its activities during this period were well documented. Its efforts demonstrate the ideological conflict between the traditionalists' nationalism and the Western ideals of the radicals. The community's activities initiated a new model of collaborative music making and *guqin* musicological research unprecedented in Chinese history. Through the declaration of nationalist ideologies in the journal *Jinyu qinkan* and the making of music in its weekly, monthly, and yearly gatherings, the Jinyu Qinshe also provides the earliest surviving comprehensive musicological documentation of the *guqin* scene in the early twentieth century. This documentation provides us with a unique opportunity to explore the subculture of a *guqin* community in Chinese urban life as the nation was facing the survival crisis of an imminent war with a Westernized foreign power.

Nationalism, Collectivism, and Individualism in the Jinyu Qinshe Community

Nationalism was the shared ideology and common pursuit of members of the Jinyu Qinshe. Collectivism provided the spiritual motivation for members to participate in gatherings and research projects. At the same time, the independence of members' different professions, their creative flair, and the democratic management of the community reflected its valuing of individualism, something that distinguished it from other traditional societies.

The community's nationalist ideal was declared in the "General Introduction" contributed by Zha Fuxi to the *Jinyu qinkan*:

> In Chinese music, *guqin* has the longest extended history. Both official and informal histories record that it was created by Paoxi 庖犧, and handed down from the Yellow Emperor. In medieval times, it was said the country was governed using rites and music, and *guqin* music was prevalent. Hence the sayings "all families were playing string instruments and reciting poems" [*jia xian hu song* 家弦戶誦] and "a gentleman does not remove *guqin* and *se* 瑟without reason" [*junzi wugu bu che qin se* 君子無故不撤琴瑟]. Since the Jin and Tang dynasties, and through the Song, Yuan, Ming, and Qing dynasties, *huyue* 胡樂 ["barbarian music"] has replaced ancient music and transformed into *yanyue* 燕樂 ["entertainment music"]. Those are *xiansuo*弦索silk music, *kunqu* 崑曲 opera, and *chuiqiang* 吹腔 wind music, then *luantan* 亂彈 and *zaju* 雜劇 operas. While other ancient music from the Yellow Emperor was lost, only *guqin* music has survived from generation to generation and stands alone. There are reasons why, for thousands of years, scholars, officials, and even ordinary people have all been enchanted by the charm of the magical power of *guqin* music. (Jinyu Qinshe, 2018: 1)

Zha then listed five reasons why *guqin* music had survived from ancient times and is superior to Western music: First, *guqin* music is not confined to the pentatonic scale. Instead, it sometimes uses the heptatonic scale and even the scale of nine notes. So, "when listening to normal Chinese music, Westerners sometimes criticize that the pitches are not tempered, but when listening to overtones and harmonics of the *guqin*, they are surprised and have no negative comments" (Jinyu Qinshe, 2018: 1). Second, "Western musicians did not see anything faster than the eighth note between the beats in Peking opera and *kunqu* opera, and consider that out of date" (Jinyu Qinshe, 2018: 2). However, according to Zha, *guqin* music is rhythmically complex, with rich fingering techniques that sometimes can be very fast. Third, the melodies of the *guqin* are composed to simulate natural sounds and express human emotions; the focus on melodies instead of lyrics contradicts the statement that "our country's music is only a branch of literature. The so-called *ci* 詞 (poetry) and *qu* 曲 (music) are all dominated by literature, and our country's music is very primitive" (Jinyu Qinshe, 2018: 2). Fourth, changes of tonality and modulation between keys are techniques frequently used in *guqin* music. It is not like the musicologist Wang Guangqi 王光祁 stated: "Westerners are very fond of transposition, but the Chinese are not" (Jinyu Qinshe, 2018: 3). And fifth, *guqin* instrument making is very refined, not only in craftsmanship but also in material selection.

> That is why we can see *guqin* instruments that have survived since antiquity, but rarely other instruments, such as *zheng* 箏, *pipa* 琵琶, *xiao* 簫, and *di* 笛. Westerners

always claim that China has no noble and grand instruments, but they do not realize that we still have playable *guqin* instruments from two thousand years ago today. (Jinyu Qinshe, 2018: 3–4)

Zha elaborated on the accompanying responsibilities of the Society:

We dare to take great pleasure in it being untrue that the Chinese have no musical arts above the usual standard. We have the one and only *guqin*. It is the duty of our *guqin* players not to leave it to future generations, but to serve the needs of the current time in embellishing, collating, promoting, and developing it. (Jinyu Qinshe, 2018: 4)

In this article, Zha frequently refers to Western music and the opinions of Westerners to support his idea that *guqin* music rises above all other Chinese music of "barbarian" origin and that it is superior to Western music, reflecting his musical nationalism and running contrary to the general trend of Westernization in the region. He considers *guqin* music a symbol of traditional Chinese heritage surpassing Western music because of its historical value and unique artistic features inherited from the time of the Yellow Emperor, features that even Westerners recognize. His musical nationalism stems from the ambition to purify this special Chinese music and from his reaction to Western hegemony in mainstream musical life.

Eric K. M. Chong has argued that there was a so-called "middle kingdom syndrome" in the breed of Chinese nationalistic discourses based on the idea of China as the cultural and political center of its region (Chong, 2018: 107). Indeed, in Zha's eyes, the so-called "barbarians" or ethnic minorities living in central imperial China's borderlands are inferior—this is clear in his claim that *guqin* music occupies a different sphere from other traditional music of non-Han-Chinese origin and even that it eclipses Western music.

The members of the Jinyu Qinshe community subscribed to a collectivist view of nationalism. Common nationalist values and goals that they found particularly salient demonstrate an orientation to collectivism, one emphasizing cohesiveness over self-interest. One aspect of this collectivism was reflected in the Society's essential regionalism. The name "Jinyu" indicates that the goal of the Society was to promote the particular *guqin* tradition of the Yushan school 虞山派 (Yushan *pai*), a regional *guqin* style that flourished in the Ming dynasty in the Changshu area of Jiangsu province, one that is local to both Suzhou and Shanghai.

Chinese regional subcultures nurtured many musical styles featuring local dialects, history, customs, and religions. In most cases, a prominent master created the particular *guqin* school that was named after a geographic region. As in other academic fields, *guqin* schools usually comprise members who followed common ideas and artistic styles. In addition to the Yushan school that flourished in the Ming dynasty, many prominent *guqin* schools emerged throughout history, including the Zhejiang school 浙派 (Zhe *pai*) in the

Song dynasty, the Guangling school 廣陵琴派 (Guangling *qin pai*) in the Qing dynasty, and the Jiuyi school九嶷派 (Jiuyi *pai*) in the period of the Republic of China.

One of the most influential *guqin* schools during the Ming and Qing dynasties, the Yushan school was named after a small mountain called Yushan in the Changshu area. At the foot of Yushan mountain is a river named Qinchuan, and a *guqin* society organized by Yan Cheng 嚴澂 (Yan Tianchi 嚴天池 1547–1625) was given the name Qinchuan Society 琴川社. Yan Cheng advocated a particular aesthetic principle of "clarity 清 (*qing*), subtlety 微 (*wei*), muted elegance 淡 (*dan*), and distance 遠 (*yuan*)" to distinguish this school from other *guqin* schools. A representative *guqin* tablature collection of the Yushan school is the *Songxianguan qinpu* 松弦館琴譜 (*Collection of Guqin Tablature of the Songxian House*, 1614), which includes an essay by Yan Cheng titled "Preface to the Collection of Qinchuan Tablature" ("Qinchuan puhui xu," 琴川譜匯序). It states the guiding principle of his school as giving full play to the music's expression without the aid of a literary text. It holds that the emotional expression of music has unique qualities to which literary text is inferior. As this implies, Yan promoted playing *guqin* solo instead of treating it as an accompaniment to singing, which was a quite popular practice during his time. He believed that "the way of sound is subtle and graceful; it may be rooted in the literary text but is not limited by it. Thus, sound is more refined than a literary text" ("音之道微妙圓通，本於文而不盡於文聲，固精於文也," Zha and Wu, 1980–2010: VIII/162). This ideal and the shifting trend from singing while playing *guqin* to playing solo only influenced Zha Fuxi during his early years of learning to play the *guqin* (Huang et al., 1995: 162). As a result of this influence, the use of the term *jinyu* in the Society's name held the following significances:

(1) It promoted Yan's ideas of emphasizing music itself instead of literary elements and the expanding of the role of *guqin* music in cultural life.
(2) Yushan *guqin* style is one of the most famous in Chinese history, and is local to Shanghai and Suzhou, where a capitalist economy flourished in the early twentieth century. The economic advantages of the local area and the subsequent rising middle classes cultivated an elite class's lifestyle that needed a regional symbol.
(3) Owing to the popularity of this regional *guqin* style, the Yushan school gradually evolved into a symbol of the broader classical *guqin* tradition. Zha mentions that "since the middle of the Wanli period of the Ming dynasty, in over seventy *guqin* handbooks, whenever origins are mentioned, they all claim to be inheritances of either the Yushan school or the Qinchuan school."[4] "Today's Yushan school" thus proclaims itself as representative of the Chinese classical *guqin* tradition.
(4) The Society's name also makes reference to the good old days of the Ming dynasty, more than three centuries ago, before the Manchurian conquest of the Han people. The Ming dynasty's *guqin* music symbolizes authentic Han Chinese

music and the classical music of "ancient" spirits. Thus, the name of the Yushan school became an ideal vehicle to promote "ancient" and "orthodox" Han Chinese culture, striking a chord with nationalists when the country's survival was at stake again.

Collectivism is also reflected in personal engagements in the collective activities of the community. For example, monthly gatherings in Suzhou required members in Shanghai to travel to Suzhou, about one hundred miles away, at a time when highway transportation was not available, and to spend the entire weekend there. This required sacrifices and dedication on the part of the members in Shanghai.

The membership dues and the donations from members also show the collectivism of the community. According to a bylaw, the community required that each member contribute one yuan each month (Jinyu Qinshe, 2018: 217). Financial ledgers published in *Jinyu qinkan* show that some members also donated extra funds. For example, out of the Suzhou branch's entire income of ¥267 in the 1936–1937 period, a figure that includes membership dues, Zha Fuxi donated ¥79, about 30 percent of the total revenue. And out of the total ¥201.80 income for the Shanghai branch, Zha donated ¥174.80, which is about 87 percent of the total revenue (Jinyu Qinshe, 2018: 299). These figures show that Zha was the largest donor toward the Society's operational expenses despite not being its wealthiest member; Zha was obviously highly dedicated to the community and took significant responsibility for maintaining its routine operations.

Individualism, as another stark feature of the Jinyu Qinshe, was always associated with democracy, with independence and self-reliance, and with interests of the individual, all of which made the Society unique in its daily operation. Unlike other traditional Chinese communities conventionally run by a centralized power figure or patron, Jinyu Qinshe was managed democratically by "the rule of law," in the form of a set of bylaws and a community board comprising a treasurer, editor, and scribe (Jinyu Qinshe, 2018: 217). The fact that almost all members did not rely on music making to earn a living was also a symbol of individualism. Members had the freedom to engage in professional work outside music. During the *yaji* gatherings, different personal interpretations of music pieces were shared among the members; several members could play the same piece, and a single member could play several pieces. Many pieces could be played both as a *guqin* solo and as a duet with another instrument, most often the *xiao* flute. The Yushan school label did not even imply that a required or singular performance style had to prevail in the community, but rather it highlighted the traditionalist ideal of the local area where the community was active. For example, the performing style of a core member Zhang Ziqian 張子謙 (1899–1991) was that of the Guangling school (which originated elsewhere, in Yangzhou), instead of that of the Yushan school. The flexibility of the performing forms and individual renditions of *guqin* pieces gave each member the freedom to develop and share their artistic talents, modes of aesthetic expression, and personal interpretations, embodying the community's respect for individuality.

From the Jinyu Qinshe, we can observe how changes in social structures were reflected in the musical life of these traditionalists and how traditional music responded to the rapid Westernization of early-twentieth-century China. In most cases, traditional music changed in response to the impact of Western culture by absorbing and adopting Western elements; examples include the Westernization of Chinese music genres, such as music for the *erhu* fiddle, which adopted many new compositions with Western elements. However, in the case of the Jinyu Qinshe, musical nationalism defied the mainstream trend of Westernization, and community members stood up to the task of safeguarding the traditional values of their musical culture. Thus, the efforts of community-making shown by Zha Fuxi and other members was a historical turning point in *guqin* music history that interweaves nationalism, collectivism, and individualism.

THE COMMUNITY MEMBERS AND THEIR SOCIAL BACKGROUND

The Jinyu Qinshe united many of the most prominent *guqin* players of twentieth-century China. In some senses, by organizing this music community and developing a new route to preserve the historical musical traditions, Zha Fuxi became one of the most prominent *guqin* figures of the time. All members of the community were traditional elites or came from the well-to-do leisure classes with aristocratic backgrounds, and they did not rely on music performance, teaching, or research to make a living. Some did not even need to take routine jobs. They were aligned with the ideal of traditional *guqin* practice of playing music for themselves rather than for audiences and did not take active roles in public musical activities (Figure 12.1). Even many years later, when the government asked Zha Fuxi to perform for audiences, he still felt very uneasy because he never thought of himself as a musician. And he considered it "shameful" when a *guqin* player did not play for himself but for other people's appreciation, something that in his mind was akin to becoming a *chuigushou* 吹鼓手, a hired wind-and-percussion-band musician at folk ceremonies, something that in a modern Chinese context also carries connotations of being a propagandist (Huang et al., 1995: 514).

The bylaws declared that the community welcomed *guqin* players of all skill levels and from all social classes, as well as those who appreciated but did not play *guqin* music (Jinyu Qinshe, 2018: 217), but most of the initial thirty members were wealthy residents of Shanghai and Suzhou who shared the same conservative cultural ideology, pastimes, aesthetics sensibilities, and social status. For example, Zhou Guanjiu 周冠九, a very wealthy Suzhou merchant, provided his residence as the venue for the *yaji* gatherings; Zhuang Jiancheng 莊劍丞 (c. 1905–53), who had many rental properties in Suzhou, used his residence as the mailing address for the Society; as already noted, Zha Fuxi provided a significant portion of the Society's financial expenditure.

The journal *Jinyu qinkan* recorded that one hundred people attended *yaji* gatherings at least once over a total of sixteen occasions, including twelve monthly gatherings

FIGURE 12.1. Gathering in the Yiyuan 怡园 garden in Suzhou, October 6, 1935 (JYQK, 2018: 6 [pictures]; credit: Jinyu Qinshe, 1938).

in Suzhou, three in Shanghai, and one radio broadcasting session also in Shanghai. According to these statistics, among the one hundred people, seventy attended once, and the other thirty regular members attended between two and eleven times. Zha Fuxi and Zhuang Jiancheng were two of the most active members, both attending eleven times. The following biographical sketches outline the personal backgrounds of the seven founding members.[5]

Zha Fuxi (also known as Zha Zhenhu 查鎮湖 and Zha Yiping 查夷平) is the principal founder of the Jinyu Qinshe, a *guqin* player, scholar, social activist, and an executive of one of China's earliest national airlines in 1930s Shanghai, with political relationships to both the Communist Party (CCP) and the Nationalist Party (KMT) in his youth. Zha was born in Yongshun county, Hunan province, where his father was appointed as a government official, away from his hometown in Xiushui county of Jiangxi province. In middle school, he learned traditional Chinese folk songs, *kunqu* opera singing, *xiao* 簫 vertical flute, *guqin*, and historical literature. He entered China's first aviation school, which was founded by Sun Yat-sen, in Guangdong in 1920 and joined the KMT, Sun's revolutionary party. Later on, Zha joined the Communist Party and was jailed for a short period after the collaboration between the CCP and KMT broke down in 1927. He then went to Shanghai to make a living and set up the Jinyu Qinshe. When the Republican government decided to start a Chinese aviation industry, Zha joined the government's transportation department as one of its earliest employees and was responsible for developing international routes.

He was also one of the central figures behind the "Uprising of the Two Airlines" 兩航起義 (Liang hang qiyi), an event in which members of two of the three leading Chinese airlines refused to have their planes flown to Taiwan in 1949 as part of the retreat of the KMT to that island. It is suggested that Zhou Enlai himself met with Zha and another executive to persuade them not to fly their aircraft to Taiwan (Yu, 2002). Zha used his political connections with the CCP to promote and preserve *guqin* music in his later life, a task no other *guqin* player was in a position to pursue in modern China.

In 1956, Zha led a *guqin* investigation group organized by the Ministry of Culture and the Chinese Musicians Association to visit ten cities across the country and collect and collate a large number of historical materials on the *guqin*. Then, under the auspices of the Beijing *Guqin* Research Association, he began a series called *Qinqu jicheng* 琴曲集成 (*Collection of* Guqin *Music*, beginning publication in 1963), which compiled and reprinted all available existing tablature scores and was finally completed with thirty-two volumes in 2010, thirty-four years after Zha's passing. A top CCP leader, Marshall Chen Yi 陈毅, endorsed Zha and the project by writing an inscription for this significant collection—a striking achievement given the *guqin*'s historical links with the social elite.[6] Zha's other seminal works include *Cunjian guqin qupu jilan* 存見古琴曲譜輯覽 (*Collection of Existing* Guqin *Music Pieces*, 1958), which gathered the titles and texts in *guqin* tablature in all extant collections; *Cunjian guqin zhifa puzi jilan* 存見古琴指法譜字集覽 (*Collection of Existing* Guqin *Fingering Characters*, 1958), which gathered all the fingering characters used in *guqin* tablature; and *Lidai qinren lu* 歷代琴人錄 (*Biography of* Guqin *Practitioners of Past Dynasties*, 1961).[7]

Zhuang Jiancheng was born in Jiangyin county, Jiangsu province, and traveled to Shanghai, Wuxi, Suzhou, and other cities to study in his youth. During the Second Sino-Japanese War, he served in the Suzhou Library and Jiangsu Provincial Library of Literature. After the war, he worked in the Jiangsu High Court and at a Shanghai textile company as a clerk. Zhuang began to study *guqin* under the tutelage of Zha Fuxi in 1935. The following year, he played a part in setting up the Jinyu Qinshe with Zha, undertaking duties in the Society's operation and collecting papers for the journal *Jinyu qinkan*. In addition, throughout his life, he attempted to restore the production of silk strings, which by that time had been discontinued. Hearing the news of Zhuang's death, Zha Fuxi referred to Zhuang as the "most accomplished student among all who have studied with me."[8]

Trustworthy historical records about Zhuang's life are scarce. The most comprehensive record is a "confession" (Zhuang, 2011: 69–76) that he seemed to have been forced to write in the first half of 1952, apparently owing to political trouble affecting him at the time. He died at a relatively young age, less than a year after writing the material, which was reorganized and published in 2011.

According to this material, Zhuang was born into a wealthy family. He owned more than twenty houses in Suzhou, most of them rented out except for the one kept as his own residence. Zhuang wrote: "I love music with my whole life. Most of my friends are capitalists, but my relationships with them are only on music matters, rarely are our connections monetary" (Zhuang, 2011: 72). In this "confession," Zhuang lists all of his acquaintances in Shanghai, many of them members of the Jinyu Qinshe, including Zhang Ziqian, Shen Caonong 沈草農 (1892–1972), Fan Boyan 樊伯炎 (1912–2001), and Wu Jinglüe 吳景略 (1907–87), and all were listed as professionals in realms outside of music. He also mentioned that he once invested some gold in Wu Jinglüe's private bank and received a bonus after the bank's dissolution after 1949. This information also suggests that Wu was successful in the financial business. From Zhuang's "confession," we also see that *guqin* performance was not a profession, and playing the instrument could not earn people a living before or immediately after the establishment of the PRC. The materials revealed that Zhuang belonged to the well-to-do social class and hence had time to engage in the stewardship of the Jinyu Qinshe with his income coming mainly from the rental of his real estate.

Peng Zhiqing 彭祉卿 (also named Peng Qingshou 彭慶壽, 1891–1944) was born into a government official's family in Luling, Hunan province. Influenced by his father, Peng began to learn the *guqin* at the age of twenty-three. Following the will of his father, he attended a law school in Hunan four years later. However, he did not practice law or go into politics. Instead, he continued to study and play the *guqin* at home and he would become famous for his playing. In 1923, the Shanxi warlord Yan Xishan 閻錫山 invited Peng to perform for him in Taiyuan. After spending two years there, Peng returned to Hunan to be a judge in a court. He then moved to Jiangxi province, becoming a judge in another court and a county mayor. He moved to Suzhou in 1933 and then worked in Shanghai. He died in Kunming in 1944 due to chronic alcoholism caused by loneliness he experienced after the death of his wife.

Li Zizhao 李子昭 (*c.* 1856–1937) was born in Chongqing county, Sichuan province, and moved to Beijing in the late Qing dynasty, where he became a famous *guqin* master over several decades. He was called to work as a professional *guqin* player in the Qingwang palace, Tianjin, and was known as the Number One Court *Guqin* Master. In the mid-autumn of 1919, the owner of Yiyuan 怡园 Garden and several other *guqin* players invited more than thirty players from around the country, including Li Zizhao, to gather in Suzhou. From that point, the Yi Yuan *Guqin* Club became a recurring gathering point for *guqin* friends in Suzhou. Li went to Shanghai in 1935 and died in 1937 at the age of eighty-one, apparently "in poverty."[9]

Zhou Guanjiu (1879–1945), born in Suzhou, was a successful merchant and antiques dealer who spent twenty years in the United Kingdom to escape political turmoil at the beginning of the Republic of China. He returned to Suzhou about 1931 after making a fortune in the antiques business in the United Kingdom. According to various resources, he provided living costs for Li Zizhao and the Buddhist *guqin* practitioner Shi Daxiu 释大休 (Zhang, 2018: 61).

According to the record in *Jinyu qinkan*, Zhou shared the same address with Li Zizhao, which suggests that Zhou provided Li's living while studying with Li.[10] *Jinyu qinkan* also indicates that Zhou's profession was in politics, commerce, and learning, and he owned a dozen rare antique *guqin* instruments from as far back as the Yuan and Ming dynasties. His hobbies included antiques authentication, gardening, keeping birds, and drinking alcohol, all typical literati pastimes in traditional society.

Reliable biographical data for the other two founding members, Wu Lansun 吳蘭蓀, and Guo Tongfu 郭同甫, are difficult to find, partly because they kept traditional literati lifestyles. Guo Tongfu used to be a county mayor and the secretary of the warlord Wu Peifu 吳佩孚, but in *Jinyu qinkan* his profession was recorded as agriculture and education. Wu Lansun's personal data is not available from the survey forms in *Jinyu qinkan*. He is the founder of the famous Wu-family style in Suzhou; scattered sources indicate that he was originally from Hanshou, Hunan province, and that he was a quartermaster in the army before moving to Suzhou in 1912 (Li and Tang, 2016: 300–301).

These biographical sketches show that all of the founding members of the community were employed in nonmusical professions, except for Li Zizhao, the only professional *guqin* player, who was eventually discarded by the Republic of China owing to his age and personal experience of serving the Qing dynasty's court. Nevertheless, they all loved *guqin* music and actively engaged in music making as a leisure activity and as an expression of nationalism.

The Jinyu Qinshe community focused not only on music making but also on community-building, theoretical discussions, ethnographic surveys, documentation, and publication. Their contemporary, the systematic musicologist, ardent New Culture advocate, and student of E. M. Hornbostel, Wang Guangqi, did not participate in *guqin* music activities but tried to reform its traditional tablature based on his understanding and admiration of Western music, with little final result. In contrast, Zha and his associates' engagement in *guqin* music practice and community-making preserved both tangible artifacts (scores and instruments) and intangible aspects (philosophy, ideology, and musical life) and made an enormous impact on the *guqin* culture in the twentieth century. Their activities can also be said to have pioneered Chinese ethnomusicological research through their unprecedented combination of applied and academic efforts.

YAJI GATHERINGS AND COMMUNITY-BUILDING

Gatherings among a relatively closed circle of upper-middle-class individuals, for the purposes of sharing artistic creativity, are called *yaji*. The practice has a long history among the elite class in Chinese society. Gatherings foster a sense of community and have been popular among the literati and aristocratic classes since at least the Tang dynasty. During *yaji*, people socialize by sharing artistic talents such as poem composition, traditional painting, calligraphy, and performing on instruments. Musical performances in *yaji* are neither ritual activities serving religious purposes nor creative activities serving commercial or entertainment needs. As the term *ya* (elegant) suggests, only specific art forms are shared. Folk arts or those with commercial or ceremonial purposes are usually not considered sufficiently elegant to be shared. The gatherings are pastime activities through which people enhance their friendships and intimacy rather than artistic performances. The *yaji* gathering plays an essential role in preserving the social ethos of the traditional arts among aristocrats and the upper-middle classes. Although early sources about *yaji* gatherings seem to describe a multimedia event in which music was not a dominant activity, in later times they became primarily musical events, designed for *guqin* players to share skills and to socialize, with participants playing *guqin* for one another without being judged on their artistic ability. There were usually no music critics nor a unified artistic standard collectively agreed upon. As a result, something beyond music—friendship and collectivism—is enhanced. Everyone is comfortable sharing and enjoying each other's artistic expression. In most cases, a well-to-do host family provides a private venue for the participants, who are usually intimate friends of the host.

Historical literature detailing *yaji* gatherings is rare. Still, several Chinese paintings from the most famous artists of the Song and Ming dynasties vividly depict the scenes. One of the best known paintings is *Xiyuan yaji tu* 西園雅集圖 (*Picture of* Yaji *in the Western Gardens*) initially created by Li Gonglin 李公麟 (1049–1106) and Mi Fu 米芾 (1051–1107). Some later masters painted variations on the same themes as well, as this gathering was among the most well-known, having taken place in 1087 in the Western Gardens of Wang Shen 王詵 (1037–c. 1093), a noted calligrapher and art connoisseur who married a daughter of the Song emperor Yingzong 英宗. Attendees included some of the most famous literati and scholars of the Song dynasty, such as Su Shi 蘇軾 (1037–1101), Huang Tingjian 黃庭堅 (1045–1105), Mi Fu, and Li Gonglin. *Guqin* and *ruan* 阮 (lute), two soft-sounding ancient Han Chinese musical instruments, appear in this painting.

In the Western ethnomusicological literature, Alan Thrasher and Larry Witzleben have investigated the activities of the Jiangnan *sizhu* music clubs of folk musicians in Shanghai (Thrasher, 2008; Witzleben, 1987), and Frederick Lau has studied the functions of music clubs in the Chinese Chaozhou diaspora in Bangkok (Lau, 2001). However, the musical activity of the *yaji* gathering had a different social function as an aspect of traditional musical life enjoyed only by the elite classes, and the subject deserves in-depth study from the perspectives of musicology, cultural studies, and sociology.

Emerging from the heavy impact of Westernization in 1930s China, the *yaji* gatherings of the Jinyu Qinshe took place during a period of political turbulence in which the *guqin* players in Shanghai and Suzhou felt alienated by the Westernization of mainstream culture. The gatherings provided opportunities for the members to socialize, comfort each other, and consolidate their nationalist ideals by bringing skills and knowledge together.

Jinyu qinkan recorded fifteen monthly gatherings, plus one live performance for a radio broadcast, although the bylaws of the community stated that there would be three types of gatherings: weekly, monthly, and yearly. For each gathering, *Jinyu qinkan* recorded the names of the attendees, the pieces they played, and the timing of each activity, including the time of arrival, the time of the *guqin* playing, and the time of the dinner party. Most *yaji* gatherings adhered to the following pattern: members arrived in early afternoon and started playing at 2:00 or 3:00 p.m., finishing before 6:00 p.m. After that, they had a dinner party about 6:00 or 7:00 p.m. in a local restaurant, another typical way of communicating and socializing in Chinese society. The Suzhou branch's first, eleventh, and twelfth *yaji* dinner parties were at Zhou Guanjiu's residence. The third was at Wu Jinglüe's house, and Zha Fuxi paid the expenses for the fifth gathering. The entire event usually ended at 9:00 p.m., when all members returned to their homes.

Four outside activities also took place during the *yaji* gatherings. One was at the third gathering in Suzhou, during which all members took a trip to pay tribute to Yan Cheng at his tomb in Changshu. According to the records, the group got together to take a bus from Suzhou to Changshu, where they were met by the local member Wu Jinglüe and one of Yan's descendants, before taking a boat to the tomb. After returning, they had dinner at Wu's residence at 7:00 p.m. The playing session began at 8:00 p.m. and continued until midnight. The members then lodged at a local inn. After sightseeing at Yushan mountain the following day and having lunch at a local scenic spot, they took the bus back to Suzhou (Jinyu Qinshe, 2018: 289–90).

The second outside event was at the fifth monthly gathering, where the Society celebrated the eightieth birthday of Li Zizhao, its eldest member, drawing a large number of participants (Figure 12.2). Many celebrated individuals participated, including the famous Buddhist scholar Zhao Puchu 趙樸初 (1907–2000) (Jinyu Qinshe, 2018: 291). The third event was a broadcast session at a Buddhist radio station in Shanghai after the seventh monthly gathering. This activity showed the Society's awareness of the importance of using mass media to transmit the *guqin* music tradition, despite the apparent contradiction to its traditional practice of retreating from public life. This gathering was

FIGURE 12.2. A gathering in Suzhou celebrating Li Zizhao's birthday, June, 1936 (JYQK: 6 [pictures]; credit: Jinyu Qinshe, 1938).

the best-attended monthly gathering, drawing fifty-nine participants (Jinyu Qinshe, 2018: 293). The fourth outside event was the Society's participation in an exhibition at the Suzhou public library. The items displayed included a portrait in oils of Yan Cheng by the well-known Chinese female painter Pan Yuliang 潘玉良 (1895–1977),[11] two *guqin* handbooks of the Yushan school, and a *guqin* instrument that used to be owned by Yan Cheng (Jinyu Qinshe, 2018: 297).

A total of forty-five *guqin* pieces were played at all the gatherings. The most popular was *Pingsha luoyan* 平沙落雁 (*Wild Geese Descend on a Sandbank*), with fifteen members playing it a total of twenty-one times. In the third monthly gathering at the Shanghai branch, six people played this one piece, which suggests it was prevalent among the community's members. In this piece, both geese and sandbanks are associated with exile. The earliest surviving version of the melody was published by a Ming prince Zhu Changfang 朱常淓 (1608–46) in his 1634 handbook *Guyin zhengzong* 古音正宗 (*Authentic Ancient Music*) as he was about to go into exile when the Manchus had almost conquered the entirety of China. Presumably owing to political reasons, ensuing Qing-dynasty publications did not mention the title's associations with exile but instead suggested that the melody expresses detachment from worldly matters or admiration for the lofty aims of wild geese. The popularity of this particular piece might hint at lofty ideals again in the context of the Han-Chinese-dominated nation facing imminent military invasion, as well as the cultural impact of foreign powers, parallel to the situation three hundred years earlier.

Other popular pieces include *Oulu wangji* 鷗鷺忘機 (*Seabirds at Peace with the World*): seven people played it a total of twelve times across ten occasions. *Xiaoxiang shuiyun* 瀟湘水雲 (*Clouds over the Xiao and Xiang Rivers*) was played by seven people eleven times. Zha Fuxi played it six times, as it was his favorite piece, and he was once even called "Zha Xiaoxiang" because of his reputation for playing it so well. Although many pieces were played on multiple occasions by many members, some other pieces were played much less regularly, such as *Si da jing* 四大景 (*Four Grand Vistas*), which was only played by Wang Zhonggao 王仲皋, although he performed it four times. *Guiqu laici* 歸去來辭 (*Come Away Home*) was only played by Wang Xingbo 汪星伯 (1893–1979) twice, and *Fengyun jihui* 風雲際會 (*The Meeting of Wind and Clouds*) was only played by Guo Tongfu twice. Another ten pieces were played only once by one member. But it might be premature to conclude they were considered inferior to the more popular ones; reasons for their fewer hearings could be that the pieces were newly recreated or particularly challenging. This was also precisely the reason why the gatherings were needed for the members to share their creativity.

The *Jinyu Qinkan* and Its Musicological Contribution

The most significant academic accomplishment of the Jinyu Qinshe was the compilation and publication of the *Jinyu qinkan*, an unprecedented achievement of Chinese musicological research that left behind a valuable resource on the history of *guqin* music culture in the early twentieth century (Figure 12.3). The journal published first-hand data about *guqin* artifacts, music, and players, and in-depth discussions of the theory and history of *guqin* music. For example, the article "Fanyin lun" 泛音论 ("On Harmonics") by Yu Dishan 余地山, a former lieutenant-general of the Republic of China, was one of the earliest academic papers in modern China discussing the frequency ratios of each of the inlay markers on the *guqin* fingerboard, expanding on ancient Chinese knowledge of the "natural joints" (Jinyu Qinshe, 2018: 85–97). It also published some newly recreated *guqin* pieces in both the traditional *jianzi pu* 减字谱 tablature and in *gongche pu* 工尺谱 notation with rhythmic elements transcribed.

Features that distinguish the journal from other musicological publications in China include the following aspects: First, the *Jinyu qinkan* documented detailed information

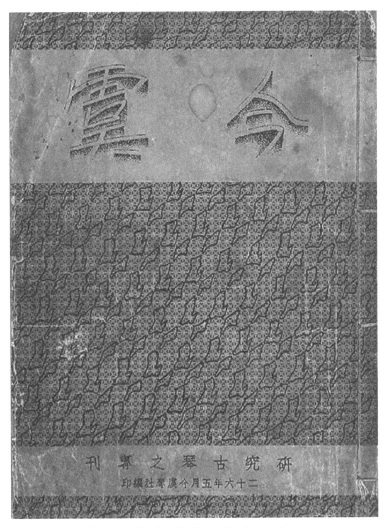

FIGURE 12.3. The cover of *Jinyu qinkan* (credit: Jinyu Qinshe, 1938).

about almost all the community's music activities between July 1936 and August 1937. The documents are invaluable ethnographic and historical sources for studying the *guqin* soundscape of one of the most Westernized regions of China at a unique historical time. Although the journal was only published once owing to the interruption of the war, it contains the only detailed information about unique historical and cultural perspectives from which we can investigate the *guqin* culture of early-twentieth-century China. Most other *guqin* handbooks compiled previously were reprints of existing historical music scores and manuals, whereas the *Jinyu qinkan* focused more on contemporary *guqin* activities and ethnographic data. Second, the journal published many in-depth research articles concerning the *guqin's* history, tuning systems, aesthetics, reviews, and playing techniques. Third, it included several recreated *dapu* 打譜 scores, which shows the community's dedication to *guqin* music creativity.

Finally, the vernacular written language *baihua wen* 白話文 had been promoted by intellectuals associated with the New Culture and May Fourth movements as a symbol of "progressive" culture over classical Chinese culture since the early 1920s. In theory, this written style allowed people with little education to read texts, articles, and books; Hu Shi had charged classical Chinese with being understood only by scholars and officials. Nevertheless, the editors of the *Jinyu qinkan* insisted on using the classical Chinese style with its traditional top-down and right-to-left typesetting, pointing to the community's conservative attitude toward cultural traditions.

In the "General Introduction" of *Jinyu qinkan*, Zha Fuxi explains, in a nationalist tone, the purpose of compiling and publishing the journal:

> We can exchange our specialties and gradually ascertain our common views so that we can make an organ for all. Thus, we shall discuss with colleagues in music circles in China and abroad to benefit all our colleagues. So Chinese music can continue on with elements of the legacies of the Yellow Emperor and Yan Emperor, which would be very fortunate. (Jinyu Qinshe, 2018: 4).

Following Zha's "General Introduction," the main content has ten sections: "Pictures," "Narration," "Discourse," "Academics," "Verification," "Music Scores," "Records," "Profiles," "Arts and Culture," and "Miscellaneous," followed by an afterword by Peng Zhiqing.

Three documents are particularly precious. One is the article "Jinyu Qinshe yinian yilai yueji jishi" 今虞琴社一年以來月集紀事 ("One Year's Chronicle of the Monthly *Yaji* Gatherings of the Jinyu Qinshe"), which is included in the "Records" section (Jinyu Qinshe, 2018: 235). This item lists the names of all participants in the fifteen *yaji* gatherings and the pieces they played. Second is the document "Qinren timing lu" 琴人題名錄 ("Directory of *Guqin* Players"), which records the address, occupation, age, instruments, and scores owned by each person. The third is the "Qinren wenxun lu" 琴人問訊錄 ("Survey of *Guqin* Players"), which includes the columns "Name," "Pieces Able to Play," "School Style," "Instruments Owned," "Scores Owned," "Works Written," "Other Musical Ability," "Other Artistic Ability," "Elegant Hobbies," and "Remarks" (Jinyu Qinshe, 2018: 254). Although some of the table's cells are blank, in the sections "Elegant Hobbies" and "Artistic Ability," we find great insight into the daily lives and social activities of the members. Many of them were traditional elites who lived a worry-free lifestyle, and most of their hobbies included Chinese painting, gardening, fishing, and drinking alcohol.

The "Records" section also documents existing *guqin* instruments from ancient times as well as those recently made—in two parts: "Gu qin zhengfang lu" 古琴徵訪錄 ("Survey of Ancient *Guqin* Instruments") and "Jin qin zhengfang lu" 今琴徵訪錄 ("Survey of Today's *Guqin* Instruments"). Both surveys have columns of "Instrument Style," "Size," "Material," "Sound," "Instrument Maker," "Owner," and so forth. The financial ledgers of the Society's Suzhou and Shanghai branches show the community's democratically managed financial matters. The journal provides some of the earliest comprehensive musicological information on *guqin* culture and the musical life of a unique community in early-twentieth-century China. The research methodologies such as documentation, survey, and analysis are used in today's ethnomusicological research. As a master *guqin* player with a strong nationalist ideal, Zha Fuxi blazed a trail for Chinese musicological efforts in preserving and safeguarding both tangible and intangible *guqin* musical heritage.

Conclusion

Facing the heavy influence of Western cultures in early-twentieth-century China, the reaction of Chinese intellectuals and music practitioners varied according to social class and affiliation. While many Western-educated elite radicals almost entirely rejected what traditional music had to offer, those in a different camp, the conservatives, promoted and embraced it, making the 1930s a high time for many traditional musical genres in Westernized Shanghai[12] and some other parts of the country.

The creation of the Jinyu Qinshe community and the publication of the *Jinyu qinkan* by Zha Fuxi and his associates were significant milestones in the *guqin* scene of early-twentieth-century China. The *Jinyu qinkan* is one of the most trusted historical sources, allowing us to understand further the life and activities of the members of this *guqin* community, which championed a nationalist ideal at a critical historical time, when the value of traditional culture was being challenged and the country was in a crisis of survival. The activities of the Jinyu Qinshe community make it possible for us to look into its fascinating musical culture by analyzing how the nationalist ideal played out in community-making and how collectivism and individualism significantly influenced the creativities of a unique music community bolstered by nationalist sentiments.

Glossary

baihua wen 白話文, vernacular written language that arose in the early twentieth century

Baoxi 庖犧, legendary emperor and creator of the *guqin*

Cai Yuanpei 蔡元培, philosopher, politician, and influential education reformer (1868–1940)

Cunjian guqin zhifa puzi jilan 存见古琴指法谱字辑览, Collection of Existing Guqin *Fingering Characters*, a mimeographed work by Zha Fuxi

Chen Duxiu 陳獨秀, reformist, educator, and cofounder of the Chinese Communist Party (1879–1942)

Chen Yi 陳毅, military marshals, former mayor of Shanghai, vice premier of the State Council and foreign minister of PRC (1901–1972).

chuigushou 吹鼓手、wind-and-percussion-band musician, or a propagandist

chuiqiang 吹腔, opera genres popular in southern China during the end of the Ming dynasty and the beginning of the Qing dynasty

ci 詞, poetry

dapu 打譜, process of recreating a composition for *guqin* from tablature

dan 淡, "muted elegance," ideal of the Qinchuan Society

di 笛, transverse bamboo flute

Fan Boyan 樊伯炎, artist, founding member of the Jinyu Qinshe (1912–2001)

Fengyun jihui 風雲際會, *The Meeting of Wind and Clouds*, composition for *guqin*

Fu Sinian 傅斯年, historian, educator, and reformist (1896–1950)

gongche pu 工尺譜, notation based on Chinese characters representing scale degrees

guqin 古琴, seven-stringed zither

Guyin zhengzong 古音正宗, *Authentic Ancient Music*, *guqin* handbook by Zhu Changfang (1634)

Guangling qin pai 廣陵琴派, Guangling school of *guqin* performance (Qing dynasty)

Guiqu laici 歸去來辭, *Come Away Home*, composition for *guqin*

Guo Tongfu 郭同甫, founding member of the Jinyu Qinshe (early twentieth century)

Hu Shi 胡适, education and language reformer (1891–1962)

huyue 胡樂, "barbarian music," historically from the western part of today's China and Central Asia

Huang Tingjian 黃庭堅, calligrapher and poet (1045–1105)

jia xian hu song 家弦戶誦, "all families were playing string instruments and reciting poems," idiom

jianzi pu 減字譜, traditional tablature for *guqin*, composed of strokes derived from Chinese characters

Jinyu qinkan 今虞琴刊, *Journal of the Jinyu* Guqin *Society* (1936–37)

Jinyu Qinshe 今虞琴社, *Guqin* Society of Today's Yushan 虞山 School

jiuju 舊劇, "old Chinese opera," target of criticism by adherents of the New Culture Movement

Jiuyi pai 九嶷派, Jiuyi school of *guqin* performance (early twentieth century)

junzi wugu bu che qin se 君子無故不撤琴瑟, "a gentleman does not remove *guqin* and *se* without reason," idiom

kunqu 崑曲, opera genre

Li Zizhao 李子昭, *guqin* performer, founding member of the Jinyu Qinshe (c. 1856–1937)

Liang hang qiyi 兩航起義, "Uprising of the Two Airlines," incident in 1949

Liang Shuming 梁漱溟, writer and philosopher (1893–1988)

Lidai qinren lu 歷代琴人錄, Biography of Guqin Practitioners of the Past Dynasties, a mimeographed work by Zha Fuxi

luantan 亂彈, category of local operas

Oulu wangji 鷗鷺忘機, *Seabirds at Peace with the World*, composition for *guqin*

Pan Yuliang 潘玉良, artist (1895–1977)

Peng Zhiqing 彭祉卿, also named Peng Qingshou 彭慶壽, founding member of the Jinyu Qinshe (1891–1944)
pipa 琵琶, lute
Pingsha luoyan 平沙落雁, *Wild Geese Descend on a Sandbank*, composition for *guqin*
Qinchuan She 琴川社, Qinchuan Society (sixteenth century) organized by Yan Cheng, model and forerunner of the Jinyu Qinshe
qing 清, clarity, ideal of the Qinchuan Society
qu 曲, music
ruan 阮, lute
Shen Caonong 沈草農, founding member of the Jinyu Qinshe (1892–1972)
shi 仕, traditional literati class
Shi Daxiu 释大休, Buddhist monk and *guqin* practitioner (1870–1932)
Si da jing 四大景, *Four Grand Vistas*, composition for *guqin*
Sima Qian 司馬遷, Han-dynasty historian (*c.* 145–*c.* 86 BCE)
Songxianguan qinpu 松弦館琴譜, *Collection of* Guqin *Tablature of the Songxian House*, *guqin* tablature compiled by Yan Cheng (1614)
Su Shi 蘇軾, poet and artist (1037–1101)
Sun Yat-sen (Sun Yixian) 孫逸仙, first president of the Republic of China (1866–1925)
Wang Guangqi 王光祁, musicologist (1891–1936)
Wang Shen 王詵, calligrapher and art connoisseur (1037–*c.* 1093)
Wang Zhonggao 王仲皋, member of the Jinyu Qinshe (early twentieth century)
Wang Xingbo 汪星伯, member of the Jinyu Qinshe (1893–1979)
wei 微, "subtlety," ideal of the Qinchuan Society
Wu Jinglüe 吳景略, *guqin* player, founding member of the Jinyu Qinshe (1907–87)
Wu Lansun 吳蘭蓀, founding member of the Jinyu Qinshe (early twentieth century)
Wu Peifu 吳佩孚, warlord of the Republic China (1916–27)
Wu-Si yundong 五四運動, May Fourth Movement (1919)
Xiyuan yaji tu 西園雅集圖, *Picture of* Yaji *in the Western Gardens*, painting by Li Gonglin 李公麟 (1049–1106) and Mi Fu 米芾 (1051–1107)
xiansuo 弦索, music for stringed instruments
xiao 簫, end-blown bamboo flute
Xiaoxiang shuiyun 瀟湘水雲, *Clouds over the Xiao and Xiang Rivers*, composition for *guqin*
Xin qingnian 新青年, *New Youth*, flagship magazine of the New Culture Movement
Xin wenhua yundong 新文化運動, New Culture Movement (1910–1920s)
yaji 雅集, "elegant gatherings," meetings of *guqin* players and like-minded supporters
Yan Cheng 嚴澂, also known as Yan Tianchi 嚴天池, founder of the Qinchuan Society (1547–1625)
yanyue 燕樂, entertainment music
Yu Dishan 余地山, lieutenant-general and member of the Jinyu Qinshe (early twentieth century)
Yushan *pai* 虞山派, Yushan school of *guqin* performance
yuan 遠, "distance," ideal of the Qinchuan Society
zaju 雜劇, historical opera genre of the Yuan dynasty
Zha Fuxi 查阜西, also known as Zha Zhenhu 查鎮湖 and Zha Yiping 查夷平, *guqin* practitioner, scholar, and social activist (1895–1976)
Zhang Ziqian 張子謙, *guqin* practitioner (1899–1991)
Zhao Puchu 趙樸初, calligrapher, religious leader, and scholar of Buddhism (1907–2000)

Zhao Yuanren 趙元任, linguist, educator, and musician (1892–1982)
Zhe *pai* 浙派, Zhejiang school of *guqin* performance (Song dynasty)
zheng 箏, zither
Zhou Guanjiu 周冠九, merchant and founding member of the Jinyu Qinshe (1879–1945)
Zhu Changfang 朱常淓, Ming prince and compiler of the *guqin* handbook *Guyin zhengzong* (*Authentic Ancient Music*) (1608–46)
Zhuang Jiancheng 莊劍丞, landlord and founding member of the Jinyu Qinshe (*c*. 1905 –1953)

Notes

1. China's failure in the First Sino-Japanese War (1894–95) was one of the essential elements that weakened the Qing dynasty. Attributing the rise of Japanese power to the Meiji Revolution and subsequent Westernization, influential Chinese scholars such as Liang Shuming considered Japan already a Westernized state (Fung, 2010: 74).
2. This publication was originally planned to be a *kan* 刊 (a periodical or journal). But Shanghai was bombarded by Japanese warplanes while the first issue was being printed, and the remaining manuscripts were lost later on because of the war. Only the first issue, with its 360 pages of contents, survived.
3. See the biographical sketch of Zha in the later part of this chapter.
4. Zha Fuxi, "Mantan *guqin*" 漫談古琴 ("A Discussion of the *Guqin*"), in Huang et al., 1995: 289.
5. These seven people signed the invitations and other initial documents (Jinyu Qinshe, 2018: 288).
6. Zha Fuxi, "Shilü shengping" 仕履生平 ("Biography"), in Huang et al., 1995: 16.
7. Zha Fuxi, "Zhongguo yinyuejia jianzhuan—Zha Fuxi" 中國音樂家簡傳—查阜西 ("Biographical Sketch of Chinese Musician: Zha Fuxi"), in Huang et al., 1995: 11; "Wo de yinyue shenghuo" 我的音樂生活 ("My Music Life"), in Huang et al., 1995: 13.
8. Zhu Fuxi, "Diao Jiancheng" 吊劍丞 ("Mourning Zhuang Jiancheng"), in Huang et al., 1995: 13.
9. Zha Fuxi, "Zuguo guqin yinyue de jinxi" 祖國古琴音樂的今昔 ("*Guqin* Music in the Past and Today in the Homeland"), in Huang et al., 1995: 457.
10. In the biographical data in *Jinyu qinkan*, Zhou indicated that he studied with Li.
11. Pan is renowned as the first woman in the country to paint in the Western style. She studied in Shanghai and Paris. Because her modernist works caused controversy and drew severe criticism in China during the 1930s, she returned to Paris in 1937 to live and work for the next forty years of her life.
12. The discussion by Jonathan Stock of the development of the local opera *huju* in early-twentieth-century Shanghai (Stock, 2003) is a good example of this phenomenon, one that paralleled the *guqin* scene discussed in the current chapter.

References

Anderson, Benedict. (2006). *Imagined Communities: Reflections on the Origin and Spread of Nationalism*. Revised edition. London: Verso.
Chong, Eric K. M. (2018). "A Review of Contemporary Chinese Nationalism Theories, Features, and Facets." In *Reimagining Nation and Nationalism in Multicultural East Asia*, edited by Sungmoon Kim and Hsin-Wen Lee, 105–22. New York: Routledge.

Fu Sinian 傅斯年. (1918a). "Xiju gailiang mianmian guan" "戲劇改良面面觀" [Drama Improvement in All Its Aspects]. *Xin qingnian* 新青年 [New Youth] 5 (4): 322–40.

Fu Sinian 傅斯年. (1918b). "Zailun xiju gailiang" "再論戲劇改良" [On Drama Improvement Again]. *Xin qingnian* 新青年 [New Youth] 5 (4): 349–60.

Fung, Edmund S. K. (2010). *The Intellectual Foundations of Chinese Modernity: Cultural and Political Thought in the Republic Era*. Cambridge, UK: Cambridge University Press.

Huang Xudong 黄旭東, Yi Hongshu 伊鴻書, Cheng Yuanmin 程源敏, Zha Kecheng 查克承, eds. (1995). *Zha Fuxi qinxue wencui* 查阜西琴學文萃 [Digest of *Guqin* Studies by Zha Fuxi]. Hangzhou: Zhongguo meishu xueyuan chubanshe.

Hu Shi 胡適. (1918). "Wenxue jinhua guannian yu xiju gailiang" "文學進化觀念與戲劇改良" [The Concept of Literary Evolution and the Improvement of Drama]. *Xin qingnian* 新青年 [New Youth] 5 (4): 308–21.

Hu Shi 胡適. (1998). "Jieshao wo ziji de sixiang" "介紹我自己的思想" [Introducing My Own Thoughts]. In *Hu Shi Wenji* 胡適文集 [The Collected Works of Hu Shi], edited by Ouyang Zhesheng 歐陽哲生, vol. 5: 507–19. Beijing: Beijing daxue chubanshe.

Jinyu Qinshe 今虞琴社, ed. (2018). *Jinyu Qinkan* 今虞琴刊 [The Journal of the Jinyu *Guqin* Society]. Reprint, Shanghai: Shanghai shehui kexueyuan chubanshe.

Lau, Frederick. (2001). "Performing Identity: Musical Expression of Thai-Chinese in Contemporary Bangkok." *Sojourn: Journal of Social Issues in Southeast Asia* 16 (1): 37–69.

Li Feng 李峰 and Tang Yulin 湯鈺林. (2016). *Suzhou lidai renwu dacidian* 蘇州歷代人物大辭典 [Dictionary of Historical People in Suzhou]. Shanghai: Shanghai cishu chubanshe.

Li Kejing 李克敬. (1991). "Lun saomang de zhanlue diwei yu Zhongguo de saomang zhanlue" "論掃盲的戰略地位與中國的掃盲戰略" [On the Strategic Position of Illiteracy Elimination and China's Strategy]. *Zhongguo shehui kexue* 中國社會科學 [China Social Science], no. 1: 49–68.

Liang Shuming 梁漱溟. (1989). "Dongxi wenhua jiqi zhexue" "東西文化及其哲學" [Eastern and Western Cultures and Their Philosophies]. In *Liang Shuming quanji* 梁漱溟全集 [The Complete Works of Liang Shuming], vol. 1: 319–547. Ji'nan: Shandong renmin chubanshe.

Merriam, Alan P. (1977). "Definitions of 'Comparative Musicology' and 'Ethnomusicology': An Historical-Theoretical Perspective." *Ethnomusicology* 21 (2): 189–204.

Stock, Jonathan P. J. (2003). *Huju: Traditional Opera in Modem Shanghai*. New York: Oxford University Press.

Thrasher, Alan. (2008). *Sizhu Instrumental Music of South China: Ethos, Theory and Practice*. Leiden: Brill.

Witzleben, J. Lawrence. (1987). "Jiangnan Sizhu Music Clubs in Shanghai: Context, Concept and Identity." *Ethnomusicology* 31 (2): 240–60.

Yu Hui 喻輝. (2017). "Guanyu Bake Kelaitun zaoqi Shanghai shenghuo shiliao de kaozheng" "關於巴克·克萊頓早期上海生活史料的考證" [Investigations of Buck Clayton's Early Life in Shanghai]. *Renmin yinyue* 人民音樂 [People's Music], no. 1: 84–87.

Yu Jianxin 于建新. (2002). "'Liang hang' qiyi mishi" "两航"起義秘史" [The Secret History of the Uprising of the "Two Airlines"], *Zhongguo dang'an bao* 中國檔案報 [China Journal of Archives] (May, 31): 1.

Zha Fuxi 查阜西, Wu Zhao 吳釗, et al., eds. (1958). *Cunjian guqin qupu jilan* 存見古琴曲譜輯覽 [Collection of Existing *Guqin* Music Tablature]. Beijing: Renmin yinyue.

Zha Fuxi 查阜西, Wu Zhao 吳釗, et al., eds. (1980–2010). *Qinqu jicheng* 琴曲集成 [Collection of *Guqin* Pieces]. Beijing: Zhonghua shuju.

Zhang Huaying 章华英. (2018). "Jindai qinseng shi daxiu jiqi qinxue chuancheng" "近代琴僧釋大休及其琴學傳承"[Modern Buddhist Guqin Practitioner Shi Daxiu and His *Guqin* Inheritance]. Zhongyang yinyue xueyuan xuebao 中央音樂學院學報 [Journal of the Central Conservatory of Music], no. 1: 55–68, 128.

Zhang Ziqian 张子谦. (2005). *Caoman suoji* 操缦琐记 [Fragmentary Recollections on *Guqin* Performance]. Beijing: Zhonghua shuju.

Zhuang Jiancheng 庄剑丞. (2011). "Guqin mingjia Zhuang Jiancheng wushiniandai de jiantao" "古琴名家莊劍丞五十年代的檢討" [A Confession of *Guqin* Player Zhuang Jianchang in the 1950s], *Shilin* 史林 [History Circles], supplementary issue: 69–76.

CHAPTER 13

A MULTIMODAL AND INTERDISCIPLINARY APPROACH TO LUO YUSHENG'S VIDEO PERFORMANCE OF *CHOUMO YINCHU* (AT BREAK OF DAY)

FRANCESCA R. SBORGI LAWSON

Introduction: Narratives

In *The Singer of Tales*—the foundational study for scholars in the field of oral performance—Albert Lord asserts that narrative singers have existed since the dawn of human consciousness, contributing richly to the intellectual and spiritual growth of humankind (1960: v). Ironically, despite the fact that Lord's title refers to the performers as singers, subsequent scholarship on oral traditions has focused almost exclusively on the uniqueness of oral communication in performance and not on singing. While the study of the oral tradition has been a fascinating and fertile topic in the area of narrative communication, the vocal, gestural, visual, and musical components of narrative performance have not received the same scholarly attention.[1]

The significance of utilizing a multimodal approach to analyzing narrative performance becomes especially clear when reviewing the body of scholarship on the earliest narrative-like communication between infants and their caregivers. Ellen Dissanayake focuses on the visual, gestural, and vocal exchanges between mothers and infants, referring to the multisensory communication as "aesthetic incunabula": the source materials for the operations used by artists in all media (2001: 336), including narrative performance. She explains how communication with infants is noteworthy because of the stylized way of repeating, exaggerating, and elaborating in visual, vocal, and gestural modalities (ibid.: 336), all of which are designed to attract, sustain, and manipulate the baby's attention (ibid.: 341). While Dissanayake speaks to the multiple modalities of exchanges between mothers and infants, Daniel Stern—one of the pioneers in mother-infant research—argues for their narrativity. Stern claims that communications between mothers and their pre-linguistic infants are actually tiny narratives with a beginning, middle, and end, including a line of dramatic tension (2002: 6), asserting that narrative thought is a universal mechanism by which both newborns and adults perceive and reflect on social behavior. Building on Stern's work, Michel Imberty explains that the wordless narratives produced by mothers and infants contain a type of quasi-plot and provide "the foundation for the thread of our personal individual life story, which later we will know how to put into words, but without which we would not be able to begin telling" (2011: 14). Gratier and Trevarthen also propose that everyone who sings, recites poetry, or speaks is engaging in human vocalization that is constructed around the need to tell a story (2008: 132).

Steven Pinker also makes a case for the universal appeal of narrative, but he centers his argument on literary fiction rather than on the proto-narrative exchanges between infants and their mothers. Using evolutionary theory to make his point about storytelling, Pinker claims:

> People tell stories. All over the world, and probably for as long as they have existed, people invent characters and recount their fictitious exploits . . . Considering the costs in time, foregone opportunities to engage in practical pursuits, and the dangers of confusing fantasy with reality, our longing to lose ourselves in fiction is a big puzzle for anyone seeking to understand human beings. All the more so from a Darwinian perspective, as one might have expected natural selection to have weeded out any inclination to engage in imaginary worlds rather than the real ones. (2007: 162)

If we accept Ian Cross's claim that "the effects of evolution are most evident in infant rather than in mature, enculturated behaviours" (2003: 24), then the research on the proto-narratives in mother-infant communication would seem to make an even more persuasive claim for the evolutionary significance of narrative than the mature, enculturated genres of literary fiction. Narrative fiction might be seen as an example of a complex genre that still draws upon both the narrativity and the aesthetic incunabula inherent in the primordial mother-infant interaction.

Hence, telling stories seems to be integral to human communication from the earliest stages and is present in all cultures throughout all time periods. Further, much of the time storytellers use visual, vocal, literary, and gestural elements. This chapter argues for the need to consider the multimodality of narrative performance and demonstrates how a single case study can draw upon research from a wide variety of academic disciplines. Given the centrality of narrative traditions throughout time and place, a multimodal and interdisciplinary approach gives this important topic its proper due and shows how the study of narratives—and Chinese narratives in particular—remains a productive and exciting area for research in the twenty-first century. I direct my discussion to a short piece performed by Luo Yusheng 駱玉笙 (1914–2002), one of the most celebrated narrative singers from the city of Tianjin, an important center for the narrative arts in northern China.

Luo Yusheng

By the beginning of the twentieth century, an increasing number of female performers became narrative singers in northern cities in Republican China (1912–49). One of the greatest, Luo Yusheng, is the featured artist in this case study that highlights Beijing drumsong (*Jingyun dagu* 京韻大鼓), a narrative genre in which the performer sings the story and plays a *gu* 鼓 drum and *ban* 板 wooden clapper during musical interludes, accompanied by three instrumentalists on *sanxian* 三弦 lute, *sihu* 四胡 fiddle, and *pipa* 琵琶 lute (Stevens, 1975: 137–46). As the adopted daughter of an itinerant street performer named Luo Caiwu 駱彩舞, Luo was originally named Xiao Caiwu ("Little Caiwu") by her adoptive father, a moniker that reflected his desire for her to follow in his footsteps and be a money-maker for him (Xue, 1984: 25). She became inordinately good at imitating not only her father but also all the other singers she heard, as she performed in a variety of venues as well (ibid.: 29). By the age of nine, due to her unusually low and resonant voice, she had begun studying the *laosheng* 老生—the mature male role—in the Beijing opera tradition. At age seventeen, influenced by the artistry of Liu Baoquan 劉寶全 (1868–1942), she decided to study Beijing drumsong. Two of Liu's contemporaries, Bai Yunpeng 白雲鵬 (1874–1952) and Bai Fengming 白鳳鳴 (1909–80), also became role models for the young female performer. Luo eventually became the disciple of Han Yonglu 韓永祿 (1876–1943), Liu Baoquan's "string master" (*xianshi* 弦師), who was able to train her according to the best traditions of the Liu, Bai, and Shao Bai schools of Beijing drumsong.[2]

Luo Yusheng's performances at age forty-six of *Choumo yinchu* 醜末寅初 (*At Break of Day*) (Luo, 1960) and *Jian'ge wen ling* 劍閣聞鈴 (*Listening to the Bells at Sword Pavilion*) (Luo, 1961) are significant because we have video footage of her at the peak of her professional career. By 1960 she had established herself as one of the greatest and most influential drumsingers in Tianjin, and these two televised performances document her enormously wide vocal range, exquisitely executed vocal ornamentation, near perfect diction, tasteful gestural movements, and overall ability to lend great emotional depth to her performances. China Television (CTV) was prescient enough to record her at this point in her career, setting the gold standard for subsequent artists to follow.

Moreover, the 1960 and 1961 recordings were made before the Cultural Revolution erupted in 1966, after which traditional performances were essentially banned for a decade. Because of her chameleon-like ability to adapt to changing political agendas, Luo continued as a singer from 1966 to 1976, changing her repertoire to accommodate the political sensibilities of the Cultural Revolution—and further ensured her success by finding her footing as a political leader. But the pieces that were appropriate to the zeitgeist of the decade did not withstand the test of time. After the end of the Cultural Revolution, she, like many other performers who had established themselves before the period of extreme socialism, returned to the traditional repertoire that had originally made her famous.

The video of *Jian'ge wen ling* represents her masterwork, and I have analyzed the music and text at some length elsewhere (Lawson, 2017: 61–67, 80–86), so I will not consider that work in this chapter. By contrast, *Choumo yinchu* (hereafter, *Choumo*) is neither as musically nor as textually complex as *Jian'ge wen ling*, but its shorter length permits a close analysis of the gestural and pictorial aspects of performance, in addition to the musical and textual. Moreover, *Choumo* was sung by virtually all the famous performers of Beijing drumsong, signaling its widespread popularity among all narrative-arts aficionados in Tianjin, and it will be the focal point of the following analysis.

The Story

The film theorist Seymour Chatman offers a clear explanation as to what he argues is the most fundamental feature in narrative, namely the distinction between the story and the discourse: "The story is the *what* in a narrative that is depicted, discourse the *how*" (1978: 19). In the case of Beijing drumsong performance, the distinction between story and discourse provides a good entry point for the present discussion. Unlike most stories in Chinese narrative traditions, *Choumo* does not have a plot with a villain and a hero, but it does have an omniscient and omnipresent narrator who documents the cosmic and human actions that take place at the break of day.

In her doctoral dissertation on Beijing drumsong, Catherine Stevens refers to the piece as an example of playful enumeration built around a list (1975: 99–100), but I would also argue that describing the individuals encountered at the break of day is actually more than playful enumeration. At its most basic level, *Choumo* might be seen as what the artificial-intelligence researcher David Gelernter calls a "theme-circling narrative," as opposed to a plot-centered narrative (2016: 24–25). He explains that "a dream, or the performance of a dream-like scene, is a theme-circle, a collection of scenes or incidents all attracted by the same memory cue" (2016: 245). The time of *Choumo*—at the break of day—signals the end of sleep and the onset of wakefulness—a time when dreams may be recalled. If, as Gelernter claims, dreams are theme-circling narratives where the theme is an emotion or an emotion-steeped image (2016: 98), then one might argue that the dream-like narrative portrayed in *Choumo* also has a theme, namely the feelings and sensations of the early morning. Daybreak is meanwhile also a time when the cosmos awakens and nudges its terrestrial beings into action, suggesting great anticipation and a desire for fulfillment and prosperity.

Choumo might also be seen as a story about time and temporality, providing a platform for the narrator's real-time descriptions of nine different individuals performing their early-morning tasks: the watchman at the drum tower, the scholar, the fisherman, the woodcutter, the Buddhist monk, the farmer, the student, the lady, and the cowherd. Each vignette exists on its own as a temporal description of the individual, and yet the overall piece is communicated from the vantage point of the narrator, whose perspective imposes another overarching temporal framework as she describes each vignette.

Further, the story also communicates a message about cosmic resonance and social harmony. In her book about music and cosmology in China, Erica Fox Brindley explains: "harmony, along with other integral concepts like balance and resonance, emerged as a concept intrinsic to the operations and functioning of the cosmos" (2012: 157). She also argues that humans are not merely passive components of a harmonious universe; rather, "they join into a unique relationship that not only elevates themselves and enhances the cosmos but [also] brings peace, harmony, and prosperity to the world around them as well" (ibid.: 158).

Although Brindley's explanations about harmony derive from an early period in Chinese history (sixth through second centuries BCE), I suggest that the following small piece exemplifies this same notion about cosmic harmony in the description of an iconic rural village in the late nineteenth or early twentieth century. As the story begins, we are privy to the narrator's view of the last great cosmic performance of the night sky before the sun rises over an elm tree, which is the first reference to earthly rather than celestial time and space. Significantly, the worldview expressed in this piece champions working-class people, as opposed to members of the elite ruling class, since the text trivializes the harried scholar and the bumbling student by portraying them as comic, even frivolous, characters in the social drama of the village. Nevertheless, the overarching message seems to be that all members of society—be they flawed or functional—contribute in some meaningful way to the world order.

THE DISCOURSE: A MULTIMODAL APPROACH

If the story is a dream-like narrative that speaks to the idea of human participation in cosmic harmony, how might the discourse portray such a story? In a theme-circling narrative like *Choumo*, the visual, musical, and gestural elements of the discourse are particularly important because of their ability to arouse emotions. Gelernter makes the case that normal spoken language is a poor way to tell people what we are feeling (2016: 118–19), as people comprehend emotions from observing bodily gestures and facial expressions and from listening to the tone of voice (ibid.: 243). Building on this idea, the success of narrative performance is due to the way gesture and musical voice enhance the emotions associated with the message of the lyrics, which are set poetically, further heightening the emotional power of the performance.

The Poetic Element

In the transformation of a story into a drumsong performance, the one who usually initiates the process is the author, who specializes in the poetic and musical conventions of the genre (Lawson, 2011: 82–83). In the case of *Choumo*, the lyrics are listed as "traditional" (Tao, 1983: table of contents), meaning that the piece is not attributed to a particular author. Nonetheless, the lyrics conform to poetic principles common to other pieces written in the genre and also allow for enough leeway for the singer—who becomes a second author—to freely embellish and add her personal touch.

Stevens describes the basic structure of Beijing drumsong as a poetic form composed of seven characters per line, organized in couplets (Stevens, 1975: 111–26),[3] and I have adopted her strategy of using "T" to designate the top line and "B" the bottom line for each couplet. As a short piece, *Choumo* has only nine couplets (as opposed to thirty-eight in *Jian'ge wen ling*), divided into two sections, with the second section beginning after the short instrumental interlude following the fourth couplet. Each piece in the Beijing drumsong tradition is uniquely rendered, and one of the characteristic features of *Choumo* is unusually long B lines. In each couplet, the T line is a rather simple and straightforward line that introduces the character, while the B line is a more complex description of the unique characteristics of the individual. In this piece, the B lines are often elongated by using common literary techniques, such as *dingzhenti* 頂針體 ("thimbling") (Stevens, 1975: 116), a practice in which the last word of a phrase becomes the first word of the following phrase. The following analysis of the poetry proceeds couplet by couplet, explaining how the story is told through poetic conventions peculiar to the Beijing drumsong tradition.

The first couplet is about the waning lights of the evening sky, using richly poetic language. As seen below, the list of short phrases about the night sky features the *dingzhenti* technique in the second, third, and fourth lines of B-1. Further, the alliteration in two pairs of repeated characters in *miaomiao mangmang* (B-1, line 5) and *huanghuang huhu* (line 6)—as well as the simpler rendition of two different alliterative pairs *mimi zaza* (line 7)—adds another layer of poetic richness to the rendition.

> T-1 醜末寅初日轉扶桑。
> *At break of day as the sun comes over the Sacred Elm;*
> B-1 我猛抬頭見
> *I look up and there, far off,*
> 天上的星
> *A sky full of stars,*
> 星共鬥
> *Stars of the Dipper,*
> 鬥和辰
> *Dipper of the galaxy,*
> 渺渺茫茫
> *Misted and blurred,*

恍恍惚惚
Now there, now gone,
密密雜雜
Dense and close;
直沖霄漢減去輝煌。
Straight up it thrusts, up to the heavens, carrying off their glitter.

The second couplet introduces the watchman, who is derelict in his duties. In B-2, instead of hearing him strike the watch block, shake the small bell, strike the gong, and hit the large bell, all of which are designed to signal the time of day, we hear his thunderous snoring. The technique called *duoju* 垛句 or "piled-up phrases," in which short, repetitive phrases are added to the middle of the line (Stevens, 1975: 118–19), is another literary technique to elongate phrases and is used to communicate the watchman's neglect in lines 2 through 5 of B-2. The narrator playfully teases the audience by listing the absence of different sounds, building suspense by delaying the audience from learning the reason why the watchman is not performing his duties: he is still fast asleep. Luo's mellifluous voice provides the melodic narrative that compensates for the absent sounds of the watchtower and mediates the deafening sounds of the watchman's snoring in our auditory imagination.

T-2 一輪明月朝西墜
A cartwheel of a moon sinks to the west—
B-2 我聽也聽不見在那花鼓樵樓上，
I can't hear from the drum watchtower;
梆兒聽不見敲，
I can't hear the watch-block being struck.
鐘兒聽不見撞，
I can't hear the little bell being shaken,
鑼兒聽不見篩，
I can't hear the gong being rapped,
鈴兒聽不見晃，
I can't hear the big bell being hit;
那些值更的人兒他沉睡如雷，夢入了黃粱。
For the watchman in charge sleeps thunderously, deep within his dreams.

While the watchman fails to signal the time of day, the cock does not. Rather than describe a human agent, T-3 opens with a crowing rooster. Wakened by the sound, the scholar, who appears to have overslept (possibly because of the sleeping watchman), hurriedly gets ready for his appointment in a nearby village. Occupying one of the highest positions in Chinese society, a scholar is usually also a government official, so portraying him as someone who nearly misses his meeting humanizes him. The humorous consequences of oversleeping are apparently not enough to seriously disrupt him from carrying out his responsibilities, so this incident is simply a small ripple in an otherwise ordinary day.

T-3 架上金雞不住的連聲唱。
The farmhouse cock keeps up a continuous song.
B-3 千門開
All doors open,
萬戶放
Each gate swings wide,
這才驚動了行路之人
The scholar on his journey,
急急
In a nervous hurry
忙忙
All in a fluster
打點行囊
Gathering up his traveling bag
出離了店房，夠奔了前面那一座村莊。
Exits by the inn door, he hurries to the village that's ahead.

A fisherman is introduced in T-4, and in B-4 we learn that he rocks back and forth, trying to maintain his balance while holding his fishing pole and scaring a group of egrets and pairs of Mandarin ducks in the process. The visual image of the wobbly fisherman and the poetic description of the frightened egrets and annoyed ducks as they wildly flap their wings heighten the narrator's depiction of both the sights and the sounds associated with the scene.

T-4 漁翁出艙解開了纜。
The fisherman leaves his cabin to untie his boat;
B-4 拿起了篙，
He takes up his pole,
駕起了小航，
Climbs aboard his boat,
漂漂搖搖，
Rocking and floating,
晃裡晃蕩，
Shaking to and fro,
驚動了水中的那些鷺鷥，
Scaring the egrets in the water,
對對的鴛鴦，
Pair on pair of Mandarin ducks,
撲攏攏兩翅兒忙，
"Pulengleng" is the sound of twinned wings working busily
飛過了揚子江。
As they fly across the Yangtze River.

The fifth couplet begins the second half of this piece, in which the narrator introduces the woodsman, another member of the working class. In this vignette, the mists and clouds are described as covering and then revealing trees on a hillside in much the same way as often depicted visually in a Chinese landscape painting. As part of the description of the hillside, we also encounter a temple in which a monk strikes a wooden fish, burns incense, and prays to Buddha. Another example of *dingzhenti*, in which the narrator begins a new line with the last word of the previous line, is used in line 2 through the beginning of line 6 of B-5.

T-5 打柴的樵夫就把高山上。
The woodsman gathering firewood goes high in the hills.
B-5 遙望見
I look up and there, far off,
山長著青雲
The clouds so pale
雲罩著青松
Clouds covering green pines,
松藏著古寺
Pines hiding the old temple,
寺裡隱著山僧，
The temple sheltering a hillside monk:
老僧在佛堂上把木魚敲的響乒乓
The hillside monk in Buddha's hall strikes the wooden fish, bing-bang
他是念佛燒香。
As he calls on Buddha he sets the incense burning too.

The sixth couplet, about the farmer, is explicit about the way he demonstrates his ability to bring prosperity to his world and to those around him. He is a good example of a human agent who, as Brindley describes, is an integral participant in the course of the cosmos itself (2012: 158). The active role of such individuals ensures the proper movements of the cosmos, allowing everyone to benefit from the bounty of the seasons. The farmer exemplifies how humans can serve as a vital link in the mutually defining process of cosmic and human interaction (2012: 159).

T-6 農夫清晨早下地。
The farmer, in the dawn, goes early to his fields.
B-6 拉過了牛，
He leads the ox over,
套上了犁，
Fits on the plow,
一到南窪去種地
He goes right to the south paddy to plow and plant,
耕的是春種秋收，
He plows for spring planting, autumn harvest,
冬藏閉戶，封上那一份錢糧。

Winter harvest and filled storehouse, keeping his own portion of cash and grain.

Unlike the farmer, the student is mockingly portrayed as a bungling novice who—like the scholar in the third couplet—has overslept, also possibly due to the failure of the sleeping watchman. The student wears the clothes of his station, but his actions betray his lack of focus as he stumbles into his study. Here, as in the vignette about the scholar, the portrayal is mildly derisive but the behavior is not egregious enough to seriously interrupt his studies.

T-7 念書的學生走出了大門外。
The student leaves his bedroom.
B-7 我只見他
Look at him ,
頭戴方巾
Scholar's hat set on his head,
身穿蘭衫腰
Long blue gown on his back,
腰系絲條
Frog buttons clinch his waist,
足下蹬著福履
Embroidered shoes encase his feet,
懷裡抱著書包
A bag of books clutched to his breast,
一步三搖
Three shakes to every step,
腳步兒倉惶走進書房。
Tripping over both feet, he goes into his study.

The lady described in the eighth couplet is a member of the elite class, a *jiaren* (佳人) or "beauty." Although the narrator does not provide any qualities or duties associated with this character, except a description of her morning toilette, it is possible that this *jiaren* is an example of the iconic figure whom Keith McMahon describes as smart, capable, chaste, and, in some cases, better than her male counterpart, the *caizi* (才子), in terms of literary talent, moral fiber, and wit (1994: 227). The portrayal of the oversleeping scholar in the third couplet and of the aspiring student clumsily making his way to the study in the seventh couplet suggest a dichotomy between the harried scholar/bumbling student and the poised—and perhaps highly intelligent and capable—lady.

T-8 繡房的佳人要早起。
The beauty in her chamber must rise early;
B-8 我只見他
Look at her, she
面對菱花
Faces her table mirror,
雲分兩鬢

Parts her cloud-like hair,
鬢邊戴著鮮花,
Sets fresh flowers at her temples,
花枝招展,
Like the flowers' opening freshness
她是俏梳椿。
She is enticingly made up.

We see the greatest degree of personal freedom in the final vignette, about the buffalo-herding boy. When he is not singing, free and unfettered, he is playing a rustic tune on his flute. An example where musical interests take over from the text, the long fourteen-measure melisma sung on the final syllable (*yao*, 遙) in B-9 metonymically represents that swaying tune.[4] The piece concludes with B-9¹, an additional line that ends the piece with a short but lively description of the boy as he rounds the curving brook. A work that begins with a description emphasizing the visual magnificence of the waning night sky ends with a lengthy musical portrayal of the cowherd's pastoral tune.

T-9　牧牛童兒不住地連聲唱。
　　　The boy herding buffalo sings without cease;
B-9　我只見他,
　　　Look at him,
　　　頭戴著斗笠,
　　　A straw rainhat on his head,
　　　身披蓑衣,
　　　A straw raincoat on his back,
　　　下穿水褲,
　　　Rain trousers on his legs,
　　　足下蹬著草鞋,
　　　Grass sandals on his feet,
　　　腕掛藤鞭,
　　　A whip dangles from his wrist,
　　　倒騎牛背
　　　Facing backwards as he rides,
　　　口橫短笛吹得是自在逍遙
　　　His flute on his lips, he plays with easy freedom.

B-9¹　吹出來的山歌兒是野調無腔這才越過了小溪旁。
　　　He plays a rustic and unknown tune as he rounds the curving brook.

The depiction of these nine individuals, some of whom are comically yet forgivingly portrayed, provides a picture in which the worker and the scholar, the cowherd and the lady, all have roles to fulfill in the proper functioning of society. But the poetry describing these characters is only the skeleton on which Luo Yusheng fleshes out her portrayal of the scene. The musical rendition provides the next level of detail in appreciating all the elements in the multimodal discourse of *Choumo yinchu*.

The Musical Rendition

Given the stated importance of the text in Beijing drumsong (Lawson, 2011: 82–83), one might wonder why one would go to the trouble of painstakingly setting it to music. Why not simply recite the text, particularly when rendering a text melodically can compete with the proper portrayal of linguistic tone? Certainly, there are genres in which the performer declaims at least part of the story in spoken language. However, most of the narrative genres involve vocalizing on some level because audiences revel in the way music enhances the story and makes it more aesthetically pleasing. Like a chef who tastes, savors, and appraises the success of a new dish, Tianjinese audiences are keenly aware of nuances in the singing of each syllable, and they listen carefully to enjoy the way in which the musical rendition heightens and plays with the lyrics (Lawson, 2017: 72). Audiences expect that a performer "first says the words and then sings the melody" (*xian nianzi hou changqiang*), meaning that the words of the story are paramount in a narrative performance. Nevertheless, it is also true that audiences come to hear the musical rendition of the story.

The desire for a musically enhanced articulation of poetry might be seen as an example of what Ellen Dissanayake refers to as "artifying" or "making special," meaning that humans "intentionally shape, embellish, and otherwise fashion aspects of their world to make these more than ordinary" (1999: 30). By setting lyrics to music, one could argue that narrators make spoken words extraordinary through their musical rendition, thereby satisfying the Chinese audience's expectation for musically satisfying performances that go beyond the ordinary communication of a storyline, an expectation that Dissanayake would claim is universal (1999: 37).

I have transcribed and analyzed the way texts are set to music in Beijing drumsong elsewhere (Lawson, 2011: 84–93), so I will only briefly summarize that discussion here. There are two major melody-types associated with Beijing drumsong, only one of which is used in this short piece. The melody-type used in *Choumo* is known as *pingqiang* 平腔, which Luo always performs in *manban* 慢板 or "slow meter." With the exception of the first two T lines, which are a showcase for the performer's virtuosity (Stevens, 1975: 159), the rest of the T lines, each of which introduces a new character in the story, exhibit the same melodic arc and cadences.

Figure 13.1 illustrates the way word tone is portrayed in T lines 3 through 6, and corresponding places in the video recording are noted for each opening syllable. Notice the difference in the opening word for each line: fourth-tone *jia* in T-3 (minute 1:59), second-tone *yu* in T-4 (2:32), third-tone *da* in T-5 (3:41), and second-tone *nong* in T-6 (4:16). With the exception of *nong* in T-6, word tones are accurately portrayed in each opening word—either in the melody itself or through the use of preceding grace notes. In T-6, the initial grace note goes counter to the upward direction of the second tone, but the subsequent upward-moving melody counteracts the brief appearance of the seemingly errant grace note preceding *nong*. I suggest that this anomaly is designed to break up the predictability of the otherwise linguistically correct setting of word tone in the

FIGURE 13.1. Melody and song text marked with speech tone, *Choumo yinchu* lines T-3, T-4, T-5, and T-6, as sung by Luo Yusheng, 1960.

other syllables—and, since the melody clearly moves upward on *nong* anyway, the direction of second tone is, nonetheless, clearly portrayed.

Compared to the cursory introductory T lines, the B lines are much more varied because the poetic rendition is more complex in the B lines—where, for example, one finds the poetic techniques such as *dingzhenti* and *duoju*. Consequently, the musical realization of the B lines is much more varied than that of the T lines, changing dramatically with each couplet. As an example, B-1, which features the *dingzhenti* technique in describing the night sky, is contrasted with B-2, which includes the list of absent sounds in the watchtower, set according to the *duoju* technique.

In Figure 13.2, note how the melody picks up where the previous repeated syllable leaves off on the syllables *xing* and *dou* in measures 3 and 4 of line B-1 (0:58–1:03). That phrase is then followed by a choppier, more disjunct melody in the following alliterative phrases *miaomiao mangmang huanghuang huhu mimizaza* in measures 5 through 8 (1:04–1:11), providing melodic balance.

A different kind of musical setting occurs in B-2; the technique of *duoju* features repetitive musical motifs for each of the absent sounds in the watchtower: two eighth notes, four sixteenth notes, followed by a two-beat break in measures 3 through 6 (1:35–1:43). After the list of absent sounds, we hear a freer, more sweeping and more ornamented melody in measures 7 through 13 (1:43–1:58) as a contrast to the previous *duoju* section.

Significantly, each B line is musically more varied than the shorter, syllabic T lines because the text is longer and more complex. The relationship of T to B lines varies in this piece—in fact, every piece written in the *duoju* tradition will have its own unique

FIGURE 13.2. Line B-1 from *Choumo yinchu* sung by Luo Yusheng, 1960.

FIGURE 13.3. Line B-2 from *Choumo yinchu* sung by Luo Yusheng, 1961.

relationship between the upper and lower lines of couplets. As a general rule, word tone is accurately portrayed, especially at the beginnings of words and at the beginnings of lines, making the lines semantically intelligible; however, once the meaning has been established, performers tend to embellish vocally in order to create a musically satisfying dimension to the performance as a way of balancing the accurate linguistic portrayal of word tone.

The flexible use of melodic and rhythmic formulae in setting lyrics in the Beijing drumsong tradition speaks to the notion of "floating intentionality," a concept proposed by Ian Cross. Cross explains that while musical meanings appear intimately bound to the contexts in which they are experienced (2003: 18), music is nonetheless still flexible. Since music, unlike language, does not declare specific meaning, it has the ability to continually transform itself. At the same time, music can also provide a unifying framework that binds disparate elements in the setting of lyrics. The use of the *pingqiang* melody-type is an example of a floating intentionality that is flexible enough to fit any text written according to the general conventions of the genre; nevertheless, once a particular text has been set to music, the resulting musical setting becomes intimately associated with the poetic lyrics and links together the different elements of the story. As Ruth Herbert explains, music is a particularly effective mediator of experience, able to bind and blend together elements of external awareness that might otherwise be perceptually separated (2011: 196–97). By setting the lyrics to music, the nine individual's in *Choumo* become linked through the use of key, meter, and the unique settings of musical formulae.

In addition to providing a unifying musical framework for the piece, the musical rendition serves other purposes as well. Herbert explains that "music's frequent coupling with words . . . makes it an effective medium for the processing of imagining, reminiscing, and reflecting that may or may not possess a partially linguistic quality" (2011: 195). Moreover, she explains that as a multimodal experience, music can be conceptualized as a composite of different types of conscious and non-conscious experience, any one of which may be dominant at a certain moment (ibid.: 195). For example, the musical interlude and the vocal melisma on the last syllable of B-9 offer what Herbert would refer to as a freedom from verbal language: "an alternative mental space in which the listener does not have to decode precise meaning" (ibid.: 196–97). The interlude certainly provides this mental space by offering a time and a space for reflection, exploring the imagery just presented and anticipating the next part of the piece. The vocal melisma at the end of the piece is another place where wordless musical beauty becomes paramount, temporarily allowing the listener to enter a different psychological time frame. This is the place where the listener can reflect on the boy's song and, as Herbert suggests, imagine, reminisce, and reflect.

Finally, the musical rendition offers a chance to reify the poetic description of sounds of the early morning, transforming the acoustical world at daybreak into music. The references to sound in the poetic text constitute an important element of the discourse, and the musical component emerges naturally from the lyrics: the snoring watchman (and even the absence of sounds from the watchtower), the crowing cock, and the onomatopoeic sound of duck wings are just some such sounds. Although Luo does not imitate any of these sounds directly, her singing (as opposed to verbal declamation) provides a melodic rendering of a world that is already rife with sounds, adding another layer of sonic beauty. A brief instrumental interlude follows the fourth couplet, providing a short opportunity for Luo to rest her voice and for the audience to reflect on the performance thus far.

After summoning up a rich soundscape, in the second half of the piece, Luo switches to highlighting other senses, with "*bing-bang*" in couplet 5, an onomatopoeic reference to the monk striking a wooden fish, as the only mention of sound. Instead of describing additional sounds in couplets 5 through 8, Luo's vocal treatment of the narrative relies primarily on a literary description of visual images, including a brief olfactory reference to the monk burning incense. The temporary absence from describing sounds during much of the second half of the piece is balanced with couplet 9, in which Luo showcases the cowherd's song and flute playing, creating an impactful return to music in the final couplet. Thus, the final part of the story provides an opportunity for Luo to sing the boy's wordless tune, providing a cadenza-like, musically significant ending to the performance.

In sum, the musical rendition "artifies" the lyrics, binds the poetic descriptions of nine individuals into one coherent piece, provides opportunities for shifts in consciousness, and enhances the auditory dimensions of the story through Luo's melodic (as opposed to verbal) rendition of the lyrics. Musical elements are further enhanced and supplemented by Luo's gestural movements and her directions for the camera's focus on a landscape painting.

The Visual Component: Pictorial and Gestural Elements

Gestures, which may include pointing to (or focusing a camera on) paintings, are integral to Luo's performance, and research on gesture suggests good reasons for Luo's predisposition to using both gesture and visual aids in her performance. As Steven Mithen explains, "gestures play a complementary role to spoken utterances, rather than being merely derivative or supplementary. So, gestures are not used simply to help the speaker retrieve words from his or her mental dictionary; they provide information that cannot be derived from the spoken utterance alone" (2006: 155). David McNeill further explains that "utterances possess two sides, only one of which is speech; the other is imagery, actional and visuo-spatial. To exclude the gestural side, as has been traditional, is tantamount to ignoring half of the message of the brain" (2000: 139). Consequently, if body movement is crucial to language, then it would make sense that gesture would play a key role in the musical rendition of a story.[5]

The practice of incorporating painting with gestural communication in Chinese narrative performance has its roots in early Buddhist storytelling that dates back to the genre of popular Buddhist folk narratives from the Tang dynasty (618–906). Victor Mair (1989) provides the most comprehensive study of *bianwen* 變文, the first recorded Chinese vernacular narratives, which were derived from a type of Buddhist storytelling with pictures. After the initial popularity of Buddhist storytelling in the Tang period, Chinese storytelling became secularized and popularized on stages in urban centers and in rural areas throughout the country. A great narrative tradition emerged over the next millennium, with the particular role of pictures in performance assuming a new level of importance in the seventeenth century with the advent of printing technology.

Explaining the importance of pictures in Chinese storytelling since the seventeenth century, Boris Riftin asserts that popular prints were created to illustrate the plots of novels, plays, and stories already known to Chinese audiences and that there was a strong correlation between the subjects of oral storytelling and the flourishing of popular prints (2010: 194). The proximity of one of the important centers of popular print production in Yangliuqing to one of the great centers of narrative-arts performance in Tianjin suggests that the visual and storytelling arts may have fed one another in Tianjin, the city where Luo established herself as a consummate storyteller.

In my field research in the People's Republic of China during the 1980s and 1990s, I did not personally encounter narrative performance with pictures except in two examples of video footage from the 1960s, both of which feature Luo Yusheng performing beside large paintings to which the camera turns at appropriate times throughout her performance (see Figure 13.4).

The performance was choreographed with the painting in mind, a point that lends some credence to Mair's and Riftin's arguments about the role of painting in performance. The pictorial and gestural elements are inextricably and carefully combined, demonstrating thoughtful planning in crafting the visual dimension of her story. The performance opens with the camera focused on a large, approximately four-by-six-foot Chinese landscape painting, set off by a black frame. The painting hangs on a wall behind Luo and her drum, which, according to standard practice, sits on a stand. The instrumental accompanists—playing the *sanxian*, *sihu*, and *pipa*—are not visible at any time during the entire seven-minute performance.

The camera alternates between focusing solely on the painting—with Luo out of sight—and focusing on Luo's gestures as she sketches out the movements of the characters in her story, using her drumstick as an extension of her arm. Stokoe (2000: 388) defines the term "gesture" to mean a hand-arm movement that symbolizes something else; Luo's use of the drumstick is an important component of her hand-arm gesturing, as though she were using a paintbrush to create the visual cues that complement her vocal portrayals.

FIGURE 13.4. Luo Yusheng's *Choumo* performance in front of a painting that depicts a morning scene. (Illustrator: Ian Ferguson)

Each time the camera focuses on Luo, it is from a different angle. Sometimes the camera is focused directly in front of her, with the painting in the background; other times, it is focused on her at different angles to the painting, all the while featuring her bodily movements from different points of vantage. Although the recording is a result of a combination of her performance choices, camerawork, and postproduction, it seems likely that Luo decided when to feature her gestures and when to foreground the painting because of the way she self-consciously emphasizes bodily movements when the camera is focused directly on her. Couplets 1, 3, 5, 7, and 8 showcase the painting, whereas couplets 2, 4, 6, and 9 highlight Luo as she energetically portrays her characters with the use of her full body and her drumstick.

One couplet that lends itself to featuring interesting bodily gestures is couplet 4, about the fisherman. As Luo describes the fisherman wobbling back and forth on the boat, she mimics his quavering movements as though she were riding on choppy waters while singing *piaopiao yaoyao huangli huangdang*, words that describe his jerking movements as he tries to balance himself (2:45–2:50). Moving both arms as if to point to the pair of Mandarin ducks near the boat, she imitates the gesture of their flapping wings while singing the onomatopoeic *pulengleng* (3:06–3:08). Luo also emphasizes the word *mang* (meaning "busy") (3:09–3:10) with some additional fast vibrato, which enhances her description of the wings. After moving her arms in grand gestures, she then retreats to the drum (3:14) while singing one measure of non-lexical syllables before the instrumental interlude, which ends the couplet about the fisherman in the great Yangzi river.

By contrast, Luo's production foregrounds the painting when her descriptions involve less visually interesting bodily activity. Focusing on the painting temporarily allows the viewer/listener to concentrate on the details of the painting while still enjoying the poetic and musical rendition of the story. For example, in couplet 7, the camera settles in on a close-up of the student as he leaves his bedroom (4:55). Throughout the couplet, the camera moves back slowly to reveal his destination, namely his study. Similarly, in couplet 8, the camera focuses on the beauty sitting at her window (5:28), slowly zooming in closer to her face as she does her morning toilette.

For a dramatic ending to the piece, Luo features both her bodily gestures and the painting more or less equally in couplet 9. In this final couplet, the audience first sees Luo narrating the story about the young cowherd (5:59), followed by a shot of the cowherd riding backward on his cow (6:35), before showcasing her dramatic gestures at the end of the piece (7:08–7:22). After a brief performance on the drum (7:23–25), she ceremoniously puts her clapper and drumstick on the drum and bows. By alternating the focus between her bodily movements and the painting, Luo provides visual variety in her narrative and guides the audience's multisensory experience of the narrative.

Conclusion

Beijing drumsong is an important narrative genre in the city of Tianjin, and Luo's rendition of *Choumo* represents one of the greatest examples of the art form. The story highlights quintessentially Chinese ideas about cosmic and earthly harmony, portrayed by the actions of characters from an imaginary rural village. While iconic in many ways, the story is also unusual because it does not have a hero or a plot. Instead, as a theme-circling narrative about the transition from night to morning, *Choumo* is a celebration of sights and sounds, making the story particularly well suited to multimodal discourse. Luo's musical rendition of the poetry, her bodily movements, and her liberal use of a painting all serve to "artify" the story through musical and visual elements, allowing for full expression of the emotions associated with the sensations of early morning. Moreover, the textual, musical, gestural, and pictorial components of the performance solicit interdisciplinary connections with diverse fields, such as mother-infant communication, biomusicology, art history, artificial intelligence, and embodied cognition, thereby suggesting new and interesting directions for future work.

Glossary

Bai Fengming 白鳳鳴, Beijing drumsong singer (1909–80)
Bai Yunpeng 白雲鵬, Beijing drumsong singer (1874–1952)
ban 板, wood clapper
bianwen 變文, vernacular Buddhist narratives
caizi 才子, "talented person," a scholar in classical tales
Choumo yinchu 醜末寅初, *At Break of Day*, Beijing drumsong composition
dingzhenti 頂針體, "thimbling," poetic device
duoju 垛句, "piled up phrases," song-structure term
gu 鼓, drum
Han Yonglu 韓永祿, Beijing drumsong singer (1876–1943)
jiaren 佳人, a beautiful woman in classical tales
Jian'ge wen ling 劍閣聞鈴, *Listening to the Bells at Sword Pavilion*, Beijing drumsong composition
Jingyun dagu 京韻大鼓, Beijing drumsong
laosheng 老生, mature male role in traditional opera
Liu Baoquan 劉寶全, Beijing drumsong singer (1868–1942)
Luo Yusheng 駱玉笙, Beijing drumsong singer (1914–2002)
Luo Caiwu 駱彩舞, itinerant performer in Shanghai and Beijing (early twentieth century)
manban 慢板, slow meter
pipa 琵琶, four-stringed lute
pingqiang 平腔, melody-type in Beijing drumsong
sanxian 三弦, three-stringed lute
sihu 四胡, four-stringed fiddle
xianshi 弦師, string master in traditional opera and narrative

Notes

1. Important exceptions include Mair (1988, 1989), Jeffery (1992), Treitler (2003), and Busse Berger (2005).

2. For a discussion of those who influenced her musical style, see Tao (1983: 69) and Liu (1983: 94–103).
3. Below, I have adapted Stevens's English translation of *Choumo*, with her permission (Lawson, 2011: no. 14).
4. Musical aspects of the performance are discussed below.
5. Research on the social nature of embodied musical performance is growing in the field of ethnomusicology, rooted in the study of both performers and listeners (Becker, 2010; Taylor, 2003; Hahn, 2007; Weidman, 2012).

References

Becker, Judith. (2010). "Exploring the Habitus of Listening." In *Handbook of Music and Emotion: Theory, Research, Applications*, edited by Patrik N. Juslin and John A. Sloboda, 127–57. Oxford: Oxford University Press.

Brindley, Erica Fox. (2012). *Music, Cosmology, and the Politics of Harmony in Early China*. Albany, NY: SUNY Press.

Busse Berger, Anna Maria. (2005). *Medieval Music and the Art of Memory*. Berkeley: University of California Press.

Chatman, Seymour. (1978). *Story and Discourse: Narrative Structure in Fiction and Film*. Ithaca, NY: Cornell University Press.

Cross, Ian. (2003). "Music and Biocultural Evolution." In *The Cultural Study of Music: A Critical Introduction*, edited by Trevor Herbert, Martin Clayton, and Richard Middleton, 19–30. London: Routledge.

Dissanayake, Ellen. (1999). "'Making Special': An Undescribed Human Universal and the Core of a Behavior of Art." In *Biopoetics: Evolutionary Explorations in the Arts*, edited by Brett Cooke and Frederick Turner, 27–46. Lexington, KY: ICUS.

Dissanayake, Ellen. (2001). "Aesthetic Incunabula." *Philosophy and Literature* 25 (2): 335–46.

Gelernter, David. (2016). *The Tides of Mind: Uncovering the Spectrum of Consciousness*. New York: W. W. Norton.

Gratier, Maya, and Colwyn Trevarthen. (2008). "Musical Narrative and Motives for Culture in Mother-infant Vocal Interaction." *Journal of Consciousness Studies* 15 (10–11): 122–58.

Hahn, Tomie. (2007). *Sensational Knowledge: Embodying Culture Through Japanese Dance*. Middletown, CT: Wesleyan University Press.

Herbert, Ruth. (2011). *Everyday Music Listening: Absorption, Dissociation and Trancing*. Farnham, UK: Ashgate.

Imberty, Michel. (2011). "Music, Linguistics, and Cognition." In *Music and the Mind: Essays in Honour of John Sloboda*, edited by Irène Deliège and Jane W. Davidson, 3–16. Oxford: Oxford University Press.

Jeffery, Peter. (1992). *Re-Envisioning Past Musical Cultures: Ethnomusicology in the Study of Gregorian Chant*. Chicago: University of Chicago Press.

Lawson, Francesca. (2011). *The Narrative Arts of Tianjin: Between Music and Language*. Farnham, UK: Ashgate.

Lawson, Francesca. (2017). *The Women of Quyi: Liminal Voices and Androgynous Bodies*. New York: Routledge.

Liu, Shufang 劉書方. (1983). "Luo Yusheng changqiang yanjiu" "骆玉笙唱腔研究" [A Study of Luo Yusheng's Melodic Style]. *Yinyue yanjiu* 音樂研究 [Music Research], no. 3: 94–103.

Lord, Albert B. *The Singer of Tales*. (1960). Cambridge, MA: Harvard University Press.
Luo, Yusheng 骆玉笙. (1960). *Jingyun dagu "Choumo yinchu" Luo Yusheng* 京韵大鼓《丑末寅初》骆玉笙 [Beijing Drum-song, "Choumo yinchu," Luo Yusheng] 1960. Accessed May 20, 2023. https://www.youtube.com/watch?v=AGePThVcrNM.
Luo, Yusheng 骆玉笙. (1962). *Jingyun dagu "Jiange wenling" Luo Yusheng* 京韵大鼓《劍閣聞鈴》骆玉笙 [Beijing Drum-song, "Jiange wenling," Luo Yusheng]. Accessed December 2, 2017. Accessed May 20, 2023. https://www.youtube.com/watch?v=ZsxEYKPIYJs.
Luo, Yusheng 骆玉笙. (2002). *Jingyun dagu "Choumo yinchu"* 京韵大鼓《丑末寅初》 [Beijing Drumsong, "The Ending of Chou and the Beginning of Yin"]. *Beijing Musical Storytelling Collection*, vol. 1. Beijing: China Record Company.
Mair, Victor H. (1988). *Painting and Performance: Chinese Picture Recitation and Its Indian Genesis*. Honolulu: University of Hawai'i Press.
Mair, Victor H. (1989). *T'ang Transformation Texts*. Cambridge, MA: Harvard University Press.
McMahon, Keith. (1994). "The Classic 'Beauty-Scholar' Romance and the Superiority of the Talented Woman." In *Body, Subject and Power in China*, edited by Angela Zito and Tani E. Barlow, 227–52. Chicago: University of Chicago Press.
McNeill, David. (2000). *Gesture in Thought*. Cambridge, UK: Cambridge University Press.
Mithen, Steven. (2006). *The Singing Neanderthals: The Origins of Music, Language, Mind, and Body*. Cambridge, MA: Harvard University Press.
Pinker, Steven. (2007). "Toward a Consilient Study of Literature." *Philosophy and Literature* 31: 161–77.
Riftin, Boris. "Chinese Performing Arts and Popular Prints." In *The Interplay of the Oral and the Written in Chinese Popular Literature*, edited by Vibeke Børdahl and Margaret B. Wan, 187–221. Oslo: Nordic Institute of Asian Studies, 2010.
Stern, Daniel N. *The First Relationship: Infant and Mother*. Cambridge, MA: Harvard University Press, 2002.
Stevens, Catherine. (1975). "Peking Drumsinging." PhD diss., Harvard University.
Stokoe, William C.. (2000). "Gesture to Sign (Language)." In *Language and Gesture*, edited by David McNeill, 388–99. Cambridge, UK: Cambridge University Press.
Tao Dun 陶鈍, ed. (1983). *Luo Yusheng yanchang Jingyun dagu xuan* 骆玉笙演唱京韻大鼓選 [Selections of Beijing Drumsong as Performed by Luo Yusheng]. Tianjin: Baihua wenyi chubanshe.
Taylor, Diana. (2003). *The Archive and the Repertoire: Performing Cultural Memory in the Americas*. Durham, NC: Duke University Press.
Treitler, Leo. (2003). *With Voice and Pen: Coming to Know Medieval Song and How It Was Made*. Oxford: Oxford University Press.
Weidman, Amanda. (2012). "The Ethnographer as Apprentice: Embodying Sociomusical Knowledge in South India." *Anthropology and Humanism* 37 (2): 214–35.
Xue, Baokun 薛寶琨. (1984). *Luo Yusheng he tade Jingyun dagu* 骆玉笙和她的京韻大鼓 [Luo Yusheng and Her Beijing Drumsong]. Harbin: Heilongjiang renmin chubanshe, 1984.

CHAPTER 14

THE EMERGENCE OF TAIWANESE NEW *XIQU*
A Case Study on Chichiao Musical Theater

HSIEH HSIAO-MEI

Introduction

Gezaixi 歌仔戲 (traditional Taiwanese musical theater) was the only dramatic form purely and proudly "made in Taiwan," distinguished from other *xiqu* 戲曲 (traditional opera) performances that were brought to the island by its Chinese immigrants. Unlike earlier operas such as *nanguanxi* 南管戲 and *beiguanxi* 北管戲, which used dialects incomprehensible to most people, *gezaixi* employed a language used by the majority of the population in Taiwan, a southern Fujian dialect with an accent mixed from those of Quanzhou and Zhangzhou, the places from which most immigrants had come. Its dialogue and lyrics were generally more colloquial, tinged with a sense of humor that spoke to ordinary people. Such accessibility thus enabled *gezaixi* to become the most popular entertainment in the first half of the twentieth century on the island.

Scholarship on early *gezaixi* has been very limited due to the lack of official attention paid to the genre. The Taiwanese scholar Zeng Yongyi's *Taiwan gezaixi de fazhan yu bianqian* 臺灣歌仔戲的發展與變遷 (*The Transformation and Development of Gezaixi*, 1988) is the first book dedicated entirely to *gezaixi* in Taiwan. Zeng coins, defines, and periodizes *gezaixi* as old *gezaixi*, indoor *gezaixi*, film *gezaixi*, radio *gezaixi*, TV *gezaixi*, and outdoor *gezaixi*. This basic schema remains influential although not unquestioned; generally, subsequent research on *gezaixi* has followed Zeng's naming and categorization. The research on local traditional opera in Taiwan has grown rapidly ever since, mostly due to the rise of Taiwanese consciousness after the lifting of martial law in 1987. The growth in advanced education and the attention to indigenous culture have resulted in an increasing number of graduate students delving into this field. Overall, established scholars are inclined to provide macro analyses of *gezaixi*, whereas graduate theses, especially those written after the later 1990s, tend to focus on specific subjects.

The subject of my master's thesis of 2000 is the subgenre of *gezaixi* called *opela* 胡撇仔, a hybrid form engaging multicultural, especially Japanese, elements. Due to its "impure" nature, *opela* had been overlooked and was rarely discussed at that time. My research attempted to redefine *opela* by examining the Japanese colonial influence and by collecting and analyzing its repertoire among the plebian outdoor theater companies.[1] Chen Youxin's study (2010) subsequently added more historical research, considering also the development of *opela* after the turn of the millennium. The two volumes of Lin Heyi's research (2016) resulted from that author's fieldwork over ten years and illuminate the merits of outdoor *gezaixi*'s improvisational nature. Lin analyzes how the improvisational and actor-centered performance functions—that is, how the *mubiao* 幕表 (scenario, or scene-outline) is constructed and instructed, how the actors create their characters based on the scenario, how performers (actors and musicians included) interact with one another, and how they develop and hone their skills. The improvisational theater foregrounds the actor's personal style and charisma.

While *opela* embodies *gezaixi*'s improvisational and flexible features, in the new millennium, the participation of the literati produced a new type of *opela* that is well-scripted and rehearsed under direction. Built on the publications above, this chapter adopts a broader perspective, reconsidering the development of *opela* from a pejorative term to an empowering phrase and exploring the ramification its evolution from *opela* to new *opela* and then to *xiqu* musical. The case study of Chichiao Musical Theater (Qiqiao Jutuan 奇巧劇團), with its productions that blurred the boundaries of *gezaixi* and Henan *banzi* 河南梆子 (the main music in traditional Henan opera, *yuju* 豫劇) and so broke the boundaries between modern and traditional theater, exemplifies the emergence of new *xiqu* in Taiwan, which is not confined within the music of any specific regional operatic genre.

OPELA: THE GRASSROOTS NEGOTIATION OF MODERNITY AND ITS DOUBLE MEANINGS

Religious performance of theater has long been prevalent in Taiwan, and it still sustains most of Taiwan's *xiqu* activities. *Gezaixi* dominated the indoor commercial theater market until the 1960s, when it began to yield to cinema. Displaced performers then turned to and took over the outdoor theater market, where they perform religious theater, now being joined by the performers of *budaixi* 布袋戲 (glove puppetry) and *dianzi huache* 電子花車 (vaudeville performed on trucks), and by film projectionists. This religious outdoor *gezaixi* is mostly funded by temples, local guilds, and individuals. It is usually staged on a temporary wooden pavilion or platform in front of the temple to celebrate the god's birthday or to show the gratitude of the community or of particular individuals. The entire event consists of daytime and nightime performances: in the daytime, a ritual play lasting about thirty minutes is followed by a two-hour-long show, in which *gulu* 古路 (old-style) plays are staged, featuring historical or legendary tales; in the three-hour-long nightly show, *opela*-style performances are more common on stage and usually attract more spectators than the *gulu* plays. *Opela* scores combine Western and Eastern influences, and productions blend traditional Taiwanese, Japanese, and Western visual aesthetics. Foreign musical instruments in *opela* include jazz drums, trumpet, saxophone, and electric piano, creating a jazzy atmosphere for the night. The plots are usually a hybrid of melodrama and swordsman fantasy, featuring themes of love and vengeance. It is not uncommon to see a character wearing a kimono or a cowboy suit and switching between traditional *gezaixi* tunes and contemporary pop songs, with the story set in premodern China.

Opela has long been a controversial term: a Japanese transliteration of "opera," it is also negatively associated with a Taiwanese phrase *o-be-pe-pe-le* (doing something perfunctorily). The double meanings of *opela* address two historical periods in Taiwan: the period of Japanese colonial influence on Taiwanese theater (1895–1945) and the semi-colonial experience under the totalitarian rule of the Nationalist Party during the martial-law era (1945–87).

The performance hybridity of *gezaixi* can be traced to the Imperial Subject Movement (Japanese, *Kōminka undo* 皇民化運動) during the Japanese colonial period in Taiwan, when outdoor religious performances were banned and indoor performances censored. When the Sino-Japanese War was at its height (1937–45), the Japanese colonizers suppressed traditional theater in Taiwan and encouraged the staging of Japanese historical-period drama, Imperial Subject plays, and *xinju* 新劇 ("new drama"; that is, spoken drama). Records show that *gezaixi* troupes hired Japanese actors to perform or instruct Taiwanese actors on how to perform Japanese historical-period drama or *xinju* (Chen Youxin, 2010: 51). However, neither Japanese period drama nor *xinju* were popular with audiences, and, therefore, Taiwanese performers inserted popular songs and even sneaked in traditional *gezaixi* tunes. Subsequently, Taiwanese performers came up with *gailiang xi* 改良戲 (reformed plays) which assumed the look of the approved forms (i.e., actors wore kimonos or Western suits and the ensemble included Western musical instruments), but the story remained based on those of traditional repertoire.[2] The tactic allowed performers and spectators to stay connected to their familiar entertainments and bypass the authorities' censorship. At the same time, it provided performers with an opportunity to experience different performance styles. Though later the Japanese left Taiwan following their defeat in World War II, the experience stayed. *Gezaixi* practitioners continued to consciously turn for inspiration to foreign, especially Japanese, forms of performance culture, such as Takarazuka Revue and Japanese historical-period film, and they gradually developed the unique style now known as *opela*.

As a hybrid performance style of Japanese, Western, and Taiwanese aesthetics and musical traditions, and a product of the assimilation policy during Japanese colonial rule, *opela* was originally the response of grassroots artists to a repressive regime, but it grew into a popular form of entertainment in postwar Taiwan. During this time, the mixed format also became a site where performers navigated modernity in the commercial theater, with the compromising reformation of the colonial period reshaped as a conscious experiment on the part of *gezaixi* practitioners to draw in more spectators. Thus, *opela* developed fully as a subgenre of *gezaixi*.

As a matter of fact, the modernization of *gezaixi* began during the postwar era, when it flourished in indoor theaters. Take music, for example: the use of popular music in *gezaixi* has been a constant factor. On the scripts of the Gongleshe 拱樂社, a commercially successful theater company during the 1950s to 1960s, quite a few stage directions note: "make entrance to a popular song," with the choice of the song depending on what was popular at the time. Most of the time it was Taiwanese, and occasionally it was in Mandarin or Japanese (Liu Nanfang, 2016: 145). When *gezaixi* withdrew from indoor theaters and turned to outdoor religious venues, street *gezaixi* performers inherited much from the *gezaixi* of the previous golden age, including its repertoire and performance style. *Opela* today uses quite a few popular songs. In traditional theater, actors recite a poem to introduce themselves or express their emotions as they make their entrance and exit, whereas in *opela* the convention of reciting entrance and exit poems is replaced by singing popular songs. Some songs are effective in characterization and plot development, and as a result certain musical conventions are established. For instance, when a female character is unwillingly deflowered, she sings "U ia hue" 雨夜花 ("A Flower on a Rainy Night"), and when a male character is drunk and in despair, he sings "Tsiuhio e sim tsiann" 酒後的心聲 ("In Wine, Truth" or "A Drunken Voice").

In outdoor *gezaixi* today, performers present traditional repertoire during the afternoon show and present bolder experiments in the evening *opela*. Because *opela* has been long defined derogatorily as *o-be-pe-pe-le* because of its mixed (and thus "impure") performance style, its original meaning, the Japanese transliteration of the word "opera," has been forgotten. The reason behind this change of association and conception has a lot to do with the Nationalist Party's cultural policy and state ideology, which had regulated Taiwan during the martial-law era. The Nationalist government took over Taiwan in 1945 and then came to Taiwan in 1949. Since then and up to the early 1990s, state patronage of traditional opera went exclusively to *jingju* 京劇 (Beijing opera) in order to enhance the nation's claims of legitimacy over China, albeit in exile (Guy, 2005: 4–5). Mandarin became the "national language" while most people in Taiwan were originally fluent in Taiwanese and Japanese, and *jingju* enjoyed the status of "national opera," priding itself on preserving tradition and cultural essence. Because "Chineseness" was officially heightened, intellectuals tended to ignore *gezaixi* despite its vitality in Taiwanese society. In this political and cultural climate, both the performers and the spectators inevitably internalized such a cultural hierarchy, which then shaped their aesthetic perceptions. Thus, an ideal model for traditional arts was constructed and fortified according to the image of *jingju*.[3]

Since state patronage went to *jingju*, the rest of the traditional operatic genres had to compete for financial support from non-governmental sources. To a great extent, a context of free-market competition arose among and between these genres. It was under such circumstances that *gezaixi* in Taiwan evolved, surviving as the "fittest" genre among its various peers and incorporating the strengths of other dramatic forms, inasmuch as the troupes of such genres as *luantanxi* 亂彈戲 and *gaojiaxi* 高甲戲 eventually disbanded and/or reassembled as *gezaixi* troupes. Doing so allowed performers from these genres to bring into *gezaixi* the training and features of their original genres, thereby further enriching the performance of *gezaixi*. Such circumstances also mean that *gezaixi* in Taiwan is constantly in the making and often referred to as a hodgepodge. Following available resources and media, it evolved into subgenres such as film *gezaixi*, radio *gezaixi*, TV *gezaixi*, outdoor (temple) *gezaixi*, and mainstage *gezaixi*. Mainstage *gezaixi*, or *gongyan* 公演 as most professional practitioners call it, is produced with a larger budget and incorporates a fuller script and sound, lighting, stage, and costume design, and it is usually subsidized by cultural foundations or governmental organizations. Today, TV *gezaixi*, outdoor *gezaixi*, and mainstage *gezaixi* are the most common modes of *gezaixi* in Taiwan.

In the post-martial-law era, Taiwan began to move away from the Chinese identity that had been imposed on its people by the Nationalist regime and to embrace an identity that is a blend of Austronesian and Chinese cultures shaped by the colonial rulers from the Netherlands, Spain, Japan, and China. The legitimacy of *jingju* in Taiwan was challenged. The indigenous *gezaixi* came to represent authentic Taiwanese culture and later, after the turn of the millennium, *opela* moved to the forefront and began to receive recognition, as the ruling Nationalist Party was brought down for the first time in the presidential election in 2000, marking the peak of a soaring Taiwanese awareness. Moreover, as Taiwan has been confronted with the impacts of Western and Japanese cultures in the age of globalization, it further suffers from anxiety about Sinicization. The identity of Taiwan is therefore torn between the concepts of not only "the West" and "tradition" but "China" and "Taiwan" as well. As a result, there has been a search for authentic Taiwanese characteristics distinct from mainland Chinese influences. Taiwanese society thus began to recognize the raw and vigorous creativity of *opela* and to value its connection to Taiwanese colonial history. The change of its image in the twenty-first century is "a response within the realm of the performing arts to the trend of reconstructing Taiwanese history" (Hsieh, 2007: 103–4).

New *Opela*: The Intervention of the Intellectuals

Teri J. Silvio (2009) states that interaction between *opela* and the Little Theater Movement[4] played an important part in *opela*'s destigmatization. She proposes the term "new *opela*," using works of the Golden Bough Theater (Jinzhi Yanshe 金枝演社), a modern theater company, and the Formosa Chunfeng Opera Troupe, an amateur traditional theater company, as examples to explain how new *opela* cites particular elements of *opela*'s bricolage and places them within a new discursive context. In new *opela*, *opela* stands for the contemporary actors' idea of what Taiwanese society was like during the 1950s to 1970s.[5]

In my opinion, we need to highlight the intervention of the literati in any discussion of new *opela*. Taiwanese intellectuals changed the look and disposition of *opela* as they became involved in productions. The Formosa Chunfeng Troupe (Chunfeng Gejutuan 春風歌劇團) is an amateur theater company formed by young *gezaixi* fans. Originally formed by members of a college-student club, the ensemble founded the troupe after graduation in 2003. Their new *opela*, *The Venetian Twins* (*Weinisi shuang bao an* 威尼斯雙胞案), which premiered in 2007, was nominated for the prestigious Taishin Arts Award that year. A successful adaptation of Carlo Goldoni's comedy of the same name, this example shows that the troupe is versed in both Taiwanese and Western performance traditions and was willing to instill new ideas in *gezaixi* theater by trying out various new combinations. Stock characters and plots of mistaken identity are common features to both *opela* and commedia dell'arte, and thus local audiences could easily resonate with the adaptation. The production team also utilized the spontaneous and playful spirit of *opela* and employed updated cultural elements, such as the practice of cosplay, or costumed role play. They achieved this by setting the main characters as *otaku* (a Japanese term for people with obsessive interests, usually related to anime and manga fandom), *fujoshi* (a Japanese term for girls who enjoy reading stories about romantic relations between boys), and juvenile delinquents. The participation of college graduates has redefined *opela* and its aesthetics, incorporating pop elements and the vocabulary characteristic of a younger generation.

Chen Youxin (2010) notes that in new *opela*, *opela* has begun to undergo a refining process. Normally, *opela* was a type of improvised theater. Actors ad libbed their lines based on a scenario or scene-outline. Improvisatory theater allowed the actor to take part in the performance as not only an actor but also a playwright and a director. *Opela* thus provided great room for a good actress to fully wield her talent and charisma. The downside was that if actors were not disciplined enough and forgot or skipped certain elements, confusion or plot contradictions would result. In new *opela*, plays are scripted and accompanied by financial support from the government and from cultural foundations. The subsidy from the National Culture and Arts Foundation, for instance, ensures that funded troupes have specific budgets for a playwright, director, music designer, and others, encouraging troupes to work with professionals from modern theater and thus catalyzing the further refining of *opela* (Chen, 2010: 252–54).

The example of the Formosa Chunfeng Troupe cited above shows changes initiated within an amateur theater company. Another example is offered by Chunmei Opera Troupe (Chunmei Gejutuan 春美歌劇團), a professional theater company that usually performs for temple festivals. Chunmei's *Youth Dream* (*Qingchun meimeng* 青春美夢), funded by the National Culture and Arts Foundation and that premiered in 2005, was produced in memory of Zhang Weixian 張維賢 (1905–77), a Taiwanese *xinju* (modern spoken drama) pioneer. It is a play in three acts, representing three phases of Zhang's youth: his passion for theater and ideals for society before going abroad, his study of *xinju* in Japan, and his return to Taiwan. *Youth Dream* is set in Taiwan during the Japanese governance, when the new and old cultures overlapped and collided, and it talks about the new form of theater, called *xinju*, and about a vanguard figure. In this context, the use of pop music, Japanese songs, kimonos, Western dress, and other foreign elements are reasonable choices for staging the story. The playwrights chose to use a storyline familiar to *gezaixi* spectators, centering on the romance of the male and female protagonists and weaving in comic relief, provided by the clown role. With the melodramatic story, the playwrights developed a more profound theme, introducing both the new theater pioneer and Taiwan's colonial history. *Youth Dream* is different from previous *opela* works, which usually appear ahistorical and illogical and were sometimes criticized for their random and spontaneous mixture of alien elements.

We should understand *opela* as a grassroots phenomenon, as a way *gezaixi* practitioners came up with to remain relevant to society, despite the restrictions of first Japanese and then Nationalist governmental authorities. *Gezaixi* practitioners in Taiwan had carried out their own experiments at coping with modernity without any support from the government. The incorporation of modern elements into traditional theater occurred at the grassroots level because, before the 1990s, the Nationalist Party in Taiwan seemed preoccupied with the preservation of tradition rather than the urgency of adapting to the times. Over the decades, however, *gezaixi* performers explored their understanding of modernity and kept adjusting their performances. In afternoon shows, these street-opera performers practiced and preserved traditional plays, but the nightly *opela* was like a theatrical laboratory for them. They continued to add music, acting styles, costumes, and language that they considered more modern, and they observed the responses of the audience. Due to their limited budgets and talents, the plebian experiments were oftentimes crude and unsophisticated, but the experiences that the street performers accumulated became the basis for future artists' developments. Therefore, when theater practitioners encounter projects such as *Youth Dream* or *The Venetian Twins* that incorporate contemporary or foreign themes, they know where to turn. In *opela*, they can easily find, say, a jazzy style of music composition, more natural physical movements, and a variety of costume conventions. Most importantly, future *xiqu* practitioners can find in *opela* a way to connect to their spectators even when they take an experimental path.

CHICHIAO MUSICAL THEATER

It was in this context that Chichiao Musical Theater, founded in 2004, gradually came to the fore. Though it is registered as a modern theater company, it is famous for its dexterous fusion of various *xiqu* genres, music genres, and languages. The works of Chichiao are sometimes compared to *opela*, yet its ambition and artistic sensibility push well beyond it. Traditional *opela* are sung and spoken in Taiwanese, but Chichaio's writing is mainly in Mandarin, with Taiwanese and Henan dialects interspersed throughout. Likewise, its music incorporates *gezaixi*, Henan *bangzi*, and pop music. The mishmash of genres and languages reflects Taiwan's multilingual, multiethnic society, but even more remarkable is the way these distinct elements complement each other and strengthen a production's narrative.

This cross-genre approach is illustrated by *Kaohsiung Happy Go* (*Zhaodi Fuxing dagou qu* 招弟復興打狗趣, 2008), which centers on a Taiwanese-mainlander couple in a military dependents' village in Kaohsiung. Ripe with jokes based on differences in accents and languages, the work presents an authentic picture of the community. The dialogues are in both Taiwanese and Mandarin (since one of the couple speaks Taiwanese and the other Mandarin), and the music is a collection of various tunes from *gezaixi*, Henan *bangzi*, and Huangmei opera (*huangmeixi* 黃梅戲).[6] *Who's the Boss* (*Jinlan qing shei shi laoda* 金蘭情誰是老大, 2011) depicts the conflicts between two gangs, and each is distinguished by its language: Mandarin and Taiwanese. The bilingual script, with a larger portion in Mandarin, not only is consistent with the plot but also, again, reflects the bilingual situation in Taiwan. The music juxtaposes pop music, Henan *bangzi*, and *gezaixi*. This music, and associated movements, are among those that still strike a chord with Taiwanese viewers, allowing the actors to take center stage and display their artistry at will.

Chichiao's 2013 production, *The Police Chalk Circle* (*Polishi huilan ji* 波麗士灰闌記), is an adaptation of the German playwright Bertolt Brecht's (1898–1956) *The Caucasian Chalk Circle* (1948). It showcased the company's ability to navigate languages and genres with ease. Bold musical experiments were attached seamlessly to the narrative. The transition from one musical genre to the next was deft, allowing each to illuminate the others. For example, in a court scene, the defendant sings *gezai* tunes while the judge responds using material from Henan *bangzi*. Each genre carries the weight of each character's perspectives, such that the resulting dialogues are between not only the characters but also the two musical styles. Furthermore, a popular music singing style is cleverly engaged. For instance, in a scene where the female protagonist, after having rescued the governor's child in a civil war and raised the child in spite of all difficulties, is confronted by both her lover and the officer with the question as to whether the child is hers, the protagonist is torn between answering yes or no to each man: if she says yes, she will lose her lover, but if she says no, the officer will take the child away. At this time, the witnessing narrator, played by a pop singer dressed in white, stands aside and sings a soft-rock song composed for this play. Her vocal texture and rendering and her musical style differ from those of the rest of the actor-singers, all of whom employ *xiqu*-based styles (albeit often rearranged with soft-rock elements). The narrator thus stands beyond the structure of the play, which is itself designed as a play within a play. Her singing comments not only on the Chalk Circle story but also the Police story, and thus she serves as a third frame or layer of the drama. Like a playwright, she seems omniscient. Her voice delivers a sense of sad sympathy and at the same time creates a sense of detached sobriety.

Music remains the biggest challenge for experimentation in *xiqu*. With *The Police Chalk Circle,* Li Changlei 李常磊 (b. 1977), an independent musician, began to work with the troupe and co-design music with He Yuguang 何玉光 (b. 1969), a *xiqu* musician. New songs in this play, such as the theme song and the narrator/pop singer's songs, were composed by Li while He Yuguang took care of arranging the songs that used traditional tunes. The participation of Li has added a sophisticated soft-rock flavor to the company's shows since then. In Chichiao's next production, *Oh My Buddha! Oh My God* (*Wo keneng buwei duhua ni* 我可能不會度化你) in 2015, Li Changlei played guitar and keyboard, and at the same time he also performed in roles on stage, as a bartender and a nurse. In this production, he arranged *gezaixi* and *yuju* (traditional Henan opera) tunes in a mixture of hip-pop, soft-rock, and bossa-nova styles. This fusion was apparently a success, winning the praise of several critics.

Chichiao's ability to incorporate vastly different *xiqu* genres into the narrative rests upon the upbringing of its leading personnel. The company's director, Liu Jianguo (b. 1981), and its lead actress, Liu Jianhua (b. 1977), are daughters of Wang Hailing 王海玲 (b. 1952), an illustrious *yuju* diva in Taiwan. Having grown up in the rehearsal studios, where they lived and breathed traditional musical theater, they create works that often blend genres and languages, especially *gezaixi* and Henan *bangzi*. Liu Jianhua is now a principal actress in the Taiwan Bangzi Opera Company (*Taiwan Yuju Tuan* 臺灣豫劇團), the island's premiere Henan opera troupe. With her clear, sonorous voice and her dashing appearance, she is known as "the prince of Henan opera." (In both *gezaixi* and Henan *bangzi* in Taiwan, young male characters are often played by female performers.) Meanwhile, Liu Jianguo, as a writer and director, has injected a contemporary and humanistic spirit into Taiwan's traditional opera scene with works that are both comedic and thought provoking. Even though they grew up with the *yuju* troupe, their mother deliberately kept them from learning traditional opera. More than two decades later, when she saw the girls' strong interest and unwavering passion, she finally changed her mind and gave her support. Because the two sisters are not classically trained, they are able to bring new ideas and perspectives to *xiqu*, and they have made the successful transition from amateur theater fans to true professionals. As Taiwan's traditional theater modernizes and seeks to remain relevant in contemporary society, they have shown the audience a multitude of possibilities.

The first piece in Chichiao's *opela* theater series is *The Roseman Warrior* (*Meigui xia* 玫瑰俠, 2014), adapted from a famous *opela* drama entitled *The Roseman Bandit* (*Meiqui zei* 玫瑰賊). It is set in contemporary Taiwan. Rich and handsome, Jin, the CEO of Four-Star Technology (played by Liu Jianhua, as the male lead) arrives late for a charity dinner party. His driver enters, reporting to him that there is a secret mission for him to undertake. In the next scene, we see a masked hero saving a beauty (the female lead), who falls in love with him. A typical *gezaixi* narrative pattern is thus established, with *sheng* 生 (male lead), *dan* 旦 (female lead), and *chou* 丑 (clown; here, the driver, the hero's sidekick): the romance between *sheng* and *dan* is sprinkled with comic elements provided by the *chou*. In traditional dramas and conventional *opela*, the *chou* is regularly the *sheng*'s devoted follower, serving as the *sheng*'s onstage foil. Thus, it is natural that spectators assume Jin to be the masked hero, Roseman. But what is interesting about Chichiao's adaptation is that, after seemingly reproducing the conventional narrative norms of *opela*, the playwright then subverts and questions these norms, creating the main suspense and conflict of the play. The audience gradually begins to wonder if the plain-looking driver is in fact the masked Roseman, a suspicion that turns out to be true. A debate about truth and appearance thus unfolds. It demonstrates that most people choose to believe what they would like to believe, being easily deluded by glamorous appearances. *The Roseman Warrior* is thus an imitation and "repetition with critical distance" (Hutcheon, 1985: 20).

Kurama Tengu

The second piece in the Chichiao Musical Theater's *opela* theater series was a production of *Kurama Tengu* (鞍馬天狗), which premiered at the end of 2016. A *tengu* 天狗 (literally, "heavenly dog") is a long-nosed spirit with human and avian characteristics, found in ancient Japanese legends. In 1924, Jirō Osaragi (1897–1973) published a novel that was set in the late Togugawa period and tells the story of a masked samurai, Ono Munefusa, who wipes out evil under the identity Kurama Tengu. Jirō's *Kurama Tengu* series became so popular that it was made into manga, movies, and television series in Japan, and it is also widely known in Taiwan (Chen Mingpan, 2012: 32–41), where records show that the *Kurama Tengu* films were already released in the 1930s (Chen Youxin, 2010: 80–81). Today, *gezaixi* plays featuring masked swordsmen and the idea of double identities typically have little to do with Jirō Osaragi's original series, despite some having "Tengu" in their titles.

Loosely adapted from the story by Jirō Osaragi,[7] Chichiao's *Kurama Tengu* vaguely reminds us of the original tale: Kurama Tengu/Munefusa allies himself with Katsura's faction to oppose the Shinsengumi special police. However, the playwright-director Liu Jianguo transposes the setting from the Tokugawa era to the kingdom of Yusha, a fictional place in an unspecified time period. Yusha is invaded and taken over by a military regime, but there are still people who seek to overthrow the new government and recover their kingdom. The new regime commissions a secret organization, Shinsengumi, to destroy the protagonist Munefusa and his friends, who are a group of loyalists seeking to avenge the loss of their family and nation.

Changes of language help to delineate a frame for the story. A monk serves as both the narrator and a confidante to the protagonist. He narrates the story to the audience in Mandarin; when he is a character in the play, he interacts with other characters in Taiwanese. Meanwhile, choices of music genre help to develop the characters. Taiwanese language and *gezaixi* music are the basis for the play, whereas Mandarin and Henan *bangzi* accompany the supernatural character Tengu, further distinguishing his non-human or demonic characteristics.

The monk tells Munefusa's story to the audience, gradually piecing together and restoring the truth. Munefusa claims that he is invincible because he is assisted by the sacred monster Tengu, who reveals himself only to Munefusa and often teleports him to the wilderness in moments of stress. The monk later discovers that the reason why Munefusa is often lost and finds his way to the temple at Mt. Kurama is because he and his younger sister took refuge here from pursuing soldiers years ago, and his sister died in a fire set by the soldiers at the temple. Young Munefusa survived the fire and is guilt-ridden. Therefore, Munefusa is driven by vengeance and becomes the number-one enemy for the new regime. As the story unfolds, Tengu turns out to be entirely a figment of Munefusa's imagination. The revelation of the truth is the climax of the drama. The *tengu* thus becomes a metaphor: it is a legend created by the subaltern and the underprivileged. The oppressed need a faith like this to support them in action, so that they can fight back against an unbeatable foe and face the consequences calmly. Although the monk discovers that Tengu does not exist in reality, he ends the story with a soothing interpretation, narrating:

> The monk understands that in less than fifteen minutes, they will all die in this maze. The small, feeble fire of resistance is doomed to be quashed mercilessly by the firm, strong militant forces. At the desperate moment when they are about to be gruesomely killed by the Shinsengumi, he sees the magnificent spirit Tengu.[8] (Liu Jianguo, 2016a)

In the finale, as the warriors fight their battle in slow motion, Tengu flies in on a wire, fabulously descending like a *deus ex machina* to rescue the dying loyalists. Is the *tengu* real or imaginary? The monk finds out the truth, but in the end he chooses to believe and decides to tell Munefusa's tale and pass on the story, and he sings in Mandarin: "Do you believe in a tale like this?" This open ending leaves the spectators to decide whether they believe in the legend of the *tengu*.[9]

In Jirō Osaragi's *Kurama Tengu*, Tengu never appears as a supernatural being. Chichiao's Tengu appears as a half-deity, half-demonic figure that is neither good nor evil, laughing off the killings and troubles in the mortal world. The reason why Tengu is willing to assist Munefusa is that he is bored and craves a bit of fun in his endless life. The lyrics of the recurring theme song "Tengu Nursery Rhyme" ("Tiangou Tongyao" 天狗童謠) state: "Do not cry if you are lost./ It is the *tengu* that takes you away./ The lost person is in the clouds./ It is the *tengu* that takes him away." What the innocent voice sings is in fact a traumatic experience. The *tengu* is also a story that Munefusa and his sister shared as a child, and it embodies the protagonist's willpower. According to the playwright-director's notes in the playbill, the story "is more than a revenge tale about the two rivaling forces. Tengu is not simply a god that endows the protagonist with superpowers. For a young man who is adrift in his grief and regret, he found in Tengu a safe harbor for his soul" (Liu Jianguo, 2016b). With the company of the creature, he is able to "fend off cruel reality, and finds the courage to go on with his life." When a child is lost in the woods, people say that he is spirited away, that Tengu is harboring the child, as "Tengu Nursery Rhyme" suggests. The song further points to those who are "disappeared" during the transition of political power. Their families can only comfort themselves and ease the pain with such thoughts as that their loved ones have been taken away by gods.

The adaptation minimizes these political messages by presenting the story in a highly entertaining, visually and aurally satisfying style. Traditional Japanese musical instruments such as *shakuhachi* 尺八 (end-blown flute) and *shamisen* 三昧線 (three-stringed lute) crisscross with Chinese *erhu* 二胡 (two-stringed fiddle) and *pipa* 琵琶 (four-stringed lute). Traditional gongs and drums alternate with jazz drums. The opening music begins with the mellow and gentle but penetrating sound of the *shakuhachi*, and the innocent voice of a child slowly sings the theme song: "Green mountains and meandering roads,/ with a *tengu* in the woods." The song then turns into a passionate variation, accompanied by *shamisen*, jazz drums, electric guitar, and *erhu*. The rock version of the theme song is interspersed with sounds of swords clashing. The main characters make their first entrance one by one in a fight, striking a pose and then exiting. With the aid of spectacular projection technology, the prologue resembles the way a film usually introduces its characters. The shift of music genres is determined by the action, going back and forth among Henan *bangzi*, *gezaixi*, soft rock, and Japanese traditional music styles. The production team also includes a martial-arts choreographer, who is an expert in both Chinese martial arts and Japanese *kendō*. This explains why the martial-arts movements of the main actors are sharp and impressive. After the drama ends, there is an additional thirty-minute show, with the ensemble singing and dancing lavishly. This merry and entertaining spectacle deliberately lightens the sorrow of the play's ending, preventing the audience from remaining too emotionally involved in the drama. It is a typical Brechtian technique of alienation.

On the surface, the play appears to be a nationalist melodrama, but the characterization is not dualistic. The villainous Shinsengumi squad is not depicted as abominable and vile, nor is the loyalist resistance group portrayed as haggard and destitute. Instead, both are equally stylish and gorgeous. As Xu Renhao states in his critique, it is this highly entertaining feature that reduces the righteous sentiments common in patriotic melodrama and keeps the work from turning into merely an outlet for postcolonial rage (Xu, 2017: 71). He continues:

> In the story rewritten by Liu Jianguo, the people of the kingdom of Yusha are a group of slaves without a nation who are forced to give up their original language and costumes. This intentional "meta" arrangement refers back again to the colonial memory of the hybrid aesthetics of *opela*. For me, it is this meta-dramatic design that creates a critical space. *Kurama Tengu* does not intend to point out friends and foes for postcolonial Taiwan. Rather, it opens up a space for the audience to contemplate "cultural ownership" in a time of vibrant cross-cultural exchanges. (ibid.: 71)

Indeed, the production shows great affinity for Japanese culture. The additional show pays tribute to the Takarazuka Revue, not to mention the fact that the play is filled with Japanese elements such as costumes, sword fighting, ninja, *enka*-style music compositions,[10] and Japanese musical instruments. During the curtain call, the troupe invited the ex-curator of the Jirō Osaragi Memorial Museum to give a speech. All this reflects how well-received Japanese culture is among the new generation in Taiwan.

Aesthetically, the production does not intend to critique Japanese colonial history in Taiwan, nor does it emphasize nationalism in its narrative. It pays more attention to how an individual manages at a time of power transition. The character Hizikata of the villainous party thinks that he does not kill for the sake of killing but rather to strengthen the new regime, and he admires Munefusa's courage and ability and spares his life in a fight. In the same vein, the hero Munefusa admits that his action is not driven by the holy idea of recovering the nation but rather by a personal desire for revenge. The climax of Chichiao's *Kurama Tengu* lies in the revelation of whether Tengu exists, and thus its point is not about heroic deeds performed while wearing a mask but rather about unmasking and confronting oneself. Tengu is Munefusa's repressed self: wild, untamed, and proud. The playwright appropriates the image of a masked hero in Japanese pop culture and a Japanese legendary figure, Kurama Tengu, to encapsulate the pain of an individual and an era. Liu's interpretation gives the tale entirely new meanings.

Linda Hutcheon points out an important idea of postmodernism, "the presence of the past" (Hutcheon, 1988: 4). She argues that there is a common feature in postmodern artistic works: that their innovation comes from their "historical parody." What these artists are doing is critically rewriting the past, instead of revisiting the past nostalgically (ibid.: 5). If Teri Silvio observes a nostalgic return in the *opela* works of the Golden Bough Theater and the Formosa Chunfeng Opera Troupe, in my opinion, Chichiao's *opela* series revisits the past, critically rewriting *opela*'s narrative and performance tradition. I do not intend to label these works with postmodernism here, as such categorization is not of my concern in this chapter. However, the notion proposed by Hutcheon is recognizable in what characterizes Chichiao's *opela* theater—that is, its critical rewriting and reinventing of tradition. Its first piece in the *opela* series, *Roseman Warrior*, is based on an *opela* classic, *The Roseman Bandit*. The adaptation investigates our illusions and disillusions about a superhero and our fantasies and disappointments about romantic love. It not only subverts our expectations for the stock characters in *gezaixi* but also questions our imagination of heroes. In *Kurama Tengu*, the playwright rewrites a Japanese story that was once material for imperial-subject plays in colonial Taiwan. Looking back at Taiwan's colonial history, the adaptation opens up more possibilities for us to reimagine the sign of the *tengu*, and it reexamines the Japanese colonial legacy in Taiwan.

New *opela*, such as the Chunmei Opera Troupe's *Youth Dream* and the Formosa Chunfeng Troupe's *The Venetian Twins*, repackages *opela* through the intervention of the literati, positioning the unique performance aesthetics of *opela* in an appropriate narrative. In new *opela*, Taiwanese and *gezaixi* music is still the base, whereas language used in Chichiao's works showcases the multilingual society of contemporary Taiwan, in which Mandarin and Taiwanese exist in tandem. Musically, Chichiao incorporates the *xiqu* genres that are still active in Taiwan, mainly *gezaixi* and Henan *bangzi*, adding new compositions, often in a soft-rock style. Taking inspiration from popular culture, its productions cross the boundaries of musical genres and theater genres effortlessly, fusing together seemingly incompatible elements seamlessly. The company is not confined within any single *xiqu* genre, and the change of musical genres in *Kurama Tengu* is driven by actions in the narrative. Even though *opela* provides the foundational artistic material for Chichiao Musical Theater, the term is no longer sufficient to define its productions. The phrases "Taiwanese new *xiqu*" or "*xiqu* musical" are probably closer to its performance aesthetics. However, the revolutionary practices and success of the company are indebted to the long trial-and-error struggles of the modern plebian *gezaixi* troupes, the outcomes of which have allowed Chichiao's members to quickly find theatrical vocabulary and materials to work with and have paved a way for *opela* spectators to accept its aesthetics with ease and deeply enjoy its performances.

I attended a conference hosted by the National Academy of Chinese Theatre Arts in 2015 in Beijing and talked about the experimental *xiqu* in Taiwan. The attendees were particularly impressed by Chichiao's musical achievements. The modernization of *xiqu* in China has a bottom line: the music of each *difangxi* 地方戲 (regional opera) has to remain pure; mixing types of music is not encouraged since it runs the risk of diluting the distinctiveness of each local opera.[11] However, in the case of Chichiao, the experiment in music has come naturally. The juxtaposition of languages and music genres in its works are smoothly arranged. While the free style of *opela* provided the foundation for artistic experiments in the vein of Chichiao's productions, the uniquely immersive upbringing of the two founders, who know well the strengths and weaknesses of *xiqu* in contemporary Taiwan and are able to shed innovative light, also explains why they are capable of breaking the boundaries of traditional operatic genres and of coming up with a new type of performance genre: Taiwanese new *xiqu*, or *xiqu* musical, in which various types of *xiqu* music and modern music coexist harmoniously.

Glossary

[J] = Japanese terms; [T] = Taiwanese terms

beiguanxi 北管戲, traditional opera genre
budaixi 布袋戲, traditional glove puppetry
Chichiao Musical Theater (Qiqiao Jutuan) 奇巧劇團, Taiwanese theater company (founded 2004)
chou 丑, clown role in traditional opera
Chunfeng Gejutuan 春風歌劇團, Formosa Chunfeng Troupe
Chunmei Gejutuan 春美歌劇團, Chunmei Opera Troupe
dan 旦, female role in traditional opera
difangxi 地方戲, regional opera
dianzi huache 電子花車, vaudeville performed on trucks
enka [J] 演歌, style of Japanese popular song (1950s onward)
erhu 二胡, two-stringed fiddle
gailiang xi 改良戲, reformed plays
gaojiaxi 高甲戲, opera tradition from Taiwan and Fujian
gezaixi 歌仔戲, traditional Taiwanese opera
gongyan 公演, "mainstage," category of professional *gezaixi* shows with a larger budget
Gongleshe 拱樂社, theater company founded in 1934 and active during the 1950s–1960s

gulu 古路, old-style plays in *gezaixi* local opera
He Yuguang 何玉光, musician (b. 1969)
Henan *bangzi* 河南梆子, main music in traditional Henan opera
huangmeixi 黃梅戲, traditional Huangmei opera
Jinlan qing shei shi laoda 金蘭情誰是老大, *Who's the Boss*, new *opela* composition (2011)
Jinzhi Yanshe 金枝演社, Golden Bough Theater
jingju 京劇, Beijing opera
Jirō Osaragi [J] 大佛次郎, Japanese author (1897–1973)
kendō [J] 劍道, Japanese sword fighting
Kōminka undo [J] 皇民化運動, Imperial Subject Movement, 1936–45, intended to assimilate Japan's East Asia colonies
Kurama Tengu [J] 鞍馬天狗, *opela* production based on Japanese legend and novel (2016)
Li Changlei 李常磊, musician (b. 1977)
Liu Jianguo 劉建幗, director of Chichiao Musical Theater (b. 1981)
Liu Jianhua 劉建華, lead actress at Chichiao Musical Theater and Taiwan Yuju Tuan (b. 1977)
luantanxi 亂彈戲, local opera tradition found historically in Taiwan
Meigui xia 玫瑰俠, *Roseman Warrior*, new *opela* theater adaptation (2014)
Meigui zei 玫瑰賊, *Roseman Bandit*, *opela* drama (late twentieth century)
mubiao 幕表, scene-outline used in improvisatory theater
nanguanxi 南管戲, traditional opera genre
opela [T] 胡撇仔, *gezaixi* plays from the Japanese colonial period and after
pipa 琵琶, four-stringed lute
Polishi huilan ji 波麗士灰闌記, *The Police Chalk Circle*, new *opela* composition (2013) based on Brecht's *The Caucasian Chalk Circle* (1948)
Qingchun meimeng 青春美夢, *Youth Dream*, new *opela* (2005)
shakuhachi [J] 尺八, end-blown Japanese flute
shamisen [J] 三味線, three-stringed Japanese lute
sheng 生, male role in traditional opera
shizhuang xi 時裝戲, modern-costumed drama (early twentieth century)
Taiwan Yuju Tuan 臺灣豫劇團, Taiwan Bangzi Opera Company
"Tiangou Tongyao" 天狗童謠, "Tengu Nursery Rhyme," song in *Kurama Tengu*
"Tsiuhio e sim tsiann" [T] ("Jiuhou de xinsheng") 酒後的心聲, "In Wine, Truth" or "A Drunken Voice," popular song (1990s)
"U ia hue" [T] ("Yu ye hua") 雨夜花, "A Flower on a Rainy Night," Taiwanese popular song (1933)
Wang Hailing 王海玲, *yuju* actress (b. 1952)
Weinisi shuang bao an 威尼斯雙胞案, *The Venetian Twins*, new *opela* based on Glodoni's comedy (2007)
Wo keneng buwei duhua ni 我可能不會度化你, *Oh My Buddha! Oh My God*, new *opela* composition (2015)
xiao juchang yundong 小劇場運動, experimental theater movement (beginning in the 1980s)
xinju 新劇, modern spoken dramas (first half of the twentieth century)
xiqu 戲曲, general term for traditional Chinese theater
yuju 豫劇, traditional Henan opera
Zhang Weixian 張維賢, *xinju* pioneer (1905–77)
Zhaodi Fuxing dagou qu 招弟復興打狗趣, *Kaohsiung Happy Go*, new *opela* composition (2008)

Notes

1. My research in the following years also looked at *opela*, and the scope was extended to *gezaixi* in China. See for example, Hsieh, 2002 and 2008.
2. Performers of traditional forms of Taiwanese theater such as puppetry and *gezaixi* had no choice but to change to the forms of *xinju*, *gailiangju*, or Japanese period plays. In his memoirs, the *gezaixi* performer Xiao Shouli recalls that during this period of time, in rural places where police departments were short-staffed, *gezaixi* was still staged, with someone keeping watch. If a police officer showed up, performers had to change their costumes and titles at once, "from Emperor to Prime Minister" and "from Clerk to Chancellor." "If we put on a *gezaixi* show, we had to prepare two versions. On the arrival of the Japanese cop, we changed our costumes into modern style and sang contemporary songs" (Wu and Wang, 1999: 36–37). Likewise, in the puppet master Li Tianlu's memoirs, "the so-called 'period drama puppetry' is to put Japanese costumes on the puppets and speak Japanese in the play. We used Western music on vinyl. They are imperial-subject plays, with puppets fighting with *katana*" (Zeng, 1991: 97).
3. The Chinese-chauvinistic inculcation was so successful that many *gezaixi* performers felt disrespected for their occupation and suffered from inferior treatment. It was no wonder that they discriminated against *opela*. Among the twenty-six troupes in Taipei that I observed in 1998 and 1999, two refused to stage *opela* in their nightly show, and the members were very proud of their persistence in staging the *gulu* plays despite the trend. The old-style *gulu* plays retained more features of the superior-status Beijing opera. By performing Beijing opera imitations, *gezaixi* players subconsciously ascended from their disenfranchised and marginalized position to one of legitimacy.
4. The Little Theater Movement (*xiao juchang yundong* 小劇場運動) in Taiwan usually refers to the experimental theater movement beginning in the 1980s.
5. Silvio's paper focuses on the narrative construction of time and space and on the nostalgic world the actors create in their works. I do not intend to discuss the Golden Bough Theater's works here because, in my opinion, the "*opela* series" of the Golden Bough, a theater company that stages modern drama, hardly uses any *gezaixi* elements in the performance. *Opela* is more of an artistic concept for the company. The so-called "spirit of *opela*" that Golden Bough Theater seeks to retain is "a kind of freedom that is receding from the lives of contemporary middle-class Taiwanese"; see Silvio, 2009: 70, 72, for the citation.
6. Huangmei opera originated in Anhui province, China, and had become popular in Taiwan due to the prominence of Huangmei opera films produced in Hong Kong in the 1960s. This troupe's connection with Henan *bangzi* is explained below.
7. Chichiao Musical Theater received permission to adapt the story from the Jirō Osaragi Museum and the Japanese Literary and Arts Association on the condition that the adaptation did not undermine the heroic image of the original *Kurama Tengu* (email interview with the company's manager Chen Jinhui, October 12, 2017).
8. The unpublished script is provided by Chichiao Musical Theater and the translation is my own.
9. In Liu Jianguo's adaptation, Yusha is under the governance of the militant regime, and its people are forced to change many of their traditions, including their names, dress, words, and weapons. The people of Yusha, including the hero, strive to overthrow the military regime and recover their kingdom. The characters in this production wear Japanese

clothing, the costume of the new regime. Thus, it becomes clear that the story of Yusha implies Taiwan's colonial history under Japanese rule, and the change of name and dress refers to Japan's implementation of the assimilation policy in Taiwan.
10. *Enka* 演歌 is a style of Japanese popular song from the 1950s onward. *Enka* songs are often used in outdoor *opela*.
11. Drama in Chinese conceptions has long been associated primarily with music and singing, as the term *xiqu* literally means "play" (*xi*) and "melody" (*qu*). Music generated from mostly rhymed verse in the play, and in regional dialects with different tones and inflections, resulted in different songs and melodies. Consequently, *difangxi* has remained classified primarily by its music. As William Dolby points out, "After about 1500 the history of drama in China becomes a history of types of music rather than genres of plays, or, more accurately perhaps, the music tends more wholly to characterize the genre" (Dolby, 1976: 90).

References

Chen Mingpan 陳銘磻. (2012). *Wo zai Jingdu xun fang wenxue zu ji* 我在京都尋訪文學足跡 [My Quest for Literary Footprints in Kyoto]. Taipei: Yueguo wenhua.

Chen Youxin 陳幼馨. (2010). *Taiwan gezaixi de yi xiang shi jie: "Hu pie zai" biaoyan yishu jincheng* 臺灣歌仔戲的異想世界：「胡撇仔」表演藝術進程 [The Imaginative World of Taiwan's *Gezaixi*: The Development of the Performing Arts of "Opela"]. Taipei: Daoxiang chubanshe.

Dolby, William. (1976). *A History of Chinese Drama*. London: Elek Books.

Guy, Nancy. (2005). *Peking Opera and Politics in Taiwan*. Urbana: University of Illinois Press.

Hsieh Hsiao-mei 謝筱玫. (2002). "Opela ji qi lishi yuanyou" "胡撇仔" [Opela: Its Definition and Historical Development]. *Zhongwai wenxue* 中外文學 [Chung Wai Literary Quarterly] 31 (1): 157–74.

Hsieh Hsiao-mei 謝筱玫. (2007). "Cong jingzhi dao hupie: Guozu rentong xia de Taiwan gezaixi lunshu" "從精緻到胡撇：國族認同下的台灣歌仔戲論述" [From Refined to Opela: Discourses on *Gezaixi* under the Changing Taiwanese National Identity]. *Minsu quyi* 民俗曲藝 [Ritual, Theatre, and Folklore] 155: 79–110.

Hsieh Hsiao-mei 謝筱玫. (2008). "Across the Strait: History, Performance, and *Gezaixi* in China and Taiwan." PhD diss., Northwestern University.

Hutcheon, Linda. (1985). *A Theory of Parody: The Teachings of Twentieth-century Art Forms*. New York: Methuen.

Hutcheon, Linda. (1988). *A Poetics of Postmodernism: History, Theory, Fiction*. New York: Routledge.

Lin Heyi 林鶴宜. (2016). *Dongfang jixing juchang: gezaixi "zuo huo xi"* 東方即興劇場：歌仔戲「做活戲」 [Taiwanese Improvisational Theater: Performing "Living Plays" in *Gezaixi*]. Taipei: Guoli Taiwan daxue chuban zhongxin.

Liu Jianguo 劉建幗. (2016a). *Kurama Tengu* 鞍馬天狗 Unpublished script, May 15, 2017. Microsoft Word File.

Liu Jianguo 劉建幗. (2016b). Playbill for Chichiao Musical Theater's *Kurama Tengu*. Kaohsiung City Dadong Arts Center, Nov. 18–19, 2016.

Liu Nanfang 劉南芳. (2016). "Liuxing gequ zai Taiwan gezaixi zhong xingcheng de taolu yu yingxiang" "流行歌曲在臺灣歌仔戲中形成的套路與影響" [The Formulated Acting

Techniques Generated from Popular Music and the Influence of Popular Music on Taiwan's *Gezaixi*]. *Xiju xuekan* 戲劇學刊 [Theatre Journal] 24: 7–43.

Silvio, Teri J. 司黛蕊. 2009. "Huaijiu de gongtongti yu zai hecheng de ziwo: Jinzhi Yanshe yu Taiwan Chunfeng Gejutuan de xin hupeizai xi" "懷舊的共同體與再合成的自我：金枝演社與臺灣春風歌劇團的新胡撇仔戲" [The Nostalgic Community and the Reintegrated Individual: The "New Opela" Performances of the Golden Bough Theater and the Formosa Chunfeng Opera Troupe]. *Xiju yanjiu* 戲劇研究 [Journal of Theater Studies] 4: 45–74.

Wu Shaomi 吳紹蜜 and Wang Peidi 王佩迪. (1999). *Xiao Shouli shengming shi* 蕭守梨生命史 [A Life History of Xiao Shouli]. Taipei: Chuantong yishu zhongxin choubeichu.

Xu Renhao 許仁豪. (2017). "Soushen yu qiudao" "搜神與求道" [Seeking Gods and Looking for Truth]. *Biaoyan yishu zazhi* 表演藝術雜誌 [Performing Arts Review] 289: 70–71.

Zeng Yongyi 曾永義. 1988. *Taiwan gezaixi de fazhan yu bianqian* 臺灣歌仔戲的發展與變遷 [The Development and Change of *Gezaixi* in Taiwan]. Taipei: Lianjing chuban gongsi.

Zeng Yuwen 曾郁雯. 1991. *Ximeng rensheng: Li Tianlu huiyilu* 戲夢人生：李天祿回憶錄 [All the World is a Stage: A Memoir of Li Tianlu]. Taipei: Yuanliu chuban gongsi.

CHAPTER 15

HYBRIDITY IN THE MODERN CHINESE ORCHESTRAL MUSIC (*GUOYUE*) OF TAIWAN

CHING-YI CHEN

Introduction

GUOYUE 國樂, which literally translates as "national music," refers to the modern Chinese orchestral music of Taiwan.¹ Chinese musicians and the Chinese Nationalist Party (Kuomintang; hereafter, KMT) introduced *guoyue* to Taiwan after 1949. The 1990s saw the onset of significant political, social, and economic changes in Taiwan that continue to affect musicians today. In addition, reaching the Taiwanese population has posed ongoing challenges to those in the *guoyue* profession, which manifested in various musical practices undergoing negotiation and reconstruction over time. Frequent cross-cultural exchange has led to the gradual incorporation into the *guoyue* system of aspects of Taiwan's indigenous and regional cultures and of other cultural ingredients from further afield, resulting in its hybridization through trends of diversification and cross-cultural contact.

Until recently, the *guoyue* musical style of China and of Chinese diasporic communities was largely ignored by scholars in China and the West. For some such researchers, *guoyue* did not fit well enough into the category of "traditional" and was therefore disregarded, and many of those studying Western art or popular music in East Asia saw it as insufficiently "modern." In Taiwan, meanwhile, there have been times when it would have been against the prevailing political ideology to question whether this musical style could be considered culturally authentic. In fact, over the past nearly seventy years of activity, *guoyue* composers and performers have developed a Taiwanese musical style quite distinct from that of the genre's Chinese origin. Today, *guoyue* engenders considerable creativity and diversity by drawing on pan-Chinese, indigenous, and other cultural expressions, and thus it interweaves traditional and modern characteristics and elements of musical transculturation. Therefore, it is essential to understand the character of this hybrid orchestral style in Taiwan according to its own terms, rather than focusing on arguments over its "authenticity." This chapter provides a brief overview of *guoyue*'s development, particularly in relation to Taiwan's social, cultural, and political contexts, and examines the complex hybridities found in contemporary artistic productions of Chinese orchestral music. By exploring *guoyue*'s development in this way, we see an emerging expression of the Taiwanese spirit that appropriates and hybridizes characteristics of Chinese, Taiwanese, and other cultures.

Hybridity and Music

Before discussing the transformational effects of political and cultural development on the national music of China and Taiwan, it is essential to define "hybridity" in order to access the concepts implied by this term in discussions of contemporary *guoyue* in Taiwan. Hybridity is a crucial concept employed in many academic disciplines, including biology, anthropology, linguistics, cultural studies, musicology, and ethnomusicology. It is essentially the combination—or in scientific terms, the crossbreeding—of two types, resulting in the creation of new species (Ashcroft, Griffiths, and Tiffin, 2007: 108). Through the concept of hybridity, researchers can study the processes leading to the development of successful hybrid species.

The notion of hybridity is often used to depict a contact place in a diaspora, one that reveals cultural mixtures where communities come into contact with other communities in the dominant society. For example, Nikos Papastergiadis argued that, in the contexts of Europe, the Americas, and Australia, "as 'ethnic elites' came to prominence within the cultural and political circles of the dominant society, they began to argue in favour of new models for representing the process of cultural interaction, and to demonstrate the negative consequences of insisting upon the denial of the emergent forms of cultural identity" (Papastergiadis, 2000: 3). But if the term "hybridity" is now widely used, theorists have also criticized usages that fail to consider inequality between visitor and host in a migrant setting.

One attempt to better account for such inequalities is elaborated by the noted postcolonial theorist Homi K. Bhabha in his book *The Location of Culture* (1994). According to Bhabha, although hybridity provides a contact space for multiple cultures to engage in cross-culturalism, it results from cultural ambivalence. This contact space can be viewed as a "third space" that involves unequal distribution of power and emphasizes the interdependence of the subjective constructs of colonizer and colonized (see, for example, Ashcroft, Griffiths, and Tiffin, 2007: 118; Watkins, 2010: 108). As Bhabha further explains, this third space may arise from a colonial or postcolonial origin, leading to the recognition of cultural diversity not through the exoticism of multiculturalism but via the articulation of hybridity in culture. Bhabha argues that "hybrid agencies find their voice in a dialectic that does not seek cultural supremacy or sovereignty" (Bhabha, 1996:

58). Music scholar Tina K. Ramnarine takes up Bhabha's concept of hybridity, suggesting that we assess its workings on a global scale and avoid conventional oversimplifications of cultural contact or cultural exchange as merely the question as to how the different cultures mix:

> In rejecting an understanding of hybridity as the simple result of cultural interaction, I have been guided by Bhabha's view that hybridity is not "a third term that resolves the tension between two cultures" but that it presents an interruption to assumptions of difference that mark power stratifications and an intervention in the "exercise of authority." This is a reading of Bhabha that is central to my project but that departs from a more habitual emphasis on his notions of the transformative powers of the third space, ambivalence, and mimicry. (Ramnarine, 2007: 32–33)

Cross-cultural contact continually highlights differences that result in new forms. Emerging hybridity is a result of power intervention that involves the unstable and uncertain imbalance of diasporic contexts. Following Ramnarine, one possible interpretation of the development of Chinese orchestral music in Taiwan is that the power interventions of the state, public cultural institutions, and elites led to hybridity in these cultural productions. But the explanation of the details of this process is not straightforward; in the following two sections, I discuss the historical development of *guoyue* in Taiwan to elaborate on this interpretation. My approach stems from the suggestion that hybridity expresses cultural ambivalence, cultural differences, and cultural encounters in *guoyue* performances and that the concept of hybridity as articulated in Taiwan involves the subversion of prominent cultural edifices. Hybridity provides a channel for studying the recent *guoyue* phenomenon of crossovers created to avoid the centralizations of either a Chinese consciousness or a Western-oriented direction.

My approach to hybridity theory is also informed by several studies exploring the relationship between hybridity and music in East Asian contexts. Examples include Gregory Lee's "The 'East is Red' Goes Pop" (1995), which explores the interrelationships between commodification, nationalism, and hybridity in Chinese popular music. Lee regards hybridity as a social reality that has been under development in Chinese cultural contexts for at least a century. Meanwhile, in a study of male cross-dressing shows in Taiwan, Wu Chao-jung also notes hybridity at play (2007). He proposes a theoretical framework that focuses on mimicry and drag parody, polyphony and carnival, and pastiche, heterotopias, and hybrid identity. In this setting, Wu argues that hybridity becomes a democratic action expressed in the selecting of the various musical materials and diversely designed programs for these shows. Finally, Lee Watkins has traced how musical performance becomes a vehicle for the embodiment of hybridity in the expression of everyday experiences that interweave racial and social status among Filipino musicians in Hong Kong (2010). From this perspective, hybridity is not only an aesthetic choice but also a mode of social action, articulating the cultural perceptions of Filipino musicians' encounters on the diasporic stage.

These studies point toward hybridity as a characteristic with a lengthy history, one with a democratic potential in situations of diaspora and postcolonial readjustment. It is something musicians turn to when they wish to explore the imbalances of race, social status, social agency, identity, power, and authority. In Taiwan, hybridity is certainly a crucial component of colonial and postcolonial experience. Moreover, examining hybridity discourse can help us trace the development of *guoyue* in different periods and under the effects of different political and cultural interactions.

THE COLONIAL SITUATION IN TAIWAN BEFORE 1945

From 1624 to 1945, Taiwan was under the colonial rule of the Dutch empire, the pro-Ming-dynasty kingdom, Qing-dynasty China, and the empire of Japan. Taiwan experienced its first wave of Western colonial settlement during the Dutch occupation of 1624 to 1662. In 1683, the Qing dynasty launched a campaign and was successful in expelling Ming-dynasty loyalists and conquering Taiwan. In 1895, Taiwan attempted to declare full independence from China and sought to gain military support from its ally, the United States. However, this attempt was unsuccessful in preventing Japan from beginning an occupation in 1895, one that made Taiwan a police state for fifty years. In 1945, Japanese colonial rule ended, and Taiwanese people at the time believed this would lead to liberation as they were absorbed into the administration of the Republic of China, led by the KMT and led by Chiang Kai-shek (1887–1975). However, after losing the Chinese Civil War to the armies of the Communist Party of China (CPC), Chiang and his remaining forces retreated to Taiwan in 1949.

Throughout this 325-year period, Han Chinese immigrants gradually moved to Taiwan in increasingly large numbers due to changes in the political and social milieus, and in search of economic betterment. Settling in Taiwan, Chinese immigrants experienced few differences from their previous lives in China. They sought means to maintain social connections to Chinese culture and customs, bringing Chinese opera, the ensemble genre *nanguan* or *nanyin* 南管/南音, and traditional Chinese instrumental music to the unfamiliar habitat of Taiwan, all of which became sources of comforting nostalgia.

At the beginning of the Japanese colonial period, the Japanese government was relatively tolerant and did not systematically suppress Taiwanese culture. Many musical genres existed, including those of Taiwanese aboriginals and Han Chinese such as *guoyue*,[2] traditional folk music, Guangdong music, *nanguan* 南管, *beiguan* 北管, Buddhist music, Daoist music, *gezaixi* 歌仔戲, and traditional Confucian ritual music. The earliest record of *guoyue* performances in Taiwan dates back to the early twentieth century. The *Taiwan Nichinichi Shinpō* 臺灣日日新報, a newspaper of the Taiwanese government under Japanese colonial rule, is a particularly vital source of information that reveals the emergence of *guoyue* activity and details the names of performers and the traditional Chinese musical instruments used: *guqin* 古琴, *zheng* 箏, *pipa* 琵琶, *huqin* 胡琴, and *sanxian* 三弦. The first *guoyue* performance in Taiwan was held in 1905, long before the Datong Yuehui 大同樂會, often seen as the founding institution for such music, was established in Shanghai in the 1920s.[3] *Guoyue* activity, then, began earlier in Taiwan than in China (Wu, 2013: 13–15). Moreover, local Taiwanese music flourished during the early twentieth century.

Another important influence on the development of Taiwanese music was the implementation of Western music education under Japanese rule. The first official schools in Taiwan to offer music courses were the teacher-training schools, or *shifan xuexiao* 師範學校 (literally, "normal schools"), where Western music and its systems were taught to primary- and secondary-school students. The Japanese moved to dominate Taiwan's national infrastructure and further strengthen its cultural connections with Japan, and opportunities were offered to some musicians to study Western music in Japan. This move had a marked and residual influence on Taiwanese music; the effect is particularly apparent when comparisons are made with China, where educational connections with Japan were more muted due to rivalry and conflict between the two countries.

The Japanese government began to exert tighter control over Taiwanese culture after 1936. Their main intention was to turn the Taiwanese into loyal and law-abiding subjects to the Japanese emperor, in a process referred to as the *Kōminka undo* 皇民化運動 ("Kōminka movement"), which effectively aimed to eradicate Taiwanese roots and undermine national attachment. The foundation of the movement was the suppression of Mandarin and local Taiwanese dialects, which were prohibited from use in public and in schools. Students were taught in Japanese and schools heavily promoted Japanese culture. Increasing tension among the local population resulted in confrontations with the Japanese government (Ho, 2006: 121), which was perceived as using the education system and cultural agenda to colonize the Taiwanese people and force them to become more Japanese (Fell, 2005: 7–8). This movement sparked an awakening of nationalism, and anticolonial sentiments were stoked by several decades of Japanese intrusion into Taiwan. Nevertheless, many Taiwanese had to speak Japanese to receive an education, and they were thus influenced by Japanese culture.

THE POSTCOLONIAL SITUATION IN TAIWAN AFTER 1945

From the 1950s to 1980s, the KMT government attempted to develop a homogeneous traditional Chinese culture encompassing traditional Chinese philosophy, namely Confucianism and Daoism, to cultivate a national Chinese identity without considering cultural and ethnic diversity. By the mid-1990s, the KMT government, led by the Taiwan-born president Lee Teng-Hui (1923–2020), had proposed the slogan "New Taiwanese" to refer to both mainland Chinese and Taiwanese people living within the territory of Taiwan (Ho, 2006). Nevertheless, a trend toward "Taiwanese consciousness" (*taiwan yishi*) came to the surface, and once it did so state policy gradually began to emphasize homegrown Taiwanese culture, although to varying degrees under different presidencies. As such, the development of Taiwan's *guoyue* remained substantially affected by political ideologies, and its musical orientation shifted with each regime change.

In 1945, the KMT took control of Taiwan, expelling Japanese control in accordance with the Cairo Agreement. In 1948, the KMT government held an international exposition that saw the first orchestral-model *guoyue* performance in Taipei, as well as many other performances. The *guoyue* performance was given by the Zhongyang Guangbo Diantai Guoyue Zu 中央廣播電台國樂組 (Central Broadcasting Station of China, Chinese Orchestra).

By 1949, the KMT had lost control in China, resulting in the fleeing of the KMT government to Taiwan in 1949 in the form of a mass emigration of intellectuals, musicians, educators, high-ranking officers, and military personnel alongside the party. The party's leader Chiang Kai-shek declared martial law in 1949, a move that brought suffering to all the Taiwanese people (including the Indigenous populations of Taiwan and the Han Chinese who had settled there before 1945). Martial law led to tighter control of politics, education policies, the military, and the media. The KMT prohibited the establishment of new political parties and restricted freedom of speech. Any form of dissent was suppressed, and people who criticized government policies were arrested. In the 1950s, the authoritarian KMT government declared the political ideal of "Constructing Taiwan, Fighting Against Communism, and Rebuilding the Nation," which was adopted as the government's guiding policy for ruling Taiwan (Liu, 2007: 49–50). Early in its rule, the KMT asserted that a loss of confidence had led to the defeat in China; the party proposed a reformative ideology to "retake China," which became the guiding principle for cultural activity.

The KMT government built a set of ideologies through which to rebuild Taiwan. First, it attempted to construct a Chinese nation and imposed a new national identity onto Taiwanese and mainlanders alike; this was a nation-building process of unification for Taiwan. Traditional Chinese culture was employed to help Taiwanese people and Chinese exiles in Taiwan attain or maintain a cultural and national identity and to indoctrinate Taiwanese people into loyalty to the KMT government. The idea that China was the homeland to which the Taiwanese people wished to return was imposed on the population. As Wachman remarked, the state's political strategy was to "sinicize," which meant imposing Han Chinese identity onto the Taiwanese people through the one-language (i.e., Mandarin) policy and political ideology taught in primary education (Wachman, 1994: 9). Not only did Mandarin Chinese become the only language spoken and taught at all levels of governmental and educational institutions; in addition, the KMT government attempted to suppress the development of Taiwanese local culture by allowing only Mandarin to be spoken in public between 1945 and 1987 (Ho, 2006: 121). These measures were followed by social oppression and persecution of local language and culture, such as through the restrictions placed upon local and ethnic Taiwanese minority songs.

Second, the KMT dominated the field of public culture, and Chinese nationalists established a central network of cultural institutions. Cultural ideology had long been used in the public sector to support the KMT's political agenda. All cultural and artistic forms, including literature, theater, film, and broadcasting, became cultural tools of the government. The KMT reorganized all cultural institutions to become parts of the government system. Therefore, artists had to gear their efforts toward cooperating with national policy. The regime's formulation of cultural policies was anchored in the promotion of traditional Chinese culture to achieve the construction of an identity that would facilitate the underlying political control of the Taiwanese people. For instance, in 1953, Chiang Kai-shek issued his first cultural address to complete Sun Yat-sen's "Three Principles of the People," which was also incorporated in the nationalist curriculum for education and promoted anti-communist propaganda (Winckler, 1994: 30). Unsurprisingly, *guoyue* acquired legitimacy as part of traditional Chinese culture and drew support from the KMT (Wang, 2003: 102).

Guoyue became a leading traditional Chinese musical genre in Taiwan and was officially encouraged by *guoyue* pioneers and the government. Several members of the Zhongguang Guoyue Tuan 中廣國樂團, including Gao Ziming 高子銘 (1907–73), Sun Peichang 孫培章 (1920–94), Wang Peilun 王沛綸 (1908–72), and Huang Lanying 黃蘭英, had moved to Taiwan with the KMT and subsequently reorganized the ensemble and provided *guoyue* training courses for people to develop their musicianship skills in Taiwan. This group has enthusiastically and actively promoted *guoyue* since its inception. It was these musicians, through actively performing *guoyue* and teaching Chinese musical instruments, that enhanced the development of *guoyue* among local communities and gradually embedded it into daily life in Taiwan. Their influence led to the sequential establishment of many Chinese orchestras in public and private organizations, schools, and military units: these included the Zhonghua Guoyue Tuan 中華國樂團, Zhengzhuan Guoyue She 政專國樂社, Zhongxin Guoyue She 中信國樂社, Chen Zhong Guoyue She 晨鐘國樂社, and Xunfeng Guoyue She 薰風國樂社, as well as Dapeng Guoyue Dui 大鵬國樂隊 in the Air Force, Haijun Guoyue Dui 海軍國樂隊 in the Navy, Huijun Luzhan Dui Guoyue Dui 海軍陸戰隊國樂隊 in the Marines, and the Luguang Guoyue She 陸光國樂社 in the Army. Ultimately, the objective of these Chinese orchestras was to preserve and develop *guoyue* through frequent interaction among all of the groups. In addition, the Zhonghua Guoyue Xuehui 中華國樂會 (Chinese Music Association, Taiwan) was established by Gao Ziming and He Mingzhong 何名忠 in 1953; its goal was to promote and preserve traditional Chinese culture and provides impetus for the development of Chinese music education in Taiwan (Liu, 2007: 51–52).

The birth and early development of *guoyue* in Taiwan reveals that memories and nostalgia were the sentiments that the nationalists and musicians aimed to induce among the public. Despite changes in place and time, *guoyue* can invoke memories key to fostering loyalty to an "imagined community," as proposed by Benedict Anderson. Anderson (1983) claims that a nation is a construction rather than a discovery of certain ethnic realities, an imagined political community that can be understood in terms of how people imagine or perceive their nation. The nationalists and musicians recognized the transcendental power of *guoyue* to arouse such nostalgic feelings among the public and engender a collective imagination of their previous homeland of China. This constituted the onset of *guoyue* promotion by the KMT in educational and cultural institutions. Its ability to promote cultural nationalism helped it become one of the most vibrant traditional musical genres in Taiwan at this time.

THE REVIVAL OF CHINA'S MUSICAL CULTURE

During the Cultural Revolution in China (1966–76), much traditional Chinese culture was regarded as bourgeois and immoral. The CPC's attempt to eradicate feudal superstition from Chinese music and culture stimulated the KMT in Taiwan to become more aggressive in their promotion of what they perceived as traditional Chinese culture, in turn. To counter the Cultural Revolution, a large-scale cultural propaganda drive known as *Zhonghua wenhua fuxing yundong* 中華文化復興運動 ("Chinese cultural renaissance movement") was implemented from the 1960s to the 1970s to restore traditional Chinese culture (Mittler, 1997: 187). The drive, which influenced the subsequent development of *guoyue*, became a means of maintaining the orthodoxy and legitimacy of the KMT regime; Chinese nationalists in Taiwan portrayed themselves as the guardians of traditional Chinese culture, and this bolstered their claim of legitimate rule over China. From the perspective of cultural policy, music was required to represent traditional Chinese culture in forms such as *guoju* 國劇 ("national opera," which indicated the genre known in the mainland as *jingju* 京劇, i.e., Beijing opera) and *guoyue* (national music), each of which was heavily supported in schools, amateur clubs, and the army by the KMT government throughout the period in question.

The cultural policy of the KMT government, meanwhile, discouraged and suppressed traditional local Taiwanese music and gradually fueled the rise of a Chinese consciousness in Taiwan. The government controlled this ideology through various institutions, including measures to disseminate this identity into everyday life, to continually remind people that they were Chinese. As noted by Nancy Guy, the KMT not only has never maintained a troupe that performs a Taiwanese genre of traditional opera, such as a *gezaixi* ensemble, but also has actively discouraged through its policies the performance of Taiwanese opera for decades (Guy, 2005: 154; see also, Wang, 2003: 98, 104).

The development of *guoyue* education in the formal curriculum and as an extracurricular activity was increasingly emphasized by the KMT government, leading to the establishment of Chinese orchestras in many schools. To cultivate professional talent for *guoyue*, Chinese music departments were established at National Taiwan Academy of Fine Arts (now National Taiwan University of Arts) in 1957 and by Zhuang Ben-li 莊本立 at the Chinese Culture Academy (now the Chinese Culture University) in 1969; the latter began to recruit increasingly large numbers of students to learn traditional Chinese instruments. In the 1960s, many universities, high schools, and elementary

FIGURE 15.1. Cheng Si Sum鄭思森 conducting a school orchestra in a national *guoyue* competition, 1973.

(Photo: courtesy of the Taipei Chinese Orchestra)

schools also began providing training in traditional Chinese instruments as extracurricular activities, and the Ministry of Education encouraged these institutions to establish modern Chinese orchestras. These orchestras became the most popular extracurricular activity for students, and they helped students to develop their Chinese cultural understanding. According to a survey conducted by the Chinese Music Association in 1985, among educational institutions spanning elementary schools to universities, 262 schools had established modern Chinese orchestras by that time (Lin, 2003, p. 32). Consequently, there was the prospect for schools to engage in a national *guoyue* competition, which provided further opportunities for the development of the genre in Taiwan (Lu, 2003, pp. 174–75) (see Figure 15.1). *Guoyue* clearly played a significant role in nourishing national Chinese identity and pride through education (Liu, 2007: 113–15).

THE EXPLORATION AND APPROPRIATION OF TAIWAN'S MUSICAL CULTURE

Because *guoyue* can be considered a medium for promoting traditional Chinese culture under the socio-political environment of the period in question, the development

FIGURE 15.2. Taipei Chinese Orchestra performing at the National Concert Hall, 2019.
(Photo: courtesy of the Taipei Chinese Orchestra)

of professional Chinese orchestras in Taiwan received especially strong political support, and this facilitated the establishment of a small number of professional Chinese orchestras dedicated to performing and developing exquisite traditional Chinese music. The first such orchestra to be founded was the Taibei Shili Guoyue Tuan 臺北市立國樂團 (Taipei Chinese Orchestra, TCO), established in 1979 by the Department of Cultural Affairs of Taipei City Government (see Figure 15.2). The second was the; Guojia Guoyue Tuan 國家國樂團 (National Chinese Orchestra, NCO), established by the Ministry of Education in 1984.[4] The third was the Goxiong Shi Guoyue Tuan 高雄市國樂團 (Kaohsiung Chinese Orchestra, KCO), established in 1989 and supported by the Education Bureau of Kaohsiung City Government.[5] The fourth was the Tainan Shi Minzu Guanxian Yuetuan 臺南市民族管絃樂團 (Tainan City Traditional Orchestra, NCTO), established in 2000 by the Tainan City Government (see Figure 15.3). With strong financial backing from Taipei City Government, the TCO held more than fifty regular and outreach concerts each year. By contrast, the NCO and NCTO, supported by their respective local governments, did not have access to large amounts of funding. Because of these limitations, some Chinese orchestras were able to hold only one annual concert while others such as the NCO managed a maximum of twelve concerts a year. Evidence suggests that access to subsidies from central and local governments influenced the development of modern Chinese orchestras; however, the extent of this influence is difficult to assess.

FIGURE 15.3. Tainan City Traditional Orchestra in musical-theater crossover performance "First Street Episode," Concert Hall of Tainan Municipal Cultural Center, October 1–2, 2016.

(Photo: courtesy of the Tainan City Traditional Orchestra)

From 1949 and up to the lifting of martial law in 1987, Taiwan had barely any political or cultural contact with China. The KMT government continued to control the spread of music from China and prevented cultural exchange between the two sides. Therefore, *guoyue* musicians needed to be careful about what they learned and performed and where they obtained musical material. Musicians were not allowed to play any compositions that contained references to communist ideology. In addition, use of songs, scores, or instruments from China was forbidden (as confirmed in interviews with Chen Ru-chi 陳如祁 and Su Wen-ching 蘇文慶).[6] However, Taiwan's *guoyue* environment was not mature enough to produce sufficient resources for every need. Consequently, *guoyue* musicians acquired musical resources through alternative methods involving scores, cassette tapes, and musical instruments. The simplest of these methods was the transcription of *guoyue* music by musicians who listened to pirate radio stations in Taiwan. During the period of musical prohibition, the performance of songs from China was regarded as treason; consequently, musicians adopted the method of creating new titles for pieces to prevent any reference to their Chinese origin and to pretend that the music had not come from China. Another method was to import musical resources or to request travelers, friends, or family members to bring back such materials from their visits to locations such as Malaysia, Singapore, and Hong Kong. Because of these methods, although the KMT government severely limited cultural exchange between Taiwan and China, it was unable to exert total control over *guoyue* exchanges between the two sides.

There is another sense in which Taiwan's *guoyue* faced challenges in relation to political and economic changes in its society in the 1980s. Taiwan's diplomatic recognition as the Republic of China came into question because the "One China" policy of the People's Republic of China (PRC) claimed that there could only be one China, with Taiwan forming one of its provinces. In 1979, the United States of America accepted the "One China" policy, and thus recognized the PRC as the sole legitimate government of China. This led to heated debates on the legitimacy of Taiwan as a nation within the PRC and KMT (Dumbaugh, 2009). Subsequent radical political transition inevitably influenced the direction of cultural development in Taiwan; in particular, breaking away from a model of centralization enabled localized cultural policies to gradually take shape. In addition, Taiwan's policy toward China relaxed and became increasingly liberalized, resulting in more frequent cross-strait interaction. Many professional musicians and Chinese orchestras from China came to Taiwan to perform or participate in academic and cultural exchanges featuring *guoyue*. Moreover, an increasing number of professional musicians and students in Taiwan endeavored to develop advanced playing skills and thus frequently traveled to China for instruction from masters. Such interaction directly influenced the techniques, methods, and even concepts of playing Chinese instruments and thus in turn influenced the direction of *guoyue* development. This enabled Chinese orchestras in Taiwan to integrate Chinese and native materials and pedagogies on a large scale. Exchanging ideas generated more musical compositions and introduced advanced skills to the genre.

A major increase in Western musical influence was also seen in Taiwan in the 1980s because of the high number of Taiwanese musicians studying Western classical music, first in Taiwan and subsequently in Western countries or Japan. After completing their studies, some musicians remained overseas while some returned to Taiwan. One of the composers and conductors, Chen Tscheng-hsiung 陳澄雄 (b. 1941), active as TCO director at this time, encouraged the TCO performers to read from Western musical staves instead of from Chinese simplified notation, giving the orchestra the possibility to create and coordinate large-size compositions. Chen made substantial efforts to direct Chinese orchestral music toward symphonization, which required considerable variety in compositional style and instrumentation, the advancement of playing skills, and the expansion of the Chinese orchestral structure.

Regarding political influence, in 1986, the Democratic Progressive Party (hereafter, DPP)[7] became the first party in Taiwan to stand as opposition to the KMT. Taiwan remained under martial law until a number of Taiwanese political intellectuals began to campaign for democracy. In 1987, Chiang Ching-kuo (1910–88), then the president of Taiwan, lifted martial law, thereby bringing about a revival of traditional Taiwanese culture in resistance to Chinese nationalism. The *bentuhua yundong* 本土化運動 ("localization movement") promoted culture that came from Taiwan itself or had strong roots there prior to 1945, its goal being to prove that Taiwanese and Chinese cultures were unique and nonhomogeneous.[8] The DPP quickly capitalized on this movement and used it to promote the party's political campaign. National identity again began to concern Taiwanese people when the DPP mobilized its supporters to pursue cultural independence. This pursuit entailed a form of "de-sinicization," an attempt to de-emphasize notions and perceptions of Chinese culture and its influence on the island. Because of the localization movement in the 1990s, a Taiwanese identity emerged and became dominant throughout the nation. This new identity was infused into Taiwan's local languages, literature, political debates, and culture, and it inevitably influenced *guoyue*. Modern Chinese orchestras began to organize their music differently in the face of this shift, from promoting Chinese identities to promoting Taiwanese ones. Such groups expressed their musical ideologies in a variety of manners.

After the DPP candidate Chen Shui-bian was elected president in 2000, localization became a mainstream activity, and the government began to heavily promote homegrown culture in Taiwan. Subsidies for Chinese orchestras decreased during Chen's presidency; the endorsement of localization was effectively a process of weakening Chinese influence, and *guoyue* suffered due to its preceding associations with the KMT's program of emphasizing Chinese heritage. However, the DPP government did not abolish *guoyue*, possibly because by this time it had become accepted as the national music of Taiwan, and thus its outright removal would have created a void in the Taiwanese national identity. Under these circumstances, materials derived from Indigenous populations and from the musical traditions of the regional Hokkien- and Hakka-speaking populations—who were well represented in Taiwan and long predated the KMT's rise there—gained greater access to support and became more popular, and *guoyue* composers increasingly used such materials as compositional resources, in turn. A review of the NCTO's CD and VCD albums in 2012, for instance, reveals that the orchestra focused on Hakka, Hokkien, and Indigenous elements, and mostly performed works produced by Taiwanese composers, thereby moving toward localization and reflecting the DPP's affirmation of multiculturalism in Taiwan. By contrast, the CD and VCD albums of the TCO produced between 1994 and 2006 placed more emphasis on Han Chinese elements, such as Chinese New Year celebration music, and featured a variety of traditional Chinese instrumental music, including Buddhist music, silk and bamboo music, and Chinese opera music (Chen, 2012: 116–18). The prominent Taiwanese composer Chang Yong-ching 張永欽, who enjoyed regular commissions from many Chinese orchestras and from the Zhonghua Guoyue Xuehui 中華國樂學會 (Chinese Music Association, Taiwan), asserted that localization became an essential step in his musical creations at this time.[9] As such, *guoyue* musicians during this period were forced to seriously reconsider the position of their genre in Taiwan. They realized that simply using material from China was no longer possible; such material would have to be fused with local musical elements to produce new compositions.

When the KMT regained power again in 2008, its new cultural policy avoided the issue of ethnicity and tended to focus on achieving a balance between globalization and localization. President Ma Ying-jeou aimed to promote harmony among all of Taiwan's communities rather than to exacerbate conflicts within Taiwan or with China. To some extent, he was able to resolve some long-standing disputes between descendants of the KMT migrants who came to Taiwan between 1945 and 1949 and those Taiwanese whose families had longer roots in Taiwan. Ma's hope was to move beyond localization alone by encouraging the cultivation of Taiwan in relation to the globalized world

(Chen, 2013, pp. 18–19. *Guoyue* performances that applied his principles from 2008 to 2016 can thus be described as a veiled means of promoting "ethnoconvergence." This relates to Mikhail Epstein's utopian ideology, which "envisions a utopia of cultural wholeness and describes transculturation in the context as a multidimensional space that appears gradually over the course of historical time" (Epstein, 1995, p. 14). Musically speaking, a representative result can be observed in the TCO's concerts after 2008 as the orchestra moved into *kuajie* 跨界 renditions (a new type of *guoyue* performance that is characterized by its cross-cultural mixture of different musical genres and art forms such as traditional and contemporary opera, dance, and Western-style spoken theater). Although not without criticisms, this new type of performance was accepted by a wide Taiwanese demographic and has provided some economic benefit for the TCO as well.[10]

The current (DPP) Taiwanese government has added one further ingredient to their earlier emphasis on re-localization and de-sinicization as a strategy for cultural development. President Tsai Ing-wen (elected in 2016) announced a "New Southbound" policy of fostering cultural exchange and expanding ties with Southeast Asian countries. In 2017, many Chinese orchestras in Taiwan, including the NCO, were invited to Malaysia by Chinese orchestras there, to cultivate mutual understanding and cultural exchange between the two countries.

Conclusion

Taiwan and China have overlapping but distinct musical styles and repertoires. In the case of *guoyue*—and despite its Chinese origins and periods of considerable interaction with Chinese models and with Chinese expertise—hybridity and interconnections with other cultural resources have been highly significant. Over the past few decades, Taiwanese society has witnessed processes of sinicization, localization, Taiwanization, re-sinicization, and new Taiwanization or re-localization. These have greatly influenced the development of modern Chinese orchestral music as the orchestras served variously as voices for the government's cultural institutions in constructing a national identity at home and as national voices for Taiwan for overseas audiences. A non-static musical identity has thus remained under continuous development within *guoyue* culture, with each cycle of change bringing new attention toward the possibilities or the risks of hybridity in ways that remain distinct from the situation of *guoyue* in China. In Taiwan, *guoyue* musical practice has opened up a "third space" that serves as a territory of negotiation for adaptation, resistance, and appropriation as musicians in *guoyue* have become inextricably entangled with others around them in local and global contexts.

An investigation into *guoyue* reveals how this musical genre in Taiwan has endured numerous changes while musicians have taken on contrasting cultural ideas over the past seventy years. Overall, the music has shifted from embodying an earlier sense of Chinese tradition and identity to evoking two differing visions of Taiwanese identity. Within this latter identity construct, two variants are currently competing: in one, an emphasis is placed on localization, which favors the reconstruction of a national identity through reference to genres already well established in Taiwan. In the other end, hybridity (cross-cultural and cross-field performance) is the result, which seems to favor musical experimentation and innovation through highly sophisticated performances. Here, the expression through music of multiethnic roots and ideas appears to transcend Taiwanese reality and any evident socio-political negotiation. While one notion treats *guoyue* as a symbol of cultural heritage, the other approaches it as a commodity—a commercial product that shapes everyday life—through which musicians exhibit creativity and innovation in order to attract wider audiences. As will be recalled from the opening of this chapter, hybridity is not necessarily a completely positive aspect: it may signal a loss of cultural "authenticity" (Pieterse, 1995) and involve an unequal power relationship (Kraidy, 2002). However, the positive connotations of hybridity include fluidity of position and transcendence of differences (Lo, 2002). The TCO led the move toward crossover performances, and despite facing criticism concerning its perceived authenticity as Chinese orchestra music, these efforts open up a whole dimension of creative possibilities, including the potential for dialogue with other cultures. By contrast, the concert themes of other Chinese orchestras marked a transition from original *guoyue* to a more "sophisticated" style with greater emphasis on localization than on purely traditional Chinese elements. These two trends have occurred simultaneously, which has provided Taiwanese audiences with a greater choice of concert types.

Glossary

Note: Some terms follow historical romanizations and romanizations used in Taiwan.

bentuhua yundong 本土化運動, de-sinicization movement
beiguan 北管, traditional music genre widespread in Taiwan
Chang Yong-ching 張永欽, composer, conductor, educator, and musician (b. 1969)
Chen Ru-chi 陳如祁, composer, conductor, educator, and performer; former vice conductor of the TCO (b. 1955)
Chen Tscheng-hsiung 陳澄雄, director and conductor of the Taipei Chinese Orchestra, 1984–91 (b. 1941)
Chen Zhong Guoyue She 晨鐘國樂社, Chinese music club formed in 1951 by Zhuang Ben-li
Cheng Si Sum 鄭思森, composer and conductor; leader of First Label Chinese Orchestra, (1944–86)
cui tai qing 催台青 or 吹台青, policy to appoint young elites in Taiwan to serve in important governmental positions
Dapeng Guoyue Dui 大鵬國樂隊, Chinese orchestra established in 1950 by Yang Zuoren for Taiwan's Air Force
Datong Yuehui 大同樂會, Datong Music Society, founded in the 1920s by Zheng Jinwen (1871–1935)
Gao Ziming 高子銘, *dizi* player and a founder of the Zhongguang Guoyue Tuan (1907–73)
gezaixi 歌仔戲, traditional Taiwanese opera genre

guoju 國劇, "national opera," designation given to Beijing opera in Taiwan after the KMT's defeat in China in 1949

guqin 古琴, plucked string Chinese musical instrument

guoyue 國樂, literally, "national music"; in context, music for Chinese orchestra, for ensembles, or for solo traditional instruments

Haijun Guoyue Dui 海軍國樂隊, Navy Chinese Orchestra; affiliated with the Navy (established 1954)

Huijun Luzhan Dui Guoyue Dui 海軍陸戰隊國樂隊, Marines Chinese Orchestra (established 1952)

He Mingzhong 何名忠, a founder of the Zhongxin Chinese Music Society and the Chinese Music Association

Huang Lanying 黃蘭英, *yangqin* player; a founder of the Zhongguang Guoyue Tuan

huqin 胡琴, family of Chinese two-stringed fiddles

Jiangnan sizhu 江南絲竹, genre of traditional Chinese instrumental music in Shanghai and nearby

jingju 京劇, traditional Beijing opera

Kōminka undo 皇民化運動 (Japanese), "Kōminka movement," Japanization program launched in 1937

kuajie 跨界, new *guoyue* form introduced to Taiwan after 2008

Luguang Guoyue She 陸光國樂社, Lukuang Chinese Music Club; affiliated to Army Headquarters (established 1965)

nanguan / nanyin 南音 / 南管, classical music genre popular in Taiwan and Southeast Asia

pipa 琵琶, plucked string Chinese musical instrument

sanxian 三弦, "three strings," fretless plucked Chinese instrument

Su Wen-ching 蘇文慶, performer, composer, and conductor (b. 1958)

Sun Peichang 孫培章, *pipa* player and a founder of the Zhongguang Guoyue Tuan (1920–94)

shifan xuexiao 師範學校, "normal school," teacher-training college

Taiwan Nichinichi Shinpō 臺灣日日新報, *Taiwan Daily News*, official newspaper (published 1898–1944)

Wang Peilun 王沛綸, composer and cofounder of the Zhongguang Guoyue Tuan (1908–1972)

Xunfeng Guoyue Tuan 薰風國樂團, National Taiwan University Chinese Orchestra (established 1952)

zheng 箏, plucked musical instrument

Zhengzhuan Guoyue She 政專國樂社, Zhengzhuan Chinese Music Society (established 1951)

Zhongguang Guoyue Tuan 中廣國樂團, Chinese musical ensemble established at the Central Broadcasting Station in Nanjing, 1935; some musicians moved to Taiwan after 1949, forming the Broadcasting Corporation of China (BCC) Chinese Orchestra

Zhonghua Guoyue Tuan 中華國樂團, Chinese orchestra (established 1958)

Zhonghua Guoyue Hui 中華國樂會, Chinese Music Association Taiwan (established 1953), which renamed itself Zhonghua Guoyue Xuehui 中華國樂學會 in 1982

Zhonghua wenhua fuxing yundong 中華文化復興運動, "Chinese cultural renaissance movement" (launched 1966)

Zhongxin Guoyue She 中信國樂社, Zhongxin Chinese Music Society (established 1952)

Zhongyang Guangbo Diantai Guoyue Zu 中央廣播電台國樂組, Music Department of the Chinese Orchestra of the Central Broadcasting Station (established in Nanjing, 1935; moved to Chongqing, 1937)

Zhuang Ben-li 莊本立, ethnomusicologist and reformer of Chinese instruments (1924–2001)

Notes

1. The term *guoyue* is simultaneously used for a broad category of Chinese music that includes various styles of folk music as well as newly composed or arranged music for traditional instruments, including solo and small ensemble repertory. This chapter is primarily concerned with the orchestral repertory.
2. During this period, the term *guoyue* mainly referred to traditional Chinese instrumental music that was usually performed by solo musicians rather than ensembles.
3. The Datong Yuehui was the first musical group to be formed and established in Shanghai in the 1920s that was dedicated to the modernizing of traditional Chinese musical instruments and the rearranging of traditional Chinese instrumental compositions, and so a direct antecedent for the modern Chinese orchestra (Lau, 2008: 210).
4. The NCO has been under the governance of the Council for Cultural Affairs since 2008.
5. The KCO became the in-house orchestra of the Kaohsiung Music Center in 2000 and was incorporated into the Kaohsiung Philharmonic Cultural and Arts Foundation in 2009.
6. Chen Ru-chi is the former vice conductor of the TCO, and Su Wen-ching is the former conductor of the NCO. Interviews were conducted on January 3, 2007, and January 10, 2010, respectively.
7. Taiwanese nationalism forms the root ideology of the DPP, with a pro-independence political tilt that became stronger in the late 1980s with the democratization of domestic politics.
8. Localization is a political ideology and local characteristic in Taiwan. This term was used by Chiang Ching-kuo (son of Chiang Kai-shek), leader of the KMT, who believed that for Taiwan's long-term development, future Taiwanese generations must be cultivated to breed officers able to work in government departments under the slogan *cui tai qing* 催台青. However, *cui tai qing* turned to advocating the *bentuhua yundong*, which was an integral socio-political movement initiated by DPP intellectuals against the pro-China KMT government.
9. Interview, Chang Yong-ching, Taipei, on September 3, 2009.
10. Currently, performances by modern Chinese orchestras can be categorized into three types: cross-cultural (mixing music from various cultures); cross-field (mixing music with traditional or contemporary opera, dance, spoken theater, and fine arts); and multimedia (mixing music with digital content such as film and animation).

References

Anderson, Benedict. (1983). *Imagined Communities: Reflections on the Origin and Spread of Nationalism*. London: Verso.

Ashcroft, Bill, Gareth Griffiths, and Helen Tiffin. (2007). *Postcolonial Studies: The Key Concepts*. New York: Routledge.

Bhabha, Homi K. (1994). *The Location of Culture*. London: Routledge.

Bhabha, Homi K. (1996). "Culture's In-Between." In *Questions of Cultural Identity*, edited by Stuart Hall and Paul du Gay, 53–60. London: Sage Publications.

Chen Ching-yi 陳靜儀. (2012). "Musical Hybridity: Guoyue and Chinese Orchestra in Taiwan." PhD diss., University of Sheffield, UK.

Chen Ching-yi 陳靜儀. (2013). "Wenhua huiliu—yi Taiwan er ge gonggong bumen guoyue tuan de yinyue xianxiang wei li" "文化匯流：以台灣二個公部門國樂團的音樂現象為例" [Transculturation: The Musical Phenomenon of Two Governmental Funded Chinese

Orchestras in Taiwan]. *Taiwan yinyue yanjiu* 台灣音樂研究 [Formosan Journal of Music Research] 17: 39–66.

Dumbaugh, Kerry. (2009). "Taiwan's Political Status: Historical Background and Its Implications for U.S. Policy." *CRS Report for Congress*. Retrieved from https://fas.org/sgp/crs/row/RS22388.pdf

Epstein, Mikhail. (1995). *After the Future: The Paradoxes of Postmodernism and Contemporary Russian Culture*. Cambridge, MA: University of Massachusetts Press.

Fell, Dafydd. (2005). *Party Politics in Taiwan: Party Change and the Democratic Evolution of Taiwan, 1991–2004*. London: Routledge.

Guy, Nancy. (2005). *Peking Opera and Politics in Taiwan*. Urbana: University of Illinois Press.

Ho Wai-chung. (2006). "A Historical Review of Popular Music and Social Change in Taiwan." *Asian Journal of Social Science* 34 (1): 120–47.

Kraidy, Marwan M. (2002). "Hybridity in Cultural Globalization." *Communication Theory* 12 (3): 316–39.

Lau, Frederick. (2008). *Music in China: Experiencing Music, Expressing Culture*. New York: Oxford University Press.

Lee, Gregory. (1995). "The 'East is Red' Goes Pop: Commodification, Hybridity and Nationalism in Chinese Popular Song and Its Televisual Performance." *Popular Music* 14 (1): 95–110.

Lin, Yi-feng 林一鳳. (2003). "Taiwan zhuanye guoyue tuan yingyun zhi yanjiu—yi Kaohsiung Shi Guoyue Tuan wei li" "台灣專業國樂團營運之研究—以高雄市立國樂團為例" [Organizational Development of Professional Chinese Orchestra in Taiwan—A Case Study of Kaohsiung City Chinese Orchestra]. MA thesis, Nanhua University.

Liu, Wen-hsiang 劉文祥. (2007). "Lunshu Taiwan xiandai guoyue di lishi mailuo yu fazhan zhengzhi tizhi xia di yinyue wenhua yanbian" "論述台灣現代國樂的歷史脈絡與發展" [The Historical Thread and the Development of Modern Chinese Music in Taiwan (1900–present): The Cultural Evolution of Music through Regimes]. MA thesis, Tainan University.

Lo, Shih-hung. (2002). "Diaspora Regime into Nation: Mediating Hybrid Nationhood in Taiwan." *The Public* 9 (1): 65–84.

Lu Yu-xiu 呂鈺秀. (2003). *Taiwan yinyue shi* 台灣音樂史 [History of Taiwanese Music]. Taipei: Wunan tushu chuban.

Mittler, Barbara. (1997). *Dangerous Tunes: The Politics of Chinese Music in Hong Kong, Taiwan, and the People's Republic of China*. Wiesbaden: Harrassowitz.

Papastergiadis, Nikos. (2000). *The Turbulence of Migration: Globalization, Deterritorialization and Hybridity*. Cambridge, UK: Polity Press.

Pieterse, Jan N. (1995). "Globalization as Hybridization." In *Global Modernities*, edited by Mike Featherstone, Scott Lash, and Roland Robertson, 45–68. London: Sage.

Ramnarine, Tina K. (2007). *Beautiful Cosmos: Performance and Belonging in the Caribbean Diaspora*. London: Pluto Press.

Wachman, Alan M. (1994). *Taiwan: National Identity and Democratization*. Armonk, NY: M. E. Sharpe.

Wang Ying-fen 王櫻芬. (2003). "Yeyu yinyue shetuan yu zhengfu jieru: Yi zhan hou taiwan nanguan yue jie wei li." "業餘音樂社團與政府介入：以戰後臺灣南管樂界為例" [Amateur Music Clubs and State Intervention: The Case of Nanguan Music in Postwar Taiwan]. *Minsu quyi* [Ritual, Theatre, and Folklore] 141: 95–167.

Watkins, Lee W. (2010). "Brown, Black, Yellow, White: Filipino Musicianship in Hong Kong and Their Hybridized Sociability." *Humanities Diliman: A Philippine Journal of Humanities* 7 (1): 58–84.

Winckler, Edwin A. (1994). "Cultural Policy in Postwar Taiwan." In *Cultural Change in Postwar Taiwan*, edited by Stevan Harrell and Huang Chun-chieh, 22–46. Boulder, CO: Westview Press.

Wu Chao-jung. (2007). "Performing Postmodern Taiwan: Gender, Cultural Hybridity, and the Male Cross-Dressing Show." PhD diss., Wesleyan University.

Wu Gan-bo 吳贛伯. (2013). *Jin bainian Taiwan guoyue shi* 近百年臺灣國樂史 [One Hundred Years of History of National Music in Taiwan]. Taipei: Boyang wenhua shiye youxian gongsi.

CHAPTER 16

TRENDS IN THE GLOBALIZATION OF *PIPA* MUSIC

BEN WU

Introduction

The *pipa* 琵琶, a pear-shaped, four-stringed plucked lute, is a traditional instrument with a long history. Its primitive form was introduced into China from central Asia through the Silk Road in the fourth century (Yang, 1981: 163). This chapter reviews the music of *pipa* in general before examining new trends of *pipa* music in recent decades; specifically, the significance of globalization in *pipa* music.

Pipa Music: Tradition and Modern Composition

The earliest recorded uses of *pipa* were as ensemble instruments accompanying singing and dancing for entertainment in imperial and noble courts in China. The first evidence indicating that *pipa* was also used as a solo instrument comes from the Tang dynasty (618–907). Later, it became a major accompanying instrument for several genres of narrative singing and traditional Chinese opera. It was also used in various instrumental ensembles.[1]

Traditionally, solo *pipa* music was performed by two disparate social groups: literati and musicians of low social status. Literati used *pipa* for leisure, as means of self-cultivation and entertainment, whereas musicians of low social status played *pipa* for a living, on streets or in teahouses (Wu, 1992).

The living tradition of solo *pipa* music can be traced back to the early nineteenth century, as the earliest extant collection of *pipa* compositions was printed in 1819 (Hua, 1819). Later, a few other collections of *pipa* music were also printed. Scores in these collections were in traditional *gongche* 工尺 notation, which used Chinese characters to represent musical notes. Editors of these collections were literati *pipa* players although the collections often included pieces mainly played by folk musicians of low social status. In addition, there are a few handwritten collections of *pipa* pieces in *gongche* notation dated to the nineteenth and early twentieth centuries.

Pipa compositions within these traditional collections were divided into *daqu* 大曲 ("large piece") and *xiaoqu* 小曲 ("small piece") categories based on length. Approximately thirty large pieces and one hundred fifty small pieces were included in these early-nineteenth-century collections. A large piece usually contained multiple sections, whereas most small pieces only had one section and a metric structure of sixty-eight *ban* 板 (beats or measures). Both large and small pieces were further divided into *wen* 文 (civil) and *wu* 武 (martial) categories. Civil pieces tended to be refined and elegant, and they were played at lower tempos with soft dynamics, whereas martial pieces were often powerful and mighty, played at faster tempos with louder dynamics.

The original composers of traditional *pipa* pieces are unknown. Although there were musical scores, the compositions were mainly transmitted orally, and scores were only used as an aid to memory. When performing the pieces, players could add their own creative elements, including occasional improvisational segments. Therefore, a commonly played traditional piece usually had different versions attributed to different schools and players. These early recorded *pipa* pieces followed traditional Chinese musical style, including employment of the *gong* 宮, *shang* 商, *jue* 角, *zhi* 徵, and *yu* 羽 modes, the five-tone and various seven-tone scales, and various typical structural features (such as the use of a series of short tunes to construct a large piece). Western musical influence was not found in traditional *pipa* music (Wu, 2001).

At roughly the beginning of the twentieth century, China entered its modern era. Although the year 1911 (when the last imperial dynasty, the Qing, collapsed) is often taken as a division point between ancient and modern China, social and cultural changes, including changes in *pipa* music, were in fact arising continuously.

Pipa music in the modern era can be divided into three periods. From 1911 to 1949, modern intellectuals began to add their influence to that of the traditional literati and lower-class *pipa* musicians (Wu, 1992). These intellectuals learned *pipa* from traditional literati while also being influenced by Western music, which was being introduced into China at that time. They rearranged *pipa* frets based on the twelve-note equal temperament system (Wu, 1990), and they began using strings made from metal or nylon instead of the traditional twisted silk. They also used Western cipher and staff notation to record *pipa* music, eventually shifting the transmission of *pipa* music from mainly involving an oral process to primarily written forms. New pieces were composed to depict contemporary events and sentiments.

Liu Tianhua 劉天華 (1895–1932) is representative of the category of modern, intellectual *pipa* composers and players, and his solo piece *Gaijin cao* 改進操 (*Exercise for*

Improvement) is exemplary of their compositions (Liu, 1933). The name of the piece came from Liu's idea that Chinese music needed to improve, and his music tries to exercise this idea. The piece has links to traditional *pipa* style, and certain foreign influences such as polyphonic tones based on Western harmony can also be found. In addition to *Gaijin cao*, Liu composed two other *pipa* solo pieces and fifteen *pipa* etudes. These are the earliest formally composed *pipa* etudes. Traditionally, literati and musicians of low social status had played small pieces or folk songs for practice.

The second period of modern *pipa* music dates roughly from 1949 to 1976 and is closely tied to the formation and early years of the People's Republic of China. In this period, *pipa* was performed primarily by professional urban players under government sponsorship. They learned the instrument from traditional literati, modern intellectuals, or other professional players, and they usually worked in professional performing troupes or music conservatories. They played both traditional and modern composed pieces, and their major performance arenas were concerts and mass-media events. Apart from in these contexts, *pipa* traditions also survived in folk instrumental ensembles, such as those for accompanying narrative songs.

In this period, about twenty to thirty *pipa* pieces were composed or adapted from folk songs or other composed songs. Some of these pieces have become well known and are now considered classics, such as *Yizu wuqu* 彝族舞曲 (*Dance of the Yi Tribe*) by Wang Huiran 王惠然 from 1960, *Langyashan wu zhuangshi* 狼牙山五壯士 (*Five Heroes on the Langya Mountain*) by Lü Shao'en 呂紹恩 from 1960, and *Caoyuan xiao jiemei* 草原小姐妹 (*Little Sisters of the Grassland*) by Wu Zuqiang 吳祖強, Wang Yanqiao 王燕樵 and Liu Dehai 劉德海 from 1973 (Wu, 2003).

Despite preserving links to traditional Chinese music, the *pipa* music of the second modern period reveals stronger Western influences, as compared to the music composed earlier. For example, the piece *Yizu wuqu* has an ABA structure, which is not commonly found in traditional Chinese music and is typically considered Western in origin. The piece also used polyphonic harmony and chords in arpeggiated form. The piece *Caoyuan xiao jiemei* was a concerto for solo *pipa* and Western orchestra, and it was the first composition of that type. Among the three composers of the piece, Wu Zuqiang and Wang Yanqiao were professional composers, and Liu Dehai was a professional *pipa* player.

The third period of the modern *pipa* era dates roughly from 1976 to the present. The "reform and opening-up" policy of the Chinese government led to a relative flourishing of music composition and performance, including those of *pipa*. Well-known solo compositions in this period include *Chun yu* 春雨 (*Spring Rain*) by Wen Bo 文博 and Zhu Yi 朱毅 from 1982, *Lao tong* 老童 (*Old Child*) by Liu Dehai from 1984, *Weishui qing* 渭水情 (*Emotion on the Wei River*) by Ren Hongxiang 任鴻翔 from 1984, *Zhao ling liu jun* 昭陵六駿 (*Six Horses in the Zhao Tomb*) by Liu Dehai from 2001, and *Shan zhi wu* 山之舞 (*Dance of the Mountains*) by Chen Yin 陳音 from 2007. Concertos for *pipa* and Chinese orchestra in this period include *Hua Mulan* 花木蘭 by Gu Guanren 顧冠仁 from 1979, and *Chunqiu* 春秋 (*Spring and Autumn*) by Tang Jianping 唐建平 from 1994. Concertos for *pipa* and Western orchestra include *Wujiang hen* 烏江恨 (*Regret on the Wujiang River*) by Yang Liqing 楊立青 from 1986, among others.

Pipa music of this period was more diverse stylistically than in the previous two periods. In general, most compositions kept the traditional Chinese style in many ways, including in their modes, scales, and general structural schemes while involving Western elements. In addition to European styles of the nineteenth century, such as Romantic and national idioms, avant-garde styles were also adapted.

Aside from practices in mainland China, the composition and performance of *pipa* music also flourished in Taiwan and Hong Kong. Well-known compositions include the *pipa* concerto *Gongfu* 功夫 (*Kung Fu*) by Doming Lam 林樂培 in Hong Kong from 1987, the *pipa* solo *Qianzhang sao* 千章掃 (*Features of Cursive Calligraphy*) by Law Wing-fai 羅永暉 in Hong Kong from 1997, and another *pipa* concerto *Yangjia jiang* 楊家將 (*Generals of the Yang Family*) by Zhong Yaoguang 鍾耀光 in Taiwan from 2003. These compositions were, in general, stylistically similar to those in mainland China.

One contributing factor to the popularization of *pipa* music was the establishment in the 1980s of formal Chinese-instrument-performance examination-board systems, which included *pipa* as a testable instrument. The most famous system is that of the Central Conservatory of Music in Beijing, which has ten grade levels for *pipa* and gives students the opportunity to take yearly examinations for certification. These testing systems encouraged young people to learn traditional Chinese instruments, including *pipa*, especially as many universities have developed preferential admissions policies toward candidates with high-level performance certificates.

This contemporary period has also seen the unprecedented emergence of well-known *pipa* players who have traveled and settled abroad, continuing their careers in *pipa* music in lands where the instrument was foreign. Who are they and what have they accomplished? The following sections focus on trends in recent decades related to *pipa* music abroad.

Active *Pipa* Players and Diverse Forms of Performance Abroad

At the end of the 1970s and in the years immediately following the institution of the Chinese government's "reform and opening-up" policy, a group of Chinese instrumentalists moved and settled abroad. This group included well-known *pipa* players who stayed active in performance. With the change in environment, new features that would prove significant for *pipa* music appeared in their performances.

Many of the well-known expatriate *pipa* players shared similar backgrounds and career trajectories. They began learning *pipa* early in their childhoods in China, often with famous *pipa* pedagogues, such as Lin Shicheng 林石城 (1922–2005) or Liu Dehai. While still in China, these artists earned relative fame and various awards for their *pipa* performances. After moving abroad, they remained active in *pipa* performance, continuing to play solo in various ensembles. They engaged in *pipa* composition, in roles ranging from consulting to composing their own pieces. These musicians also participated in *pipa* performance education, whether teaching at amateur schools, offering university or college classes, or giving masterclass lectures. In addition to playing locally, they often toured country-wide or internationally to spread their art. As a result, many of these artists have gained further accolades for their performance, composition, and education while abroad.

In general, active *pipa* players abroad expanded their repertoire to incorporate more diverse performance forms than those common in China, due to the different audiences and performance environments they encountered. These major performance forms of *pipa* music will be examined below, along with introductions to the *pipa* players abroad who most frequently employ or exemplify each form. The transliterations and orderings of players' first and last names are presented as shown on their professional websites (listed in the Appendix).

Whether in China or abroad, solo *pipa* performances remain the primary method to showcase the instrument. But in the early twenty-first century, multimedia recitals and concerts have developed as variants of traditional solo performances; two prominent works with multimedia dimensions are *Ancient Dances* by the musician Wu Man 吳蠻 and the composer Chen Yi 陳怡 (premiered in 2005), and *Tales of Pipa* by the musician Yang Jing 楊靜 (premiered in 2016). Taking its inspiration from three works by the famous Chinese poet Li Bai 李白 (701–62), *Ancient Dances* contains three movements "Cheering," "Longing," and "Wondering." The piece consists of *pipa* solo accompanied by percussion instruments and video art incorporating Chinese calligraphy and paintings. The performer and cocomposer of *Ancient Dances*, Wu Man, was born in Hangzhou. She graduated from the Central Conservatory of Music in Beijing and became the first recipient of a master's degree in *pipa* performance at the conservatory. Wu moved to the United States in 1990 and currently lives in San Diego. She has collaborated with several Western instrumental ensembles, including the Kronos Quartet, and she became a founding and active member of Yo-Yo Ma's Silk Road Project. In 2013, she was named Instrumentalist of the Year by Musical America, becoming the first performer of a non-Western instrument to receive this award. The other multimedia work, *Tales of Pipa*, comprises five parts with nine pieces, each of which sees the solo *pipa* accompanied by floating images and musical soundtracks. The five parts lead listeners through the development of *pipa* music in history, from ancient tales to contemporary compositions. Yang Jing, the composer and performer of *Tales of Pipa*, was born in Henan. After graduating from the Shanghai Conservatory of Music with a major in *pipa* performance, she became a *pipa* soloist with the Central Chinese Orchestra in Beijing. Yang moved to Japan in 1998 and then to Switzerland in 2003. She began studying composition in Switzerland and eventually achieved a master's degree in composition and theory at the Bern University of Arts. She established the European Chinese Ensemble and both composes and plays for the ensemble.

Pipa musicians abroad have not only experimented with novel recital forms for solo performances but also harnessed special types and historical variants of the instrument. These instrumental variations include the five-string *pipa*, the *nanyin* 南音

pipa, and the conventional *pipa* with silk strings. Aside from its extra string, the five-string *pipa* is otherwise similar in shape and composition to a conventional *pipa*. It was introduced to the plains of China through the Silk Road in the fourth century, and it became a frequently used instrument in the Tang dynasty, along with the historical form of the more conventional four-stringed *pipa*. It was later introduced to Japan, and the Shoso-in Repository in Nara still holds such an instrument from the Tang dynasty. The five-string *pipa* was lost in China roughly from the tenth century, but the four-stringed form survived. Modern musicians have been trying to recreate the five-string *pipa*, and one successful reconstruction was made by the musician Cheng Yu程玉in the United Kingdom in 2005. Born in Beijing, Cheng Yu graduated from the Xi'an Conservatory of Music, with a major in *pipa* performance. She became a *pipa* soloist with the Central Chinese Orchestra in Beijing before moving to the United Kingdom in 1990 and settling in London. She achieved a master's degree and a PhD in ethnomusicology at the School of Oriental and African Studies, University of London. After reconstructing her five-string *pipa*, Cheng Yu played it in recitals in London, Seoul, and Taipei from 2005 to 2007. She also participated in the composition and adaptation of the pieces performed in the concerts, including the solo *Wang Zhaojun* composed with Stephen Dydo. She is also a cofounder of the UK Chinese Ensemble.

Nanyin, a traditional vocal and instrumental genre in southern Fujian and Taiwan, uses *nanyin pipa* as one of its primary instruments. *Nanyin pipa* displays some historical features and playing skills that are no longer used on the conventional *pipa*. The most obvious difference is that the conventional *pipa* is held vertically, whereas the *nanyin pipa* is held horizontally, just as the conventional *pipa* was before and during the Tang dynasty. Due to this difference, the plucking skills are also different. Min Xiao-Fen 閔小芬, a *pipa* musician based in the United States, has occasionally played *nanyin pipa*. Born in Nanjing, she learned *pipa* from her father and well-known *pipa* master, the professor Min Jiqian 閔季騫. She became a *pipa* soloist with the Nanjing Chinese Orchestra before moving to the United States in 1992. Currently living in New York, she established the Blue Pipa Trio, which combines *pipa* and Western instruments. She has also played *pipa* in other ensembles of instruments from Europe, Asia, and Africa. The piece *Nanyin pipa: Operas Murmuring* on her compact disc, *Dim Sum*, is an original composition that uses *nanyin pipa* and her own lyric-less vocals. It conveys her impressions of traditional *nanyin* music and style without reference to a specific traditional piece. On the same CD, another piece, *Tang Song, Water Sounds*, also uses *nanyin pipa* as its main instrument.

As discussed earlier, the traditional *pipa* used strings made of twisted silk, but the modern *pipa* now uses metal or nylon strings. This change is a trade-off, as metal or nylon strings can generate a louder volume, but they lose the traditional timbre produced by silk strings. Therefore, some musicians, within and outside of China, retain use of silk strings when ancient or traditional pieces are played, so restoring the traditional timbre. One example of this is occurred when the musician Zhou Yi 周懿 played *Two Pieces of the Tang Dynasty*, as transcribed by Ye Dong 葉棟 based on ancient Tang-dynasty scores, in a New York concert in 2016. Zhou Yi was born in Shanghai and graduated from the Shanghai Conservatory of Music, with a major in *pipa* performance.

Zhou moved to the United States in 1998 and settled in New York. She was a cofounder of the Ba Ban Chinese Music Society of New York, which performs Chinese music regularly. She has also participated in several operatic and musical theater premieres with *pipa* in the orchestra.

The *pipa* concerto is an extensively encountered form in the globalized arena, and many *pipa* players abroad have played them with symphony orchestras. For example, Changlu Wu 吳長璐 performed Han Lankui 韓蘭魁's *Qilian kuangxiang* 祁連狂想 (*Rhapsody on the Qilian Mountain*, 1995) with the Houston Symphony in 2015. As one of the few concertos composed in China that have been performed abroad, this piece combines Chinese folk tunes with European nationalist conventions of structure, harmony, and instrumentation. Changlu Wu was born in Jiangsu and graduated from the Shanghai Conservatory of Music, with a major in *pipa* performance. Wu moved to the United States in 1990 and settled in Houston. While remaining active in *pipa* performance, she established the Changlu Wu School of Music and taught *pipa*, *zheng* 箏 (bridged zither), and piano there. She also founded the North America Youth Chinese Orchestra, aimed at teaching Chinese instruments to children of primary, middle, and high school ages. Other examples of *pipa* concertos performed abroad include Tan Dun 譚盾's *Concerto for String Orchestra and Pipa* premiered by Wu Man and the Seattle Symphony Orchestra in 2001, and Zhao Jiping's 趙季平 *Pipa Concerto No. 2*, which was premiered by Wu Man and the Sydney Symphony Orchestra in 2013.

Alongside conventional concertos that feature solo *pipa* and orchestra or string ensemble, concertos for *pipa* and one or more additional primary instruments have also been composed. Bernd Franke's *Mirror and Circle* for *pipa*, violoncello, and Chinese orchestra is one such example. It was premiered by the *pipa* musician Ya Dong 董亞, the cellist Peter Bruns, and the National Chinese Orchestra of Taiwan in 2014. In this work, the interactions between *pipa* and violoncello symbolize those of Eastern and Western cultures as they engage in dialogue, collide, compete, and play in unison. While the composition uses a Taiwanese folk song as its major melodic source, it also employs avant-garde methods and styles. Ya Dong was born in Shanghai. After graduating from the Shanghai Conservatory of Music with a major in *pipa* performance, she became an instructor of *pipa* at the same conservatory. Dong moved to Germany in 1987 and settled in Darmstadt, Hesse. She and a cofounder established the Ancient Wind ensemble, which performs both traditional and modern Chinese music.

Another unique concerto-form composition involving *pipa* is the *Four Seasons*, a concerto adapted by Mychael Danna based on Vivaldi's *Four Seasons* concertos. Composed for the Tafelmusik Baroque Orchestra, it features *pipa*, violin, Indian sarangi, and Inuit throat-singing, with the musician Wen Zhao 趙文欣 on *pipa*. After its premiere in Canada, it has been played internationally since 1997. A documentary film featuring the piece, *The Four Seasons Mosaic*, was made by Media Headquarters in 2004. Wen Zhao was born in Beijing and graduated from the China Conservatory of Music, with a major in *pipa* performance. Zhao moved to the United Kingdom in 1989, studying music and playing *pipa* there. In 1997, she relocated to Canada and settled in Toronto. She was a cofounder of the Lute Legends Ensemble, which contains three plucked-string instruments from China, Europe, and Central Asia. Other examples of this compositional form include: Eric Gaudibert's *Double Concerto* for *pipa*, *dizi* 笛子 (bamboo flute), and orchestra, which was premiered by Lingling Yu 俞玲玲, Dai Ya 戴亞, and the Shanghai Philharmonic Orchestra in 2010; and Vincent Ho's *Rejuvenation: A Taoist Journey* for *pipa*, orchestra, and narrator, which was premiered by Wu Man and the Toronto Symphony Orchestra in 2017.

Ensembles involving the *pipa* can be divided into two broad categories: those in which a *pipa* is played with other Chinese instruments and those in which it is joined by instruments of Western and/or other cultures. Of course, the former is considered more traditional, and many such pieces have been composed in mainland China. Instruments often used with *pipa* include *erhu* 二胡 (bowed fiddle), *zheng*, *dizi*, *ruan* 阮 (long-neck lute), and *yangqin* 揚琴 (dulcimer). Performance forms include duos, trios, and ensembles of more instruments. One example of a more traditional Chinese instrumental duo is that of *pipa* and *erhu*, a collection of pieces for which was recorded by Lingling Yu and Guo Gan 果敢 in 2011 on a CD entitled *Yue Luo* 月落 (*Moonset*) (Yu and Guo, 2011). All of the pieces in the collection are from the traditional repertory of Jiangnan *sizhu* 江南絲竹 ("silk and bamboo" ensemble music in the lower Yangtze river valley). The *pipa* artist Lingling Yu has also performed a duo for *pipa* and *dizi* (played by Zeng Ming 曾明), with pieces adapted from the traditional Chinese *kunqu* 崑曲 opera by the two players. Lingling Yu was born in Hangzhou. After graduating from the China Conservatory of Music, with a major in *pipa* performance, she became an instructor of music at Tsinghua University in Beijing. She moved to Switzerland in 1998 and settled in Geneva. There, she has participated in various ensembles, including Ensemble Dialog, with instruments from Western and Asian traditions.

An example of larger ensemble music involving *pipa* and other Chinese instruments is the quintet for *pipa*, *dizi*, *erhu*, *zheng*, and percussion by the musician Yihan Chen 陳一涵 and her partners. They performed Zhou Long 周龍's 2004 composition *Mount a Long Wind*, recorded by Music from China for YouTube in 2015. The piece symbolizes a journey "to mount a long wind and break the heavy waves" with a combination of Chinese and avant-garde styles. Yihan Chen was born in Wenzhou. After graduating from the China Conservatory of Music, with a major in *pipa* performance, she became a *pipa* instructor at the middle school affiliated with the same conservatory. After moving to the United States in 1999, Chen settled in Simsbury, Connecticut. She joined Music from China in New York, which performs Chinese instrumental music regularly.

Ensembles in which *pipa* is played with instruments of Western and/or other cultures are relatively new, as fewer opportunities existed historically to develop such ensembles in China. As with ensembles using only Chinese instruments, ensembles using *pipa* and non-Chinese instruments vary in size, from duos and trios to much larger groups. A common instrumental combination in the duo form is *pipa* and guitar. Several *pipa* players have performed in duos of this makeup, including the musician Qiu Xia He 何秋霞. Born in Baoji, He graduated from the Xi'an Conservatory of Music, having majored in *pipa* performance. Afterward, she became a *pipa* instructor at the same conservatory. She moved to Canada in 1989 and settled in Vancouver. She established the Silk Road Music ensemble (not to be confused with Yo-Yo Ma's Silk Road Project), which pioneered Chinese-Western musical fusions. In addition, she has participated in various other ensembles including the Jou Tou ensemble of "world music." Within the Silk Road Music ensemble, Qiu Xia He and her major partner André Thibault performed duets of *pipa* and guitar. On their 2012 album *Standing Out*, there are several pieces of this form composed or adapted by the two players. These pieces display a combination of Chinese and North American, especially Acadian styles, possibly related to André Thibault's Acadian/French Canadian roots.

The musicians Yang Wei 楊惟 and Ed Sweeney have also contributed in the area of duets for *pipa* and guitar. Yang Wei was born in Shanghai. After learning *pipa* from several famous pedagogues, he became a *pipa* soloist in the Shanghai Chinese Orchestra. Yang moved to the United States in 1996 and settled in Chicago. As a well-known *pipa* player and teacher, in 2013 he was invited by the Chinese Music Department at the National Taiwan University of the Arts in Taipei to be a visiting professor. Yang and Sweeney played duets of *pipa* and guitar or banjo on the CD, *What Lies Ahead*, released in 2015. The pieces are based on either traditional Chinese tunes or American folk songs, adapted to the duet form. For example, "Old Six Beats" is a traditional Chinese tune that they adapted for *pipa* and banjo, and "Home on the Range" is a classic western folk song adapted for *pipa* and guitar.

Pipa is also involved in duos with various other instruments. Liu Fang 劉芳 played duets of *pipa* and violin with Malcolm Goldstein, the pair releasing a double-CD set *Along the Way* in 2010 (Liu and Goldstein, 2010). Among the pieces on disc 1, three are duets composed by the two players, and all of the pieces on disc 2 are duets based on freestyle improvisations. In addition to traditional Chinese and European styles, avant-garde material is prominent, especially in the improvisations. Liu Fang was born in Kunming. After graduating from the Shanghai Conservatory of Music, with a major in *pipa* and *zheng* performance, she became a soloist with the Kunming Song and Dance Troupe. Liu moved to Canada in 1996 and settled in Montreal. She mainly performs *pipa* and *zheng* solo at concerts in Canada and Europe, and she also participates in duos and trios of *pipa* and instruments from Europe, Asia, and Africa.

In addition, trios involving *pipa* and other instruments are also commonly performed. For example, a trio of *pipa*, sitar, and tabla—performed by Gao Hong 高虹, Shubhendra Rao, and Ty Burhoe—premiered the piece *Morning*, which was composed by the three performers at a concert in Minneapolis that was recorded for YouTube in 2007. The piece harnesses a combination of Chinese and Indian styles, with sitar and tabla being major instruments of traditional Indian music. Gao Hong was born in Luoyang, Henan province. After graduating from the Central Conservatory of Music in Beijing, with a major in *pipa* performance, she became a *pipa* soloist with the Beijing Song and Dance Troupe. Gao moved to the United States in 1994 and settled in Eagan, Minnesota. She teaches *pipa* at Carleton College and is the director of the college's Chinese Music Ensemble and the Global Music Ensemble. She wrote the book *Hal Leonard Chinese Pipa Method*, which was published in 2016.

Another example is the Yadong Guan Trio, with *pipa* by Yadong Guan 管亞東, guitar by Bruno Roussel, and violoncello by Christophe Lobel. They played pieces adapted from Western or Chinese works, such as *The Girl with Flaxen Hair* by Claude Debussy, and *The Moon Represents My Heart* by Weng Ching-hsi 翁清溪. Yadong Guan was born in Beijing and graduated from the Music College, Minzu University of China, with a major in *pipa* performance. Guan moved to Canada in 1997. After achieving a master's degree in composition from Université Laval, she settled in Ottawa. She established the Yadong Guan Trio, and she also plays *pipa* in other ensembles of Chinese and Western instruments. Meanwhile, she works as a performance instructor for *pipa* at Carleton University.

One further example is the Manring Garcia Ma Trio, which had Jie Ma 馬捷 playing *pipa* or *ruan*, Michael Manring playing fretless or fretted basses, and Christopher Garcia playing multiple percussion instruments. The pieces they performed were all composed by members of the trio in an intercultural style, with the mix of instruments originating in Europe, America, Asia, and Africa. Jie Ma was born in Lanzhou, Gansu province. After graduating from the Tianjin Conservatory of Music, with a major in *pipa* and *ruan* performance, she became an instructor at Liaoning Normal University. Ma moved to the United States in 2004 and currently lives in Los Angeles. She has participated in several ensembles of *pipa* and "world instruments," such as the Manring Garcia Ma Trio.

In addition to duos and trios, there are various kinds of larger ensembles that involve *pipa* alongside instruments of other cultures. Among them, *pipa* and Western string quartet has been a rather common form. Examples harnessing this form include three compositions written for and premiered by Wu Man—Terry Riley's *The Cusp of Magic* of 2005, Philip Glass's *China* of 2015, and Wu Man's own *Four Chinese Paintings*, also of 2015—and two compositions written for and premiered by Lingling Yu in 2017, *Like Rain . . .* by Bun-Ching Lam 林品晶 and *Sounding Landscapes "Alpstein"* by Fabian Müller.

Along with chamber-music forms, *pipa* has also been used in orchestras for operas, musical theater, and film soundtracks. With Chinese stories becoming the themes of several operas in recent decades, several Chinese instruments, including *pipa*, have been employed in their realization. The following are a few examples: Wu Man played *pipa* for Bun-Ching Lam's *The Child God* in 1998, and for Philip Glass's *The Sound of a Voice* of 2003; Zhou Yi played *pipa* for Huang Ruo 黃若's *Dr. Sun Yat-Sen* in 2011 and for the same composer's *Paradise Interrupted* in 2016. Likewise, a few musical-theater pieces added *pipa* to their orchestras; examples include Huang Ruo's *The Dance and the Railroad*, which premiered in 2013, and Sean Hagerty's *Around the World in 80 Days*, which premiered in 2014. Both of these works had Zhou Yi playing *pipa* in the orchestra. *Pipa* has also been used in film soundtracks in recent decades. Liu Fang has played *pipa* for five films, including Andrzej Gwizdalski's short drama *The Players* in 2011 and Christian Lara's drama *Summer in Provence* in 2012, and Liu also composed the soundtrack for each of these films. Wu Man played *pipa* for two films directed by Ang Lee: *The Wedding Banquet* (1993) and *Eat Drink Man Woman* (1994). Qiu Xia He did the same for John Milton Branton's short film *Tears of a Lotus* in 1998 and Erik Paulsson's televised documentary movie *Island of Shadows: D'Arcy Island Leper Colony, 1891–1924* in 2000.

Although the examples above are by no means exhaustive, they paint a picture of the diversity and extent of *pipa* performance abroad. In addition to the well-known active players introduced, there are many other musicians who play *pipa* outside of China, all of whom contribute in numerous ways to the spreading of *pipa* music worldwide. These musicians perform diverse repertoires. Among them, *pipa* solos, use of the *pipa* in ensembles of Chinese instruments, and *pipa* concertos with Chinese orchestras were all developed in China before being introduced abroad. In overseas contexts, these forms have functioned to introduce Chinese music to foreign audiences, even when the pieces played also include Western influences. Generally, however, the musical styles of such compositions are similar to those heard in China, as discussed in the first section of this chapter.

Pipa performance forms primarily developed abroad include *pipa* concertos accompanied by Western orchestra (although *pipa* concertos with Western orchestra first appeared in China in the 1970s) and *pipa* as a part of ensembles of instruments from multiple cultures. These combinations perhaps make it easier for audiences to appreciate *pipa* music. The musical styles of these compositions are also very diverse, perhaps because the origins of the instruments used are also rather diverse. In such ensembles, *pipa* mainly serves to represent Chinese elements or styles against a background of other cultural styles represented by the other instruments, although, of course, each composition in this genre has its unique stylistic characteristics.

The same is mostly true when the *pipa* is used outside China in orchestras for opera, musical theater, and film soundtracks. Its usage mainly revolves around the contents or stories of the works relating to China. Utilization of *pipa* in these productions brings an intrinsically Chinese element to the musical sound. Meanwhile, multimedia recitals and concerts take advantage of modern technology in the accompaniments they pair with *pipa*, perhaps with the subconscious goal of updating the sound of this ancient instrument so that it might interest contemporary audiences.

COMMONLY PERFORMED AND REPRESENTATIVE COMPOSITIONS

Both traditional and modern *pipa* compositions are performed abroad. When the focus is on tradition, the selection is biased toward very famous pieces, including but not limited to *Shimian maifu* 十面埋伏 (*Ambush from All Directions*), *Xiyang xiaogu* 夕陽簫鼓 (*Flute and Drum at Sunset*), and *Long chuan* 龍船 (*Dragon Boats*). Note should also be made of a recently rediscovered traditional piece, *Poxi xiangzheng* 婆媳相爭 (*Mother-in-law Arguing with Daughter-in-law*). The piece had been previously mentioned in legends about *pipa*, but until recently, no score existed for it. Contemporary players did not know how the piece sounded until 1996, when it was recreated by the famous *pipa* master Lin Shicheng based on memory. At that time, Lin and one of his students,

Gao Hong, were touring in the United States, and Lin taught the piece to Gao, face-to-face. Later, Gao performed and recorded the piece, finally making it available to the public. Although the events inspiring and depicted by the piece may be trite and banal—perhaps that's why Lin had neither performed nor taught it publicly before this time—it contains unique passages that imitate the sounds of an argument between an old woman and a young woman, demanding considerable technical skill from the musician (Yang, 2011). Regarding modern composed works, a few well-known ones made in earlier periods are often selected, for instance, *Yizu wuqu* and *Tianshan zhichun* 天山之春 (*Spring on the Tianshan Mountains*) composed for *rewapu* 热瓦普 (long-necked lute) by Wusimanjiang 烏斯滿江 and Yu Lichun 俞禮純 in 1961 and adapted for *pipa* by Wang Fandi 王範地 in 1964.

What deserves more attention are the new works composed for *pipa* players abroad in recent decades. These compositions can be divided into two broad categories: those composed by professional composers and those by well-known *pipa* players. For the first category, eight commonly performed and representative compositions by eight different composers are presented here in the order of their premieres. This list is by no means exhaustive, but the eight works are examples that shed light on the many outstanding compositions in this field.

Chen Yi's *The Points* is a famous solo piece fingered and premiered by Wu Man in 1991. According to the composer, its name *The Points* carries a double meaning. First, a point is one of the eight standard brush strokes in Chinese calligraphy, an artistic feature that captured Wu's musical imagination. Second, the title also captures the essence of plucked string music, in that each note can be considered a point.[2] Links to traditional Chinese styles can be found in the composition's rhythmic patterns and its employment of techniques similar to those used in traditional martial pieces. The influence of avant-garde styles too is obvious in musical expressions, such as the arrangement of tonality and enharmonic chords. Many other players, including Lingling Yu and Zhou Yi, have also played this piece.

Zhou Long's *King Chu Doffs His Armor* (*Bawang xiejia* 霸王卸甲) for *pipa* and orchestra from 1991 was arranged from the traditional martial piece of the same name. The original piece describes the failure of the king Chu at the famous battle against the warlord Liu Bang in 202 BCE, including the king's personal feelings when separated from his favorite concubine. Zhou Long's work extends the essence of the original piece through the cooperation of *pipa* and orchestra. It was premiered by Wu Man and the Women's Philharmonic of San Francisco in 1991, and it has also been performed by other players and orchestras later.

Tan Dun's *Ghost Opera* for string quartet, *pipa*, water, paper, stone, and metal was composed for the Kronos Quartet and Wu Man in 1994. The work was inspired by the composer's memories of watching traditional Chinese opera based on ghost stories in Chinese rural areas. In addition to *pipa* and the normal instruments of the string quartet, the work also contains vocals, one-stringed lute, bowed gong, cymbals, tam-tam, Tibetan bells, water bowl, paper whistle, and stones, with minimal sets of lighting. It has five movements: "Act I. Bach, Monks, and Shakespeare Meet in Water," "Act II.

Earth Dance," "Act III. Dialogue with 'Little Cabbage' " ("Little Cabbage" or "Xiao baicai" 小白菜 is a Chinese folk song), "Act IV. Metal and Stone," and "Act V. Song of Paper." The work combines all of the instruments together, mixing traditional Chinese, classical European, and avant-garde styles (see further, Young, 2007). Recorded and released on CD by Nonesuch Records (Tan, 1997), the composition has also been performed by Lingling Yu and Zhou Yi with other string quartets in Europe and America respectively.

Lou Harrison's *Concerto for Pipa and String Orchestra* was composed for Wu Man, and she and Stuttgart Chamber Orchestra premiered the piece in 1997. A recording of this composition performed by Wu Man and the Chicago Symphony Orchestra appears on the label CSO Resound (2009). It contains seven movements with the following titles, all referring to certain meanings of the music: "I. Allegro"; "II. Bits and Pieces: Troika"; "III. Bits and Pieces: Three Sharing"; "IV. Bits and Pieces: Wind and Plumb"; "V. Bits and Pieces: Neapolitan"; "VI. Threnody for Richard Locke"; "VII. Estampie." The overall style of the work is a combination of traditional European and avant-garde styles, although Chinese styles can also be identified, mainly in the *pipa* part, from time to time.

Bright Sheng 盛宗亮's *Three Songs for Violoncello and Pipa* was written for Yo-Yo Ma and Wu Man and premiered at the White House in 1999. According to the composer, the work was based on three popular folk melodies that the composer heard while growing up in China: "Seasons" is a folk song in the northwestern area, "Little Cabbage" is from the north of the country, and "Tibetan Dance" is based on the melody of a well-known Tibetan folk dance. The work combines the sounds of the violoncello and *pipa* with traditional Chinese and avant-garde techniques and styles. The work has subsequently also been performed by Zhou Yi.

Bun-Ching Lam's *Song of the Pipa* is a *pipa* concerto premiered by Wu Man and the New Jersey Symphony Orchestra in 2001. According to the program notes on Bun-Ching Lam's website, it is based on the poem of the same title, "Pipa xing" 琵琶行 by the famous Tang-dynasty poet Bai Juyi 白居易 (772–846 CE). Lam adds: "It is intended to be a 'translation' of the words into music rather than literal illustrations. It takes on the spirit; the progress and the pace of Bai's poem unfolds slowly, like a scroll."[3] The work is of a predominantly Western avant-garde style, although Chinese elements can also be recognized in the *pipa* part. The composition was also performed by Zhou Yi later.

Qin Wenchen 秦文琛's *Pipa Words* (*Pipa ci* 琵琶辭) is a *pipa* solo commissioned by Lingling Yu, composed in 2006. While it inherits some features of traditional civil and martial pieces, the work explores new expressions for the instrument, especially various overtones and noises generated by special playing techniques. It presents new timbres, rhythmic patterns, and a distinct structure, mixing the styles of traditional Chinese and avant-garde music. The composition's overseas premiere was performed by Lingling Yu, and it has also been played by several other players in various locations since.

Huang Ruo's *Flow I & II* for *pipa* and mixed ensemble was premiered by Zhou Yi and Ensemble FIRE in 2013. The ensemble comprises a vocalist, violin, violoncello, bassoon, and percussion.[4] The style of the work is basically a combination of Chinese folk-song-like melodies with rock rhythms and dynamics. The vocal part has no lyrics but rather is sung with excited emotions while the *pipa* mainly plays melodies.

The other major category of new works of *pipa* music abroad consists of works composed by well-known *pipa* players, mostly for their own performance. Below are a few representative compositions in this category. Yang Jing has composed a large number of works for *pipa* with various forms and styles. Her pieces *Pinsu* 品訴 (*Disclosure*) and *Jiu lianyu* 九連钰 (*Nine Jade Chains*) composed in the years before she lived abroad still form the core of her solo recitals. She has also written pieces for *pipa* in ensembles. For example, *Identity* is a piece for a quartet of *pipa*, violin, viola, and violoncello, which premiered in Zurich in 2017.[5] The piece primarily consists of dialogues and interactions between *pipa* and the other instruments, as if they are talking about each other's identities. The whole ensemble also occasionally unifies, as if to express the identity of the entire group. Although the whole piece has an avant-garde sound, traditional Chinese elements can still be identified, especially in the *pipa* part.

Wu Man has composed *pipa* pieces of various forms and styles. Examples of her compositions can be found on the CD, *Pipa: From a Distance* (Wu, 2003), a collection of ten *pipa* pieces of her own composition. One of Wu Man's latest compositions is the ensemble piece *Green (Vincent's Tune)* on the CD, *Sing Me Home*, released by Yo-Yo Ma and the Silk Road Ensemble (Ma, 2016). According to the composer, when Vincent (Wu Man's son) was four years old, he would often run around singing this tune. Wu Man was so struck by his melody that she turned it into a composition as a way to capture his youth and the wonderful times they spent together.[6] While the *pipa* part in the piece reflects a typically Chinese style, the ensemble more generally mixes styles of different cultures and harnesses several modern techniques.

Gao Hong's solo *Flying Dragon*, written in 2003, is inspired by her Chinese zodiac sign. According to Gao's talk about the piece, in a YouTube video, a fortune teller told Gao's mother that Gao was a flying dragon, based on the time and date of her birth. Her life has paralleled some of the characteristics associated with a flying dragon: constantly on the move and never knowing what the future will bring. In the composition, Gao explores the mixed emotions and confusion brought on by her nomadic lifestyle. She reflects upon the constant struggles and challenges in a life filled with both hardship and happiness as well as a constant need for inner strength.[7] The piece was released by Innova Recordings (Gao, 2003) and was adapted to become a *pipa* concerto, performed by Gao Hong and the St. Olaf Orchestra in 2011.

Min Xiao-Fen interweaves various themes of traditional Chinese music with sounds of jazz, blues, and contemporary Western music in her compositions. Her works rely on diverse forms and sounds, establishing clearly her voice as a composer. The latest of such efforts is the CD, *Mao, Monk and Me* (Min, 2017). It features her treatments of jazz standards played by Thelonious Monk mixed with historical Chinese counterparts, including reformed Beijing operas and folk songs that Min heard in China during Mao's Cultural Revolution (1966–76). For example, the piece *My Monk's Dream* combines music of Beijing opera with improvisations learned from Monk's recording.[8] It presents Min's impressions of Beijing opera using special *pipa* techniques and her own lyric-less vocals to imitate the tunes and percussive sounds of the genre. Another CD, *Dim Sum* (Min, 2012), also contains pieces composed or arranged by Min, mixing styles of traditional Chinese music, blues, and jazz.

Qiu Xia He's compositions are all written for various ensembles with *pipa*. Her major ensemble, Silk Road Music, based in Vancouver, released the CD, *Endless*, "a collection of traditional Chinese, Irish, and Quebecois folk and classical numbers and original compositions based on Brazilian, jazz, and Celtic music" (He, 1998). The piece *Clouds— Irish Impressions* on the CD is for *pipa*, guitar, and percussion. Qiu Xia He composed it after she toured in Ireland and was deeply impressed by the country's beauty and folk music. The musical style combines Chinese and Celtic music.[9] The piece was also arranged as a triple concerto for *pipa*, guitar, and percussion for Silk Road Music and the University of British Columbia Symphony Orchestra in 2012.

As stated earlier, many well-known *pipa* players abroad have engaged in *pipa* composition to various degrees and in various ways. One important form is improvisation during performance. Another similar but distinct method of participating in *pipa* composition is the addition of specific fingering and playing techniques by *pipa* players, which are often not included when a piece is written by a professional composer. Wu Man often improvised parts when she played in the ensemble of the Silk Road Project. Jie Ma plays an improvised section in the solo piece *Bubble* (2016), which she also composed and performed. Likewise, Liu Fang improvised with her partner in the duet for *pipa* and violin, introduced earlier. In addition to works composed by *pipa* players, many others written by professional composers also contain dedicated improvisational sections.

As we can see, compositions by both professional composers and *pipa* players have multiple and diverse musical styles, and many of them combine musical genres across geographic boundaries and time periods. Generally, elements of traditional Chinese music are prominent, the *pipa*'s timbre and melodies imbuing a piece with an inherently Chinese style. Meanwhile, traditional European and avant-garde features can often be found in the overall structure, harmony, polyphonic texture, and special effects. Features of other musical styles from around the world are incorporated by the addition of instruments of other nations and cultures. These features have been combined in various compositions, giving them multicultural features.

Summary of Trends and Their Significance

Based on the descriptions, observations, and discussions laid out in the preceding sections, trends in the *pipa* music of recent decades and their significance can be summarized as follows.

1) Roughly since the 1980s, a number of well-known *pipa* players from mainland China have gone abroad and settled in North America, Europe, and other places worldwide. While abroad, they have stayed active in *pipa* performance and teaching. As a result, they have introduced *pipa* and its music to many people across the world who may not have known the instrument or its music before.

2) As audiences and performance environments have changed, *pipa* players abroad have had more opportunities to collaborate with musicians of other countries. Interaction between the *pipa* and the instruments of other cultures has generated new and diverse performance forms, and the *pipa* has become a part of numerous multicultural ensembles, which has made the *pipa* more internationally visible as an instrument of "world music."

3) Compared to *pipa* performances in China during the same period, improvisation has become a more prominent feature of *pipa* performance abroad. Although improvisation is an important feature in the history of *pipa*, its use has become less common in China due to the ready availability of written scores and musicians' subsequent reliance on them. However, there has been some degree of reverse influence recently, for instance with Wu Man teaching a Global Musician Workshop to mainland Chinese students in the Central Conservatory of Music in Beijing in 2017, an event in which multicultural music and improvisation were heavily emphasized.

4) New compositions for *pipa*, many of which are written for players abroad, have enriched music around the world. They are diverse and novel in terms of performance forms and musical styles. Some of the new forms have developed into conventions of their own. These include duos of *pipa* and guitar, quintets of *pipa* and Western string quartet, and concertos for *pipa* and orchestra.

In addition to the trends outlined above, other important developments should be considered, including the following:

1) Foreign students have been going to China to learn Chinese instruments, including *pipa*. Although the number of foreign students learning *pipa* is not large, there are some such students almost every year. Most of them come from Asian countries, including Japan, South Korea, Malaysia, Singapore, and Indonesia. In addition, students from Taiwan, Hong Kong, and Macao have also traveled to mainland China to learn *pipa*. Aside from traditional term-long courses, the Central Conservatory of Music and the Shanghai Conservatory of Music also offer summer schools in Chinese music, where overseas students have learned to play *pipa*, among other Chinese instruments.

2) Chinese-instrument exam-board systems have been introduced in a few other countries, including the United States, Canada, and Singapore. In each case, this has involved cooperation between a local institute and the Central Conservatory of Music in Beijing. *Pipa* is one of the testable instruments in these systems, encouraging young students in these countries to learn Chinese instruments and to help them ascertain their playing level. Some universities and colleges have also offered favorable admission policies to candidates who have obtained high levels of instrumental performance, popularizing the testing system.[10]

3) The gradual expansion of the network of Confucius Institutes worldwide has provided a set of institutional bases that sometimes include instruction in Chinese musical instruments, and dance, alongside language studies.

All of these trends indicate the several ways in which *pipa* music is on a path of globalization. Looking back on the instrument's history, the ancient *pipa* of the Tang dynasty had already been globalized to certain degree. At that time, scholars from Japan came to the Tang-dynasty capital city, Chang'an, learned *pipa*, and took the instrument back to Japan, where it remains in use in the present day, under the name *biwa*. It is believed that the Korean *bipa* and the Vietnamese *dàn tỳ bà* are also related to the Chinese *pipa*, and each was possibly introduced from ancient China as well.

Although the modern globalization of *pipa* seems to have begun in the 1980s, changes to the instrument and its music in the early twentieth century sowed the seeds for this process. These changes include reforms to the arrangement of frets to be based on twelve-tone equal temperament, strings being made from the more commonly available metal or nylon rather than silk, and scores shifting from *gongche* to Western cipher or staff notations. These changes made the *pipa* more approachable to Western-educated musicians and easier to combine with instruments of Western and other cultures.

Compared to other major Chinese instruments, such as *qin* 琴 (seven-stringed zither), *zheng*, *erhu*, *dizi*, and *yangqin*, the *pipa* stands out for the extent of its globalized resonances. It has probably the largest numbers of players overseas, the most new compositions, and the richest range of new performance forms with instruments of other cultures. Although the reasons for this phenomenon can only be speculated, and they are largely beyond the scope of this chapter, it is worth raising the possibility that the *pipa*'s history may have contributed to its globalization. As stated earlier, the *pipa* was introduced into China from Central Asia through the Silk Road in the fourth century. Since the *pipa*, Western lute, and guitar have the same ancestor, it is relatively easy for them to play together and for musicians who have knowledge of one instrument to transfer their interest and skills to another. This perhaps also accounts for the popularity of *pipa* and guitar duos overseas.

Although the origin of guitar can be traced back to Central Asia, it came into its modern shape in Europe, and the contemporary form has now been popularized everywhere in the world. Is it possible that *pipa* is following in the guitar's footsteps and will become similarly universal? The answer remains to be seen. Regardless, the globalization of the *pipa* allows more audiences around the world enjoy its music and is actively introducing uniquely Chinese elements to the music of other cultures. However, concern exists that traditional features of the instrument may be fully or partially lost through the processes of globalization. Therefore, attention needs to be invested in how best to avoid loss of traditional repertoire, skills, and styles associated with the instrument. Fortunately, many *pipa* musicians are keenly aware of this, devoting time to the maintenance of traditional features. The interest displayed by musicians abroad in reconstructing and using more ancient forms of *pipa*—such as the five-string *pipa*, the *nanyin pipa*, and the silk-stringed *pipa*—is an illustrative example of this initiative to maintain *pipa* traditions. Attempts to revive ancient or "lost" pieces such as *Poxi xiangzheng* is another example. Overall, the globalization of *pipa* is still in progress. *Pipa* music is likely to become richer through its multicultural entanglements, and greater numbers of people across the world will enjoy its music.

Appendix: Artist Websites

Changlu Wu: http://www.nayco.org/about/
Cheng Yu: http://www.ukchinesemusic.com/cy.htm
Gao Hong: http://www.chinesepipa.com/
Jie Ma: http://www.majiepipa.com/
Lingling Yu: http://www.linglingyu.org/biograph-of-lingling-yu-traditional-chinese-music/?lang=en
Liu Fang: http://www.philmultic.com/English/index.html
Min Xiao-Fen: http://minxiaofenbluepipa.org/
Qiu Xia He: http://silkroadmusic.ca/who-is-silk-road-music/qiu-xia-he
Wu Man: http://www.wumanpipa.org/about/bio-en.html
Yadong Guan: https://www.yadongguan.com
Yang Jing: https://www.yangjingmusic.com/
Yang Wei: http://pipasensation.com/en/about-yang/
Yihan Chen: http://www.yihanchenmusic.com/
Zhou Yi: http://www.instantencore.com/contributor/bio.aspx?CId=5126166

Glossary

Bai Juyi 白居易, poet (772–846 CE)
ban 板, beat or measure
Bawang xiejia 霸王卸甲, traditional *pipa* solo piece
Bright Sheng 盛宗亮, composer (b. 1955)
Bun-Ching Lam 林品晶, composer (b. 1954)
Caoyuan xiao jiemei 草原小姐妹, *Little Sisters of the Grassland*, composition by Wu Zuqiang, Wang Yanqiao, and Liu Dehai (1973)
Changlu Wu 吳長璐, *pipa* performer (b. 1968)
Chen Yi 陳怡, composer (b. 1953)
Chen Yin 陳音, *pipa* performer and composer (b. 1962)
Cheng Yu 程玉, *pipa* performer (contemporary)
Chun yu 春雨, *Spring Rain*, composition by Wen Bo and Zhu Yi (1982)
Chunqiu 春秋, *Spring and Autumn*, composition by Tang Jianping (1994)
daqu 大曲, "great pieces," traditional category of longer-duration solo repertory
Dai Ya 戴亞, *dizi* performer (b. 1964)
dizi 笛子, bamboo flute
Doming Lam 林樂培, composer (b. 1926)
erhu 二胡, two-stringed fiddle
Gaijin cao 改進操, *Exercise for Improvement*, composition by Liu Tianhua (1927)
Gao Hong 高虹, *pipa* performer (b. 1968)
gong 宮, *shang* 商, *jue* 角, *zhi* 徵, and *yu* 羽, five pitches of a pentatonic scale and the corresponding modes
gongche 工尺, traditional notation using simple Chinese characters to represent musical notes
Gongfu 功夫, *Kung Fu*, composition by Doming Lam (1987)

Gu Guanren 顧冠仁, composer (b. 1942)
Guo Gan 果敢, *erhu* performer (b. 1968)
Han Lankui 韓蘭魁, composer (b. 1959)
Hua Mulan 花木蘭, composition by Gu Guanren (1979)
Hua Qiuping 华秋苹, compiler of edition of *pipa* scores (1819)
Huang Ruo 黃若, composer (b. 1976)
Jiangnan *sizhu* 江南絲竹, "silk and bamboo" ensemble music of the lower Yangtze river region
Jie Ma 馬捷, *pipa* performer (b. 1978)
Jiu lianyu 九連钰, solo *pipa* composition by Yang Jing (1986)
kunqu 崑曲, genre of traditional opera
Langyashan wu zhuangshi 狼牙山五壮士, *Five Heroes on the Langya Mountain*, composition by Lü Shao'en (1960)
Lao tong 老童, *Old Child*, composition by Liu Dehai (1984)
Law Wing-fai 羅永暉, composer (b. 1970)
Li Bai 李白, poet (701–62)
Lin Shicheng 林石城, *pipa* performer and educator (1922–2005)
Lingling Yu 俞玲玲, *pipa* performer (contemporary)
Liu Dehai 劉德海, *pipa* performer and composer (1937–2020)
Liu Fang 劉芳, *pipa* performer (b. 1974)
Liu Tianhua 劉天華, *pipa* composer and player (1895–1932)
Long chuan 龍船, *Dragon Boats*, traditional *pipa* solo piece
Lü Shao'en 吕绍恩, composer (b. 1935)
Min Jiqian 閔季騫, multi-instrumentalist and educator (1923–2020)
Min Xiao-Fen 闵小芬, *pipa* performer (b. 1959)
nanyin 南音, traditional vocal and instrumental genre from Fujian and Taiwan
pipa 琵琶, pear-shaped, four-stringed plucked lute
Pipa ci 琵琶辭, *Pipa Words*, *pipa* solo by Qin Wenchen (2006)
Pinsu 品訴, *Disclosure*, *pipa* solo by Yang Jing (1986)
Poxi xiangzheng 婆媳相爭, *Mother-in-law Arguing with Daughter-in-law*, recreated traditional *pipa* solo
Qianzhang sao 千章掃, *Features of Cursive Calligraphy*, composition by Law Wing-fai (1997)
Qilian kuangxiang 祁連狂想, *Rhapsody on the Qilian Mountain*, composition by Han Lankui (1995)
qin 琴, seven-stringed zither
Qin Wenchen 秦文琛, composer (b. 1966)
Qiu Xia He 何秋霞, *pipa* performer (b. 1966)
rewapu 热瓦普, long-necked lute
Ren Hongxiang 任鴻翔, *pipa* performer and composer (1942–99)
ruan 阮, long-necked lute
Shan zhi wu 山之舞, *Dance of the Mountains*, composition by Chen Yin (2007)
Shimian maifu 十面埋伏, *Ambush from All Directions*, prominent traditional *pipa* solo
Tan Dun 譚盾, composer (b. 1957)
Tang Jianping 唐建平, composer (b. 1955)
Tianshan zhichun 天山之春, composition for *pipa* by Wusimanjiang and Yu Lichun (1961), rearranged for *pipa* by Wang Fandi (1964)
Wang Fandi 王範地, *pipa* performer and educator (1933–2017)
Wang Huiran 王惠然, composer (b. 1936)

Wang Yanqiao 王燕樵, composer (b. 1937)
Weishui qing 渭水情, *Emotion on the Wei River*, composition by Ren Hongxiang (1984)
wen 文, subdivision of "civil" repertory
Wen Bo 文博, composer (contemporary)
Wen Zhao 趙文欣, or Zhao Wenxin, *pipa* performer (b. 1967)
Weng Ching-hsi 翁清溪, composer (1939–2012)
Wujiang hen 烏江恨, *Regret on the Wujiang River*, composition by Yang Liqing (1986)
Wusimanjiang 烏斯滿江, *rewapu* player (1932–90)
Wu Man 吳蠻, *pipa* perfomer (b. 1963)
Wu Zuqiang 吳祖強, composer (b. 1927)
wu 武, subdivision of "martial" repertory
"Xiao baicai" 小白菜, "Little Cabbage," folk song
xiaoqu 小曲, "small pieces," traditional category for shorter-duration repertory
Xiyang xiaogu 夕陽簫鼓, *Flute and Drum at Sunset*, solo *pipa* composition
Ya Dong 董亞, *pipa* performer (contemporary)
Yadong Guan 管亞東, *pipa* performer (contemporary)
Yang Jing 楊靜, *pipa* performer and composer (b. 1964)
Yang Liqing 楊立青, composer (1942–2013)
Yang Wei 楊惟, *pipa* performer (b. 1960)
Yangjia jiang 楊家將, *Generals of the Yang Family*, composition by Zhong Yaoguang (2003)
yangqin 揚琴, dulcimer
Ye Dong 葉棟, musicologist (1930–89)
Yihan Chen 陳一涵, *pipa* performer (contemporary)
Yizu wuqu 彝族舞曲, *Dance of the Yi Tribe*, composition by Wang Huiran (1960)
Yu Lichun 俞禮純, composer (contemporary)
Zeng Ming 曾明, *dizi* performer (b. 1962)
Zhao Jiping 趙季平, composer (b. 1945)
Zhao ling liu jun 昭陵六駿, *Six Horses in the Zhao Tomb*, composition by Liu Dehai (2001)
zheng 箏, bridged zither
Zhong Yaoguang 锺耀光, composer (b. 1956)
Zhou Long 周龍, composer (b. 1953)
Zhou Yi 周懿, *pipa* performer (contemporary)
Zhu Yi 朱毅, composer (contemporary)

Notes

1. For more information about *pipa* in ancient history, see related sections of Yang, 1981.
2. A program note for the piece is provided at: https://www.sheetmusicplus.com/title/points-sheet-music/1790416.
3. The program note is at: http://www.bunchinglam.com/programnotes.htm.
4. A performance of Huang Ruo's *Flow I & II* is on YouTube at: https://www.youtube.com/watch?v=_BF0_OiUh1c.
5. A performance of Yang Jing's *Identity* is on YouTube at: https://www.youtube.com/watch?v=zgL2IRM1wTE.
6. A performance of Wu Man's *Green (Vincent's Tune)* is on YouTube at: https://www.youtube.com/watch?v=a_l9gBvOU00.

7. A performance of Gao Hong's *Flying Dragon* is on YouTube at: https://www.youtube.com/watch?v=hCdHGFfqSmA.
8. A performance of Min Xiao-Fen's *My Monk's Dream* is on YouTube at: https://www.youtube.com/watch?v=jCoGSnLf3EI.
9. Qiu Xia He's *Clouds – Irish Impressions* is on YouTube at: https://www.youtube.com/watch?v=yOBkPvFCDHU.
10. Details of the examinations in the United States are at http://www.uscycs.org/; those in Canada are available via https://www.bccma.net/; and those in Singapore, https://www.nafa.edu.sg/chinese-instruments-graded-examinations.

References

Chicago Symphony Orchestra. (2009). *Traditions and Transformations—Sounds of Silk Road Chicago*. CSO Resound CSOR901801, compact disc.

Gao Hong. (2003). *Flying Dragon: Gao Hong and Friends Around the World*. Innova Records 595, compact disc.

Gao Hong. (2016). *Chinese Pipa Method*. Milwaukee: Hal Leonard.

He Qiuxia. (1998). *Silk Road Music: Endless*. Jericho Beach Music JBM 9801-2, compact disc.

Hua Qiuping 華秋蘋. (1819). *Pipa pu* 琵琶譜 (*Pipa* Score). Wuxi.

Lam, Joseph. (2007). "Music, Globalization, and the Chinese Self." *The Macalester International Roundtable* 2, 1–30. Accessed November 17, 2021. http://digitalcommons.macalester.edu/intlrdtable/2..

Liu Fang and Malcolm Goldstein. (2010). *Along the Way: Duo Pipa & Violin*. Philmultic PMPCD809, compact disc.

Ma, Yo-Yo. (2016). *Yo-Yo Ma: Sing Me Home, Silk Road Ensemble*. Sony Music Classical 88875181012, compact disc.

Min Xiao-Fen. (2012) *Dim Sum*. Blue Pipa BB008, compact disc.

Min Xiao-Fen. (2017). *Mao, Monk and Me*. _____, compact disc.

Tan Dun. (1997). *Tan Dun: Ghost Opera. Kronos Quartet, Wu Man, Pipa*. Nonesuch 79445, compact disc.

Wu Ben 吳犇. (1990). "Jindai *pipa* zhuwei gaige de jige wenti" "近代琵琶柱位改革的幾個問題" [On the Reforms of the *Pipa*'s Frets in Modern Times]. *Zhongguo yinyue* 中國音樂 [Chinese Music], no. 3: 16–17.

Wu Ben 吳犇. (1992). "*Pipa* yinyue yu qi shehui beijing" "琵琶音樂與其社會背景" [*Pipa* Music and Its Social Background]. *Zhongguo yinyuexue* 中國音樂學 [Musicology in China] 27: 57–67.

Wu Ben 吳犇. (2001). "China, Living Traditions, Han Instrumental Music, Solo Traditions: Pipa." In *The New Grove Dictionary of Music and Musicians*, second edition, edited by Stanley Sadie, 5: 681–82, 684.

Wu Ben 吳犇. (2003). "Chinese *Pipa* Pieces Composed in the 20th Century." *Intercultural Music* 5: 69–82.

Wu Man. (2003). *Wu Man – Pipa: From a Distance*. Naxos World 76037-2, compact disc.

Yang Shufang 楊淑芳. (2011). "Lun pudongpai pipa de jinghua 'poxi xiangzheng'" "论浦东派琵琶的精华《婆媳相争》" [On the Famous Piece of the Pudong *Pipa* School "Mother-in-law Arguing with Daughter-in-law"]. *Wenyi zhengming* 文艺争鸣 [Discussion on Literature and Arts], no. 12: 153–56.

Yang Yinliu 楊蔭瀏. (1981). *Zhongguo gudai yinyue shigao* 中國古代音樂史稿 [A Draft History of Ancient Chinese Music]. Beijing: Renmin yinyue chubanshe.

Young, Samson. (2007). "Reconsidering Cultural Politics in the Analysis of Contemporary Chinese Music: The Case of *Ghost Opera*." *Contemporary Music Review* 26 (5–6): 605–18.

Yu, Lingling, and Guo Gan. (2011). *Yue Luo: Jiangnan Sizhu Music*. Felmay FY8185, compact disc.

PART III

CROSS-CUTTING ISSUES IN CONTEMPORARY SETTINGS

CHAPTER 17

HUMANISM IN RED

A New Mainstream Narrative in the Pop Songs of 1980s China

LIJUAN QIAN

INTRODUCTION: THE RISE OF HUMANISM IN 1980S CHINA

The articulation of humanism has been a recurrent theme historically in various genres of Chinese literature and the arts. One such well-known case is the classic sixteenth-century novel, *Journey to the West* (*Xi you ji* 西遊記), which stresses the issues of freedom, standing up to unjust authority, the loss of belief, and the importance of self-direction. Latterly, adaptations from this novel have continued to hint at a strong desire for humanist expression, even during periods when China has seen tight central governance. A recent interpretation with nationwide impact, particularly among young people, is the online novel *Wu Kong's Biography* (*Wukong zhuan* 悟空傳, written by Zeng Yu 曾雨, pseudonym Jin Hezai 今何在, 2016, originally published online in installments in 2000) (Liao, 2017). The great popularity of the novel led to the release of a film version, *Wu Kong*, in 2017. This movie's theme song "Equaling Heaven" ("Qi tian" 齊天, composed and sung by Hua Chenyu 華晨宇, lyrics by Jin Hezai) became a real hit in the Chinese popular music scene. It was also performed by the Tibetan singer Zahi Bingzuo 紮西平措, the 2017 winner of *The Voice of China* (*Zhongguo hao shengyin* 中國好聲音) in his final song-battle in that show (Qian, 2017: 57–58), and again by Hua Chenyu himself in the TV talent show *Singer* (*Geshou* 歌手) in 2018. The humanism articulated in the song lyrics closely matches that of the novels and movie:

> The young and wild don't want to live in vain,
> Who will give me something to believe in? ...
> I can still smile ...
> What is fate? I say fate is determined by the heart.[1]

Humanist articulations are part of a trend in Chinese pop song that dates back to the 1980s, when that genre first re-appeared as an indigenous entertainment genre within China. As the decade was a transitional phrase, during which multiple pre-existing and newly emerging social, political, and cultural forces came into negotiation with one other, it's not surprising that the pop songs of this time drew on varied musical and cultural inspirations.[2] Indeed the ideas of humanism were actively brought forward by two generations of pop musicians, one middle-aged and the other younger, as an articulation of their generational identities.[3] This chapter explores the contribution these pop musicians made in seeking to balance self-expressiveness and political engagement in a nation gradually materializing from a long revolutionary period but not yet fully integrated into cultural and commercial globalization. How did these musicians narrate humanist issues—such as personal choice, the questioning of one's beliefs, and the role of self-direction—in pop songs?

The 1980s generally saw Chinese intellectuals place great emphasis on new practices in cultural fields. The wider attempt to push China into modernization drove intellectuals to search for the cultural causes that had resulted in backwardness in the economy, politics, science, and technology (Gan, 2006: 4). Among the various types of cultural ethos that exerted major influence on Chinese intellectuals and associated musicians were an existing Marxist humanism and the newly imported existential humanism of Jean-Paul Sartre (Lin and Li, 1994).

While Marxist humanism emphasized historical determination and objectivity, Sartre characterizes existential humanism as "the relation of transcendence as constitutive of man with subjectivity," adding that "what is at the very heart and centre of existentialism, is the absolute character of the free commitment, by which every man realises himself in realising a type of humanity" (1973: 47). The Chinese translators of Sartre's work argued that existential humanism encouraged and inspired European intellectuals spiritually as they recovered from the trauma of World War II (Zhou and Tang, 1988: 2), hinting that it might hold the same function for Chinese intellectuals after their long suffering during the Cultural Revolution. Much literature produced during the period, particularly the movement of Scar Literature (*shanghen wenxue* 傷痕文學), echoed this ideological trend, showing the importance of the "creative self" and of the expression of an "un-alienated" human nature (*ren xing* 人性) (Wang, 1996: 32, 34). Instances include the novels *Teacher in Charge of a Class* (*Banzhuren* 班主任) (Liu, 1979) and *Stones in the Wall* (*Ren a, ren* 人啊, 人) (Dai, 1980).

In fact, the contesting of individualism in existential humanism and collectivism in Marxist humanism appears as a main characteristic in the humanist articulation in the field of culture at this time. As pointed out by Barmé, "During the 1980s, the issue of individualism—the philosophical and political importance of the autonomous self—enjoyed only a short period of relatively open contention... and... provoked government bans and denunciations from 1983 onward" (1999: 239). Chinese readers from the beginning learned that Sartre's philosophy was controversial. For instance, it propagated self-transcendence and self-realization, emphasizing subjectivity rather than the objectivity of the Marxist humanism that was dominant in China (Wang, 1996: 28). Those radical intellectuals who advocated existential humanism thus aroused severe criticism from those responsible for orthodox ideological policy. Nevertheless, irrespective of the underlying difference between Marxist and existential humanist ideologies, a main tendency for Chinese intellectuals in this decade was to turn to humanism to relieve their memories of suffering and to emancipate themselves from their own feelings of alienation.

THE RISE OF HUMANISM IN 1980S CHINESE POP SONGS

The composer Fu Lin 付林, active in Chinese popular-music circles since the 1980s, described the composers in his generation as used to writing songs with "conceptual words" (*gainian ci* 概念詞) (Fu Lin, interview, Beijing, September 1, 2008). Fu's notion of "conceptual words" here has a double meaning. It has a strong association with the symbolic words used in revolutionary songs; for instance, the revolutionary youth very often used the symbolism of the sun to hint at their passion for Chairman Mao (Wagner, 1995). Its second meaning points to Chinese traditional literati aesthetics, where it was also customary to objectify emotions through use of such metaphors. An example is found in this excerpt from the lyrics of "The Sentiment of the Leaves for the Root" ("Lüye dui gende qingyi" 綠葉對根的情誼, 1986):[4]

Do not ask me where I am going,	*Buyao wen wo dao nali qu,*
my heart longs for you;	*wode xin yizhe ni;*
...	...
I am one of your leaves,	*Wo shi nide yi pian lüye,*
My root is in your soil,	*wode gen zai nide tudi,*

Fu understood the rock song "I Have Nothing" ("Yi wu suo you" 壹無所有, 1986) by Cui Jian 崔健, the most influential rock musician of the 1980s, as signifying a breakthrough in the way "conceptual words" were used to express emotion as occurring in a state of direct "outcry." Although Cui himself has stated that "I Have Nothing" is merely a male-female love song, this piece has been widely taken by Chinese scholars as emblematic of humanist expression in 1980s' pop songs, pointing to its messages of human nature, existence, and self-consciousness (Jin Zhaojun 金兆钧, interview, Beijing, August 23, 2008). It was also taken by several Western scholars as a marginal cultural expression that contained an anti-state message. For instance, Baranovitch interprets the title phrase, "I have nothing," as the articulation of spiritual and material impoverishment of Cui's disillusioned generation (2003: 32–33), and Jones hears it as an allegory of the deprivation of the generation's emotional and political rights (1992: 137):

> I want to give you my aspiration,   *Wo yao gei ni wode zhuiqiu,*
> and my freedom,   *haiyou wode ziyou.*
> but you always laugh at me,   *ke ni que zongshi xiao wo,*
> saying I have nothing.   *yi wu suo you.* (Ling, 1994: 409)

Yet, in pointing to Cui as countercultural antihero and breakthrough songwriter, current research apparently neglects several pre-existing and newly emergent pop-song genres that also signal the rise of humanism in the decade. Compared to an older generation who had been taught to devote themselves to serve the nation through personal sacrifice, the young generation appeared to doubt the value of this devotion after their exposure to the influence of Western humanism. The various newly emerged song genres during the period represent the ways young musicians articulated humanism in their evolving understandings. Significantly, these songs mostly appeared within mainstream expressive culture and attempted "positive" political engagement. Examples explored in more depth in this chapter are a pop-style lyrical song (*shuqing gequ* 抒情歌曲)[5] "Blood-Stained Dignity" ("Xuerande fengcai" 血染的風采, 1986), a public-welfare song (*gongyi gequ* 公益歌曲) "Fill the World with Love" ("Rang shijie chongman ai" 讓世界充滿愛, 1986), and a "northwest wind" song (*xibei feng* 西北風) "My Beloved Hometown" ("Wo reliande guxiang" 我熱戀的故鄉, 1987).[6]

Signaling Humanist Transition: "Blood-Stained Dignity"

"Blood-Stained Dignity" was a state-commissioned song written in 1986 to commemorate the soldiers who died in the Sino-Vietnamese War (1979–91). Instead of the middle-aged musicians usually assigned to write official songs, it was written by two young men, the musician Su Yue 蘇越 and the lyricist Chen Zhe 陳哲. Chen had lost a close friend in that war. For this reason, the lyrics had actually been finished before the song was formally commissioned (Chen Zhe, interview, Beijing, December 29, 2009). The content of the song can be read as a conversation between a couple about to be separated. In verse 1 (excepted below), the soldier comforts his partner, telling her not to be sorrowful if he dies because he will have devoted his love to his country. (In verse 2, the woman answers she will not be sad if it happens because she understands his devotion.)

> I may not be back anymore   *Ruguo wo gao bie,*
> after I say goodbye,   *jiang buzai huilai,*
> Can you understand?   *ni shifou lijie?*
> Can you understand?   *ni shifou mingbai?* (Li, 1992: 183–184)

Publicized as an official song, this piece was first performed at the 1987 Chinese Spring Festival Party. Xu Liang 徐良, the male singer, was a surviving hero from the war. In the performance, Xu wore an army uniform and sat in a wheelchair, prominently displaying the fact that he had lost a leg. Although Xu's singing was consistent with the official-song style—which he had trained in as a student at the Sichuan Conservatory of Music—his facial expressions were unlike those of such professional musicians, whose actions are normally somewhat exaggerated onstage. Plain and restrained, his eyes shining with tears, Xu's performance reminded the audiences that they were encountering a real story with real emotions. Meanwhile, the female singer Wang Hong 王虹, who had just won the 1986 National Young Singers TV Competition, wore a sober dark suit rather than her usual stage costumes, and her singing style and stage movements also showed an attempt to imitate the official-song style. Behind them, seven men in white clothes, danced with red Chinese national flags, circling the stage. The whole performance emanated a strong state-sponsored flavor.

Musically speaking, "Blood-Stained Dignity" has an origin in the lyrical songs of the 1950s, appearing as an example of a de-localized Chinese folk-song style in which specific local origins are hard to distinguish (Fu Lin, interview, Beijing, September 1, 2008). It meanwhile adds characteristics of pop song in its compositional technique, vocal style, and arrangement, which altogether suggest a sorrowful mood. This is achieved in the melodic line in the first part, which remains simple, moving by small intervals. The phrases are short and neat, using a rhythmic mode (Figure 17.1) and its variants (see the vocal part in Figure 17.2); they repeat the 2+2+4 phrase mode of measures 9 to 16 as the music for measures 17 to 24. In measures 9 to 10 and 13 to 14, the melody outlines minor

FIGURE 17.1. Rhythmic mode in "Blood-Stained Dignity."

FIGURE 17.2. "Blood-Stained Dignity," measures 1–24 (Li, 1992: 183–84).

FIGURE 17.3. Voice and *erhu* interaction in "Blood-Stained Dignity," measures 13–20.

triads. The melodic progression mainly remains stable, avoiding big leaps. Exceptions appear only when the lyrics pose the questions "Can you understand?" and "Will you expect me forever?" (Figure 17.2, measures 13–14, 21–22), where octave leaps are used to suggest restrained sorrow. The Chinese two-stringed fiddle *erhu* 二胡 always appears at the ends of phrases, where it varies the melody of the phrase (Figure 17.3). The sorrowful timbre of the *erhu* enhances the sad feeling between the couple. Besides the clear melodic line, it is hard to hear an accompanying texture of harmony, which strengthens the narrative and lyrical function of the song.[7]

Unlike typical works in the official-song category, "Blood-Stained Dignity" maintains a gentle and calm tone to narrate the mood of its military subject. More conventionally in revolutionary films and songs, such themes are treated affirmatively and forcibly through vigorous sounds and exaggerated images, suggesting that heroic triumph is about to unfold from concerted action. Yet China has a long history of describing a wider set of heroic archetypes and valuing the spiritual qualities of a real hero. In 96 BCE, for instance, the historian Sima Qian wrote in the "Biographies of Assassins" ("Cike liezhuan" 刺客列傳) section of the *Historical Records* (*Shiji*, 史記): "The desolate gale freezes River Yi. The doomed hero has made his death wish" (1989: 895). This same kind of death wish is expressed in a very calm and elegant way in "Blood-Stained Dignity," as its lyricist Chen Zhe explained:

> I thought, "Don't be so stupid, don't be so false, people are not so noble. They just do what they have to do." It [going to the battlefield] was for our home [nation], for everyone.... In such a moment, the strong power that belongs to a man is revealed, very plain, but very determined. After the Tiananmen demonstrations, I realized that it was a kind of high, lofty human nature that the Chinese people pursued at that time. (Chen Zhe, interview, Beijing, December 29, 2009)

If many soldiers in the front line of the war thought this song expressed the real feeling and meaning they experienced when they faced death, the song's combination of seemingly authentic human expression and message of lofty beliefs in fighting for justice endowed it with a blurred patriotic meaning that extended beyond its original propagandistic function in relation to the Sino-Vietnamese war and allowed singers and listeners alike to draw new meanings over time from the second section of its lyrics: "If it happens, do not be sorrowful, the flag of the republic shows our blood-stained dignity." For instance, in the 1989 Tiananmen demonstrations, when soldiers and students fought one another, both groups sang this song, each believing that they were sacrificing themselves for the greater benefit of the nation.[8]

In the social background of the mid- and late 1980s, using a grief-stricken tone to express patriotism not only brought Chinese audiences to recall the suffering they had endured during the Cultural Revolution but also functioned as a way for them to question the unacceptable realities of the present. Intellectual groups were worried both by the backward economy as compared to that of the Western world and by the decline in culture as compared to China's previous history. Feeling sorrow for the decline of the nation rather than for individual suffering obviously draws on the ideology and values of the traditional Chinese literati. The highly controversial TV documentary series *River Elegy* (*He shang* 河殤) (Su and Wang, 1988) explains why they conceived this pessimistic and sorrowful mood.

> Nowadays, the intellectuals are finally getting rid of the stigma of the "stinking ninth" (*chou laojiu* 臭老九).[9] Their social status seems much higher than before. But poor economic conditions and spiritual depression and distortion still accompany them. Did spiritual depression result from the turbulent modern history or the poverty and backwardness during recent decades? They may not be the only causes. Behind them, it is the spiritual pain of the nation. The whole pain is for the decline of civilization.[10]

Finding a Universal Language: "Fill the World with Love"

Another officially approved song, "Fill the World with Love" was written to celebrate the International Year of Peace in 1986, directly inspired by the pop song from the United States, "We Are the World" (1985) and the subsequent Taiwanese version "Tomorrow Will Be Better" ("Mingtian hui geng hao" 明天會更好, 1985). The head editor of China Audio and Video Head Office (Zhongguo Luyin Luxiang Chuban Zongshe), Wu Haigang 吳海崗, invited a composition group to write lyrics for this purpose. The assigned team copied the aim of raising money for public welfare and the group-singing format of these two song examples (Chen Zhe, interview, December 29, 2009). This song was designed to be performed by 108 pop singers, the first time a big group of pop singers had gathered together in any such official performance (You, 2019: 346).[11]

Its published notation names five lyricists: Chen Zhe, lyricist of "Blood-Stained Dignity," was overall coordinator; Guo Feng 郭峰 gave advice on revisions; Sun Ming 孫銘 and Liu Xiaolin 劉小林 each contributed to several lines of Part I of the song; and Wang Jian 王健, the only middle-aged composer in the team, provided a draft, of which only the title was finally retained (Lin, 1994: 665).[12] The practice of "collective composition" was commonly found during the Cultural Revolution and has multiple meanings in the Chinese context, but its prime aim was to avoid any emergence of a distinctive musical style belonging to any particular composer or area and thereby enhance the official song's supposedly universal national characteristics.

Because four out of the five composition members were young musicians, "Fill the World with Love" was positioned as an articulation of the younger generation during the mid-1980s. Following a long period of spiritual suffering during the Cultural Revolution and in the quickly changing social transformations that ensued from the subsequent "reform and opening-up" policy, many Chinese welcomed the opportunity to introspect on the past and look for spiritual guidance as to where they should go (Xu Peidong 徐沛東, interview, Beijing, August 27, 2008). Members of the younger generation conceived a feeling of loss and a concomitant need for self-comfort and self-direction. Chen Zhe added his own words on this point:

> At that time, [the spirit] of young people was wandering.... [The revolutionary faith of] Mao Zedong was gone and the new belief hadn't been set yet.... The temporary small shops run by entrepreneurs crowded across the square outside People's Hall. They hosted different exhibitions and sold clothes. That was the general scene at the time. That means all things belonging to the past were gone. Unlike today, at that time, you were not someone, you were nothing. (Chen Zhe, interview, Beijing, December 29, 2009)

To accommodate these thoughts, this song was designed as a large-scale song suite of 16 minutes and 45 seconds, far longer than the average pop song. Its overall structure of three parts can be heard as a narrative of the whole experience of the transitional period. Part I (see Figure 17.4) expresses retrospection on past experiences, referring to the Cultural Revolution. Here, phrases like "far away," "decades before," and "the past is already behind us" refer to the attitude of the young generation toward a painful collective memory, suggesting people's spirits were gradually recovering from the destructiveness of the Cultural Revolution. Part II opens with a very soft and delicate description of the people's efforts at mutual comfort, which points out the needs of the current generation. The song's use of a chorus suggests the role of social cohesion, in helping the young generation to heal their gloomy memories of the past, and shares their experiences more collectively with audiences who may have had common experiences. Part III uses a lively tone to depict a future scenario in which everyone will share true love. Here, the sentence "let the world fill with true love" is repeated several times, to stress the main theme—of conceiving love—to finish the whole narrative.

In contrast to official songs of a previous era that loudly declaim hate (for class enemies or other targets) or love (for Communist leaders or labor heroes), the song relied on gentle and calm means of expression. In Part II, for example, the instrumentation maintains a quiet and soft feeling, avoiding a dense texture or an assertive arrangement in the melody.[13] A four-bar piano introduction features three descending pentatonic-scale steps. Verse I—sung by all the children and female singers—maintains

Part I

(Verse)

When I think back, it seems far away,	*Xiangqilai shi nayang yaoyuan,*
as if it happened decades before,	*fangfu dou yishi congqian,*
the dream has never been broken,	*na buceng pomiede menghuan,*
it is still deep inside my heart.	*yiran yincangzai xinjian.*
Who is it calling without words,	*Shi shui zai momo huhuan,*
triggering the passion in our hearts,	*jiqile xinzhongde bolan,*
we may never realize,	*yexu hai cong wei ganjue,*
the past is already behind us.	*women yijing zouguo zuotian.*

(Chorus)

O, year by year,	*O, yinian you yinian,*
we move toward tomorrow,	*o, women zou xiang mingtian,*
...	...

Part II

(Verse)

Gently placing my hands on your face,	*Qingqingde pengzhe nide lian,*
to wipe away your tears;	*wei ni ba yanlei ca gan;*
my heart belongs to you forever,	*zhe ke xin yongyuan shuyu ni,*
which tells me I am not alone.	*gaosu wo buzai gudan.*
Gazing deeply in your eyes,	*Shenshende ningwang nide yan,*
without needing to say any more;	*bu xuyao gengduode yuyan;*
holding your hand tightly,	*jinjinde wozhu nide shou,*
this warmth still does not change.	*zhe wennuan yijiu wei gaibian.*

FIGURE 17.4. Lyrics to "Fill the World with Love" (Lin, 1994: 667–70).

(repeat once)

(Chorus)

We share the joy,	*Women tong huanle,*
we share the suffering,	*women tong renshou,*
we have the same expectation;	*women huaizhe tongyangde qidai*
we share wind and rain,	*women gong fengyu,*
we share the aspiration,	*women gong zhuiqiu,*
we treasure the same love.	*Women zhengcun tongyiyangde ai.*
Regardless whether acquainted or not,	*Wulun ni wo ke ceng xiangshi,*
regardless near or far away,	*wulun zai yanqian zai tianbian,*
bless you sincerely,	*zhenxinde wei ni zhuyuan,*
may you be happy and secure.	*zhuyuan ni xingfu ping'an.*

(repeat once)

Part III

(Verse I)

You are coming and he is coming,	*Ni zou lai, ta zou lai,*
we are coming together,	*women zoudao yiqi lai,*
in the colorful world,	*zai zhe bingfende shijie li,*
we feel thrilled.	*xinchao zai pengpai.*
You are coming and he is coming,	*Ni zou lai, ta zou lai,*
we are coming together,	*dajia zou dao yiqi lai,*
in the colorful world,	*zai zhe bingfende shijie li,*
there is infinite love.	*you wuxiande ai.*

(Chorus)

Ah, let the world,	*A, rang zhe shijie,*
fill with true love,	*you zhenxinde ai,*
ah, let the world,	*a, rang zhe shijie,*
be full of sentiment and love.	*chongman qing he ai.*

(repeated once in verses I and II, and three times in verse III)

Ah, year by year,	*A, yi nian you yi nian,*
Ah, we welcome tomorrow	*A, women yingjie mingtian.*

(repeated four times)

FIGURE 17.4. Continued

a very stable and smooth vocal line, over a simple piano accompaniment that provides an arpeggio at the end of each word. The melody and arrangement of the interlude are the same as those of the introduction. String instruments play sustained chords on the first beat of every measure. As a whole, every aspect of the music, from its arrangement to its vocal style, contributes to sustaining the intended soft, gentle, and smooth feeling.

As the performance of the song would be the first time young pop musicians would lend their voices to an officially approved public event like this in China, the senior administrators in the China Audio and Video Head Office reminded the composition team about the political sensitivity of the song, mentioning that it would need approval by state cultural officers in advance of the performance. To address such a political demand, the songwriters adopted the theme of love, which was already accepted both by an older generation, who stood in a dominant political position, and by a younger generation, who were eager to voice their real feelings. The theme of love acted as a cohesive force for both generations, even though they may have brought different understandings and interpretations to the term "love" itself. The older generation was accustomed to the concept of love being directed toward the Communist Party, the nation, or one's career aspirations and treated mainly as a lofty kind of love. The young musicians, meanwhile, were pursuing a kind of general love among human beings, which included mutual love, care, trust, and help; the love they envisaged also extended to the celebration of self-identity and of the value of the individual, two notions that had long been targets of oppression and alienation.

Another cohesive facet of the song among these prospective listeners was its combination of the signs of individual and collective ideologies. Reviewing the lyrics shows this fusion of individualism ("I," "my," "your," "you," and "he") and collectivism ("we," "share," and "world"). Moreover, even the singular terms can be interpreted as referring to the whole generation rather than to just one person or group. Hearing the lyrics this way draws on a point made by two Western scholars in their analyses of Cui Jian's "I Have Nothing." In his analysis, Andrew Jones argues that, "The singer's 'I' becomes *our* 'I,' and then merges with a collective 'we' " (1992: 138). Timothy Brace also suggests that substituting "We have nothing" for "I have nothing" at each occurrence of the lyric describes "the feeling of today's Chinese youth" (1991: 63, 54). This way of listening links songs like "I Have Nothing" and "Fill the World with Love" to an ideology already apparent in revolutionary songs: the leftist songwriters of the 1930s "almost invariably chose to write of the struggles of workers, oppressed women, and exploited children in terms of a collective 'we' " (Jones, 2001: 123).

The first live performance of the song in Beijing Worker's Stadium also suggests such an incorporation of individualism and collectivism. Given a chance to show their personal styles, singers were arranged to take turns singing each line in the verses of Parts I and III. The different vocal styles can be heard in these solos, including the rougher sonorities of rock, the thinner and more nasal timbres used in folk song, and a vocality typical of Western and Chinese pop. The singers were arranged seemingly randomly on the stage, rather than in a neat line or in clear order. Some had the most fashionable hairstyles at that time, and some wore sunglasses. After every short solo, the live audience of more than ten thousand warmly cheered. All these factors emphasized each singer's individuality.[14] To build a collective identity, meanwhile, all the singers wore identical jackets—males in yellow and females in pink—with an identical T-shirt underneath. In the chorus sections, the singers downplayed their personal styles to produce a blended, harmonious sound. The male performers stood shoulder to shoulder, and the female performers held hands with each other. Most of them lifted their arms together at the end.

"Fill the World with Love" was the beginning of a new genre of public-welfare songs, one that addresses the goodwill of the general population toward the rebuilding of shared ethical values and spiritual needs. Similar songs afterward include "The Devotion of Love" ("Aide fengxian" 愛的奉獻, 1989), "Longing" ("Kewang" 渴望, 1990), and "Peace be with You" ("Zhu ni ping'an" 祝妳平安, 1996).[15]

Healing Historical Scars: "My Beloved Hometown"

Unlike both "Blood-Stained Dignity" and "Fill the World with Love," the "northwest wind" song "My Beloved Hometown" came from a non-official context. However, the song shares characteristics with those others written during this transitional period, providing a third perspective on the ways that 1980s songwriters handled the juxtaposition and negotiation of individual desires and social forces. Having a sense of Scar Literature is a way to understand the seemingly contradictory expressions of "northwest wind" songs. Scar Literature is a style that emerged at the end of the 1970s and has been described as being largely negative in portraying the sufferings and trauma of educated people during the Cultural Revolution (Chen, 1996: 160–61). To a large extent, the genre was tolerated and accepted by the Chinese Communist Party because its prime concerns are love and faith; its practitioners "embraced love as a key to solving social problems" (Liu, 2003: 24).

Like Scar Literature, "northwest wind" songs were strongly affected by the established expressions of Socialist Realism, which encouraged them to adopt a positive stance from which to praise the much-enhanced material conditions of the 1980s as compared with those of before 1949 or, subsequently, during the Cultural Revolution. Songs like "My Beloved Hometown" shift to a worried tone when faced with portraying the reality of underdevelopment, which has been read as endowing the song with an anti-state political meaning by several Western scholars (for instance, Brace, 1992: 162). Indeed, the first part of the lyrics directly describes the hometown as a poor rural place with low straw huts, bitter well water, and a small dry stream. The northwestern folk vocal style plus the timbre of the Chinese traditional double-reed instrument *suona* 嗩吶 strengthen the feeling of desolation:

My hometown is not at all beautiful,	*Wode jiaxiang bing bu mei,*
low straw huts and bitter well water,	*di'aide cao fang kusede jing shui,*
one small stream that often gets dry,	*yitiao shichang ganhede xiao he,*

I continue to long for the small village.　　*yilianzai xiao cun zhouwei.* (Lin, 1994: 534–36; English translation from Baranovitch, 2003: 21)

Such concerns were familiar to the songwriters and those around them too. "My Beloved Hometown" was written in a private music salon called Damucang 大木倉沙龍 in 1987.[16] Before the draft of the lyrics was shown to other musicians, the salon's manager Liu Weiren 劉偉仁 approached the lyricist Meng Guangzheng (Figure 17.5) to check whether he dared to release such a work. Meng explained: "I visited my wife's hometown, and I found it didn't look as beautiful as I had been told. But I wish the village can become pretty." The composer Xu Peidong (Figure 17.6) was interested in the draft. In their collaboration, the lyricist and musician incorporated the multiple ideologies of the time into the song in a way that they hoped might not raise

FIGURE 17.5. Meng Guangzheng in Damucang salon (© Liu Weiren, used by permission).

FIGURE 17.6. Xu Peidong (right) in Damucang salon

(© Liu Weiren, used by permission).

official objections but would nevertheless develop a new pop-song style. For instance, the first line of the lyrics was originally, "My hometown is not such a beautiful place" using the word "place" (*difang* 地方). Yet "place" was a keyword in official songs, such as "In the Place of Peach Blossoms in Full Bloom" ("Zai na taohua shengkaide difang" 在那桃花盛開的地方), where it always carried a positive gloss. In order to avoid running counter to that official norm, Xu Peidong changed the phrase to be more straightforward: "My hometown is not at all beautiful" (Xu Peidong, interview, Beijing, August 27, 2008).

Meng and Xu also took efforts in the song to adopt the overall shape of Socialist Realist artworks, in which, as noted, a negative opening can be deployed if it is followed by a more positive presentation of mainstream ideology. Thus, in Part II of the song, and after a slow and sentimental salute, "O, hometown, hometown," the feeling shifts to the expression of deep sentiments for the hometown: "I kiss and kiss the soil of my hometown never too much; I love and love the water of my hometown never too much." This transition was then followed by a slogan-like expression: "I will use my sincerity and perspiration, to change you into a fertile land with beautiful water." The music suggests the same contradiction. Although the beginning seems to express a worrying and sad feeling, the main arrangement uses a happy, disco-oriented rhythm.[17] Overall, this song suggests that the listener can expect a happy and promising future if they apply love and faith to any current worrying realities; thus the song identifies itself as mainstream, albeit a new way of working with those values and symbols.

These features of "My Beloved Hometown" are typical of the other "northwest wind" songs: two-part lyrics, with the larger early part expressing worry and sadness and the final part positively embracing the future; a combination of a sad, nostalgic melodic tone and a contemporary, upbeat rhythmic mode and instrumentation. For instance, "The Moon of the Fifteenth Is Rounder Than That of the Sixteenth" ("Shiwude yueliang shiliu yuan" 十五的月亮十六圓, 1987) and "Yellow Plateau" ("Huang tu gao po" 黃土高坡, 1988) both echo these same general social concepts of universal love and revolutionary faith.

Conclusion: Breakthrough as a "New" Mainstream

The emergence of individualism in the pop songs of the 1980s marks the rise of humanism in China and shows that it extended significantly beyond the minority musical space of rock music. In contrast to a collectivist ideology in which people were expected to behave in set ways, putting the homeland and the party line above their personal doubts or desires, pop musicians created a new narrative that offered comfort with regard to the painful memories and spiritual wounds of the past. The songs explored in this chapter—"Blood-Stained Dignity," "Fill the World with Love," and "My Beloved Hometown"—indicate how these musicians projected their feelings of sadness, confusion, and worry in a calm, soft, and direct way, and their emergent articulation of self-direction can be seen as an important indicator of how Chinese intellectuals of that period hoped to find and build a new future for themselves and for the nation by enlisting mainstream expressive and political channels. They thus stand apart from songs like "I Have Nothing," which shared the same ideological position but did not present collaboration with mainstream state forces as a means forward.

With the tumultuous events of June 1989, these collaborative dreams were for the most part shattered, and the pop-music mainstream in China turned slowly but inexorably toward commercial-entertainment ends, but, for a few years in the late 1980s, pop musicians' songs pushed onto the political stage. They enabled young people to assert their equality with the older generation and began to take over the function of revolutionary songs in embracing social issues, ideological connections, and spiritual guidance. For instance, immediately after the premiere of "Fill the World with Love" on May 9, 1986, an official newspaper assessed the performance as a political articulation of important social issues, gathering together pop singers who, it claimed, usually behaved like "a heap of loose sand."[18] Following this official statement on the song, music critics and scholars began to re-evaluate the role of pop songs. For instance, the scholar Liang

Maochun claimed that "Pop [*tongsu* 通俗] songs are best suited to expressing the key issues of the times, including political issues" (Liang, 1987).

The content assessed here may help address Western misapprehensions of the history of Chinese music, which can both overestimate the social impact of rock and under-recognize the progressive political content of certain mainstream songs in the mid- and late 1980s. It also suggests that it may be worth a close look at examples of mainstream popular music of other periods and the ways these reflect (or deny) the ideologies of their creators and draw together (or propel apart) different generations of listeners. Chinese intellectuals may no longer be setting the pace in mainstream songwriting, and the social disruption of the Cultural Revolution is certainly receding, but this does not automatically mean that those writing and performing subsequent sets of repertory possess less complicated ideologies or future ambitions.

Glossary

"Aide fengxian" 愛的奉獻, "The Devotion of Love," popular song of the public-welfare type (1989)
Cai Guoxing 蔡國慶, singer (b. 1966)
Chen Zhe 陳哲, lyricist (b. 1955)
chou laojiu 臭老九, "stinking ninth," label given to intellectuals during the Cultural Revolution
Cui Jian 崔健, singer and songwriter (b. 1961)
Damucang 大木倉沙龍, Beijing music salon (mid-1980s)
difang 地方, place
erhu 二胡, two-stringed fiddle
Fu Lin 付林, composer (b. 1946)
gainian ci 概念詞, "conceptual words," specific song lyrics that symbolize and objectify emotion
gang tai gequ 港臺歌曲, popular songs from Hong Kong and Taiwan
Geshou 歌手, *Singer* (formerly *Wo shi geshou* 我是歌手, *I Am a Singer*) TV show (first aired 2013)
gongyi gequ 公益歌曲, public-welfare song genre (1980s)
Gu Jianfen 谷建芬, composer (b. 1935)
Guo Feng 郭峰, singer and songwriter (b. 1962)
He shang 河殤, *River Elegy*, TV series (1988)
Hua Chenyu 華晨宇, singer and songwriter (b. 1990)
"Huang tu gao po" 黃土高坡, "Yellow Plateau," popular song (1988)
Huang Shiqi 黃奇石, songwriter (b. 1940s)
Jin Hezai 今何在, pseudonym of online novelist Zeng Yu 曾雨 (b. 1977)
Jin Zhaojun 金兆鈞, music critic (b. 1958)
"Kewang" 渴望, "Longing," popular song of the public-welfare type (1990)
Lei Lei 雷蕾, songwriter (b. 1952)
Liu Qing 劉青, composer (b. 1960s)
Liu Shizhao 劉詩召, composer (b. 1936)
Liu Weiren 劉偉仁, manager of Damucang salon (active 1980s)
Liu Xiaolin 劉小林, lyricist (b. 1950s)
"Lüye dui gende qingyi" 綠葉對根的情誼, "The Sentiment of the Leaves for the Root," popular song, music by Gu Jianfen and lyrics by Wang Jian (1986)

Mao Aming 毛阿敏, singer (b. 1963)
"Mingtian hui geng hao" 明天會更好, "Tomorrow Will Be Better," Taiwanese popular song (1985)
"Qi tian" 齊天, "Equaling Heaven," movie theme song (2017)
qingchu jingshen wuran 清除精神污染, "resist spiritual pollution," political campaign (1983–84)
"Rang shijie chongman ai" 讓世界充滿愛, "Fill the World with Love," popular song (1986)
ren xing 人性, human nature
shanghen wenxue 傷痕文學, Scar Literature, genre recounting sufferings of the Cultural Revolution period (initiated late 1970s)
Shiji 史記, *Historical Records*, compiled by Sima Qian
"Shiwude yueliang shiliu yuan" 十五的月亮十六圓, "The Moon of the Fifteenth Is Rounder Than That of the Sixteenth," popular song (1987)
shuqing gequ 抒情歌曲, folk and lyrical song genre
Sima Qian 司馬遷, historian (*c*. 145–87 BCE)
Su Yue 蘇越, composer (*c*. 1955–2018)
Sun Ming 孫銘, lyricist (b. 1950s)
Sun Yue 孫悅, singer (b. 1972)
suona 嗩吶, double-reed instrument
tongsu 通俗, popular song genre
Wang Hong 王虹, singer (active 1980s)
Wang Jian 王健, lyricist (b. 1928–2021)
Wei Wei 韋唯, singer (b. 1963)
"Wo reliande guxiang" 我熱戀的故鄉, "My Beloved Hometown," popular song (1987)
Wu Haigang 吳海岗, editor at China Audio and Video (b. 1950s)
Wukong zhuan 悟空傳, *Biography of Wu Kong*, online novel by Jin Hezai and film (2000, 2017 respectively)
xibei feng 西北風, "northwest wind," popular song genre
Xi you ji 西遊記, *Journey to the West*, classic novel by Wu Cheng'en (*c*. 1592)
Xu Liang 徐良, singer (b. 1961)
Xu Peidong 徐沛東, composer (b. 1954)
"Xuerande fengcai" 血染的風采, "Blood-Stained Dignity," popular song (1986)
Yi Ming 易茗, lyricist (b. 1952)
"Yi wu suo you" 壹無所有, "I Have Nothing," popular song by Cui Jian (1986)
Yishu rensheng 藝術人生, *Life of an Artist*, China Central TV program (2012)
Zahi Bingzuo 紮西平措, Tibetan singer (b. 1986)
"Zai na taohua shengkaide difang" 在那桃花盛開的地方, "In the Place of Peach Blossoms in Full Bloom," popular song (1980)
Zhongguo hao shengyin 中國好聲音, *The Voice of China*, TV show (first aired, 2012)
"Zhu ni ping'an" 祝妳平安, "Peace be with You," popular song of the public-welfare type (1996)

Notes

1. All translations of song titles, lyrics, related interview notes, and TV documents, are the author's own, unless stated otherwise.
2. Chinese pop songs of the 1980s were close but not identical to Western pop songs at that time. Melodically, these songs were rooted in the Chinese folk song and lyrical song (*shuqing gequ*), which were well known in the revolutionary era and earlier, for instance, in

the adoption of a de-localized traditional music style and a preference for high pitches and fast speeds. Meanwhile, they were rhythmically and instrumentally updated to Western popular-music ideals to appeal to the interests and aesthetics of ordinary people. As such, the 1980s pop songs can be seen as transitional between the style of the lyrical songs of the revolutionary era and the more radically Westernized pop song styles of the 1990s and afterward.

3. The middle-aged musicians were those born in the 1930s and 1940s, and they introduced and launched local pop-music writing in the early 1980s. Their works combined the melodic writing of revolutionary songs with some aspects of Western pop music in rhythm, vocal style, or instrumentation. On this foundation and with the support of the middle-aged musicians, a younger generation of pop musicians (born in the 1950s and 1960s) emerged from the mid-1980s onward.
4. A cipher notation is available at 绿叶对根的情意_简谱_搜谱网 (sooopu.com), accessed Jan 3, 2023.
5. Generally speaking, official lyrical song during the 1980s developed from the lyrical songs of the 1950s and 1960s, which emphasized emotional expression, showing this characteristic via expressive melodies and highly skilled compositional synthesis of Chinese classical music, traditional folk music, and Western musical techniques. The lyrics usually praise the prosperity of the nation and the people's merits (Qian, 2011: 46–58, 253).
6. "Blood-Stained Dignity" was written in 1986, with lyrics by Chen Zhe and music by Su Yue. The term "northwest wind" refers to the style of northwestern China. The genre combines folk characteristics (mainly melodic patterns and vocal delivery) of the region with a strong, fast, disco-rock beat in the "easy listening" style typical of the so-called *gang tai* 港臺歌曲 pop songs of Hong Kong and Taiwan during this period (Baranovitch, 2003: 19).
7. The notation in Figures 17.1–17.3 is transcribed from a live performance at the televised 1987 Spring Festival celebrations, on YouTube, https://www.youtube.com/watch?v=4ka-zqQ5vHI, accessed December 16, 2020.
8. This description stems from documentaries on the Tiananmen Square protests and also from interviews with musicians who have claimed they were onsite during the protests.
9. "Stinking ninth" was a term of abuse applied by ultra-leftists to educated people, especially during the Cultural Revolution; see Schwarcz (1994: 177).
10. The team also produced a book of the same title (Su and Wang, 1988). *River Elegy* is available for viewing on YouTube, at https://www.youtube.com/watch?v=YpCmGc7AP1Q; this statement occurs at 1:46:56, accessed December 14, 2020.
11. In a campaign of 1983–84, "resist spiritual pollution" (*qingchu jingshen wuran* 清除精神污染), there was a rule that no more than three popular musicians were allowed to play in any official performance.
12. Wang Jian was also the lyricist of "The Sentiment of the Leaves for the Root," discussed above. It is interesting to note that the song's romantic title ("Fill the World with Love") came from this middle-aged woman rather than from any of the four younger male lyricists.
13. Film of the live performance is available on YouTube, at https://www.youtube.com/watch?v=kCQBXZMcYPA, accessed December 14, 2020.
14. Interview with Cai Guoqing 蔡國慶, one of the 108 singers in the performance, on the program *Life of an Artist* (*Yishu rensheng* 藝術人生), China Central Television 3, October 4, 2012.

15. "The Devotion of Love" 愛的奉獻, lyrics by Huang Shiqi 黃奇石, music by Liu Shizhao 劉詩召, sung by Wei Wei 韋唯; "Longing" 渴望, lyrics by Yi Ming 易茗, music by Lei Lei 雷蕾, sung by Mao Aming 毛阿敏; "Peace be with You" 祝你平安, lyrics and music by Liu Qing 劉青, sung by Sun Yue 孫悅.
16. The Damucang salon was held in the outskirts of Beijing every two weeks for about two years from March 14, 1987. The role of the salon was to encourage innovative songwriting. Composers, lyricists, and singers nationwide were invited there to communicate, share new works, and find potential collaborators.
17. The song is on YouTube, https://www.youtube.com/watch?v=jGGPE2QJs7E, accessed December 17, 2020.
18. The description of the article's content is from the recollections of my interviewee Chen Zhe, Beijing, December 29, 2009. For a better understanding of the description of "a heap of sand" in the Chinese context, see Poole (1993).

References

Baranovitch, Nimrod. (2003). *China's New Voices: Popular Music, Ethnicity, Gender, and Politics, 1978–1997*. Berkeley: University of California Press.

Barmé, Geremie R. (1999). *In the Red: On Contemporary Chinese Culture*. New York: Columbia University Press.

Brace, Timothy. (1991). "Popular Music in Contemporary Beijing: Modernism and Cultural Identity." *Asian Music* 22 (2): 43–63.

Brace, Timothy. (1992). "Modernization and Music in Contemporary China: Crisis, Identity, and the Politics of Style." PhD diss., University of Texas at Austin.

Chen Xiaomei. (1996). "The Disappearance of Truth: From Realism to Modernism in China." In *In the Party Spirit, Socialist Realism and Literary Practice in the Soviet Union, East Germany and China*, edited by Hilary Chung, Michael Falchikov, Bonnie S. McDougall, and Karin McPherson, 158–65. Amsterdam: Rodopi.

Dai Houying 戴厚英. (1980). *Ren a ren* 人啊，人 [Stones in the Wall]. Guangzhou: Huacheng chubanshe.

Gan Yang 甘陽. ([1985] 2006). "Bashi niandai zhongguowenhua taolun wuti" "八十年代中國文化討論五題" [Five Issues about Chinese Culture in the 1980s]. In *Gu jin Zhong xi zhi zheng* 古今中西之爭 [The Debates Crossing Ancient and Present, Western and China], edited by Gan Yang, 25–29. Beijing: Shenghuo, dushu, xinzhi Sanlian shudian.

Jin Hezai 今何在. (2016). *Wu kong zhuan* 悟空傳 [Biography of Wu Kong]. Beijing: Beijing lianhe chuban gongsi.

Jones, Andrew F. (1992). *Like a Knife: Ideology and Genre in Contemporary Chinese Popular Music*. Ithaca, NY: Cornell East Asia Institute.

Jones, Andrew F. (2001). *Yellow Music: Media Culture and Colonial Modernity in the Chinese Jazz Age*. Durham, NC: Duke University Press.

Li Yuchen 李雨辰, ed. (1992). *Zhongguo xiandai youxiu gequ jicheng: Shuqing gequ, 1978–1990* 中國現代優秀歌曲集成：抒情歌曲 1978–1990 [A Collection of Excellent Contemporary Chinese Songs: Lyrical Songs, 1978–1990]. Shenyang: Chunfeng wenyi chubanshe.

Liang Maochun 梁茂春. (1987). "Tongsu gequde zhongyao shouhuo: Ping gequ 'Rang shijie chongman ai'" "通俗歌曲的重要收獲：評歌曲 '讓世界充滿愛'" [The Achievement of the Pop Song: "Fill the World with Love"]. *Beijing yinyue bao*, May 20: unpaginated.

Liao, Shannon. (2017). "China's Biggest Movie Is Based on an Internet Novel." *The Verge*, July 19, 2017. Accessed December 1, 2020. https://www.theverge.com/2017/7/19/15998458/wu-kong-sun-china-journey-to-the-west.

Lin Tongqi and Li Minghua. (1994). "Subjectivity: Marxism and 'The Spiritual' in China Since Mao." *Philosophy East and West* 44 (4): 609–46.

Ling Ruilan 淩瑞蘭, ed. (1994). *Zhongguo xiandai youxiu gequ jicheng: Tongsu gequ, 1978–1990* 中國現代優秀歌曲集成：通俗歌曲1978–1990 [A Collection of Excellent Contemporary Chinese Songs: Pop Songs 1978–1990]. Shenyang: Chunfeng wenyi chubanshe.

Liu Jianmei. (2003). *Revolution Plus Love: Literary History, Women's Bodies, and Thematic Repetition in Twentieth-Century China*. Honolulu: University of Hawai'i Press.

Liu Xinwu 劉心武. (1979). *Banzhuren* 班主任 [Teacher in Charge of a Class]. Beijing: Zhongguo qingnian chubanshe.

Poole, Teresa. (1993). "On Top of a Heap of Loose Sand: As China's Economy Overheats, Its Elusive Political Leaders Cannot Keep Pace, says Teresa Poole." *The Independent*, August 19, 1993. Accessed December 23, 2020. https://www.independent.co.uk/voices/on-top-of-a-heap-of-loose-sand-as-china-s-economy-overheats-its-elusive-political-leaders-cannot-keep-pace-says-teresa-poole-1462253.html, unpaginated.

Qian, Lijuan. (2011). "Pop Song Composition in China in the 1980s: An Elite Synthesis for the Mainstream." PhD diss., University of Sheffield.

Qian, Lijuan. (2017). "Which Identity Matters? Competing Ethnicity in Chinese TV Music Contests." *The World of Music* (New Series) 6 (2): 57–82.

Sartre, Jean-Paul. (1973). *Existentialism and Humanism (L'existentialisme est un humanisme)*. Translation and introduction by Philip Mairet. London: Methuen. First published, Paris: Editions Nagel, 1946.

Schwarcz, Vera. (1994). "Memory and Commemoration: The Chinese Search for a Livable Past." In *Popular Protest and Political Cultural in Modern China*, edited by Jeffery N. Wasserstrom and Elizabeth Perry, 170–83. San Francisco: Westview Press.

Sima Qian 司馬遷. (1989). *Shi ji juan 86* 史記卷八十六 [Historical Records, scroll 86]. In *Si bu bei yao* 四部備要 [Four Scripts], edited by Lu Feikui 陆费逵, 895. Beijing: Zhonghua shuju.

Su Xiangkang 蘇曉康 and Wang Luxiang 王魯湘, eds. (1988). *He shang* 河殤 [River Elegy]. Beijing: Dangdai chubanshe.

Tang Yongkuan 湯永寬. (1988). "Sate, yi wei 'chuyu zuopai yu youpaide jiaocha huoli zhixiade zhexuejia'" "薩特，壹位'處於左派與右派的交叉火力之下的哲學家'" [Sartre, A Philosopher "under Joint Pressure from the Leftwing and the Rightwing"]. In *Cunzaizhuyi shi yi zhong rendaozhuyi* 存在主義是壹種人道主義 [Existentialism Is a Humanism], translated by Zhou Xuliang 周煦良 and Tang Yongkuan, 1–7. Shanghai: Shanghai yi wen chubanshe.

Wagner, Vivian. (1995). "Songs of the Red Guards: Keywords Set to Music," selective summary of MA thesis, University of Heidelberg. Accessed February 27, 2020. http://academics.wellesley.edu/Polisci/wj/China/CRSongs/wagner-redguards_songs.html.

Wang Jing. (1996). *High Cultural Fever: Politics, Aesthetics, and Ideology in Deng's China*. Berkeley: University of California Press.

You Jingbo 尤靜波. (2019). *Zhongguo Liuxing yinyue jian shi* 中國流行音樂簡史 [A Brief History of Chinese Popular Music]. Shanghai: Shanghai yinyue chubanshe.

CHAPTER 18

STAGING RACE AND SEXUALITY ACROSS BORDERS

Marketing Pop Singer Coco Lee

GRACE WANG

Introduction

STEPPING onto the stage for her final performance of the popular singing competition *I am a Singer* (*Wo shi geshou* 我是歌手) in 2016, Coco Lee (Li Wen 李玟, subsequently called Coco) stood resplendent in a red couture cheongsam, the very same outfit she had worn during her performance of the theme song from the film *Crouching Tiger, Hidden Dragon* at the 2001 Oscars ceremony in Hollywood. Restaging this career triumph for *I am a Singer*, the singer hoped to secure the audience votes necessary to capture victory in the reality-television singing competition. With arms outstretched in a wave of undulating movements, Coco commanded the stage with her rendition of "A Love Before Time" ("Yueguang airen" 月光愛人); lingering camera shots of audience members and fellow singer-contestants wiping away tears helped punctuate for television viewers the emotive impact of her live performance. This performance, as framed through the reality-television show, marked a return of sorts for the singer—back to the performing spotlight through a reminder (or introduction) to viewers of the internationalism of her career as a Chinese singer.

While Coco's final performance on *I am a Singer* played on audience nostalgia, the show also critically reframed it for Chinese contexts. During the 2001 Oscars performance, the singer performed against a backdrop of kung-fu fighters dancing in choreographed sequence, signaling her difference and distance from the Hollywood elite in the audience. Taking the stage after Coco's performance, the actor Steve Martin quipped, "I love to see dancers when they get hopped up on caffeine," effectively reducing Chineseness and martial-arts imagery into a punchline. Repeating this performance fifteen years later on *I am a Singer*, Coco made a few critical changes. Rather than offer an English rendition with a Western orchestra, she took center stage with little background distraction, singing in Mandarin with a small ensemble of Chinese instrumentalists. The same red cheongsam, in this context, came to represent a symbol of Chinese achievement—a "red coat of armor" (*hongse zhanpao* 紅色戰袍) as described in some media reports. Moreover, her ability to fit, once again, into the slender 21-inch cheongsam of her youth made manifest the singer's intense discipline, diligence, and drive toward self-improvement, both in the long arc of her musical career and in her continued painstaking body maintenance through diet and exercise. In this way, her eventual triumph on the reality-television singing competition placed her victory and image within neoliberal and quality (*suzhi* 素質) discourse in China.[1]

As Coco is a singer who has worked across American and Chinese musical contexts, her musical career surfaces the complex dynamics of race, gender, and nation undergirding these musical landscapes and the position of Chinese Americans within them. If her performance at the Oscars underscores the orientalist logic that frames the reception of Chinese and Chinese American singers on the global stage, Coco's celebrity persona on *I Am a Singer* shows how internationalism can be repackaged as a symbol of Chinese pride. This chapter uses Coco's musical career as a case study to explore the translation of Chineseness as it travels across American and Chinese popular-music markets, paying particular attention to the multidirectional traffic of ideas about race, gender, and sexuality that accompany global movements in popular music. Focusing on two moments from the singer's career—her attempt to crossover into the US market in the early 2000s and her victory on the hit reality-TV singing competition *I am a Singer* in 2016—this chapter examines the hegemony of Anglo-American popular music within changing global coordinates of power marked by the rise of China's market. It analyzes how Coco's crossover bid brings to the surface both essentialist ideas of Chineseness circulating in the United States and the extent to which the singer capitalizes on racialized performances of Black and Latina female sexuality to sell her music and public persona in Chinese contexts. These racial dynamics, while central in American popular music, have often been overlooked in studies of Chinese forms. The focus on the transnational circulation and politics of race illuminates reasons for the still-limited success that Chinese singers have found while attempting to break into international and American markets. At the same time, Coco's participation on *I Am a Singer* also emphasizes the multidirectional influences in repertoire, performance styles, and musical arrangements of a singing competition show, which involved performers from such places as Korea, Taiwan, Hong Kong, China, Singapore, Kazakhstan, the Philippines, and the United States.

Throughout her career in Asia, Coco has skillfully marketed her hybrid Chineseness and internationalism to enhance her appeal. These same traits are highlighted in the singer's life narrative as presented on the reality-television show. Born in Hong Kong, she moved to San Francisco as a child, growing up immersed in American popular culture. While she originally intended to follow her mother's footsteps and pursue a career in medicine, her plans were diverted when she placed second in a singing competition in Hong Kong and soon after secured a recording contract. She did not find fame, however, until moving to Taiwan, where she learned Mandarin and quickly adapted to the cultural and musical aesthetics of Mandopop. In the 1990s, as Coco began securing fame and accolades in Taiwan's pop-music industry, her difference—from her colorful outfits to her provocative dance moves, changing hair colors, boisterous laugh, and her intimate familiarity with musical genres like soul, R&B, and hip-hop—represented a marketable form of capital. After signing with Sony Music Taiwan in 1996, she scored huge hits with Mandarin albums such as *DiDaDi* and *Sunny Day: Feeling Good*. As her stardom in regional markets in Asia grew, Sony Music executives located in Coco the potential to expand her global reach and usher in a wave of Asian artists to the American public. Coco's familiarity with American pop music and vocal styles, coupled with her charisma and performing experience, situated her well to crossover into US markets. In 2000, with an eye toward American pop-music stardom and the backing of an intense promotional campaign by Sony Music (whose Latinx artists had recently achieved enormous commercial success in the United States), Coco released her first US-produced album.

Crossing Over into US Markets

When Coco began hitting the US radio and talk-show circuit in 2000 to promote her first English-language album, the moment seemed ripe for an Asian or Asian American singer to match the chart-topping success enjoyed by Latinx pop singers such as Ricky Martin, Jennifer Lopez, Enrique Iglesias, and Marc Anthony in the late 1990s. The collective popularity of these singers—euphemistically dubbed a "Latin explosion" or "Latin invasion"—foretold an opening in the US pop market that might extend beyond its usual Black-White racial binary. As Coco was a Sony Music artist like many of the top-selling Latinx crossover stars, her fluency in English and American culture positioned her as an ideal candidate to usher a parallel "Asian explosion" into the American mainstream. Indeed, she appeared groomed to follow the career trajectory paved by Jennifer Lopez, whose hit album *On the Six* (1999) similarly combined an urban persona with sexy dance moves, high production value, generic platitudes about love, and R&B dance-club tracks and pop ballads.

From Martin's swiveling hips to Lopez's shimmying booty, the Latin explosion in American popular music drew on familiar stereotypes about the intoxicating spice, heat, and sensuality of both the music and people. In her critique of the "Latin music boom," Maria Elena Cepeda (2000) notes how the tropicalization of Latinx musicians intertwined visuality, embodied sexuality, and sound. Superficially layering polyrhythms onto the US pop vernacular, the Latin music boom signaled a profitable strategy to sell ethnic and music signifiers to a mass market through pleasurable hints of Latinx difference. As the cultural critic George Lipsitz notes, "What the mainstream wants is a kind of flavor of otherness without the history, the political implications and the specific [cultural] connections that actually produce the music itself" (as quoted in

Gurza, 2004). It followed that Coco could tread a similar path toward commercial success by tapping into marketable modes of Chineseness in the United States.

Yet, what would constitute commercially appealing ideas about Chineseness to mainstream US audiences was not entirely clear. While Coco's marketing appeared to follow the racial and gendered scripts of successful Latinx female singers—playing up a sexy, urban vibe that capitalized on the pleasurable otherness—she lacked an "ethnic" pop-music tradition that might influence her particular brand of pop. That is, the influence and audible trace of music traditions such as Latin jazz, salsa, and merengue in the American pop vernacular meant that American audiences already held some familiarity with Latin music. The same, however, could not be said about Chinese pop music. In the early 2000s, most Americans did not have any sense of Mandopop, and those that did frequently derided it as sappy, saccharine, and derivative—as an inferior copy of American pop music (Moskowitz, 2009: 72–75). Assessing the potential for Mandopop to crossover to American audiences, a *Wall Street Journal* article from 2000 cited limitations in the "drippy" genre itself, describing Mandopop as "essentially a mix of syrupy ballads and tinkly melodies that end up in karaoke lounges" (Tam, 2000). Moreover, tropes of sonic orientalism meant to signal Chineseness in the US mass-media landscape—from the gong to pentatonic riffs to "ching chong" vocalizations—merely exacerbated existing racial stereotypes. Thus, despite being an established pop star in Asia, Coco could not easily draw on her overseas fame to intrigue American audiences or cull musical influence from Mandopop. This helps to explain why, unlike Latinx artists, whose English-language albums tended to include (albeit toned-down) Latin beats and some Spanish in their lyrics, Coco's album *Just No Other Way* of 1999 contained no linguistic or cultural references (even superficially) to her Chineseness.

The de-emphasis on Coco's internationalism and Chineseness during her crossover bid into the US market stands in contrast to the capital placed on her foreign upbringing during the early stages of the singer's career in Taiwan. By the 1990s, Taiwan's music industry had become adept at marketing Chinese Americans like the L.A. Boyz, Vanness Wu, David Tao, Leehom Wang, and Coco Lee as distant yet familiar vehicles to repackage the style and feeling of American popular music into their own hybrid blend of Mandopop. These Chinese American singers were, themselves, an embodiment of this mixture of Chineseness tinged with internationalism and Western modernity that became emblematic for much of Mandopop's appeal. Taiwan's pop-music industry marketed these singers as creative and innovative, introducing new fashions and music styles such as hip-hop, R&B, and soul to local audiences. Such sentiments are echoed by Roger Lee, then a music executive at Magic Stone Records, who notes: "Record companies like us are constantly looking for artists with original ideas, new looks, or creative styles. And we find that a lot of ABCs [American-born Chinese], because of their background and upbringing, are more likely than local artists to possess these qualities, which are important assets in making innovative music" (Chang, 2002). Coco's vocal range and penchant for melisma invited direct comparison to singers like Whitney Houston and Mariah Carey, including monikers hailing her as the "Chinese Mariah Carey." As a performer based in Taiwan, where everyday interactions with

African Americans remained fairly limited, Coco could claim an intimate attachment to the youthful edginess, creativity, and "cool" of what was sometimes referred to as "Black music" (*heiren yinyue* 黑人音樂) without facing questions about musical authenticity, Black experience, and/or anti-Black racism in the United States; her American upbringing was sufficient to legitimate her claim to "Black music." Crossing into the American market, however, necessitated an engagement with the racial history and politics of the US popular-music industry and the place of Chinese and Chinese Americans within it.

While Chinese Americans and Asian Americans broadly have always made music of almost every conceivable kind, they continue to remain outside of the authenticating links connecting race with musical ownership and expression in the United States. Viewed as entering genres such as hip-hop, R&B, pop, and jazz from the outside and as lacking a rich musical tradition of their own, Asian American musicians have adopted a variety of musical and marketing strategies for navigating their place and presence in different musical cultures (Fellezs, 2007; Sharma, 2010; Tiongson, 2013; Wang, 2007, 2015; Wong, 2004; Zheng, 2010). Some artists have attempted to de-emphasize Asian ethnicity by fostering a sense of ambiguity around their race. In the late 1990s, for instance, the Filipino American singer Jocelyn Enriquez capitalized on the racial ambiguity of her appearance and surname to affiliate herself with African American and Latinx communities (the prevailing ethnicity associated with the genres in which she performed). As Elizabeth Pisares elaborates:

> [Enriquez] was accused of passing herself off first as Latina, and then as black to attract listeners who would not accept someone as Asian American performing Latin freestyle, house, or R&B. . . . [H]er dark complexion, angular features, and Spanish surname allowed her visual representation to be maneuvered between prescribed Latina and black images that define dance-music genres. (Pisares, 2006: 173)

Other artists, in contrast, explicitly highlighted their ethnicity strategically to disarm critics (Wong, 2004: 56). For example, in his debut album, *The Rest is History*, MC Jin (the first Asian American rapper signed to a major label) adopted an unapologetic and assertive "I'm Chinese" stance as a way to preempt critiques about being Chinese in a musical culture that accrues authenticity and cultural capital through Blackness. Negotiating a musical terrain marked by the absence of other Chinese or Asian American rappers, Jin emphasized his ethnicity linguistically and thematically, by including Cantonese raps and critiquing prevailing assumptions about Chinese emasculation and weakness. Despite the limited commercial impact of Enriquez and MC Jin, their strategies to navigate Anglo-American musical cultures not considered their own find echoes in Coco's marketing campaign by Sony Music. Collectively, these musicians point to the continued challenges that Asian American artists encounter while navigating the racialized terrain of US popular music and the nation more broadly.

The sense of outsider status negatively attached to Coco's Chineseness thus made her celebrity in Asia a conundrum in her marketing strategy in the United States. For while Coco's fame in Asia would appear to be an asset, it also highlighted her Asian and Chinese difference, an aspect of identity explicitly de-emphasized in her American album. As a result, there often emerged a lack of clarity for marketing and managing racialized perceptions of Coco's ethnicity or capitalizing on her success in Asia. This lack of clarity became evident, for example, on CNN, which introduced Coco as a pop star from Asia intent on "taking her blend of urban music and Asian pop stateside" (CNN, 2000). Yet, the album itself, which featured a familiar blend of R&B, hip-hop, and soul-tinged dance tracks and pop ballads, did not seem to contain linguistic or musical influences from Asian pop. None of the tracks made any thematic reference to her Chinese ethnicity. And finally, the album's cover image obscured visual markers of Coco's Chineseness. With eyes cast downward and a cascade of reddish curls tumbling down her face, the image diverted attention from her ethnicity: "She could be taken for a light-skinned African American or Blasian [multiracial Black and Asian]" (Stratton, 2015). In this way, her Chinese difference became subsumed under the Black-White racial logic of American popular music.

Similarly, in the music video for the album's lead-off single, *Do You Want My Love*, a blonde-haired Coco dances against a backdrop of African American and other ethnically ambiguous dancers in dark club and dance-studio scenes; none of the background dancers are visually legible as Asian. And while the camera lingers on her torso and hips as Coco dances suggestively with other male club-goers, her "urban sexy vibe" aligns more closely with the performance of African American or Latina sexuality in R&B videos. Significantly, her visual presentation does not riff on orientalized visions of Chinese women as submissive "China dolls" or overly erotic vixens. The image of Coco sidling up to Black and Brown male dancers in dark clubs thus complements the racial politics of the dance-and-R&B feel of her music while shifting attention away from her Chineseness.

Striving to gain inclusion in a popular-music landscape marked by the absence of Asian Americans, musical artists are tacitly encouraged to align Chineseness with Blackness and other communities of color in the United States, which can function to close the distance that listeners may feel between a singer's ethnicity and musical style. In interviews, Coco makes these Afro-Asian connections explicit, emphasizing the affinity and support she enjoys from the African American community and the structural similarities between the two racial minority groups. As the singer affirms, "I have received huge support from the African American community. The rappers in the L.A. studios loved me. They're like, 'My mother loves you, my cousin likes you, my whole family likes you too.' They went nuts. They had to struggle to get in the industry, so we had common bonds" (Short and Drake, 2000). Defining Chinese Americans as a racial minority group that shares a similar history of exclusion with African Americans allows her to frame their (collective) "struggle to get in the industry" within the discourse of multicultural inclusion into the nation. Moreover, Coco attempts to convert the love she feels from African American musicians into a stamp of legitimacy that authenticates her musicality and rightful belonging in such genres as R&B, hip-hop, and soul. As Coco elaborates: "I worked with Macy Gray's US songwriter Darryl Swann and he said, 'Coco, you've got some soul.' I'm like: 'Some?' And he's like, 'Coming from a brother, if I say you've got soul, trust me girl, you've got soul.'"[2] Here, Coco inherits the elusive quality of soul—implicitly understood as the property of African Americans—through proxy, a "brother" whose praise confers credibility to her musical offerings.

Prevailing racial narratives of Chinese and Chinese Americans as "model minorities" in the US cultural context hindered any easy claims Coco could make to having "soul." Model-minority narratives link Chinese Americans to diligence, discipline, and high academic achievement, depleting them of creativity, originality, and the "coolness and born-in-the-U.S.A. authenticity required for American pop stardom" (Navarro, 2007). Ironically, these latter qualities represent some of the same characteristics granted to Chinese Americans or American-born Chinese in Taiwan's Mandopop. Much has been written about the ideological function of model-minority narratives in the United States to castigate "deficient" minority groups like African Americans for lacking the "proper" cultural values to succeed in a meritocratic nation (Kim, 1999; Palumbo-Liu, 1999). Coco's claims of closeness and acceptance by the African American community can, on the one hand, work against the anti-Black racism embedded in model-minority narratives. On the other hand, they also strain credibility, a seeming superficial grab at the "cool" and musical authenticity granted to African American communities given the seeming lack of sustained reflection on the costs of anti-Black racism in the United States.

Coco's attempt to position herself as a minoritized American subject with ties to African Americans was further undercut by media references to her stardom in Asia, which positioned the singer as entering the United States (and its popular music) from the outside. Such perceptions of her outsider status merely exacerbated prevailing stereotypes of Chinese Americans as "forever foreign," regardless of their citizenship or generational status. Coco's marketing manager at the time conceded, too, that Coco faced a significant hurdle overcoming the perception that Chinese Americans are "foreigners who won't appeal to pop audiences" (Rodriguez-Valdes, 2000). Thus, while Coco repeatedly noted in interviews that her bid to crossover into US markets represented a "homecoming"—a return to her roots as a California girl, a cheerleader in high school, and an avid fan of the Los Angeles Lakers—references to the fame she enjoyed in Asia reinforced the more familiar view of Chinese Americans as not-American. And while Coco's upbringing in Hong Kong and the United States activated notions of transnational hybridity and internationalism that enhanced her appeal in Chinese-speaking markets, narratives claiming her belonging in pop-music industries in both America and Taiwan fueled confusion in an American media landscape that was not well versed in bicultural, bilingual, and border-crossing Chinese American identities (Chiao, 2009). Witness, for example, the ways that Coco's muddled marketing strategy created confusion even for Lisa Ling, a Chinese American talk-show host conversant in Asian American politics. Appearing on the daytime talk show *The View*, Ling fumbled her introduction of the singer, admitting that she became temporarily confused while reading her teleprompter, which described the singer both as Asian American and the "Mariah Carey of Asia" (YouTube, 2011). This confusion speaks to the limitations of American mainstream media to fully present Chinese American identity as encompassing a wide range of bilingual and bicultural sensibilities.

The negative critical reception of Coco's album did little to help the singer's already daunting prospect of reaching a mainstream American audience. Critics universally panned the album as lacking individuality and personality. Such traits, while not specifically racialized, echo long-standing discourses attached to Asian people, perhaps particularly Chinese people, in the United States, surfacing the latent orientalist underpinnings that accompany global movements in popular music. *Entertainment Weekly* assailed the singer's album as derivative: "From its drama-queen ballads to its limpest of R&B moves, from its Mariah-wannabe mannerisms to its contrived hip-hop to its defiantly banal song titles . . . Lee's US debut *Just No Other Way* is [a] monstrously impersonal product. It gives assembly lines such a bad name, Ford should sue" (Browne, 2000). *Rolling Stone* similarly lambasted the album as "slick bubble gum"—a second-rate, sickly sweet confection that will leave American audiences wanting. As the review continued, while the "Mariah Carey of Taiwan" may have "scored huge hits across the Chinese-speaking world with a sound and a look that owe, well, a lot to Mariah," American audiences demand more: "[Lee] doesn't have the bracing grooves that could make her flexible, pretty voice stand out, or even a great hook or catchphrase. All she has are a hundred borrowed vocal mannerisms and a bunch of tunes made with cookie cutters that are blunt from overuse" (Wolk, 2000). Indeed, the moniker "Mariah Carey of Taiwan" may have already proved damning, constructing Coco as a "karaoke" version of the original. The quality of the album's tracks notwithstanding, it is worth pausing on the descriptors woven into Coco's reviews: impersonal, cookie cutter, borrowed, wannabe, and assembly line. The hegemonic presumptions within these terms underscore the conundrum that Chinese and Chinese American artists confront navigating the racist and self-servingly orientalist assumptions embedded in global movements of popular music. For artists like Lee, assimilating to anglophone models of popular music invite critiques of derivativeness, but failing to do so would reaffirm the racial logic of Chinese foreignness and irrelevance.

Coco's crossover attempt ultimately fell short of expectations. Her first album sold a disappointing forty thousand copies according to Nielson Soundscan, and only one single, "Do You Want My Love," made an appearance on the Billboard chart, which tracks the popularity of songs and albums in the United States. And while it may be tempting to point to the musical shortcomings of Lee's album as the sole reason for its commercial flop, to do so would elide the extent to which racist perceptions and expectations about Chineseness and Chinese popular music influenced her critical reception, marketing, and entrance into US markets. Much like the Latin music boom reinforced racialized imagery of sultry Latina singers, Coco's crossover attempt intersected with broader racial and musical narratives about Chinese and Chinese Americans in the United States. The emphasis of her success in Mandopop was dismissed, writ large, by critics as musically wanting, and her fame in Asia located her as coming from a place of inferiority—or, at the very least, as a singer who would need to overcome those impressions. Indeed, the perception of moving from a place of less to one of more—from

Mandopop to US popular music—is rooted in the term "crossover," which, as Reebee Garafalo notes, suggests a "movement from marginal to mainstream, from secondary market to mainstream market" (quoted in Cepeda, 2000: 16).

At the same time, the hegemony of Anglo-American popular music in global music markets allowed Coco to leverage her crossover experience in English-language markets, despite tepid sales, to enhance her career and brand. Indeed, Coco's internationalism—including a focus on her American "success" and performance at the Oscars ceremony—continues to be centrally incorporated into her narrative arc, as evident on *I am a Singer*. At the same time, the reality-TV show contextualizes Coco's international achievements with the pride she feels in her Chineseness and her desire to raise the international profile of Chinese singers. Rather than a California girl whose minoritized status in the United States connects her structurally and affectively to African Americans—a biographical narrative that never quite resonated with American audiences and would hold even less resonance for Chinese audiences—Coco's narrative on *I am a Singer* and her career more broadly tap into essentialist notions of pan-Chineseness. Her home, family upbringing, and core values remain Chinese, regardless of her upbringing, citizenship, and/or residence in the United States.

Coco's Triumph on *I am a Singer*

First aired in 2013, *I am a Singer* is a popular reality-TV singing competition broadcast on Hunan Television. Based on a Korean format of the same name, the show features established artists performing on the same stage for a studio audience, whose votes determine the ranking of the singers each week and the eventual winner. During the fourth season, Coco's competitors hailed from China, Hong Kong, Taiwan, and South Korea and included sentimental favorites like the Mandopop singer Jeff Chang (Zhang Xinzhe 張信哲) and the Cantopop singer Hacken Lee (李克勤), as well as younger performers such as the Taiwanese singer-songwriter Lala Hsu (Xu Jiaying 徐佳瑩) and the K-pop artist Hwang Chi-yeul (황치열). These competitors have enjoyed varying levels of fame during their career and many, like Coco, are no longer at the peak of their popularity. Thus, rather than a "stepping stone toward a musical career, *I am a Singer* operates on a different logic: the audience adjudicates if the singer is worthy of stardom" (Wang and de Kloet, 2016: 293). Being "worthy" is tied to the singer's performance—their voice, stage presence, dancing, and overall aesthetic style—as well as the narrative crafted around their public persona and character.

In the first glimpse that viewers have of Coco in the fourth season of *I am a Singer* (airing from January to April 2016), she is in her living room, practicing with the pop legend Lionel Richie. As viewers are informed that Coco worked on preparing for the show through the Christmas and New Year vacations, the show establishes her persona as that of a workaholic and perfectionist, someone willing to sacrifice her holidays to deliver her best performance for fans and the show. "Killing it, killing it," Richie gushes to the camera as the singer improvises some melismatic embellishments to his classic hit song, "Say You, Say Me." Reflecting on her musical path in an interview segment that follows, Coco recounts launching her career after achieving success on a TV singing competition in Hong Kong and her eagerness, twenty years later, to embark on what she called the second phase of her musical career. "You only live once," Coco offers, first in English and then in Chinese, her penchant for sprinkling English phrases into conversation serving to remind viewers of (or to introduce younger ones to) an American internationalism that defines her music and style.

Early on, the show establishes Coco as the apparent favorite to win the competition. Backstage handlers clamor to work with her, and fellow contestants declare Coco's performance their favorite of the night. And yet, in what might seem to be a surprising twist (and good television drama), the studio audience ranks Coco's performance near the bottom, placing her in jeopardy of being eliminated from the competition. Indeed, for a reality-TV show that depends upon the drama of competition to retain viewers over the course of a season, having the winner appear a foregone conclusion would not make for compelling viewing. Allowing the audience, rather than expert judges or critics, to have the final vote allows the reality-TV show to present itself as an equalizing platform. Like her fellow contestants, Coco cannot simply rely on past successes, audience nostalgia, and/or earlier career triumphs. Nor can her dense network of high-profile connections—her apparent friendship with global celebrities or her marriage to a wealthy foreign husband—leverage a desired outcome. Rather, in a nod to fair and democratized competition, the show suggests that like the other contestants, she must earn her spot with the audience each week.[3]

Through stylized drama and the heightened realism that marks the reality-TV format, *I am a Singer* unfolds the multiple pressures placed on singers to master various aspects of making music. Each episode devotes equal air time to the singers' practice and preparation, their actual performance, and the slow unveiling of that week's results. The extensive coverage devoted to this backstage work makes visible the labor and dedication behind each of the singers' seamless performances. Easily recognizable stock characters and storylines are developed in successive episodes, particularly through interview clips that purportedly offer glimpses into the performers' motivations and thought processes. At the same time, given the popularity of reality-TV shows in China, most of the competitors were already somewhat versed in the format and performative expectations placed on participants within this genre of entertainment. Before appearing on *I Am a Singer*, for instance, Coco had served as a guest judge on *Chinese Idol*, *Voice of China*, and *Asia's Next Top Model*. Thus, for a media-conversant performer like Coco, her narrative arc on *I am a Singer* is likely the result of both self-conscious crafting as well as careful scripting and editing by television producers.

In her analysis of reality-TV talent shows in China, Ling Yang emphasizes the extent to which Chinese fans map narratives of individual triumph in these shows onto the broader goals of the nation. As she elaborates, "unlike the more individualistic 'transformation stories' or 'success myths' in Western *Idols*, Chinese fans consciously link the fate of individuals with the fate of the nation in the changing global system" (2014: 528).

This helps account for the emphasis on the ways that contestants embody such characteristics as hard work, tenacity, and discipline, as they correlate with the flexible skills needed to succeed in a competitive global system. Attaining success on these shows, in this sense, is tethered less to innate talent or luck than to perseverance, motivation, and discipline. These traits are repeatedly valorized on *I Am a Singer*, where contestants sing and dance through illness and physical pain. At the same time, the contestants link their desire to push through obstacles with the goal of self-improvement, prioritizing social harmony over individual competitiveness against each other. The singers constantly model support and encouragement to others, repudiating a zero-sum perspective of individual achievement (Wei, 2014). In this way, the show structures competition less as a contest between the contestants and more as an opportunity for self-improvement and cultivation—values that align with neoliberal logic and *suzhi* discourse in China.

While the show officially identifies Coco as a Hong Kong singer, her upbringing, career trajectory, and language of song selections (she sings primarily in Mandarin and English) places her at a distance from other Hong Kong singers, stretching that definition significantly (Cheung, 2017: 100). Indeed, her narrative arc on the show depicts her Chineseness as hybrid and international, highlighting her collaboration with global pop icons like Michael Jackson, the purported respect for Chinese people she has garnered through awards and accolades from the West, and the intense pressure she places on herself to positively represent Chinese people to the world. She builds upon the sexiness and personal physical appeal associated with her image, adapting her embodiment of sexuality as sanctioned by Americanness during her youth into a media narrative that emphasizes discipline and diligence on the reality-television show.

Crafting Coco's Sexiness for Chinese Stages

When Coco emerged on Taiwan's pop-music scene during the 1990s, her marketing focused on her exceptionalism—her distinctive laugh, changing hair color, and provocative dance moves, and the English with which she peppered her songs and interviews—which translated into a form of capital linked to modernity and internationalism (or more specifically Americanism). Her upbringing in the United States allowed her to claim closer intimacy with both American popular music and the expressions of sexuality reflected in its performance styles. As Chih-Chieh Liu notes in her analysis of Coco's dancing body, local Taiwan media portrayed Coco's "sexy hips" as natural and effortless, an apparently seamless extension of her Chinese American body. Her rocking bottom represented an "awe-inspiring corporeal spectacle which 'naturally' epitomizes her Chinese American identity and the idea of 'sexiness'" (2014: 269). Known among local crowds for "the sexiest body in the sexiest outfits on top of her Ricky-Martin-style butt movements," the seeming ease with which Coco inhabited the sexiness of popular US pop singers represented both an aspirational and exceptional sign of her difference (Ho, 2003: 327). This difference, as the Singaporean producer-songwriter Li Sisong reflects, provided the singer with certain freedoms: "The only one who gets away with the sex-bomb look and sex-bomb voice is Coco Lee. And that's because she's from America; people here know that and make an exception for her. [Asian audiences] let her sing according to a different standard" (Tan, 2013: 203). And while her "sex bomb" style drew upon racialized understandings of Black and Latina female sexuality in the American popular imagination, Coco's performance of sexuality translated broadly as "American" on the Taiwanese stage.

As the singer's fame expanded beyond Taiwan, the international spotlight that her celebrity brought to the country also helped sanction her overt performances of sexuality. As Ho notes, given the island's complex political standing, "Taiwan's desire for international recognition has often hinged upon other means of cultural representation"; in this way, celebrities like Coco "are seen as serving the noble cause of the nation-state building project" (2003: 327). Coco's recognition in a wider international context shielded her from the moral critique and consternation placed on sexual displays deemed crass and "low class" (for example, as embodied by "betel-nut girls," the young, scantily clad women who can be found on the roadsides of Taiwan selling betel nut, a mild stimulant, to working-class men).

At the same time, it is clear that Coco calibrated her expression of sexuality to culturally marketable ideas of sexiness in Taiwan's pop-music landscape, steering her image in interviews away from suggestions of sex and eroticism. Her public persona, in that sense, aligned with other popular female singers from Taiwan, Hong Kong, and Japan during the 1990s, who counterbalanced their performances of sexuality with a narrative of innocence and purity (Ho, 2003: 326). Thus, while her provocative clothing and dance pushed boundaries onstage, she invokes her mother offstage to emphasize her Chinese upbringing despite growing up in the United States, framing her Chineseness through her mother's enforcement of discipline and strict codes of chastity. She even pivots to her mother as well when questioned about her image. For instance, when asked in a 2000 interview whether she considers herself to be sexy, Coco responds: "My mom thinks I have a nice shape, and I don't mind wearing clothes to show my body. Women's curves are a beautiful thing, but I'm not trying to sell sex" (Short and Drake, 2000). Functioning as a gendered stand-in for the nation, Coco's mother "sinocizes her 'American-ness' and desexualizes possible connections to eroticism" (Liu, 2014: 280). The implicit approval of her onstage choices by her chastity-preserving mother allows the singer to claim ownership over her body and clothing styles while also diluting its link to coarser implications of selling sex. Such generic platitudes about celebrating women's curves—and, more broadly, body acceptance—emerge in other interviews, where she emphasizes neoliberal virtues of self-esteem and individual worth. Responding to a question by Malaysia's *Star Online*, for example, Coco muses: "All women have a sexy side.... We must have confidence in everything we do and that's what makes us sexy" (YouTube, 2013). Disassociating being sexy from individual sexuality or eroticism, Coco packages herself as selecting from the best of both cultures. Her American upbringing infuses her image with creativity, passion, and distinctiveness while her references to Chineseness ground her image in chastity, discipline, and diligence, thus containing her perceived distance from local audiences. Moreover, the singer offers an imagination of Chineseness and internationalism within consumer-driven models of modernity based on a broadening of self-expression and ideas of self through fashion, beauty, and style (Hershatter, 2007: 47). This positioning of Chinese American identity as modern and cool—a formulation that, in many ways, mirrors the pastiche, glossy hybridity of Taiwan's Mandopop—stands in clear contrast with the marketing of Coco's identity in American popular music as a racial-minority subject claiming structural and cultural alignment with other people of color in the United States.

On *I am a Singer*, Coco draws on her existing public persona of sexiness, internationalism, and hybridity while adapting it for the reality-TV competition stage and audience. The expert judges on the show comment on the freedom and abandonment with which Coco expresses herself in her musical phrasing and dance. The singer, in turn, counterbalances her onstage performance with an oft-repeated narrative that constructs her (even as a married woman in her forties) as a "mama's girl" who continues to seek parental approval. At the same time, the show highlights her parents—particularly the spectral presence of a father she never knew—to embody the roots of her work ethic rather than a foil for her sexiness. Dramatically dedicating her performance to her father in the fourth episode of the show, Coco demonstrates to the camera a strong desire to show her father that she had matured into a "not lazy" and "good daughter," explicitly linking her industriousness and filiality with an attempt to compensate for paternal loss.

In similar fashion, the show depicts the singer's personal physical appeal with a narrative of work and discipline. Her performance of sexiness, rather than being a natural outgrowth of her Americanness, is secured by practice and labor. At the end of each live performance on *I Am a Singer*, Coco bows deeply—marking the break from her onstage performance to her offstage persona—expressing gratitude to her guests, band, and audience for their continued support. On social-media forums such as Sina Weibo, commenters note how Coco's display of humility reflects her "good education" and upbringing. The show tracks Coco meticulously rehearsing every aspect of her vocal choices and dance moves, leaving no detail to chance. The focus on the disciplined labor that each performance entails shifts emphasis away from a discourse of the "natural" sexiness embodied by Coco's dancing form. Rather, through a narrative focus on diligence, politeness, and constant self-improvement, *I am a Singer* locates her sexy image within the neoliberal logic and *suzhi* discourse in China. Her sexiness is folded into a narrative of training and discipline—the culmination of hard work and sacrifice.

It may be that the re-articulation of Coco's body through the framework of practice and discipline maps onto her narrative as a singer moving into the next phase of her musical career. When Coco participated in *I Am a Singer*, she was in her early forties, an age when a woman's sexiness is not necessarily assumed or desired. Throughout the season, her fellow contestants threw light-hearted jabs about her age, jokingly calling her *dama* 大媽, or an older woman (negatively associated in this context with someone retired or with more leisure time and money). At the same time, her age amplified the admiration of her body, converting it into an aspirational commodity symbolizing health, sacrifice, and attractiveness that others might attain through their own rigor and inner qualities of self-control and discipline. News articles and chatter on social-media platforms such as Tianya and Sina Weibo commented on the intensity of her daily workouts and strict diet regimen, speculating on a purported five hundred or seven hundred daily sit-ups and a two-hour daily workout. The energy, fitness, and vitality displayed through her dancing body and "wasp waist" (*huangfeng yao* 黃蜂腰) particularly within the context of her chronological age, represented the physical manifestation of sacrifice and discipline. The rigor of her body maintenance thus found reward in her ability in the final performance to fit, once again, into the original 21-inch red cheongsam worn for her 2001 Oscars performance and the victory voted her by the audience. Here, we can place narratives circulating about Coco's body within ideas that emerged in urban, post-reform China that Susan Brownwell terms "body culture": the "daily practice of health, hygiene, fitness, beauty, and dress, and decoration" as well as "the means by which the body is trained and displayed to express a particular lifestyle" (Brownwell quoted in Hershatter, 2007: 41). For Coco, the health and fitness of her body became indicators, more broadly, of the health of an inner self—her "healthy" sexuality, consumption habits, and moral character. The ways in which *I Am a Singer* folds discourses of sexuality within narratives of diligence and hard work highlights the multiple meanings placed on the female body. Bodily attributes such as a "wasp waist" and "electric hips" link a gendered idealization of the female body with a moral discourse of quality and inner character.

In her final performance on *I Am a Singer*, Coco emerges triumphant. Performing in the red cheongsam, she signals her Chinese pride for a Chinese audience and physically manifests her discipline, hard work, and quality of character. If her performance at the Oscars ceremony represented a gesture outward—to win respect for Chinese people on the global stage and to show that Chinese can sing or, at the very least, do more than martial arts—her performance on *I Am a Singer* recasts that career highlight inward toward a nationalist Chinese context. Her "red coat of armor" signals the rising status of China and Chinese people in the world, re-centering Chineseness rather than foreign affirmation. Moreover, Coco's duet in the final episode with the African American R&B/hip-hop singer Akon is demonstrative of the interest that American pop acts have in the mainland Chinese market. Her internationalism, in this instance, allows her to act as an intermediary for American pop singers interested in expanding their appeal in Chinese markets.

Conclusion

Coco's musical career—from the height of her popularity in Taiwan's Mandopop scene during the 1990s to her attempt to embody a significant global force in American popular music and again in Chinese contexts through popular singing competitions like *I Am a Singer*—points to the multidirectional currents affecting Chinese popular music. While China's market and popular-music industry may eventually grow to eclipse and overtake Western-based models of globalism, the longstanding hegemony and allure of Anglo-American popular music continues to beckon Chinese singers. For those looking to expand beyond international markets in Asia, Coco continues to serve as a site of comparison, both as an existing benchmark of success and of the particular challenges that Chinese singers confront in Anglo-American popular music. For example, years later in 2016, a BBC story discussing the attempts of the Chinese pop star Jane Zhang (Zhang Liangying 張靚穎) to become "China's first global pop star" used Coco as a point of contrast, citing her as "one of the most successful Chinese singers trying to enter the international market" (Tsoi, 2016). Yet even without direct reference to Coco, the recursiveness of the questions posed about Chinese singers like Zhang reveal the persistent racial and gendered dynamics that continue to frame the presence of Chinese singers in Anglo-American popular-music markets: Singing in English, how would Zhang retain her distinctiveness from Western or American artists? Which cultural aspects of Chineseness would lend a (marketable) sonic uniqueness to her brand of pop music, particularly since this music does not originate from Asia? And how did she navigate relationships with African American musicians and producers, particularly given the influence of hip-hop and R&B in her own musical offerings? That these questions about the marketability of Chinese pop stars in the United States linger, even in the face of enormous changes in the Chinese and US music industries and shifting power coordinates in US-China relations, invites closer investigation into the entrenched racial and musical beliefs about Chineseness and Chinese singers as they circulate in the United States. Moreover, as the case study of Coco highlights, qualities valued in popular singers in Chinese markets continue to remain at odds with the branding of an American pop star. On *I Am a Singer*, Coco's cultivated public persona of discipline, diligence, and sexuality echoes rather than contests dominant perceptions of Chinese in the United States, whether as model minorities or as culturally different. Such traits remain in dissonance with perceptions of pop music stardom in the American cultural imagination.

While the moment of attempted crossover of Chinese singers into US and global markets places into sharper relief the often-unacknowledged Afro-Asian connections and borrowings in Chinese popular music, questions ranging from the appropriation of hip-hop iconography and African American and Latinx sexuality to the translation of American racial politics are relevant in Chinese contexts as well. The strong presence of "Black music" in Mandopop and the transnational cultural politics of race in Chinese contexts represent potential areas of further study, building upon and extending existing research in other genres and East Asian popular music (see, for example, Jones, 2001; Condry, 2006; Anderson, 2016). At the same time, Coco's participation in *I Am a Singer* also underscores the rich cross-dialogue between popular music and media industries in Asia, including Japan, Korea, China, Hong Kong, and Taiwan, among others. The growth of the Chinese market and the music and entertainment industry has made it a desirable destination for aspiring pop stars across Asia and, to an extent, those in the United States. These sites of commercial entertainment, and the media narratives constructed around (and by) popular singers, make them rich sites of analysis for the politics of gender, race, and nation. Moreover, as Coco's enormously successful career in Asia shows, the continued deferment of a Chinese or Asian "explosion" in American popular music does not necessarily represent a limitation but rather a re-imagining of the global markets, in which one seeks and finds fame and musical belonging. Rather than attempting to embody an incoming global force for American popular music, Coco charts a path for finding respect and inclusion in Chinese markets that is distinctively Chinese American.

Glossary

Chang, Jeff (Zhang Xinzhe 張信哲), singer (b. 1967)
dama 大媽, older woman
heiren yinyue 黑人音樂, "Black music"
hongse zhanpao 紅色戰袍, "red coat of armor," reference to Coco Lee's cheongsam
Hsu, Lala (Xu Jiaying 徐佳瑩), singer and songwriter (b. 1984)
huangfeng yao 黃蜂腰, "wasp waist"
Hwang Chi-yeul 황치열, K-pop singer (b. 1982)
Lee, Coco (Li Wen 李玟), singer (b. 1975)
Lee, Hacken (Li Keqin 李克勤), singer and actor (b. 1967)
suzhi 素質, quality
Wo shi geshou 我是歌手, *I am a Singer*, TV singing competition (first aired 2013, subsequently renamed *Geshou*)
"Yueguang airen" 月光愛人, "A Love Before Time," theme song from the film *Crouching Tiger, Hidden Dragon* (2000)
Zhang, Jane (Zhang Liangying 張靚穎), singer (b. 1984)

Notes

1. *Suzhi*, loosely translated as "quality," is a key concept in Chinese governance and encompasses "qualities of civility, self-discipline and modernity . . . a sense and sensibility of the self's value in the market economy" (Yan, 2003: 494). The widespread usage of *suzhi* discourse by the 1980s functions broadly to rationalize cultural and economic hierarchies in China. The dichotomy between "backwardness and development," used to denigrate the "low quality" of Chinese rural laborers hindering Chinese modernization, expands to include intimate physical and psychological details of personhood, from consumption habits to body management and middle-class desires for social mobility (Anagnost, 2004: 190).
2. It is also worth noting how Coco repeats these stories, too, within Chinese contexts, often as a way to articulate the hurdles and eventual acceptance (and success) she achieved in the US market. For instance, relaying an anecdote from her early days promoting *Just No Other Way* in the United States, the singer notes the deep skepticism she faced from DJs: "They didn't believe a singer from China could sing R&B, so I just sang right away without any accompaniment. . . . Their faces would be frozen for a second, and then they clapped while smiling at me. I knew I'd made it" (Nan, 2013).
3. This narrative remains in play, despite knowledge of state regulation of television shows, including the tight eye on reality-TV talent shows with audience engagement (Yang, 2014) and some suspicion among Hong Kong viewers that the results were somewhat predetermined to prevent a Cantopop singer from winning the show (Cheung, 2017).

REFERENCES

Anagnost, Ann. (2004). "The Corporeal Politics of Quality (*Suzhi*)," *Public Culture* 16 (2004): 189–208.

Anderson, Crystal. (2016). "Hybrid Hallyu: The African American Tradition in K-pop." In *Global Asian American Cultures*, edited by Shilpa Davé, Leilani Nishime, and Tasha Oren, 290–303. New York: NYU Press.

Browne, David. (2000). "Just No Other Way." *Entertainment Weekly*, March 3, 2000, issue 528: 74.

Cepeda, María Elena. (2000). "Mucho Loco for Ricky Martin; Or the Politics of Chronology, Crossover, and Language within the Latin(o) Music 'Boom.'" *Popular Music and Society* 24 (3): 55–71.

Cheung, Carlos K. F. (2017). "Trans-border Televisual Musicscape: Regionalizing Reality TV *I am a Singer* in China and Hong Kong." *Global Media and China* 2 (1): 90–108.

Chiao, Christine. (2009). "Coco Lee: The Case of the Incomplete Crossover." *UCLA International Institute*, July 31, 2009. Accessed June 12, 2018. http://international.ucla.edu/institute/article/110971.

CNN. (2000). "Coco Lee is Coming Home." *Showbiz Tonight*. Broadcast. March 1, 2000.

Condry, Ian. (2006). *Hip-Hop Japan: Rap and the Paths of Cultural Globalization*. Durham, NC: Duke University Press.

Fellezs, Kevin. (2007). "Silenced but Not Silent: Asian Americans and Jazz." In *Alien Encounters: Popular Culture in Asian America*, edited by Mimi Thi Nguyen and Thuy Linh Nguyen Tu, 69–110. Durham, NC: Duke University Press.

Gurza, Agustin. (2004). "1999 was the Year of the Latin Explosion." *Los Angeles Times*, August 15, 2004, E1.

Hershatter, Gail. (2007). *Women in China's Long Twentieth Century*. Berkeley: University of California Press.

Ho, Josephine. (2003). "From Spice Girls to Enjo Kosai: Formations of Teenage Girls' Sexualities in Taiwan." *Inter-Asia Cultural Studies* 4 (2): 325–36.

Jones, Andrew. (2001). *Yellow Music: Media, Culture, and Colonial Modernity in the Chinese Jazz Age*. Durham, NC: Duke University Press.

Kim, Claire Jean. (1999). "The Racial Triangulation of Asian Americans." *Politics & Society* 27 (1): 105–38.

Liu, Chih-Chieh. (2014). "Denaturalizing Coco's 'Sexy' Hips: Contradictions and Reversals of the Dancing Body of a Chinese American Superstar in Mandopop." In *The Oxford Handbook of Dance and the Popular Screen*, edited by Melissa Blanco Borelli, 268–88. Oxford: Oxford University Press.

Moskowitz, Marc L. (2009). "Mandopop Under Siege: Culturally Bound Criticisms of Taiwan's Pop Music." *Popular Music* 28 (1): 69–83.

Nan, Chen. (2013). "Veteran Pop Star Back in the Spotlight." *China Daily*, July 5, 2013.

Navarro, Mireya. (2007). "Trying to Crack the Hot 100." *New York Times*, March 4, 2007., 9: 1.

Palumbo-Liu, David. (1999). *Asian/American: Historical Crossings of a Racial Frontier*. Stanford, CA: Stanford University Press.

Pisares, Elizabeth. (2006). "Do You Mis(recognize) Me: Filipino Americans in Popular Music and the Problem of Invisibility." In *Positively No Filipinos Allowed: Building Communities and Discourse*, edited by Antonio T. Tiongson Jr., Ed Gutierrez, and Ric Gutierrez, 172–98. Philadelphia: Temple University Press.

Rodriguez-Valdes, Alisa. (2000). "Coco Lee Hits the Ground Running." *Los Angeles Times*, February 17, 2000, CAL: 62.

Sharma, Nitasha. (2010). *Hip Hop Desis: South Asian Americans, Blackness and a Global Race Consciousness.* Durham, NC: Duke University Press.

Short, Stephen, and Kate Drake. (2000). "Everyone Remembers a Name Like Coco." *Time Asia*, November 20, 2000. Accessed June 12, 2018. http://edition.cnn.com/ASIANOW/time/features/interviews/2000/11/20/int.coco_lee.html.

Stratton, Jon. (2015). "Popular Music, Race and Identity." In *The Sage Handbook of Popular Music*, edited by Andy Bennett and Steve Waksman, 381–400. Los Angeles: Sage.

Tam, Pui-Wing. (2000). "Here Comes Asia's Ricky and Mariah—Not Just for Karaoke Anymore, Mandarin Pop Could be the Next Crossover Sensation." *Wall Street Journal*, March 31, 2000, B1.

Tan, Shzr Ee. (2013). "An Interview with Li Sisong, Producer and Songwriter." In *Gender in Chinese Music*, edited by Rachel A. Harris, Rowan Pease, and Shzr Ee Tan, 201–4. Rochester, NY: University of Rochester Press.

Tiongson, Jr., Antonio T. (2013). *Filipinos Represent: DJs, Authenticity, and the Hip Hop Nation.* Minneapolis: University of Minnesota Press.

Tsoi, Grace. (2016). "Could Jane Zhang become China's First Global Pop Star?" *BBC Chinese*, December 21, 2016. Accessed June 12, 2018. https://www.bbc.com/news/world-asia-china-38179767.

Wang, Grace. (2015). *Soundtracks of Asian America: Navigating Race through Musical Performance.* Durham, NC: Duke University Press.

Wang, Oliver. (2007). "Rapping and Repping Asian: Race, Authenticity, and the Asian American MC." In *Alien Encounters: Popular Culture in Asian America*, edited by Mimi Thi Nguyen and Thuy Linh Nguyen Tu, 35–68. Durham, NC: Duke University Press.

Wang, Qian, and Jeroen de Kloet. (2016). "From 'Nothing to My Name' to 'I Am a Singer': Market, Capital, and Politics in the Chinese Music Industry." In *Handbook of Cultural and Creative Industries in China*, edited by Michael Keane, 293–310. Northampton, MA: Edward Elgar Publishing.

Wei, Junhow. (2014). "Mass Media and the Localization of Emotional Display: The Case of China's Next Top Model." *American Journal of Cultural Sociology* 2 (2): 197–220.

Wolk, Douglas. (2000). "Just No Other Way." *Rolling Stone*, March 30, 2000, issue 837: 64.

Wong, Deborah. (2004). *Speak It Louder: Asian Americans Making Music.* New York: Routledge.

Yan Hairong. (2003). "Neoliberal Governmentality and Neohumanism: Organizing Suzhi/Value Flow through Labor Recruitment Networks." *Cultural Anthropology* 18 (4): 493–523.

Yang, Ling. (2014). "Reality Talent Shows in China: Transnational Format, Affective Engagement, and the Chinese Dream." In *A Companion to Reality Television*, edited by Laurie Ouellette, 516–40. San Francisco, CA: John Wiley and Sons.

YouTube. (2011). "Coco Lee - abc, The View." February 10, 2011. Accessed June 12, 2018. https://www.youtube.com/watch?v=bInnSV7IHSk.

YouTube. (2013). "Coco Lee 5: What Makes Me Sexy." July 25, 2013. Accessed June 12, 2018. https://www.youtube.com/watch?v=w8mpYfcZYvg.

Zheng, Su. (2010). *Claiming Diaspora: Music, Transnationalism, and Cultural Politics in Asian/Chinese America.* New York: Oxford University Press.

CHAPTER 19

RE-IMAGINING CHINA'S WOMEN PIANISTS

Yuja Wang and Zhu Xiao-Mei

SHZR EE TAN

INTRODUCTION

As China has been aggressively pushing programs for cultural diplomacy around the world via music, two women pianists hailing from the territory's diaspora—Yuja Wang 王羽佳 and Zhu Xiao-Mei 朱曉玫—have emerged in the recent spotlight; the first enjoying widespread international success, and the second becoming a cult figure in China while physically residing in Europe. On concert platforms, Wang (born 1987), who established her career in North America, regularly pits her short body (clad in controversial skin-tight clothes) for visual flourish against the piano, performing heavy-weight pieces from Russian repertoire. In contrast, Zhu (born 1949) lives and plays in self-imposed obscurity as a survivor of the Cultural Revolution, finding meditative solace through recording projects involving the music of J. S. Bach.

At first glance, the performance styles of these two pianists present stark alternatives to oft-seen images of Chinese musical femininity, epitomized by concert pianists such as Chen Sa 陳薩, Jane Xie 解靜嫻, Zhang Zuo 左章, and innumerable others. Stereotyped as long-haired, musical swots who haunt the corridors of studios and conservatoires around the world, they are imagined as conscientiously putting in multiple-hour shifts at the keyboard in anticipation of concert appearances in flowing ball gowns. This version of femininity can be understood as stemming from the notion of the traditional *shunü*, or virtuous Confucian lady (Zhao, 2017). Seen in slightly different guises through the ages via Chinese literature, painting, pop culture, and other media, such figures are often depicted as demure, sylph-like women skilled in both the domestic arts and musical pursuits befitting the middle class, such as playing the *qin* (seven-stringed zither) or *pipa* (pear-shaped four-stringed lute). In mainstream Chinese societies, these women have come to be idealized and are traditionally cast as orthodox, conservative models of subservient Chinese femininity. In musical terms, this conservatism has been deployed by women pianists who channel notions of Chinese virtue through their quiet, conscientious search for perfectionism in musicianship. This is the case even as they play up to, or against, rivaling—and often racist—tropes (Brown, 2020) of Chinese pianists as emotionless, robotic performers (Yang, 2007: 14) or, in the case of male superstars such as Lang Lang, as spectacular showmen. Complementing my earlier work on Chinese masculinities on the piano (Tan, 2013), this chapter on Yuja Wang and Zhu Xiao-Mei investigates intersectional issues of sexuality, ethnic identity, artistic "authenticity," and class in the making of new Chinese musical femininities.

With the pianists Wang and Zhu, any traditionally established gender identities are side-stepped through different possibilities for the production of agendered (and sometimes desexed) personas in their expression of distinctly different personas. While the two artists' external representations may constitute superficial marketing veneers, visual aspects of their identities are closely integrated into their musical expressions and—holistically understood—wider, embodied performance dynamics. These in turn reveal their personal as well as their audiences' constructions and expectations of their different qualities as icons, which hinge on societal and cultural/subcultural notions of not only gender but also taste, class, Chineseness, and Asian cosmopolitanism.

Here, I argue that while Wang's lightning fingers and cut-out clothes (emphasizing her small frame) highlight her latent sexuality, they also ironically promote her as an eternally pre-pubescent—and, by extension, a desexed—child: an infantilized wunderkind. Not so similarly, but working nearer the other end of the age spectrum, Zhu's sage-like stage affectations and shapeless dresses mark her as asexual and nun-like, even as she has been proclaimed as an old-school "Chinese lady."[1] A common characteristic of these two cases lies in the protagonists' forging of their individual—and still developing—femininities partly through, paradoxically, a desexed, asexual, and agendered filter. In this chapter, I investigate how the two musicians navigate around stereotypical tropes of Chinese musicianship in dramatically different and effective (if also self-essentializing) ways. Indeed, at the same time that Wang and Zhu construct gendered and agendered versions of their external selves, they also wittingly and unwittingly subvert race-inflected images of Chinese performers within and beyond China. How did Wang and Zhu come to be women piano icons of their time? How are their femininities enacted in performance of sound, musicality, and gesture? How do their different personas relate to wider Chinese pop (and imagined) elite culture?

Yuja Wang and the Trope of Youthful Vigor

It makes sense to consider the case of Yuja Wang first, because of its direct challenge to orthodox constructions of Chinese femininity, detailed above. Born in Beijing to a dancer and a percussionist, Wang began studying the piano at the age of six, almost immediately entering the junior program of the city's prestigious Central Conservatory of Music. In the 1990s and 2000s, her constant appearances as a child and teenager on the international competition circuit (where she won major awards) helped to cement her initial reputation as a wunderkind. One of the earliest turning points in her career, however, was her admission to the Curtis Institute of Music at the age of fifteen to study with the pedagogue Gary Graffman, also the teacher of fellow Chinese piano superstar, Lang Lang. In 2007, she attracted international attention when she stepped in to cover for the Argentine piano legend Marta Argerich in a performance with the Boston Symphony Orchestra. In 2009, Wang signed a recording contract with the long-established German company Deutsche Grammophon, with which she has released four albums of music by Romantic and late-Romantic composers. Holding more than fifty engagements with orchestras around the world each year, Wang is an internationally recognized name today, coming to rival in visibility her slightly senior compatriot, Lang Lang. While she is technically based in New York, the pianist's shifting concert schedule sees her exercise her cosmopolitanism as a superstar, jet-setting from one big city to another.

At the forefront of Wang's visibility lies its literal element. Her pianism is exothermic and commanding, gesturally large, and packed with frenetic energy. This is seen not only in her chosen repertoire of Brahms, Rachmaninov, Scriabin, and other composers who make virtuosic demands of serious showmanship and technique from the performer but also in her vivid, dramatic, and direction-fueled execution of the pieces and her manipulation of sound. *The New York Times*, for example, hailed her 2011 debut at Carnegie Hall, playing Prokofiev's Piano Sonata No. 6, as channeling

> barbaric, propulsive, harmonically brittle outbursts into a formal four-movement sonata structure. In most readings, intriguing tension results from hearing music of such aggressive modernism reined in by Neo-Classical constraints. Ms. Wang reconciled these conflicting elements through a performance of impressive clarity and detail. (Tommasini, 2011)

Likewise, the *San Francisco Chronicle* appeared equally stupefied by Wang in 2012, calling her, "quite simply, the most dazzlingly, uncannily gifted pianist in the concert world today, and there's nothing left to do but sit back, listen, and marvel at her artistry" (Kosman, 2012).

In her birthplace of China, far beyond garnering musical accolades, Wang has been turned into a national icon of sorts by the mainstream as well as the semi-academic press (Yang, 2017; Su, 2016; Duan, 2013). Commenting on her performance of Rachmaninov's Third Piano Concerto, the *People's Daily* wrote in 2011: "Recognized as one of the hardest works to play, this piece is considered the King of Piano Concertos. However, Yu Jia's impeccable playing as always was hugely appreciated by the crowd" (Anonymous, 2011).

In spite or because of her pianism, her ability to dispatch heavy, large-scale repertoire with well-known musical institutions from around the world, it might be argued that Wang's quintessential and more widely celebrated performances are those of slighter solo works. These are encore pieces captured in short video recordings, easily disseminated over the Internet. Shunned by professional critics who see these bite-sized departures as a somewhat schizophrenic betrayal of her deeper musicality (Tommasini, 2011), these video clips are clearly welcomed by Wang's audiences and have rendered her a meme of her own. Almost as if tailor-made for the age of social media, they have gained her even broader fame beyond the elite circles of classical live performance. Played at fiendish speeds and conveniently timed to be about one to three minutes in length, they cater to the attention spans of fans on websites such as YouTube and the Chinese-owned bilibili.com and qq.com. The pieces range from Art Tatum's arrangement of "Tea For Two," to Arcadi Volodos's transcription of Mozart's "Rondo alla Turca," to Rachmaninov's transcription of Rimsky-Korsakov's "Flight of the Bumblebee."[2] To be sure, most of these video clips do not originate as made-only-for-Internet devices; many of the recorded performances were encores captured in situ at Wang's live concert appearances. However, comments that accompany the clips show that these performances have reached viewers beyond the usual audience at concert halls and classical-music fans. As critiques on the Internet go, her playing—while often awed at—is not always hailed as a triumph. Many of the comments focus on her technical prowess, musical dynamism, and choice of dress.

One interesting aspect of the reception of Wang's performances is the comparative absence of complaints over her obvious demonstration of extreme technical facility, a topic which has otherwise been a point of contention for pianists such as Lang Lang and Li Yundi. With these two pianists, their dexterities at the piano—sometimes deemed executed at the expense of musicianship—have been channeled into tropes about empty showmanship. More harshly, they hint at race-inflected stereotypes about "robotic" and "mechanical" musical identities forged through state hothouse programs (Tan, 2013). While critics outside of China now and then acknowledge that Wang may not necessarily have plumbed for the profound in all of her performances, they have also tended not to directly accuse her of facile display, as they have with Lang and Li. Such an apparent cutting of slack for Wang might well stem from honest observations of her genuinely different approach to musicality, even if these have been tellingly described as a function of her perceived youth. *The New York Times*, again, wrote of her interpretation of Beethoven in 2016: "This was not a probing or profound *Hammerklavier*. But I admired Ms. Wang's combination of youthful energy and musical integrity" (Tommasini, 2016).

Indeed, if any controversy was to be found in Wang's performances, it would be in audience reactions to her stage attire, as well as her own pronouncements on choice of concert and everyday dress. Frequently found on and off stage in stiletto heels and close-fitting mini-dresses, with hemlines and skirt-slits rising well above her knees, Wang favors designers such as Hervé Léger, a Parisian known for his "bandage" dresses made out of figure-hugging strips of cloth wrapped tightly around the body. Elsewhere, she has also been known to sport couture featuring strategic cut-out shapes, exposing her back or her legs. These outer presentations of Wang's pianistic identity have as much been assumed by fans to be made on behalf of her sexual identity as they are surely also reflections of broader societal and subcultural attitudes toward Wang's Chineseness, gender, age, pianism, and musicality.

The *Los Angeles Times*'s critic Mark Swed notoriously drew disapproval for his review of Wang's 2011 concert at the Hollywood Bowl. Swed's words pre-empted the political backlash to everyday sexism that would erupt six years later in the wake of the Harvey Weinstein scandal and the #MeToo campaign on social media:

> But it was Yuja Wang's orange dress for which Tuesday night is likely to remembered. . . . Her dress Tuesday was so short and tight that had there been any less of it, the Bowl might have been forced to restrict admission to any music lover under 18 not accompanied by an adult. Had her heels been any higher, walking, to say nothing of her sensitive pedaling, would have been unfeasible. (Swed, 2011)

Reactions to the above review did not stop *The New Criterion*'s critic Jay Nordlinger from commenting on another concert, as recently as in 2018, that Wang's "usual concert attire, namely stripper-wear . . . could not possibly have seen her wearing less without being arrested" (Nordlinger, 2018).

To be sure, in whispers across concert-hall cafes and in piano studios, in official reviews generated by other mainstream media, on fan websites, and on social-media platforms around the world (including in China), scrutiny of Wang's virtuosic prowess continued to be almost always prefaced by mentions of her very-tight skirts, her showing of skin, and the particular colors or brands of her gowns.[3]

Wang herself has spoken in public about her choice of clothing, describing with some ambivalence how she places value on both freedom of physical movement on stage and freedom of aesthetics plus social mores in her performance of visual and personal identity. Proclaiming herself to be a fan of fashion, she was unashamed of citing her choice of clothing as an indispensable part of her image and a key element of her wider performance approach as a musician. Speaking to the *Telegraph* in 2014, she countered:

> It's just natural for me. I am 26 years old so I dress for 26. I can dress in long skirts when I am 40. Anyway I have many different styles, I don't only wear short. I don't understand why I have to explain this, I just do what is natural for me. (Hewett, 2014)

Re-gendering the Eternal Wunderkind, Woman-Child, and Enfant Terrible

A simplistic reading of Wang's strategic dress sense and her audiences' obsession over it would put the debate in terms of how her outer form is a reflection of her sexuality. Indeed, Wang herself stated to *The Guardian* in 2017: "If the music is beautiful and sensual, why not dress to fit? It's about power and persuasion" (Maddocks, 2017).

A literal mapping of the pianist's clothing style to a purely erotic dimension of her broader persona, however, does little to aid the understanding of a more holistic construction—and consumption—of Wang's projected persona. Tellingly, most of the diatribes (within and beyond China on mainstream and social media) generated about this topic rarely address her sexuality directly. Here, they do not quite describe her as "sexy" or "hot" in the same way that magazines, news websites, and blogs might openly label a pop idol. Instead, reports and comments tend to administer the literary equivalent of raising an eyebrow in relation to Wang's lack of coverage of skin in public contexts. They focus on her choice of concert gear as an infraction of an unofficial moral code—whatever this might mean for audiences of Western art music or for her general fans.

Such apparent demonstrations of relative conservatism reflect how genre operates in the wider world of Western classical music, where "a set of musical events (real or possible)" have their course "governed by a definite set of socially accepted rules" (Fabbri, 1981: 52). Indeed, one might say that social mores or the doxa of writing styles in this world tend to dictate the use of particular language or sense of dress more attuned to a middle-of-the-road code of practice; it is not often that classical-music performers wear clothes with cut-out segments or have their sexuality commentated about in direct prose redolent of unmitigated objectification. The fact that moral dimensions of Wang's depth of character have been questioned on account of (interpretations of) her dress choices reveals as much of the biases of critics (and the broader music scenes that they co-construct with Wang) as it sheds light on Wang's intended performative persona. However, a fuller reading of Wang's performance dynamics has to be gained from understanding these alleged displays of fervent sexuality as part of broader, holistically embodied performances that project at the same time cultural and individual identity. The classic Butlerian and Schechnerian views are of course that all gender is performed (Butler, 1990; Schechner 1988), and in Wang's case, music and gesture both function as the medium of performance, even as they are also process and product. This much has been written about in specific literature on music and embodiment (Crossley, 2015; Clayton, Dueck, and Leante, 2013; Downey, 2002). Where the costuming of the body, however, and its resulting implications for gestural movement within a specific context is located in relation to nested performances of assumed gender and sexuality, Wang presents a deceptive case. In fact, peeling away the first layer of commentary on her alleged performances of sex via her costumes, one might argue the opposite at the next level: that her performances end up desexing her image to a large extent. Wang's cut-out clothes serve less to enhance her curves than to emphasize her compact stature, presenting her as an eternal child prodigy; she commented, recalling a newspaper that described her as a "'Twenty-Eight-year-old Wunderkind.' Isn't that an oxymoron?" (Malcolm, 2016).

Certainly, the pianist herself has historically been extremely conscious of her small size, complaining that couture dresses on her tiny frame tended to end up evoking a sleazy image: "It's hard to find clothes because I'm so petite" (Kovan, 2017). Here, it is crucial to understand that statement and the re-gendering of Wang specifically through live performance, rather than only through analyzing sound recordings or deconstructing still images. This is due to the gestural dynamics and visual effervescence found in her fully embodied persona, only found in real-time appreciation of her presence and movements. Her body-hugging clothes distill her visual charisma into a small, focused bundle of energy. This pixie-like frame is in turn pitted in dramatic contrast against the seven-foot Steinway and Bösendorfer pianos she regularly performs on—metaphorical monster machines. The technically demanding pieces that are at the heart of Wang's performative duels, then, are dispatched with grand, action-packed flourishes. I contend that the ensuing suggestion of performative dissonances, set up in the contrasting visages of child-versus-beast or pixie-versus-monster, make for a particular kind of titillating entertainment resembling a battle between David and Goliath rather than an overt display of a particularly sexualized or womanly femininity. One might in fact even extrapolate that the physical condensation and reconstruction of Wang into the paradoxical figure of a twenty-eight-year-old wunderkind—more child than woman, more Puck-like fairy than siren—might well have also rendered her to a large extent sexless in the public gaze.

Zachary Woolfe of *The New York Times*, for example, in 2013 confessed "that while perhaps 90 percent of my attention was on her precise yet exuberant playing, a crucial 10 was on her skintight flame-colored dress." He elaborated further:

> Her alluring, surprising clothes don't just echo the allure and surprise of her musicianship, though they certainly do that. More crucial, the tiny dresses and spiky heels draw your focus to how petite Ms. Wang is, how stark the contrast between her body and the forcefulness she achieves at her instrument. That contrast creates drama. It turns a recital into a performance. (Woolfe, 2013)

The *New Yorker* later picked up on this same comment, anatomizing Wang's appeal and her consciousness about it as something to be found in her self-proclaimed small frame, rather than a curvaceous body:

> But in fact Yuja's penchant for the riskily short and clingy has less to do with allegiance to the dress code of her generation than with an awareness of her own "supersmallness," as she calls it. She knows that small tight clothes bring out her beauty and large loose garments don't. But she is not just a woman who knows how to dress. She is a woman who is constantly experimenting with how to dress when she is playing on a concert stage. She is keenly aware—as many soloists affect not to be—that she is being looked at as well as listened to. (Malcolm, 2016)

Malcolm's article had earlier described Wang, tackling Beethoven's "Hammerklavier" Sonata, as "a dominatrix or a lion tamer's assistant. She had come to tame the beast of a piece, this half-naked woman in sadistic high heels. Take that, and that, Beethoven!"

Taken collectively, the quotes from above shed light on the media reception of Wang's persona: it rests on a distinctly fetishized body, with dress apparently an organic extension of the self that is "embedded within the social world and fundamental to microsocial order" (Entwistle, 2000: 325). The comments on Wang reflect as much on the people who view and listen to her as they do on the pianist who has been turned into an object. She has become the vehicle by which consumers of her artistry can plumb for particular meanings in spectacles that see her received, at one extreme, in a somewhat pedophiliac way—as a child-woman, a sexual, asexual, yet fiercely human sprite. Writing on *hanliu* and K-pop idols consumed in China, Rowan Pease (2009: 164) situates a different kind of infantilization within the broader structures of cultural power-play and fans' ownership and co-construction of their idols. In the case of Wang, an element of self-essentializing is perhaps in effect. She boldly invites the spectating of her duel with the piano and, in so doing, establishes a new power dynamic with her audiences.

Of interest is how the baring of skin becomes an embodied vehicle for the metaphoric baring of one's soul, the revealing of Wang's psychological being. This is an idea with which Wang herself, as well as critics, have been happy to play. Speaking to *The Guardian* in 2017, she again rationalized wearing skin-tight clothes: "Perhaps it's a little sadomasochistic of me. But if I'm going to get naked with my music, I may as well be comfortable while I'm at it" (Maddocks, 2017). Wang's sense of body-aliveness enhanced through costume is clearly an element channeled frequently in performances. Speaking to *Elle* in 2017, she said:

> In my twenties, I'd put on my tight Hervé Léger dress and heels, and it looked like I was going to the bar. Concertgoers think, Classical music—it's really serious. There are lots of rules, and the dress code, which I broke, was one of them. It's irrelevant to what we're doing. It's just a piece of cloth, but once it's on my body, it boosts my confidence, and that translates to the music. (Kovan, 2017)

What, then, of this confidence in the enfant terrible figure that Wang creates? Drawing upon the work of Erving Goffman (1956) concerning the presentation of self, and that of Phillip Auslander (2006) on musical personae, it is tempting to observe the pianist's deliberate representations of a full, "organic" self through various lenses of obverse imaging. The phenomenon can be seen in her railing against "the multiple, layered frames" (Auslander, 2006: 104) and social contracts assumed of not only the classical-music genre but also other performative "laminations" (ibid.: 105) that hint at different facets of her identity: her countering of known and established images of Chineseness, femininity, masculinity, classical pianism, and humanity.

In Wang's flashy—almost brash—countenance, she is the antidote to traditional images of conservative feminine subservience found in imagined, traditional China. Her slinky dresses and provocative hemlines—perhaps more commonly seen in a pop arena, and that she describes as "modern and edgy" (Malcolm, 2016) rather than sexy or revealing—are calculated to break taboos of the concert hall, where evening dresses, even if skin-tight, do not show much skin and where black tie is the norm. Her fiery gestures on stage—sometimes described as passionate and sensuous—plus her lively personality in interviews move against the grain of stereotypes of Chinese pianists as machine-like technicians. Her small frame, coupled with large gestures, plays with the child-woman dissonance. Finally, her casual approach toward dealing with audiences, co-workers, fans, the press, and the media—all seen in her seemingly flippant quips on fashion, "trashy" literature, partying, mobile-phone usage, and Communist pragmatism in China—invokes her technology-savvy generation's sensibilities and tendency toward the carelessly informal. These create a stark contrast with the imagined circumspection of elder colleagues such as Emanuel Ax, Charles Dutoit, Maurizio Pollini, and Murray Perahia, all of whom she has frequently been compared to or who are conductors with whom she works.

Taken together, Wang's various appearances as a woman figure of international reputation, standing for a particular version of Chineseness (intended or not), present a formidable counterweight to the established cultural tropes of Chinese masculinity and pianistic success informed by her compatriots Lang Lang and Li Yundi. To be sure, from a positivist and feminist viewpoint, Wang is no more a female answer to Lang or Li than the two male artists can realistically be thought of as versions of, or reactions against, particular kinds of masculinities found on the other side of an artificial East-versus-West debate. Mina Yang and Mari Yoshihara both tackle this broader issue, looking at the different ways in which ethnically East Asian classical musicians self-essentialize in terms of curating repertoire and projecting particular gender identities (Yang, 2007: 2; Yoshihara, 2008: 83), and at the same time assert new cultural and socio-economic belongings (Yoshihara, 2008: 167–69). Indeed, taking an intersectional approach and pushing the gendered projection, interpretation, and consumption of Wang to further fringes, it is similarly possible to see how the trajectories that the pianist has covered in her career on behalf of her distinct brand of ambivalent femininity hint at broader transcendental issues of ethnicity, age, and (as I discuss later) social class via genre.

Zhu Xiao-Mei as Asexual Sage

In my analysis of Yuja Wang, it is no coincidence that the majority of media and audience pronouncements, as well as my reflections on my in-person and recorded experiences of her concerts and interviews, have so far come from outside of China. This is a function of Wang's international presence, one built on considerable exposure in the concert halls of cosmopolitan cities around the world. This aspect of Wang's career as a Chinese pianist—and as a brand—is discussed toward the end of the chapter. However, for now, I turn to consider a contrasting example of Chinese pianistic femininity, that of Wang's compatriot, Zhu Xiao-Mei.

Unlike Wang, Zhu's recent celebrity has been honed largely within China. Based in Paris, Zhu was born in Shanghai in 1949 to a family of artists. Like Wang, Zhu was talent-spotted at an early age; she played on national television while only eight years old, entering the Central Conservatory in Beijing at ten. In comparison to Wang, however, Zhu's fledgling career—as with many artists and intellectuals in her generation—was interrupted by the Cultural Revolution. During this period, she was sent to a labor camp in Zhangjiakou, Hebei, where she re-acquainted herself with the music of J. S. Bach (Zhu, 2007; Wallace, 2015). This experience was to prove seminal in the pianist's artistic, psychological, and intellectual coming of age. As Zhu relates, her recent and late career success was ultimately a result of, and a response to, the years she had lost during her twenties and afterward. Her time in the labor camp was crucial to her formulation of a meditative approach toward playing Baroque music, and it saw her learn to weave into her playing various philosophies evoking the timelessness and equanimity found in ancient Chinese classics.

Following the end of the Cultural Revolution, in 1979 Zhu left China for the United States and Boston's New England Conservatory, where she eventually obtained a master's degree in piano performance. This led to a short stint teaching the instrument at a music center in Vermont, after which she made a definitive move to Paris. In Europe, Zhu remained out of the relative spotlight until an ironic turn in the expansion of social media within China transformed her almost overnight into a cult figure (Wang, 2017). While she continues to earn her main living as a teacher at the Paris Conservatoire, Zhu has recently become an emblem of a particular brand of poignant Chinese pianism, by dint of her alleged hermitism, now celebrated by emerging generations of Chinese musical connoisseurs as a form of new Chinese mysticism.

In her eternal bob and drab-colored, shapeless robes, Zhu manifests a femininity opposite in many ways to Wang's. Her image is made subdued and asexual by her seniority. On stage and in videos, she speaks deliberately and moves slowly, as if preternaturally tracing the movements of a *taiji* master, channeling sagely wisdom, and shunning the bright lights of platforms provided by glamorous concert appearances with big orchestras. Zhu almost exclusively plays and records J. S. Bach, frequently speaking of the composer and her communing with his music as an exercise in philosophical and spiritual practice, as if akin to executing a Chinese ink painting, as noted in a documentary film by Michel Mollard titled *The Return is the Movement of Tao* (2014), inspired by Zhu's performances and recordings of Bach's *Goldberg Variations*.

At a recital in Hong Kong in the same year, in a post-concert chat with the audience, Zhu put forward the idea that Bach would have been Buddhist if he had come to know about the religion. Speaking later, in Chinese, to the *Financial Times* in Hong Kong, she remarked of the comment (author's translation):

> I was only joking with the audience. But, in saying this, there's also a logic. Bach wrote a well-known piece called *The Art of Fugue*; he didn't finish it. His son said that this was because his father was ill. But I have doubts, I think he meant to leave it unfinished. There's a Chinese saying: *liu bai* 留白 [leaving blank]. It's a persuasive saying. I've always wondered about this piece, which is almost written save its conclusion. Why did Bach not complete it? He was a conscientious composer who was clear about what he wanted, surely an end [in the score] would indicate an end [in the intended music]? I feel that Bach was capable of thinking about Eastern philosophy. (Zhang, 2014)

Interestingly, it was only after her departure from China that Zhu began exploring Chinese thought more thoroughly. She re-encountered Lao Zi and Daoism in the context of her heightened identity as a Chinese person living in the diaspora in Paris. Describing her interpretation of the *Goldberg Variations* to *The Irish Times* in 2015, in French-accented English, she compared the work to an aspect of the teachings of Lao Zi (or Lao Tzu):

> For me, as for that most famous Chinese philosopher Lao Tzu, something most important in my life is water. And I feel Bach's music is like water. His name actually refers to water—it's no accident . . . . The *Goldberg Variations* is like the water in a river. At the end it's not finished: it goes back to the beginning. The water continues to flow. (Wallace, 2015)

Speaking to *Peng Bai, The Paper* in 2014, she commented more specifically in Chinese about the connection between Bach and the early Daoists' ethos for social cohesion, betraying a transcultural attempt to link the composer with mystical aspects of Chinese philosophy:

> Actually, Chinese people listen to and understand Bach best; he is very much like China's Lao Zi and Zhuang Zi. Bach wrote counterpoint—many disparate voices playing at the same time, yet still coming together in *hexie* 和諧 [harmony]. I feel that our current society is in need of this type of spirit. If only different peoples could, like Bach's music, come together in flow and exchange, we would have a harmonious society. This concept is very important. (Liao with Wang, 2014)

In China, Zhu's approaches to thinking about and performing Bach have been met by sympathetic ears among audiences and critics, who appear to have found similar spiritual experiences in her performances and recordings. The Chinese critic Tian Yimiao, for example, enthused that her *Goldberg Variations* encompassed "both elegance and vulgarity, complexity in its difficulty, full of many diverse wonderful things. And thus Bach became a kind of *xiulian* [ascetic practice]" (Tian, 2017). In use of this particular term, Tian refers to the Daoist practice of seeking refinement through self-cultivation.

More widely, commentators on the Chinese Internet have praised Zhu's interpretations for their "sincere simplicity," "unassuming attitude," and "sense of stillness and balance." That is not to say that Zhu never receives criticism from her Chinese listeners. In spite of oft-verbalized respect for Zhu's artistic "authenticity," critics have also been known to simultaneously fault her performances for technical issues in phrasing, pedaling, or dynamic control. Yet, as Tang Chuanye 唐川頁 put it, evoking the Japanese ethos of *wabi sabi* in a post to a discussion thread, the imperfections become perfections in themselves.[4]

Two points are worth raising for further discussion in relation to the last few quotes by and about Zhu. First, while very little is said about Zhu as a specifically female persona, there are projections of, and assumptions about, her wider identity—ideas concerning gender ambivalence and asexual sagacity, even de-sensualized nunhood. These are seen in how Zhu herself brushes off queries about her intentionally modest sense of dress, with subsequent media feting her disinterest as a value in itself. Indeed, if any fetishization of a particular identity was to be found here, it would be in the act of disembodying Zhu, refocusing attention onto her austere, intellectual, and spiritual life, rendered lofty and immaterial against the notion of banal physicality.

Of course, this idea becomes indefensible when Zhu's refusal to dress in a particular way, or to deal with the alleged superficiality of her image, itself reflects heightened bodily and gestural awareness. In her pursuit of sound and thought as abstract essences, she deliberately embodies quiet poses, languid gestures, stillness in phrasing, and quietude in tone production. On stage and in videos, she consciously displays a deliberate style of musical embodiment that neatly fits into her projected identity. While dissonances created by coexisting and competing attributes of woman-versus-child and fairy-versus-monster are to be found in Wang's youthful persona, Zhu's expression of gender ambivalence tends toward the opposite. Paralleling Peggy Phelan's descriptions of a "broken symmetry" in which the (female or racially identified) self becomes a default Other as a result of structural inequalities (Phelan, 1993: 25–27), they are somewhat disarticulated and hint at absence rather than presence; Zhu is "unmarked," potentially androgynous, and, in her stolid and unwavering occupation of the other end of the age spectrum, rendered asexual in her womanhood.

A second point arising from the quotes above lies in Zhu's choice of the word *hexie* in her interview with the *Financial Times*. The term has been adapted for specific usage within China, via a concept borrowed from Confucianist philosophy by the former Chinese president, Hu Jintao. Initially coined by Hu in the mid-2000s to signify political stability across the diverse and populous nation, *hexie* has since acquired connotations of authoritarian censorship and the enforced abiding to government-prescribed narratives. Returning to Zhu, then: to be sure, in interviews elsewhere, the pianist appears to steer clear of politics in conversation, preferring to subsume such discussions (as with discussions of her everyday life) into abstract talk of philosophy and spirituality. Yet, whether or not the pianist meant to direct a courteous nod to the Chinese government in this particular interview in Hong Kong, and in the context of a series of recitals in China, her life story itself has certainly been plumbed for different political discourses by both marketing agents and a rising new demographic of young, middle-class fans.

Repackaging a "Non-commercial" Commodity: Class, Taste, and China's New Connoisseurs

Zhu's reception in China has occurred not only through her promotion as an enigmatic, cult figure. While the pianist has had limited success as a performer of live concerts in her longstanding home of Paris, she has come to be celebrated, via her recordings, only relatively recently in the land of her birth. This has occurred not only through the promotion of her current sage-like persona but also through recounting her past life travails as a China-born artist who was once a victim of persecution during the Cultural Revolution.

Zhu herself has played a part in telling this particular story, publishing an autobiographical novella in which she describes the horrors of being sent to a labor camp after watching the disintegration of her family, as one relative after another was denounced and persecuted. In the same work, she tells of rediscovering her love for Bach and the joy of playing the composer in secret, an act of meditative resistance and a reclaiming of her humanity (Zhu, 2007).

While Zhu's book has been published and circulated in Europe, its contents are directly familiar to many in her audiences in China. Of particular interest to them is not so much the trauma she has suffered but rather the reconciliation of the pianist today to tragic events of the past and how she has subsequently transcended them via the adoption of ancient Chinese metaphysics. The idea of Zhu as an undiscovered treasure living in relative obscurity, hidden in plain sight in the cosmopolitan everyday of Paris, has no doubt also added to the romanticism of her image as an artistic hermit—at least as suggested by the publicity and press photos that usually place her scarf-clad figure in dreamy autumn scenes. As with Yuja Wang's audiences, whose comments on the younger pianist's visage betray perspectives on social mores particular to a specific subcultural scene, the sudden popularity of Zhu—largely exclusive to China—reflects the emerging tastes of new classes of audiences and consumers of Western art music in a territory experiencing rapid economic progress.

Wang Weida (2017: 210) ascribes Zhu's success to the recent rise of a discerning and self-consciously learned group of critic-cum-bloggers led by the Sheep Bone Group (Qianggu quan 腔骨圈), which is active in the consumption and appreciation of Western art music in China's bigger cities.[5] As he explains, these armchair reviewers who "discovered" Zhu actively disseminate their comments on music and the arts via fast expanding social-media platforms such as WeChat and Weibo. Styling themselves as intellectuals and connoisseurs, they command surprisingly large followings with younger and newly converted music fans who find it difficult to engage with more technical reviews in the mainstream press penned by elder, conservatory-trained critics. Writing in colloquial language, this newer generation of critics-of-critics see themselves as champions of "true" classical music in China, searching for quality instead of quantity. They aim at safeguarding taste and aesthetics amid new Western art-music scenes emerging across the country, each rising to fulfill the new musical desires of a rapidly developing middle class. Positioning their audiences as a class above China's new petite bourgeoisie, these new critics shun concerts that feature crowd-pleasing Strauss waltzes and marathon Chopin preludes, which make up the staple repertoire in the concert halls of China's second- and third-tier cities. As far as these carefully discriminating aficionados are concerned, such events cater only to the spectacle-seeking hoi polloi as opposed to lovers of profound art. To the new critics, a better demonstration of refined taste would be found in authentically appreciating the unspoiled gem of an unflashy performer such as Zhu, whose association with the relatively austere music of J. S. Bach and whose pursuits of noble simplicity in Chinese philosophers mirror their self-images as ascetic intellectuals.

It is clear here that Zhu has become a prime target of fetishization. I argue that this fetishization functions along class lines, played out in a classic scenario in which demonstrations of aesthetic tastes act as signifiers of social position (Bourdieu, 1984: 5–6). Interestingly, as a result of Zhu's perceived non-commercial value due to her "outlier" ethic, among would-be musical snobs in China she has paradoxically become a hugely successful commercial product, much as indie rock, for example, has ironically become a "hidden product of consumer capitalism" (Keightley, 2001: 129). Tickets to Zhu's most recent solo recital in Beijing—a rare event—reportedly cost as much as 2,000 RMB in 2014. Zhu herself appeared surprised at the development, late in life, expressing bemusement at the ironies involved. This was evident in her interview with the Chinese publication *Peng Bai, The Paper* in 2014:

> ZHU: I never expected China to have developed so quickly; my audiences were all young people; they love classical music to the extent of it being a craze. A boy came all the way from Hengyang in Hunan; he bought a ticket worth 2000 RMB. I felt precious on his behalf. Can someone love classical music so much that he'd have to pay for the transport, hotel costs too? He must have used up at least a whole month's salary. When I see him, I see hope for China.
> REPORTER: Apart from fans who exceed your expectations, what else did you find different [about China]?
> ZHU: All the big cities in China have concert halls. There's a crisis now in Europe; it's poverty everywhere, crumbling and in disrepair. China is coming up in the world now; this sort of power fills me with pride. When the Chinese economy develops to a certain level, we can then find possibilities for cultural and artistic development.
> REPORTER: You've also said in the past that the music scenes in China were developing somewhat impetuously.
> ZHU: This is inevitable. It's not like making money; it's easy to get rich overnight. But cultural development requires several generations of communal searching, building up of critical interest. Interest is important.
> REPORTER: Why do fans love you so much?
> ZHU: I think they've promoted me to the high extremes. So, everyone's been cheated and lied to.
> REPORTER: Living overseas for thirty-five years, in China you've just about become a "legend." (Liao with Wang, 2014)

This excerpt hints at the paradox of Zhu's commercial success—an astonishment even to herself, as a non-commercial artist who has resisted being turned into a commodity. More importantly, the interview exposes Zhu's popularity among an expanding class of audiences, alongside China's economic-cultural development. Zhu's quotes on Chinese pride shed light on her surreptitiously nationalist sentiments as she relates again to a world she may have once forsaken while living in semi-exile in the diaspora—a world now seen to burgeon with new opportunities. An interesting aspect of this re-relation is its impact on her reception: Zhu's fans also value her for the nostalgia of seeing a Chinese artist once persecuted during the Cultural Revolution now making her way back to the homeland in a new dawn of Chinese cultural success domestically and around the world.

Transnational Chineseness and Artistic "Authenticity": Mediatization and Markets

The issue of Chinese nationalism demands further discussion here, in this chapter's penultimate section. Where the past few sections on Yuja Wang and Zhu Xiao-Mei have touched mainly on gender articulations and re-projections of the two pianists' musical identities, there is also analysis to be made of their performances and reception on another level, one of intersectionality in relation to ethnicity and nationality. Are there, for example, any distinctive "Chinese" elements to be read in Wang and Zhu's musical artistry, whether or not in engagement with their gender identities? What does "Chineseness" here mean in relation to birthplace, current residence, transnational networks, and domestic success in the "mainland" versus attaining an international spotlight? Where do self-essentialism, cultural authenticity, and cosmopolitan double-consciousness come into play?

Such questions have to be answered in consideration of a grid of further factors, not least the important role played by the (social) mediatization of both pianists, and also in an analysis of the marketing of their iconic personas to a range of specific demographics. As with other piano icons who have become well-known in the Chinese world, the question of Wang and Zhu's "Chineseness" has to be unpacked in terms of broader transnational identities and cultural- and politico-economic flows. While both performers were born in China, they have since established their careers in the cosmopolitan cities of New York and Paris respectively. One might even argue that the critical formation of their early to mature creative identities developed outside of China, in conservatories in the United States.

Broadening this discussion to the emergence of dual or multiple identities into discourses of transnationalism, Lau and Everett also point out that "the concepts of hybridity, identity politics, and globalization have . . . proved extremely useful in our efforts to locate the various subject positions in the critical reception of art music that integrates East Asian and contemporary Western idioms" (2004: xvii). Instead of dismantling the "dualism of East and West," they seek to "investigate how the notions of East and West are constructed, circulated, and utilized" (2004: xvii). As transnationals who do not so much identify as culturally, geographically, or artistically rooted in the "center" or "margin," or in the "East" or the "West," but rather traverse different spatial nodes, Wang and Zhu continue to fly back and forth not just between Europe or the United States and China but also around the world (the former to a larger extent than the latter). One would imagine their personas to be in constant flux and situationally constructed to whatever broader cultural currents they encounter, react to, or consciously try to influence. Aihwa Ong, writing more theoretically, puts the to-and-fro shifting and remaking of contextual identities succinctly: "Non-Western cultures are not disappearing but are adjusting in very complex ways to global processes and remaking their own modernities" (Ong, 1999: 240).

This unpacking of race, place, and experience in understanding the artistic evolution of Wang and Zhu in terms of a desired, stable "musical authenticity," attached to whatever notion of a "Chinese style" of playing "non-Chinese music" that can be read via the empty signifier of skin color, then, has to be re-examined in view of both musicians' self-essentializing (ironically in reaction to existing stereotypes) for different marketplaces. These displays of "honest musicianship" go beyond how Mari Yoshihara understands Asian musicians to deliberately circumvent issues of cultural authenticity by evoking a cultural blankness or even universality or internationality in the context of Western art music (Yoshihara, 2008: 200). The performative stylizations hit harder at the idea of artistic authenticity, often critiqued by popular-music scholars as the somewhat naïve pursuit of an ultimately constructed myth (Frith, 1986, Moore, 2002).

As already described, both Wang and Zhu consciously disrupt mainstream versions of Chinese femininity, one equated to subservient womanhood, in almost opposite ways. Their spirited performances—channeling energy dynamics from opposite ends of the exothermic and endothermic spectrum—challenge stereotypes of Chinese musicians as robotic or mechanically passionless. At the same time, in their production of alternative versions of Chinese pianism, they have unwittingly reinforced other kinds of ethnic stereotypes: of the genius child virtuoso and of the philosopher-sage. To this end, both performers have been received among different audiences as, ironically, remaining authentic to their imagined, innate artistry. Zhu's aspirations toward the purest form of ancient wisdom via music are unquestioned as noble aims in themselves. Wang's capricious expending of terrifying energy is celebrated not as inauthenticity but rather as a genuine artistic trait, woven organically into her image as a youthful zephyr of the keyboard. To be sure, there are always slippages between the persons, personas, and personalities intended by Wang and Zhu, caught in between what Auslander (2006) describes more theoretically in terms of the contextual differences between genre framing and different interactive social dynamics.

In the spirit of a Barthian query, one might ask here, then: to what extent are the public personas of Wang and Zhu—gendered or otherwise—co-constructed in the ears and minds of their audiences and fans? Any putative answer will have to consider not only the recorded albums and live aspects of their performance portfolios but also the roles different kinds of social media play in furthering their public presence. Here, the two artists operate in slightly different worlds, and this in turn reflects on their different transnational reaches. Wang is successful within and beyond China and is a regular, recognized presence on world stages. She has seen her primary means of engaging with an already global (if elite) public via concerts amplified through widespread interest generated by the short video clips of her encore pieces. A 102-second video of her rendition of "Flight of The Bumblebee" in 2008 (see note 2), for example, had received almost 5.7 million views on YouTube by March 2018, with commentators remarking humorously (and less humorously) on her prowess. Figure 19.1 shows examples of commentators taking metaphorical and literal swipes at her speed, her "satanic" abilities, and her Asian ethnicity.

Wang also has established a reasonably active Internet profile beyond YouTube. She has a more extensive presence on niche websites dedicated to Western art music, such as medici.tv. Here, fuller, high-definition recordings of her concerto or long-recital appearances can be viewed, complementing the lower-resolution versions

3 years ago

Term: Holy fuck
Pronunciation: /ˈhōlē/ /fək/
Definition: (1) An exclamation of one's incredulity or lack of cognition, often as the result of observing some previously inconcieved act or occurrence.
(2) See Yuja Wang.

REPLY   529   👍 👎

View all 7 replies ∨

3 years ago

Fun Fact: She won that piano from Satan after defeating him in a musical duel.

REPLY   230   👍 👎

View all 2 replies ∨

1 year ago

Too slow: should be 10x faster

REPLY   11   👍 👎

View all 2 replies ∨

3 years ago

Roses are red, violets are blue, there's always an Asian who's better than you.

REPLY   471   👍 👎

FIGURE 19.1. Criticism of Yuja Wang on YouTube.

of both the short clips and more extended recitals found on YouTube. In addition, Wang has also given numerous video interviews, interspersed with piano playing, to TV stations and a whole range of media outlets, including fashion-oriented ones. However, YouTube remains one of the main places where her viral videos are disseminated. Optimized for sharing on parallel platforms such as Facebook, Twitter, Buzzfeed, Reddit, and music blogs, these video memes open and close loops of re-mediation from Wang's live recordings—via strategic excerpting—to live-audiences-turned-online-fans-turned-new-offline-audiences, when they seek to see her in the flesh in a concert hall.

YouTube has been banned in China for some time, but many of the same clips, in addition to those retrieved from concert footage in China, can also be found on Chinese websites such as bilibili.com, youku, baidu.com and iqiyi.com. One difference between footage residing on websites outside and within China can be found in the latter's slight emphasis on components of idol culture otherwise found widely across pop-music industries in China and its diaspora. Here, there is more press and fan fixation on Wang's love life, her hairstyle, her hobbies, her astrological signs, and, of course, her clothes. In this sense, the China-generated fan world for Wang recalls the earlier treatment of another Chinese superstar, Li Yundi, whose huge (if lately decreasing) popularity in China once hinged upon his articulation of a transnational J-pop-idol image (Tan, 2013). In fact, in her initial years of fame, Wang was more concerned about being compared to the then-bigger name, Lang Lang. An interview transcript illustrates how, already at an early stage of her career, the pianist was clued into the intersectional issues of ethnicity, personal style, her fetishized size, and the creative issue of carving out an artistic niche on her own terms:

XIN JING PAPER: What do you get asked the most?
WANG: Lang Lang . . . the same teacher stuff and whatever, when I'm overseas, what's the difference between studying in China and outside China, why so many Chinese kids are learning the piano and so good at it.
XIN JING PAPER: And your answer is?
WANG: As for the question on Lang Lang, my answer is: I don't like to be framed and put in this category. Although we are both Asians, went to the same school, had the same teacher, our personalities are very different; we are completely different artists. I feel that my Chinese teachers are full of passion and poetry; my teachers overseas are good with theory and analysis. Chinese kids are good with the piano because Chinese teachers are good at striking a good foundation, and there is just so much talent in China. I tell people that the piano in China is like sports in the United States; it's very popular (laughs).
XIN JING PAPER: Your first album was very modern.
WANG: With my first album I wanted to make a statement, so all the pieces on it are very "edgy." Because everyone looks at me and thinks I'm a little Asian girl, weak and tiny on the outside. It's precisely the kind of stereotype I want to break.[6]

This Q&A style of interview remains a common format in mainstream-media interviews with Wang published in Chinese and disseminated on the Chinese Internet. However, mainstream media, taken as a whole, is only one of the many platforms that fans use to engage with their icon. In the world of blogs, WeChat discussion groups, Weibo conversations, and social media at large, musical "street cred" is better demonstrated. On this front, it is the unlikely icon of Zhu who has cornered the market of "exclusivity," by positioning herself as a "secret discovery." While a representative YouTube video by Zhu had amassed just over than sixty thousand views outside China by March 2018,[7] on social media within China, including on blogs, "friendship groups," and instant-messaging platforms, she remains a topic of heated debate. This has come to pass both in relation to her alleged hidden genius and, more recently, in connection to a backlash against her sudden rise to fame, with some pointing to the potential overhyping of her talent. On zhihu.com, for example, ever-expanding threads with cascading tributaries of comments discuss in fine detail everything from Zhu's love of Chinese ink painting to her use of rubato, to the "true" spirit of Bach, to her cult status and the questionable foundations of her fame (Figure 19.2).

如何评价朱晓玫演奏的哥德堡变奏曲？

OK，写了这么多，其实就想说明"音乐=人生"这么个浅显易懂的道理。巴赫是最均衡的。他之后的作曲家，分别在"人生"的某（些）方面，做了夸张化处理。比如贝多芬的英雄主义，肖邦的诗意……但是，若以包罗万象而论，则巴赫的"人生"显然最贴近真实的"人生"……写到这里，猛然发觉电脑上通过XXXX元的音箱放出来的《哥德堡变奏曲》却也如本文一般，进入了尾声。此时抬头一看，朱晓玫女士脸上松弛的肌肉依旧随着音乐抖动，但不知为何，此时，我却觉得，她变得顺眼了许多。

编辑于 2015-10-21 16:01

▲ 赞同 127 ▼   ● 25 条评论   ✓ 分享   ★ 收藏   ♥ 喜欢   收起 ∧

知乎用户

5 人赞同了该回答

水墨 灵动

发布于 2014-04-02 03:57

▲ 赞同 5 ▼   ● 1 条评论   ✓ 分享   ★ 收藏   ♥ 喜欢

知乎用户

16 人赞同了该回答

什么时候Rubato成了弊端了？ 不会有人想要把现代钢琴的特点和演奏技法全都抛弃仅仅为了"还原古乐"效果吧？那还不如直接用古乐器，何必在现代钢琴上费劲儿呢？既然用了现代钢琴，就发挥一些现代钢琴的特色么，自然演奏技法也得现代一点

FIGURE 19.2. Zhihu discussion thread on Zhu Xiao-Mei's interpretation of the "Goldberg Variations."

The trend for appreciation of Zhu, Wang Weida (2017: 192–212) explains, is the result of a suddenly developing social-media industry in China coinciding with the equally rapid—and outwardly focused—expansion of nascent Western art-music industries in China. Wang describes this as a natural consequence of new, emerging classes of classical-music fans who want to demonstrate themselves—via increasingly esoteric musical taste—to be more socially mobile than the next. Ultimately, and coming full circle back to the question of Chineseness, such congruent developments in the fields of media networks and economic development have to be understood within the larger contexts of new nationalisms and transnationalisms that have risen in China and beyond. These in turn, to an extent, have been influenced by as well as affected the careers and reception of Yuja Wang and Zhu Xiao-Mei.

Conclusion

Yuja Wang, a fixture on the international stage and whose concerts, like Zhu's, sell out constantly in China, arguably functions as a de facto instrument of cultural diplomacy overseas, rather than domestically. Yet, unlike her compatriot Lang Lang, who has graced large state events such as the Beijing Olympics opening ceremony of 2008, Wang has not participated in major government-endorsed extravaganzas. Her offhand comments about China's cultural power have veered toward pragmatic ambivalence; she almost casually acknowledges the political-economic success of the nation as a foregone conclusion while bemoaning hyperefficient musical-training systems or restrictive cultural contexts, all amid chatting happily about topics from cheap literature to haute couture to boyfriends. Like others in her generation of upwardly mobile twenty- and thirty-somethings, Wang has experienced multiple opportunities for international travel, including extensive periods of touring and working overseas in tandem with China's foreign economic and investment policies. She is, therefore, reasonably clued into global trends, spending much of her life in hotels and airport lounges when not in New York.

Wang speaks to an extremely elite generation of Chinese audiences who are comfortable as transnationals in their constant zig-zagging between China and the world's major cities and who are aspiring cosmopolitans, in their absorption of new materially enhanced lifestyles (at least in the worlds of fashion, food, and hospitality). But Wang also operates beyond this zone of Chinese transnationality: she is a known name among a different class of elite fans within global and multiple Chinese diasporas, people whose lives have been entrenched for at least a few generations in various cities and communities around the world. Likely schooled in Western art music as a matter of upbringing, as part of the Chinese diasporic experience (Yoshihara, 2008: 30–34), these audiences make up a secondary category of her appreciators. Forming yet another subgroup within an even broader global network of classical-music fans around the world, they see themselves as equally cosmopolitan members of the international elite world.

With the pianist Zhu Xiao-Mei, the situation is somewhat different and must be contextualized within a different sense of transnational Chineseness, one imagined on local terms within China. Zhu's global profile as a pianist is limited to her pedagogical presence at the Paris Conservatoire. However, the very fact of her relative obscurity in a kind of self-exile within one of Europe's major classical-music centers is the key reason for her extraordinary force as an icon within China. Zhu's image speaks to a new trans-local bourgeoisie-within-bourgeoisie, which buys into her aura for both nationalist and class-conscious reasons. She is an anti-success story for her fans in China, who may not have the means to jet-set between Beijing, Shanghai, New York, and Paris but in their imaginations construct a cosmopolitan Chinese piano world on her behalf. Shrouded in the Byronic romance of old-school journeying, exploration, and personal soul-searching away from "home," this is a nostalgia- and nationalism-laced world, where Zhu's return to her "roots," in literal form for homecoming concerts and metaphorically through re-invention of herself via "ancient" literature and philosophy, is celebrated as a demonstration of a new quiet Chinese cultural power.

The irony here is that Zhu's old-school artistic charms have been discovered and have come to turn her into the cult success that she is today by means of new domestic media technologies disseminated across the vast and developing Chinese Internet. These state-controlled technologies and networks enable the mushrooming of very specific communities within China, under the circumstances of increasing state censorship and blocking of parallel platforms from outside of China. Paradoxically here, China's transnationalisms are developing but clipped in growth. Unlike the audiences of Wang, who presumably attend her concerts in the course of regular events at Lincoln Center or the Barbican, Zhu's fans hail from cities all across the "mainland," traveling long distances simply to listen to and watch her, even as they may be intimately and soulfully connected to the artist through prior, repeated listenings and viewings of her recorded performances.

One might ask: Do the worlds of Wang and Zhu collide? And what do they say about the broader impact of the individuals as pianists, women, commercial successes, brands, and as persons of Chinese ethnicity of contrasting generations? The obvious answer is that there will always be many points of overlap, given the sprawling and intersectional networks of connections developing in communities, industries, institutions, and scenes across and beyond China. Such transformations can only have occurred in tandem with the ease of airplane travel within and beyond the country, following rising incomes and economic development, and also with the telescoping of imagined and real communities thanks to the World Wide—as well as the not-quite-world-wide—Web. Indeed, often on Chinese websites that are reasonably easily accessed outside of China (sometimes mirrored on websites in Hong Kong), there are constant debates and discussions comparing the two performers and assessing them against their male compatriots.[8] These comparisons are intersectional in how they asymmetrically include or exclude certain socio-economic classes, or classes of citizenship, and how they are uneven in the flows of music, information, and human and other resources across and beyond China's borders. In their similar, different, and interlinked ways, both Wang and

Zhu exist within and shape the dynamics of emerging communities of Chinese citizens and members of multiple Chinese diasporas, where the scales of national, transnational, cosmopolitan, and international networks begin to reduce in size or even contextually collapse. As larger-than-life figures—who, in their imagined casual and everyday existences, are also normalized as regular—they make new meanings for Chinese musicians, women, and culture as a whole.

Glossary

Chen Sa 陳薩, pianist (b. 1979)
hexie 和諧, harmony
Jane Xie (Xie Jingxian 解静娴), pianist (b. 1983)
Lang Lang 郎朗, pianist (b. 1982)
Li Yundi 李雲迪, pianist (b. 1982)
liu bai 留白, "leaving blank"
Qianggu quan 腔骨圈, Sheep Bone Group, group of music critics operating on Weibo China
wabi sabi 侘寂 [Japanese], doctrine of seeking perfection in imperfection
xiulian 修煉, Daoist practice of asceticism
Yuja Wang (Wang Yujia 王羽佳), pianist (b. 1987)
Zhang Zuo (Zuo Zhang 左章), pianist (b. 1988)
Zhu Xiao-Mei 朱曉玫, pianist (b. 1949)

Notes

1. Blogpost by yutu3041. "Shui hai jide Gu Shengying—zhongyu youle houjizhe—Zhu Xiao-Mei" "誰還記得顧聖嬰—終於有了後繼者—朱曉玫" [Who Still Remembers Gu Shengying—There's Finally a Successor—Zhu Xiao-Mei], posted August 22, 2012. Accessed March 6, 2018. http://www.360doc.com/content/13/1122/03/1397577_331182146.shtml.
2. "Yuja Wang – Tea For Two (Encore)," https://www.youtube.com/watch?v=MCUjdgdqE90; "Yuja Wang – Mozart – Turkish March," https://www.youtube.com/watch?v=NJdzGLK3gfc; and "Yuja Wang plays the Flight of the Bumble-Bee (Vol du Bourdon)," https://www.youtube.com/watch?v=8alxBofd_eQ, all accessed March 6, 2018.
3. See, for example: "Wang Yuja: wo zhi xiang yu yinyue chiluo xiangjian" "王羽佳：我只想與音樂赤裸相見" [Wang Yuja: I Only Want to Get Naked with the Music], posted September 22, 2017. Accessed March 6, 2018. http://www.sohu.com/a/193845253_636365; "Ni you duoshao muguang bei tade zhuozhuang xiyin?" "你有多少目光被她的著裝吸引" [How Often Has Your Eye been Stolen by Her Glamour?' posted November 17, 2016. Accessed March 6, 2018. http://www.360doc.com/content/16/1117/22/11548039_607387860.shtml.
4. "Ruhe pingjia Zhu Xiao-Mei yanzou de Gedebao bianzouqu?" "如何評價朱曉玫演奏的哥德堡變奏曲?" [How Does One Critique Zhu Xiao-Mei's Performance of the Goldberg Variations?]. Accessed March 6, 2018. https://www.zhihu.com/question/20248783.

5. The moniker of the self-named Sheep Bone Group derives from the habit of a clique of friends-turned-music-critics in China emerging in the 2010s, who would often congregate for a bowl of sheep bone soup after live concerts to discuss their opinions of each performance. Members of this group would then post their thoughts on larger private and semi-public WeChat and Weibo chat groups.
6. The passage is from an interview in the *Beijing News* (*Xinjing bao* 新京報) copied into the Music Piano Room blog post. "Wang Yujia: Wo he Lang Lang hen buyiyang" "王羽佳：我和郎朗很不一樣" [Wang Yuja: I'm Very Different from Lang Lang], Feburary 24, 2014. Accessed August 24, 2021. http://blog.sina.com.cn/s/blog_5db528530101byss.html.
7. "J. S. Bach – Goldberg Variations, Zhu Xiao-Mei (Piano) + 'The Return is the Movement of Tao.'" Accessed March 6, 2018. https://www.youtube.com/watch?v=Cq2EtAK38xk.
8. For example: "Cou ge renao, ye fa zhang Zhu Xiao-Mei ayi" "湊個熱鬧，也發張朱曉玫阿姨" [Joining in the Fun, Also Sending One of Aunty Zhu Xiao-Mei]. Accessed August 24, 2021. https://www.douban.com/group/topic/26994173/?cid=311605572.

References

Anonymous. (2011). "Huaren gangqin Meinü Wang Yuja chuan chaoduanqun yanzou zai meiyinfa zhenglun" "華人鋼琴美女王羽佳穿超短裙演奏在美引發爭論" [Chinese Piano Beauty Wang Yuja Wears a Short Skirt in the United States Inviting Controversy], *Renmin ribao* 人民日報 [People's Daily], August 15, 2011.

Auslander, Philip. (2006). "Musical Personae." *The Drama Review* 50 (1): 100–119.

Bourdieu, Pierre. (1984). *Distinction: A Social Critique of the Judgment of Taste*, translated by Richard Nice. London: Routledge and Kegan Paul.

Brown, Geoff. (2020). "Yuja Wang: John Adams Review—A Showcase for Pianist Wang's Flying Fingers, but Ultimately Superficial." *The Times*, April 24, 2020. Accessed August 24, 2021. https://www.thetimes.co.uk/article/yuja-wang-john-adams-review-a-showcase-for-pianist-wangs-flying-fingers-but-ultimately-superficial-67wb83s7x.

Butler, Judith. (1990). *Gender Trouble: Feminism and the Subversion of Identity*. London: Routledge.

Clayton, Martin, Byron Dueck, and Laura Leante, eds. (2013). *Experience and Meaning in Music Performance*. Oxford: Oxford University Press.

Crossley, Nick. (2015). "Music Worlds and Body Techniques: On the Embodiment of Musicking." *Cultural Sociology* 9 (4): 471–92.

Downey, Greg. (2002). "Listening to Capoeira: Phenomenology, Embodiment, and the Materiality of Music." *Ethnomusicology* 46 (3): 487–509.

Duan, Zhaoxu. (2013). "Wang Yujia: Gudian yu xiandai de canlan zhisheng." "王羽佳:古典與現代的燦爛之聲" [Wang Yuja: Brilliant Sounds of the Classical and Modern]. *Renmin yinyue* 人民音樂 [People's Music], no. 3: 8–13

Entwistle, Joanne. (2000). "Fashion and the Fleshy Body: Dress as Embodied Practice." *Fashion Theory* 4 (3): 323–347.

Everett, Yayoi Uno, and Frederick Lau. 2004. "Introduction." In *Locating East Asia in Western Art Music*, edited by Yayoi Uno Everett and Fred Lau, xv–xxi. Middletown, CT: Wesleyan University Press.

Fabbri, Franco. (1981). "A Theory of Musical Genres: Two Applications." In *Popular Music Perspectives*, edited by David Horn and Philip Tagg, 52–81. Gothenburg: International Association for the Study of Popular Music.

Frith, Simon. (1986). "Art Versus Technology: The Strange Case of Popular Music." *Media, Culture & Society* 8 (3): 263–79.

Goffman, Erving. (1956). *The Presentation of Self in Everyday Life*. New York: Random House.

Hewett, Ivan. (2014). "Yuja Wang Interview: 'I Can Wear Long Skirts When I'm 40.'" *Telegraph*, February 5, 2014.

Keightley, Keir. (2001). "Reconsidering Rock." In *The Cambridge Companion to Rock and Pop*, edited by Simon Frith, Will Straw, and John Street, 109–42. Cambridge, UK: Cambridge University Press.

Kosman, Joshua. (2012). "S. F. Symphony Review: Wang's Awesome Rachmaninoff." *San Francisco Chronicle*, June 19, 2012.

Kovan, Brianna. (2017). "Piano Phenomenon Yuja Wang is Breaking Classical Music Taboos." *Elle*, May 24, 2017.

Liao Yang 廖陽 with Wang Xinyi 王心怡. (2014). "Gangqinjia Zhu Xiao-Mei de fennu: Weishenme Zhongguo de Wenhua yao he zhuanqian lianxi zaiyiqi?" "鋼琴家朱曉玫的憤怒：為什麼中國的文化要和賺錢聯繫在一起？" [The Angst of Pianist Zhu Xiao-Mei: Why Does Chinese Culture Have to be Linked to Making Money?]. *Peng Bai, The Paper*, November 10, 2014. Accessed March 6, 2018. http://www.thepaper.cn/newsDetail_forward_1277055.

Maddocks, Fiona. (2017). "Interview. Yuja Wang: If the Music is Beautiful and Sensual, Why Not Dress to Fit?" *The Guardian*, April 9, 2017.

Malcolm, Janet. (2016). "Yuja Wang and the Art of Performance: The Piano Prodigy is Known for the Brilliance of Her Playing and for Her Dramatic Outfits." *The New Yorker*, September 5, 2016.

Mollard, Michel. (2014). *The Return Is the Movement of Tao*. DVD. Leipzig: Accentus Music.

Moore, Allan. (2002). "Authenticity as Authentication." *Popular Music* 21 (2): 209–23.

Nordlinger, Jay. (2018). "The Yuja 'n' Jaap Show." *The New Criterion*, March 5, 2018.

Ong, Aihwa. 1999. *Flexible Citizenship: The Cultural Logics of Transnationality*. Durham, NC: Duke University of Press.

Pease, Rowan. 2009. "Korean Pop Music in China: Nationality, Authenticity, and Gender." In *Cultural Studies and Cultural Industries in Northeast Asia: What a Difference a Region Makes*, edited by Chris Berry, Nicola Liscutin, and Jonathan D. Mackintosh, 151–68. Hong Kong: Hong Kong University Press.

Phelan, Peggy. (1993). *Unmarked: The Politics of Performance*. London: Routledge.

Schechner, Richard. (1988). *Performance Theory*. London: Routledge

Su, Lin. 2016. "Jinglinbande yanzou yu reqingruhuo de biaoxianli—lingting Wang Yujia gangqin duzou yinyuehui" "精靈般的演奏與熱情如火的表現力—聆聽王羽佳鋼琴獨奏音樂會" [Performance of a Sprite and Passionate Expression—Listening to Wang Yujia's Solo Piano Recital]. *Yishu pingjian* 藝術評鑑 [Art Appraisal], no. 10: 24–25.

Swed, Mark. (2011). "Music Review: Yuja Wang and Lionel Bringuier at the Hollywood Bowl." *Los Angeles Times*, August 3, 2011.

Tan, Shzr Ee. (2013). "New Chinese Masculinities on the Piano: Lang Lang and Li Yundi." In *Gender in Chinese Music*, edited by Rachel Harris, Rowan Pease, and Shzr Ee Tan, 132–51. Rochester, NY: University of Rochester Press.

Tian Yimiao 田藝苗. (2017). "Zhu Xiao-Mei: Jiandan shi ziyou" "朱曉玫：簡單即是自由" [Zhu Xiao-Mei: Simplicity is Freedom]. *Sohu*, June 16, 2017. Accessed March 6, 2018. http://www.sohu.com/a/149250503_303962.

Tommasini, Anthony. (2011). "Flaunting Virtuosity (And More)." *The New York Times*, October 21, 2011.

Tommasini, Anthony. (2016). "Review: Yuja Wang Tackles Beethoven's 'Hammerklavier,' Assured to a Fault." *The New York Times*, May 16, 2016.

Wallace, Arminta. (2015). "Pianist Zhu Xiao-Mei: The Tao of Bach." *The Irish Times*, August 1, 2015.

Wang Weida. (2017). "Western Art Music in Post-Socialist China." PhD diss., Royal Holloway University of London.

Woolfe, Zachary. (2013). "Restrained, Then Madly Lyrical: The Pianist as Spring Mechanism." *The New York Times*, May 17, 2013.

Yang, Mina. (2007). "East Meets West in the Concert Hall: Asians and Classical Music in the Century of Imperialism, Post-Colonialism, and Multiculturalism." *Asian Music* 38 (1): 1–30.

Yang, Xiaolong 楊小龍. (2017). "Yuyi wucai, jiayin jicheng—ping Wang Yujia gangqin duzou yinyue hui." "羽翼五彩，佳音即成—評王羽佳鋼琴獨奏音樂會" [Colorful Wings and Ideal Sounds—A Review of Wang Yujia's Solo Piano Recital]. *Gangqin yishu* 鋼琴藝術 [Piano Artistry], no. 2: 55–59.

Yoshihara, Mari. (2008). *Musicians from A Different Shore: Asians and Asian Americans in Classical Music*. Philadelphia: Temple University Press.

Zhang Lifen. (2014). "Yu Zhu Xiao-Mei gongjin zaocan" "與朱曉玫共進早餐" [Breakfast with Zhu Xiao-Mei]. *Financial Times*, Chinese edition, November 7, 2014.

Zhao, Dong. (2017). "The Christian Bodhisattva in China: Sinicization of the Virgin Mary in Chinese Literature." In *Representations of the Blessed Virgin Mary in World Literature and Art*, edited by Elina V. Shabli, 95–110. London: Lexington Books.

Zhu, Xiao-Mei. (2007). *La Rivière et son secret. Des camps de Mao à Jean-Sebastien Bach: le destin d'une femme d'exception* [The River and Its Secret. From the Camps of Mao to Johann Sebastian Bach: The Destiny of an Exceptional Woman]. Paris: Éditions Robert Laffont.

CHAPTER 20

LIVENESS AND MEDIATION IN CHINESE ART MUSIC

From The Map *to the* Qingming Festival

GERMÁN GIL-CURIEL

Introduction

THE exact meaning of liveness and mediation in music remains much debated. The discussion is usually framed around the exact limits of each term, "liveness" and "mediation," the inherently overlapping boundaries of which have only grown more blurred since the rise of digital technology. According to Katja Kwastek, the term "liveness" was first used in the context of the media in the 1930s, when radio broadcasting had become widespread. Although storage media such as the phonograph record had existed for many years, it was only with the arrival of radio that listeners were no longer able to distinguish between a direct broadcast of a performance and a broadcast of a recording. Consequently, direct broadcasting was now designated as "live broadcasting." Thus, the term "liveness" entered the vocabulary at the moment it became possible to simulate "here and now" communication using the mediation of new storage and broadcasting technology (Kwastek, 2015: 117). While the phrase "live recording" places the focus on the production of data, "live broadcasting" emphasizes the process of transmission, and the "live concert" prioritizes the moment of performance and reception (ibid.: 118). If, as Philip Auslander (1999) has pointed out, the sense of the term "liveness" has changed once and again according to the growing diffusion of interactive media, more recent technology has enabled various new mixes and combinations, such that earlier distinctions between live and mediated have become less useful. This is clear, for instance, in the case of opera, where new forms of media and technology have transformed the spatiotemporal experience. Stage directors "have transformed the settings of classical and grand operas by generating postmodern collisions of time and place" (Everett,

2015: xi), even involving digital technology to project film projections, which has become an indispensable constituent of the contemporary operatic mise en scène.

An alternative, non-technology-focused meaning for the term "liveness" has been proposed by Peter Brook, who highlights how liveness is produced through processes that emerge during reception by an audience, since spectators bring qualities of liveness into being through the nature of their attention. Brook contends that while in general the term "live" connotes all sorts of positive meanings, with the qualities of vibrancy, immediacy, relevancy, and realness among others usually ascribed to it, not all live experiences are actually such. Instead, sometimes they are "routine, mundane, disappointing . . . sometimes, they are deadly." In this sense, for Brook, "liveness" should be understood not as the opposite of "mediated," but rather as the opposite of "deadliness," that is, "a failed relationship between performance and audience" (cited in Reason and Lindelof, 2016: 1–2). From Brook's perspective, what is important about liveness resides not in some essential or ontological characteristic of the performance itself but rather in the relationship between performance and audience. In a live performance, the main point is an interaction of "mutual surprises" between audience and performer(s). It is a real encounter in which both parties experience something that takes place between them, includes them both, is accessible only to them, and leaves them both changed, even if only fleetingly.

In this chapter, I use the term "total art" to encompass the ways in which liveness and mediation can be understood in Chinese music, following Auslander and Brook, while placing the arts and the connections between them at the center. In particular, I do so through the case of *The Map: Concerto for Cello, Video, and Orchestra* (*"Ditu" wei datiqin, luxiang, jiyueduikaixiezouqu* 《地圖》為大提琴、錄像及樂隊嘅協奏曲, 2002; hereafter, *The Map*) by Tan Dun 譚盾, which I analyze in the first part of the chapter. I discuss how Tan Dun transforms the settings of the performance by generating the postmodern collisions of time and place, alluded to by Yayoi Uno Everett, involving digital technology, not only to screen film projections but also to bring a variety of music traditions—Chinese and Western, old and new—into dialogue with each other and with nature, which is incorporated into the scenery and, in some cases, serves as instruments, as very much a "live" part of the performance. I also argue that viewing *The Map* can result in a notoriously "live" experience, as defined by Brook, in the way that it elicits audience attention.

In the second part of the chapter, I use the term "mediation" to highlight the role of the arts and their connections. I refer here to the process whereby a work of art is transformed when passing from one medium to another, considering in particular the passage from painting into music in the case of *Along the River during the Qingming Festival* (*Qingming shanghe tu* 清明上河圖). Originally painted by Zhang Zeduan 張擇端 during the reign of the emperor Huizong of the Song dynasty (1100–26), it was recast in 2006 as *Chinese Symphonic Picture along the River during the Qingming Festival* (*Zhongguo yin hua Qingming shanghe tu* 中國音畫清明上河圖, hereafter *Qingming Symphonic Picture*) composed by Shi Zhiyou 史志有. Drawing from the work of Linda Hutcheon on inter-medial adaptation as a cultural meme (Hutcheon, 2007: 31–32),

I contend that mediation is the precondition to liveness, in the sense of keeping and transmitting the meaning and relevance of a fundamental piece of culture over time. I argue that music can be treated as a (re)mediation of social values, imaginings, and experience. The chapter concludes with a summary of the main points made and a discussion of how the theoretical frameworks introduced in the case studies are particularly useful for analyzing liveness and mediation in music in the Chinese context, specifying their advantages and highlighting their potential in further research on the topic.

Tan Dun and *The Map*: Live and Mediated Performance as "Total Art"

The term Gesamtkunstwerk, attributed to Richard Wagner, has been used to describe an artwork that reintegrates theater, music, and the visual arts of ancient Greek drama into opera and eventually into cinema, therefore regarded as "total" in that sense. According to Anke Finger and Danielle Follet, three kinds of practices of blending are associated with the Gesamtkunstwerk concept: the aesthetic, which promotes the blending of "the different arts and genres, as in multimedia, operatic, and synesthetic creations"; the political, which blends art and society, intertwined with the first; and finally, the metaphysical, which aspires to a sort of borderlessness, "a merging of present, empirical reality with a non-present, or not-yet-present, envisioned totality" (2011: 4). While this theory was developed in the West and emerges from a Western perspective, I will argue here that it can also be very fruitfully applied to understand liveness and mediation in the Chinese context.

The history of this seminal aesthetic concept has been labyrinthine, and it now has a "heterogeneous historical identity that manifests itself in the real similarities between various works and artistic projects that arise in quite different contexts" (Finger and Follet, 2011: 2). But despite its Wagnerian roots, the concept has given birth to new theories and multimedia concepts through time, such as synesthesia or correspondence of the arts, and more recently new perceptions of the nature of intermedia, on the basis of a variety of amalgamation of artworks. As instances of this correspondence, let us remember that in China paintings were often called "silent poems" as they conveyed feelings not easily put into words, and during the Han dynasty (202 BCE–220 CE), the court delegated the management of both music and poetry to the Music Bureau, on account of their perceived equivalence (Knight, 2012: 25–26).

A long-time practitioner of total art, Tan Dun is probably the most renowned contemporary Chinese composer. His vast oeuvre comprises operas, visual music, an orchestral theater series, organic music with orchestra or with voices[1], symphonic works, concertos, solo music, ensemble works, an oratorio and chorus, ritual music, film soundtracks, and multimedia creations. His stage devices and multimedia approaches, as displayed in his operas, orchestral works, and dance/ballet music—for example, *Ghost Opera* (*Guixi*

鬼戲, 1994), *Marco Polo* (*Makeboluo* 馬可波羅, 1995), and *The Map*—have been widely discussed. Tan Dun is also one of the most celebrated Chinese pioneer composers of hybrid music, drawing from Eastern and Western traditions, thereby adding a particular cultural dimension to his own totalizing, blending impulse. His visual music, as the main protagonist in his multimedia installations, brings traditional ethnic music into dialogue with the latest technology. Its multimedia presentations involve music with nature, theatrical performance, dance, architecture, landscape, and cinema, with each medium providing a unique contribution. But his work is also truly innovative in that it mixes the technological with the traditional, interweaving the visual with the auditory, as a pertinent example of total art (Gil-Curiel, 2016b: 122–23). Tan Dun's brand of total art draws on theatrical, dance, and organic elements, against a backdrop of natural scenarios. For instance, his *Water Heavens* (2010) performance for strings, water, *pipa* 琵琶, and voice—part of his "Visual Music" series related to water—takes place in an old Chinese pavilion, based on the composer's concept of "architectural music":

> A stream of water flows into the hall, forming a pond surrounded by the audience, creating the stage of *Water Heavens*. In this ancient house, a drop of water falls from high above through the oculus bringing out the musical dialogue of Zen music and Bach. . . . In *Water Heavens* music can be seen and architecture can be heard. (Tan Dun cited in Gil-Curiel, 2016a: 75)

As explained by Tan, the concept behind this architectural music relies on the fact that the hall's structure is similar to that of an ancient two-story house. The wooden structure of the upper floor reveals a Ming-dynasty-style house, whereas the iron pillars and steel floor of the lower level resemble an industrial space with a distinct German Bauhaus style. During the performance, the river flows in and out through the house, linking the interior and exterior space, as a symbol of the purification of spirit and soul. "The combination of the different Ming and Bauhaus styles, as well as the contrasting sounds of water, iron, and other natural instruments completes my 'architectural music' wonderland where heaven and man become one" (Tan, cited in Law, 2013). This strongly recalls the metaphysical dimension of total art, as mentioned above. Tan Dun notes his ultimate goal for *Water Heavens* as being to create a space where the architecture could become an instrument that could be heard and played.

His work entitled *The Map*, a concerto for cello, video, and orchestra filmed in an ancient village in Tan's home province of Hunan, furnishes an excellent example of how Tan Dun's brand of total artwork combines the live and the mediated. Experimentation that led to this concerto began on two separate trips to Hunan, in 1999 and 2001, during which Tan Dun employed ethnic source material and turned it into abstract sonorities, sometimes keeping the source material in its pure state on a video screen while simultaneously exploring its timbres orchestrally. In March 2004 he took this further by arranging a performance of the resulting composition by the Shanghai Symphony Orchestra in rural Hunan. Documentary footage depicting the lives of Chinese ethnic minorities, including the Tujia 土家, Miao 苗, and Dong 侗, and also musical performances by them, was played on a screen at the location where the orchestral musicians were playing the cello concerto. Thus, the musicians onsite interacted with the ethnic-minority musicians onscreen, in a duet of live and recorded performances (see Gil-Curiel, 2016a: 74–75). More than thirty thousand villagers from the area came to the performance (Melvin and Cai, 2004: 332) (see Figure 20.1). For many, it was their first time ever to attend a symphony concert, and so the event turned out to be "live" in very much the sense described by Brook above.

Tan Dun described *The Map* as being about minority cultures in China, looking at the past as well as the future. But instead of taking a curatorial approach that seeks to preserve a tradition at the expense of its vitality, he sought to bring ethnic rural tradition literally into counterpoint with the modern urban avant-garde. He put it thus:

> *The Map* is a multimedia concerto grosso. I wanted to discover the counterpoint between different media, different time-spaces, and different cultures. The structures and musical textures are designed to create antiphonal music by building a counterpoint between the cello solo and video, orchestra and video, solo and ensemble, text and sound, and multichannel video and live playing of stone. Metaphorically, the orchestra becomes nature, the soloist symbolizes people, and video represents tradition...
>
> Actually my greatest wish in composing *The Map* was to meld technology and tradition. *Through tradition, technology can be humanized; through technology, tradition can be renewed* and passed on. Today, ancient cultural traditions vanish every day, everywhere. If artists embrace the past and the future within their hearts, miracles will arrive. (Interview with Tan Dun, cited in Smith, 2004, emphasis mine)

FIGURE 20.1. On-site musicians interact with on-screen ethnic-minority performers, for an audience of more than 30,000 villagers.

(Still from *Tan Dun: The Map*. DVD. Deutsche Gramophone, 2004)

These ideas of Tan Dun's are evident in each of the movements of *The Map*, as I briefly summarize below, paying attention to the cultural issues involved in each section as well as the Chinese and Western musical instruments and their aesthetic impact.

The Map includes several video clips, one for each of the sequences featured. It begins with video footage of a piece called "Nuo: Ghost Dance and Cry-Singing," which juxtaposes contrasting musical elements of rural Hunan, namely the sorrowful pleas of professional mourners with the jubilant percussion of ancient Nuo opera 儺戲 (*nuoxi*), a kind of masked performance in which the boundaries between theater and religious ritual are blurred. It continues with leaf blowing, which young Tujia men do as a means of courtship. By blowing a stream of air over the edge of the leaf's surface, a Tujia man can communicate a surprisingly broad range of emotional states. Next is "Daliuzi" ("Cymbal Coloring"), in which percussionists establish a collaborative rapport in order to produce a wide range of sonorities imitating the sounds of nature. By the time the video clip for this sequence begins, the entire orchestra—first percussion, then brass, then winds, then strings—has already "framed the rhythm and timbre with a full instrumental realization of the sonorities, allowing live and taped performances to come together in multimedia counterpoint at the end" (Smith, 2004).

"Daliuzi" is followed by "Miao Suona," a movement modeled on the music of a more rustic version of the Han double-reed instrument *suona* 嗩吶, which requires a delicate balance of fingering and breathing to control pitch and volume. Again, the orchestra and solo cello first set the mood with phrasing and ornamentation derived from *suona* playing styles, and then the videotaped performance begins. The trope of having two participants use music to appear to communicate with one another is employed again in "Feige" (飛歌, literally, "flying song"), borrowed from a form of Miao antiphonal singing of the same name (in Mandarin). This example is one of several in which women figure prominently in *The Map*.[2] Similarly, in the piece called "Tongue Singing" played near the end, a quintet of Dong women perform using a rare example of polyphonic folk singing, a vocal technique reminiscent of those found, for instance, in Slavic nations. Their refrain uses rapid tongue articulations that imitate the sound of cicadas, as the form highlights a vocal leader accompanied by slow-moving drones, like a medieval European organum, with singular vocal techniques that imitate the sounds of nature.

The only two movements lacking a full videotaped field recording are the "Interlude" and "Stone Drums." The "Interlude" opens with a scrolling text introducing the story behind *The Map*, amid a symphonic backdrop that explores a range of modernist orchestral sonorities. This is followed by "Stone Drums." Instead of a field recording, the video shown is of Tan Dun himself, emulating the movements of a Ba Gua master whom he had met earlier and whose performance had greatly impressed him.

The Map concludes with "Qeej" which features the *lusheng* 蘆笙, a free-reed mouth organ most characteristic of the Miao, Dong, and other ethnic minorities in southwestern China. (The instrument is known in some of their languages as *qeej*). It is regularly featured in village celebrations, with melodies that are related to specific ritual dances. Here, it is placed into dialogue with the cello. Throughout this movement, the recorded component becomes in essence an additional instrumental section, which Tan folds into the orchestra.

By composing for a European orchestra while incorporating the unique perspectives of different cultures and idiosyncratic personal roots, Tan renews the orchestra. In sum, the three types of boundary-blurring characteristics of total art mentioned above—the aesthetic, which blurs boundaries between genres; the political, which blends art and society; and the metaphysical, which aspires to a sort of borderlessness—are present in *The Map*. The combinations of live and mediated, traditional and modern (even avant-garde), ethnic and cosmopolitan, present and absent, and East and West are all brought together into a meaningful unity that audiences might well have perceived as live in the sense of an encounter, a contingent moment open to surprises. Be that as it may, *The Map* was highly successful and has subsequently been performed numerous times in Europe and the US.

Along the River during the Qingming Festival: Liveness and Mediation from Painting to Music (and into Virtual Reality)

Scholars such as Linda Hutcheon have theorized the phenomenon of adaptation across the media in terms of cultural units that evolve and mutate, with the prior work of art enjoying, as it were, an afterlife in new incarnations (Hutcheon, 2007: 176). She proposes three qualities as needed for high survival value in these works of art—longevity, fecundity, and copying fidelity—although she acknowledges that, in a cultural context, copying means changing with each repetition (ibid.: 167). In this section of the chapter, I borrow from this theory to discuss *Along the River during the Qingming Festival* (*Qingming shanghe tu*), a work of art that began its life as a painting, then was turned into a "Chinese symphonic picture" (*Zhongguo yinhua* 中國音畫), and is at the moment of writing being converted into a virtual-reality digital experience that will allow users to "enter" its world, in which music constitutes a large part.

Source: The Painting

The painting's Chinese title can be translated as "Scenes along the River during the Qingming Festival." It is a monumental masterpiece on a light-colored silk scroll, 528 centimeters long and 24.8 centimeters high, running from right to left as is typical of this genre of painting from the Northern Song dynasty. It was made by the famous court painter Zhang Zeduan (1085–1145)—a native of Dongwu, today's Zhucheng, in Shandong province. The quality of longevity is thus evident in this case.

Using a traditional Chinese realistic manner of painting in detail, this work of art focuses on everyday life. It depicts the natural scenery along the banks of the Bian river and social activities during the early twelfth century, a very prosperous period of Chinese history, during the celebration of the Qingming festival. The Song dynasty was a period when commerce began to flourish in the cities. At the time Bianjing became the capital of Song China, "businesses and shops gradually began to invade traditionally residential areas, with stores and wine shops springing up in city streets, bringing newfound trade and prosperity with them. *Qingming shanghe tu* vividly depicts this new prosperity of the merging cities of the period" (Wu and Wallace, 2008: unpaginated). The painting thus conjures a parallel situation to the present, suggesting an ideal time to "copy" this cultural product with high fidelity in musical (and other visual) forms.

Qingming shanghe tu has three sections. The first, with its focus on the coming spring, sets the tone for the entire painting. Along with budding willow trees and travelers setting out on journeys, there are people on sedan chairs returning from visits to their ancestors' graves. The second section depicts the Bian river, especially the boats that are seen plying back and forth under the Rainbow bridge. Various carriages, horses, and throngs of people can be seen. The final section shows the streets overflowing with traffic and pedestrians, typical of the hustle and bustle of the flourishing city of Bianjing. A magnificent, imposing city gate is at the center, with crisscrossing streets and buildings clustered on each side. The bridge, ships, carriages, wine shops, teahouses, temples, and stores of all kinds are depicted in meticulous detail. Every imaginable trade and a great diversity of busy characters—such as physicians, fortune tellers, seers, monks, jugglers, storytellers, official scholars, innkeepers, and barbers—are depicted here.

In sum, considered one of the most important works in Chinese art history, *Qingming shanghe tu* is a masterpiece of realism that restores to life the pulse of a thriving historical town, interweaving small scenes into a unified whole. Consequently, ever since its creation, the painting has seen a great number of counterfeits, replicas, and copies circulating, and it has even often gone missing. In fact, according to official records, there have been so many different versions of the painting in existence at any one time that it is difficult to state which one is the original by Zhang Zeduan.

Mediated by Music: The Symphonic Picture

There are some similarities, and also important differences, between the form of the piece I describe here and the symphonic poem that flourished during the Romantic period in the second half of the nineteenth century and developed into a form of program music in the West. Among the similarities, first, both seek to bring to the mind of the listener a semantic field circumscribed by the words of the title, which is to be used as an interpretative framework for the music. Although a given meaning may not be intrinsic to the musical sounds in question, it is a fact that music as listened to by an audience is not detached from how it is contextualized; it comes as music with a title that already proposes a way of hearing the sounds themselves. As the painting is set in Bianjing, Shi

Zhiyou's composition musically evokes local particularities of the history and culture of Henan, employing, for example, instruments such as the *fangsheng* 方笙 and *suona* and material from Henan traditional opera genres (including *yuju* 豫劇, *quju* 曲劇, *yuediao* 越調, and *sipingxi* 西平戲), folk songs, and other sources.

Second, both Western symphonic poems and the *Qingming Symphonic Picture*, in addition to their titles, employ a set of conventions, such as: identifying participants by highly differentiated melodies, rhythms, or instrumentation; using specific musical forms as emblems of transformation and struggle; military motifs to convey a sense of victory. The *Qingming Symphonic Picture* is structured around three main categories taken from the painting, namely: characters, actions (also referred to as "activities and tasks"), and places (or "sceneries and settings"). New sections are sometimes introduced through reference to one or another of these categories, and the title of each piece is also meant to indicate how it is to be interpreted by listeners. The symphony comprises sixteen such pieces with pictorial referents found in order from right to left, as would be encountered when viewing the scroll, plus an overture and a finale (eighteen pieces in total). Here I discuss three illustrative examples, one of each category.

Among the characters, there is a piece entitled "Fellow Townsmen." In the painting, local townsmen are seen having a conversation under the willows of the south bank of the Bian river. Musically, they are coded as being from Henan, with one of their voices represented by a *zhuihu* 墜胡,[3] "full of the Henan accent and local charms" (Shi, 2006: unpaginated). The second voice is represented by an *erhu* 二胡, with music based on the melody of a local folk song.

Among the "activities and tasks," a tableau entitled "Fighting with Waves" features a fierce harp glissando that leads the movement into a burst of tension. The warning of what will be a fight between a boatman and the waves is conveyed by the brass, and a heart-quaking battle seems to immediately begin. The sound is determined, and it conveys a sense that victory will be achieved. Toward the end, the orchestra and the *erhu* respectively play a triumphal rhythm. And among the "sceneries and settings" category, the Bian river takes center stage. The introduction via the flowing figure of the celeste is meant to depict the silver waves of the river in the sunshine, and the bass strings play the river's leitmotif. The *erhu* offers an ode to the mother river, accompanied by the wave-like figure in the upper strings. When the motif enters the second half of the section, the music again takes a wave-like shape. The rest of the pieces are similarly structured.

The third similarity between the symphonic poem and the *Qingming Symphonic Picture* is related to the community-building potential associated with the form. In the nineteenth century, the symphonic poem was often used in Western music to advance particular ideological and nationalistic agendas, helping in effect to reshape history. It is used in a similar way in the *Qingming Symphonic Picture*. In the words of the composer Shi Zhiyou, "adapting the scroll painting into a Chinese 'symphonic picture' revitalized, after about nine hundred years, an instant of historical Chinese ancestry through music" (Shi, 2006: unpaginated).

The overall theme of growing prosperity noted above, bound to the idea of national pride, is emphasized by the characters, actions, and places chosen. The magnificent city gates (Figure 20.2), which are featured prominently on the painting, also have a

FIGURE 20.2. The Magnificent City Gates (detail from *Along the River during the Qing Ming Festival*), musically rendered by *suona* in the *Qingming Symphonic Picture*.

movement devoted to them in the symphonic picture, in which the *suona*, an instrument generally associated "with the more flamboyant musical styles of northern China" (Wang et al., 2019: 162), takes a preponderant role. Among the characters, for instance in the "Fellow Townsmen" segment discussed earlier, the expressive *erhu* rhythm is said to indicate "the two men's common wish for [an] affluent life" (Shi, 2006: unpaginated). Similarly, the movement entitled "Serving Guests," taking place at an inn, aims to bring to mind a lavish banquet. It begins with the string section playing an agile pizzicato, setting a joyful mood for listeners. Wide-leaping intervals on the *gehu* 革胡 (literally, "revolutionary *huqin*") are described by the composer as meant to foreground the sharing of wine and food. At the climax of the movement, the successive transitions between the motifs add many unexpected colors to the music, as the various flavors of the meals would. The movement enters a phase of modulation and comparison in its middle part, associated with the scene inside the inn. The dialogue between orchestra and *gehu* would seem to echo the diners' conversation. Other characters selected are the trading team and the fortune teller, whose cheerful and lively *banhu* 板胡 fiddle and *zhuihu* tunes convey good fortune.

In addition to the theme of prosperity, the community-building potential is evident in the type of actions that were selected for musical rendering: small talk by townspeople and the sharing of a meal are among activities considered by anthropologists and psychologists to be crucial for social bonding (Morgan, 2015; Dunbar, 2017). Pondering one's future in the "community of history and destiny" (Anderson, 1983: 19) that is a nation also frames the fortune teller's patron as a member of that community. The significance of these pieces is highlighted by the fact that they were chosen from among a vast number of possibilities: in total, there are 800 human figures, 390 buildings, 28 boats, 60 animals, 28 vehicles, and about 170 trees, all vividly depicted.

Having considered the similarities between symphonic poems and this symphonic picture, let us now consider the differences. First and most important for my argument here is that, in terms of source material, the symphonic poem was mainly used to recreate history and its battles, with nature (including the seasons and natural features like mountains or oceans) as a secondary set of topics, thus making reference primarily to reality. And while among the arts, literature enjoyed primacy of place in program music—and thus program music remained intimately tied to developments in opera and the theater—visual arts, such as painting or sculpture, were only rarely references for program music (Kregor, 2015: 4). In this sense, the *Qingming Symphonic Picture* can be considered more of a remediation than its Western counterparts, as it is directly related to the visual arts while aspiring to be considered a musical version of the visual work, rather than merely an illustration of it.[4] The introductory guide to the piece reads thus: "After hundreds of years, the 'Riverside Scene at Qingming Festival' is *now developed* into a Chinese symphonic picture, *musically giving rebirth to all details of the painting in focus*" (Shi, 2006: unpaginated, my emphasis). Second, and related to this, whereas the overwhelming majority of programmatic compositions take a single perspective of a subjective experience as their aesthetic basis, the *Qingming Symphonic Picture* attempts to convey multiple perspectives. This may be related to the fact that "the Chinese artists of the past were cleverly adept at linking scenery viewed from different viewpoints" (Law, 2016: 147), a feature of scrolls, in particular, known as "floating perspective." Musically, this becomes a specifically Chinese feature of Shi's version.

More recently, the scroll was digitized, incorporating into the representation process the traditional arts of painting and music along with the contemporary technology of digital animation.[5] The animated version of the painting, occupying a full wall about thirty times the size of the original scroll, was shown for a three-month period in the Shanghai World Expo in 2010 at the China Pavilion. The final 3D, animated, viewer-interactive digital version is entitled *River of Wisdom*. Subsequently, it was exhibited in Hong Kong (2010), Macau (2011), Taiwan (2011), and Singapore (2012). In this way, the Song-period artwork continues to live, through mediation, its prolific afterlives.

Conclusion

This chapter has discussed the concepts of liveness and mediation in Chinese music from two different perspectives. First, it employed the conceptual framework of the total artwork, which considers a work of art as comprising various arts and media. I have argued that this concept is useful to discuss the way that liveness and mediation is employed by Tan Dun, with specific reference to his composition *The Map*, in which the music of Chinese ethnic minorities is brought into dialogue with an orchestra by means of a screen showing recorded footage of their performances, to which the musicians on the stage respond. Indeed, music has never been alone (as the following case made clear).

Second, I have argued that mediation can also be understood as the process whereby a work of art is adapted, or translated, from one medium into another one, gaining additional liveness in the process. I have discussed this using the painting entitled *Along the River during the Qingming Festival* and the symphonic picture made after it. On the one hand, I have paid attention to similarities between this work and the symphonic poems of the nineteenth century in Western music, noting the use of conventions and intentions. On the other, I have also highlighted specifically Chinese characteristics of this symphonic picture and noted how it is these precisely that make it a worthy case study for a discussion of liveness and mediation in music, since the stated aim was not merely to illustrate but rather to become a version of the visual artwork, rendered in musical form.

As these two cases have made clear, both the term "total art," with its focus on blending and removing boundaries, and the concept of adaptation or remediation, place the arts and media, and the relations between them, at the center. In doing so, they help to transcend the conceptualization of liveness and mediation as binary oppositions, inherent in one approach that focuses on technology (liveness as the opposite of mediation, with all its complexities) and another that considers engagement between audience and performer (liveness as the opposite of a boring performance). Instead, liveness and mediation are shown to be inextricably connected, with the latter being the precondition for the former, as liveness refers to living blocks of culture (memes to Dawkins, (1976) 2016: 245) that require mediation to be transmitted, disseminated, and renewed.

I have suggested here that the pieces comprising *The Map* and the *Qingming Symphonic Picture* transmit, disseminate, and renew such living cultural blocks through their musical mediations. The music of the ethnic minorities of China and the characters, activities, and sceneries of the painting *Along the River during the Qingming Festival* are cultural blocks that come alive when musically performed, that are disseminated when heard and viewed, and that are renewed through the compositions with which they enter into dialogue (such as *The Map*, from the audience perspective) and through the musical translations and their written descriptions (in the symphonic picture).

Moreover, this approach explicitly focuses on the transgenerational dimension of the transmission of culture; that is its liveness, achieved through mediation. There is no binary opposition here as the culture lives on. When liveness is conceptualized as the opposite of the mediation, or as the opposite of disengagement, the focus is instead on the "here and now," the time of encountering the performance. It is in this sense that I contend that total art and inter-semiotic translation are especially suitable frameworks to conceptualize liveness and mediation in the Chinese context: a sort of yin/yang of music.

Glossary

banhu 板胡, two-stringed fiddle
"Ditu" wei datiqin, luxiang, ji yuedui kai xiezouqu 《地圖》為大提琴、錄像及樂隊嘅協奏曲, *The Map: Concerto for Cello, Video, and Orchestra*, composition by Tan Dun (2002)
Dong 侗, minority population featured in *The Map*
erhu 二胡, two-stringed fiddle
fangsheng 方笙, "square *sheng*," mouth organ with a squarish design from Henan province
feige 飛歌, "flying song," genre of Miao antiphonal song
gehu 革胡, literally, "revolutionary *huqin*"
Guixi 鬼戲, *Ghost Opera*, composition by Tan Dun (1994)
huqin 胡琴, family of mostly two-stringed fiddle-type instruments
lusheng 蘆笙, free-reed mouth organ of groups including the Miao and Dong
Makeboluo 馬可波羅, *Marco Polo*, composition by Tan Dun (1995)
Miao 苗, minority population featured in *The Map*
nüshu 女書, phonetic writing system used exclusively among women in Jiangyong county, Hunan province
nuoxi 儺戲, genre of folk opera connected to exorcism rites
pipa 琵琶, four-stringed lute
Qingming shanghe tu 清明上河圖, *Along the River during the Qingming Festival*, painting by Zhang Zeduan completed during the reign of the emperor Huizong (1100–26)
quju 曲劇, genre of traditional opera in Henan
ruan 阮, lute with fretted neck, circular body, and four strings
Shi Zhiyou 史志有, composer (1956–2020)
sipingxi 西平戲, genre of traditional opera in Henan
suona 嗩吶, double-reed instrument
Tan Dun 譚盾, composer (b. 1957)
Tujia 土家, minority population featured in *The Map*
Wang Zhongbing 王仲炳, musician who redesigned and reintroduced the *ruan* (mid-twentieth century)

Notes

1. According to Tan Dun, organic music "concerns both matters of everyday life and matters of the heart. These ideas find their origin in the animistic notion that material objects have spirits residing in them, an idea ever-present in the old village where I grew up in China. Paper can talk to the violin, the violin to water. Water can communicate with trees, and trees with the moon, and so on. In other words, every little thing in the totality of things, the entire universe, has a life and a soul" (Smith, 2004).

2. In other recent multimedia work such as *Nüshu: The Secret Songs of Women* (2013) a thirteen-movement work for video, solo harp, and orchestra, Tan Dun continues the research begun in Hunan. The work captures the sounds of *nüshu* 女書 script, a phonetic writing system devised by women speakers of the Shaozhou Tuhua dialect, who had not been allowed to receive formal education. Tan Dun's research has aimed to rescue what is considered a dying language, resulting in a series of short films of women singing songs written in *nüshu*. These are then presented alongside the orchestral performance. As with

The Map, the songs in the video are used in counterpoint to live music, continuing Tan's tendency to use live and mediated performance for "total art" blending.

3. The *zhuihu* is part of the *huqin* (胡琴) family of Chinese two-stringed fiddles of varying constructions, many of which are played with the bow hair inserted between the strings. The *zhuihu* has a metal soundbox and a fretless fingerboard. The *erhu* is the most well-known *huqin*, both inside and outside of China, and it makes up the largest section of the modern Chinese orchestra.
4. Another interesting case of collaboration between painting and music in the Chinese context is related to the *ruan* 阮 (a lute with a fretted neck, a circular body, and four strings), the popularity of which declined after the Song dynasty: in the 1950s, Zhang Zirui 張子銳 and Wang Zhongbing 王仲炳 reinvented the *ruan* to fulfill the needs of the modern orchestra "using ancient paintings for reference" (Wang et al., 2019: 375).
5. Another clear example of animating paintings in which music is essential can be found in Peter Greenaway's project entitled "Classical Paintings Revisited." For instance, *The Wedding at Cana* by Paolo Veronese is set to a soundtrack, consisting of superimposing digital imagery and projections, such as close-up images of faces and diagrams onto the painting, showing interrelations and similarities between cinema and painting (Gil-Curiel, 2016b: 123–24).

REFERENCES

Anderson, Benedict. (1983). *Imagined Communities: Reflections on the Origins and Spread of Nationalism*. London: Verso.
Auslander, Philip. (1999). *Liveness: Performance in a Mediated Culture*. London: Routledge.
Dawkins, Richard. ([1976] 2016). *The Selfish Gene*. Oxford: Oxford University Press.
Dunbar, R. I. M. (2017). "Breaking Bread: The Functions of Social Eating." *Adaptive Human Behavior and Physiology* 3: 198–211.
Everett, Yayoi Uno. (2015). *Reconfiguring Myth and Narrative in Contemporary Opera*. Bloomington: Indiana University Press.
Finger, Anke, and Danielle Follet. (2011). *The Aesthetics of the Total Artwork*. Baltimore: Johns Hopkins University Press.
Gil-Curiel, Germán. (2016a). "Chinese Identity: Poetics of Cinema and Music in Hero." In *Film Music in 'Minor' Cinemas*, edited by Germán Gil-Curiel, 71–89. New York: Bloomsbury.
Gil-Curiel, Germán. (2016b). "The Future of the Arts: Intermediality." In *The Future of Professional Fields: Views from the Mexican Diaspora in Europe*, edited by Red Global MX Europe, 121–28. Dublin: Red Global MX Europe.
Hutcheon, Linda. (2007). *A Theory of Adaptation*. London: Routledge.
Knight, Sabina. (2012). *Chinese Literature*. Oxford: Oxford University Press.
Kwastek, Katja. (2015). *Aesthetics of Interaction in Digital Art*. Cambridge, MA: MIT Press.
Kregor, Jonathan. (2015). *Program Music*. Cambridge, UK: Cambridge University Press.
Law, Sophia Suk-Mun. (2013). *Dialogues with Tan Dun*. Accessed November 10, 2017. http://tandun.com/visual-music/water-heavens/ [no longer available].
Law, Sophia Suk-Mun. (2016). *Reading Chinese Painting: Beyond Forms and Colors, a Comparative Approach to Art Appreciation*. New York: Better Link Press.
Melvin, Sheila, and Jindong Cai. (2004). *Rhapsody in Red: How Western Classical Music Became Chinese*. New York: Algora Publishing.

Morgan, Kelly. (2015). *Chitchat and Small Talk Could Serve an Evolutionary Need to Bond with Others*. Accessed August 17, 2021. https://www.princeton.edu/news/2015/12/14/chitchat-and-small-talk-could-serve-evolutionary-need-bond-others.

Reason, Matthew, and Anja Molle Lindelof. (2016). *Experiencing Liveness in Contemporary Performance*. New York:Routledge.

Shi, Zhiyou. (2006). "Chinese Symphonic Picture: Riverside Scene at Qingming Festival." *Symphony Guide*. CD Liner Notes. Guangzhou: Guangdong yinyue chubanshe.

Smith, Ken. (2004). *Tan Dun*. Accessed November 10, 2017. http://tandun.com/composition/the-map-concerto-for-cello-video-and-orchestra/ [no longer available].

Wang, Chenwei, Junyi Chow, and Samuel Wong. (2019). *The Teng Guide to the Chinese Orchestra*. Singapore: World Scientific.

Wu, Ying, and Patrick Wallace, eds. (2008). *Qingming shanghe tu: Scenes along the River during the Qingming Festival, by Zhang Zeduan*. Shanghai: Better Link Press.

CHAPTER 21

THE AMATEUR AND THE PROFESSIONAL IN WUHAN'S PARK POP

SAMUEL HORLOR

INTRODUCTION

NAN'ANZUI Riverside Park 南岸嘴江灘公園 in Wuhan is the location for a cluster of four stages holding the nightly pop-singing shows known by some participants as "passion square" (*jiqing guangchang* 激情廣場). Pedestrians descend into the park from one of the city's major bridges, and a few refreshment stalls at the foot of the steps trade on the flow of audience members who channel past them on their way to the stages. Pausing to buy a bottle of water, I am curious to know how the woman behind the stand in front of me thinks of the music that feeds her business; they are amateur (*yeyu* 業餘) performances, she begins in reply to my enquiry, before explaining that people toss money to musicians who "make their living from singing" (*yi changge wei sheng* 以唱歌為生) (anonymous, personal communication, May 11, 2014).[1] The stallholder is not the only person I speak to at and around shows for whom "amateur" is an immediate point of reference when describing *jiqing guangchang*, and there is obviously no contradiction in her mind to also characterize the performances with a focus on money exchange. Indeed, ideas about the amateur—and its counterpart, the professional (*zhuanye* 專業)—serve to orient people far more widely as they participate in and represent contemporary and historical Chinese musical practices. But evident from this brief conversation is that common-sense distinctions based on "making a living" do not always tell the full story as to what each term implies.

To describe oneself or others as amateur or professional is to comment on more than individual economic circumstances. In different contexts, it may be to position someone in terms of heredity, social standing, and life trajectory. It can imply judgment on musical skills, training, and transmission; point to different functions, contexts, and technologies of performance; and denote particular modes of self-presentation and creativity. It can also reveal much about changing musical economies and shifting ways in which music is valued in a society. *Jiqing guangchang*'s place in each of these conversations is not fixed in the kind of formal theorizing that might surround a classical genre, nor is it made solid in a folklore with continuity across generations of participants or devotees. The specific form of performances I observed in 2014 represents perhaps only a fleeting emergence in the mundane life of Wuhan, destined to dissolve into the changing landscape of this provincial capital having left little tangible impact beyond the lives of those immediately involved. The case study, therefore, is less encumbered by established sets of connotations for the labels amateur and professional, even if these labels can indeed be meaningful to some people. It leaves open the possibility of, rather than aligning individuals squarely with one or the other, considering a broader range of facets of musical experiences and how they are bound up in the two notions, thus entertaining that real-life situations may comprise complex interrelations between amateur and professional qualities or modes. The case study, then, presents a challenge to scholarship that is less inclined to critically tackle wider contemporary discourses that implicitly valorize one over the other.

Amateur and Professional Musicians

Insofar as *jiqing guangchang* performers sing for money, it may be intuitive to call them professional musicians. About a dozen performers are associated with each of these park stages, and they spend evenings taking turns to sing spells of two or three classic pop songs for audiences of up to about a hundred people; their primary goal is to attract cash tips from spectators who they get to know individually across numerous encounters from evening to evening. Convention in the park dictates that gifts be offered in multiples of 100 yuan (about 16 US dollars in 2014), and most singers receive at least several hundred yuan in total during each of two or three turns on the stage. Various people at the shows estimated for me a monthly income for singers of about 10,000 yuan, and this seems plausible even for the lowest earners; the figure is already three to five times higher than wages I saw advertised for entry-level service jobs around the city at the time (Horlor, 2019a: 4). But while a *jiqing guangchang* performance lasts two or three hours, being a performer is truly a full-time occupation. Most of the dozens who I met in Wuhan told me they sing at two sessions every day; an equally significant part of their work occurs away from the public gaze, as they spend time sharing meals, late-night snacks, karaoke sessions, and other forms of social contact with their audience benefactors in groups and one-to-one, developing the relationships that spawn the gifts (Horlor, 2019a).

Making a living by working full-time in music is the basis for the primary common understanding of the term "professional musician" in English, and in mainland Chinese contexts of the past seventy years, employment by a government entity such as a state troupe has been central to defining a professional musician (Bryant, 2004: 4). But the utility of these intuitive formulations can sometimes be complicated by considering the great variety of economic circumstances experienced by real people in different musical contexts. Broadly speaking, the ideas of earning a living and working in music can be highly ambiguous, with each showing various degrees, grey areas, and fluctuations (Finnegan, 1989: 13). Playing for money is incorporated in several ambivalent ways, for instance, into the lives of the musicians who Stephen Jones encountered in a northern Chinese village: shawm-band members "perform for a fee while remaining peasants at least in name" (Jones, 2004: 385), and it is normal for ritual ensembles to perform "purely as a social duty within one's own village, but to receive a fee for performing in other villages" (Jones, 1995: 81). Whether members of these ensembles earn a living as professionals is an unresolved question, not least as judged from multiple viewpoints within the local context. Further complications emerge when considering, more widely, that sometimes paid and unpaid musicians perform together, that some find their main occupation in music but end up out of pocket when travel and other costs are factored in, and that musicians' career trajectories often take them between different economic statuses over time (Finnegan, 1989: 12–13). Ambiguities might perhaps be accommodated by considering amateur and professional as ideal types on opposite ends of a continuum of real practices. This is a model, though, that seems to have been proposed more out of convenience—as a way of clarifying a study's subject matter (Finnegan, 1989; Cottrell, 2004)—than as a theoretically purposeful contribution to the issue. Continuum models, of course, have the weakness of implying a zero-sum relationship between the two ideals: something that is more amateur is necessarily less professional, and vice versa. Of greater interest to me in this chapter is showing how a practice or an occasion might simultaneously display amateur and professional facets that are independent from each other or that are related in more complex ways.

Perhaps, however, these complexities only suggest that distinctions between the amateur and the professional are unhelpful or of purely academic interest. Reports from Chinese musical worlds like that of Jiangnan *sizhu* 江南絲竹 ("silk and bamboo" ensemble music), where there are "no rigid lines [to] separate the amateur and professional musician," may do little to suggest otherwise (Witzleben, 1987: 248). Here, instrumentalists from humble walks of life mix and play as equals with conservatory teacher-performers in public teahouses, free from the negative judgments on the skills and attitudes attached to *yeyu* musicians in some other contexts (see Lau, 1991: 46). But to downplay the importance of the amateur-professional divide would be to ignore that it does indeed hold deep significance for people in many contexts as they understand and represent music making and their involvements. Amateur and professional labels often hold "emotive overtones" that entwine the notions in people's sense of self and in how they identify with and distinguish themselves from others (Finnegan, 1989: 13). Sometimes this even breeds antagonistic relations between people aligned with each of the two realms; in the rural northern Chinese setting again, Jones describes how long-running feuds between a ritual association and a paid instrumental group shape village musical life, with the latter accused of profiting inappropriately from borrowing the former's instruments (and sometimes of damaging them) (Jones, 2004: 228).

Similar emotive identity negotiation may be in evidence as, in fact, almost all *jiqing guangchang* singers in Wuhan reject, when I suggest it in conversation, that their substantial income makes them professionals. Instead, they take pride in their *yeyu* status, the term literally meaning doing something "in addition to work" (Coderre, 2016: 68). One singer insists on this designation even though she explains that she is frequently absent from *jiqing guangchang* sessions due to other commitments as a wedding singer (A-wen, personal communication, October 16, 2014). Another goes further, defining her work status to me as unemployed (*shiye* 失業, literally, having "lost work"); although performing is her primary occupation, she does not count it as a job because she has never studied music formally or worked for a state entity—the implication perhaps is that she sees her situation as only a temporary one (Ganzi, personal communication, May 7, 2014).

While these comments express a casual modesty, they also hint at the particular social, and ultimately financial, gains at stake for singers insisting on amateur status in this context. Singers do not simply sell a stage presentation to their patrons but harness their wider personas and ongoing interpersonal interactions to develop a rapport with these individuals; money follows not from expressions of unusual skill or star quality but rather from an intimacy that accompanies demonstrations of their relatability and worthiness of support. I think of *jiqing guangchang*'s money orientations as part of a gift economy rather than as embedded in a transactional system (Horlor, 2019a); performers draw on an assemblage of skills and attributes wider than those directly related to singing on a stage. Ideas of musical specialism go hand-in-hand with professionalism in some wider ethnomusicology theory (Merriam, 1964: 124), but like Daoist ritual specialists in rural China, whose music is valued for its contribution to ritual occasions rather than as an object of detached aesthetic contemplation (Jones, 2004: 174), *jiqing guangchang* singers are less specialist musicians and more experts in promoting a particular set of modes of social experience.

I was a little taken aback, though, when one individual who I considered among the weaker performers contradicted most of her colleagues by insisting to me that she was a professional singer. Taozi had been pointed out to me by fellow show regulars as someone whose means of extracting cash extended into sexual contact with patrons; indeed, I found a widespread general perception that these shows had a hidden sexual dimension, whether or not these suspicions were widely warranted (Horlor, 2019a: 17). Perhaps Taozi's reputation left her with more to be gained than many of her colleagues from emphasizing a specialist musical role (at least to me). Sex is another of the themes bound up in ideas of both the amateur and the professional more widely. On the one hand, "the lingering taint of the popular musician's (particularly the female vocalist's) traditional association with unorthodox pleasures" is connected in twentieth-century history to a lack of formal (or professional) musical training (Jones, 2001: 29). Earlier in history, on the other hand, an "unsavory aura" was cast around those considered to be professional actors in the operatic art of *kunqu* 崑曲, as a result of their associations with male courtesanship (Li Mark, 1990: 96).

Indeed, the overlap with perceptions of morality here points to perhaps the strongest emotive connotations bound up in the amateur-professional duality in Chinese musical history. The "amateur ideal" is a phrase summarizing the attitude of scholar-officials and literati of imperial times when practicing various arts in the pursuit of self-cultivation (Thrasher, 1980: 89). Typically playing instruments such as the *qin* 琴 seven-string zither, these members of elite society made music "not so much for an audience as for the performer's own enlightenment and enjoyment" (Yung, 2009: 66). Detached from commercial and other concerns, these practices manifest Confucian and Daoist notions of the beauty found in "recapturing of old and refined themes reflecting the social harmony of traditional culture" and expressing them in understated ways (Thrasher, 1980: 88)—in other words, this was "refined music" (*yayue* 雅樂) (Jones, 2001: 29). This version of amateurism is so central to the development of Chinese artistic culture as to be thought readable even in the basic forms of its instrumental music: "[I]ts standard of performance (regarding pitch accuracy, temperament, embellishment and formality in presentation) is often surprisingly flexible, no doubt owing in large part to the extent of amateur participation in its recreation" (Thrasher, 1985: 3). For reasons I return to later, though, amateur may be less helpful a description here than generalist or universalist, especially as "contempt for specialisation" is a defining feature in the attitude of the all-around scholar-officials (Mackerras, 1973: 2), one they share, in a sense, with the socially, rather than specifically musically, oriented *jiqing guangchang* singers.

In complement to the amateur ideal, though, the typical narrative of modern scholarship presents professional musicians as historically aligned with the vulgar or "common music" (*suyue* 俗樂) (Jones, 2001: 29). Only in the past century have various developments brought greater social legitimacy to professional rather than amateur musicians. Growing Chinese nationalist sentiments and concern for forging distinct national culture is linked to the establishment of systems of formal musical training along Western lines, changing performance contexts, and the commodification of musical products, a corollary being "the creation of an entirely new occupational category—the professional musician" (Jones, 2001: 29). In Chinese contexts, as in various others around the world, the narrative is of a newly imported focus on individuality, "scientific" qualities, and Western ideas of music ontology—"revolutionary changes in the very conceptions of what music is and is about" (Turino, 2008: 148). In this framework, while the professional now carries forward musical standards, the amateur is no longer associated with refinement and quality, instead taking on disparaging connotations of an apparently Western outlook: to be unpaid, or perhaps institutionally unattached, is to be inferior, to be amateurish (Mackerras, 1973: 3).

When people orient themselves with reference to the amateur and the professional, then, they reflect fluid conceptions surrounding fundamental issues of value in music. Likewise, they identify themselves or disparage others with reference to matters of ritual service, social intimacy, sexual morality, refinement and cultivation, musical skill and flexibility, and so on. In other words, the notions do far more than simply evoke individual economic categorizations. To adequately explore this broadened outlook demands more systematic consideration of the amateur and the professional, not just in the experience of musicians but also as formative of particular kinds of musical occasions where contrasting social realms are placed at stake.

Musical Occasions with Amateur and Professional Qualities

Taken holistically and as threshold to a wider social picture, *jiqing guangchang* performances exemplify the musical occasion comprised of a mixture of amateur and professional qualities. The stages in Nan'anzui Riverside Park are unusual in comparison with most others in Wuhan, where organizers bring out equipment to street corners or derelict spots each day, and singers work hard during the first few songs to attract loose circles of people around them, establishing an arrangement they intend to hold for the rest of the session. In the park, there are four fixed arenas, each with raised stages, relatively modern sound systems and stage lighting, and covered audience spaces (Figure 21.1). Arriving at just before 7 p.m. on May 9, 2014, I find a substantial audience already gathering; most are perched on plastic stools, and a few tables with

Figure 21.1. One of the *jiqing guangchang* stages in Nan'anzui Riverside Park, with a pre-show video playing on the screens.

(Photo by author, May 9, 2014)

more comfortable chairs near the front are strictly reserved for spectators already established as VIPs through a history of generous giving. Galvanizing the audience's attention toward the front of the arena even before the singing begins are three giant screens showing a Hollywood action movie, the original English audio playing as loudly as in a cinema. After a while, the film cuts off suddenly, and a man in his forties wearing a smart jacket enters the stage to flaring smoke machines, flashing lights, and music from the live band. Reminiscent of a TV gala host, he gives a lavish welcome speech, promising an evening of fun and happiness; he then breaks into the song "Three Hundred Sixty-Five Blessings" ("Sanbai liushiwu ge zhufu" 三百六十五個祝福, 1991), originally by Cai Guoqing 蔡國慶, before finally taking up his core role of introducing the first of the evening's young woman performers.

As the main part of the show begins, an important tone has already been set by several markers of the professional. The movie used to gather and warm-up the crowd, the emcee's personal presentation and welcome, the spectacle of the stage show, and the introductory song all serve to orient those in attendance toward a common communicative vocabulary rooted in the norms of popular song and mainstream media performance. Most fundamentally perhaps, spoken and sung utterances coming from the stage exclusively use Mandarin, the national lingua franca; this is just one sense in which the prevalent expressive mode shares important foundations with those of the commercial pop industry and wider institutionalized national life. Indeed, all of the songs performed come from the pop canon of the 1980s onward, the most widely inclusive repertory for this middle-aged and older target public and one central to a genre of popular music in some ways defined by professionalism. Gregory Booth and Terry Lee Kuhn make precisely this point when separating the fundamental "economic support system" of popular musics from those of classical and folk musics (Booth and Kuhn, 1990: 419). Professionalism, they argue, is the ideal state in the former, even for people on the fringes of the main economic system, as *jiqing guangchang* singers may be: "[T]he models being imitated by dilettantes are, indeed, professional. Professionalism may be said to be, on one very important level, the measure of success for a pop musician" (Booth and Kuhn, 1990: 428). In a literal sense, *jiqing guangchang* singers are invariably humble in the ambitions they reveal to me; they are not under any illusions about launching careers as pop stars but simply out to support their children or relatives. But the point is a broader one: the singing and wider presentation of the shows set up *jiqing guangchang* to be judged in the language and according to the standards of practices shaped by formalized economic models. In this sense, the professional is a foundational quality upon which *jiqing guangchang* is built.

Meanwhile, the shows display elements of an "amateur organizational ethos" (Lee, 2007: 409). Frederick Lau could be talking about *jiqing guangchang* when he describes a performance for tourists in Guangdong province: "The homey set-up and casual ambiance immediately caught one's attention. . . . [T]his performance was informal; it lacked the ritualized and polished quality often associated with professional troupes" (Lau, 1998: 123). The impressive technology of the *jiqing guangchang* stage show that I witness in the park by no means precludes looser moments from permeating the presentation.

The giant video screens display the pre-show movie in triplicate, the projectors not properly calibrated for rendering one continuous image, and barriers to this Chinese-speaking audience following the English-language movie are reinforced by the garbled mix of English and Spanish subtitles on screen; it is apparently no secret that this is a pirated copy of the film. Likewise, when the singing begins, the otherwise slick emcee maintains the street-corner *jiqing guangchang* custom of indiscriminately booming out over the current song calls for the next singer to get ready (*zhunbei* 准备) for her turn on the stage, obviously not concerned to conceal this kind of background organizational work from the audience (Horlor, 2019b: 14). Just as identifying with amateur status is part of the singers' process of developing intimacy with potential patrons, too much of the professional polish of a TV or concert-hall production may run counter to the kind of personal atmosphere being built.

A useful reference point in approaching this melding of amateur and professional qualities is Thomas Turino's distinction between participatory and presentational performance (Turino, 2008). These terms are offered as ideal types for two kinds of performance practices, the former based on collective and inclusive involvement in producing sound and the latter about specialist performers making musical offerings to others in primarily listening roles. The unusual material and technological setup in the park may align these *jiqing guangchang* shows more with archetypal presentational performances in a concert hall or pop arena. Although nowhere do *jiqing guangchang* audiences ever participate directly in the singing, the fixed stage and video screens at this location add particular encouragement for counterposed performer and audience positions to emerge, with spatial and orientational patterns laid down before the actual show begins. The main impact of this arrangement is that, unlike during the singing on street corners, the potential for indirect participation is reduced. Gift-givers cannot enter the stage area to place money directly into a singer's hand; instead they mainly deliver it via off-stage helpers. So, the performances feed less off the spontaneity of direct interpersonal interaction.

Links with presentational and participatory performance modes are an important part of how amateur and professional qualities are read in broader musical occasions, especially in the context of shifting historical circumstances of the past century. Jones emphasizes the connection in China: "Urban *professional* performances on stage for a seated 'audience' are largely a product of the period since 1949, having little in common with traditional music-making" (Jones, 1995: 82, emphasis added). While informal performing to other group members within a rehearsal is "the most representative of traditional amateur music making," stage performance contexts are certainly not unknown in Chinese music history, especially in urban entertainment genres and opera (Thrasher, 1985: 9).[2] The focus on different modes of performance reveals, among other things, that the amateur and the professional have important spatial and material dimensions. In the park sessions that I attended, with technology and convention dividing space into zones for performers, audiences, and VIP guests, there is a degree of order and predictability in how people come into contact with each other. Perhaps this points to a professional mode, with performance unfolding in planned and regulated ways. Indeed, these are qualities Casey Man Kong Lum associates with the professional in the context of karaoke-club singing in Chinese American diaspora settings. Lum notes that the memberships of high-ranking business professionals generate a "corporate managerial mannerism expressed in the organization of these clubs," a professionalism in participants' wider lives associated with a formality and disciplined character in their free-time gatherings (Lum, 1996: 61). It is also a reminder that amateur and professional status can be bound up in the relative physical positioning of people in space. In rural temple fairs and funerals, for example, amateur ritual groups occupy the central ritual space and "vulgar" professional groups are merely "watchdogs at the gate" (Jones, 2004: 324). On another level, the amateur nature of whole genres, like the campus songs of the 1970s and 1980s, is imagined as tied to their development by students in the school campuses (*xiaoyuan* 校園) of Taiwan (Moskowitz, 2010: 34) and Singapore (Kong, 1996: 107). The genres' histories see musicians initially "contained within the spaces of amateur music-making" until new commercial orientations encourage showmanship with more expansive reach (Kong, 1996: 123).[3] And since the archetypal amateur ideal is bound up with music being made in private spaces (such as the home or the court), *jiqing guangchang*'s freely accessible public settings, and its outward-looking inclusivity, may be read as another professional quality.

Looking at the implications of different performance modes also helps to connect the focus on the broader musical occasion back to the earlier discussion about individual economic circumstances. The developed infrastructure of the park stages is correlated here with the convention for gifts to be given in higher amounts and, in turn, with shows attracting some singers with commercial performing experiences. The only instance of a performer in Wuhan approaching me speaking English (rather than Mandarin) was at one of these park stages: a young woman who called herself Julie told me that she had sung professionally for six years with a Filipino band in the major cities of Shanghai, Hangzhou, and Xiamen, but had come to *jiqing guangchang* three months ago to be within a few hours of her hometown (personal communication, October 23, 2014). Others from outside Wuhan told me that they had become aware of these stages via a group on the QQ social-media platform used by performing artists for sharing news of work opportunities. In some senses, then, the technological and material circumstances of these stages—and the hints toward professional qualities, as far as they are aligned with presentational modes of performance—can be mapped onto the economic involvements of participants.

But if the alignment of amateur with participation, and of professional with presentation, has so far suggested a drift in *jiqing guangchang* toward the latter pairing, how does this perspective add to the idea that the qualities meld to form these musical occasions? Most significantly, it opens up the topic to a discussion of musical features and modes of creativity, a territory revealing how participatory (amateur) qualities can thrive even in conditions that elsewhere encourage more presentational (professional) modes. In general, *jiqing guangchang* singers are conservative in their rendering of songs in performance, perhaps bringing to mind typical karaoke singers, insofar as they follow famous recordings closely, especially when the park performers are constrained by the accompaniment of a recorded backing track instead of the live band, as many choose (Horlor, 2019c: 20–22). There is, then, less evidence of the professional musician's "emphasis on individual creativity and virtuosity" that comes through strongly in international discussions of popular musics (Booth and Kuhn, 1990: 428) and in various Chinese music contexts, where this mode is contrasted with the traditional and conservative orientation of amateurs (Jones, 2004: 16; Lee, 2007: 8; Rees, 1998: 151; Wang, 2003: 153; Witzleben, 1987: 246; Yung, 2009: 81).[4] In fact, the ways in which individual innovation is manifest most strongly in *jiqing guangchang* singing bring to mind some of the musical features that Turino links to participatory modes, especially the centrality of long extended grooves, unstable endings, and repeated patterns (Turino, 2008: 150). Singers here play with the structure of songs, often jumping back to the beginning, moving to another one halfway through, or merging two together, all directly in response to the mood of the crowd and to the amounts of money flowing (Horlor, 2019c: 27). Their primary avenue of creativity and spontaneity, then, looks to the embeddedness of the musical performance in a social occasion, rather than prioritizing a kind of innovation aimed at a listener deeply contemplating an artistic product (despite the more presentational elements of the shows already highlighted).

As all of this shows, the economic experiences of individual musicians are both linked to, and manifestations of, a far broader array of issues. While for almost all *jiqing guangchang* singers it is advantageous to identify most strongly with ideas of the amateur, the musical material, norms of expressive communication, modes of creativity, and the spatial, material, and technological circumstances of the shows have complicated relationships with amateur and professional qualities—often intersecting with those of participatory and presentational performance modes. While these qualities are visible to an extent when looking at musicians individually, their melding shapes the performances as arenas for certain patterns of sociality involving not just singers but also a variety of other actors.

Linking the Amateur and the Professional

Standing on the periphery of the audience at the largest *jiqing guangchang* stage in this park cluster, I talk to a fellow spectator, a man in his forties. Singers not currently on stage circulate all around, approaching us regularly with offers of cigarettes and soft drinks, a key part of the hosting role that drives their income from the gift economy. The man tells me that, on his way to the session earlier in the evening, he stopped off at a karaoke stand to sing a few numbers. Beside the refreshment stall I passed on my way into the park at the beginning of the chapter, I skirted around groups of men playing pool under the shelter of the bridge (Figure 21.2), and just beyond them were a couple

FIGURE 21.2. Refreshment stall and pool tables under the bridge at the entry to Nan'anzui Riverside Park.

(Photo by author, May 11, 2014)

of decades-old television sets, each with a handful of people gathered around on plastic stools. This is where my companion paid 10 yuan (about $1.60 US dollars) to take the microphone for three songs. Every time I pass stands like this, I hear snippets of numbers such as "The Most Dazzling National Style" ("Zui xuan minzu feng" 最炫民族風, 2009) by Fenghuang Chuanqi 鳳凰傳奇, or "Still Together in Spirit" ("Ouduan silian" 藕斷絲連, 2008) by Chen Rui 陳瑞, familiar to me as mainstays of *jiqing guangchang*.

It is a reminder that karaoke and *jiqing guangchang* are linked—if not consciously in dialogue, then in reference to the system of popular musics I characterized earlier as fundamentally professional in orientation. But as both a singer and an audience member tonight, the man's trajectory within the system raises the prospect of drawing out a greater sense of synergy, rather than contradiction, from the picture of merging amateur and professional qualities that I have painted so far.

The term *jiqing guangchang* clearly links this kind of show to wider street leisure, particularly the square-dancing (*guangchang wu* 廣場舞) exercise gatherings enjoyed ubiquitously by older people in urban China. These activities take place in similar public spaces, including city squares, or *guangchang*; this term is common to both. But, like the karaoke singer, the square dancer may be out primarily for pleasure, not committed in the same way as the *jiqing guangchang* singer to their activity, or indeed to performance in the same sense. Certain scholarship on Chinese and other contemporary musical practices uses the ideas of leisure and the amateur more or less interchangeably (for example, Wang, 2003: 96), and karaoke is sometimes described as an amateur phenomenon (Katz, 2011: 467). But influential sociological perspectives actually argue to exclude those engaged in leisure pursuits from the amateur category. In the 1970s, Robert Stebbins put forward a distinction: "Amateurs are people who engage in activities that, for other people, constitute work roles. One cannot be an amateur butterfly catcher or matchbook collector; no opportunity for full-time employment exists here" (Stebbins, 1977: 588). As I suggested when discussing the amateur ideal earlier, perhaps this means that the Confucian scholar-official did not play the *qin* as an amateur (considering that the category of professional *qin* player is a later emergence) but rather as a generalist, a universalist, or indeed to use a word more typical in comparable historical anglophone contexts, a "gentleman" (Stebbins, 1977: 583). Likewise, to the extent that *jiqing guangchang* singers are aligned with amateur qualities, there is clearly a meaningful distinction to be made between their version of amateurism and the leisure-oriented singing of my audience companion.

Rather than revisit the problem of labeling individuals, however, the main point here comes from acknowledging the nuances of different roles in an activity and that different kinds of participants may be defined largely in reference to one another. Stebbins frames this as a system in which professionals, amateurs, and—crucially—publics interact. Amateurs usually perform for audiences or publics whose membership overlaps with those of professionals, and, as I have already suggested, this is the phenomenon that orients *jiqing guangchang* singers to the standards set by industry professionals. But Stebbins sees particular significance in amateurs also composing part of the professional's public. Being less restricted by the need to maintain highly tuned skills in one specialist area, the amateur in a genre such as *kunqu* can experiment with several roles or even with learning from several different teachers (Li Mark, 1990: 103). They bring their generalist, but nonetheless direct, appreciations of the genre's demands to their appraisals of professionals' performances, motivating the latter to maintain standards and providing a wider perspective that regulates the genre's broader directions (Stebbins 1977: 587). Perhaps, then, there is a level upon which my karaoke-singing fellow audience member plays the amateur to the *jiqing guangchang* singer's professional.

His roles tonight certainly highlight that more people than just the primary musicians are "active and skilled participants" in the musical occasion and of relevance when considering amateur and professional qualities (Finnegan, 1989: 15). The historical record tends to offer only limited evidence of the impact of the people in the background of many of the genres I have referred to so far (Li Mark, 1990: 99), part of the tendency to privilege the experience of the headline musician when considering this topic. But I have already touched on how, in *jiqing guangchang* musical occasions, the emcees contribute to the prevailing expressive tone and how direct exchange with audience members shapes the singers' balancing of participatory and presentational performance qualities. Likewise, backing musicians, organizers, and helpers are clearly present in the equation in various ways. The experience of the keyboard player in one of the accompanying bands, for example, reinforces Stebbins's idea of the two modes being linked and mutually constituted. This middle-aged man is keen to harness my help in learning some *zhuanye* (here best translated as "specialist") skills on the piano (Horlor, 2019c: 26), the implication being that his usual accompanying role is not of that standard (even though he and his colleagues routinely and impressively access memory of a vast range of songs with virtually no warning). Stebbins's larger system of connected amateur and professional modes acknowledges the importance of individuals' attitudes and trajectories over time; perhaps the keyboard player's ambition to take his skills to another level makes him a "preprofessional," just as the performance history of Julie, the English-speaking singer I met earlier, might make her a "postprofessional" (Stebbins, 1977: 595). Indeed, the wider perspective stressing interconnections rather than hard binary distinctions also raises the possibility of amateur and professional giving way to a greater range of nuanced categories; audiences of storytelling-and-singing (*pingtan* 評彈) in Suzhou, for instance, include connoisseurs (*hangjia* 行家), enthusiasts (*pingtan mi* 評彈迷), aficionados (*aihaozhe* 愛好者), habitués (*changke* 常客), and fans (*piaoyou/fensi* 票友/粉絲), all with different qualities of engagement and positions against amateur and professional ideal types (Shi, 2016: 151).

Musical material and creativity also routinely flow between realms. Lawrence Witzleben describes how compositions originating in the professional sphere of Jiangnan *sizhu* concert repertory can become incorporated into the amateur world of teahouse music making, with initially disapproving musicians there eventually adapting them to the norms of that context (Witzleben, 1987: 246–47). In economic senses, too, it is worth noting that a major part of a professional musician's role may be to train, organize, and perform with amateurs—the two are by no means separate in their routine activity. Indeed, in China of the late 1920s, the professionalization of Western classical-music education, performance, and publishing lay the infrastructure for an explosion in amateur activity, especially in the form of music societies (Jones, 2001: 43). There are knock-on effects on emotive levels of identity negotiation, too. Jonathan Stock notes that the improving social status of professional operatic actors in Shanghai in the first part of the twentieth century was partly because "the rise of the amateur performer from a good background lent esteem to all those involved in dramatic engagements" (Stock, 2003: 97). These examples are enough to make clear that it is not exceptional but in fact quite usual in real-life practices for amateurs and professionals to work in direct concert rather than tension, in realms such as musical material, economic activity, and emotive meaning.

The most crucial consequence of this idea is to undermine any impression that real musical practices may be taken as pure or isolated in either their amateur or professional qualities. The broader lens I have advocated challenges the idealization of one or other mode. Lau frames this point with reference to the contemporary culture of bamboo-flute (*dizi* 笛子) music, in which the idea of amateurism is tightly bound up in the genre description "folk" (*minjian* 民間). Whereas this label may bring to mind disinterestedness from commercial or institutional entanglements, the reality Lau finds is strikingly different: "[T]he most prominent feature of *minjian* activities in contemporary China is the official role in structuring and supervising all cultural activities and scholarly activities and not the voluntary unstructured impression" portrayed by earlier scholars (Lau, 1991: 48). Notions of the amateur and the professional have the potential to become explicitly or implicitly vested with value, by scholars just as much as by other actors in musical worlds. To conclude the discussion, then, it is worth briefly considering how this issue plays out in the *jiqing guangchang* context and how this may comment more widely on Chinese music scholarship.

DE-IDEALIZING THE AMATEUR

The half-dozen or so clusters of *jiqing guangchang* shows in their relatively out-of-the-way spots of Wuhan in 2014 were, in many ways, swallowed up by the vastness of this city. Perhaps as meaningful a marker of the amateur as any I have discussed so far is what they share with Ruth Finnegan's well-known case study on musicians in an English town: they are largely "hidden" from wider recognition (Finnegan, 1989). On one rare occasion, in May 2014, a photograph and brief description of a *jiqing guangchang* performance appeared as a color piece on online news platforms. The described scene centers on a "spontaneously organized group of *aihaozhe* [music enthusiasts]" (China News Service, 2014). The word *aihaozhe* aligns the singers most with the leisure fringes of amateur activity, their main preoccupation apparently being to "cultivate their interest while at the same time bringing everyone joy" (ibid.). Phrases like this present the activity in a positive light, and the piece's title adds to the image of its wholesomeness, describing this as a "grassroots stage" (*caogen wutai* 草根舞臺)—although "grassroots" is not a term I found in most *jiqing guangchang* participants' vocabulary. Singers are presented as "gratefully calling out 'thanks big brother for your support'" when men present them with flowers (ibid.), a representation striking in its contrast with the sexual innuendo I found in general perceptions of the shows' reward practices.

As notions with weight in personal and group identity, the amateur and the professional have potential to become bound up in sentimental discourses. In this news piece, for instance, positive markers of the amateur (at least in the sense that it incorporates what Stebbins would call leisure) share a language with the spontaneous, the uncommercial, and the disinterested, thus perhaps calling to mind a certain purity in the experience. In contrast, in various other contexts, the professional designation can function as a barrier, "an exclusionary principle and tactic that aims to delegitimate certain performance idioms along the lines of race, class, and gender, among others" (Salvato, 2009: 69). A key challenge for scholarship is to properly recognize the amateur and the professional as territories of constructing otherness, as notions evoked at the service of ends and agendas, benevolent or otherwise. Research geared to reinforcing rather than critically examining these interpretations may end up stealthily elaborating a position on what should be valued in musical practices rather than exploring the complexities of real-life experience. My approach in this chapter, taking the object of study to be the musical occasion comprising a melding of amateur and professional qualities, is meant to transcend reliance on hard distinctions in the labeling of musicians as either amateur or professional. This approach is enhanced rather than compromised by acknowledging real-life ambiguity.

Sometimes scholars make a deliberate point of intervening in judgments of value that are bound up with the topic of this chapter. In his discussions of participatory and presentational performance, for example, Turino purposefully expresses concerns that the former mode, linked to amateur activity, may become underappreciated in society, recommending that "all fields continue to be equally valued and available for the contributions they can make to social life" (Turino, 2008: 154). There are comparable arguments for the re-evaluation of amateur or leisure modes in contexts such as karaoke, too. Robert Drew advocates for their overlooked seriousness: "The realm of leisure/pleasure is not inconsequential, or 'necessary' only for the re-creation of the capacity to work in waged labour. It contains its own work, its own 'art-work,' symbolic work which is about the formation and expression of identity" (Paul Willis, quoted in Drew, 1997: 465). Similarly, Jones argues unapologetically that amateur ceremonial music is left out of "the official image of Chinese music, widely disseminated through its monopoly of the media, [of] the secular professional entertainment music of the towns" (Jones, 1995: 10).

Potentially more problematic, though, is when the valorization of the amateur and its associated qualities is not accompanied by the same upfront agenda of correcting perceived distortions. Scholarship of this kind, by trustingly aligning the amateur with notions such as refinement, community, and democratization, may end up mystifying or romanticizing the subject. The disinterested sophistication of the historical elite's amateur ideal, in particular, can become one of the established "truths" of Chinese musical culture, against which other practices and modes are judged. Perhaps the biographical approach exemplified by Bell Yung's portrait of his *qin* teacher, Tsar Teh-yun 蔡德允, can lend itself to reinforcing this kind of discourse: "Tsar Laoshi has quietly but fiercely defended the age-old tradition of keeping *qin* within lofty literatus ideals and practices, free from societal demands and financial pressure, and has passed this tradition on to her students" (Yung, 2009: 81). These celebrations of the amateur ideal may conceal that the historical record from which the ideas emerge is itself far from disinterested. It might, in fact, be taken as evidence of a "self-conscious musical antiquarianism" having shaped perceptions of Chinese musical history (Jones, 1995: 39) or, as Lau puts it, as a manifestation of how "the elite buttressed their position in the social hierarchy by propagating and promoting their own values and cultural practices while disparaging those of subordinate groups" (Lau, 1991: 40). Perhaps the amateur ideal is best thought of as an "invented tradition" functioning primarily to legitimize a present-day elite (Walser, 1992: 265) rather than as something meaningfully comparable to the realities of any contemporary practice, where disinterested bubbles do not exist.

Another notion aligned with the amateur in similarly positive terms is community. In particular, the word is sometimes used as a shorthand for the kinds of sociality associated with what is considered amateur music making. In rehearsals among Chinese-opera practitioners in Singapore, for instance, "[t]he focus is on presenting a persuasive performance through communal interaction, rather than a focus on individual technicalities. Indeed, by extending their technical proficiency as a means of educating and relating to others, the amateur performer fosters 'a community of spirit'" (Lee, 2007: 409). The growing emphasis upon presentational qualities of performance noted in modern contexts is lamented in some quarters as detrimental to communal modes of interacting. But the desirability of these modes can also be presented as self-evident and uncomplicated. In Taiwan, for instance, Wang Ying-Fen speaks out against "a deterioration of the *nanguan* (南管) community both in terms of its musical quality and its members' pride and identity as amateur musicians" (Wang 2003: 97). Loss of certain kinds of sociality means fewer opportunities for participants to achieve "*nanguan*'s ideal of 'harmony in differences'" (Wang 2003: 151). But sentiments like this do not fully account for the key idea that I have sought to explore in this chapter: real practices may not have these kinds of uncomplicated alignments with qualities associated with the amateur (and the professional). Indeed, to idealize community as a quality of amateur activity is perhaps to ignore its flip side: the exclusion that is the inevitable counterpart of belonging. Jones describes the boisterous, alcohol-fueled sociality of amateur playing in the village context: "[T]he Music Association is now one of very few formal opportunities for people (or rather men) to get together socially, for social networks to be enjoyed wider than those of the family" (Jones, 2004: 248). His parentheses hinting at the marginal role of women in amateur music in this context is a warning of the complexities hidden behind this inviting image of communal sociality.

Often, these complexities may be revealed only with reference to historical contexts upon which a more skeptical outlook is normalized. During the radically politicized period of the Cultural Revolution (1966–76), for example, the term "amateur" was "incredibly elastic—and this elasticity was fundamentally a function of its political desirability" (Coderre, 2016: 68). The idea among political leaders was that music would become democratized, "accessible to the entire population, and everyone could become revolutionary through music" (Clark, Pang, and Tsai, 2016: 3). But this positivity rings hollow with knowledge of the destruction and suffering that are now more often associated with this period of history. So-called democratization is a theme of the contemporary online (especially social-media) environment, too, where control over creative work is apparently spread to the hands of the amateur in ways impossible with traditional media (Zhao, 2016). "Amateur participation in professional industries is today routinely positioned as, if not unequivocally 'good,' then at least an essentially positive development" (Hamilton, 2013: 178), but this carries the potential for those with commercial ambitions or corporate sponsorship to profit from dubiously associating themselves with the amateur (Salvato, 2009: 69). Likewise, in writing on the recent popularity in China of "original ecology folk songs" (*yuanshengtai min'ge* 原生態民歌)—performances that claim to present "authentic," untrained qualities—Rowan Pease highlights the mechanisms of formal training and economics that are unashamedly mobilized to produce singers who can pass themselves off as local tradition-bearers (Pease, 2013: 195). These examples caution us against too readily reinforcing wider valorization of the amateur as synonymous with refinement, community, or democratization.

CONCLUSION

This chapter has argued for a more comprehensive and ambivalent view of the amateur and the professional. It is realistic to think of the two notions as describing more than just the economic circumstances of individual musicians. Labeling people along these lines, in fact, says something about features of a musician's background or personal qualities, their modes of expression and creativity, the involvements of other participants in musical performance, the nature of the performance context and its embeddedness in wider economic systems, and the values of musical cultures. To talk instead about the qualities of musical occasions acknowledges that real situations do not exist in a pure realm of either an amateur or a professional mode. Instead, they are complex sums of these qualities, the occasions constituted by amateur and professional orientations that are linked in wider systems of overlapping publics. Amateur and professional distinctions are certainly meaningful to people in some but not all situations of Chinese music, but it is also important to acknowledge how these meanings result from various interests, agendas, or simplifications, thus confounding inclinations to valorize either amateur or professional modes. *Jiqing guangchang* park performances instead show that real musical occasions of contemporary Chinese life depend in their fundamental natures upon the melding of these two qualities.

GLOSSARY

aihaozhe 愛好者, aficionados, enthusiasts
Cai Guoqing 蔡國慶, singer (b. 1968)

caogen wutai 草根舞臺, "grassroots stage"
changke 常客, habitués
Chen Rui 陳瑞, singer (b. 1976)
dizi 笛子, bamboo flute
Fenghuang Chuanqi 鳳凰傳奇, Phoenix Legend, pop duo (formed 2004)
guangchang wu 廣場舞, "square dancing"
hangjia 行家, connoisseurs
jiqing guangchang 激情廣場, "passion square," local name for stages for pop singing in Nan'anzui Riverside Park and elsewhere in Wuhan
Jiangnan *sizhu* 江南絲竹, "silk and bamboo" ensemble music tradition
kunqu 崑曲, traditional opera genre
minjian 民間, folk
Nan'anzui Jiangtan Gongyuan 南岸嘴江灘公園, Nan'anzui Riverside Park, Wuhan
nanguan 南管, genre of traditional ensemble music in Taiwan
"Ouduan silian" 藕斷絲連, "Still Together in Spirit," pop song performed by Chen Rui (2008)
piaoyou/fensi 票友/粉絲, fans
pingtan 評彈, storytelling-and-singing genre from Suzhou
pingtan mi 評彈迷, enthusiasts of *pingtan*
qin 琴, seven-string zither
"Sanbai liushiwu ge zhufu" 三百六十五個祝福, "Three Hundred Sixty-Five Blessings," pop song by Cai Guoqing (1991)
shiye 失業, unemployed
suyue 俗樂, "common music"
Tsar Teh-yun (Cai Deyun) 蔡德允, *qin* player, poet, and calligrapher (1905–2007)
xiaoyuan 校園, school campus
yayue 雅樂, "refined music"
yeyu 業餘, amateur
yuanshengtai min'ge 原生態民歌, "original ecology folk songs"
zhuanye 專業, professional
"Zui xuan minzu feng" 最炫民族風, "The Most Dazzling National Style," pop song by Fenghuang Chuanqi (2009)

Notes

1. All research consultants are given pseudonyms in this account. This chapter is based on research in Wuhan in the spring and fall of 2014, where participant observation at more than fifty *jiqing guangchang* performances around the city formed part of my wider ethnographic engagements with the lives of singers, instrumental musicians, audience members, and other participants.
2. Moves to staged performance contexts have been linked strongly to government cultural policies concerned with protecting and harnessing local heritage, both within China and beyond. While in the Taiwanese genre of *nanguan* 南管 this has been framed as a professionalizing tendency, and one linked to "commodification, vulgarization, and theatricalization" (Wang, 2003: 152), in the Chinese-opera world in Singapore, it is actually amateur groups that have become associated with presentational qualities, advanced technology, and spectacular stage shows (Lee, 2007: 412–13). Modern technology is

not only linked to performance becoming more presentational, however; in Cantonese opera in Hong Kong, it has been credited with bringing the genre significant new participatory dimensions, through an explosion of karaoke-singing gatherings (Katz, 2011: 468).

3. Among the various other related realms in which participatory and presentational qualities can be read are the materiality and corporeality of music making. Recent staged performances of the *qin* music once archetypal of the amateur ideal see the music shaped by the instrument's material development, including in the use of louder metal strings (Yung, 2009: 80–81). And in Jiangnan *sizhu*, distinctions between teahouse and stage performance are accentuated by the emergence in the latter's players of more expansive bodily expression, to the extent that "[t]o participate in the amateur music-making, a professional must modify his accustomed approach to performing or feel conspicuously out of place" (Witzleben, 1987: 246).

4. In the background is the common-sense idea that higher skill level is a major factor in what separates professionals from amateurs (Mackerras, 1973: 2). This sentiment is not always endorsed by those deeply embedded in musical worlds. Experienced amateurs of the storytelling-and-singing genre *pingtan* 評彈 in Suzhou, for example, see themselves as far above the level of the younger generation of conservatory-trained storytellers and consider this a worrying indication of a form in decline (Shi, 2016: 197); see also Li Mark for a similar discussion about *kunqu* (1990: 97).

References

Booth, Gregory, and Terry Lee Kuhn. (1990). "Economic and Transmission Factors as Essential Elements in the Definition of Folk, Art, and Pop Music." *Musical Quarterly* 74 (3): 411–38.

Bryant, Lei Ouyang. (2004). "'New Songs of the Battlefield': Songs and Memories of the Chinese Cultural Revolution." PhD diss., University of Pittsburgh.

China News Service. (2014). "Wuhan gongyuan li de 'caogen wutai'" "武漢公園裡的'草根舞臺'" [A Wuhan Park's "Grassroots Stage"]. *Zhongguo xinwen wang* 中國新聞網 [China News Service], May 3, 2014. Accessed September 25, 2019. http://www.chinanews.com/tp/2014/05-03/6126786.shtml.

Clark, Paul, Laikwan Pang, and Tsan-Huang Tsai. (2016). "Introduction." In *Listening to China's Cultural Revolution: Music, Politics, and Cultural Continuities*, edited by Paul Clark, Laikwan Pang, and Tsan-Huang Tsai, 1–8. New York: Palgrave Macmillan.

Coderre, Laurence. (2016). "Breaking Bad: Sabotaging the Production of the Hero in the Amateur Performance of *Yangbanxi*." In *Listening to China's Cultural Revolution: Music, Politics, and Cultural Continuities*, edited by Paul Clark, Laikwan Pang, and Tsan-Huang Tsai, 65–83. New York: Palgrave Macmillan.

Cottrell, Stephen. (2004). *Professional Music-Making in London: Ethnography and Experience*. Aldershot, UK: Ashgate.

Drew, Robert. (1997). "Embracing the Role of Amateur: How Karaoke Bar Patrons Become Regular Performers." *Journal of Contemporary Ethnography* 25 (4): 449–68.

Finnegan, Ruth. (1989). *The Hidden Musicians: Music-Making in an English Town*. Cambridge, UK: Cambridge University Press.

Hamilton, Caroline. (2013). "Symbolic Amateurs: On the Discourse of Amateurism in Contemporary Media Culture." *Cultural Studies Review* 19 (1): 177–92.

Horlor, Samuel. (2019a). "Neutralizing Temporary Inequities in Moral Status: Chinese Street Singers and the Gift Economy." *Asian Music* 50 (2): 3–32.

Horlor, Samuel. (2019b). "Permeable Frames: Intersections of the Performance, the Everyday, and the Ethical in Chinese Street Singing." *Ethnomusicology Forum* 28 (1): 3–25.

Horlor, Samuel. (2019c). "Popular Song Afterlives: Oral Transmission and Mundane Creativity in Street Performances of Chinese Pop Classics." *Journal of World Popular Music* 6 (1): 10–31.

Jones, Andrew. (2001). *Yellow Music: Media Culture and Colonial Modernity in the Chinese Jazz Age*. Durham, NC: Duke University Press.

Jones, Stephen. (1995). *Folk Music of China: Living Instrumental Traditions*. Oxford: Oxford University Press.

Jones, Stephen. (2004). *Plucking the Winds: Lives of Village Musicians in Old and New China*. Leiden: CHIME.

Katz, Mark. (2011). "The Amateur in the Age of Mechanical Music." In *The Oxford Handbook of Sound Studies*, edited by Trevor Pinch and Karin Bijsterveld, 459–79. Oxford: Oxford University Press.

Kong, Lily. (1996). "Making 'Music at the Margins'? A Social and Cultural Analysis of *Xinyao* in Singapore." *Asian Studies Review* 19 (3): 99–124.

Lau, Frederick. (1991). "Music and Musicians of the Traditional Chinese 'Dizi' in the People's Republic of China." DMA diss., University of Illinois at Urbana-Champaign.

Lau, Frederick. (1998). "'Packaging Identity through Sound': Tourist Performances in Contemporary China." *Journal of Musicological Research* 17 (2): 113–34.

Lee Tong Soon. (2007). "Chinese Theatre, Confucianism, and Nationalism: Amateur Chinese Opera Tradition in Singapore." *Asian Theatre Journal* 24 (2): 397–421.

Li Mark, Lindy. (1990). "The Role of Avocational Performers in the Preservation of *Kunqu*." *Chinoperl Papers* 15: 95–114.

Lum, Casey Man Kong. (1996). *In Search of a Voice: Karaoke and the Construction of Identity in Chinese America*. Mahwah, NJ: Lawrence Erlbaum Associates.

Mackerras, Colin. (1973). *Amateur Theatre in China, 1949–1966*. Canberra: Australian National University Press.

Merriam, Alan. (1964). *The Anthropology of Music*. Evanston, IL: Northwestern University Press.

Moskowitz, Marc. (2010). *Cries of Joy, Songs of Sorrow: Chinese Pop Music and its Cultural Connotations*. Honolulu: University of Hawai'i Press.

Pease, Rowan. (2013). "Broken Voices: Ethnic Singing and Gender." In *Gender in Chinese Music*, edited by Rachel Harris, Rowan Pease, and Shzr Ee Tan, 181–200. Rochester, NY: University of Rochester Press.

Rees, Helen. (1998). "'Authenticity' and the Foreign Audience for Traditional Music in Southwest China." *Journal of Musicological Research* 17 (2): 135–61.

Salvato, Nick. (2009). "Out of Hand: YouTube Amateurs and Professionals." *TDR: The Drama Review* T203: 67–83.

Shi Yinyun. (2016). "Performing Local Identity in a Contemporary Urban Society: A Study of Ping-Tan Narrative Vocal Tradition in Suzhou, China." PhD diss., Durham University.

Stebbins, Robert. (1977). "The Amateur: Two Sociological Definitions." *Pacific Sociological Review* 20: 582–606.

Stock, Jonathan. (2003). *Huju: Traditional Opera in Modern Shanghai*. Oxford: Oxford University Press.

Thrasher, Alan R. (1980). "Foundations of Chinese Music: A Study of Ethics and Aesthetics." PhD diss., Wesleyan University.

Thrasher, Alan R. (1985). "The Role of Music in Chinese Culture." *World of Music* 27 (1): 3–18.

Turino, Thomas. (2008). *Music as Social Life: The Politics of Participation*. Chicago: University of Chicago Press.

Walser, Robert. (1992). "Eruptions: Heavy Metal Appropriations of Classical Virtuosity." *Popular Music* 11 (3): 263–308.

Wang Ying-Fen. (2003). "Amateur Music Clubs and State Intervention: The Case of *Nanguan* Music in Postwar Taiwan." *Journal of Chinese Ritual, Theatre and Folklore* 141: 95–167.

Witzleben, J. Lawrence. (1987). "*Jiangnan Sizhu* Music Clubs in Shanghai: Context, Concept and Identity." *Ethnomusicology* 31 (2): 240–60.

Yung, Bell. (2009). "Tsar Teh-yun at Age 100: A Life of Qin Music, Poetry, and Calligraphy." In *Lives in Chinese Music*, edited by Helen Rees, 65–90. Urbana: University of Illinois Press.

Zhao, Elaine Jing. (2016). "Professionalization of Amateur Production in Online Screen Entertainment in China: Hopes, Frustrations, and Uncertainties." *International Journal of Communication* 10: 5444–62.

CHAPTER 22

"MINORITIES" AND THE MAINSTREAM

The Musical Place of the Non-Han Peoples in Modern China

CHUEN-FUNG WONG

Introduction

Peoples and cultures subsumed indiscriminately under the category of "minority nationalities" (*shaoshu minzu* 少數民族)[1] in China today inhabit a relationship with the majority Han that is often fraught with colonial implications. Amid its growing consumption inside and outside the post-socialist state, the music of China's non-Han peoples is increasingly audible in the global stage (Wong, 2017), often inextricably connected with China's own identity project in modern times. Notwithstanding the vast diversity of contexts and modes of expression, the performing arts of the fifty-five officially recognized "minority nationalities" are often conceived en masse as an exterior in China. This is related, in no small measure, to discourses of otherness that have manifested in almost every aspect of the non-Han performing arts and informed much of official staged performance since the mid-twentieth century. It is hard to overstate that modern China's geographical and racial Others have been listened to as primarily "musical," often relegated through a number of acoustic identifiers to the stereotype of joyful entertainers, singing, playing, and dancing to music that is primarily festive and amusing. This is best epitomized by the notorious cliché "good-at-singing-and-dancing" (*nengge shanwu* 能歌善舞)—what Helen Rees has called "the motif of music-making minority" (2000: 23–27)—a discursive trope that has rendered non-Han bodies as artistically skilled producers of sounds that invoke instant, corporeal pleasure. The inborn musicality that marks the non-Han peoples articulates a stark contrast to senses of historicity and refinement often attributed to the traditional music of the Han—notably in genres such as Peking opera (*jingju* 京劇), *kunqu* 崑曲 singing, the *qin* 琴 zither, and *pipa* 琵琶 plucked lute, as well as chamber styles in the "silk-and-bamboo" (*sizhu* 絲竹) traditions. In many important ways, hearing the music (and noise) of the non-Han peoples has been a fundamental means through which many in the modern Chinese audience come to recognize their fellow citizens and imagine their ethnic ways of life—and accordingly create their sense of a national self.

This is not to suggest that the music of the non-Han has always been perceived as stylistically homogenous. In modern China's multinational musical imagination, indeed, each "minority" group finds itself routinely identified with a certain reified set of sonic and choreographic icons. Musical instruments, which are among the most visible of these stereotypes, are good examples here: the Hmong (Miao) are often seen playing the mouth organ *qeej* (*lusheng* 蘆笙); the "horse-head" fiddle *morin khuur* (*matouqin* 馬頭琴) stands for the Mongolian; the plucked lute *dombra* (*dongbula* 東不拉) for the Kazakh; and the plucked lute *rawap* (*rewapu* 熱瓦普) for the Uyghur; to name a few. Such fixing of music and physical objects into readily identifiable sonic tropes has played an important role in the state's assimilationist modernization schemes. Paul Clark (2008: 256), for example, argues in his research of performing arts during the Cultural Revolution (1966–76) that the homogenization of local "minority" art into "easily recognized versions of their originals" provided Chinese audiences in the 1950s and early 1960s with certain familiar "dance moves or musical sounds or tropes as signifying particular ethnic groups" and "standardized, easily recognized signs of ethnic diversity and assertion of multicultural tolerance." These sonic and choreographic icons were then "valued as providing a ready, even shorthand way to assert a Chinese version of modern culture" (ibid.: 256). The musical otherness in performing arts, in other words, has been actively sought for pragmatic ends that go beyond representational needs.

The senses of alterity invoked in "minority" performing arts should therefore be understood not only in their perception by the mainstream Chinese audience. To be sure, colonial imaginaries of enticing women, delicious fruits, colorful costumes, and unrestrained life have contributed to and informed modern China's musical fetishization of the non-Han peoples and places. It is also true that, to many Han musicians and audiences, the label "minority music" often appears in the realm of entertainment as undifferentiated, miscellaneous, and somewhat nullified. Yet to understand the performing arts of the non-Han as operating merely as blank signifiers that are void of contextual substance and artistic integrity is also to overlook the cultural work that has been enabled and effected in the process. This chapter is concerned with non-Han indigenous music as it has become minoritized in a shared yet divergent process of cultural enlightenment with the Han over the past few decades in mainland China. My analyses here are informed—and perhaps also to some extent constrained—by my research on the music of the Uyghur, who are Turkic-speaking Central Asians in the far northwestern province of Xinjiang. Stylistically remote from mainstream Han Chinese genres, Uyghur and other non-Han music in Xinjiang offer unique cases to examine the state's assimilationist policies and strategies of resistance by the local musicians. As Chinese composers and musicians continue to claim inspirations in their encounter with the land and the peoples in far-flung non-Han territories, questions that problematize concepts of hybridity and otherness also become particularly relevant. The basic argument here is that the minority/majority binary that has loomed so large in Chinese music scholarship and performance today is fundamentally a modern construct, manifested through a symbiotic musical relationship between the "minorities" and the mainstream. The shifting senses of belonging is also contingent upon such a relationship as musicians and audiences envision their own musical futures.

"Minorities"

It would be inaccurate at best to understand the music of many non-Han peoples as existing in a primordial state, uncontaminated by outside influences before they became "minority music" under the new People's Republic in the mid-twentieth century. In northwestern China, reformist cultural movements overlaid with nationalist sentiments began to take shape at the turn of the twentieth century across the Sino-Russian borders. Late nineteenth-century collections of Uyghur Taranchi songs and folk literature by the Russian folklorist Nikolai Pantusov (1849–1909), for example, served as raw materials and models for the burgeoning identities of the modern Uyghur nation in the 1920s (Pantusov, 1890; see also Brophy, 2016: 222). Ideals of modernist reform embraced by Central Asian Jadidists in the early twentieth century may also have contributed to the formation of Uyghur national culture through music (Harris, 2017: 38, quoting Mukkadas Mijit, 2016: 32). The new Uyghur musical dramas produced in Ghulja (Yining) in the 1930s and 1940s (Memtimin Hoshur, 2014), the introduction of non-indigenous instruments (such as the modernized, plucked lute *chaplima rawap* and the violin, which is still known by its Russian name *iskripka* among Uyghur musicians today), as well as the early modern ensemble formats introduced from the Soviet Central Asia also marked the beginning of a new cultural era before substantial Chinese influence (Abdushükür Muhemmet'imin, 1997: 340–46; see also Harris, 2008: 29–33).

Yet, not until the Communist takeover in 1949 did the music of the Uyghur and other non-Han peoples partake, reluctantly or otherwise, in a substantial process of cultural renewal as they became incorporated into the socialist state and subsumed as its internal Others. China's post-1949 "minority" cultural policy has been characterized by the coalescence of—and fluctuation between—two seemingly conflicting principles. The first revolves around the Soviet-derived concept of autonomy for "minority" nationalities, as manifested in the various levels of administrative territories as well as the official status and specific rights given to members of the fifty-five recognized non-Han groups. Few would disagree that, while political autonomy is largely titular, the multiculturalist celebration of diversity has been the official line and indoctrinated in various aspects of the life of the non-Han peoples. In the performing arts, this is evident in the substantial state sponsorship of music and dance, as implemented in the many folkloric singing-and-dancing troupes established in non-Han territories throughout the 1950s (Rees, 2001: 479–80); large-scale ethnographic research projects to document and preserve their music (Wong, 2009); as well as educational institutions established to impart their performing arts. Such assertive implementation of pluralistic policy has allowed a certain level of tolerance that may appear at odds with attempts of aggressive assimilation, as seen, for example, during the Cultural Revolution (Wong, 2016: 147–65) and recently with mass detention and the eradication of Uyghur culture and identity (Millward, 2019).

The second principle of China's "minority" cultural policy is rooted in the notorious, centuries-old belief that the "barbaric" tribes residing on the imperial periphery have never existed at a state of civilization comparable to the Han Chinese and the Sinicized non-Han in China proper (such as the Manchu during the Qing empire). Such chauvinism continued to resonate in much of the twentieth century and beyond and served as an integral discourse of Chinese modernity. As many have argued, the portrayal of the non-Han peoples as yet-to-be-enlightened primitives has served China's self-fashioning as advanced and progressive in the course of becoming a modern nation (Gladney, 1999: 57–61). In the performing arts, the relational construction of Han and Chinese modernist nationalism has relied on the active policing of music and dance such that, as Gardner Bovingdon (2010: 7–8) puts it, these have become "not mere misrepresentations" but instead the "very stuff of politics." Until rather recently, the Central Asian soundscape of Uyghur and a number of other non-Han music traditions in the northwest has been characterized, to different extents, as possessing deficient qualities and aesthetics that await improvement: sympathetic timbre on some indigenous instruments as undesired noise; diatonic fretting and unequal temperament as unscientific; oral transmission and the absence of notation as defective; heterophonic texture and small-size chamber-ensemble formats as simplistic.[2]

The Han people—whose homogeneity, to be clear, is itself a questionable modern construct—often emerge as enlightened incomers whose benevolent help has introduced modern social institutions and cultural devices to raise the non-Han to a higher level of civilization—what Stevan Harrell has called China's "civilizing project" for the "minorities" (1995: 4). In music, this is best manifested in the state-sponsored, modernist reform project systematized after 1949 across the entire country. Operated with the ostensible goal to enlighten the non-Han peoples, the project introduced to local traditional music such European concert-music procedures as functional harmony, equal-tempered tuning, grandiose orchestral textures and formats, solo virtuosity, sanitized timbres, standardized repertoire, written notation, as well as professionalized training and performing troupes. In the case of Uyghur and other non-Han music in the northwest, conservatory-style music institutions were established in the 1950s and 1960s; the most high-profile of these, the Faculty of Music at the Xinjiang Arts Institute, which was initiated in the late 1950s in the provincial capital Urumqi, has established a curriculum of training professional Uyghur performers, composers, and music educators in the conservatory setting. A good number of graduates from these institutions are often employed in the various provincial and county-level song-and-dance troupes across the territory. These professional performing ensembles are established and run by local governments of various administrative levels; the most prestigious is the autonomous region's Xinjiang Song-and-Dance Troupe (founded in 1962), which has assumed the role of recreating traditional music in progressive, grandiose styles.

The advent of the music conservatory as the chief site for music transmission and the government-run performing troupe as the emblem of professionalism also brought about changes in how musicality is conceived. Some of the finest non-Han musicians were enlisted in these state institutions as performers, instructors, composers, and researchers. Under the new system, the traditional guru of the past was transformed from a versatile multi-instrumentalist and/or master vocalist to often no more than a member of a performing troupe, the "work unit" (Uyghur: *orun*), responsible for a designated instrumental or vocal part or for an assigned task as composer or arranger. In most cases, the work unit has also been something musicians depend on to receive a modest salary, health and housing benefits, and political teachings—a structure that remains effectively in place in Xinjiang and a number of other non-Han territories today, where performing artists are under the strictest control and most vulnerable to political persecution.

The new system and its embrace of professionalism have also worked to decontextualize traditional performance practices and to cultivate a new kind of technicality (and listening habit) for the musical body. In essence, it obliterated the music's indigenous folk or religious contexts as well as a kind of time-honored, in-group professionalism. In Uyghur music, this is exemplified by the case of a number of reworked traditional pieces in the modern concert repertoire, as frequently performed by professional musicians today. Some of the better-known examples include solos for the *rawap* plucked lute, such as *Yaru* and *Tashway*; traditional Ili-style pieces for the *tembur* plucked lute, such as the much-performed *Ejem*; as well as an instrumental genre known as *merghul*, which originally appeared as postludes to poetic songs in the classical *On Ikki Muqam* (*Twelve Muqam*) and were later rearranged for specific solo instruments. These rearranged pieces are commonly distinguished from their originals—which are now referred to as *yerlik* (local) or *kona* (old)—as they feature rapid runs, long and amplified tremolos, arpeggiated figures, chord-like patterns, and a broader range and are normatively performed with equal-tempered scales, exaggerated dynamic contrast, standardized length, regularized rhythm (and meter), and sometimes set to orchestral arrangements. A good example here is the instrumental *merghul* taken from the first *dastan* song of "Oshshaq Muqam"; its virtuosic rearrangement is frequently performed as a showcasing concert piece for the *ghéjek* fiddle.[3]

As described elsewhere (Wong, 2018: 60–61), I was somewhat surprised to learn that Uyghur musicians who have been trained in the traditional and the professional styles—and thus are proficient in both—consistently claimed that the older version was more challenging to learn. I was explicitly discouraged from learning the older version of these pieces until after I had learned the newer versions. This is certainly not because the new versions are less technically demanding; indeed, quite the opposite is true. The actual reason is that these new arrangements—most of them descriptively notated and readily printed in published scores—require little concern for performing practices that are spontaneous and contingent, such as ornamentation and some degree of interaction. They also appear to be more exact and predictable, and they demand little of the musician's cultivation or immersion in the tradition. This way, the orality assumed in traditional music making was diminished and replaced by standardized notation, model recording, "ethnic" attire and uniform, modified instruments, as well as the concert-stage setting—technologies of modern performance that seek to establish regularity and transparency. At work here is also a kind of reconstitution of meaning and cultural memory in these newly created musical "texts": instrumental music was taken out of its poetic and often sacred contexts to be refashioned as somewhat autonomous "works," ready for the re-inscription of new stories about "minority" progress and cultural enlightenment in the modern era. Examples of such musical and discursive reframing that I have examined include the composition *Méning Rawabim* and the rearranged version of *Tashway* (Wong, 2012 and 2018), both created for the solo *rawap* by the modernist composer Qurban Ibrahim (1922–98) in the early 1960s and intimately connected to the interpretation by the virtuoso Dawut Awut (1939–2007), who is remembered today as a pioneer reformer for a treasured national instrument.

Diverging views and personal preferences surely exist among local musicians and audiences of different musical experiences and listening habits. While non-conservatory-trained musicians often maintain different degrees of reservation over professionalized and concertized preferences (for example, Light, 2008: 194–200), modernist musicians and composers are sometimes critical of content they perceive as obsolete and unscientific in traditional music.[4] Yet it is interesting to note that, by and large, musical modernity has rarely been approached as a troubled condition or national crisis, in ways that have characterized, for instance, the enduring debate on the "Westernization" of Chinese music among Chinese academics and musicians today. It would not be unfair to say that, to many non-Han musicians, rarely has musical modernity meant the passive acceptance of unwanted outside (that is, Chinese) influence or the erasure of cultural heritage. Indeed, the notion of outstanding masters or musical geniuses who are virtuosic is not without parallels in the past and in traditional Uyghur music making today; nor was it uncommon in traditional practice for individual songs or instrumental music to be performed as stand-alone pieces detached from their original contexts. What is new here is the coexistence of the traditional and the modern in musical life, as well as the self-consciousness associated with such binaries as old/new and traditional/modern, which sometimes appear less as actual styles and more as discursive frames. The national pride often embedded in such cultural expression of progress is also notable: a number of high-profile Uyghur virtuosi, such as the late *satar* (bowed lute) and *tembur* soloist Nurmuhemmet Tursun (1957–2004), the *ghéjek* soloist Ekrem Ömer (1963–2012), and the aforementioned Dawut Awut even attained status as national heroes. To many in the audiences of these contemporary masters, modernist creativity in their works is often viewed as pinnacle rather than troubled disruption or controversial moment in the development of their national music (see Méhmanjan Rozi and Turghan Shawdun, 1995: 85–90, 249–54).

To briefly conclude, it is the coalescence of these two principles of "minority" cultural policy—that is, a multiculturalist celebration of ethnic diversity and a Han-Chinese-led cultural enlightenment project to "civilize" the "minorities"—that has forged a unique space for subaltern musical modernity over the past nearly seven decades in China. Non-Han elites often consider themselves keen participants and sometimes even leaders—and less often as reluctant victims—of a cultural renewal project that, at its core, is integral to their own national history. The sense of progress embodied in the modern soundscape also represents a promising strategy for indigenous music, which has long been perceived as primitive, to sublimate its marginality to a national collectivity that is advanced and modern (Wong, 2018: 62–63). As the anthropologist Louisa Schein observes in the case of the ethnic Hmong in southwestern China, concepts of progress are rarely antithetical to the Hmong's pursuit of ethno-national interests. In performing modernity, non-Han actors "confounded their consignment to the role of the impoverished, rural, tradition bearers and strove to make membership in the prestigious category of modernity less exclusive, more negotiable" (Schein, 2000: 223). It is thus useful to consider cultural modernity and subaltern empowerment in the same breath, and to understand modernity not as a top-down, overwhelming condition but rather as a consciousness that is generative and adaptable. For non-Han elites, the ability to traverse between the old and the new is often a preferred strategy to engage prejudices, stereotyping, and other forms of discrimination.

THE MAINSTREAM

The other side of the minority/mainstream symbiosis relates to the representation of otherness, as briefly noted in the opening of this chapter. Perhaps the most prominent and influential outcome of such colonial enterprise is the sizable oeuvre of exotic-styled compositions written for Chinese musical instruments since the early 1950s. Composers of this genre claim inspirations through encountering "minority" peoples and places—via films, recordings, "field trips" to the borderlands, or actual experience as settlers—and employ recognizable stylistic devices and contextual tropes that invite exotic imagination in their works. Of importance here is not only the representation strategies and narratives but also the modernist musical languages and techniques formulated in these primarily Han Chinese compositions. The broader thesis of this part of the chapter is that musical exoticism should be approached as being how a Chinese nation on its way to becoming modern has sought to musically domesticate its neighboring peoples and cultures. I suggest that the adaptation of the real or imagined non-Han styles has enriched the expressive capacity of recently reengineered Chinese musical instruments; it also expanded the musical vocabularies and the range of compositional options for modern Chinese music.

The vast majority of these works—which altogether are estimated to account for nearly a quarter of Chinese instrumental works written since the 1950s—is intended to be performed on traditional Han instruments that have undergone considerable modification in the modern era. They are also squarely among some of the most performed concert pieces for the showcasing of virtuosic technical brilliance. Rarely have less "reformed" instruments, such as the *qin* seven-string zither and the *xiao* 簫 vertical bamboo flute, been assigned pieces of explicit exotic styles. To be clear, there certainly exists a comparable genre of traditional music of the premodern era that alludes to imaginaries of the imperial borderland. Legends of Lady Wang Zhaojun (c. 52 BCE–c. 15 BCE), a court lady of the Han empire who was married off to a tribal chief of the "barbaric" Hun in exchange for peace, for example, have been a favorite poetic theme for a good number of these pieces, the famous *pipa* suite *Saishang qü* (*Song of the Frontier* 塞上曲) being the best-known example. Yet this genre of frontier-themed music (and poetry) is distinguished from its modern counterpart by one important aspect: it was mostly prescriptive and stylistically indistinguishable from other genres in Chinese music. References to the remote peoples and places relied primarily on the music's programmatic context rather than realist strategies, such as exotic scales, irregular meters, and the like. The realism in the representation of otherness in post-1950s Chinese compositions is thus a uniquely modern approach whose implications deserve close examination.

"Minority"-themed compositions abound in modern Chinese instrumental music. To use compositions inspired by Uyghur and other non-Han peoples in Xinjiang as an example, most performers of Chinese instruments today—most notably those of the *zheng* 箏 zither, *erhu* 二胡 fiddle, *di* 笛 flute, *pipa*, *yangqin* 揚琴 dulcimer, and *ruan* 阮 lute (and their modern orchestral varieties)—are equipped with a repertoire of pieces with titles such as *Joyful Xinjiang* (*Huanle de Xinjiang* 歡樂的新疆, 1960s), *Festivals on the Tianshan Mountain* (*Jieri de Tianshan* 節日的天山, 1970s), *The Sun Shines on Tashkurgan* (*Yangguang zhaoyao zhe Tashiku'ergan*, 1976), *The Grapes Are Ripe* (*Putao shoule* 葡萄熟了, 1980), to name a few of the best known. These compositions frequently employ a range of compositional devices—purportedly derived and appropriated from non-Han music—to invoke the exotic landscape and ethnic life of far northwestern China, including: syncopated rhythms and irregular meters that recall "ethnic dances"; accidentals in an otherwise largely pentatonic or diatonic scale, most often the sharpened fourth and the flatted seventh; tonal ambiguity between the tonic and subdominant areas; as well as cadenza-like, virtuosic, festive passages. Consistent with the twentieth-century realist turn in Chinese art and literature, these composers and musicians seek to represent the "real presence" of the non-Han peoples by formulating a lexicon of exotic musical language. In reality, whether these devices and styles accurately mimic Uyghur and other non-Han music is often not a major concern, as long as the exotic flavors are easily discernible and compatible with concepts of "minority" imagined by the mainstream Chinese audience. The authenticity of these largely fictive "minority styles" rarely been subjected to critical scrutiny, and many among the untroubled Chinese musicians and audiences take them as genuine and reflective of ethnic ways of life. What is important in such reification of musical difference is the formulation of what Jonathan Bellman has called the "exotic equation," one that strikes a "balance of familiar and unfamiliar: just enough 'there' to spice the 'here' but remain comprehensible in making the point" (Bellman, 1998: xii).

A good example here is the category of "minority"-style compositions written for the *erhu*, a bowed fiddle stemming from regional traditions of eastern and southern China and identified as a potential instrument to realize the reformist ideals by early modernist musicians beginning in the 1910s and 1920s. The best known of these reformers is Liu Tianhua 劉天華 (1895–1932), who famously modeled the techniques and styles of the modern *erhu* after the European violin and initiated a solo tradition for what had otherwise been primarily an ensemble or accompanying instrument in the past. Attempts to emulate Western art music not only continued but also intensified and systematized after 1949, and composers looked further to the music of the newly incorporated non-Han peoples for inspiration and opportunities to expand the range of expressivity on this renewed Chinese instrument. Efforts then began to identify instruments and styles in non-Han and other regional Han traditions that are physically and acoustically comparable to the *erhu*. The Mongolian *morin khuur* horse-head fiddle emerged as a favorite choice. A number of modernist Chinese instrumental compositions written for the *erhu* as a solo instrument since the late 1950s claimed Mongolian styles as sources of inspiration. Images of steppes and horses abound in these realist musical works, in which the *erhu* is made to explore a range of technical possibilities in order to mimic the figures of galloping or trotting horses, as the *morin khuur* does, or to capture the broad, expansive Inner Asian steppes like the singing of Mongolian *urtin duu*, or "long song." Some of the best known of these include the modern classic *Horse Racing* (*Sai ma* 賽馬), written in 1959 by the multi-instrumentalist Huang Haihuai 黃海懷 (1935–67; Huang died at the age of thirty-two at the onset of the Cultural Revolution, soon after being sent for "re-education"); *New Herdsmen on the Steppes* (*Caoyuan xin mumin* 草原新牧民), written in 1975 by the soloist Liu Changfu 劉長福 (b. 1944); as well as *Galloping War Horses* (*Zhanma benteng* 戰馬奔騰), written in 1976 by Chen Yaoxing 陳耀星 (b. 1941).

An immediate product of such appropriation is the creation of a series of techniques and expressions that are believed to be idiomatic to the *morin khuur* and absent in the traditional music of the *erhu* and other Chinese bowed strings. These include chains of long, uninterrupted trills (*zhanyin* 顫音) and trills that alternate between notes that are a third apart (*san du zhan yin* 三度顫音) as well as glissando figures that imitate horse neighing. Likewise, on the right-hand, new techniques such as jeté (ricochet) bowing (*pao gong* 拋弓) and percussive bowing (*ji gong* 擊弓) were created to imitate horse galloping. Use of pizzicato and rolling fingers (using multiple fingers successively to repeat the same note) became more extensive and systematic.[5] Composers also made use of rare modal scales or modulation in order to invoke exotic sensibilities; well-known examples include *Song of the Morin Khuur* (*Matouqin zhi ge* 馬頭琴之歌) composed in 1962 by Xia Zhongtang 夏中湯 and, again, *Galloping War Horses*. Similar cases can be found in the new "minority"-themed compositions written for the *pipa* since the late 1950s, which explored a range of tremolo (*yaozhi* 搖指) techniques for all the right-hand fingers to imitate sustained melodies and legato phrasing (Yuan, 1987: 223). Significantly, most of these new incorporated techniques then became standard and were broadly applied to pieces that are thematically related or unrelated to the non-Han.

It would not be an exaggeration to say that the modern, national attributes of the *erhu* and other "improved" Chinese instruments are acquired partly through their versatility in reproducing a wide variety of non-Han and regional Han styles. It is the *erhu*, the modern national instrument—rather than its premodern or regional varieties, such as the northern *banhu* 板胡, Cantonese *gaohu* 高胡, coconut-shell *yehu* 椰胡, among other bowed strings—that has been the focus of these modernist experiments.[6] The appropriation of non-Han styles should thus be understood as part of a project that is intimately connected to the modernization of Chinese national music. Another well-known example here is *On the Steppes* (*Caoyuan shang* 草原上), a solo written in 1956 by the composer and instrumentalist Liu Mingyuan 劉明源 (1931–96) for the *zhonghu* 中胡, the "middle-range" fiddle that was created in the 1940s and conceived to be an alto-range *erhu*. The instrument is normatively tuned a fifth below the *erhu* and has served in the Chinese orchestra as the equivalent to the viola in the Western orchestra. Liu is said to have been inspired by a performance of *urtin duu* singing and the horse-head fiddle on an official visit to Mongolia in 1954 and other trips to Inner Mongolia. He then composed the first solo for a newly created instrument based on styles of Mongolian music, partly because the horse-head fiddle is of a comparable range and timbre to the *zhonghu*. Several ornamentations and bowing techniques mentioned above are applied extensively in this piece (see Chen, 2012).

It is remarkable to note that it took a "minority"-style composition to launch the solo profile of a newly created Han Chinese instrument. The same is true also for the thirty-six-pipe keyed mouth organ, *jiajian sheng* 加鍵笙. This is an alto version of the traditional seventeen-pipe *sheng* 笙 constructed to fill the middle range of the orchestral texture. A thirty-two-pipe prototype was first built in 1963, leading to a series of experiments that eventually brought about a standardized thirty-six-pipe version in the early 1980s. The first solo composed for this newly minted instrument was titled *Tastes of Dai Village* (*Dai xiang fengqing* 傣鄉風情, 1985), written by its creator Wang Huizhong 王惠中 (b. 1942) based on folk musical elements of the Dai peoples residing on the Sino-Burmese border in Yunnan. A variant of this modern instrument, with a circular rather than rectangular wind-chest—the thirty-six-pipe keyed circular mouth organ (*jiajian yuan sheng*)—was created in approximately the same period by Zhang Zhiliang 張之良 (b. 1940), who also wrote its first solo, *Joyful Steppes* (*Huanle de caoyuan* 歡樂的草原) (1977), based on Kazakh music from northwestern China. Likewise, the first composition that established the *ruan*, a Chinese plucked lute reinvented in the 1950s as a solo instrument, is a concerto titled *Remembrance of Yunnan* (*Yunnan huiyi* 雲南回憶), composed in 1987 by Liu Xing 劉星 (b. 1962) based on "minority" folk elements from Yunnan.

Meanwhile, the issue of authenticity looms large when composers claim to be inspired by and borrow from a non-Han style or instrument. The question is not so much about stylistic fidelity as it is about the sounds and gestures that are deliberately imagined as authentic and thus chosen to serve the purpose. Elsewhere I have written about the musical image of otherness as projected in the much-performed solo, *The Grapes Are Ripe*, composed by Zhou Wei 周維 (b. 1960) for the *erhu* in 1980 (Wong, 2011). This showpiece is marked by its extensive use of codified and highly exoticist musical language that is said to reference Uyghur traditional music. It features explicit tonal ambiguity, frequent use of accidentals, upbeat phrases, and syncopated rhythms—stylistic features that are common in stereotypical "minority"-style compositions but have little in common with traditional Uyghur music. In particular, the *erhu* is made to mimic the Uyghur spike fiddle *ghéjek* in its musical portrayal of a grape-picking Uyghur woman, seen through a characteristic Han masculinist gaze.

As such examples reveal, the "minority" sound source that Chinese composers perceive or present as authentically "ethnic" is very often an outcome of reformist experiments in the modern period. The Uyghur *ghéjek* commonly used in staged concerts and conservatory teaching today is an instrument that has gone through aggressive modifications since the mid-1950s. Premodern types of *ghéjek* are fretless and feature a thick horse-hair melodic string alongside more than a half-dozen sympathetic strings. To achieve a sanitized timbre, reformists in the 1960s and 1970s removed all the sympathetic strings and the melodic string and replaced them with four steel melodic strings (normatively tuned in fourths) played over an added fretless fingerboard—a clear attempt to emulate the Western violin. The animal skin that originally covered the spherical resonating box was replaced by a thin wood board at the front, and a python skin (stretched over a small wood frame that is not visible from the outside) was placed inside the resonating box, which produced an invented "ethnic" sound through its nasal timbre. Finger and bowing techniques of the modern *ghéjek* are greatly indebted to influences from the Western violin and the Chinese *erhu* (Wong, 2018: 55–56). In some sense, the sounds of the *ghéjek* invoked in *The Grapes Are Ripe* belong to an utterly different stylistic category, one that is neither traditional Uyghur nor entirely Western or Chinese. The very "minority music" that Chinese composers seek to borrow and appropriate in their works is thus very often a mediated creation of the imagination, a concocted authenticity that is shaped simultaneously by exoticism and reformist ideals, deliberately chosen to serve purposes that go beyond mere representation.

Conclusion

This chapter has shed light on how China's musical encounters with its marginal peoples and cultures have been deeply implicated in discourses of cultural enlightenment that have characterized the music of both the "minorities" and the mainstream Chinese today. On the one hand, the music of the non-Han peoples is involved in a dual minoritizing process, one that simultaneously celebrates its contribution to multiethnic diversity and seeks to rectify its perceived primitivity. As Timothy Taylor writes (2007: 70–71), "Political and geographic margins are peculiarly energetic sites where meanings are made, remade, altered, transformed, and altered again. . . . It becomes clear that marginality—either as positionality or in representations—plays a pivotal role in forming and altering worldviews and thus, among other things, aesthetic processes." Marginality in non-Han performing arts has certainly served as a major source for creativity in the music of both the non-Han peoples and the Han Chinese. On the other hand, as non-Han elites re-appropriated the state's enlightenment scheme for their own nationalist aims, Chinese musicians' adaptation of largely fabricated "minority styles" also enriched the language of modern Chinese music and instruments by expanding their vocabularies and expressive ranges. The emergence of modern Chinese techniques and styles is thus closely connected with the representation of "minority" otherness in Chinese music. Referencing his famous *pipa* arrangements of "minority" compositions (including that of the *rawap* solo *Spring on Tianshan Mountains* [*Tianshan zhi chun* 天山之春] in 1961), the renowned pipa soloist Wang Fandi 王范地 (1933–2017) explained that "it has been my goal to inherit and develop the music of the *pipa*.... [I]n order to enrich the performing techniques of the *pipa* and to diversify its styles, I seriously learned [to play] the *rawap* and other minority instruments" (Wang, 2003: 50–51). The aspiration to "advance" Chinese music through stylistic borrowing from non-Han traditions as expressed here is far from rare; similar views are broadly shared among modern Chinese composers and musicians.

It would thus not be a stretch to assert that Chinese music would not be the same as we hear and play it today without the non-Han peoples partaking in its modern renewal. Exoticism is rarely a mere act of representation; the otherizing strategies employed in these works help the audience to arrive at a perspective, through which the exotic is made comprehensible and becomes part of the self. The "minority" elements in these Chinese compositions and instruments are aestheticized in order for them to be perceived as natural, and they are eventually incorporated as normative in Chinese music. A good number of these works have become extremely popular over the past few decades inside and outside China precisely because they are artistically powerful and convincing. Their lasting success should resist untroubled analysis that looks at the music simply as the outcome of some successful compositional procedures that merely "sound good." Rather, it speaks to China's continued troubled relationship with its ethnic neighbors and marginalized peoples as well as the ways in which the modern Chinese musical self has been predicated on its conception of "minority" otherness.

Glossary

banhu 板胡, fiddle with a wooden soundboard
Caoyuan shang 草原上, *On the Steppes*, composition by Liu Mingyuan (1956)
Caoyuan xin mumin 草原新牧民, *New Herdsmen on the Steppes*, composition by Liu Changfu (1975)
Chen Gang 陳鋼, violinist, composer, and arranger (b. 1935)
Chen Yaoxing 陳耀星, composer (b. 1941)
Dai xiang fengqing 傣鄉風情, composition for *jiajian sheng* by Wang Huizhong (1985)
dastan داستان, Uyghur narrative singing, or a section in a *muqam* suite

Dawut Awut داۋۇت ئاۋۇت, *rawap* virtuoso (1939–2007)
di 笛, horizontal flute
dombra (Kazakh) (Chinese: *dongbula* 東不拉), plucked lute
Ejem ئەجەم, traditional Ili-style Uyghur composition
Ekrem Ömer ئەكرەم ئۆمەر, *ghéjek* soloist (1963–2012)
erhu 二胡, fiddle
gaohu 高胡, Cantonese form of two-stringed fiddle
ghéjek غېجەك (Chinese: *aijieke* 艾捷克), spike fiddle
Huanle de caoyuan 歡樂的草原, *Joyful Steppes*, composition by Zhang Zhiliang (1977)
Huanle de Xinjiang 歡樂的新疆, *Joyful Xinjiang*, composition for *yangqin* by Zhou Deming (1960s)
Huang Haihuai 黃海懷, composer and multi-instrumentalist (1935–67)
iskripka ئىسكرىپكا, violin
ji gong 擊弓, percussive bowing
jiajian sheng 加鍵笙, added-key mouth organ (1960s)
jiajian yuan sheng 加鍵圓笙, added-key circular mouth organ (1970s)
Jieri de Tianshan 節日的天山, *Festivals on the Tianshan Mountain*, composition by Jiang Wentao 姜文濤 and Cao Ling 曹玲 (1970s)
jingju 京劇, Beijing opera
kona كونا, "old," designation for repertory in its original form
kunqu 崑曲, traditional opera genre
Liu Beimao 劉北茂, performer and composer (1903–81)
Liu Changfu 劉長福, performer and composer (b. 1944)
Liu Mingyuan 劉明源, performer and composer (1931–96)
Liu Tianhua 劉天華, music reformer (1895–1932)
Liu Xing 劉星, composer (b. 1962)
Matouqin zhi ge 馬頭琴之歌, composition by Xia Zhongtang (1962)
Méning Rawabim مېنىڭ راۋابىم, a modern Uyghur composition by Qurban Ibrahim (1963)
merghul مەرغۇل, an instrumental postlude added to a song, or instrumental pieces
morin khuur (Mongol) (Chinese: *matouqin* 馬頭琴), "horse-head" fiddle
nengge shanwu 能歌善舞, "good-at-singing-and-dancing," idiom regularly applied to minority populations in China
Nurmuhemmet Tursun نۇرمۇھەممەت تۇرسۇن, *satar* and *tembur* performer (1957–2004)
On Ikki Muqam ئون ئىككى مۇقام, classical repertory of the *Twelve Muqam*
pao gong 拋弓, jeté (ricochet) bowing
pipa 琵琶, four-stringed lute
Putao shoule 葡萄熟了, *The Grapes Are Ripe*, composition for *erhu* by Zhou Wei (1980)
qeej (Hmong) (Chinese: *lusheng* 蘆笙), mouth organ
qin 琴, seven-stringed zither
Qurban Ibrahim قۇربان ئىبراھىم, composer (1922–98)
rawap راۋاپ (Chinese: *rewapu* 熱瓦普), plucked lute
ruan 阮, lute
Sai ma 賽馬 (1959), *Horse Racing*, composition by Huang Haihuai (1959)
Saishang qü 塞上曲, *Song of the Frontier*, suite for *pipa*
san du zhanyin 三度顫音, trill alternating notes a third apart
satar ساتار (Chinese: *sata'er* 薩它爾), long-necked bowed lute
shaoshu minzu 少數民族, "minority nationalities"

sheng 笙, mouth organ
sizhu 絲竹, "silk and bamboo," category of instrumental ensemble traditions
Tashway تاشۋاي, solo for *rawap*
tembur تەمبۇر (Chinese: *tanbuo'er* 彈撥兒), plucked lute
Tianshan zhi chun 天山之春, arrangement of *rawap* solo for *pipa* by Wang Fandi (1961)
urtin duu (Mongol) (Chinese: *changdiao* 長調), "long song," Mongolian vocal tradition
Wang Fandi 王范地, *pipa* performer and arranger (1933–2017)
Wang Huizhong 王惠中, instrument reformer and composer (b. 1942)
Xia Zhongtang 夏中湯, composer (b. 1939)
xiao 簫, vertical flute
Xiao huagu 小花鼓, *Small Flower Drum*, composition for *erhu* by Liu Beimao (1943)
Yangguang zhaoyao zhe Tashiku'ergan 陽光照耀著塔什庫爾干, *The Sun Shines on Tashkurgan*, arrangement for violin by Chen Gang (1976)
yangqin 揚琴, dulcimer
yaozhi 搖指, tremolo
yehu 椰胡, two-stringed fiddle with coconut-shell resonator
yerlik يەرلىك, "local," designation for repertory in its original form
Yaru يارۇ, traditional Uyghur composition, a solo for *rawap*
Yunnan huiyi 雲南回憶, concerto for *ruan* by Liu Xing (1987)
Zhanma benteng 戰馬奔騰, *New Herdsmen on the Steppes*, composition by Chen Yaoxing (1976)
zhanyin 顫音, trill
Zhang Zhiliang 張之良, instrument reformer and composer (b. 1940)
zheng 箏, zither
zhonghu 中胡, mid-pitched fiddle created in the 1940s
Zhou Deming 周德明, composer (latter part of the twentieth century)
Zhou Wei 周維, composer (b. 1961)

Notes

1. I generally avoid using the term "minority" to refer to the peoples identified as such in post-1950s China. The Uyghur, Tibetans, and other non-Han peoples are the majority of their homeland, and there is nothing "minor" about their art, music, and culture. The sense of inferiority that comes with the term (and its Chinese equivalent, *shaoshu minzu*) should also be critically approached. When quotation marks are placed on the term "minority" in this essay, I am typically referring to minoritizing discourses.
2. These views were prevalent particularly during the period from the 1950s through the 1980s; see Wan Tongshu (1986: 93–103) for an example regarding the modernization of Uyghur musical instruments.
3. For a published notation used for conservatory teaching, see Abdukérim Osman (2008: 172–76). For a recording of the piece played in an overtly virtuosic style, as is standard today in concert performances, refer to *The Music of Uygur Nationality* (1996), which features members of the Xinjiang Song-and-Dance Troupe, the top state-sponsored ensemble.
4. The latter view is held by quite a number of urban musicians I have interviewed, including the composer and educator Tursunjan Létip (b. 1951), who is also critical of the modern

canonization of the classical *muqam* (in various interviews from 2009 to 2013). Some of his views can be seen in Létip, 1997; and 2002: 3–14.

5. The first use of pizzicato on the *erhu* was likely in *Small Flower Drum* (*Xiao huagu* 小花鼓), a miniature composed in 1943 by Liu Beimao 劉北茂 (1903–81), the brother of Liu Tianhua. But its application as a brief left-hand double-stroke that begins the piece is an utterly different technique from how it is used in post-1950s compositions. Similarly, the technique of rolling fingers first appeared in solos written by Liu Tianhua in the late 1920s but was not systematically used in later compositions.

6. Some of these local varieties, such as the Cantonese high-pitched fiddle, *gaohu*, are indeed modern creations from different periods of the twentieth century and yet maintain regional identities that are distinguished from the national status of the *erhu*.

REFERENCES

Abdukérim Osman. (2008). *Ghéjek Dersliki* [Ghéjek Lessons]. Vol. 1. Ürümchi: Shinjang ma'arip neshriyati.

Abdushükür Muhemmet'imin. (1997). *Uyghur Muqam Xezinisi* [Treasure of Uyghur Muqam]. Ürümchi: Shinjang Dashösi (Uniwérsitéti) neshriyati.

Bellman, Jonathan. (1998). "Introduction." In *The Exotic in Western Music*, edited by Jonathan Bellman, ix–xiii. Boston: Northeastern University Press.

Bovingdon, Gardner. (2010). *The Uyghurs: Strangers in Their Own Land*. New York: Columbia University Press.

Brophy, David. (2016). *Uyghur Nation: Reform and Revolution on the Russia-China Frontier*. Cambridge, MA: Harvard University Press.

Chen Yu-Hsuan. (2012). "Zhonghu qū 'Caoyuan shang' yü 'Zan ge' zhi yanjiu" "中胡曲「草原上」與「贊歌」之研究" [A Study on the Zhonghu Compositions "On the Steppes" and "Song of Praise"]. Thesis, National Taiwan Normal University.

Clark, Paul. (2008). *The Chinese Cultural Revolution: A History*. Cambridge, UK: Cambridge University Press.

Gladney, Dru. (1999). "Representing Nationality in China: Refiguring Majority/Minority Identities." In *Consuming Ethnicity and Nationalism: Asian Experiences*, edited by Kosaku Yashino, 48–88. Honolulu: University of Hawai'i Press.

Harrell, Stevan. (1995). "Introduction: Civilizing Projects and the Reactions to Them." In *Cultural Encounters on China's Ethnic Frontiers*, edited by Steven Harrell, 1–36. Seattle: University of Washington Press.

Harris, Rachel. (2008). *The Making of a Musical Canon in Chinese Central Asia: The Uyghur Twelve Muqam*. Aldershot, UK: Ashgate.

Harris, Rachel. (2017). "The New Battleground: Song-and-Dance in China's Muslim Borderlands." *World of Music* 6 (2): 35–55.

Light, Nathan. (2008). *Intimate Heritage: Creating Uyghur Muqam Song in Xinjiang*. Berlin: Lit Verlag.

Méhmanjan Rozi and Turghan Shawdun. (1995). *Muqam töhpiklarliri* [Muqam's Contributors]. Ürümchi: Shinjang xelq neshriyati.

Memtimin Hoshur. (2014). *Ili Uyghur Tiyatirining Chiliqi* [Ili Uyghur Theater]. Ürümchi: Shinjang yashlar-ösmüler neshriyati.

Millward, James. (2019). "'Reeducating' Xinjiang's Muslims." *New York Review of Books*, February 7, 2019. Accessed December 2, 2021. https://www.nybooks.com/articles/2019/02/07/reeducating-xinjiangs-muslims/.

Mukaddas Mijit. (2016). "La mise en scène du patrimoine musical ouïghour: Construction d'une identité scénique" [Staging Uyghur Musical Heritage: Construction of Stage Identity]. PhD diss., Université Paris Ouest Nanterre La Défense.

Music of Uygur Nationality. (1996). Compact disc. Taipei: Cradle Records.

Pantusov, Nikolai. (1890). *Taranchinskiia piesni* [Taranchi Songs]. St. Petersburg: Tip. Imp. Akademii nauk.

Rees, Helen. (2000). *Echoes of History: Naxi Music in Modern China*. Oxford: Oxford University Press.

Rees, Helen. (2001). "Cultural Policy, Music Scholarship, and Recent Development." In *Garland Encyclopedia of World Music 7 (East Asia: China, Japan, and Korea)*, edited by Robert Provine, Yosihiko Tokumaru, and J. Lawrence Witzleben, 478–83. New York: Routledge.

Schein, Louisa. (2000). *Minority Rules: The Miao and the Feminine in China's Cultural Politics*. Durham, ND: Duke University Press.

Taylor, Timothy. (2007). *Beyond Exoticism: Western Music and the World*. Durham, NC: Duke University Press.

Tursunjan Létip. (1997). *Uyghur chalghu eswabliri* [Uyghur Musical Instruments]. Ürümchi: Shinjang Uniwérsitéti neshriyati.

Tursunjan Létip. (2002). "Uyghur muqamliri peqet 'on ikki' mu" [Are There Only Twelve Uyghur Muqam]. *Shinjang sen'iti* [Xinjiang Arts] 1: 3–14.

Wan Tongshu. (1986). "Yueqi de xin fazhan" "樂器的新發展" [New Development of Musical Instruments]. In *Weiwu'er zu yueqi* 維吾爾樂器 [Uyghur Musical Instruments], 93–103. Ürümchi: Xinjiang renmin chubanshe.

Wang Fandi 王范地. (2003). *Yanghe ji* 養和集. Hong Kong: Wide Code Wah Shui Publishers.

Wong Chuen-Fung. (2009). "The Value of Missing Tunes: Scholarship on Uyghur Minority Music in Northwest China." *Fontes Artis Musicae* 56 (3): 241–53.

Wong Chuen-Fung. (2011). "Representing the Minority Other in Chinese Music." In *Reading Chinese Music and Beyond*, edited by Joys Cheung and King Chung Wong, 121–45. Hong Kong: Chinese Civilisation Centre, City University of Hong Kong.

Wong Chuen-Fung. (2012). "Reinventing the Central Asian Rawap in Modern China: Musical Stereotypes, Minority Modernity, and Uyghur Instrumental Music." *Asian Music* 43 (1): 34–63.

Wong Chuen-Fung. (2016). "The West is Red: Uyghur Adaptation of The Legend of the Red Lantern (Qizil Chiragh) during China's Cultural Revolution." In *Listening to China's Cultural Revolution: Music, Audiences, and Legacies*, edited by Paul Clark, Laikwan Pang, and Tsanhuang Tsai, 147–66. London: Palgrave Macmillan.

Wong Chuen-Fung. (2017). "Intercultural Encounters, Global Circulations, and the 'Original Ecology' Style of Uyghur Music in the Late Twentieth Century and Beyond." In *Sketches of China*, edited by Bernhard Hanneken, 211–24. Berlin: Verlag für Wissenschaft und Bildung.

Wong Chuen-Fung. (2018). "Modernist Reform, Virtuosity, and Uyghur Instrumental Music in Chinese Central Asia." *Ethnomusicology Reader Volume Two*, edited by Jennifer Post, 53–64. New York: Routledge.

Yuan Jingfang 袁靜芳. (1987). *Minzu qiyüe* 民族器樂 [National Instrumental Music]. Beijing: Renmin yinyue chubanshe.

CHAPTER 23

"KITA ANAK MALAYSIA" ("WE ARE THE CHILDREN OF MALAYSIA")

Performing Multicultural Chinese Identities

TAN SOOI BENG

INTRODUCTION

THE Penang-born popular folk singer, songwriter, and film star Ah Gu (or Ah Niu 阿牛)[1] took the stage by storm with his multilingual song "Speak My Language" in 1998. This song touched the hearts of many, exemplifying ongoing dialogues about what it means to be Chinese and what comprises Chineseness among those who were born in and have made multiethnic Malaysia their home.

In "Speak My Language," Ah Gu asks "What is my culture? What should it be?" Educated in Chinese-language schools, Ah Gu speaks Mandarin as his main language. However, to communicate with fellow Chinese or Malaysians from Malay- or English-language schools, he has to use "broken *rojak* Market English." *Rojak*, a type of mixed fruit salad tossed in local chili paste, is employed as a metaphor for the mixing of cultures and languages.

> I speak Hokkien and Mandarin
> And I like eating Wantan Mee, Instant Mee
> Why do I have to speak other language[s]
> While I am talking to my people?
>
> Tell me please what is my culture?
> Tell me please what should it be?
> Tell me please where is my future?

> North, South, West, or East? [...]
> I am just looking for my ID
> So don't blame me
> For my broken Rojak Market English [...]
> (Ah Gu, "Speak My Language," 1998)[2]

Malaysia is a multiethnic, multireligious country with a population of 28.3 million (Department of Statistics, 2010). The Chinese comprise 24.6 percent of this population and are varied in composition, forming one of the largest Chinese communities outside of China. Their forefathers came from various parts of Fujian and Guangdong; they belong to different dialect groups, such as Hokkien, Cantonese, Hakka, Teochew, and Hainanese. However, they all call themselves Malaysian Chinese, or *huaren* 華人 ("Chinese people"), a term translated into Hokkien as "Tenglang," into Cantonese as "Tongyan," and so on. In response to Ah Gu's question, it is the nature of intercultural contact, place of residence, and educational backgrounds that determine the lingua franca of the Chinese in Malaysia.[3]

Malaysian Chinese identities have been, and continue to be, experienced in numerous and active ways. Wang Gungwu (1991), a prominent scholar of the Chinese inside and outside of China, has argued that it is essential to avoid defining a standard or static version of Chinese identity; the Chinese who have settled overseas tend to adopt multiple identities. As they mediate the different cultures and worlds they live in, their performances and identities are defined by heterogeneity and hybridity rather than by essence or purity (Hall, 1990: 235). These identities change and can only be understood within the context of the socio-political and historical conditions of the particular period and place that shaped their formation.

Musical works, the performing arts, and languages are involved in dynamic processes of creating and recreating manifold Chinese identities. It is inevitable that the Chinese who live in multiethnic societies adapt to and mix the cultures of others around them. Yet, in the process of crossing borders, references to selected Chinese cultural markers are maintained. The boundaries of these markers are, however, not fixed but flexible. For instance, Southeast Asian Chinese who no longer speak or write Chinese might express their identities through cultural activities such as playing Chinese musical instruments or singing Chinese songs in English, Malay, or other local languages.

This chapter takes a transnational approach, looking at different ways of being Chinese in Malaysia by going beyond the China-centered models typical of Chinese-diaspora studies (Hau, 2014; Tan and Rao, 2016; Wang, 1999). I not only look at interactions between the Chinese based in the Malaysian states and in China but also take into account interactions among the Chinese in Malaysia, people of other ethnic descent in the country, and other international musicians. Furthermore, Singapore has been included in the analysis as it was part of British Malaya. Nevertheless, it is not possible for this chapter to be exhaustive in considering all of the different forms of musical cultures and ethnicities at stake since the time the Chinese arrived in Malaysia.[4] I focus on the syncretic musical practices of particular Chinese musicians from three periods:

the colonial, post-independence, and transnational globalized eras. These music-makers actively navigate their way through the socio-political conditions of the historical moments in which they live. Their creations are also influenced by factors such as class, education, cultural contact with other ethnic groups, and national state policies.

The Peranakan Chinese in Early Twentieth-Century British Malaya

The first Chinese who came to Malaya were mainly traders from Fujian province. They settled in the ports of Malacca, Penang, Singapore, and Kelantan as early as the sixteenth century. They intermarried with local women and adapted to the Malay sociocultural environment. By the nineteenth century, there had emerged a group of local-born Chinese who spoke a type of Malay patois and adopted certain features of Malay dress, cooking, and music; they were known as Baba (referring to men), Nyonya (referring to women), or Peranakan (meaning local-born). During the colonial period, the local-born Chinese in the Straits Settlements of Malacca, Penang, and Singapore formed an influential class of businessmen who called themselves the Straits Chinese; they acted as intermediaries between the British and the Malays and served on local councils. Educated in the English-language schools set up by the British, many Straits Chinese were employed in British government offices or as teachers in the schools (Tan Chee Beng, 2004).

In the 1920s and 1930s, the local-born Peranakan adopted Malay forms of musical and theatrical expression, including *bangsawan* theater and the *ronggeng* social dance, but they held onto Chinese rituals with their percussion music, as well as to festivals of the lunar calendar, as markers of Chinese identity (Tan Sooi Beng, 2016). The English-educated Peranakan were also adept at playing the piano, guitar, violin, saxophone, and other Western instruments, and they took part in English theater.[5]

The various traditions of Malay *pantun* (quatrain verse) singing in *dondang sayang* and *kronchong*,[6] and the chanting of Hokkien rhymes, illustrate how the Peranakan in the Straits Settlements embraced syncretism in their music. They adopted local Malay folk music, rhythmic patterns, textures, and verse singing, incorporated Western and Malay instruments, and used Western triads, scales, and strophic form—but they also retained their Hokkien rhymes for educating younger generations.

Malay *Dondang Sayang*

Dondang sayang is an elaborate form of Malay poetry or *pantun* singing, popular among the Peranakan of the Straits Settlements. Singers try to outwit each other in repartee style, using *pantun* to debate topics of interest such as love, good deeds, business, fruits, or the sea in the Baba Malay patois. Performances can last many hours depending on the abilities of the singers. The Gunong Sayang Association of Singapore, which was set up in 1910, was the first *dondang sayang* association in the Straits Settlements, and it played an important role in disseminating the tradition. Members of the association not only performed but also published collections of *dondang sayang pantun*. Koh Hoon Teck, one of the founders of the Gunong Sayang Association of Singapore, compiled five volumes of *Panton Dondang Sayang Baba Baba Pranakan* (*Dondang Sayang Verses by the Baba Baba Peranakan*), published in 1911 and reprinted in 1916 and 1920. Koh's own company, located at 83 and 84 Bras Bash Road, Singapore, published the verses. This company also sold books, stationary, postcards, toiletries, perfume, and newspapers (Koh, 1916: 103).

The following *dondang sayang pantun* about *Budi* (*Good Deeds*, 1920) printed by Koh's company shows the use of Baba Malay spelling. As in the Malay *pantun*, each line of the verse ends with a rhyming "A" sound. The first two lines of the verse are allegorical suggestions of the meaning made explicit in the last two lines:

Pulo pandan jauh ka-tenga	Pandan island is far away in the center of the sea
Gunung Daik bercabang tiga	Daik Mountain has three ranges
Anchor badan dikandong tana	The body rots when one is buried
Budi yang baik dikenang juga	Good deeds will still be remembered (Koh, 1920: 16)

Prominent *dondang sayang* singers such as Koh Hoon Teck were recorded in the 1930s by gramophone companies such as His Master's Voice (HMV) and Pagoda.[7] The musical transcription of *Dondang Sayang Tanaman I* (*Dondang Sayang about Plants I*, Pagoda, V 3770, sung by Miss Piah, Mr. Poh Tiang Swee, and Mr. Koh Hoon Teck) illustrates the use of a Western violin, Malay *rebana* frame drum, and Malay gong. Believed to be influenced by the Portuguese who came to Southeast Asia in the sixteenth century, this ensemble also accompanies the Malay folk social dance called *ronggeng*, where men and women dance without touching one another (Tan Sooi Beng, 1993).

A characteristic melody known as the *dondang sayang* tune (adapted from Malay *dondang sayang*) accompanies the improvisation of the *pantun*. A typical five-measure melody begins all *dondang sayang* repartee singing, which can last for several hours depending on the abilities of the vocalists (Figure 23.1).

The rhythm played by the frame drum (*rebana*) and the placements of the gong beats resemble the Malay *asli* rhythmic pattern from the *ronggeng* dance repertoire. As in traditional Malay music, the vocalist sings in heterophony with the violin, or *biola* in Malay (Figure 23.2).

Kronchong from the Dutch East Indies

Peranakan musical groups such as the Gaylads, Sunbeam Musical Party, Moonlight Minstrels, and Mayfair Musical Party promoted other syncretic forms of Malay and

Dondang Sayang 1

FIGURE 23.1. Typical *dondang sayang* melodic introduction from *Dondang Sayang Tanaman 1* (Pagoda V3770), sung by Miss Piah, Mr. Poh Tiang Swee, and Mr. Koh Hoon Teck.

English songs in Penang, Melaka, and Singapore (*Straits Echo*, July 28, 1931; *Times of Malaya*, August 23, 1934). These musical groups performed *kronchong* and Malay folk tunes in Baba Malay, and minstrel songs in English, at special concerts and exhibitions.

It is said that Portuguese sailors brought the *kronchong* to Batavia (locally known as Betawi, now Jakarta) in the sixteenth century. The earlier ensembles were mainly string bands comprising violin, guitar, ukulele, mandolin, and banjo, but flute and double bass were added later. *Kronchong* music was featured in the *komedi stambul* musical theater of Java, but it was subsequently adapted by the Malay *bangsawan* performers and Straits Chinese musical parties, by way of traveling singers from the Dutch East Indies (Tan Sooi Beng, 1993).

As with the *dondang sayang*, gramophone companies such as HMV and Pagoda recorded *kronchong* in Singapore. Lim Seng Hooi (abbreviated to H.S.L.) was the Straits Chinese owner of the Criterion Press of Penang, which printed songbooks, such as *Penghiboran Hati* (H.S.L., 1924), and sold them to the public. The Criterion Press also printed local newspapers such as the English daily *Straits Echo*, the Malay weekly *Chahaya Pulau Pinang*, and the Chinese daily *Penang Sin Poe*. The Western notation and Baba Malay verses of the sixteen *kronchong* songs printed in *Penghiboran Hati* further show the eclectic nature of the song repertoire of the Peranakan. As the song titles in the book suggest, the melodies were adapted from *stambul* (a type of musical theater), popular *kronchong* recorded by 78-RPM recording companies as well as other local folk songs.[8] The melodies were notated for violin or mandolin, with chords for guitar.

Dondang Sayang 1

FIGURE 23.2. Score of voice and violin performing in heterophony and accompanied by the *asli* rhythmic pattern in *Dondang Sayang Tanaman 1* (Pagoda V3770), sung by Miss Piah, Mr. Poh Tiang Swee, and Mr. Koh Hoon Teck.

Figure 23.3a displays the strophic melody of *Kronchong Weltevreden* (named after a colonial district of old Batavia) for violin or mandolin, published in *Penghiboran Hati* (H.S.L., 1924). The score begins with a four-measure introduction, and then there is a sixteen-measure melody that follows an ABCD structure. The guitar chords notated in Example 23.3b show a fundamental harmony based on the I, IV, and V chords of popular recordings of the early twentieth century (Yampolsky, 2010: 30).

Hokkien Rhymes in Penang Hokkien

Unlike the Peranakan in Malacca and Singapore who spoke Baba Malay, those in Penang retained Hokkien as their language of communication with other dialect groups and with the new Chinese immigrants who came in large numbers in the late nineteenth century (these newcomers, or *sinkeh*, are discussed in the following section). Hokkien rhymes were recited by the elders to entertain and to teach their children about Chinese values, customs, and appropriate behavior. However, the Penang-style Hokkien differed from the Hokkien in Fujian as Malay and English words had been added. It continues to be spoken by the diverse Chinese population in Penang and is the lingua franca among the Chinese in Medan and Phuket, who had close trade links with Penang in the past.

The Hokkien rhymes were either two- or four-line verses recited to specific rhythms or sung using Malay folk melodies. As a child, I enjoyed the rhymes chanted by my grandmother; many of these rhymes have since been compiled and published by Chee (2008) and Kwok (2005). My grandmother would recite the funny rhyme below with her grandchildren so that we would not be afraid of the dark when there was a blackout. The lines under the words indicate eighth-note values while the words without lines have a quarter-note duration:

Am bong bong, *Ah mah tui ah* kong, 暗濛濛，阿嬤追阿公，
Ah kong pek k'ee chang, *Ah ma ch'uei bou* lang. 阿公爬上樹，阿嬤找不[到]人.

It is all dark, Grandma chases Grandpa
Grandpa climbs up a tree, Grandma cannot find him.

On the first and fifteenth day of Chinese New Year, grandmothers often sang the following rhyme to the tune of the Malay folk song, "Trek Tek Tek," to remind the young Nyonya ladies to pray to the deities for prosperity and stability throughout the new year. The fifteenth day of the Chinese lunar calendar is also the equivalent of Valentine's Day for the Chinese, an opportunity for unmarried Baba to see the Nyonya dressed up and touring the town in horse-drawn carriages. The verse below

FIGURES 23.3. (a–b) Handwritten musical score of *Kronchong Weltevreden* for violin or mandolin with guitar accompaniment, published in *Penghiboran Hati* (H.S.L. 1924).

FIGURE 23.3. Continued

was recited in Penang Hokkien, with the Malay word *suka* added in the penultimate line:

<u>Ch'ei</u> it <u>chap</u> goh, <u>Nyonya</u> chaboh pai <u>angkong</u>, 　　初一十五，娘惹拜神，
<u>T'nee</u> eh <u>bou</u> chui, <u>Long chong</u> hu <u>luan luan</u> chong. 　　池裡沒水，全部魚亂亂沖，
<u>Ah</u> nya <u>ah chee</u>, <u>Achnua</u> lu <u>aneh</u> gong? 　　姐妹們，你們為什麼要這麼講，
<u>Pneh pneh suka</u>, <u>Mm</u> bien <u>knia</u> lang kong. 　　彼此喜歡，就不用怕人講。

Nyonya ladies pray on the first and fifteenth day
The fishes will rush around if there is no water in the tank
Ladies and sisters, why are you so foolish?
If people love each other, do not fear what people say. (Chee, 2008: 12)

THE NEWCOMERS (*SINKEH*) IN BRITISH MALAYA

In the mid-nineteenth century, large numbers of Chinese people of Hokkien, Teochew, Cantonese, Hakka, Hainanese, and other dialect groups migrated to British Malaya to work in tin mines, open farms, or establish businesses. They were known as the *sinkeh* 新客 (newcomers). Unlike the local-born Peranakan, who created their syncretic forms of music, these Chinese immigrants brought their own performing and martial arts from China.

Professional opera and puppet-theater troupes from China toured the different parts of Malaya and entertained the *sinkeh*. Some performers remained and set up their own troupes. Chinese opera and puppet theater were also performed as offerings to celebrate the birthdays of Chinese deities at temple festivals and during lunar-calendar festivals, such as the seventh month Phor Tor (Hungry Ghost) festival, which is a local version of the Zhongyuan festival (中元節). These festivals fortified a sense of community and fulfilled the spiritual needs of the immigrants in the new land.

Newspapers of the 1930s inform us that the *kotai* 歌台 ("song stage") performed at amusement parks was another popular form of entertainment that was enjoyed by the *sinkeh*. Some examples include Keat's Magical and Vaudeville Show, which featured "hula-hula dancing and magical arts," and the Cherry Blossom Music and Operatic Show, which attracted "capacity houses" with its "excellent performance and beautiful girls" and "modern orchestra, singing and dancing" at the Fun and Frolic Park (*Straits Echo*, November 20, 1933; February 5, 1934). Among the popular songs performed by the traveling troupes were the Mandarin *shidaiqu* 時代曲 ("songs of the times") known locally as *laogu* ("old songs"); they featured songs by singers such as Zhou Xuan 周璇 and Bai Guang 白光 that were trendy in Shanghai and Hong Kong in the 1930s and 1940s.

Additionally, amateur cultural organizations, and martial-arts and lion-dance associations, were set up in the towns. Organized as part of Chinese voluntary or clan associations that took care of the needs of the Chinese immigrants, these Chinese cultural organizations provided places for the *sinkeh* to socialize, entertain one another, and practice their culture. One of the popular activities at these associations was the improvisation of opera tunes and Teochew, Hokkien, Cantonese, and Hakka folk tunes of the provinces from which the Chinese immigrants originated. Playing what was known as *difang yinyue* 地方音樂 ("regional music"), ensembles usually consisted of bowed fiddles (*erhu* 二胡, *yehu* 椰胡), plucked lutes (*pipa* 琵琶, *yueqin* 月琴), transverse and vertical flutes (*dizi* 笛子, *xiao* 簫), mouth organ (*sheng* 笙), and percussion of drums, gongs, cymbals, and small bells (*gu* 鼓, *luo* 鑼, *bo* 撥, *ling* 鈴 respectively). It was reported that regular music-practice sessions were held at the Penang Chinese Ladies Chin Woo Association, the Toi Sun Union, and other clubs (*Straits Echo*, March 16, 1935).

Besides promoting friendship and entertainment, the amateur clubs played important roles in fundraising for specific purposes, and they kept people in touch with life in China. The Perak Chinese Amateur Dramatic Association staged Chinese operas to collect money to aid the Anglo-Chinese School Building Fund, "to provide relief to clerks thrown out of employment as a result of the depression," and to help flood victims of Canton (*Times of Malaya*, March 28, 1913; June 18, 1932; *Star*, January 26, 1987).

NATION-STATE POLICIES AND THE SEARCH FOR NATIONAL IDENTITIES, 1950S–1980S

Most performance activities halted when the Japanese invaded Malaya in 1942. After the war, Chinese performing arts continued to decline as Malaya experienced a breakdown of political and economic stability due to food shortages, unemployment, and labor unrest. The British imposed censorship on all performances, including Chinese cultural activities, during the twelve-year Communist insurgency, which began in 1948 and was known as the Emergency.

In 1957, Malaya became independent, but the following three decades were characterized by struggles as the Chinese found themselves citizens of a state attempting to unify the multiethnic population through the introduction of Malay as the national language and other pro-native policies. Communication with and travel to and from China were curtailed following the formation of the Communist state. The Chinese in Malaysia debated the function of the arts in society, responded to nation-state policies, and searched for forms of Malaysian national identity. This period also saw the coming together of diverse groups of Chinese to promote selected forms of performing arts as markers of Chineseness, in response to fear of being assimilated by the state. Even the Baba gradually became more Sinicized (while keeping their mixed identities) as they lost their special status under British rule and were categorized as Chinese in the new nation.

The eighty-seven-year-old Lee Soo Sheng 呂書成, who performed, conducted, and composed for the *huayue tuan* (Chinese orchestra) in Keat Hwa primary and secondary schools and the Dejiao Hui 德教會 (Moral Uplifting Society) in Alor Star, recalls his experiences during this turbulent period (personal communication, Alor Star, Kedah, November 1, 2003). Born in 1931, Lee attended the Chinese Keat Hwa Primary School in Alor Star and then the Chung Ling Secondary School in Penang. He learned the harmonica in Chung Ling and initiated a harmonica band when he returned to teach in his primary school in the 1950s.

Lee explained that during the 1950s and 1960s, Chinese cultural associations continued to have important social functions, providing opportunities for Chinese youths—especially lower-class youths—to socialize and learn the arts. As in China, Hong Kong, and Taiwan, heated debates about the meanings and uses of culture occurred in these associations. They identified themselves either as organizations promoting "art for the people" or "art for art's sake"; both kinds were critical of the influence of "yellow culture," or popular music. On the one hand, groups that advocated "art for the people" promoted art portraying social realities. Their aim was to raise awareness of the plight of the downtrodden, through music, dance, and drama that depicted the lives of plantation workers, fishermen, and the working class. On the other hand, those who advocated "art for art's sake" viewed their activity as essentially aesthetic, their aim being to promote interest in and raise the quality of the Chinese performing arts. The audiences of both groups consisted solely of Chinese who were educated in Mandarin schools, Mandarin being the language of communication around the practices (see Tan Sooi Beng, 2000a). Lee emphasized that, to the government, both groups were perceived as threats to national security:

> In the 1950s and early 1960s, during the Emergency and post-Emergency periods, many Chinese cultural activities were considered pro-Communist and banned by the Malaysian government. It was difficult to get permits to give public concerts. My own harmonica band was banned. I was disappointed as harmonica playing had nothing to do with politics.

Lee then joined the Teochew *difang yinyue* music group at the Dejiao Hui and learned how to play Chinese musical instruments.

In the 1960s, the "art for art's sake" and "art for the people" groups began to consolidate, prompted by the introduction of the modern Chinese orchestra, which had become the national orchestra of China, as popularized in Hong Kong and Taiwan.[9] The modern Chinese orchestra comprised sections of bowed strings, plucked strings, winds, and percussion, all seated like a Western orchestra and led by a conductor. Chinese musicians from Malaysia who had studied in Hong Kong were attracted to the new sounds of the modern Chinese orchestra, which combined Western and Chinese elements; they brought newly improved instruments, scores, and recordings of new pieces when they returned to Malaysia. The Dejiao Hui in Alor Star established its *huayue tuan* in 1964, the Penang Philharmonic Society followed in 1971, and the Jit Sin Secondary School Chinese Musical Instrument Society in Seberang Perai was initiated in 1968 (Tan Sooi Beng, 2000b).

The new orchestra stirred excitement among the different classes of Chinese musicians, not to mention Lee. In 1964, he joined the *huayue tuan* of the Dejiao Hui in Alor Star; he later arranged and composed music for the orchestra. "Even then, the authorities banned my first composition, *A Song for All*, when the Chinese students of a national university used it as their theme song for social protest," Lee commented.

Subsequently, the 1970s and 1980s witnessed further consolidation of Chinese performing groups and certain Chinese traditions, such as lion and dragon dances, operas, and festivals. The different types of Chinese came together to assert their common identity; they felt the New Economic Policy introduced in 1971 to restructure society discriminated in favor of the Bumiputra (comprising Malays and other indigenous people) with regard to admission into universities and public service, the granting of scholarships, the issuing of licenses for operating businesses, and so on. Moreover, the National Culture Policy was perceived as assimilationist and designed to bring about the demise of cultures the government identified as "non-indigenous." As Chinese cultural groups were not eligible to receive funding from the government, they raised their own funds for sustaining Chinese schools and culture in the country (for an in-depth discussion, see Tan Sooi Beng, 2000a). Lee stressed that the Chinese orchestra developed further as a self-conscious marker of Chineseness, with it already having become popular among Chinese youths and school children. By then, many Chinese secondary schools had founded their own orchestras, often sponsored by well-to-do Chinese patrons.

Nevertheless, Lee underscored that all performing-arts groups were aware of the need for local relevance. Chinese cultural groups incorporated some Malay and Indian folk music and dances, and Malaysian dramatic themes, into their performances. The Chinese orchestra largely followed contemporary trends in China and Hong Kong, but local compositions based on Malay folk and popular songs were also created. Malaysian Chinese identity called for the use of Malay folk melodies, rhythms, images, and other elements as its markers.

Lee himself arranged more than one hundred pieces for the Chinese orchestra, including Malay folk and patriotic songs. He explained: "I am inspired by people's daily activities, events as well as sounds of the environment. I create music that promotes the values and cultures of the multiethnic society and the beauty of Malaysia." Regarding the arrangement of the patriotic song "Tanah Pusaka" ("Land of Inheritance," composed by Ahmad Merican), Lee elucidated: "I wanted to show the beautiful melody and the image of a wide paddy field that represents the idea of freedom and a place that is undisturbed by problems such noise pollution; an ideal place for the people of [the state of] Kedah."[10] He continued, "*Potong Padi* [*Harvesting Paddy*] is based on a folk song about cutting paddy in the Malay villages."

Figure 23.4 is a short excerpt from *Joget Anak Udang* (*Joget Dance Music*) that illustrates how Lee combined Malay and Western musical elements in his arrangements for the Chinese orchestra. *Joget Anak Udang* employs the characteristic *joget* dance rhythm of triplet quavers versus duple quavers. The string instruments use the typical Chinese heterophonic style, but Western I, IV, and V triads are employed.

Lee also plays with the tone colors of the Chinese orchestra's instruments. As in many Chinese pieces, the flute (*dizi*) is used to represent birdcalls in his arrangement of "Burung Kakak" ("Cockatoo Bird"),[11] a children's song from Indonesia that is popular in Malaysia. As a tribute to his contributions in the development of *huayue tuan* music in Malaysia, Lee's compositions were recorded for a compact disc called *Songs*

Joget Anak Udang

FIGURE 23.4. Notation of four measures of *Joget Anak Udang* showing the use of three against two notes and simple triads.

for All (named after his first composition); the pieces were performed by the China Broadcasting Traditional Orchestra (Lee, 1996).

LIBERALIZATION AND GLOBALIZATION AT THE TURN OF THE TWENTY-FIRST CENTURY

Compared to the 1970s and early 1980s, some liberalization appears in government policies toward non-Malay language and culture in the 1990s. Cultural performances during National Day celebrations and Citrawarna (Colors of Malaysia, a festival to attract tourists) feature multiethnic dances and music, albeit with the versions of Chinese dances and music standardized (see Tan Sooi Beng, 2003). Since the turn of the twenty-first century, musicians have been able to travel to and from China, Hong Kong, and Taiwan; there is a fair amount of cultural exchange between the Chinese groups of the various countries. With increased travel and communication through the mass media, computer technology, and collaborations, some cultural groups are beginning to draw inspiration from other parts of the world as well.

A transnational form of Chineseness based on multiculturalism seems to be the trend. With the liberalization of policies, Chinese musicians are no longer preoccupied with the politics of creating a national identity. They collaborate with other theater, dance, and visual-arts practitioners of various ethnic backgrounds and from other countries to initiate new forms, content, and vocabulary in performance. Multidimensional works, including theatrical performances, videos, and installations, have also emerged. Chinese musicians perform in different spaces to different kinds of mixed audiences, including international ones. Musical creations and audiences spill over boundaries of ethnicity, language, space, and state. Nevertheless, certain Chinese instruments and elements that are flexible in definition are maintained as sonic markers of Chineseness.

As shown in the examples below, it is not surprising that all of these groups use social media and YouTube to reach a wider multiethnic and international audience.

The Dama Orchestra, which was established as a *huayue tuan* by Khor Seng Chew 许成就 (a *pipa* and guitar expert) in early 1993, typifies this trend. Due to a shortage of funding and audience support at the turn of the new millennium, Dama decided to transform itself, seeking to appeal to larger audiences including the English- or Malay-educated Chinese middle-class. The recontextualization of globalized, multicultural popular hits of yesteryear has put the Dama Orchestra on the world map.

In a recent musical-theater performance entitled "Yours Musically" (2016), Dama offered a repertoire of popular songs from the past two decades, sung in Chinese, English, Malay, Indian, and other languages.[12] Their multilingual songs included "Empress Wu" and "Butterfly Lovers" (from their previous musical-theater productions), P. Ramlee's "Getaran Jiwa," Sudirman's "Balik Kampung," the theme song of the Hindustani film *Kuch Kuch Hota Hai*, and "Dancing Queen" from the film *Mama Mia!*

Dama has also popularized the *shidaiqu* as theater, through the staging of "Spring Kisses Lover's Tears" (1997), "The Songs in Me" (2000), "Memories" (2004), and "Le Cabaret Shanghai" (2004). These Mandarin oldies were sung by classically trained sopranos such as Phoon Sook Peng, Angela Chock, and Tan Soo Suan. Chinese instruments *erhu*, *dizi*, *pipa*, and *yangqin* were blended with Western percussion, double bass, and keyboard. English narration promoted understanding among non-Chinese-speaking audiences; lighting and costume designs enhanced the productions visually. Dama's new repertoire represents a hybrid Malaysian Chinese identity, mixing Malay, Chinese, Indian, Western, and other influences (Loo and Loo, 2014).

Similarly, Hands Percussion, formed by Bernard Goh in 1997, has presented contemporary theatrical drumming that merges the Chinese *shigu* 獅鼓 (lion drum) with Indonesian *gamelan* gongs, and Malay *gendang* and *kompang*, as well as Western and African drums, to audiences in Malaysia and overseas. In an interview with the independent radio station BFM, Goh, currently the group's artistic director, explained that the performers challenge themselves to "explore cutting-edge and unconventional drumming without losing the group's Malaysian identity."[13] They not only cross but also push the boundaries of playing percussion and drums. *Rhythm Ride* (2016), for instance, explores complex rhythms on the *gamelan* gongs and lion drums, using creative performance methods and stylized movements.[14]

To take the group's experimentation to a higher level, Hands Percussion collaborates with international and local musicians. The Wind of Nomads Concert (2017) featured African and Asian percussion, the result of a three-year collaboration between Hands and Dafra Drums of Burkina Faso, West Africa. The concert showcased unique outcomes achieved from combining the African djembe, other percussion instruments, and the lion drum. "Percussion Paradise" (2017), a celebration of the group's twentieth anniversary, presented collaborations with Norway's Sisu Percussion, the marimba player Tan Su Yin, and the Kelantanese musician Mat Din (*Star Metro*, September 26, 2017).[15]

Likewise, Ombak Potehi, which I initiated in 2014, has attempted to revitalize Hokkien glove-puppet theater in Penang by way of introducing multiethnic characters, costumes, dialogue, and music.[16] By traversing ethnic and cultural boundaries, the theatrical and musical content is more accessible to people of different races, gender, ages, and income levels. Moreover, the group believes that the performing arts can educate and promote the sharing of cultures among the diverse peoples of Penang. In the performance of *Kisah Pulau Pinang* (*Penang Story*, 2017), we tried to capture the daily lives, activities, and interethnic relationships of cosmopolitan society, through revisiting major historical events in colonial Penang prior to the Japanese occupation in 1942. The performance featured the mixing of Hokkien, Malay, Indian-Muslim, and Chinese Peranakan songs and dialogue. Based on interviews in the multiethnic communities in Penang, it illustrates a people's history of Penang not found in textbooks. This is a history of people of various races interacting in marketplaces and coffee shops, mixing cultures and languages.[17] *Kisah Pulau Pinang* drew in three thousand people of different races to the five public shows held at the George Town and Butterworth Fringe Festivals and Heritage Celebrations in Penang in 2017.

In popular music, the BM Boys (comprising Vincent Ng Boon Seng, Ho Ying Khee, Bonnie Ang Swie Chien, Tan Ming Yih, Tan Chin Teik, Cheng Kai Yong, and Goh Pin Aun, who all grew up in Bukit Mertajam, or BM) have sought to cross cultural borders by adding local elements and instrumentation to global popular-music productions. In an interview (personal communication, Kuala Lumpur, December 13, 2002), Vincent Ng, the leader and composer of the group, highlighted the campus-folk-song movement of Taiwan, which promoted original songwriting using acoustic instruments such as the guitar, as key inspiration for members, who were studying at Universiti Malaya in the 1990s.[18] "We chose the name BM Boys to show our love for the town that we were born and grew up in," Ng continued. The campus folk movement began in the 1970s, at a time when Taiwanese students were asking questions about what it meant to be Taiwanese Chinese after the expulsion of Taiwan from the United Nations. They also wanted to develop a distinctively Taiwanese music, to counter the domination of Anglo-American pop (Yang, 1994).

In like manner, the BM Boys attempted to create Chinese pop that was uniquely Malaysian, through their lyrics and musical instrumentation. They added Chinese, Indian, and Malay drums to Chinese instruments, such as the *dizi* and *erhu*, and the Western guitar. They sang in Mandarin but often used different Chinese dialects, including Teochew, Hokkien, and Hakka, and some Malay as well. Vincent Ng explained, "I wanted to show that Malaysian Chinese have the ability to speak many different dialects and that is part of being Malaysian. The texts are about our own society, the daily lives of the Malaysian Chinese and their thinking."

The BM Boys consciously adapted Malay folk tunes and social-dance music in their songs. "Tong Nian Xiong" 童年頌 ("Song for Childhood," from the album *Tong Nian Xiong*; BM Boys, 1995) is sung in Mandarin using the Malay *inang* dance rhythm. It incorporates the Malay folk song "Lenggang Lenggang Kangkong," sung in Malay, which reminds the singers of good times they enjoyed together when young: "In our video clip, we wanted to show the natural beauty of the Malaysian environment such as the paddy fields, the hills, and the caves; we enjoyed playing games such as flying kites and playing with marbles." Parts of the song are accompanied by handclaps commonly employed in *dikir barat* and by rhythms played on the Malay frame drum, *kompang*.[19] Lyrical interludes are performed by the *erhu*.

The BM Boys are also known for their lyrics, which deal with social concerns and the environment. "Nang Si Chit Keh Nang" 俺是一家人 ("We are One Family," from the album *BM Boys*, 1997) stresses that all Malaysians (whether Malay or Chinese, rich or poor) should live together in harmony, show tolerance, communicate with one another, and work hard together, as they are one family. The song is sung in the Teochew dialect:

The stars are in the sky, people are on earth　　　天頂心 土下人
It does not matter where you come from　　　莫管汝是 乜籍人
You play the Malay drum, I carry the Chinese lantern　　　汝打鼓 我提燈籠
Lighting this earth.　　　照著光明叼世間.

We are one family　　　俺是一家人
It does not matter if you have money　　　莫管汝有鐳無鐳 日子甬怨歎
You must work hard to earn money　　　要有出力去拼賺
Only then can one eat and be independent . . .　　　正有吃有得企

The BM Boys reiterated that Malaysia, and not China, is their home in the song "Kita Anak Malaysia" ("We are the Children of Malaysia," 2009). While they appreciate and maintain their Chinese ancestry, they also foster a multicultural identity with the common ethic of "working together and striving forward." As shown in the video clip, the song features Malay and Chinese drum accompaniment and is set against the tranquil scenery of the sea and bamboo groves.[20]

Finally, transnational Malaysian Chinese pop musicians who travel widely between Malaysia, Singapore, Taiwan, Hong Kong, and China do not sever ties with their multicultural homeland. Wee Meng Chee 黃明志 (b. 1983, Johore), popularly known as Namewee, the high-profile Malaysian Chinese composer, recording artist, singer, and film maker, is a case in point. He uses the genre of hip-hop, music videos, and YouTube to make social commentaries about life, politics, and injustices in Malaysia. Namewee shot to fame in Malaysia after releasing a contentious song entitled "Negarakuku," in which he raps over the national anthem of Malaysia, "Negaraku" ("My Country"). In the video, he raises issues about police corruption, inefficient public services, and affirmative action in Malaysia. He emphasizes how Chinese-educated students like himself have to study overseas as their Chinese-school certificates are not recognized for entry into national universities in Malaysia. In 2018—a year of the dog, following the Chinese zodiac—he was remanded for four days and interrogated at the police station after he released the music video "Like a Dog" in conjunction with Chinese New Year. The police claimed that his lyrics about corruption and images of the dog (seen as impure in

Islam) could "cause disharmony, or feelings of hatred." In the song, Malaysian dogs were barking *mari mari, wang wang* ("come come, money money" in Malay).[21]

Despite the controversial music videos, Namewee also highlights that there is a natural desire for the Chinese to integrate with other communities as fellow Malaysians. In "Ali, AhKao, and Muthu" (referring to common nicknames for Malay, Chinese, and Indians in Malaysia) of 2017, Namewee collaborates with well-known Indian and Malay singers such as David Arumugam and Aniq respectively. They underscore how the different ethnic groups in the villages grow up together and can remain friends for life if there is no political intervention. In 2019, he changed the images of the song to challenge all Malaysians to come together to fight the COVID-19 pandemic.

Conclusion

This chapter highlights narratives about Chinese musicians' attempts to create music that is distinctively Chinese and Malaysian, from the early twentieth century through the turn of the new millennium. These performers and composers have made music at different times, in changing contexts, and with varying agendas; their narratives often intertwine, but at other times they conflict. Particularly engaging, though, is the sense of dialogue and continuity that emerges from their various accounts. The stories articulate an ongoing struggle to forge identities that are Malaysian and yet Chinese.

The narratives point to Malaysian Chinese identities that are varied and determined by place, time, transcultural interaction, types of education, status in society, and individual agency. These identities are often informed by contradictions and challenges only graspable with reference to particular socio-political and historical contexts. During the colonial period, the local-born Peranakan adapted music of Malaysia, the Dutch East Indies, and Europe while the *sinkeh* brought cultural practices from China. After independence, the Chinese who had become citizens of Malaysia maintained Chinese rituals and cultural expressions, but they also searched for national identities. Despite differences and contestations evident during this era, there was a general understanding among composers that Malay markers—such as folk songs and dance rhythms, and images of the village, paddy fields, and the peaceful Malaysian environment—made the works Malaysian. At the turn of the new millennium, with globalization and the liberalization of national policies, Chinese musicians have revised their notions of Chineseness in transnational directions. Yet their identities are entrenched in the Malaysian experience of multiculturalism and multilingualism. Fusion blurs distinctions between various ethnic groups and makes cultural products more accessible to all. Nevertheless, new hybrid forms continue to make references to specific Chinese cultural markers, which have malleable qualities.

The narratives also elucidate the openness and valor of the Malaysian Chinese as they accept difference. Throughout the periods studied, Malaysian Chinese musicians and composers have shown consistent openness to outside influences; they fuse musical

FIGURE 23.5. Multiethnic characters and costumes in localized Potehi glove-puppet theater, representing the children of Malaysia.

(Photo by Tan Sooi Beng)

elements of different parts of Asia and the West, and they express their own Malaysian styles by absorbing all kinds of local multicultural elements. Malaysian Chinese identities have evolved historically and will continue to do so. As the world becomes increasingly globalized, the Chinese live multiple cultural identities and transnational subjectivities, just as their ancestors did in the borderless world prior to British colonization. Contemporary Chinese musicians in Malaysia have incorporated lived historical experiences, struggles against essentialism, and a striving for cultural representation as equal subjects in a plural society (Figure 23.5). Chinese music, then, is a site in which Chinese Malaysians can nurture an inclusive future. Kita Anak Malaysia!

Acknowledgments

I thank Lee Soo Sheng and Vincent Ng for the interviews and Kang Su Kheng for the musical transcriptions.

Glossary

Note: Some terms follow Hokkien dialect romanizations

"A-Niu he A-Hua de gushi" 阿牛和阿花的故事, "The Story of Ah Niu and Ah Hua," song by Tan Kheng Seong (1997)
Bai Guang 白光, singer and film actress (1921–99)
"Bolixin" 玻璃心, "Fragile," song by Wee Meng Chee (2021)
bo 撥, cymbals
Dejiao Hui 德教會, Moral Uplifting Society based in Alor Star
difang yinyue 地方音樂, "regional music," ensemble music drawing on regional traditions
dizi 笛子, transverse flute
erhu 二胡, two-stringed fiddle
gu 鼓, drum
huaren 華人, Chinese
huayue tuan 華樂團, Chinese orchestra
Khor Seng Chew 许成就, music director and producer, Dama orchestra
kotai 歌台, "song stage"
laogu 老歌, "old songs," local name for *shidaiqu*
Lee Soo Sheng 呂書成, composer and musician (b. 1931)
ling 鈴, small bell
luo 鑼, gong
pipa 琵琶, four-stringed lute
sheng 笙, mouth organ
shidaiqu 時代曲, "songs of the times," Mandarin song genre in the first half of the twentieth century
shigu 獅鼓, lion drum
sinkeh 新客, mid-nineteenth-century Chinese migrants to British Malaya
Tan Kheng Seong (Chen Qingxiang) 陳慶祥, singer, songwriter, and actor, also known as Ah Gu (A-Niu) 阿牛 (b. 1976)
"Tong Nian Xiong" 童年頌, "Song for Childhood," song by the BM Boys (1995)
Wee Meng Chee 黄明志, singer, songwriter, filmmaker, and actor, also known as Namewee (b. 1983)
xiao 簫, vertical flute
yehu 椰胡, two-stringed fiddle with a coconut-shell resonator
yueqin 月琴, round-bodied lute
Zhongyuan festival (中元節)
Zhou Xuan 周璇, singer and film actress (1920–57)

Notes

1. Born in Kampung Benggali, Province Wellesley, Ah Gu (meaning "bull" in Hokkien) is the nickname for the singer-composer Tan Kheng Seong, stemming from his hit song "The Story of Ah Niu and Ah Hua" ("A-Niu he A-Hua de gushi" 阿牛和阿花的故事, 1997). Ah Gu is known for his country-folk songs (sung in Mandarin, Hokkien, Teochew, or Cantonese) laced with humor. In these songs, Ah Gu takes listeners back to nature and the village community that he misses. He recorded with the independent company Rock Records and Tapes based in Taipei at the turn of the millennium and has since ventured into film and acting.
2. This song is available on YouTube, at https://www.youtube.com/watch?v=3wFdELvhdbU, accessed December 9, 2021.

3. See Tan Chee Beng (2004) for a discussion of the different types of Chinese and their identities in Malaysia. Tan compares the Chinese cultures and religious practices in Malaysia with those in other parts of Asia where Chinese live.
4. See Tan Sooi Beng (2000a) for a more in-depth analysis of the historical development of different forms of performing arts in relation to socio-economic and political changes in Malaysia of the twentieth century.
5. I have analyzed the cosmopolitan performing arts of the Straits Chinese, including minstrel shows, Peranakan theater (*wayang peranakan*), Malay opera (*bangsawan*), Malay social-dance and music (*ronggeng*), and English theater, in Tan Sooi Beng (2016).
6. The spelling of the term *kronchong* varies from place to place. Variations include *kroncong* and *keroncong*. But the Peranakan in the Straits Settlements use *kronchong* in their published scores.
7. Polyphon Werke AG of Germany produced records in British Malaya using labels such as Hindenburg and Pagoda. The two companies catered more to the Chinese Peranakan communities and recorded their eclectic wedding music and *dondang sayang*. His Master's Voice or the Gramophone Company of the United Kingdom focused more on Malay songs. See Murray et al. (2013) for examples of the recorded music and for brief descriptions of Peranakan wedding music and *dondang sayang*.
8. Yampolsky (2010) analyzes the origins and musical changes in Javanese *kroncong* captured in 78-RPM recordings of the genre in the first half of the twentieth century. The article also provides a summary of the various types of *kroncong*, outlining their instrumentation and musical styles. It should be noted that Yampolsky's notation of the recorded popular *kroncong* shows similar chord structures as those in *Kronchong Weltevreden*, although he begins the repeated stanza on chord I, after the chord V7 in the introduction.
9. See Tan Sooi Beng (2000b) for a detailed account of the development of the *huayue tuan* in Malaysia.
10. "Tanah Pusaka" was rearranged for a bigger orchestra and performed by the joint Keat Hwa Secondary School Chinese orchestra and other Chinese orchestras at the Dewan Filharmonik Petronas in 2011. The invited Malay guest singer Nur Farahin Mahadi sang the song, and Goh Suk Liang conducted the piece. A video clip of the performance is available on Facebook, at https://www.facebook.com/khssco/videos/10150284483234648/, accessed December 9, 2021.
11. See Matusky and Tan (2017: 348, 410, 411) for analysis, listening notes, and notation of "Burung Kakak" by Lee Soo Sheng. An excerpt of an audio recording of the piece is on CD-2 (track 23) that accompanies the book.
12. Promotional video clips of Dama can be found on YouTube, at https://www.youtube.com/watch?v=mX-CtTjkN-g and https://www.youtube.com/watch?v=LtfAo_pEhFI, both accessed December 3, 2021.
13. The interview is on the BFM website, at https://www.bfm.my/podcast/the-bigger-picture/front-row/bernard-goh-hands-percussion-paradise, dated September 21, 2017, accessed December 3, 2021.
14. A brief extract of *Rhythm Ride* is available on YouTube, at https://www.youtube.com/watch?v=EAPzry81fMo, accessed December 3, 2021.
15. For these examples, see clips on You Tube, https://www.youtube.com/watch?v=HPt3PjiFTN4, https://www.youtube.com/watch?v=C5AQxPmcbMc, and https://www.youtube.com/watch?v=fSw0eXiI7WY, all accessed December 3, 2021.

16. Ombak Potehi is the training arm of Ombak-Ombak ARTStudio, an arts collective. Ombak Potehi comprises young artists who are concerned about reviving the endangered *potehi* plus some additional supporters, such as myself. Although the *potehi* is still performed during temple celebrations, audiences for the shows have declined over time, as young people are unable to understand the classical Hokkien used and unfamiliar with the stories that are performed. Ombak Potehi apprentices have studied the traditional theatrical and musical techniques with a traditional group called Beng Geok Hong Puppet Troupe.
17. *Penang Insider*, June 29, 2017, accessed December 3, 2021, http://www.penang-insider.com/penang-potehi-on-stage. Parts I and II of *Kisah Pulau Pinang* are available on YouTube, at https://www.youtube.com/watch?v=ClodcmAjnyU and https://www.youtube.com/watch?v=BmObd64ojIA respectively, both accessed December 3, 2021.
18. The Alternative Music Group, a band comprising Chow Kam Leong, Chong Sang Teck, and Yu Di, played a central role in promoting the unplugged Chinese campus-folk-song style. The group created Halo Productions, which produces its own records and those of talented Chinese singer-songwriters. Realizing that there was no venue for Chinese youths to gather and listen to music, the Alternative Music Group started the Halo Café, a music cafe for alternative folk musicians to perform. The BM Boys, Ah Gu, and Michael and Victor, who have succeeded in Taiwan and Hong Kong, played at the Halo Café in the early days of their careers (*Star*, October 4, 1998).
19. *Dikir barat* is a form of social music from Kelantan. Performers are divided into two groups to sing about topical issues in antiphonal style (see Matusky and Tan, 2017). The video of the song "Tong Nian Xiong" is available on YouTube, at https://www.youtube.com/watch?v=EFpgtQJxymc, accessed December 3, 2021.
20. See video on YouTube, at https://www.youtube.com/watch?v=-iDTI1KPwZk, accessed December 3, 2021.
21. "Malaysiakini," February 23, 2018. https://www.malaysiakini.com/news/413204, accessed December 9, 2021. On YouTube, "Negarakuku" is available at https://www.youtube.com/watch?v=gyiBvJtJ5Z4; "Ali, AhKao, and Muthu" at https://www.youtube.com/watch?v=nVjvTJ6sEEc (2017) and https://www.youtube.com/watch?v=Ok3rtvotwHA (2019), accessed December 9, 2021. Namewee has been banned in mainland China because of his music video "Fragile" ("Bolixin" 玻璃心), a duet with Kimberley Chen, a Taiwan-based Australian singer. The song lampoons socio-political issues in China and has become viral. See *Malay Mail*, November 16, 2021, https://www.malaymail.com/news/showbiz/2021/11/16/malaysian-rapper-namewee-defends-china-satire-fragile-as-views-hit-30-milli/2021202, accessed December 9 2021.

References

Ah Gu 阿牛. (1998). *Chang Ge Gei Ni Ting* 唱歌給你聽 [Sing a Song for You]. Compact disc. Taipei: Rock Records and Tapes.

BM Boys. (1995). *Tong Nian Xiong* 童年頌 [Song for Childhood]. Kuala Lumpur: Follow Me Records.

BM Boys. (1997). *Fangyan chuangzuo* 方言創作 [Dialect Song Competition]. Kuala Lumpur: Follow Me Records.

Chee, Johnny. (2008). *A Tapestry of Baba Poetry*. 3rd ed., with compact disc. Penang: Overseas Printing Resources.

Department of Statistics. (2010). *Population and Housing Census of Malaysia*. Kuala Lumpur, Department of Statistics.

Hall, Stuart. (1990). "Cultural Identity and Diaspora." In *Identity: Community, Culture, Difference*, edited by Jonathan Rutherford, 222–37. London: Lawrence and Wishart.

Hao, Caroline. (2014). *The Chinese Question; Ethnicity, Nation and Region in and beyond the Philippines*. Manila: Ateneo de Manila University Press.

Koh Hoon Teck. (1916). *Dondang Sayang Baba Baba Pranakan, Vol. II* [Dondang Sayang Verses by the Baba Baba Peranakan, vol. 2]. 2nd ed. Singapore: Koh and Company.

Koh Hoon Teck. (1920). *Panton Dondang Sayang Baba Baba Pranakan, Vol. 1* [Dondang Sayang verses by the Baba Baba Peranakan, vol. 1]. 3rd ed. Singapore: Koh and Company.

Kwok, Raymond. (2005). *Ch'arm Ch'arm Rhymes and Ditties*. Penang: Macro Dragon.

Lee Soo Sheng. (1996). *Songs for All*. Kedah: Irama Padi Studio Management, IRP 001, compact disc.

Lim Seng Hooi (H.S.L.). (1924). *Penghiboran Hati* [Entertaining the Heart]. Penang: Criterion Press.

Loo Fung Ying and Loo Fung Chiat. (2014). "Dama Orchestra's Shidaiqu Recontextualized in Theatre." *Asian Theatre Journal* 31 (2): 558–73.

Matusky, Patricia, and Tan, Sooi Beng. (2017). *The Music of Malaysia. The Classical, Folk and Syncretic Traditions*. 2nd ed. London: Routledge.

Murray, David, Jason Gibbs, David Harnish, Terry Miller, Tan Sooi Beng, and Kit Young. (2013). *Longing for the Past: The 78 RPM Era in Southeast Asia*. Atlanta: Dust-to-Digital.

Tan Chee-Beng. (2004). *Chinese Overseas: Comparative Cultural Issues*. Hong Kong: Hong Kong University Press.

Tan Sooi Beng. (1990). "The Performing Arts in Malaysia: State and Society." *Asian Music* 21 (1): 137–70.

Tan Sooi Beng. (1993). *Bangsawan: A Social and Stylistic History of Popular Malay Opera*. Singapore: Oxford University Press.

Tan Sooi Beng. (2000a). "The Chinese Performing Arts and Cultural Activities in Malaysia." In *The Chinese in Malaysia*, edited by Lee Kam Hing and Tan Chee-Beng, 316–41. Kuala Lumpur: Oxford University Press.

Tan Sooi Beng. (2000b). "The Huayue Tuan (Chinese Orchestra) in Malaysia: Adapting to Survive." *Asian Music* 31 (2): 107–28.

Tan Sooi Beng. (2003). "Multi-Culturalism or One National Culture: Cultural Centralization and the Recreation of the Traditional Performing Arts in Malaysia." *Journal of Chinese Ritual, Theatre and Folklore* 141: 237–60.

Tan Sooi Beng. (2016). "Cosmopolitan Identities: Evolving Musical Cultures of the Straits-born Chinese of Pre-World War II Malaya." *Ethnomusicology Forum* 25 (1): 35–57.

Tan Sooi Beng and Nancy Yunhwa Rao. (2016). "Introduction—Emergent Sino-Soundscapes: Musical Pasts, Transnationalism and Multiple Identities." *Ethnomusicology Forum* 25 (1): 4–13.

Wang Gungwu. (1991). "The Study of Chinese Identities in Southeast Asia." In *China and the Chinese Overseas*, edited by Wang Gungwu, 222–39. Singapore: Times Academic Press.

Wang Gungwu. (1999). *China and Southeast Asia: Myths, Threats and Culture*. Singapore: World Scientific, Singapore University Press.

Yampolsky, Philip. (2010). "Kroncong Revisited: New Evidence from Old Sources." *Archipel* 79: 7–56.

Yang, Fang-Chih Irene. (1994). "The History of Popular Music in Taiwan." *Popular Music and Society* 18 (3): 53–66.

CHAPTER 24

CONCLUSIONS

New Directions in Chinese Music Research

JONATHAN P. J. STOCK

INTRODUCTION

From one perspective, this volume may well comprise the largest single research source on Chinese music published in English to date.[1] Its chapters collectively exemplify significant Chinese musical histories and contemporaneities, setting topics arising within the current boundaries of the People's Republic of China alongside those that carry resonances of that nation but occur elsewhere. These case studies are replete with new conceptions and analytical insights, and collectively they advance study in this area by no small dimension. Yet, from another perspective, this book can also be understood as primarily a fresh interjection in a conversation that has been ongoing for a long while—in the "Introduction," Yu Hui describes the *Shijing* 詩經 as our volume's earliest (known) predecessor. If that would have been an intimidating comparison to bring to mind while writing a chapter, it does at least imply that this conversation might be expected to go on a lot longer—climate change, species degradation, pandemics, and human conflicts permitting.

The present volume is certainly very far from being a complete orientation to China's musical history or a systematic guide to all of its principal contemporary musical realities. Instead of providing encyclopedic information on a myriad of musical traditions, genres, instruments, musicians, compositions, and music-related principles, we present new and diverse writing from leading researchers that addresses how we deal with China's music history and with the variegated styles, traditions, and practices identified as somehow musically Chinese in the present. In line with other volumes in Oxford's Handbook series, it is thus a book about research. Our central ambition is to advance our field by capturing the energetic, multidisciplinary actualities of where we are now, producing a set of essays that function as a dynamic springboard that propels study onward and upward in the years to come.

We might employ the term "Chinese music studies" to describe all of the research that occurs within this broad area. But research on Chinese music is currently targeted at readerships across multiple languages, and it is published in numerous, distinct disciplinary forums. In anglophone settings, on the one hand, there is hardly a discipline of Chinese music studies with a recognized core of established intellectual frameworks and methodological norms; in sinophone circles, on the other hand, the subject area is claimed by several competing disciplinary visions, each with its own emphases. From this perspective, and when we talk with one another about Chinese music in either of those settings, we can sometimes feel like strangers driven together by coincidence (*ping shui xiang feng* 萍水相逢; literally, "duckweed joining up by chance"). This book thus offers a rare opportunity for us to recognize shared concerns and, through doing so, work together to build a more explicit disciplinary infrastructure for Chinese music studies.

In the writing below, I discuss prospects for Chinese music studies as a discipline that will need to operate effectively across multiple languages in a world where linguistic identities are both contested and unequal. That discussion allows me to identify conditions that deserve further attention, not least the seemingly contradictory trends that simultaneously push for the paying of greater attention to insider voices and the ever-increasing role of English as a medium for international scholarly exchange. I raise thoughts on translation, theory production, coauthoring, and critical engagement and on how these are contributory parts of a viable, incisive, and inclusive disciplinary future. I then identify some sample areas where we seem already very well prepared to form core disciplinary pillars for Chinese music studies: global music history, diaspora, decolonization, and intangible cultural heritage. These are not the only possibilities at play in the field as it presently stands or even just within the confines of this volume, of course. Accordingly, and prior to advancing my personal observations, I draw out themes and possibilities either implicitly or explicitly put forward by the contributor of each chapter.

Themes Raised in Each Chapter

Part I encompasses essays that address our ways of writing histories of Chinese music. Essays here exemplify the rich sets of archaeological, iconographic, and literary sources available to music historians in this part of the world and address aspects of the long tradition of Chinese music theory and its sub-area of research into musical temperament. Chapters explore the ways that both histories and historical musical practices preserve and inscribe narratives about the past and project reverberations into the present and the future. Through case studies on China's important historical bell sets and on the *qin* 琴 zither, Yang Yuanzheng (Chapter 2) shows how archaeological discoveries demand that we rethink received historical paradigms. Yang's point could be readily generalized; the expert interpretations produced in Chinese music studies deserve to be tested through empirical study, which inevitably includes in-depth discussion with musicians, instrument builders, and other culture bearers. Yu Hui and Chen Yingshi's "Theorizing 'Natural Sound'" (Chapter 3) shares this concern, asking how we might reconsider what we learn from the textual sources provided by many generations of Chinese scholars in light of what we can discover through studying the realizations of actual musical practice. Their chapter points us toward fascinating spaces where practical and theoretical consciousnesses appear to conflict and where new historical research can provide alternate musical possibilities for the thoughtful contemporary performer and listener.

Zhao Weiping's study of iconographical and literary data on two ancient foreign dance forms (Chapter 4) interrelates the theoretical and the practical in another set of ways. Zhao brings a historian's interpretative depth to these source materials—few, if any, of which were originally created to serve as scholarly source materials. He then adds his eye for telling detail as he reconstructs the postures and movements characteristic of these historical genres. Zhao's commentary on the transformation in Han society of these dances is thereby all the more revealing of the aesthetic norms of everyday entertainment in that period. Zhao's work fits well into the global history theme that I mentioned earlier, but it can also be read as an encouragement to scholars of Chinese music to attend more comprehensively to dance, movement, and the potentials and affordances of the human body, as well as to the research produced by scholars within each of those areas.

Interdisciplinary approaches to historical materials provide a foundation for Alan Lau's essay (Chapter 5) on the analysis of song structures in *kunqu* 崑曲 opera. One of Lau's key observations is that music and language work in ways that are fluid and contrasting. As such, songwriters and vocalists occupy a space that is dynamically imbued with expressive power. If Zhao's chapter implicitly pointed to the benefits we might accrue from working with dance and movement scholarship, Lau's chapter argues that we have much to learn from those in linguistics. The interface of music and language comes up regularly in chapters throughout this book; it's certainly a domain within which those in Chinese music studies can make even more of a contribution to global research.

Joseph Lam's essay (Chapter 6) takes a contrasting but complementary approach to the interplay of music and words. Lam's topic is the chanting and singing of song texts preserved in the historical classic, the *Shijing*. Rather than analyzing music structure, though, Lam is interested in the ways that these songs bear cultural narratives and shared memories while also serving as inspiration for personal expression. Since the song lyrics but not the original melodies have come to us from the *Shijing*, the songs represent a continuing tradition of creative recontextualization in new situations. Jeff Warren, writing on music and ethical responsibility, describes the situation that results and underlies Lam's case study:

> All musical experience is embodied, and points to the other bodies involved in experiencing—including listening, dancing, performing or creating—music. In other words, the experience of music provides us with a trace of others. We contact

music, experience the trace of others and leave a trace of ourselves. Music is thus never completely our own. Encounters with music involve traces of others that we must respond to. (2014: 164)

There's a rationale here for a more extensive examination within Chinese music studies of the musical ways such encounters achieve significance within both exceptional and everyday circumstances. Such an exploration could draw on a rich indigenous bibliography on morals, ethics, and aesthetics in East Asian contexts, and we might counterbalance this literature with use of ethnographic methodologies, already familiar to many of us, which lend themselves to assessment of the experiential, behavioral, and interpersonal aspects of music making across a wider range of social groups and settings than those that concerned many historical writers.

In Chapter 7, Yang Hon-Lun takes music historiography as her principal subject, asking what kinds of music histories are produced in Chinese contexts and how such sources variously reflect three distinct ways of accounting for the past: ideology, discourse, and memory. Yang crystallizes her discussions through detailed examination of the narratives put forward in recent music histories on Hong Kong and on the Cultural Revolution, each of which remains a sensitive subject in the Chinese state's evaluations. Yang does far more than point to how far historical accounts continue to serve those who control the primary channels of discourse; instead, she makes a powerful appeal that our role as researchers includes a responsibility to expose and challenge historical biases, including those operative in the present moment, and she shows how we can actively safeguard memory-keeping in our studies of music.

Part I closes with Frederick Lau's analysis of five representative moments when institutional characteristics of the modern musical system took form in China: school songs, the music conservatory, the rise of Western-style composition, musical individualism, and commercial and popular music (Chapter 8). These features (plus potential others, such as reform of national musical instruments) are shared with many other nations, but the nuances with which they occurred and the linkages between them are specific to the Chinese situation. Thus, the account offers a unique case study in the global history of music, yet it is also readily comparable to situations that occurred elsewhere.

Part II comprises an array of studies of significant musical genres and practices from across the sinophone world. Alan Thrasher provides an overview of the instrumentation of a set of regional music ensembles (Chapter 9). His account also offers orientation to foundational Chinese concepts of ensemble performance, many of which are shared in the groupings studied throughout the remainder of Part II. Crucial here is the insight that Chinese heterophony is a result not of a single organizational approach but rather of several types of variational action that occur at once, a practice that requires both experience and imagination from the musicians. The essay implicitly suggests a basis for comparative study of further heterophonic groupings, including those outside the sinophone world. It also provides grounds for close analysis of the pleasure that musicians find in playing with one another and of the interplay of aesthetics and ethics, as skilled executants make real-time decisions on what exactly to vary and how to make space so that the contributions of others can momentarily rise to the fore (see further, Witzleben, 1995).

Each subsequent chapter is more geographically and historically focused, and thus many are also accounts of processes of change. In Chapter 10, Mercedes Dujunco focuses on recreational Jiangnan *sizhu* 江南絲竹 music in Taicang, a county-level city outside Suzhou. She assesses the group's repertory and reflects on the ways that group members have expanded it by incorporating music from other regional traditions and through a carefully executed project led by the professional composer, Zhang Xiaofeng 張曉峰, in which new compositions in traditional style were introduced and memorized. As a whole, the chapter reminds us that what may look like age-old traditions can actually be quite recently established in their present formats, and the musicians involved may be actively pursuing their own pathways of evolution, development, and historical reconstruction. Dujunco's case, which she recommends as a model for similar endeavors elsewhere, hints at the huge efforts undertaken across China in intangible heritage revival and sustenance.

Du Yaxiong's chapter shares a concern with understanding shifting attitudes to intangible cultural heritage, presenting a case that addresses the folk songs of the Yugurs, a minority population found in Gansu province (Chapter 11). Du explains that since the 1980s, many Yugur have given up a nomadic existence based on herding in favor of agricultural farming and other sedentary occupations. One consequence has been the reformation and re-categorization of their singing practices; for instance, herdsmen's vocalizations used formerly to encourage mother goats to nurse their young may now be either discarded or instead sung to human audiences for entertainment, and a whole genre of "new folk song" has arisen which is also shaped toward public performance. Du describes culture as (ideally) accumulative, and it is clear that the Yugurs with whom Du has worked for several decades increasingly perceive their vocal repertory as an inheritance of songs and that they regret having lost some of them in the dramatic social changes of the past two generations. Du's chapter points to the potential for long-term relationships between researcher and community to lead to collaborative research-led action on several levels. This too would be a valuable component in a newly invigorated Chinese music studies.

In Chapter 12, Yu Hui recounts the fascinating case of the Jinyu Qinshe 今虞琴社, a body formed in Shanghai and Suzhou in the 1930s by musicians who wanted to conserve the *qin* and its music into a new social era. The Society's meetings provided temporary respite from a turbulent external environment, but they were far more than a safe space for elite socialization around reassuringly familiar music. Instead, those most active in the Society shared a nationalist and participatory outlook on the value of Chinese culture, and they encouraged new steps, such as research and broadcasting. Yu's study adds nuance to our views of modern music history in China, helping us to avoid the uncritical opposition of traditionalists versus either advocates of whole-scale Westernization or radical revolutionists. Such a case study, again, contributes to global histories of music, among other potential new directions for research.

Francesca Lawson's multimodal assessment of Beijing drumsong (*jingyun dagu* 京韻大鼓) (Chapter 13) sustains this same research aspiration of taking modernization as a topic in its own right. In her case, Lawson assesses the new realities of a prominent traditional musical genre as it became mediated by recording and broadcast technologies in the mid-twentieth century. Her research informs several issues that were important in preceding chapters too, among them the interfacing of music and language and the means through which music performance and gesture combine to form meaningful expressions of both personal artistry and broader cultural identity. Her key intellectual frame of reference, however, is provided by a turn to studies in narrative communication, derived from work on oral traditions and from that on mother-infant interactions. This diverse toolkit enables Lawson to more fully account for a performance that is thoroughly musical, textual, and visual, which in fact describes a great breadth of musical expressions worldwide, not only in Chinese-speaking parts of world.

Taiwan is of course one such site in the sinophone world and one with its distinct historical pathways, up to and through the modern period. Chapter 14, by Hsieh Hsiao-Mei, is the first chapter of two in this volume that focus on Taiwan, and Hsieh assesses the hybridized theatrical genre known in Taiwanese as *opela* 胡撇仔 (*hupeizai* in Mandarin). Hsieh traces the rise of this genre from formative influences, including those in traditional Chinese theater and more recent Japanese entertainments such as spoken dramas and the cross-dressing of Takarazuka Review. In the present century, intellectuals have become influential participants in the genre; its hybridized roots allow them considerable freedom to draw on diverse musical, literary, and dramatic sources in forming their new creations.

Chapter 15 considers the history of the modern orchestra of Chinese instruments in Taiwan. Hybridity is also a key facet that the author Chen Ching-Yi describes as she accounts for the *guoyue* 國樂 ensemble's reliance upon production of a dynamic "third space" for music making that was neither traditional nor Western. What's perhaps most striking is how malleable this third space was in Taiwanese musical practices; its potentials were rapidly reimagined as alienation from Chinese models gave way to fusion and importation and then to a self-conscious intensification of identifiably Taiwanese elements. The ironies of use of the "Chinese orchestra" to express Taiwanese distinction will be lost on few readers.

Wu Ben's chapter on the globalization of music for *pipa* 琵琶 (Chapter 16) closes Part II. Placing his discussion in the context of the longer history of solo music for the *pipa*, Wu considers the striking number of soloists now resident in North America (and elsewhere) and the key musical trends stimulated by their presence there. In such settings, the *pipa* is not only called upon to project Chinese cultural identity but also becoming reimagined as a global music instrument and so thrust into musically diverse ensembles and partnerships that occur much less regularly in China. As Wu notes, an outcome of this is a rise of improvisatory performance skills, which relates both to norms among the mixed musical environments within which migrant Chinese musicians are now seeking work and to the desire to pool creative agency. Such collective influence is relied upon by some composers in new music circles, where live art is valued for its collaborative and performative qualities, somewhat in reaction to earlier conceptualizations of performance as the dutiful recreation of fixed compositions. Wu asks the interesting question as to why *pipa* appears to have thrived in such circles more than many another Chinese instrument: Is it that the instrument, as an import from Central Asia, was already multicultural when it first reached China and so its cross-cultural potential has been there for a long time already? Might it be that the *pipa* benefits from comparison with the guitar, which has become almost ubiquitous in contemporary musical ensembles, and so it's both familiar and unfamiliar to Western audiences at once? (For myself, I wonder how far the answer relates to the specific musical entrepreneurialism of the leading *pipa* players who have settled in Canada and the United States; in Western Europe, I've seen as much new music featuring the *zheng* 箏 as that employing the *pipa*, and the *zheng* also seems a highly suitable instrument for new music, in terms of its timbral possibilities and visual appeal.) Whatever the answer, Wu's question suggests the potential for a much broader cross-cultural inquiry as to why certain instruments seem to acclimatize well to new musical and societal circumstances and what might happen to the inherited musical signifiers of Chinese identity as they become more widely regarded as features of hybridized, global music.

Part III of this volume deals with salient issues that have arisen particularly in the most recent decades. Most of the essays explicitly trace the musical consequences of intersections between what might be taken as opposing forces or perspectives. In Chapter 17, Lijuan Qian looks at the restoration of China's popular-music industry in the mid-1980s, specifically at the impact on mainstream popular music of a small number of intellectual songwriters whose individualist and self-directed humanism emerged in response to the widespread trauma of the years of the Cultural Revolution (1966–76). In fact, and notwithstanding its ubiquity, the mainstream popular music of this era has received less attention than rock music, at least among Western researchers, so Qian's essay is also a reminder for us to listen carefully to these large-scale expressions: at the very least, they capture something of the spirit of the times; at the most, they propose through the emotion-shaping structures of popular song what shape that spirit should form.

Grace Wang's essay on the singer Coco Lee (Li Wen) 李玟 also resides in the category of mainstream popular entertainment but looks instead at its cross-border dynamics (Chapter 18). Wang compares two moments when Lee attempted to work across borders: already an established star in Taiwan in the early 2000s, she attempted to break into the American market with material in English, with little success; in 2016, Lee proved victorious in the prominent Chinese TV singing contest, *I am a Singer*, reestablishing her credibility for a new generation of Chinese listeners. The comparison reveals how the preconceptions that audiences in each locale held about Lee's ethnicity intersected with their ideas about the singer's talent and her embodied representations of gender and sexuality. What resulted were almost diametrically opposed conclusions on her integrity as an artist, which says at least as much about the audiences in question as it does about Lee herself. Again, what we might take as unassumingly mainstream music proves to be rich ground for the researcher to uncover the workings (and impasses) of intercultural values in the world around us.

In Chapter 19, Tan Shzr Ee compares not two moments of performance but rather two Chinese women pianists who have found success in the wider world, Yuja Wang 王羽佳 and Zhu Xiao-Mei 朱曉玫. Tan's argument turns on the contrasting of these two women as icons, how they present themselves visually, and on how their audiences decode the tropes each pianist embodies or overturns. Tan's chapter compares the voices of critics, mostly those outside China (for Wang) and primarily those inside it (for Zhu). Even though piano performance remains a field in which liveness is centrally important, new technologies, digital formats, and online forums mediate almost all these acts of presentation and critical evaluation, such that researching them is also an act of tracing how digital media shape our cultural lives more generally.

The dualities of mediation and liveness also lie at the heart of Germán Gil-Curiel's essay on a prominent orchestral work by the contemporary composer Tan Dun 譚盾 (Chapter 20). Interestingly, Gil-Curiel takes up the term "mediation" to reflect upon how Tan transformed the historical painting *Qingming shanghe tu* 清明上河圖 (*Along the River during the Qingming Festival*) into a musical item. From this perspective, mediation is neither new nor something that occurs only through digital means—it may even be a fundamental aspect of music itself, as already suggested by Jeff Warren in the passage cited above. Finally, Gil-Curiel suggests that liveness and mediation are not binary opposites at all but rather two dimensions of musical creativity and transmission that can be combined or opposed in a range of ways. This is indeed a pungent thought that will appeal to analysts of music in sinophone settings and far beyond.

Samuel Horlor, in Chapter 21, provides a similarly provocative reconsideration of the terms "amateur" and "professional," which he illustrates through a study of the specific context of singing that occurs in numerous Chinese public squares and parks. In these settings, it is not satisfactory to identify singers as either amateur or professional. Instead, their singing displays both amateur and professional characteristics at once, and the two categories simultaneously reflect the status and ethical standing of participants, the relationships that form between vocalists and patrons, and aesthetic qualities of the music they perform. This nuanced finding is readily applicable to musical occasions across and beyond the sinophone world.

The final two chapters explore issues related to minority populations, of rather different kinds. In Chapter 22, Chuen-Fung Wong focuses on the minoritization of Uyghur music and on the ways that the Han-majority population has appropriated and processed the musical ingredients or signs of marginalized populations, reshaping them to invigorate the Han modernist reformation of the nation's music overall. In certain cases, a feedback loop has occurred, with the reformed reinventions becoming influential in "minority" areas, thus adding new layers to the question of who is imitating or representing whom. In Chapter 23, Tan Sooi Beng considers how musicians among the Chinese-minority population in Malaysia have, at various historical moments, both crossed boundaries and retained selected markers of their Chineseness in a multicultural context. As Tan points out, this is a distinctly non-Chinese way of being Chinese, a balancing act in which transnational subjectivities evoked through musical creation and listening nurture an inclusive future. If these two chapters seem to point in somewhat different directions, each recognizes that many of us sustain multiple cultural and national identities at once, a state of being that requires efforts that are essential, difficult, always in-progress, and highly characteristic of twenty-first-century society.

Languages

Music researchers since at least Charles Seeger have noted the challenges inherent in attempting to explain one expressive-communicative medium (music) through the terms and structures of another (language).[2] The inherent intangibility of musical sound as a structure or system that unfolds through real time only magnifies this issue. This may go some way to illuminate why music studies often achieve only a peripheral position in the wider academy, even though music researchers regularly explore issues and materials of broad societal relevance—evidenced in this volume by chapters that explore such themes as history, identity, group formation, gender, sexuality, and diaspora—and even though so many people in the academy and among the public are genuinely interested in music. In fact, issues relating to language provide an even more complicated context for our current work for at least two further reasons.

First, Chinese is itself very far from being a single language. Shu-mei Shih has been foundational in calling out what is at stake here. Shih notes that many languages are spoken in China but that, while we typically use the term "Chinese," we actually mean only Mandarin Chinese. This apparently innocent shorthand sustains a nationalist, Han-centric project that compresses nationality, ethnicity, and language. Drawing attention away from the multiplicities of actual practice, it veils the long-standing and continuing operations of China as an imperial state.[3] Shih writes: "The word 'Chinese,' then, has been misused to equate language with nationality and ethnicity, and official monolingualism has disregarded and suppressed linguistic heterogeneity" (2011: 715). In exploring linguistic heterogeneity, the chapters incorporated in this volume draw on sources in the classical written language of ancient treatises, the special linguistic formulations and registers of onstage singing, the habits of online discourse, and the shifting nuances of several contemporary spoken languages found within and beyond China's present borders.

Second, Chinese music research both benefits and suffers from its distribution across numerous languages. A search in October 2021 of the ProQuest Thesis and Dissertations database discovered 153,702 contributions to this field spread across sixteen languages, the ten most widely used being English, Chinese, French, Spanish, Portuguese, Turkish, German, Serbian, Dutch, and Afrikaans. Some important languages are missing from that list (suggesting major gaps in the database's coverage). A similar search on the WorldCat database turned up 128,772 items, 50,613 of which are in Chinese and 41,335 in English. Among the remainder were significant numbers in Japanese, Korean,

Italian, Russian, and Vietnamese alongside most of the other languages already listed.[4] If this diversity reflects China's international prominence and the widespread potential audiences for research in this area, a challenge for us as researchers is that few among us can become confident readers across more than a small handful of the languages listed here. The most inspiring new discoveries and interpretations may not always circulate as widely as they deserve to due to the challenges thrown up by this wide linguistic array.

That might look like a call for the acceleration of a process through which English has become the primary international language for scholarly communication in many fields, perhaps even including Chinese music studies. But English inevitably filters Chinese materials and subject positions through its own systemic and cultural norms. Moreover, the dominance of English sustains structures that disproportionately benefit those of us who have acquired acceptable academic English and, equally, hinders the global recognition of researchers who write primarily from other linguistic perspectives. Again, this might seem an issue that will in any case be resolved over time as East Asian (and other non-anglophone) researchers increasingly train in academic English so that they can offer what Sato and Sonoda, in the context of Global Asian Studies programs, have called "inside-out" viewpoints (2021). However, it is not simple to separate advanced training in scholarly English from deep inculcation into the values and norms of an anglophone-dominated academy, a step that runs against widespread moves at the present moment toward the decolonization of knowledge production.

The prospect of paying greater heed to indigenous voices is a welcome one, even while it remains vulnerable, as Shih essentially notes above, to cooption by powerful and nationalistic state forces.[5] It seems incumbent upon us all to use whatever agency we can deploy to ensure that clichéd and uncritical interpretations do not rise to the fore under the flag of decolonization. But while it's easy to point accusingly as the Chinese government attempts to project influence into new spaces (as, for instance, in the recent controversy over censorship of items in the People's Republic of China (PRC)-facing website for the Cambridge University Press journal, *China Quarterly*; see further Wong and Kwong, 2019), and while we can expect such efforts to continue, the West is hardly beyond reproach in this regard. It is exactly an extended history of Western exoticizations, orientalizations, misapprehensions, and strategic compartmentalizations that make collective action to level the playing field now so urgent. Nancy Yunhwa Rao provides a salient example, describing the "division of intellectual labor" that she perceives in the field of North American music theory, between those who study Western music and present "universalizing models and theories" and those who study non-Western musical traditions and are treated as specialists who operate within a limited frame of reference:

> First, such a division of intellectual labor allows the "theorists" to be more or less ensconced in their discipline, collecting raw data from different area studies and cultures to test or expand their universalizing models and theories, without burdening themselves to acquire the requisite knowledge about these non-Western traditions. Second, such division of intellectual labor relegates those theorists who work on non-Western music with adequate language and cultural knowledge to the

roles of area-specialists, their work marginal to the discipline of music theory, and their conceptual model or analysis not "theoretical" enough to be considered a valuable contribution to the "world of music theory." They are cultural insiders but not theorists. (Rao, 2019: 78)

This kind of structural inequity is reinforced by, and reinforces, the linguistic divisions already mentioned. For this volume, Yu Hui and I offered greater editorial support to those who take up a particularly heavy burden when asked to write in English, and we asked authors to employ within their chapters their subjects' names, music titles, and similar data in the language those people would habitually use. The present volume thus takes a step toward linguistic poly-vocality, when compared to edited collections of the preceding decade or so that, in so many other respects, offer significant inspiration to us in this project. The richly thematic *China and the West: Music, Representation, and Reception* (Yang and Saffle, 2017), for example, includes several chapters from authors with native-level proficiency in Chinese, but each such author already works in an English-speaking institutional context and has a lengthy CV of publications in English. The same is true for the valuable collection *Gender in Chinese Music* (Harris, Pease, and Tan, 2013), which includes just one chapter from a researcher who actually works in China (alongside further Chinese voices featured in interview excerpts, interwoven between the main chapters). A third set of essays that broke new ground in yet another set of ways, *Lives in Chinese Music* (Rees, 2009), similarly has just one chapter coauthored by a writer based in China (and he too is heard mostly through interview extracts).

Apart from working to include more contributors who work primarily in the sinophone contexts of the PRC or Taiwan, we encouraged each contributor to theorize, placing their new contribution within what they perceived as the most relevant contexts of prior learning (which might be in Chinese, English, other languages, or a combination of these, as appropriate to their topic). It is worth adding that we do not assume that theory building is necessarily a higher contribution than the provision of studies that address gaps in our collective knowledge. Nor do we believe that more theorizing per se will necessarily open the minds of those who currently cannot imagine that the study of music in China raises questions that have potential application elsewhere in the world (nor that studies of music in China need to be validated by how applicable they are globally). Instead, by recognizing that all of our contributors have the right to advance new theoretical interpretations of whatever kind best suits their respective topics, we aim to model a future that is intellectually heterogenous and democratically capacious.

Such a future must extend well beyond the dualities of "inside-out" and "outside-in," as identified by Sato and Sonoda. The work of Shu-mei Shih has already been mentioned. Other thinkers who can help us structure Chinese music studies to better recognize the various linguistic and subject positions that we individually and collectively embody include such diverse writers as Stuart Hall, with his sense of postcolonial identity as ruptured, discontinuous, hybridized, and always under construction (1990), and Lila Abu-Lughod, who notes the special position of "halfies," researchers "whose national or cultural identity is mixed by virtue of migration, overseas education, or parentage"

(1991: 466). The sinophone world is at least as interesting as the Caribbean or Arabic worlds and is not identical to either. It warrants further theorization by those with adept and imaginative minds.

A final cluster of implications that arise from thinking about multiplicities of linguistic actuality concerns the overlapping practices of translation, coauthoring, and critical engagement. Notwithstanding incidents like the *China Quarterly* affair, the sinophone sphere may already be leading the world in practices of translation. Examples include the direct translating of pathbreaking research sources into Chinese (such as the large collection of English-language papers on numerous ethnomusicological topics, by Cao Benye and Luo Qin, 2019) and also varied efforts at cultural translation: Guo Shuhui's bilingual introduction to Chinese traditional music in *Sounding China* (2019) is one recent example, and music recording and touring projects such as the Yandong Grand Singers' *Everyone Listen Close* (2019) can be thought of as a second type of translation work. Those of us who work primarily in English could do more to follow the lead offered by our Chinese peers and reciprocate with our own efforts at attentive cross-cultural listening and reading. There is also enough practice already undertaken to form a basis for in-depth discussions—led by Chinese scholars—of what is lost or found, gained, transformed, or re-centered through differently directed acts of translation. Such discussions could inform all of us who work across and between linguistic communities, not only in relation to music or China.

While translation is thriving (though unevenly distributed), coauthored and other forms of multiauthored works remain rare in our field. With the understandable exceptions of interview transcripts and the sharing of editorial workload, solo-authored contributions dominate each of the multiauthored volumes already cited, other recent collaborative volumes (such as Clark, Pang, and Tsai, 2016; Thrasher, 2016; Tsai, Ho, and Jian, 2020; or Guy 2021), and the tables of contents of the field's major journals, as well as this volume. At present, when coauthoring occurs in music-related research, it often arises from a team comprising a tutor and a graduate student and so may represent the combining of two researchers' perspectives on a shared topic. Broader collaborations, by contrast, have the potential to cover wider topics and develop authoritative comparisons and interdisciplinary perspectives across a larger scale. Incidentally, such collaborative work also matches the group-based production of so much music and its distribution across the contemporary world, allowing for new fusions of voices and expertise to appear. James Farrer and Andrew Field's account of dance, drink, and socializing in nocturnal Shanghai (2015) exemplifies the rich benefits of such coauthoring.

Many kinds of engaged, critical work involve thinking and writing across perceived borders and questioning assumed habits and norms. Such labor is especially available to those of us who occupy positions between linguistic or scholarly communities and whose positions allow us the relative freedom to speak out on certain matters. In a passage originally about diasporic citizens, one that resonates for many of us who research Chinese musical culture, Stuart Hall identifies the ways that some of us might bring strategic unsettlement to established scholarly assumptions and conventions:

They are people who belong to more than one world, speak more than one language (literally and metaphorically), inhabit more than one identity, have more than one home; who have learned to negotiate and translate between cultures, and who, because they are irrevocably the product of several interlocking histories and cultures, have learned to live with and indeed to speak from difference. They speak from the "in-between" of different cultures, always unsettling the assumptions of one culture from the perspective of another, and thus finding ways of being both the same as and at the same time different from the others amongst whom they live. (1995: 206)

Of course, we will need to approach any such unsettlements ethically and humanely. If Chinese music studies might be more collaborative, as I've just suggested, it also needs to be a forum where we can broach disagreement and tolerate uncertainty and divergent interpretations. The spaces between are full of new dialogic opportunities and rich in potential for the production and sharing of larger understandings.

DISCIPLINES AND NEW THEORETICAL DIRECTIONS

Just as our subject is approached from diverse linguistic positions, research on Chinese music contributes to numerous academic disciplines, from theater studies to sociology, from political science to music theory, and from Asian studies to linguistics to ethnomusicology. This breadth very well reflects the pronounced resonance of our fundamental topic: music—or perhaps better, "people making music," to adopt Jeff Titon's impactful formulation (1989)—articulates numerous dimensions of Chinese society, today as in the historical past. Even within the immediate area of Chinese music studies there are quite distinct sets of intellectual affiliation. Shen Qia explores several of these in his history of ethnomusicology in China (1999), referring, among others, to the contrasting disciplinary perspectives of folk-music research (*minjian yinyue yanjiu*), Chinese traditional music theory (*minzu yinyue lilun*), Chinese musicology (*Zhongguo yinyuexue*), and Chinese traditional musicology (*Zhongguo chuantong yinyuexue*).[6] It follows, then, that researchers within each discipline will frame their respective contributions in Chinese music research in multifarious ways, drawing on diverse approaches, discrete theoretical models and priorities, and potentially quite divergent core literatures.[7] In some cases, music may not even be a central subject so much as one topic among several others. Audiences for research in Chinese music studies are equally broadly spread and by no means all looking for the same kinds of material.

Preparation of this volume reinforced for me the observation that even authors dedicated enough to contribute chapters to such a project as this may share little proximity to one another in terms of intellectual framework or key references. Chinese music studies needs to embrace this set of frameworks and approaches, acting as a space where we expect to find not only those who already think like we do but also new interlocutors and fresh inspirations. But I think we might additionally encourage and support one another by taking up some of the best ideas that have emerged within Chinese music studies, reapplying them in our own work so that we can collectively develop core theoretical directions, even if we still mostly deploy them in our work to strategically inspire, or unsettle, readers from outside this immediate area. Here are some contexts where Chinese music studies may already offer a distinctive kind of laboratory for the development of work that can have wide potential relevance:

I. Global histories of music. Scholars in the Western world are increasingly aware that there would be significant benefits in pursuing global histories of music, but so far we have often struggled to realize such histories effectively, not least because most Western music historians only train in European languages and music. Thomas Irvine's account of the sound of the late-eighteenth- and early-nineteenth-century "Sino-Western encounter" that occurred as the Western powers sent missions to Qing-dynasty China (2020), for instance, deals with its topic only via European sources, which inevitably leaves much of the sonic encounter and the subject positions surrounding it unexamined. With their linguistic training, sinophone music historians could do a more comprehensive job, resulting in a more equitable global history of the encounter, not simply an account of Europeans overseas.

II. Diaspora, transnationalism, and their ends. We already have a particularly stimulating set of publications on Chinese music in North America (for example, Zheng, 2010; Wang, 2015; Rao, 2017). As the PRC continues to rise in global stature, new attention, and renewed scrutiny, will fall upon populations identified as Chinese, and research in these communities will acquire new resonances as a result. This work is rich in insights into the intersections between music, race, memory, class, gender, migration, erasure, and belonging. Studies like those just mentioned deserve to be not only admired but also widely emulated and extended to other locales where people of Chinese origins now reside. Their theoretical intuitions could inspire researchers of music in many further transcultural settings worldwide. Some of this work additionally develops questions about identity, nation, and personhood that would be very applicable to "home" locales, where such notions are often taken very much for granted.

III. Decolonizing music scholarship. The sinophone world is one of the world's major sites of empire and of expansive, multiethnic settlement and displacement. It also comprises a collection of territories which have been subject to waves of migration and colonization by imperial forces of northern, eastern, and western origins and where the postcolonial is very much a work in progress. All of this means that models emerging from the study of locations colonized by the European powers can cope only thinly with the sets of subject position that occur across sinophone locales. This is especially the case in relation to music in China and related societies. Power, opportunity, and status distributions intersect with, bypass, and become overwritten by those found in the wider world in a pattern that's quite distinct from that of, say, African American music or even the music of India and its widespread global diaspora (see further, Tan, 2021). We need to develop alternate paradigms that help explain what's at stake for whom in all of this.

IV. Intangible cultural heritage and applied research. The PRC and Taiwan have become significant locations for programs of intangible cultural heritage preservation and promotion. (Orientational essays for the PRC are Rees, 2012, and Zhang, 2015; Wang, 2012, provides a case study from Taiwan.) These milieus are particularly rich sites for investigation for a number of reasons, including the sheer amount of public attention they can generate and the development in China over several decades of an intricate structure of state-run supports at all ranks, from the local to the county, city, provincial, and national levels. In some cases, cultural heritage is being reshaped by the gaze of the tourist industry or by state authorities, who are hypersensitive to the expression of systems of belief that haven't been officially endorsed and are concerned over cultural-identity projections among minority populations that might counteract the state's broader policies of assimilation and homogenization. Researchers familiar with this vivid array of programs are well placed to assess the transformative impacts over time of intangible-cultural-heritage programs and structures and to move into applied research focusing on the areas that the culture bearers see as most urgently in need of attention. It is not far-fetched to imagine this sphere of research being led internationally by researchers with experience in sinophone settings.

Conclusions

Many other spaces beyond those sketched above provide possibilities for new research explorations that relate to music in, from, or associated with China. Research on musical practice might be one such space. Participatory learning of musical performance is already widely established among ethnomusicologists and other music researchers, and sinophone contexts include an ample set of traditions in which musicians create new artistic works that embody and translate new understandings (see further, McKerrell, 2021). Such a topic is also an excellent space for collaborative work, as discussed above. There are additionally numerous genres that are not well represented in this volume, and some that are not well covered in Chinese music studies more generally, which deserve greater attention.

It may seem overly modest (or self-serving) to close a large and inevitably weighty volume on Chinese music research by saying that the world needs more such research. Nevertheless, it is clear that the sinophone world is immensely complex, and music remains a key to understanding many of this sphere's historical self-constructions and its variegated contemporary values and embodiments. Notwithstanding the complexities of the world around us, it is urgent that we find the time, the stances, the inspirations, and the collaborations necessary to produce such research and thereby contribute to more balanced understandings of people making music in, from, and associated with China.

Glossary

guoyue 國樂, music for modernized folk ensemble or Chinese orchestra
Jiangnan *sizhu* 江南絲竹, Jiangnan "silk and bamboo," instrumental ensemble genre
Jinyu Qinshe 今虞琴社, *Guqin* Society of Today's Yushan 虞山 School
jingju 京劇, traditional opera genre
jingyun dagu 京韻大鼓, tradition ballad-singing genre
kunqu 崑曲, traditional opera genre
Lee, Coco (Li Wen) 李玟, popular-music singer (b. 1975)
opela 胡撇仔, hybridized music theater genre in Taiwan (pronounced *hupeizai* in Mandarin)
pipa 琵琶, pear-shaped lute
ping shui xiang feng 萍水相逢, duckweed joining up by chance (idiom)
qin 琴, seven-stringed zither
Qingming shanghe tu 清明上河圖, *Along the River during the Qingming Festival*, painting by Zhang Zeduan 張擇端 (1085–1145)
Shijing 詩經, song collection compiled by Confucius (551–479 BCE)
Tan Dun 譚盾, composer (b. 1957)
Yuja Wang (Wang Yujia) 王羽佳, pianist (b. 1987)
Zhang Xiaofeng 張曉峰, composer (b. 1931)
zheng 箏, zither
Zhu Xiao-Mei (Zhu Xiaomei) 朱曉玫, pianist (b. 1949)

Notes

1. The only exception may be the China entries in the East Asia volume of the *Garland Encyclopedia of World Music* (Provine, Tokumaru, and Witzleben, 2002), which may equate a larger total word count, although one divided over many different topics and themes.
2. Zbikowski, 1999, provides a valuable summary of the history of Seeger's lifelong engagement with this topic. Key publications by Seeger himself include Seeger, 1977a and 1977b. Speech and music are not always at odds, of course, as Seeger also noted; Lawson, 2020, offers an example with a Chinese focus of prospects for new research at this very interface.
3. Certain groups outside China are, of course, also happy to sustain the suspicion that migrants of Han ethnicity retain allegiance to the Chinese state, even after multiple generations in their present homes.
4. Search for "Chinese music" in ProQuest Dissertations & Theses A&I and in WorldCat, October 5, 2021. Both these databases are managed in the English-speaking world and likely feature disproportionately more results in English than in other languages.

5. It is also not an entirely new one in the East Asian context, as Yu Hui reminds us through his discussion of Liang Shuming's "Easternization" (see Chapter 12).
6. Yang Mu (2003) provides valuable critical reflection on these same trends.
7. Nor do those of us with closely similar disciplinary affiliations necessarily all think alike. Compare two recent bibliographies of Chinese music research prepared for Oxford Bibliographies Online, one as the "China" section of the "Music" listing, the other as the "Chinese music" section of the "Chinese studies" listing (Lam, 2017; Stock, 2018).

REFERENCES

Abu-Lughod Lila. , (1991). "Writing Against Culture." In *Recapturing Anthropology: Writing in the Present*, edited by Richard G. Fox, 137–62. Santa Fe: School of American Research Press.

Cao Benye 曹本冶 and Luo Qin 洛秦, eds. (2019). *Ethnomusicology Lilun yu fangfa: Yingwen wenxian daodu Ethnomusicology*理论与方法英文文献导读 [Ethnomusicology: Theory and Method: A Guide to Literature in English] 4 vols. Shanghai: Shanghai yinyue xueyuan chubanshe.

Clark, Paul, Laikwan Pang, and Tsan-Huang Tsai. (2016). *Listening to China's Cultural Revolution: Music, Politics, and Cultural Continuities*. Basingstoke: Palgrave Macmillan.

Farrer, James, and Andrew N. Field. (2015). *Shanghai Nightscapes: A Nocturnal Biography of a Global City*. Chicago: University of Chicago Press.

Guo Shuhui 郭树荟. (2019). *Sounding China: A Companion to Chinese Traditional Music*, 来自中国的声音:中国传统音乐概览 [Lai zi Zhongguo de shengyin: Zhongguo chuantong yinyue gailan]. Translated by Li Mingyue. Shanghai: Shanghai yinyue chubanshe.

Guy, Nancy, ed. (2021). *Resounding Taiwan: Musical Reverberations Across a Vibrant Island*. New York: Routledge.

Hall, Stuart. (1990). "Cultural Identity and Diaspora." In *Identity, Community, Culture, Difference*, edited by Jonathan Rutherford, 222–37. London: Lawrence and Wishart.

Hall, Stuart. (1995). "New Cultures for Old." In *A Place in the World? Places, Cultures, and Globalization*, edited by Doreen Massey and Pat Jess, 175–213. New York: Oxford University Press.

Harris, Rachel, Rowan Pease, and Shzr Ee Tan, eds. (2013). *Gender in Chinese Music*. Rochester, NY: University of Rochester Press.

Irvine, Thomas. (2020). *Listening to China: Sound and the Sino-Western Encounter, 1770–1839*. Chicago: University of Chicago Press.

Lam, Joseph S. C. (2017). "China." In *Oxford Bibliographies in Music*, edited by Kate Van Orden. Accessed October 11, 2021. https://www.oxfordbibliographies.com/view/document/obo-9780199757824/obo-9780199757824-0013.xml. DOI: 10.1093/OBO/9780199757824-0013.

Lawson, Francesca, R. S. (2020). "Hidden Musicality in Chinese *Xiangsheng*: A Response to the Call for Interdisciplinary Research in Studying Speech and Song." *Humanities and Social Sciences Communications* 7, article no. 24. DOI:10.1057/s41599-020-0528-y

McKerrell, Simon. (2021). "Towards Practice Research in Ethnomusicology." *Ethnomusicology Forum* 31 (2): 10–27. DOI:10.1080/17411912.2021,1964374.

Provine, Robert C., Yosihiko Tokumaru, and J. Lawrence Witzleben, eds. (2002). *The Garland Encyclopedia of World Music. Volume 7, East Asia: China, Japan and Korea*. New York: Routledge.

Rao, Nancy Y. (2017). *Chinatown Opera Theater in North America*. Urbana: University of Illinois University Press.

Rao, Nancy Y. (2019). "On Division of Intellectual Labor." *Intégral* 33: 77–81.

Rees, Helen. (2009). *Lives in Chinese Music*. Urbana: University of Illinois Press.

Rees, Helen. (2012). "Intangible Cultural Heritage in China Today: Policy and Practice in the Early Twenty-First Century." In *Music as Intangible Cultural Heritage: Policy, Ideology, and Practice in the Preservation of East Asian Traditions*, edited by Keith Howard, 23–54. Farnham, UK: Ashgate.

Sato, Jin, and Shigeto Sonoda. (2021). "Asian Studies 'Inside-Out': A Research Agenda for the Development of Global Asian Studies." *International Journal of Asian Studies* 18 (2): 207–16.

Seeger, Charles. (1977a). "The Musicological Juncture: 1976." *Ethnomusicology* 21 (2): 179–88.

Seeger, Charles. (1977b). "Speech, Music, and Speech about Music." In *Studies in Musicology, 1935–1975*, by Charles Seeger, 16–30. Berkeley: University of California Press.

Shen Qia. (1999). "Ethnomusicology in China." Translated with a response by Jonathan P. J. Stock. *Journal of Music in China* 1: 7–38.

Shih, Shu-mei. (2011). "The Concept of the Sinophone." *Proceedings of the Modern Languages Association* 126 (3): 709–18.

Stock, Jonathan P. J. 2018. "Music in China." In *Oxford Bibliographies in Chinese Studies*, edited by Tim Wright. Accessed October 11, 2021. http://www.oxfordbibliographies.com/view/document/obo-9780199920082/obo-9780199920082-0021.xml. DOI: 10.1093/OBO/9780199920082-0021.

Tan Shzr Ee. (2021). "Whose Decolonisation? Checking for Intersectionality, Lane-Policing and Academic Privilege from a Transnational (Chinese) Vantage Point." *Ethnomusicology Forum* 30 (1): 140–62. DOI: 10.1080/17411912.2021.1938447.

Thrasher, Alan R., ed. (2016). *Qupai in Chinese Music: Melodic Models in Form and Practice*. New York: Routledge.

Titon, Jeff T. (1989). "Ethnomusicology as the Study of People Making Music." Paper delivered at the annual conference of the Northeast Chapter of the Society for Ethnomusicology, Hartford, CT, April 22, 1989. Reprinted in Jeff T. Titon, *Toward a Sound Ecology: New and Selected Essays*, 27–37. Bloomington: Indiana University Press, 2020.

Tsai, Eva, Tung-hung Ho, and Miaoju Jian. (2020). *Made in Taiwan: Studies in Popular Music*. New York: Routledge.

Wang, Grace. (2015). *Soundtracks of Asian America: Navigating Race through Musical Performance*. Durham, NC: Duke University Press.

Wang Ying-fen. (2012). "Lessons from the Past: *Nanguan/Nanyin* and the Preservation of Intangible Cultural Heritage in Taiwan." In *Music as Intangible Cultural Heritage: Policy, Ideology, and Practice in the Preservation of East Asian Traditions*, edited by Keith Howard, 161–79. Farnham, UK: Ashgate.

Warren, Jeff. (2014). *Music and Ethical Responsibility*. Cambridge, UK: Cambridge University Press.

Witzleben, J. Lawrence. (1995). *Silk and Bamboo Music in Shanghai: The Jiangnan Sizhu Instrumental Ensemble Tradition*. Kent, OH: Kent State University Press.

Wong, Mathew Y. H. and Ying-ho Kwong. (2019). "Academic Censorship in China: The Case of The China Quarterly." *PS, Political Science & Politics* 52 (2): 287–92. DOI:10.1017/S1049096518002093.

Yandong Grand Singers. (2019). *Everyone Listen Close: Wanp-Wanp Jangl Kap*. Pan Records, PAN 2122, compact disc.

Yang Hon-Lun and Michael Saffler, eds. (2017). *China and the West: Music, Representation, and Reception*. Ann Arbor: University of Michigan Press.

Yang Mu. (2003). "Ethnomusicology with Chinese Characteristics." *Yearbook for Traditional Music* 35: 1–38. DOI: 10.2307/4149320.

Zbikowski, Lawrence M. (1999). "Seeger's Unitary Field Reconsidered." In *Understanding Charles Seeger, Pioneer in American Musicology*, edited by Bell Yung and Helen Rees, 130–49. Urbana: University of Illinois Press.

Zhang Boyu. (2015). "Applied Ethnomusicology in China: An Analytical Review of Practice." In *The Oxford Handbook of Applied Ethnomusicology*, edited by Svanibor Pettan and Jeff Todd Titon, 735–50. New York: Oxford University Press.

Zheng, Su. (2010). *Claiming Diaspora: Music, Transnationalism, and Cultural Politics*. New York: Oxford University Press.

Index

For the benefit of digital users, indexed terms that span two pages (e.g., 52–53) may, on occasion, appear on only one of those pages

Tables and figures are indicated by *t* and *f* following the page number. Chinese personal names are grouped by alphabetization of first character

Abu-Lughod, Lila, 501–2
Academy for the Performing Arts (Hong Kong), 142
adaptation in the arts, 422
Aerang Yinxing Jis, 236, 239–41
aesthetic blending, 418, 422
aesthetic incunabula, 271–72
African Americans, support for Coco Lee, 378–79
Ah Gu (Ah Niu, Tan Kheng Seong), 468–69, 487n.1
aihaozhe (music enthusiasts), 444
Akon, 386
"Ali, AhKao, and Muthu" (Wee Meng Chee collaborative performance), 485
Along the River during the Qingming Festival (Qingming shanghe tu), 417–18, 422–26, 427
Along the Way (CD), 337
Alternative Music Group, 489n.18
amateur ideal, 435, 445–46
amateur (*yeyu*) musicians
　de-idealizing of, 444–47
　professional musicians, distinction from, 431–36, 440–44
　qingkechuan (amateur performers), 214–15
　See also professional musicians
amateurs, definition of, 442
Americanness, Lee's, 384–85
An Lushan, 50
An Xiuzhen, 240
Analects (*Lunyu*, Confucius), 115, 134
Ancient Dances (Wu Man and Chen Yi), 333

Ancient Wind ensemble, 335
Anderson, Benedict, 247, 316–17
Anglo-American popular music, hegemony of, 374, 381
Anglo-Chinese School Building Fund, 478
Anhui province, Jiangnan region and, 201
Anlu Bell 1, 13*f*, 14*f*, 15
Anlu Bell 1 and Anlu Bell 2, 11–12
aphorisms
　from the *Analects*, 115
　from *Shijing* lyrics, 119–20
applied research, need for, 505
archaeology, value of, 23
architectural music, 418–19
Aristoxenus, 41
artistic authenticity and transnational Chineseness of Chinese women pianists, 405–10
art music. *See* liveness and mediation in Chinese art music
Art of the Fugue, The (Bach), 400
art(s)
　adaptation in, 422
　artifying, 282
　augmentation as basic process for, 243
　Western versus traditional Chinese, 248, 249
Ashina (Tujue princess), 51
audiences, liveness and, 417
Auslander, Philip, 398, 406, 416–17
authenticity, musical borrowings and, 461–62
aviation industry, Zha Fuxi and, 256–57
Awut, Dawut, 456–57

512 INDEX

Baba Malay spelling, 471
Ba Ban Chinese Music Society of New York, 334–35
Bach, J. S., 391, 399–400
badaqu (eight great pieces), 200
Bai Fengming, 273
Bai Juyi, 49–50, 167, 341
Bai Yunpeng, 273
baihua language, 159, 166
bamboo-flute (*dizi*) music, 444
"Bamboo Horse" ("Zhuma," Shen Xingong), 159
bangdi (transverse flute), 185
bangu (*danpigu*, single-skin drum), 187
bangzi (opera genre), 191
banhu (bowed string instruments), 191
banshi bianzou (metrical variation), 90
Baranovitch, Nimrod, 355
Barmé, Geremie R., 354–55
Battle of Shanghai, 250
bayin (musical instrument classification system), 199
Bazhan wu suite, 186–87, 186*f*, 187*f*
"Beifeng" ("Cold Blows the North Wind"), 110
Beijing drumsong (*Jingyun dagu*), 273, 274, 276, 282
Beijing *Guqin* Research Association, 257
Bellman, Jonathan, 459–60
bells (*bianzhong*)
    Anlu Bell 1, woodblock facsimile of inscription from, 13*f*, 14*f*
    discussion of, 10–16
    double tones from, 10–11
    shape of, 16
    striking points, 11, 12–15
    from tomb of Zeng Hou Yi, 2, 10–11, 15, 37, 136
bentuhua yundong (localization movement), 321–22
betel-nut girls, 384
"Between Memory and History: Les Lieux de Memoire" (Nora), 145
Bhabha, Homi K., 311–12
bianwen (vernacular narratives), 286
bias, historical, 146–47
"Bigong" ("The Ancestral Temple"), 111
bili (*guanzi*, reed-pipe), 185

"Bin zhi chuyan" ("When Guests are Seated, the Banquet Begins"), 118
bird songs, 116
biwa. See *pipa* (lute)
Black music (*heiren yinyue*), 376–77
blending, types of practices of, 418, 422
"Blood-Stained Dignity" ("Xuerande fengcai," Chen Zhe and Su Yue), 356–59, 357*f*, 358*f*, 370n.6
"Blooming Flowers and the Full Moon" ("Yueyuan huahao"), 170
Blue Pipa Trio, 334
BM Boys, 483–84
bo (cymbals), 188, 189
bodies
    body culture, 385–86
    embodied musical experience, 493–94
    female bodies, gendered idealization of, 385–86
    Lee's, 383–84, 385–86
    non-Han, 452–53
    Wang's embodied performances, 396–98
    Zhu's embodiments, 402
Booth, Gregory, 437
"Border Defense 9" ("Bianfang jiu"), 56
Bourdieu, Pierre, 149n.1
Bovingdon, Gardner, 455
bowed string instruments (*laxian yueqi*), 190–91
Brace, Timothy, 363
Branton, Milton, 338
Brecht, Bertolt, 299
Bright Moon Song and Dance Troupe (Mingyue gewutuan), 169, 170
Brindley, Erica Fox, 275
British Malaya
    Chinese opera in, 477
    Japanese invasion of, 478
    newcomers (*sinkeh*) in, 477–78
    Peranakan Chinese in early twentieth-century in, 470–77
    puppet-theater troupes, 477
broken *rojak* Market English, 468
Brook, Peter, 417
Brownwell, Susan, 385–86
Bruns, Peter, 335
Bubble (Ma), 343

budaixi (glove puppetry), 293–94
buffalo-herding boys, 281
Burden of History: A Historical Account of Hong Kong from Mainland China, The (*Lishi de chenzhong: Cong Xianggang kan Zhongguo dalu de Xianggang lunshu*, Wong Wang-Chi), 141
Burhoe, Ty, 337
"Burung Kakak" ("Cockatoo Bird," folk song arrangement), 480–81

cadential patterns, 80–81, 80*f*
Cai Guoqing, 436–37
Cai Yuanding, 32
Cai Yuanpei, 161, 162–63, 248, 249–50
"Caiqi" ("Gathering White Millet"), 117
Cairang Danzeng, 239
Cairo Agreement, 315
"Caishu" ("Gathering Beans"), 118
"Caiwei" ("Gathering Thorn-ferns"), 110
Cambridge School of historical music reconstruction, 81
Cambridge University Press, *China Quarterly*, 500
Caoyuan xiao jieme (*Little Sisters of the Grassland*, Wu Zuqiang, Wang Yanqiao, and Liu Dehai), 331
Caucasian Chalk Circle, The (Brecht), 299
Central Conservatory of Music (Beijing), 332, 344
Cepeda, Maria Elena, 375–76
Chan Wing-Wah, 143
Chang Yong-ching, 322
"Changdi" ("Cherry Flowers"), 110
Changlu Wu School of Music, 335
Changsha tomb no. 1195 (in Wulipai, Hunan province), 17*f*, 23
Chatman, Seymour, 274
chauvinism, as discourse of Chinese modernity, 455
checked tones, 64
Chee, Johnny, 474
Chen Ching-Yi, 310–25, 496
Chen Duxiu, 248
Chen Haitao, 52–53
Chen Ru-chi, 320, 326n.6
Chen Rui, 71–72, 94n.12, 94–95n.20

Chen Shui-bian, 322
Chen Tianguo, 196n.13
Chen Tscheng-hsiung, 321
Chen Yang, 190
Chen Yaoxing, 460
Chen Yi, 257, 340
Chen, Yihan, 336
Chen Yin, 331
Chen Yingshi, 30–43, 44n.1, 492–93
Chen Youxin, 293, 297
Chen Zhe, 356, 358, 359–60, 370n.6, 371n.18
Chen Zongzhen, 231
Cheng, King (of Zhou dynasty), 110
Cheng Si Sum, 318*f*
Cheng Yu, 333–34
Chengzu, Emperor, 113
Cherry Blossom Music and Operatic Show, 477
Cheung Sai-Bung (Zhang Shibin), 140–41
Chiang Ching-kuo, 321–22, 326n.8
Chiang Kai-shek, 313, 315, 316
Chicago Symphony Orchestra, 341
Chichiao Musical Theater, 293, 298–301, 307n.7
  See also *Kurama Tengu*; Taiwanese new *xiqu*
children's songs, 235
  See also music education
China and the West (Yang and Saffle), 501
China Audio and Video Head Office (Zhongguo Luyin Luxiang Chuban Zongshe), 359, 363
China Broadcasting Traditional Orchestra, 480–81
China Quarterly (journal), 500
Chinese Americans
  limitations of media representation of identity of, 379–80
  musicians in Taiwan, marketing of, 376–77
  musicians in US popular-music industry, 377
  as racial minority, 378–79
Chinese Communist Party. See Communist Party of China
Chinese Culture Academy (later Chinese Culture University), 317–18
Chinese diaspora, maintenance of Chinese cultural markers, 469, 470

514 INDEX

Chinese heart-minds, *Shijing* songs as expression of, 123–24
Chinese Music History (*Zhongguo yinyue shi*, Wang Guangqi), 139–40
Chinese mysticism, Zhu and, 400
Chinese Nationalist Party (Kuomintang, KMT), 310, 314–18
Chineseness
   of Lee (Coco), 374–75, 377–78, 384–85
   Malaysia and, 468, 485
   markers of, in Malaysia, 478, 480
   sonic markers of, 481–82
   transnational, 411, 481–82
   transnational, of Chinese women pianists, 405–10
   See also Lee, Coco (Li Wen)
Chinese New Year rhyme, in Penang Hokkiet, 474–77
Chinese pop music
   American audiences' lack of familiarity with, 376
   factors affecting, 386–87
   film music and, 170
   shidaiqu, 169–70
Chinese Spring Festival Party, 356–57
Chinese storytelling, 286
Chinese Symphonic Picture along the River during the Qingming Festival (*Zhongguo yin hua Qingming shanghe tu*), 417–18
Chong, Eric K. M., 252
Chong Sang Teck, 489n.18
Choumo yinchu (*At Break of Day*), 273, 274, 276–81, 283f, 284f
   See also Luo Yusheng
Chow Fan-Fu (Zhou Fanfu), 143
Chow Kam Leong, 489n.18
Chow, Rey, 142–43
Chow-Morris, Kim, 225n.6
"Chuci" ("Tribulu"), 118
chuida ensembles, 215
shuigushou (musician of wind-and-percussion band), 261
chuiguan yueqi (wind instruments), 184–87
"Chuju" ("Military Carriages"), 110
Chunmei Opera Troupe (Chunmei Gejutuan), 297–98
Chu Sui-Bing (Zhu Ruibing), 143–44

Citrawarna (Colors of Malaysia) festival, 481
clappers, 188
Clark, Paul, 453
class
   class struggle in music's evolution, 140
   fetishization of Zhou and, 404
clothing
   Coco Lee's, preferences in and critiques of, 363
   Wang Yuja's preferences in and critiques of, 394–99
   Yugurs', changes to, 238
   Zhu Xiao-Mei's, 401
Clouds (He), 343
CNN, on Coco Lee, 377–78
coauthoring, issues raised by, 502
Coco. *See* Lee, Coco (Li Wen)
coincidence (*ping shui xiang feng*), 492
Collection of New Songs and Poetry (*Xin shige ji*, Zhao), 168
Collection of School Songs, A (*Xuexiao gechangji*, Shen), 159–60
collective composition, 359–60
collectivism
   in "Fill the World with Love," 363–64
   nationalism and individualism and, in Jinyu Qinshe community, 250–55
common music (*suyue*), 435
communal drinking ritual (*xiang yinjiu li*), 111–13
communalism, in Confucianism, 165–66
Communist Party of China (CPC), 139, 256, 313, 363, 364
community, amateurism and, 446
composers, individualism of, 165–68
composition, modernities of Chinese music and, 164–65
Compositional History of the Ballet "The White-Haired Girl," A (*Balei wuju Baimaonu chuangzuo shihua*, Yang), 145, 146–47
conceptual words (*gainian ci*), 355
Concerto for Pipa and String Orchestra (Harrison), 341
Concerto for String Orchestra and Pipa (Tan Dun), 335
Confucianism, core values in, 165–66
Confucius (Kongzi), 115, 242
   See also Shijing (*Book of Songs*)

Confucius Institutes, 344
control, discourse as form of, 141
creative stimulus and expressive model, *Shijing* songs as, 119–23
Criterion Press (Penang), 472
critical engagement, issues raised by, 502–3
Cross, Ian, 272, 284–85
cross-cultural contact, hybridity resulting from, 311–12
crossover, as term, negativity of, 380–81
Cui Jian, 355–56
Cui Zundu, 34–35
cultural radicalism vs. musical conservatism, 247–50
Cultural Revolution
    amateur as term during, 446–47
    attitudes toward, 147
    impact of, 317
    Luo Yusheng's response to, 273–74
    minority art during, 453
    model operas (*yangbanxi*) of, 145–47, 150n.8
    Scar Literature (*shanghen wenxue*), 354, 364
    Zhu, impact on, 399–400
culture
    jazz culture, in Shanghai, 248
    perpetual metamorphosis of, 243
    in Taiwan, under KMT, 315–16
    Taiwanese musical culture, under Japan's occupation, 313–14
    transmission of, 427
Culture Ministry (China), 241

daduizi (musical dialogue), 208
Dafra Drums, 482
Dai Ya, 335–36
daji yueqi (percussion instruments), 187–89
daluo (gongs), 189
Dama Orchestra, 482
Damucang (music salon), 365–66, 365f, 366f, 371n.16
dance
    Bright Moon Song and Dance Troupe, 169, 170
    historical images of, 51–52, 52f, 53f, 54f
    energetic dances (*jianwu*), 60
    ronggeng (Malay folk social dance), 471
    See also *huxuan* and *huteng* dances

dangdang (basin-shaped gongs), 188–89
"Danggena" ("It is Beautiful," Aerang Yinxing Jis), 240–41
Danna, Mychael, 335–36
Daoism, Zhu Xiao-Mei and, 401
Daoist priests, 204, 212, 215–16
dapu scores (for *guqin*), 37–38, 263–64
daruan (lute), 182
Dasiyue (music training school), 138
Datong Yuehui, 326n.3
Dawu (*The Great Wu*), 139
daybreak, in *Choumo yinchu*, 274
Dayueshu (music training school), 138
deadliness of live experiences, 417
death wishes, 358
Debussy, Claude, 338
Dejiao Hui (Alor Star), 479
Democratic Progressive Party (DPP, Taiwan), 321–22, 323
democratization, as theme of contemporary online environment, 446–47
de-sinicization, 321–22
Deutsche Grammophon, 392–93
development zone, Yugur resettlement in, 237
diangu (historical anecdotes), 66
diangu (point drum), 187
dianzi huache (vaudeville performed on trucks), 293–94
diasporas
    hybridity in, 134–35, 311, 469–70
    need for music research on, 504
diet, changes to Yugurs', 237
difangxi (regional opera), music of, 305
difang yinyue (regional music), 477–78
digital animation, 426
dikir barat, 489n.19
dimi (speech), 232
Dim Sum (CD), 342
Ding Shande, 163
dingzhenti (literary technique), 276, 278–79, 283
disciplines in Chinese music research, 503–5
discourse
    on amateurism as a musical ideal, 445–46
    on Chinese music history and historiography, 135–36, 141–44, 147, 148, 156–57, 494

discourse (*cont.*)
    as frame for interpreting Coco Lee's biography, 373–74, 378–79, 382–83, 385–86, 388n.1
    of ethnic minorities as natural musicians, 452–53
    and as uncivilized, 455
    of Luo Yusheng's video performance of *Choumo yinchu* (*At Break of Day*), 274, 275–88
    of traditional vs. modern, 456–57
dish-shaped gongs, 189
Dissanayake, Ellen, 271–72, 282
diversity, multiculturalist celebration of, 454–55
dizi (*hengdi*, transverse flute), 185–86, 444
Dolby, William, 308n.11
dondang sayang (poetry singing), 470–71
Dondang Sayang Tanaman I (*Dondang Sayang about Plants I*), 471, 472f, 473f
Dongfang hong (*The East is Red*), 10, 139
Donghong Yishutuan (Donghong Arts Troupe), 213–14, 214f
"Dongmen zhici" ("The Moat at the East Gate"), 117
"Dongshan" ("March to East Hill"), 110
dongxiao (flute type), 184, 186–87, 191
Dongxi yuezhi zhi yanjiu (*Musical Systems in the East and West*, Wang Guangqi), 36–37
Dongya Yuelu Xuehui (East Asian Society for Music Theory and Intonation), 3
Double Concerto (Gaudibert), 335–36
Do You Want My Love (Lee), 378, 380–81
Draft History of Ancient Chinese Music, A (*Zhongguo gudai yinyue shigao*, Yang Yinliu), 140
Draft History of Chinese Music, A (*Zhongguo yinyue shi lunshu gao*, Cheung Sai-Bung), 140–41
drag shows in Taiwan, hybridity in, 312
Drew, Robert, 445
"Drizzle" ("Maomao yu," Li), 169–70
drums, 187
drunkenness, as subject of *Shijing* songs, 118
Du Yaxiong, 239, 239f, 495
Du You, 48, 59
Duan Anjie, 51–52

duanqiang (melodic pause), 75–76
Dujunco, Mercedes M., 199–224, 495
Dunhuang caves (grottoes), 54–55, 54f, 57, 137, 179
duoju (literary technique), 277, 283
the Dutch, occupation of Taiwan, 313
Dutch East Indies, *kronchong* from, 471–74
Dydo, Stephen, 333–34

East Asian Society for Music Theory and Intonation (Dongya Yuelu Xuehui), 3
Easternization, as term, origins of, 248–49
"'East is Red' Goes Pop, The" (Lee), 312
Edison, Thomas, 169
eight tones (*bayin*, instrument categorization), 136
Ellis, Alexander J., 44n.6
the Emergency (Communist insurgency, Malaya), 478, 479
emotions, 124, 136, 251, 253, 274, 288–89, 295, 303, 355, 356–57, 391–92, 497
    language and understanding of, 275
Endless (CD), 343
Engels, Frederick, 140
enka (popular song style), 308n.10
Enqing Zhuoma, 240
Enriquez, Jocelyn, 377
Ensemble Dialog, 336
Ensemble FIRE, 341
ensembles
    bowed strings in, 191
    percussion in, 189
    plucked strings in, 183–84
    regional-ensemble music playing, 165
    sheng-guan ritual ensembles, 184
    wind instruments in, 185–87
Entertainment Weekly, criticisms of Lee album, 380
Epstein, Mikhail, 322–23
equal temperament, 2–3, 41
erhu (fiddle)
    discussion of, 190
    in ensembles, 191
    as focus of modernist experiments, 461
    minority-style compositions for, 460
    performance practices for, 180
    types of, 197n.29

voice and *erhu* interactions in "Blood-Stained Dignity," 357–58, 358f
erxian (bowed fiddle), 183–84, 183f, 190, 191
ethnicity
 ambiguities, management of, 377–79
 ethnic groups, definition of, 230, 452–53
 ethnoconvergence, 322–23, 453, 485
 intersectionality of, 405, 408, 411–12, 481–82, 497–98, 499
 stereotypes of, 375–76, 406–7
ethnomusicology
 Chinese, 3, 230, 241, 259, 503
 description of, 247
 precepts of, 100
 Western, 3–4, 171, 260, 434
European Chinese Ensemble, 333
Everett, Yayoi Uno, 405–6, 417
Everyone Listen Close (Yandong Grand Singers), 502
"Evidence of Pitch in the Neolithic and Bronze Ages and Its Bearing on the History and Development of Chinese Musical Scales" (Huang Xiangpeng), 10
evolutionism
 history and, 139–40
 storytelling and, 272
excavated remains, description of, 9–10
existential humanism, 354
exoticism, in music and dance, 47–48, 311–12, 458–62, 463, 500
expressive model and creative stimulus, *Shijing* songs as, 119–23

Faculty of Music (Xinjiang Arts Institute), 455–56
family living, as subject of *Shijing* songs, 110
"Famu" ("Cutting Trees"), 117–18
fangman jiahua (melodic augmentation process), 207
fanjian fa (complex-simple, variation principle), 180–81, 191–92
"Fanyin lun" ("On Harmonics," Yu Dishan), 262–63
farmers, in *Choumo yinchu*, 279
Farrer, James, 502
Fei Shi, 156–57, 160
femininity
 Chinese stereotypes of, 391–92
 disruption of stereotypes of, 392–93, 398–99, 400, 406
 See also women
Feng Jiexuan, 21–22
"Feng ru song" ("Wind Entering Through the Pines"), 63–92
Fengyun jihui (*The Meeting of Wind and Clouds*), 262
fetishisms, Zhu Xiao-Mei as target of fetishization, 402–5
Field, Andrew, 502
filial piety, as subject of *Shijing* songs, 110
Filipino musicians in Hong Kong, hybridity and, 312
"Fill the World with Love" ("Rang shijie chongman ai," pop song), 359–64, 361f, 367–68
film music, 170, 338
Finger, Anke, 418
Finnegan, Ruth, 444
First Sino-Japanese War, 163, 268n.1
fishermen, in *Choumo yinchu*, 278, 288
5-limit tuning, 34, 36
"Flight of The Bumblebee," Wang's performance of, 406–7
floating intentionality, 284–85
floating perspective, 426
Flow I & II (Huang), 341
flutes, performance practices for, 180
Flying Dragon (Hong), 342
folk (*minjian*) activities, 444
Folk Music of China (Jones), 199–200
folk songs
 Hungarian, 236
 original ecology folk songs, 446–47
 short tune folk songs, 235
 traditional, for Yugur weddings, 242
 of western Yugurs, changes in, 238–42
 Wu folk songs in Jiangnan musical area, 202
 Yugur folk songs, 232–36
Follet, Danielle, 418
"For a Wonderful Future" (Du Yaxiong), 239
foreign musical dances in Chinese history. *See huxuan* and *huteng* dances
Formosa Chunfeng Opera Troupe (Chunfeng Gejutuan), 296–97
Foucault, Michel, 135–36, 141

Four Seasons (Danna), 335–36
Four Seasons Mosaic, The (documentary), 335–36
"Four Seasons Song" ("Siji ge," He), 170
Franke, Bernd, 335
Fu Lin, 355
Fu Sinian, criticisms of Chinese opera, 249
Fun and Frolic Park, 477
funeral songs (lamentations), 233, 234
"Futian" ("Bright and Extensive Fields"), 118

Gaijin cao (*Exercise for Improvement*, Liu), 330–31
gailiang xi (reformed plays), 294
Gaisberg, Fred, 169
Gang of Four (*siren bang*), 145–46, 150n.9
gang tai pop songs, 370n.6
Gansu Audio and Video Company, 239
Ganzhou Uyghurs, 231
Gao Hong, 337, 339–40, 342
Gao Houyong, 195n.4
gaohu (bowed string instruments), 190, 191
Gao Ming, 68
Gao Xuefeng, 204–6, 212–13, 226n.20
Gao You, 21–22, 23
Gao Ziming, 316
Garafalo, Reebee, 380–81
Garcia, Christopher, 338
Gaudibert, Eric, 335–36
gehu (bowed string instruments), 424–25
Gelernter, David, 274, 275
gender ambivalence, Zhu's expression of, 402
Gender in Chinese Music (Harris, Pease, and Tan), 501
Gesamtkunstwerk, 418
"Gesheng" ("The Dolichos Grow"), 101
gestures
    definition of, 287
    gestural and pictorial elements in Luo Yusheng's video performance of *Choumo yinchu*, 286–88
"Getan" ("Dolichos and Yellow Birds"), 116–17
gezaixi (traditional Taiwanese musical theater), 292, 294, 295–96, 298
gez jer (girl's songs), 233
ghak (musical dialogue), 208
ghéjek (Uyghur spike fiddle), 461–62

Ghost Opera (Tan Dun), 340–41
gift economies, 434, 440–44
Gil-Curiel, Germán, 416–28, 498
Glass, Philip, 338
globalization
    and anxiety about Sinicization, 296
    and liberalization in Malaysia, 481–85
    and localization, 322–23
    and modernities, 405–6
    and musical preservation, 91–92, 243
    of *pipa* music, 332–45
global warming, impact on Yugur lifestyles, 236–37
glove-puppet theater, 486f, 489n.16
Goffman, Erving, 398
Goh, Bernard, 482
Goh Suk Liang, 488n.10
Goldberg Variations (Bach), 401, 409f
Golden Bough Theater (Jinzhi Yanshe), 296–97, 307n.5
Goldoni, Carlo, 297
Goldstein, Malcolm, 337
gongche (musical notation), 69f, 82f, 83f, 137, 183, 262–63, 330, 345
Gongleshe theater company, 295
gongs, types of, 197n.26
good-at-singing-and-dancing (*nengge shanwu*), 452–53
Graffman, Gary, 392–93
Gramophone Company, 488n.7
Grapes Are Ripe, The (Zhou Wei), 461–62
grassroots stage (*caogen wutai*), 444
Gratier, Maya, 271–72
Grave M6, Yanchi, Ningxia, 51–52, 52f
Green (Vincent's Tune, Wu Man*)*, 342
Greenaway, Peter, 429n.5
Gu Family Music Troupe (*Gujia Yinyueban*), 216–19, 216f, 217f
Gu Feiyun, 213–14
Gu Guanren, 208–9, 216–17, 331
Gu Lijian, 206
Gu Zaixin, 216–17, 218–19
Guan, Yadong, 338
"Guanju" ("*Guanguan*, Cry the Ospreys"), 100–1, 114, 115
guanzi (*bili*, reed-pipe), 185
Guanzi (*Book of Master Guan*), 2–3, 31–32

"Gufeng" ("East Wind"), 101
guganyin (melodic skeleton), 180
guiding principles (*guilü*) of traditional performance practices, 180
Guiqu laici (*Come Away Home*), 262
guitar-*pipa* duos, 336–37, 345
gulu (old-style) plays, 293–94
Gunong Sayang Association of Singapore, 470–71
Guodian tomb no. 1 (in Hubei province), 17f, 20, 23
Guo Feng, 359–60
Guo Gan, 336
guoju (national opera), 317
Guo Moruo, 21
Guo Shuhui, 502
Guo Tongfu, 259, 262
guoyue (modern Chinese orchestral music, national music)
  challenges faced by, 321
  earliest record of performances in Taiwan, 313–14
  under KMT, 316, 317
  local Taiwanese elements in, 322
  orchestras performing, 316
  as term, meaning of, 310
  See also Jiangnan *sizhu*; modern Chinese orchestral music of Taiwan
guqin (zither)
  investigation group for research on, 257
  marker positions on fingerboard of, 36f
  music for, superiority to Western music, 251, 252
  origins of, 247–48
  photographs of players of, 256f, 261f
  pitches of marked string lengths on, in *sanfen sunyi* tuning, 40t
  ratios of marked string lengths on, 37t
  regional schools for, 252–53
  as symbol of traditional Chinese culture, 249
  tuning of open strings, 39–40
  tuning systems for, 35–41, 40t
  See also Jinyu Qinshe Society in 1930s China
"Gu qin zhengfang lu" ("Survey of Ancient *Guqin* Instruments"), 265
Guy, Nancy, 317

Guyin zhengzong (*Authentic Ancient Music*, Zhu Changfang), 262
Gwizdalski, Andrzej, 338

Hagerty, Sean, 338
hair-cutting songs, 233
halfies, 501–2
Hall, Stuart, 501–3
Hal Leonard Chinese Pipa Method (Hong), 337
Halo Café, 489n.18
Hands Percussion, 482
Han Lankui, 335
Han people, as enlightened compared with non-Han people, 455–56
Han Xiu, 53–54, 53f
Han Yonglu, 273
Hanya Xishu (Chaozhou classic suite), 183–84, 183f
"Haotian you chengming" ("Heaven Made Its Imperial Appointment"), 110
harmonic overtone series, 34, 35f
harmony, Brindley on, 275
Harrell, Stevan, 455–56
Harrison, Lou, 341
hay-cutting songs, 234
He Chengtian, 32
He Jixin, 239
He Luting, 163, 170
He Mingzhong, 316
He, Qiu Xia, 336–37, 338, 343
He Yuguang, 299–300
"Heming" ("Crane Crows"), 117
Herbert, Ruth, 284–85
heterophony
  heterophonic ideal, 191–92
  heterophonic performance practice, 180–81
  in *kunqu* and Jiangnan *sizhu*, 211–12
  See also traditional instruments and heterophonic practice
hexie (harmony), Zhu's use of term, 402
Hexi Uyghurs, 231
Historical Chronicle of the Model Operas, A ("*Yangbanxi*" *biannian shi*, Li), 145, 146, 147
Historical Record of Model Opera, A (*Yangbanxi shiji*, Shi and Zhang), 145, 146
Histories of the North (*Bei shi*), 51

historiography, as term, meaning of, 135
history
　Chinese, *Shijing* songs as, 110–14
　historical bias, 146–47
　linear progressive view of, 156
　political power and, 146
　as term, meaning of, 135
Ho, Josephine, 384
Ho, Vincent, 335–36
Hokkien Rhymes in Penang Hokkien, 474–77
Hong Kong
　Filipino musicians in, hybridity and, 312
　music scholarship in, 3
　pipa music performances in, 332
　PRC scholars' writing on, 141–44
　sovereigns of, relationship with, 142–43
Hong Kong Composers: The 1930s to the 1990s (Xianggang zuoqujia: Sanshi zhi jiushi niandai, Liang Maochun), 141–42
Hongli ji (*The Tale of Red Pear Blossoms*), 81, 82*f*
Hongwu zhengyun (rhyme dictionary), 73–74, 75*f*
Horlor, Samuel, 431–48, 498
Hou hanshu (*History of the Later Han Dynasty*), 31
Houston Symphony, 335
"How Can I Not Keep Thinking of Her?" ("Jiaowo ruhe buxiang ta," Zhao), 166–67
Hsieh Hsiao-Mei, 292–306, 496
Hu Dengtiao, 181
Hu Jintao, 402
Hu Rongrong, 146–47
Hu Shi, 166, 248, 249
Hu Yuan, 112
Hua Chenyu, 353
Huainanzi (*Book of the Prince of Huainan*), 20, 23, 31–32
Huang Haihuai, 460
Huang Jinpei, 93n.2
Huang Lanying, 316
Huang Ruo, 341
Huang Tingjian, 260
Huang Xiangpeng, 10–11, 38–39
Huang Zi, 167, 168
Huangmei opera, 307n.6
Huangnibao Autonomous District, 230

huayin (portamentos), 180
hui (marked nodes on the *qin*), 21–22, 23
huju (Shanghai opera), 211, 212
huju shalong (*huju* salons), 213–14
humanism
　in 1980s China, rise of, 353–55, 367
　in 1980s Chinese pop songs, rise of, 355–67
　existential humanism, 354
　humanist articulations in Chinese literature and art, 353–54
　Marxist humanism, 354–55
Hungarian folk songs, 236
Hungry Ghost (Phor Tor) festival, 477
huqin (bowed string instruments), 190. *See also* erhu
Hutcheon, Linda, 304, 417–18, 422
"Huteng Boy" ("Huteng er," Li Duan), 56
huteng dance, 55–59
huteng dancer, figurine of, 58–59, 58*f*
huxuan dance, 48–55, 54*f*
"*Huxuan* Girl: Against This Bad Social Custom" ("Huxuan nu: Jie jin xi ye," Bai Juyi), 49–50
hybridity
　and the Chinese orchestra, 310–24, 482
　of Chineseness and internationalism, 374–75, 379–80, 383, 405–6, 469, 485
　definitions of, 312
　in male cross-dressing shows in Taiwan, 312
　musical, in Hong Kong, 144
　positive and negative connotations of, 323–24, 453–54
　in Tang entertainments, 54
　theatrical, in Taiwan, 293, 294–95, 303
hybrid music, Tan Dun as composer of, 418–19

I am a Singer (*Wo shi geshou,* reality-TV singing competition), 373–74, 381–83
identity. *See* performing multicultural Chinese identities
Identity (Yang), 342
ideologies on Chinese music history and historiography, 137–41
"I Have Nothing" ("Yi wu suo you," rock song), 355, 363, 367
imagined communities, 247, 316–17
Imberty, Michel, 271–72

imperial exam system, 249
Imperial Subject Movement, 294
improvisation, 164–65, 192, 330, 343
improvisatory theater, 297
individualism, 165–68, 250–55, 354–55, 363–64, 367
infants, communication with, 271–72
injustice, as subject of *Shijing* songs, 110
In Memoriam (Huang), 167
Innova Recordings, 342
"In Response to Li Jiaoshu's New Poems, The Twelve *Yuefu*: *Huxuan* Girl" ("He Li Jiaoshu xin ti yuefu shi'er shou yuefu: Huxuan nu," Yuan Zhen), 48–49, 50
inside-out viewpoints, 500
institutions and music education, modernities of Chinese music and, 160–64
Instruction Book for Primary School Singing (*Xiaoxue gechang jiaoxuefa*, Shen), 160
instruments
   bowed string instruments (*laxian yueqi*), 190–91
   communication of ritual and imperial meanings by, 122–23
   Dama Orchestra's use of, 482
   for *aying yinyue* (regional music) performances, 477–78
   in ensembles with *pipa*, 336
   in *guoyue* activities, 313–14
   imported, types of, 179
   in *Kurama Tengu*, 303
   in Lee's folk song arrangements, 480–81
   modern era modifications of, 458–59
   in "My Beloved Hometown," 364
   of non-Han peoples, 453
   percussion instruments, 187–89
   plucked string instruments, 181–84
   school songs' influence on, 158
   in *shifan* music, 215
   for Uyghur music, modern concert repertoire of, 456
   Western, in ensembles with *pipa*, 336–37
   wind instruments (*chuiguan yueqi*), 184–87
   See also *erhu*; *guqin*; *pipa*; *qin*; traditional instruments and heterophonic practice
intangible cultural heritage, need for music research on, 505

Intangible Cultural Heritage Program, 220–21, 226n.26
intellectual labor, division within, 500–1
intellectuals, 296–98, 359
   See also *shi* (literati) class
internationalism, 374, 386
intimate relations, as subject of *Shijing* songs, 101
Introduction to the Development of Music in Hong Kong, An (*Xianggang yinyue fazhan gailun*, Chu), 143–44
Irvine, Thomas, 504

Japan
   Malaya, invasion of, 478
   music scholarship in, 3
   pipa in, 345
   Taiwan, Japanese culture in, 303–4
   Taiwan, occupation of, 313–14
jazz culture, in Shanghai, 248
jer (song), 232, 238–39
Ji Kang, 68
Ji Zha, 110–11
jiahua (melodic embellishment), 90, 165
jiajian sheng (mouth organ), 461
jiajian yuan sheng (mouth organ), 461
"Jiangchengzi" ("To the Tune of River City," Su Shi), 119–20
Jian'ge wen ling (*Listening to the Bells at Sword Pavilion*), 273, 274
Jiangjun ling (*General's Orders*), 218–19
Jiang Kui, 119–20, 165
Jiang Qing, 145–46
Jiangnan musical area, genres prevalent in, 202
Jiangnan province, formation of, 200–1
Jiangnan region
   as cultural region, 201
   location of, 200–4
   map of, 201f
   symbolism of, 201
Jiangnan *sizhu* (music ensembles)
   amateurs versus professionals in, 433–34
   description of, 202
   in the greater Suzhou area, 199–224
   origins of, 202–4
   performance locations for, 204
   possible decline of, 206

INDEX

Jiangnan *sizhu* (music ensembles) (*cont.*)
  regional opera music, interconnections with, 211–15
  repertory revitalization project, 206–9, 220–21
  shifan genres, comparison with, 215–19
  teahouse versus stage performances of, 449n.3
  See also Taicang
Jiangsu province, map of Suzhou metropolitan area, 205f
"Jiang yousi" ("The River has Branches"), 117
Jiang-Zhe area, 201
"Jianjia" ("Reeds and Rushes"), 101, 119–20
jianzi pu (traditional *guqin* tablature), 165
Jiaofang (music academy), 56–57, 60
jiaren (beautiful woman), 280
"Jigu" ("Drum Rolls"), 117
"Jiming" ("The Cock has Crowed"), 117
jingbo (cymbals), 188
Jing Fang, 32
jinghu (bowed string instruments), 190
jingju (Beijing opera), 295, 317
Jin Hezai (Zeng Yu), 353
"Jin qin zhengfang lu" ("Survey of Today's *Guqin* Instruments"), 265
Jinyu qinkan (journal)
  on gatherings, 260–61
  "General Introduction" to, 251, 264
  on *guqin* studies, 249
  importance of, 250, 265
  Jinyu Qinshe's nationalist ideal in, 251–52
  musicological contributions of, 262–65
  photograph of cover of, 263f
  on *yaji* gatherings, attendance at, 255
Jinyu Qinshe Society in 1930s China, 247–68
  community members' social backgrounds, 255–59
  cultural radicalism vs. musical conservatism, 247–50
  description of, 250
  Jinyu qinkan and its musicological contribution, 262–65
  nationalism, collectivism, and individualism in the Jinyu Qinshe community, 250–55
  yaji gatherings, 259–62

"Jinyu Qinshe yinian yilai yueji jishi" ("One Year's Chronicle of the Monthly *Yaji* Gatherings of the Jinyu Qinshe"), 264–65
jiqing guangchang performances, 436f, 436–42
Jirō Osaragi, 301, 302
Jit Sin Secondary School Chinese Musical Instrument Society, 479
Jiu lianyu (*Nine Jade Chains*, Yang), 342
jodatsko (rhyming poems), 232, 233–34, 239–40
Joget Anak Udang (*Joget Dance Music*), 480, 481f
Jones, Andrew, 355
Jones, Stephen
  on amateur ceremonial music, 445, 446
  on amateur-professional feuds, 433–34
  on Jiangnan *sizhu*, evolution of, 199–200, 219
  on *kunqu* performers, training of, 226n.18
  mentioned, 432–33
  on professional performances, 438–39
  on *shifan luogu*, 225n.4
Journey to the West (*Xi you ji*), 353
Jou Tou ensemble, 336–37
Joyful Steppes (*Huanle de caoyuan*, Zhang Zhiliang), 461
"Jugong" ("Chariots and Horses"), 118
"Julin" ("Approaching Chariots"), 118
just intonation, 33–35, 37–38, 41
Just No Other Way (Coco Lee album), 376, 380
"Juxia" ("Wedding Procession"), 117–18

"Kaifeng" ("Genial Wind"), 110, 116–17
Kangju (kingdom of Kang), 48
Kaohsiung Chinese Orchestra (KCO, Goxiong Shi Guoyue Tuan), 318–19
Kaohsiung Happy Go (*Zhaodi Fuxing dagou*), 299
"Kaopan" ("Hut by the Stream"), 117
karaoke, 438–39, 440–42
Keat's Magical and Vaudeville Show, 477
Khor Seng Chew, 482
King Chu Doffs His Armor (*Bawang xiejia*, Zhou Long), 340
King Hui of Chu (Yan Zhang), 11
Kisah Pulau Pinang (*Penang Story*), 483
"Kita Anak Malaysia" ("We are the Children of Malaysia," BM Boys), 484

KMT (Kuomintang, Chinese Nationalist
    Party), 310, 314–18
Kodály, Zoltán, 236
Koh Hoon Teck, 470–71
Kōminka undo (Kōminka movement), 314
Kongzi. *See* Confucius
Korea, music scholarship in, 3
kotai (song stage), 477
kronchong from Dutch East Indies, 471–74
Kronchong Weltevreden, 474, 475f
Kronos Quartet, 340–41
Kuhn, Terry Lee, 437
kunqiang melodies, 202–3
kunqu (opera genre), 63–92
    composition of, 69f, 87–92, 493
    hidden melodies from the past, 81–84
    historical and regional perspectives, 73–76
    in Jiangnan musical area, 202
    Jiangnan *sizhu*, relationship with, 211–15
    kunqu creation, complexities in, 90f
    kun recitation and singing, 71–72
    language-music interactions, 64–65, 69–80
    melodic relationships, 80–91
    origins of Jiangnan *sizhu* and, 204–5
    qupai paradigm, 65–68
    reductive analytical approaches, 84–87
    stylistic division within, 70f
    textual *qupai* and *kunqu* composition, 68
    theoretical background, 64–68
kun recitation and singing, 71–72
Kuomintang (KMT, Chinese Nationalist
    Party), 310, 314–18
Kurama Tengu, 301–5
Kuttner, Fritz, 33
Kwastek, Katja, 416–17
Kwok, Raymond, 474

ladies, in *Choumo yinchu*, 280–81
Lai Kin (Li Jian), 143
Lam, Bun-Ching, 338, 341
Lam Ching-Wah (Lin Qinghua), 143
Lam, Doming, 332
Lam, Joseph S. C., 99–127, 138, 493
Lang Lang, 392–93, 394, 399, 408, 410
languages
    bilingualism in Taiwan, 299
    Chichiao Musical Theater's use of, 298–99
    in *Kurama Tengu*, 301
    language-music interactions in *kunqu*, 64–65, 69–80
    music and, 499–503
    in Penang, 474
laosheng (opera role type), 273
Lara, Christian, 338
Latinx musicians, tropicalization of, 375–76
Latinx pop singers, success of, 375–76
Lau, Alan, 493
Lau, Frederick
    on bamboo-flute music, 444
    as chapter author, 155–73, 494
    on elites, 445–46
    on informal performances, 437–38
    research by, 260
    on transnationalism, 405–6
Lau, Kar Lun Alan, 63–92
Law Wing-fai, 332
Lawergren, Bo, 21
Lawson, Francesca R. Sborgi, 271–89, 496
laxian yueqi (bowed string instruments),
    190–91
leaf blowing, 421
Lee, Ang, 338
Lee, Coco (Li Wen), 373–88
    Chineseness of, 374–75, 377–78, 384–85
    on *I am a Singer*, 381–83
    internationalism of, 374–75, 384–85
    in US markets, 375–81
Lee, Gregory, 312
Lee, Roger, 376–77
Lee Soo Sheng, 478–79, 480–81
Lee Teng-Hui, 314–15
Legge, James, 128n.8
Lei Xuanchun, 231
Leigudun, *qin* from, 20, 21
leisure/pleasure realm, value of, 445
"Lenggang Lenggang Kangkong" (Malay folk
    song), 483–84
Létip, Tursunjan, 465–66n.4
Leung, Paul (Liang Bao'er), 143
Li Bai, 68
Li Cang, 22
Li Changlei, 299–300
Li Duan, 56
Li Gonglin, 259–60

Li Hongzhang, 155
Li Ji, 52–53
Li Jian (Lai Kin), 143
Li Jinhui, 150n.6, 169–70
Li Mark, Lindy, 88
Li Minghui, 169
Li Shan, 21–22, 23
Li Shang, 21
Li Shutong, 159
Li Sisong, 383–84
Li Song, 145, 146, 147
Li Tianlu, 307n.2
Li Wen. *See* Lee, Coco
Li Ya, 208
Li Yu, 95n.26
Li Yundi, 394, 399, 408
Li Zizhao (Number One Court *Guqin* Master), 258, 259, 261–62, 261*f*
Liang Bao'er (Paul Leung), 143
Liang, David, 164
Liang Maochun, 141–42, 367–68
Liang Qichao, 139, 165
Liang Shuming, 248
Lianhua Film Studio (Lianhua yingye gongsi), 170
liberalization and globalization at turn of the twenty-first century, 481–85
Lidai zhongding yiqi kuanzhi fatie (*Model Calligraphy of Inscriptions on Bronzes of Successive Dynasties*, Xue Shanggong), 12
lieux de memoire, 147–48
"Liezu" ("Meritorious Ancestors"), 110
Lim Seng Hooi, 472
ling (bells), 188
Lin Guangzhao (Aixuan, pseud.), 15–16
Lin Heyi, 293
Lin Qinghua (Lam Ching-Wah), 143
Lin Shengxi, 163
Lin Shicheng, 332–33, 339–40
Lin Xiyi, 15–16
Ling, Lisa, 379–80
Ling Yang, 382–83
linguistic tones (*shengdiao*), 64
Lipsitz, George, 375–76
literati. *See shi* (literati) class
Little Theater Movement (*xiao juchang yundong*), 296–97, 307n.4

Liu An, 20, 22
liu bai (leaving blank), 400
Liu Baoquan, 273
Liu Beimao, 466n.5
Liu Changfu, 460
Liu, Chih-Chieh, 383–84
Liu Ching-Chih (Liu Jingzhi), 143–44
Liu Dehai, 331, 332–33
Liu Fang, 337, 338, 343
Liu He (later Marquis of Haihun), 16–18, 18*f*, 19*f*, 22, 23
Liu Jianguo, 300, 301, 307–8n.9
Liu Jianhua, 300–1
Liu Jingzhi (Liu Ching-Chih), 143–44
Liu Mingyuan, 461
Liu Tianhua, 161–62, 163–64, 330–31, 460, 466n.5
Liu Tingxin, 239
Liu Weiren, 365–66
Liu Wu, 20, 23
Liu Xiaolin, 359–60
Liu Xin, 31
Liu Xing, 461
Liu Yanshi, 55–56
Liuhua liujie, 208–9, 209*f*, 213
live art, in new music circles, 496–97
liveness and mediation in Chinese art music, 416–28
    Along the River during the Qingming Festival, 422–26
    Tan Dun and *The Map*, 418–22
    as total art, 418–22
Lives in Chinese Music (Rees), 501
Liyuan (traditional-opera academy), 56–57, 60
liyue (rites and music system), 140
Lobel, Christophe, 338
localization, 143–44, 322, 323–24, 326n.8
Location of Culture, The (Bhabha), 311–12
Long chuan (*Dragon Boats*), 339–40
long tune folk songs, 235
Lopez, Jennifer, 375
Lord, Albert, 271
Los Angeles Times, on Yuja Wang, 395
"Love Before Time, A" ("Yueguang airen"), 373
Lü Buwei, 243–44
Lü Nan, 113–14
"Lu'e" ("Long and Large Bushes"), 110

lullabies, 235
Lülü aying (*Essential Music Theories*), 113–14
Lum, Casey Man Kong, 438–39
"Luming" (drinking song), 117–18
luo (gongs), 188–89
Luo Caiwu, 273
Luo Feng, 52–53
Luo Yusheng, 271–89
Luogu sihe (*Gongs and Drums Four Unified*), 203
lusheng (mouth organ), 421–22
Lüshi aying (*Master Lü's Spring and Autumn Annals*), 31–32, 136, 243–44
Lute Legends Ensemble, 335–36
lüxue (study of musical tuning), 31
Lüxue (*The Study of Musical Pitches*, Miao Tianrui), 37
"Lüyi" ("Green Robe"), 101, 119–20

Ma, Jie, 338, 343
Ma Ying-jeou, 322–23
Ma, Yo-Yo, 341, 342
Magnificent City Gates (detail from *Along the River during the Qing Ming Festival*), 425f
mainstage *gezaixi*, 295–96
mainstream, non-Han peoples' musical place in modern China and, 458–62
Mair, Victor, 286, 287
Malay *dondang sayang*, 470–71
Malaysia
 higher education, racism in, 484–85
 introduction of modern Chinese orchestras into, 479
 liberalization and globalization at the turn of the twenty-first century, 481–85
 Malaysian Chinese (*huaren*), 469
 National Culture Policy, 480
 See also British Malaya, performing multicultural Chinese identities
Malcolm, Janet, 397
male cross-dressing shows, 312
Malov, Sergey, 231, 236
manban (slow meter), 282
Mandarin, tones in, 65f
Mandopop, 374–75, 376–77, 387–88
 See also Popular music
"Mang" ("Men"), 101

mangpi (python skin), 190
Manring, Michael, 338
Manring Garcia Ma Trio, 338
Mao, Monk and Me (CD), 342
Mao Zedong, 138–39, 229, 243
"Maoshi daxu" ("Mao Preface to the *Shijing*"), 115, 124
Map, The: Concerto for Cello, Video, and Orchestra ("*Ditu*" *wei datiqin, luxiang, jiyueduikaixiezouqu*, Tan Dun)
 discussion of, 417, 418–22
 photograph of performance of, 420f
 as total artwork, 419–22, 420f
marginality, role of, 462–63
masculinity, 399, 461–62
Martin, Steve, 373–74
Marxist historical materialism, 140
Marxist humanism, 354–55
Mat Din, 482
Mawangdui tomb 3, Changsha, Hunan
 occupant of, 22
 qin from, 17f, 18, 19–20, 21, 23
mawei huqin (horsetail fiddle), 190
May Fourth New Cultural Movement (Wu-Si yundong), 162, 248
MC Jin, 377
McMahon, Keith, 280
McNeill, David, 286
Mecarto comma, 32
Media Headquarters, 335–36
media industries in Asia, popular music and, 387–88
mediation, 417–18, 427
 See also *Along the River during the Qingming Festival*; liveness and mediation in Chinese art music
melismas, 285
melody
 melodic leadership and support, 195n.7
 melodic relationships in *kunqu*, 80–91
 melodic variation in Jiangnan *sizhu* music, 207–8
 perception of, 95n.31
memory
 Chinese music history and historiography and, 145–48
 influence on the past, 146–47

memory (*cont.*)
   lieux de memoire, 147–48
   memory-keeping sites, 150–51n.11
   types of, 147–48
   See also the past
Meng Guangzheng, 365–67, 365f
Méning Rawabim (Qurban), 456–57
"Men Need to Have High Ambition" ("Naner zhiqi gao," Shen), 159–60
merghul (instrumental genre), 456
Merican, Ahmad, 480
metaphysical blending, 418, 422
Mi Fu, 259–60
Miao Tianrui, 36–37
middle kingdom syndrome, 251
Mikkonen, Simo, 163
Ministry of Education (Taiwan), 317–18
Min Jiqian, 334
Min Xiao-Fen, 334, 342
minorities
   minority discourse, 144
   minority music, 454–58
   minority nationalities (*shaoshu minzu*), 452–53
   model-minority narratives, Chinese Americans and, 379
   See also ethnicity
minyue (folk-music traditions), 91–92
minzu yinyue lilun (national music theory), 2–3
Mirror and Circle (Franke), 335
Mithen, Steven, 286
model operas (*yangbanxi*) of Cultural Revolution, 145–47
modeng (*xiandai*, modern), as term, 155–56
modern Chinese instrumental music, minority-themed compositions in, 459–60
modern Chinese orchestral music of Taiwan, 310–25, 479–81
   hybridity and music, 311–13
   musical culture in China, revival of, 317–18
   Taiwan's musical culture, exploration and appropriation of, 318–23
modernity and modernization
   in Chinese music, 155–73
   commodification of music in, 168–70

   composers, individualism of, 165–68
   double meanings of, grassroots negotiation of, 293–96
   impact on cultural causes, 354
   institutions and music education, 160–64
   nature of, 458
   Westernization versus, 171
Molihua (*Jasmine Flower*), 213
Mollard, Michel, 400
Mongolia
   Liu Mingyuan's visit to, 461
   as source for "exotic" musical styles, 460
Monk, Thelonious, 342
monologic historical explanations, 147
morin khuur (horse-head fiddle), 460–61
mothers, mother-infant communication, 271–72
Mount a Long Wind (Zhou Long), 336
mouth organs
   jiajian sheng, 461
   aying, 421–22
   sheng, 180, 184, 185–86
mubiao (scenario, scene-outline), 293
Mudanting (*The Peony Pavilion*, Tang Xianzu), 114, 213
Müller, Fabian, 338
multicultural Chinese identities. *See* performing multicultural Chinese identities
multimodality of music, 285
   See also Luo Yusheng
multisensory communication, 271–72
music
   as challenge for experimentation in *xiqu*, 299–300
   Chinese performance practices, 164–65
   contextualization of, 423–24
   flexibility of, 284–85
   functions of music-making, 117–18
   global histories of, need for, 504
   in *Kurama Tengu*, 301, 303, 304–5
   language, relationship to, 64
   musical Confucianism, 115–16
   musical conservatism vs. cultural radicalism, in Jinyu Qinshe Society, 247–50
   musical conventions, in *opela*, 295

musical difference, reification of, 459–60
musical exoticism, Chinese modernism and, 458
musical pitches, classification of, 35–36
musical rendition of *Choumo yinchu*, 282–86, 283*f*, 284*f*
music-language interactions in *kunqu*, 69–80
music notations, importance of, 137
music propaganda, 139
music-recording industry, 168–69
music theory, Chinese scholarly traditions of, 2–3, 30–33, 235–36, 500–1, 503
  old or ancient pieces (*guqu*), 164
  popular music, in *gezaixi*, 295
  of regional operas, 305
  text, interrelationship with, 129n.23
  traditional pieces (*chuantong qumu*), 164
musical archaeology and prehistory of music in China, 9–25
  bells, 10–16
  qin, 16–23
music communities as manifestation of nationalism. *See* Jinyu Qinshe Society in 1930s China
music education
  conservatories as chief sites for music transmission, 456
  formation of Chinese orchestras in schools in Taiwan, 317–18, 318*f*
  modernities of Chinese music and, 160–64
  modernizing of, 157
  suspension of (1920s), 162–63
  in Taiwan, 314
Music from China (New York), 336
music history and historiography in Chinese context, 134–49
  discourse of, power politics of, 141–44
  ideologies in, 137–41
  memory and, 145–48
  sources for, 136–37
Music Office (Hong Kong), 142
music societies, 443–44
muyu (woodblock type), 188, 189
"My Beloved Hometown" ("Wo reliande guxiang," pop song), 364–67
My Monk's Dream (Min), 342

"Na" ("How Admirable!"), 118
Namewee (Wee Meng Chee), 484–85, 489n.21
Nan'anzui Riverside Park (Wuhan), 431, 441*f*
nanbangzi (woodblock type), 188, 189
"Nang Si Chit Keh Nang" ("We are One Family," BM Boys), 484
nanguan (performance genre, [Fujian] *nanyin*), 181–82, 186–87, 187*f*, 446, 448–49n.2
nanyin pipa, 334
Nanyin pipa: *Operas Murmuring* (Min Xiao-Fen), 334
narratives
  discussion of, 271–73
  pictures in narrative performances, 287, 287*f*
  typical *gezaixi* narrative patterns, 300–1
  See also stories
National Academy of Chinese Theatre Arts, 305
National Academy of Music, 161, 162–64
National Chinese Orchestra (NCO, Guojia Guoyue Tuan), 318–19
National Chinese Orchestra of Taiwan, 335
National Conservatory of Music, 138
National Culture and Arts Foundation, 297
national discourse, as model narrative, 141
National Intangible Cultural Heritage, Yugur folk songs on list of, 230, 241
nationalism, 139, 250–55, 404–5
  See also Jinyu Qinshe Society in 1930s China
Nationalist Party (Taiwan), 296, 297–98
National Minorities' Music and Dance Festival (Beijing), 237
National Music Institute (China), 249–50
national music theory (*minzu yinyue lilun*), 2–3
National Taiwan Academy of Fine Arts (later National Taiwan University of Arts), 317–18
nations, as imagined communities, 316–17
natural intervals, 34
natural sound, theorization of, 30–43
  guqin, intonations and contemporary significances of, 35–41
  just intonation, theory of, 33–35
  music theory, Chinese scholarly tradition of, 30–33

"Negaraku" ("My Country," Wee Meng Chee), 484–85
neoliberal values, Coco Lee's emphasis on, 384
Nettl, Bruno, 160, 171
New Book of the Tang (*Xin Tang shu*), 48, 51–52
newcomers (*sinkeh*) in British Malaya, 477–78
New Cultural Movement (Xin wenhua yundong), 166, 248, 249
New Economic Policy (1971, Malaysia), 480
new folk songs, 238, 239, 240–41
New Jersey Symphony Orchestra, 341
new music, use of term, 150n.6
new *opela*, 296–98
New Southbound policy (Taiwan), 323
New York Times, on Wang, 393, 394
New Yorker, on Wang, 397
Ng, Vincent, 483
ni fan, wo jian; wo fan, ni jian (When you play ornately, I play simply; when I play ornately, you play simply), 208
Nie Chongyi, 15–16
nine bureaus of performance (*jiubuji*), 47–48
non-Han peoples, musical place in modern China, 452–65
    mainstream and, 458–62
    minority music, 454–58
Nora, Pierre, 135–36, 145, 147–48
Nordlinger, Jay, 395
Nor Jis, 239, 241
North America Youth Chinese Orchestra, 335
northwest wind songs, 364, 367
Number One Court *Guqin* Master (Li Zizhao), 258, 259, 261–62, 261*f*
Nuo opera (*nuoxi*), 421
Nur Farahin Mahadi, 488n.10
nursing-baby-animal songs, 234–35, 239–40
nüshu script, 428–29n.2
"Nüyue jiming" ("A Couple's Morning Dialogue"), 122

objective past, 135
objects, text versus, 15, 16
Oh My Buddha! Oh My God (*Wo keneng buwei duhua ni*), 299–300
Old Book of the Tang (*Jiu Tang shu*), 52–53, 59

Ombak Potehi (glove-puppet theater), 483, 489n.16
Ömer, Ekrem, 457
Ong, Aihwa, 405–6
onomatopoeic words, 116
On the Six (Lopez), 375
opela (*gezaixi* subgenre), 293–98
opera(s), 145–47, 182, 211–15, 338, 416–17
orchestras
    modern Chinese, introduction into Malaysia, 479
    modern Chinese, types of, 326n.10
    musical theater orchestras, *pipa* in, 338
    See also *guoyue* (modern Chinese orchestral music, national music); modern Chinese orchestral music of Taiwan
organic music, 428n.1
original ecology folk songs (*yuanshengtai min'ge*), 446–47
otherness, 452–53, 458–63
Oulu wangji (*Seabirds at Peace with the World*), 262
Out of Chaos and Coincidence: Hong Kong's Music Cultures (*Le zai diancuo zhong: Xianggang yasu yinyue wenhua*, Yu), 144
outsiders, Lee as, 379–80
Ouyang Xiu, 15, 48
overtone series, 34, 35*f*

paiban (clappers), 186–87, 188, 189
paintings, as silent poems, 418
Pan Yuliang, 268n.1
Panton Dondang Sayang Baba Baba Pranakan (*Dondang Sayang Verses by the Baba Baba Peranakan*, Koh Hoon Teck), 470–71
pantun (Malay quatrain verse), 470
Pantusov, Nikolai, 454
Paoxi, 251
Papastergiadis, Nikos, 311
park pop. See Wuhan, park pop in
passion square (*jiqing guangchang*), 431
the past
    hidden melodies from, 81–84
    objective versus subjective, 135
    postmodernism in, 304

understanding of, in PRC, 147
  See also memory
pastoral songs, 234
Paulsson, Erik, 338
Pease, Rowan, 397–98, 446–47
Peking University Music Group (later Peking University Institute of Music Transmission and Learning), 161, 162
Peking University Music Research Association, 161–62
Pelliot, Paul, 150n.5
Penang Hokkien, Hokkien Rhymes in, 474–77
Penang Philharmonic Society, 479
Peng Bai (news publication), interview with Zhu, 404–5
Peng Zhengyuan, 208–9
Peng Zhiqing (Peng Qingshou), 258
Penghiboran Hati (songbook, Lim Seng Hooi), 472
pengling (bell type), 188
pentatonic scales, 235–36
People's Daily, on Wang, 393
People's Republic of China (PRC). *See* China
Perak Chinese Amateur Dramatic Association, 478
Peranakan Chinese in early twentieth-century British Malaya, 470–77
percussion instruments (*daji yueqi*), 187–89
"Percussion Paradise" (Hands Percussion performance), 482
performance practices
  improvisation, 192
  participatory versus presentational, 438–40
  performance variation (*bianzou*), 180
  traditional, guiding principles of, 180
performance spaces, public versus private, 438–39
performing artists
  non-Han, control over, 456
  of traditional Chinese music, 164
performing multicultural Chinese identities, 468–86
  Hokkien Rhymes in Penang Hokkien, 474–77
  kronchong from Dutch East Indies, 471–74
  liberalization and globalization at the turn of the twenty-first century, 481–85

Malay *dondang aying*, 470–71
nation-state policies and the search for national identities, 478–81
newcomers (*sinkeh*) in British Malaya, 477–78
Peranakan Chinese in early twentieth-century British Malaya, 470–77
Phor Tor (Hungry Ghost) festival, 477
pianists. *See* women pianists, re-imagining of
Picken, Laurence E. R., 81, 128n.16
pictorial and gestural elements in Luo Yusheng's video performance of *Choumo yinchu*, 286–88
pictures, in narrative performances, 287, 287f, 288
pingqiang (melody type), 282, 284–85
Pingsha luoyan (*Wild Geese Descend on a Sandbank*), 262
pingtan (storytelling-and-singing genre), 202, 449n.4
Pinker, Steven, 271–72
Pinsu (*Disclosure*, Yang), 342
pipa (lute)
  ensembles involving, 336–38, 345
  foreign students of, in China, 344
  material for strings of, 334–35
  minority-themed compositions for, 460–61
  nanyin pipa, 334
  performance forms for, 335–39
  performance practices for, 180
  special types and historical variants of, 333–34
  See also pipa music
Pipa Concerto No. 2, (Zhao Jiping), 335
Pipa: From a Distance (CD), 342
Pipa ji (*The Tale of the Lute*), 68
pipa music, 329–48
  categories of, 330
  classic pieces, 331
  commonly performed and representative compositions, 339–43
  modern composition and tradition of, 329–32, 333, 335–36
  performance abroad, diverse forms of, 333–39, 343–44
  trends and significance, 343–45
  Western influences on, 331

Pisares, Elizabeth, 377
pitch substitutions, 195n.5
place, as term, connotations of, 365–66
plot-circling narratives, 274
plucked string instruments (*tanbo yueqi*), 181–84
Plum Blossoms in the Snow (*Taxue xunmei*, Huang), 167
poems and poetry
   chanting of lyrics of, 111
   dondang aying (poetry singing), 470–71
   paintings as silent poems, 418
   poetic elements of *Choumo yinchu*, 276–81
   relationship of language and music in, 64–65
   relationship to song, 115, 232
Points, The (Chen Yi), 340
Police Chalk Circle, The (*Polishi huilan ji*), 299–300
politics
   music's relationship to, 138–41
   political blending, 418, 422
   political-social tensions as subject of *Shijing* songs, 110
Polo, Marco, 3–4
Polyphon Werke AG, 488n.7
polyphony (*fudiao yinyue*), heterophony versus, 180
popular (pop) music
   Anglo-American popular music, hegemony of, 374, 381
   "Blood-Stained Dignity," 356–59
   "Fill the World with Love," 359–64
   in Hong Kong, 142–43
   humanism in, 353–67
   kronchong in Malaya, 471–74
   in Malaysia, 468–69, 477, 479, 482, 483–85
   media industries in Asia and, 169–70, 387–88
   "My Beloved Hometown," 364–67
   of 1930s China, 169–70
   of 1980s China, 353–69
   orientalist assumptions embedded in global movements of, 380
   professionalism and, 437
   in Taiwanese theater, 294, 295, 299
   in Wuhan, 431–47
   See also Lee, Coco;

postmodernism, the past in, 304
Potehi glove-puppet theater, 486*f*
Potong Padi (*Harvesting Paddy*, folk song arrangement), 480
Poxi xiangzheng (*Mother-in-law Arguing with Daughter-in-law*), 339–40
"Preface to the Collection of Qinchuan Tablature" ("Qinchuan puhui xu," Yan Cheng), 253
prehistory. *See* musical archaeology and prehistory of music in China
professionalism
   as barrier, 445
   non-Han musicians and, 456
professional musicians
   amateur musicians, distinction from, 431–36, 440–44
   as new occupational category, 435
   pipa music, performance of, 331
   Yugurs as, 239
   See also amateur (*yeyu*) musicians
program music, relationship to visual arts, 426
proper music (*yayue*), 115
public education, school songs and, 158
public-welfare songs, 364
Pythagorean comma, 44n.7

Qi, Kun, 225n.5, 226n.22
Qian Lezhi, 32
Qian, Lijuan, 353–69, 497
Qian Renkang, 160
qiangfu (song body), 77
qiangtou (song head), 77
qiangwei (song tail), 77
"Qiang youci" ("Tribulus Grows on the Wall"), 110
Qianlong, Emperor, 114
"Qifa" ("Seven Stimuli," Mei Sheng), 20, 23
"Qifu" ("Minister of War"), 110
Qilian kuangxiang (*Rhapsody on the Qilian Mountain*, Han Lankui), 335
Qin Shi Huang, 47–48
Qin Wenchen, 341
Qiu Zhilu, 114
Qin (Zhou-dynasty vassal state), 12
qin (zither)
   discussion of, 16–23

influence of unearthing of, 10
line drawings of, 17f, 18f, 19f
tablature notation for, 150n.4
Qinchuan Society, 253
Qinding Shijing yuepu (*An Imperial Anthology of Notated Music for* Shijing *Songs*), 114
Qing dynasty, conquest of Taiwan, 313
qing-gongpu (melodic guides), 82
qingkechuan (amateur performers), 214–15
"Qingmiao" ("Solemn Temple"), 110
Qingming Symphonic Picture. See *Along the River during the Qingming Festival*
qingshangyue music ensembles, 203
qingyin. See Jiangnan *sizhu*
"Qingying" ("Blue Flies"), 117
"Qinjian" ("Annotation of *Guqin*," Cui Zundu), 34–35
qin pipa (later *ruan*, lute), 182
qinqin ("Qin-kingdom lute"), 182
Qinqu jicheng (*Collection of* Guqin *Music*), 257
"Qinren timing lu" ("Directory of *Guqin* Players"), 264–65
"Qinren wenxun lu" ("Survey of *Guqin* Players"), 264–65
qu (poetic format), 68
qudi (transverse flute), 185
Qulü (*Rules for Singing* Qu [*Poetry*], Wei Liangfu), 63
qupai (labeled tunes)
 in *kunqu*, 63
 paradigm, 88–91, 90f
 text-setting and, 158–59
 textual, and *kunqu* composition, 68, 88
 textual, template of "Feng ru song," 65–66, 67f
Qurban Ibrahim, 456–57
quxiang pipa (lute), 181–82

race
 Chinese Americans as model minority, 378–79
 and Coco Lee's attempt at US market crossover, 376–77
 See also ethnicity; minorities
racism
 and ethnic minorities, 252
 in Malaysian higher education, 484–85
 in US popular music circles, 380–81

Ramnarine, Tina K., 311–12
Rao, Nancy Yunhwa, 500–1
Rao, Shubhendra, 337
Rao Zongyi, 21
rawap (plucked lute), 462–63
reality-TV format, 382–83
recording technologies, 168–69
Record of Music. See *Yueji*
red, humanism in. See humanism
red coat of armor (*hongse zhanpao*), 373–74, 386
Rees, Helen, 452–53
reform and opening-up policy, 360
regional-ensemble music playing, 165
regional opera music, interconnections with Jiangnan *sizhu*, 211–15
Rejuvenation: A Taoist Journey (Ho), 335–36
relationships, in Confucianism, 165–66
Remembrance of Yunnan (*Yunnan huiyi*, Liu Xing), 461
Ren Hongxiang, 331
resist spiritual pollution (*qingchu jingshen wuran*) campaign, 370n.11
Rest is History, The (MC Jin), 377
Return is the Movement of Tao, The (Mollard), 400
revolutionary films and songs, treatment of themes in, 358
rhythm, perception of, 95n.31
Richie, Lionel, 381–82
Riftin, Boris, 286, 287
Riley, Terry, 338
rites, music and, 137–38
ritual songs, 233
River Elegy (*He shang*, TV documentary series), 359
Rofel, Lisa, 171–72
rojak (fruit salad), 468
Rolling Stone, criticisms of Lee album, 380
romantic love, 166–67
Rong Geng, 12
ronggeng (Malay folk social dance), 471
roosters, in *Choumo yinchu*, 277–78
Roseman Bandit, The (*Meiqui zei*), 300–1, 304
Roseman Warrior, The (*Meigui xia*), 300–1, 304
Roussel, Bruno, 338
ruan (lute), 181, 182, 429n.4, 461

Ruan Hong, 214–15
Ruan Yuan, 11–12
Ruo, Huang, 338
rural areas, Jiangnan *sizhu* performances in, 204, 220
Russians
　in China, 163
　as teachers for National Academy of Music, 163

Saishang qü (*Song of the Frontier*), 458–59
sandu chuangzuo (compositional model), 68, 69f
sanfen sunyi (tuning system), 31–33, 38
San Francisco Chronicle, on Wang, 393
santur (instrument), 182–83
sanxian (lute), 182
Sar Tala, 239
Sartre, Jean-Paul, 354–55
Sato, Jim, 500, 501–2
Scar Literature (*shanghen wenxue*), 354, 364
Schein, Louisa, 458
scholars, in *Choumo yinchu*, 277–78
school song (*xuetang yuege*) genre, 157–60, 167–68, 171
Seattle Symphony Orchestra, 335
Second Sino-Japanese War, 250
Seeger, Anthony, 100
Self-Strengthening Movement (Ziqiang yundong), 160–61
self-writing, 142–43, 144
"Sentiment of the Leaves for the Root, The" ("Lüye dui gende qingyi," song), 355
Sepu (*Music for Shijing Songs with Se Zither Accompaniments*, Xiong Penglai), 113, 119
seven bureaus of performance (*qibuji*), 47–48
sexuality
　Coco Lee's sexiness, 374, 383–86
　criticisms of Yuja Wang's, 396
　jiqing guangchang singers and, 434–35
　Zhu Xiao-Mei's asexuality, 400
shangfan xiajian (complex above, simple below, variation principle), 180–81
Shanghai
　Jiangnan *sizhu* music in, 199–200, 219
　Westernization of, 248, 249
Shanghai Ballet School, 146

Shanghai Conservatory of Music, 2–3, 344
"Shanghai Night" ("Ye Shanghai," Zhou), 170
Shanghai Orchestra, 167
Shanghai Philharmonic Orchestra, 335–36
Shanghai Symphony Orchestra, 419–20
Shangshu (*Esteemed Documents*), 31
Sheep Bone Group (Qianggu quan), 403–4, 413n.5
Shen Qia, 503
Shen Xingong, 159–60, 167–68
Shen Zhibai, 37
sheng (mouth organ), 180, 184, 185–86
Sheng, Bright, 341
sheng-guan ritual ensembles, 184
Shenqi mipu (collection of *guqin* tablature), 39
Shi (kingdom), 56
shi (poetry form), 64, 65f
shi (literati) class
　disappearance of, 249
　new *opela* and, 296–98
　pastimes of, 258
　performance of solo *pipa* music, 329, 330
　yaji (gatherings), 259–60
　See also intellectuals
Shi Daxiu, 258
Shi Yonggang, 145, 146
Shi Zhiyou, 423–24
Shi Zhongqin, 146–47
shidaiqu (songs of the time), 169–70, 482
shi'erxi. See Jiangnan *sizhu*
shifan genres, comparison with Jiangnan *sizhu*, 219
shifan gu (*shifan* drum music), 215
shifan luogu (gong-and-drum music), 202, 203, 215–19
shifan xiyue. See Jiangnan *sizhu*
shigu (lion drum), 482
Shih, Shu-mei, 499
Shiji (*Historical Records*, Sima Qian), 30–31, 134
Shijing (*Book of Songs*, Confucius), 99–127
　aesthetics and morals of, 115–16
　Cheung Sai-Bung on, 140–41
　contemporary singing of, 120–23
　as creative stimulus and expressive model, 119–23
　as expression of Chinese heart-minds, 123–24

as history, 110–14
as memory, 101–10
as soundscapes, 116–19
mentioned, 2, 493
tradition of chanting and singing of, 99–100
Yu Hui on, 491
challenge for
Shimian maifu (*Ambush from All Directions*), 339–40
"Shiwei" ("Reduced"), 110
Shiyue tupu (*Illustrated Scores of* Shijing *Songs*, Lü Nan), 113–14
Shizong, Emperor, 113–14, 138
short tune folk songs, 235
Shoso-in Repository (Nara), 333–34
shouluo (gongs), 189
Shuanghaizi village, Minghua, Yugurs in, 237
"Shuli" ("Millet Fields"), 119–20
shunü (virtuous Confucian lady), 391–92
sibao (instrument), 196n.23
Si da jing (*Four Grand Vistas*), 262
sihu (bowed string instruments), 190
Silk Road Ensemble, 342
Silk Road Music ensemble, 336–37, 343
Silk Road Project, 333
Silvio, Teri J., 296–97, 304
Sima Qian, 30–31, 358
Singer of Tales, The (Lord), 271
Sing-Song Girl Red Peony (*Ge'nü hongmudan*, sound film), 170
Sinitic languages, tonal nature of, 64
sinkeh (newcomers) in British Malaya, 477–78
Sino-Vietnamese war, 356, 358–59
siren bang (Gang of Four), 145–46, 150n.9
Sisu Percussion, 482
"Siwen" ("Oh Accomplished Houji"), 122–23
sizhu. *See* Jiangnan *sizhu*
sizhu zhi xiang (hometown of silk and bamboo music). *See* Taicang
Smith, David Stanley, 167
social changes. *See* western Yugurs, social change and maintenance of musical tradition among
Socialist Realism, 364, 366–67
social media, 403–4, 406–8, 407f, 409
Song dynasty, 423
Song of the Pipa (Lam), 341

song(s)
children's songs, 235
gang tai pop songs, 370n.6
hair-cutting songs, 233
hay-cutting songs, 234
northwest wind songs, 364, 367
nursing-baby-animal songs, 234–35, 239–40
official lyrical song, 370n.5
poems versus, 232
public-welfare songs, 364
relationship to dance, 115
school song (*xuetang yuege*) genre, 157–60
story songs, 233
work songs, 234
by Zhao Yuanren, 166–67, 168
See also music education; popular music
Songs for All (CD), 480–81
Songxianguan qinpu (*Collection of* Guqin *Tablature of the Songxian House*), 253
sonic orientalism, 376
Sonoda, Shigeto, 500, 501–2
Sony Music, 377
Sony Music Taiwan, 374–75
Sopplimenti musicali (Zarlino), 34
soul, Coco Lee and, 378–79
Sounding China (Guo), 502
soundscapes, *Shijing* songs as, 116–19
sources for Chinese music history and historiography, 136–37
"Speak My Language" (Ah Gu), 468
Spring and Autumn period, disappearance of folk songs during, 242
Spring on Tianshan Mountains (*Tianshan zhi chun*, Wang Fandi), 462–63
square-dancing (*guangchang wu*) exercise gatherings, 442
stambul (musical theater type), 472
Standing Out (CD), 336–37
Star Online (news source), 384
state ceremonies, performers for, 138
state sacrifices, soundscapes of, 118
state sacrificial songs, *Shijing* songs as, 110, 111
Stebbins, Robert, 442–43
stereotypes
of Chinese musical femininity, 391–92
of women pianists, 392, 406, 408
Stern, Daniel, 271–72

Stevens, Catherine, 274, 276
Stevin, Simon, 32–33
stinking ninth (*chou laojiu*), 359, 370n.9
Stock, Jonathan P. J., 137, 140, 268n.12, 443–44, 491–506
Stokoe, William C., 287
St. Olaf Orchestra, 342
stop consonants, 93n.5
stories
    story songs, 233
    ubiquity of, 272–73
    See also narratives
Story of the Western Chamber (Xi xiang ji), 170
Straits Chinese, 470
Street Angel (Malu tianshi), 170
students, in *Choumo yinchu*, 280
Stuttgart Chamber Orchestra, 341
subjective past, 135
suernai (shawm), 185
Su Family Ensemble, 196n.13
Suijin cipu (Xie), 95n.24, 95n.25
sun, symbolism of, 355
Su'nan *chuida* (wind-and-percussion ensemble music), 202
Sunan County Cultural Bureau, 242
Sunan Yugur Autonomous County, 230
Sun Ming, 359–60
Sun Peichang, 316
Sun Yat-sen, 247–48, 256, 316
suona (shawm), 185, 421, 424–25
Su Shi, 119–20, 260
Su Sixu, 57
Su Wen-ching, 320, 326n.6
Su Yue, 356, 370n.6
suyue (vernacular music), 115–16
suzhi (quality), 388n.1
Suzhou, map of metropolitan area, 205f
    See also Jiangnan *sizhu*
Swann, Darryl, 378–79
Swed, Mark, 395
Sweeney, Ed, 336–37
Sydney Symphony Orchestra, 335
sympathetic strings, 462
symphonic poems, 424
    See also Along the River during the Qingming Festival

Taicang
    affluence in, 211
    Jianang *sizhu* repertoire in, 200, 204–9, 220
    map of, 205f
Taicang City Cultural Bureau (Taicangshi Wenhuaguan), 206–7
Taicang Jiangnan Sizhu Ensemble, 206
Taicang Jiangnan sizhu shidaqu (Ten Great Pieces of Jiangnan Sizhu in Taicang), 204–5
Taicangshi Loudong Kunqu Tangmingshe (music club), 213–14
Tainan City Traditional Orchestra (NCTO, Tainan Shi Minzu Guanxian Yuetuan), 318–19, 320f
Taipei Chinese Orchestra (TCO, Taibei Shili Guoyue Tuan), 318–19, 319f, 322–24
Taiwan
    bilingualism in, 299
    campus-folk-song movement, 438–39, 483
    China, lack of cultural exchange with, 320
    Chinese consciousness in, rise of, 317
    colonial situation before 1945, 313–14
    Japanese colonial period in, 294
    Lee (Coco) in, 374–75, 376–77, 383–85
    martial law in, 315, 321–22
    musical culture of, 134–35, 318–23, 446, 496
    music scholarship in, 3
    Nationalist government of, 295
    pipa music performances in, 181–82, 332
    postcolonial situation after 1945, 314–17
    theater, religious performance of, 293–94
    Western musical influence, increase in, 321
    See also modern Chinese orchestral music of Taiwan; Taiwanese new *xiqu*
Taiwan Bangzi Opera Company (Taiwan Yuju Tuan), 300
Taiwanese consciousness (*taiwan yishi*), 314–15
Taiwanese new *xiqu*, 292–306
    Chichiao Musical Theater, 298–301
    intellectuals, intervention of, 296–98
    Kurama Tengu, 301–5
    Modernity, grassroots negotiation of, 293–96
    new *opela*, 296–98
    opela, 293–96

Taiwan gezaixi de fazhan yu bianqian (*The Transformation and Development of Gezaixi*, Zeng Yongyi), 292–93
Taiwan Nichinichi Shinpō (newspaper), on *guoyue* activities, 313–14
Tales of Pipa (Yang Jing), 333
"Talk at the Yan'an [Yenan] Forum on Art and Literature" (Mao), 138–39
Tan Dun
　Concerto for String Orchestra and Pipa, 335
　Ghost Opera, 340–41, 418–19
　on organic music, 428n.1
　as total art composer, 418–19
　See also *Map, The: Concerto for Cello, Video, and Orchestra*
Tan Kheng Seong (Ah Gu), 487n.1
Tan, Shzr Ee, 391–412, 498
Tan, Sooi Beng, 468–86, 498–99
Tan Su Yin, 482
"Tanah Pusaka" ("Land of Inheritance," Ahmad Merican), 480
tanbo yueqi (plucked string instruments), 181–84
Tang Chuanye, 401
Tang empire
　Hu and Han music and people, integration during mid-Tang period, 54
　tribute system, 48, 50–51
Tang Jianping, 331
Tang Xianzu, 114
tanggu (hall drum), 187, 189
tangming musicians, 212, 215–16
Tang Song, Water Sounds (Min Xiao-Fen), 334
"Taoyao" ("Peach Tree"), 101, 121–22, 129n.25
Taozi (*jiqing guangchang* singer), 434–35
Tashway (Qurban), 456–57
Tastes of Dai Village (*Dai xiang fengqing*, Wang Huizhong), 461
Taylor, Timothy, 462–63
teacher-training schools (*Shifan xuexiao*), 314
technology
　substitution as basic process for, 243
　tradition and, 420
ten bureaus of performance (*shibuji*), 47–48
"Tengu Nursery Rhyme" ("Tiangou Tongyao"), 302

text(s)
　art of text-setting, school-song writing and, 158–59
　interrelationship with music, 129n.23
　music and performance and, *Shijing* songs as, 100–1
　objects versus, 15, 16
　textual sources, description of, 9
themes
　in Chinese music history, 137
　of discourse on Hong Kong's musical past, 141–42
　theme-circling narratives, 274, 288–89
theorization
　division within, 500–1
　role of, 501
Thibault, André, 336–37
third spaces, nature of, 311–12, 323
"Thoughts about Developing Chinese Music" ("Zhongguo yinyue gailiangshuo," Fei), 156–57
Thrasher, Alan R., 179–94, 225n.11, 260, 494–95
3-limit tuning, 32
"Three Principles of the People" (Sun and Chiang), 316
Three Songs for Violoncello and Pipa (Sheng), 341
Tian Yimiao, 401
Tiananmen demonstrations, 358–59
Tianchi village, 216–19, 216*f*, 220
tianci (poetry writing process), 65–66
Tianshan zhichun (*Spring on the Tianshan Mountains*, Wusimanjiang and Yu Lichun), 339–40
"Tingliao" ("Torches Burning in the Courtyard"), 118
tiqin (bowed string instruments), 191
Titon, Jeff, 503
toddling (learning-to-walk) songs, 235
tomb frescoes. See *huteng* dance
tongbo (cymbals), 188
Tongdian (*Survey of Institutions*), 179
"Tonggong" ("Red Bows"), 118
tonggu (drums), 189
"Tong Nian Xiong" ("Song for Childhood," BM Boys), 483–84

Toronto Symphony Orchestra, 335–36
total art
  live and mediated performance as, 418–22
  The Map as, 419–22, 420f
  Tan Dun's, 418–19
  as term, use of, 417
tradition, technology and, 420
traditional instruments and heterophonic practice, 179–94
  bowed string instruments (*laxian yueqi*), 190–91
  bowed strings in ensemble, 191
  heterophonic ideal, 191–92
  heterophonic performance practice, 180–81
  percussion in ensemble, 189
  percussion instruments (*daji yueqi*), 187–89
  plucked string instruments (*tanbo yueqi*), 181–84
  plucked strings in ensemble, 183–84
  wind instruments (*chuiguan yueqi*), 184–87
  wind instruments in ensemble, 185–87
traditions. *See* western Yugurs, social change and maintenance of musical tradition among
translation, issues raised by, 502
transnationalism, 405–10, 411, 504
travel, soundscapes of, 118
Trevarthen, Colwyn, 271–72
Tsai Ing-wen, 323
Tsar Teh-yun, 445–46
Tujue tribe, 51
tuning systems
  bells as validation for writings on, 136
  equal temperament, 2–3, 41
  for *guqin*, 35–41
  just intonation, 33–35, 37–38, 41
  politics and, 137
  sanfen sunyi, 31–33, 38
Tuo Likun, 242
Turino, Thomas, 438, 439–40, 445
Turkic languages, 231
Tursun, Nurmuhemmet, 457
TV, Yugurs and, 240
Twelve Shijing Songs. See *Zhao Yansu chuan fengya shiershipu*
Two Pieces of the Tang Dynasty (Ye Dong), 334–35

UK Chinese Ensemble, 333–34
United States
  Chineseness, racial and musical beliefs about, 386–87
  Lee's crossover into markets of, 374–81
  model-minority narratives in, 379
  "One China" policy, acceptance of, 321
University of British Columbia Symphony Orchestra, 343
Uprising of the Two Airlines (*Liang hang qiyi*), 257
urtin duu (Mongolian long song), 460
utterances, components of, 286
Uyghur khaganate, 230–31
Uyghurs, 454, 456–58

Venetian Twins, The (*Weinisi shuang bao an*), 297, 304–5
vernacular (licentious) music (*suyue*), 115
Veronese, Paolo, 429n.5
Victor Talking Machine Company, 169
video, Tan Dun's use of, 418–22
visual arts, relationship to program music, 426
vocal *qupai* paradigm, 66, 66f
voice-leading rules, language-music interactions and, 76–80

Wachman, Alan M., 315
Wall Street Journal, on Mandopop, 376
"Wandering Songstress, The" ("Tianya ge'nü," He), 170
Wang, Grace, 497–98
Wang Agen, 226n.20
Wang Fandi, 339–40, 462–63
Wang Guangqi, 139–40, 251, 259
Wang Guanqi, 36–37
Wang Gungwu, 469
Wang Guowei, 9, 21–22, 23
Wang Hailing, 300
Wang Hong, 356–57
Wang Hongzhi (Wong Wang-Chi), 141
Wang Houzhi, 11–13
Wang Huiran, 331
Wang Huizhong, 461
Wang Jian, 359–60, 370n.12
Wang Jian reliefs, 179
Wang Jilie, 81, 88

Wang Kefen, 52–53
Wang Peilun, 316
Wang Pu, 32
Wang Shen, 259–60
Wang Shoutai, 77, 81, 88
Wang Weida, 403–4, 410
Wang Xijue, 211
Wang Xingbo, 262
Wang Yanqiao, 331
Wang Ying-fen, 96n.36, 446
Wang, Yuja
    Chineseness, 405
    clothing, preferences in and critiques of, 394–99
    criticism of, 407f
    as eternal wunderkind, re-gendering of, 395–99
    interview with, 408–9
    performance practices of, 393
    performing persona of, media reception of, 397–98
    personas of, 396, 405–7
    reception of performances in US, 393–94
    social media and, 393–94
    stereotypes of, 392
    trope of youthful vigor and, 392–95
Wang Zhaojun, 458–59
Wang Zhongbing, 429n.4
Wang Zhonggao, 262
Wang Zichu, 18–20, 21, 22
"Wanqiu" ("Highland Wan"), 117
warfare, *Shijing* songs' evocations of, 117
Warren, Jeff, 493–94
"Watching the *Huteng* Dance at Night in Assistant Secretary Wang's Mansion" ("Wang Zhongcheng zhai ye guan wu Huteng," Liu Yanshi), 55–56
watchmen, in *Choumo yinchu*, 277
water, Zhu Xiao-Mei on, 401
Water Heavens (Tan Dun), 418–19
Watkins, Lee, 312
Wedding at Cana, The (Veronese), 429n.5
weddings
    music for, 216–19
    traditional Yugur, 242
    wedding songs, 233–34
Wee Meng Chee (Namewee), 484–85, 489n.21

Wei Liangfu, 63, 202–3, 204–5
Wei Zhiyan, 114
Weishi yuepu (*A Songbook of the Wei Family*, Wei Zhiyan), 114
Wen Bo, 331
Wen Zhao, 335–36
Weng Ching-hsi, 338
wenren (traditional scholar, literati), 63
"Wenwang" ("King Wen"), 110
"Wenwang yousheng" ("King Wen's Voice"), 118–19
wenzipu (*guqin* tablature), 37–38
West
    Chinese music research in, 3–4
    composers in, 164
    performers in, 165
    Western art music, emulation of, 460
    Western classical music, operation of genre in, 396
    Western ethnomusicology, introduction into Asia, 3
    Westernization, modernization versus, 171
western Yugurs, 229–45
    folk songs, changes in, 238–42
    folk song tradition, 232–36
    lifestyles of, 230–32, 236–38
What Lies Ahead (CD), 337
whirling dance. See *huxuan* dance
Who's the Boss (*Jinlan qing shei shi laoda*), 299
wind instruments (*chuiguan yueqi*), 184–87
Wind of Nomads Concert, 482
Winzenburg, John, 163
Witzleben, J. Lawrence, 200, 203–4, 206, 260, 443–44
women
    as amateur musicians, 446
    in *Choumo yinchu*, 280–81
    in *The Map*, 421
    objectification of, 129n.27
    See also femininity
women pianists, re-imagining of, 391–412
    transnational Chineseness and artistic authenticity, 405–10
    Wang Yuja, 392–99
    Zhu Xiao-Mei, 399–405
Women's Philharmonic of San Francisco, 340
Wong, Chuen-Fung, 452–65, 498–99

Wong Wang-Chi (Wang Hongzhi), 141
woodblocks, 188
woodsmen, in *Choumo yinchu*, 278–79
Woolfe, Zachary, 397
word tones, 282–84, 283f
work songs, 234
Wu, Ben, 329–48, 496–97
Wu, Changlu, 335
Wu Chao-jung, 312
Wu, Emperor (of Northern Zhou dynasty), 51, 139
Wu, Emperor (of Western Han dynasty), 99, 111
Wu folk songs, 202
Wu Guodong, 203, 225n.3
Wu Haigang, 359
Wu Jinglüe, 257–58, 261
Wu Kong (movie), 353
Wu Kong's Biography (*Wukong zhuan*, Zeng Yu), 353
Wu Lansun, 259
Wu Man
  compositions by, 342
  improvisations by, 343
  works premiered by, 335–36, 338, 340–41
Wu Peifu, 259
Wu Zhao, 21, 22
Wu Zhongxi, 90–91
Wu Zuqiang, 331
Wuhan, park pop in, 431–48
  amateur and professional musicians and, 432–36
  amateurs, de-idealizing of, 444–47
  amateurs and professionals, linking of, 440–44
  musical occasions with amateur and professional qualities, 436–40
wutong wood, 191
"Wuyi" ("No Clothes?," Ying Shangneng), 114
Wuzhong xiansuo (string ensemble of the Wu [region]), 202–3

Xia Zhongtang, 460–61
"Xiangshu" ("Look at a Rat"), 110
Xiangyin shiyuepu (*Music Scores for Singing Shijing Songs at the Communal Drinking Ritual*), 113–14

xiangzhan (resonating cup), 196n.25
xianshi (string poem, music genre), 183
xiansuo instrumental ensembles, 202–3
xiansuo (strings) repertoire, 183–84, 183f
xiao (vertical flute), 184
xiaobo (cymbals), 189
Xiao Caiwu. *See* Luo Yusheng
Xiao Mei, 208
Xiao Shouli, 307n.2
Xiao Youmei, 161, 162–64, 167–68
xiaoluo (gongs), 189
"Xiaomin" ("High Heaven"), 110, 119–20
"Xiaoming" ("Bright Heaven"), 110
Xiaoxiang shuiyun (*Clouds over the Xiao and Xiang Rivers*), 262
"Xiaoxing" ("Starlets"), 110, 119–20
xibapai. *See* Jiangnan *sizhu*
xi-gongpu (melodic guides), 82
Xinjiang Arts Institute, Faculty of Music, 455–56
xin Jiangnan *sizhu* (new Jiangnan silk and bamboo [music]), 208–9
Xinjiang province, Uyghur and other non-Han music in, 453
Xinjiang Song-and-Dance Troupe, 455–56
xinju (new drama), 294
Xin qingnian (*New Youth*, journal), 249
Xinyang, bells excavated in, 10
Xiong Penglai, 113
"Xiongzhi" ("Male Pheasant"), 116–17
xiqin (bowed string instrument), 190
xiqu (traditional opera), 292, 299–300
  See also Taiwanese new x*iqu*
Xiyang xiaogu (*Flute and Drum at Sunset*), 339–40
Xiyuan yaji tu (*Picture of Yaji in the Western Gardens*, Li Gonglin and Mi Fu), 259–60
xiyue. *See* Jiangnan *sizhu*
"Xizhihazhi" ("Song on the Road," Cairang), 239
"Xizhihazhi" ("Song on the Road," historical folk song), 232–33
"Xuanniao" ("Heaven Commissions the Black Swallow"), 111
Xue Shanggong, 12
xuetang yuege (school song) genre, 157–60, 165–66, 167–68, 171

Xu Jian, 21–22
Xu Li, 31, 34–35
Xu Liang, 356–57
Xu Peidong, 365–67, 366f
Xu Renhao, 303
Xu Shen, 21–22, 23

Ya Dong, 335
Yadong Guan Trio, 338
yaji (literati gatherings, elegant gatherings), 203, 255, 256f, 259–62
Yampolsky, Philip, 488n.7
Yan Cheng (Yan Tianchi), 253, 261–62
Yandong Grand Singers, 502
Yang, Hon-Lun Helan, 134–49, 163, 494
Yang, Mina, 399
Yang Jie, 145, 146–47
Yang Jing, 342
Yang Liqing, 331
Yang Wei, 336–37
Yang Yinliu
    Draft History of Ancient Chinese Music, 140
    on *guqin* tuning systems, 38, 93n.4
    Huang's article, response to, 10
    on just intonation, 37
    on *kun* recitation, 71
    on northern phonologies, 75–76
    on *shifan luogu* melodies, 226n.23
    on *Shijing* song performance procedures, 120
    voice-leading rules of, 77
Yang Yuanzheng, 9–25, 492–93
Yang Yuhuan, 50
yangbanxi (model operas) of Cultural Revolution, 145–47
yangqin (dulcimer), 182–83
"Yangzhou man" ("A Long Song on Yangzhou," Jiang Kui), 119–20
Yan Xishan, 258
Yan Zhang (King Hui of Chu), 11, 12
"Yanyan" ("Swallows"), 110, 116–17
yanyue (entertainment music), 251
Yarji (Yurgur folk singer), 237
yayue (refined music, court music, ritual category), 47–48, 435
Ye Dong, 334–35
yehu (bowed string instruments), 191

Yellow Emperor, 247–48, 251
"Yeyou sijun" ("Dead Antelope"), 101
yi, as term, meaning of, 244
Yijing (book of divination), 244
Yili jingquan tongjie (*A General Survey of Ritual*, Zhu Xi), 112
Ying Shangneng, 114
yin-yang philosophy, 180–81
Yi Yuan *Guqin* Club, 258
Yizu wuqu (*Dance of the Yi Tribe*, Wang Huiran), 339–40
Yoshihara, Mari, 399, 406
"Youbi" ("Fat and Strong Horses"), 117–18
"Yougu" ("Blind Musicians"), 110, 119
Youlan (*Solitary Orchid*), 38
"Younü tongju" ("Lady in the Carriage"), 117
Youth Dream (*Qingchun meimeng*), 297–98, 304–5
YouTube, Wang videos on, 407–8
Yu, Lingling, 335–36, 338, 340–41
Yu Di, 489n.18
Yu Dishan, 36–37, 262–63
Yu Hui
    as chapter author, 247–68, 492–93, 495
    mentioned, 507n.5
    on *Shijing*, 491
    on Yang's texts, 149n.3
Yu, Lingling, 336
Yu Siu-Wah (Yu Shaohua), 143–44
Yu Zhenfei, 71
Yuan Zhen, 48–49, 50
Yueji (*Record of Music*)
    on *Great Wu, The*, 139
    ideologies and practices mentioned in, 137–38
    on instituting music, 116
    Lüshi chunqiu, comparison with, 136
    on melodic contours, 119
    on *Shijing* songs, 115
    on singing poetic words, 124
yuelü, as term, derivation of, 30–31
Yue Luo (*Moonset*, CD), 336
Yuelü quanshu (*Complete Collection of Music Treatises*, Zhu Zaiyu), 113–14
yuelü xue (tradition of musical studies), 30–33
Yuen Ren Chao (Zhao Yuanren), 166–68
yueqin (moon lute), 182

yueshe (music clubs), 203–4
Yueshu (*Music Book*), 179
"Yugur Grassland Disappeared, The" (Nor Jis), 241
yugur jer (folk songs), 232
Yugurs
  about, 230
  languages of, 230, 231
  singers, photograph of, 239*f*
  transportation used by, 238
  See also western Yugurs, social change and maintenance of musical tradition among
Yung, Bell, 164, 165, 445–46
Yungang caves, 179
yunluo (gongs), 188–89
Yunnan, as source for minority folk elements, 461
Yushan school of *guqin* playing, 252–53

Zahi Bingzuo, 353
Zarlino, Gioseffo, 33–34, 36
Zeng Hou Yi (Marquis Yi)
  bells from tomb of, 2, 10–11, 15, 37, 136
  line drawings of *qin* from tomb of, 17*f*
Zeng Ming, 336
Zeng Yongyi, 292–93
Zeng Yu (Jin Hezai), 353
Zeng Zhimin, 157, 159
Zha Fuxi
  activities of, 259
  Cai Yuanpei and, 249–50
  donations to Jinyu Qinshe Society, 254, 255
  Jinyu qinkan, "General Introduction" to, 251, 264
  legacy of, 265
  life of, 255, 256–57
  on Jinyu Qinshe's nationalist ideal, 251–52
  pieces played by, 262
  yaji gatherings, attendance at, 255–56
  Zhuang Jiancheng and, 257
Zhang Fan, 145, 146
Zhang, Jane (Zhang Liangying), 386–87
Zhang Shibin (Cheung Sai-Bung), 140–41
Zhang Weixian, 297–98
Zhang Wen, 242
Zhang Xiaofeng, 206–9, 220, 495
Zhang Yetang, 202–3, 211

Zhang Zeduan, 417–18, 422
Zhang Zhiliang, 461
Zhang Ziqian, 254
Zhang Zirui, 429n.4
zhangu (drums), 189
Zhao Jiping, 335
Zhao Puchu, 261–62
Zhao Weiping, 47–60, 493
Zhao Yansu, 112, 113
Zhao Yansu chuan fengya shiershipu (*Twelve Shijing Folk and Banquet Songs Transmitted by Zhao Yansu*), 112, 119
Zhao Yuanren (Yuen Ren Chao), 166–68, 249–50
zheng (*santan*, zither), 181, 186–87, 496–97
Zheng Minzhong, 20, 21, 22
zheng sheng (tunes of the Zheng state), 47–48, 61n.1
Zheng Xuan, 111, 244
Zheng Zuxiang, 21–22
"Zhenwei" ("Zhen and Wei Rivers"), 101
zhiqu (song creation), 68
zhisheng fuyin. *See* heterophony
zhisheng ti. *See* heterophony
Zhong ding kuanzhi (*Zhong Bells and Ding Tripod Inscriptions*, Wang Houzhi), 11
"Zhonggu" ("Chime-bells and Drums"), 118–19
Zhongguo minjian gequ jicheng: Gansu juan (*Anthology of Folk Songs of China's Peoples: Gansu Volume*), 230
zhonghu (bowed string instruments), 185–86, 186*f*, 190, 191, 461
Zhonghua Guoyue Xuehui (Chinese Music Association, Taiwan), 316, 322
Zhonghua Liuban (Jiangnan *sizhu* composition), 185–86, 186*f*
Zhonghua wenhua fuxing yundong (Chinese cultural renaissance movement), 317
Zhonglü shu (*Book on Bell Pitches*, Liu Xin), 31
zhongruan (lute), 182
zhong (bell) sets, 10
Zhongyang Guangbo Diantai Guoyue Zu (Central Broadcasting Station of China, Chinese Orchestra)., 315
Zhong Yaoguang, 332

Zhongyuan yinyun (rhyme dictionary), 73–74, 75–76, 75*f*, 77–79, 94n.17
Zhongzhou yun (phonology type), 70, 70*f*, 71
Zhou Chenglong, 208–9
Zhou Fanfu (Chow Fan-Fu), 143
Zhou Guanjiu, 255, 258
Zhou li (*Rites of Zhou*), 118
Zhou Long, 336, 340
Zhou Wei, 461–62
Zhou Yi, 334–35, 338, 340–41
Zhu Changfang, 262
Zhu Ruibing (Chu Sui-Bing), 143–44
Zhu Xi, 33, 35–36, 112–13, 116, 124
Zhu Xiao-Mei
  as asexual sage, 399–402
  autobiographical novella, 403
  on Bach, 400, 401
  China, reception in, 402–3
  Chineseness, 405
  as cult success, 411
  discussion thread on, 409*f*
  on *Goldberg Variations*, 401
  interview with, 404–5
  personas of, 405–7
  repackaging of, 402–5
  stereotypes of, 392
  success, paradox of, 404–5
Zhu Yi, 331
Zhu Zaiyu
  equal temperament solution, discovery of, 32–34, 36, 41–42
  musical discovery of, 2–3
  tuning systems, ignorance of, 36
  Yuelü quanshu (*Complete Collection of Music Treatises*), 113–14
Zhuang Ben-li, 317–18
Zhuang Jiancheng, 255–56, 257–58
zhudiao (main melody), 180
zhuqiang (chief melodic characteristics), 81, 85, 88
Zizhu diao (*Purple Bamboo Melody*), 213
zizhu xiao (flute type), 184